THE BENDING CROSS

RAY GINGER

The Bending Cross

A BIOGRAPHY OF

Eugene Victor Debs

> Let the people take heart and hope every-
> where, for the cross is bending, the midnight
> is passing, and joy cometh with the morning.
> —*Debs in 1918*

NEW YORK / RUSSELL & RUSSELL

For the late Peter Fagan,
WHO COULD HAVE TOLD THIS STORY
FAR BETTER THAN I HAVE DONE.

ACKNOWLEDGMENTS

The author owes his sincere thanks to the following publishers and individuals for permission to reprint material in this book:

Johnson Baur, Robert F. Baur, Mrs. Annette Baur Calder, Mrs. Raymond P. Harris, and Mrs. Cecelia Baur Martin for numerous selections from the letters of Mr. and Mrs. Eugene V. Debs.

Bobbs-Merrill Company: for selections from *The Letters of James Whitcomb Riley*, edited by William Lyon Phelps, copyright 1930.

University of Chicago Press: for a selection from Ralph Chaplin, *Wobbly*, copyright 1948.

Mrs. Marguerite Debs Cooper and Mrs. Theodore Debs for selections from the letters of Theodore Debs.

Crown Publishers: for selections from Clyde R. Miller, *The Process of Persuasion*, copyright 1946.

Mrs. Clarence Darrow: for portions of a letter from Clarence Darrow to Mrs. Kate Debs, November 5, 1926.

Dodd, Mead & Company: for selections from Allan Nevins, *Grover Cleveland*, copyright 1932.

Doubleday & Company: for a selection from Joseph P. Tumulty, *Woodrow Wilson As I Know Him*, copyright 1921.

E. P. Dutton & Company: for selections from Samuel Gompers, *Seventy Years of Life and Labor*, copyright 1925.

Greenberg, Publisher: for selections from McAlister Coleman, *Eugene V. Debs*, copyright 1930.

Harcourt, Brace & Company: for selections from Heywood Broun, *It Seems to Me, 1925–1935*, copyright 1935; from Carl Sandburg, *The American Songbag*, copyright 1927; from Lincoln Steffens, *Autobiography*, copyright 1931; from *The Letters of Lincoln Steffens*, edited by Ella Winter and Granville Hicks, copyright 1938.

Harvard University Press: for a selection from *The Holmes Pollock Letters*, edited by Mark DeWolfe Howe, copyright 1941.

Henry Holt & Company: for selections from Oscar Ameringer, *If You Don't Weaken*, copyright 1940.

Houghton Mifflin Company: for selections from Henry James, *Richard Olney & His Public Service*, copyright 1923.

vii

Indiana University: for selections from Floy Ruth Painter, *That Man Debs and His Life Work,* 1929.

International Publishers: for selections from Ella Reeve Bloor, *We Are Many,* copyright 1940; from William D. Haywood, *Bill Haywood's Book,* copyright 1929.

Charles H. Kerr & Company: for selections from William H. Carwardine, *The Pullman Strike,* copyright 1894; from Arthur Morrow Lewis, *The Art of Lecturing,* copyright 1908.

Alfred A. Knopf, Inc.: for a selection from Emma Goldman, *Living My Life,* copyright 1931.

Dr. Robert L. Leslie: for selections from *Art Young: His Life and Times,* copyright 1939.

Sinclair Lewis: for a selection from his letter to Mrs. Kate Debs, April 30, 1927.

Liveright Publishing Company: for a selection from Art Young, *On My Way,* copyright 1928.

Macmillan Company: for selections from John R. Commons, *Myself,* copyright 1934; from Granville Hicks, *John Reed,* copyright 1936; from Morris Hillquit, *Loose Leaves from a Busy Life,* copyright 1934; from Ernest Poole, *The Bridge,* copyright 1940; from William Allen White, *The Editor and His People,* copyright 1924.

Princeton University Press: for a selection from Grover Cleveland, *The Government in the Chicago Strike of 1894,* copyright 1913.

G. P. Putnam's Sons: for selections from Caro Lloyd, *Henry Demarest Lloyd,* copyright 1912.

Rinehart & Company: for a selection from Floyd Dell, *Homecoming,* copyright 1933.

Carl Sandburg: for a selection from his letter to Eugene V. Debs, November 26, 1922.

Charles Scribner's Sons: for selections from Clarence Darrow, *The Story of My Life,* copyright 1932.

Scores of persons have contributed their memories and manuscript material to this story. Some of them gave much, others considerably less, but they all showed a cooperation and kindness which heightened my understanding of the Debs' traditions as they have been preserved in our own time. Without their help this book could never have attained its present form:

Louis Austin	Frank Bohn
Roger Baldwin	William E. Bohn
Oscar Baur	Alfred Bosch
Robert F. Baur	Louis B. Boudin

George D. Brewer
Earl Browder
Mrs. Annette Baur Calder
William H. Chetham
August Claessens
McAlister Coleman
Mrs. Marguerite Debs Cooper
Florence Crawford
Solon DeLeon
Chester McA. Destler
Mrs. Carabelle G. Dickey
Mrs. Edith Love Drake
Delbert Earley
Mrs. Max Ehrmann
Charles W. Ervin
Lee Walker Evans
Ed Evinger
Mr. and Mrs. Peter Fagan
S. Feinstein
Elizabeth Gurley Flynn
Philip S. Foner
H. O. Fuhrberg
Adolph Germer
Carl Haessler
Covington Hall
Mr. and Mrs. Powers Hapgood
Mrs. Raymond P. Harris
Mr. and Mrs. Frederic Heath
Fred Heinl
G. A. Hoehn
John Haynes Holmes
Mrs. Frank Anstead Hughes
John Keracher
Sol Klapman
Mrs. Yetta Land
Louis Lazarus
Algernon Lee
Lena Morrow Lewis
A. R. Markle
Mrs. Cecelia Baur Martin
Mr. and Mrs. Robert Minor
Dr. M. L. Nearing

Scott Nearing
Sam Nesin
Martin E. O'Connell
Winifred O'Connell
Frank P. O'Hare
James Oneal
John Panzner
Lesley Payne
Frank Pfister
John C. Prechtel
Howard H. Quint
Helen Ross
Mrs. Clarence Royse
Lena Schuhardt
Oswald Schuhardt
Will Schuhardt
Mr. and Mrs. Shubert Sebree
David A. Shannon
Mr. and Mrs. John R. Shannon
Harry Sheer
Upton Sinclair
Alvin G. Slemons
Mrs. Seymour Stedman
Mr. and Mrs. Maurice Sugar
Norman Thomas
Laurence Todd
Alexander Trachtenberg
Mary Heaton Vorse
Alfred Wagenknecht
Mrs. Frank Casper Wagner
Phil Wagner
Mrs. Sherman D. Wakefield
James Peter Warbasse
Harry F. Ward
Fred D. Warren
William Weinstone
Noble C. Wilson
Peter Witt
Morris H. Wolf
John M. Work
Rose Wortis
Dr. and Mrs. J. Rudolph Yung

In addition to the persons listed above as actual contributors to this volume, I applied for information from an even larger group who either refused or neglected to comply. This is not meant to imply criticism of these persons, but is merely mentioned by way of saying that I have not knowingly neglected any potential source of facts.

Miss Agnes Inglis of the Joseph A. Labadie Collection at the University of Michigan rendered invaluable assistance for more than a year; the Rand School of Social Science for two months; Mrs. Hazel Hopper, Mr. Howard H. Peckham, and their colleagues at the Indiana State Library for several weeks. I have also used material from the following depositories: University of Chicago Library, Chicago Historical Society, John Crerar Library of Chicago, Library of Congress, Fairbanks Library of Terre Haute, Illinois Historical Society, New York City Public Library, Wisconsin Historical Society, and the Yale University Library. In each case the institution's staff has shown extreme skill and consideration in making data available for my use.

Portions of the manuscript have been read, always with incisiveness and compassion, by Dr. Arno L. Bader and Dr. L. G. VanderVelde of the University of Michigan, Prof. Joseph H. Friend of Cleveland College, David A. Shannon of the Carnegie Institute of Technology, Harry Barnard, Mary B. Land and Louis H. Pollak. Without doubt they have reservations about the result, and any faults rest with the author rather than with his critics.

Finally, at the risk of seeming impertinent or ungenerous, I want to record that I am hugely beholden to my wife, Ann Fagan Ginger, who has served as bulwark and helpmeet through it all.

Ray Ginger

CLEVELAND, OHIO
NOVEMBER, 1948

CONTENTS

Part i.   The Railroad Brotherhoods   1

Part ii.   The American Railway Union   85

Part iii.   American Socialism   185

Part iv.   World Socialism   315

Selected Chapter Sources   460

Bibliography   489

Index   502

Part I.

The Railroad Brotherhoods

As sure as a man will raise his hand by some
instinct, to shield himself against a blow,
so surely will workingmen, instinctively,
periodically, gather into unions. The
Union is the arm that Labor instinctively throws up to screen
its head. DANIEL DELEON

CHAPTER I

◻

[1]

IN LATE MAY, 1851, a flatboat swung ponderously away from the western bank of the Wabash River and nosed into the dock at the foot of Main Street.[1] Daniel and Marguerite Debs gazed with apprehension at the frontier town of Terre Haute, Indiana, their new home. Already a bleaching sun and thousands of hooves had ground the Terre Haute streets into a heavy brown dust. Dust settled in Daniel's beard; it covered his six-foot frame; particles landed on his long, straight nose and muddied in the sweat. The man stirred. Bad luck had followed him since leaving his native Alsace nearly three years earlier; Terre Haute seemed to offer a last chance. At first sight that chance was anything but reassuring.

A restless stream of French-Canadian trappers, Welsh and Scotch-Irish farmers, German merchants from the Old Country, had been pouring into western Indiana for thirty years. They found a region of immense opportunity. A stream of wealth was sweated from the rich bottomland. Days and months and years formed a restless cycle: plant corn in the spring, harvest in the autumn, feed the hogs and ship the pork on flatboats to New Orleans. Men made money and bought land and made more money and nobody cared much about other things. There was no time for sanitation, or gentle living, or even rest. It was raw, new country, and a man was a fool to miss his chance.

By 1850 more than fifty thousand hogs a year were being slaughtered in the butcheries which spread their stench along the banks of the Wabash. Livestock were pastured on the courthouse lawn, tied to the wooden fences, or left to wander at will through the streets. Men wore boots, carried guns, spat tobacco juice carelessly across flour barrels. The town was goaded by a

[1] Throughout this work, all facts have been carefully checked, and all quotations are deemed authenic.

3

single passion: get yours, get it quick, make it grow. Terre Haute was a strange place for a refined, philosophical immigrant.

[2]

JEAN DANIEL DEBS (everyone called him Daniel, never Jean) was born at Colmar, Alsace, on December 4, 1820. His father, owner of textile mills and meat markets, member of exclusive clubs, sent Daniel to school in Paris and Waldersbach, where the boy gained a deep love of French and German romanticists— Goethe, Schiller, Eugène Sue, Victor Hugo. For two and a half centuries, members of the Debs family had been among the men of affairs in Colmar, but Daniel grew away from commercial activities. His ancestors were bakers, merchants, surveyors, surgeons; he an expert on the latest poetry and a connoisseur of fine prints. To complete this heresy, Daniel obstinately continued to court Marguerite Marie Bettrich, who worked in one of his father's mills. The family quarrel was bitter: the father insisted that their social position must be maintained, and Daniel replied that his private life was a matter that he alone must decide. The wrangling persisted until the father suddenly died in the spring of 1848.

Now Daniel was free to go his own way, and his first thought was of America. Immersed in the ferment of his own life, the young emigrant unconsciously was swept along by another ferment that touched many lives. The streets of nearly every capitol in Europe had learned the bitterness of blood and treachery and shattered hope. In France and Germany, Hungary and Austria, the workers had thrust boldly for control of the government, but the business classes had deserted the uprisings to side with the aristocracy. The revolutions were smashed by rulers who struck back savagely. These events were almost unnoticed by the young emigrant. Although his ancestors had led the French Revolution in Colmar, his father had deserted politics for money-making, and Daniel's mind was filled with his own problems—the death of his father, his love for Marguerite, his future in America.

The political refugees who were determined to rebuild their

lives in America were fleeing without money or goods; Daniel
was well dressed and his wallet filled with bank notes. The
seventy-one day voyage, however, allowed ample time for an
American businessman to fleece Daniel of his savings, and he
landed penniless in New York City on January 20, 1849. At
once he began to write daily to "Daisy," as he called Marguerite,
begging her to join him; for months she daily refused, tormented
by the fear that the difference in their training would make a
happy marriage impossible. At last resorting to the dramatic,
Daniel swore he would commit suicide if his beloved did not
come to this country. Daisy arrived in New York on September
11 and they were married two days later.

The ill fortune which had been heralded by the loss of Daniel's
savings haunted the couple. A daughter died within a short
while after her birth. In grief, Daisy and Daniel moved west-
ward to Cincinnati, and their furniture, shipped by flatboat
down the Ohio River, drifted past its destination to New Orleans
and was never recovered. It was then that Daisy and Daniel
decided to settle at the large French community in Terre Haute.

[*3*]

In 1851, Terre Haute held fewer than six thousand people. Daniel found that he could cross the town in less than fifteen minutes, starting at the covered county bridge over the river, walking
a block north to Main Street, and then less than a mile east to
the Wabash and Erie Canal. But due to its location at the inter-
section of the river, the canal, and the National Road, the town
was growing rapidly. Daniel had little trouble finding a job in
one of the packing houses; from dawn to dusk he stuck to the
miserable, grueling labor. Wages were low and the lunches which
Daisy carried to her husband were often too meager for a man
who worked fourteen hours a day with his hands and his back.
Blow followed blow; another daughter died before she could be
named. Daniel left the packing house before the unsanitary conditions there completely broke his health. He tried job after job,
and finally went to work laying ties on the Vandalia, the first
railroad to come through Terre Haute. After two days, no longer

able to hold the pick handle which had worn huge blisters on his hands, he was laid off. The endless struggle went on, one ill-paid job after another, and no rest.

Then, at last, a daughter was born who lived, and she was given the same two names as her mother, Marie Marguerite. But Daisy and Daniel feared greatly for the life of their child. Sanitation was unknown. Hogs and cattle wandered through the town. Garbage was thrown into the streets. Stagnant water in the canal was an ideal breeding place for mosquitoes, so that malaria epidemics swept the population. Yellow fever was a constant threat during the long and hot summers. Doctors were few; medical facilities were primitive. Unexplained deaths were often attributed to "chills and fever" or to "vapors rising from the newly plowed ground." Money was dear, but the life of a baby was cheap in Terre Haute. So in the spring of 1854, when an ague epidemic threatened, the young parents hastily retreated to New York.

Another daughter was born soon after they reached Brooklyn, and Daniel quickly found that supporting two children in the East was at least as difficult as feeding one on the frontier. That autumn, when the ague epidemic had passed, the Debs family returned to Terre Haute. This time Daisy found a means of livelihood; she invested the last forty dollars of family savings in a stock of groceries and opened a store in the front room of their house. Daniel was heartbroken; he thought the venture would surely fail and leave them penniless. But the young couple were well liked by the French colony in Terre Haute and Daniel had learned the butcher trade from his father. Within a few months the family was earning a decent living.

In the two-story frame house and store on North Fourth Street, their first son was born November 5, 1855. Daniel, thinking that he had found in the writings of Eugène Sue and Victor Hugo a tradition of reason and justice by which men should live, named his son Eugene Victor Debs. The older children had been baptized Roman Catholics, but Daisy had failed to find in Terre Haute the serene security of her cathedral in Colmar. Her ensuing doubts were promoted by her Protestant husband. The last ties were severed before Eugene was born, and he began life unblessed by the sanctions of organized religion.

The frontier village was pleasant for a young child. Broad meadows furnished an ideal place for picnics, and the wooded western shore of the Wabash promised a thousand adventures. Small boats could be floated in the puddles which formed in the clay streets, and the canal, now seldom used for larger traffic, was a half block from the Debs' house. If a child survived, he had his chance for success and happiness; but life itself was uncertain. Several times Eugene Debs, buried under blankets yet shaking with fever, spent horrible days and nights suffering from the Wabash shakers, a type of ague.

In 1861, when Eugene Debs was five years old, the Civil War began. Before the war there was little antislavery feeling around Terre Haute, for most of the population was Southern-born, and the region's exports moved through Southern territory to New Orleans. The 1851 state constitution deprived all Negroes of the right to vote, and the 1860 elections sent to Congress from Terre Haute Daniel W. Voorhees, whose viewpoint on slavery had been flatly expressed: "Property in slaves is not to be distinguished from other kinds of property protected by the Constitution." But after the shots at Fort Sumter, most men in Terre Haute united to defend the Union. Recruiting offices were flooded; Indiana's quota was filled more than twice within a week. A camp was organized on the outskirts of the town, and a preacher there took as his text: "In the name of our God we set up our banners."

The blockade of the Mississippi and increased transport needs made Terre Haute into a booming railroad center, and Eugene spent many afternoons idly watching troop trains move through the town. To him the locomotive, beckoning toward a future where brave men conquered danger, seemed more, far more, than a mere dirty engine towing a string of dirty cars. Men wearing blue denim jackets and engineers' caps swaggered through the streets, and small boys dreamed of becoming railroad engineers.

Proslavery sentiment lasted throughout the war, each election posing anew the question of whether Indiana would remain in the Union. Politics, always a serious matter in the rural Midwest, reached a fierce crescendo of partisanship. One Fourth of July two separate celebrations were held, one by the Union faction, which Daniel favored, and another by the Confederate sympathizers. The entire town feared a clash between the two, but the day passed peacefully. On another occasion the city was thrown into panic by reports of the swift advance of Morgan's Confederate Raiders, who actually crossed the Ohio River but did not reach as far north as Terre Haute. To fend off such threats, the people organized a secret Loyalty League and a home guard, which paraded through the streets and drilled on the meadows outside of the town. Each day brought new dangers and new triumphs; the times were exciting enough to stir the imagination of any boy. Eugene was too young to puzzle over the meaning of the conflict; it was an unknown monster that seemed to spout glory and death with the same mouth. Not until many years later did Debs see a giant shining through the gray fog of doubts and treachery:

History may be searched in vain for an example of noble heroism and sublime self-sacrifice equal to that of Old John Brown.
From the beginning of his career to its close he had but one idea and one ideal, and that was to destroy chattel slavery; and in that cause he sealed his devotion with his noble blood. Realizing that his work was done, he passed serenely, almost with joy, from the scenes of men.
His calmness upon the gallows was awe-inspiring; his exaltation supreme.

Had it not been for the determination of Daniel Debs, his son might have spent the war years sitting around the store listening to the tales of battle. But to Daniel's educated mind, moving with ease among the French and German classics, education was the sole piety, and he was greatly concerned about the training of his children. The first public school in Terre Haute, begun in 1853, suspended the next year for lack of funds; the father had small faith in it when it reopened in 1860. Daniel, whose grocery business flourished to the point where the family moved to a larger house at Eleventh Street and Wabash Avenue, chose instead to send Eugene to the Old Seminary School, a private institute on Sixth Street.

The boy, with a marvelous memory and a desire to learn, quickly became bored with the endless repetition of lessons in reading, writing, and ciphering, and decided that the best thing about school was the candy store in the little frame shack down the street. He greatly preferred Sunday evenings at home, when Daniel acted as tutor. Gazing at the large busts of Voltaire and Rousseau, Eugene quietly listened to passages from Racine, Corneille, or the favorite, Hugo, and sometimes Goethe or Schiller. Thus he learned both French and German, and slowly absorbed the democratic traditions of Europe. He learned that men had hungered for freedom, written about it, fought and bled for it on a thousand dusky hills, long before the Civil War in America.

But there was no danger of Eugene's becoming lost in the past; the present was too imminent, too tawdry, too colorful. Only two blocks away, lining Wabash Street just west of the canal, was a double chain of saloons, whorehouses, cheap hotels. Before men dared to sleep in the local boardinghouses they drew a bolt across the door to their room. The shameless gambling, cheating, and all-night carousing drew forth sermons from the ministry, but not even the newspapers took such sermons seriously. As one local paper pointed out, "To live up to the reverend gentleman's standard the whole business world would have to be revolutionized."

It was so common for children to spend Sunday afternoon on the streets that a nondenominational mission school was started in the armory. The school's recruiting officer combed the town for boys loitering or playing marbles, and brought them to the services. Students at first received picture cards for attendance, an enticement that was hurriedly dropped when it was discovered that several boys were gambling for the picture cards by pitching pennies.

Eugene Debs, by spending Sunday at home, evaded both delinquency and mission school. Daniel was his usual companion; his mother and the girls were too busy cooking and sewing. A preference for classicism, which Daniel had learned from the

French dramatists and Daisy from the Catholic Church, required that all life be adorned with ritual. Countless hours were lavished on the chores of making clothing immaculate and meals grandiose, and always through the confusion moved Daisy—small, gentle, but complete master of each development. Sunday dinner was lifted into high ceremony, performed with gaiety but after the prescribed fashion. The huge mirth and the fine manner became for Eugene the structure of existence, until nothing could be done without an added flourish. This was even true of the hunting trips that he often took with Daniel. Equipment was always perfect when they marched off in quest of mushrooms; good dogs and a flawless shotgun went with them after snipe and prairie chickens. On these trips the boy learned the names of animals and flowers, the best swimming places, how thick the ice had to be before it was safe for skating. By comparison, pitching pennies was dull and mission school highly unpleasant.

Only once was Eugene inside a church, the day he ventured into St. Joseph's Cathedral. Years later he remembered the terrifying experience:

The priest delivered an address on Hell. I shall never forget it as long as I live. He pictured a thousand demons and devils with horns and bristling tails, clutching pitchforks steeped in brimstone, and threatening to consume all who did not accept the interpretation of Christianity as given by the priest. I left that church with a rich and royal hatred of the priest as a person, and a loathing for the church as an institution, and I vowed that I would never go inside a church again.

Because Eugene Debs thought that the church should preach love like Christ, not fear like a hangman, the vow was kept. On the flyleaf of a Bible which he received in 1868 as a prize in a spelling contest, his teacher had written: "Read and obey." Debs later commented tersely: "I never did either."

The end of the Civil War, although it may have gratified Daniel's ideals, gravely damaged his income. Trade fell off sharply at the store. Soldiers returning from the front were unable to find jobs. Wages, which had lagged behind rising prices throughout the war, dropped even farther. A business slump was beginning, and there were now six children in the family. Daisy had borne five more babies but only three had lived—Eugenie, Emma, and Theodore. Eugene, the only boy except for a year-old baby, was forced to spend much of his time clerking in the store. It was dull drudgery, for when you had learned that butter was a dime a pound, spring chickens a dime each, string beans a nickel a quart, you knew about all there was to know. The boy leaned on the counter and listened wistfully to the trains passing two blocks away.

A hope for relief from boredom came when he transferred to the public grammar school in 1867, and again when he began high school in 1869. But both times the hope proved vain; the schools offered only more reading, more writing, more ciphering. Even boyhood sports were lost to him because Daniel worked long hours in the store and Daisy said that he was too big to play marbles. One night Eugene accompanied his father to a vaudeville show and yearned to become a song-and-dance man, but the fancy soon wore off.

Always his thoughts kept returning to the men in blue denim jackets and engineers' caps. The closing years of the decade, in which freight engines crossed the continent to California, saw four new railroads lay their ties into Terre Haute. The population grew to sixteen thousand; by 1870 there were only three larger cities in Indiana. And in that same year, when he was fourteen years old, Eugene Debs quit high school. His parents opposed this decision, but he was eager to take some responsibility for feeding the large family, and he also still felt the lure of the railroad. Even Daniel was forced to admit that his son would never succeed in business—the boy's work at the store had been marked by over-weights and liberal credit—so the father agreed to ask a fellow Alsatian who worked in the paint-shop of the Vandalia line if there were vacancies there. Just a few months earlier the Vandalia shops had received their first important additions since their construction in 1853. The old enginehouse was now the erecting department; an enlarged roundhouse, a car shed, paintshops, a boiler department, a tinshop, a large planing mill, and a blacksmith shop were all standing. Terre Haute now had a labor shortage in contrast to the unemployment of 1866, and it was possible for a boy to find work.

On May 23, 1870, Eugene Debs—lean, six feet tall, with angular power—began cleaning grease from the trucks of freight engines. Now at last he was a railroader, but the haze of glamor grew thin at close range. The shops were cold and damp, the hours long and monotonous; the potash which he used to loosen the grease ate into his hands until they were raw and bled across the knuckles. For fifty cents a day he was compelled to be a whipping boy, take orders from everybody, stand for abuse and profanity and constant goading by men who were themselves goaded by other men. Two days' wages were spent to buy a paint scraper, and that evening he carved his name on the blade, up near the handle. He kept the tool until he died, a symbol of labor at fifty cents a day. At dusk his aching muscles dragged him home to a pallet stuffed with straw in the drafty attic which he now shared with Theodore; the next morning stiff legs were scarcely able to carry him back to the job. But he kept working from a sense of duty, grim stamina, delight in the roaring loco-motives, a joy at the pride in Daisy's eyes when he carried home his weekly pay check, the vain bluster with which he paraded in front of his admiring brother, Theodore. And then came pro-motions. He was sent out with a crew to paint every switch on the seventy miles of track between Terre Haute and Indianap-olis. Later he was permitted to paint simple stripes on car bodies, and finally to make lettering on locomotives.

For years Eugene Debs had been known as one of the most likeable boys in Terre Haute. His manner was open-handed and genuine in a way that demanded the same treatment. He did small favors for the women in the community and helped their husbands to repair buggy wheels or haul wood, but his generos-ity was usually directed toward the younger children. His pockets loaded with candy from his father's store, he passed it out with both hands to everybody he met. Word got around that he was an expert at making kites, and that he was eager to teach people how to fly them. As soon as Theodore was old enough to walk easily, the older brother taught him to ice-skate and to build rafts, took him for long tramps in the surrounding hills. Eugene's glamorous tales about railroading may have been prompted by a desire for personal recognition, but this possibility did not lessen Theodore's gratitude. Theodore came to have a blind, unqualified adoration of his older brother.

When Eugene began to paint signs for the railroad, his services to the community acquired a much greater value. The neighbors soon learned that Eugene Debs would paint a sign, any kind of sign, and wouldn't charge a penny for his work. This ability brought the young railroader added prestige, and it also gave him deep pride in his craftsmanship. He painted signs in black on large boards and then nailed on a wooden border. Even if Debs had no stencils and drew the letters freehand, they were round and fair. This printing, easily recognized as a professional job, was in strong contrast to Debs' writing, which sprawled forceful and ugly across the page. The printing, not the writing, was most typical of the man's viewpoint. Later in life, he frequently announced that incompetence was the best possible reason to fire a workman.

Eugene Debs' kindliness, which remained a dominant motive in his life, was rooted in his earliest memories. Daniel was known as a stern and retiring man, an unyielding disciplinarian. Even Daisy sometimes raised her hand in retribution against the children. But punishment was rare, and came only when it was deserved. Daniel Debs, who often seemed disagreeable to the outside world, was deeply revered by his children, and the reverence for Daniel was matched by their worship of Daisy. Although Daniel kept free of what he considered women's work around the house, this immunity did not extend to his sons. Eugene Debs spent so many hours helping Daisy in the kitchen that he became an excellent cook, an avocation that he enjoyed for the rest of his life. That enjoyment came partly from the memories of his parents' home and the affection that prevailed there. In 1899, Daisy and Daniel Debs celebrated their golden wedding anniversary in Terre Haute, with all their children present, and Eugene Debs paid tribute to his parents: "I can but say in the name of my sisters and my brothers and those younger in the bonds of family allegiance to our father . . . that we tender him our warmest congratulations upon this rare occasion. When we greet him our hearts are in our hands; when we kiss his time-furrowed cheeks our hearts are on our lips, and when we congratulate him upon this, his golden wedding anniversary, our hearts are in our words." Debs, however flowery his expression, was utterly sincere when he said on that occasion: "There are two words in our language forever sacred to memory— Mother and Home! Home, the heaven upon earth, and mother its presiding angel."

However, other men have loved their family and friends only to show cold indifference to those alien to themselves. Debs' moral strength came from his acceptance of responsibility for the welfare of strangers, and the reason again lies in his childhood. The home of Daniel Debs contained two books that left an enduring mark on his oldest son. Eugene automatically read the works of Schiller, who applauded the deeds of generous young men when they declared open warfare against all ugliness and cruelty. "The Hostage," written by this great German romanticist, remained Debs' favorite poem. Even more important was *Les Misérables*, Victor Hugo's story of Jean Valjean. Valjean, completely brutalized by poverty, stole a loaf of bread in order to feed his family, and was redeemed by the gentle friendship of a girl and a priest. *Les Misérables* captured Debs' emotions. He read it time after time throughout his life, and each time he swore his allegiance to its central theme. He talked about it constantly. He recommended it equally to his friends and to casual acquaintances.

Just a week before Christmas, 1871, the young railroader was forced to take a long step forward. On that night, while he was painting stripes on a car, the engineer from the yard engine snorted into the shop. The engineer's profane explosion ended with the statement that his damfool fireman had been too drunk to come to work, and that he needed somebody to shovel coal. Then he noticed the tall boy with the jutting jaw and the shock of thick brown hair. At that moment Eugene Debs, with his consent or without it, became à fireman. For the first time he

climbed onto a switch engine as a member of its crew. For the
first time he knew the biting cold on one side and the fury of heat
on the other, knew the smell of snow blowing through an open
cab.

He was soon given a job firing over the road from Terre Haute
to Indianapolis. His wages, which had been a dollar a night on
the switch engine, went even higher. He insisted on using the
extra money to go to business college every afternoon, crowding
his sleep into a few morning hours. His mother felt grave concern
over the boy's health, but Eugene drove himself because he
knew no other way to live. Daisy could understand that; for
all of her gentle ways and slight stature, she was the same res-
olute woman who had launched the Debs' grocery.

The young fireman continued to spend at home those rare
hours which were not needed for work, sleep, or school. The
Debs were such a close-knit family that they were called "clan-
nish" in a town sensitive to real or imagined snobbery. The
neighbors made other charges against Daniel. They said he was
grouchy. They could not understand his mushroom-hunting
and often remarked: "There goes that crazy Frenchman after
toadstools again." His position in the largely German community was made even more difficult in 1870 by the Franco-
Prussian War, which found Daniel an ardent advocate of the
French cause. But in 1871 Daniel gladly agreed to the marriage
of his oldest daughter Marie to John G. Heinl, a young German
immigrant who had come to Terre Haute a few years earlier
and had opened one of the first greenhouses in the town.

There were moments, during the years he worked on the railroad, when Eugene Debs thought he might have made a mistake
in leaving school. Eugene tried to study at home, but he found
it very difficult. His job took most of his time and energy, and
there were always chores to be done for his mother and for the
neighbors. He found it impossible to turn down any request for
help, and his reading in literature and railroad technology
seemed to move slowly. It was small consolation to know that
the local schools taught only the most elementary of subjects,
Eugene Debs continued to mourn his own lack of knowledge,

and he persuaded himself that this was due to his own action. In the spring of 1873, when his class graduated from high school, Debs lay on his bed and cried with anguish.

The following autumn he suffered an even greater blow. Investigation of the Credit Mobilier scandals by a Congressional committee had revealed widespread fraud in railroad construction, fraud in which Congressmen pulled the strings and shared the profits. Stockholders, panic-stricken by the danger to their investments, dumped their securities recklessly onto the market. Creditors clamored for their funds at railroad offices and banks. The largest financial house in America, Jay Cooke & Company, closed its doors on September 18; bankruptcy had been caused by overinvestment in the Northern Pacific Railroad. The price of farm products fell rapidly, but every price drop seemed to cause the piles of rotting corn and wheat to grow. Wages were slashed to the starvation level, but every wage cut seemed to throw more men out of work. The railroads shut down almost completely, and Eugene Debs was laid off by the Vandalia.

There were no railroad jobs in Terre Haute, and Debs rode the freights over the Chicago and Eastern Illinois to Evansville. Daisy had pleaded with him to stay at home, but Eugene had insisted that he was a locomotive fireman and intended to find work in his own trade. It was unpleasant to leave the security and prestige that he had known in Terre Haute; it became even more unpleasant when he was unable to find work in Evansville. He was apprehensive as he caught a freight car for St. Louis, but good luck came back to him, and there he was hired as a locomotive fireman.

St. Louis was the largest city that Debs had ever seen. It was also the city of greatest unhappiness. The depression prostrated the metropolitan workers. In a town like Terre Haute, most men owned their own homes and raised food in truck gardens, but food and shelter were fearful worries to the workingmen of St. Louis. Families were expelled from their homes and wandered aimlessly through the streets. Men left their wives and children behind them while they went elsewhere in search of work. Clapboard shanties began to spring up along the mud flats of the Mississippi River. Small children played in the mud, rolled in it, ate it. Eugene Debs saw these things; the plight of Jean Valjean was not, after all, merely a horrible dream in Victor Hugo's mind.

From these experiences Debs learned that his frustrations were not personal cares to be cherished in lonely bitterness. More than a dozen years passed before he began to understand the events of 1873. Nearly thirty years passed before he advocated a remedy. But he could already have said, as he did say later: "When I rise it will be with the ranks, and not from the ranks." This identification with workingmen implied faith in all workingmen, a confidence that they would move forward by virtue of their own courage and unity. Debs trusted these people so fully because he knew them so well. He had seen hungry families divide their food with the neighbors. That was enough for him.

The young fireman proved his basic soundness by his actions in St. Louis. Even when thus uprooted from his home and normal routine, he kept his balance and continued his studies. He read anything and everything, with no goal except a vague desire for more knowledge. He soon became an amateur authority on railroading. He remembered long sections of the French and German classics all his life. His engineer, with whom he shared a sleeping room during this period, would wake up, after the two men had returned from a long trip and gone wearily to bed, to find his roommate reading. He thought Debs quite considerate to have shaded the candle, but he always snorted that the young fireman was "a damn fool." Debs merely laughed, agreed that he probably was, and went ahead with his reading. Thirty years later, the engineer had changed his mind: "I still believe there was a damned fool in that room, but I know now that it wasn't Debs."

Debs' railroad career was abruptly terminated in 1874. His mother had been concerned for his safety since he first became a fireman. Now that his lanky figure no longer tramped in her kitchen each night, Daisy's concern had become panic, a justified feeling. Several railroads used unsafe equipment in order to cut their operating costs. Worn rails, merely turned over rather than replaced, broke under added strain. Defective boilers often exploded, setting fire to the wooden coaches. Faulty trestles collapsed under passing trains. A poor coupling system caused many railroaders to be smashed between cars. Injuries and deaths among train crews were so common that the newspapers paid little attention unless several passengers were also killed.

Finally, in the autumn of 1874, one of Eugene's friends slipped under a locomotive and was killed. That proved too much for Daisy, who wrote a letter to her son pleading with him to come home. The boy was confused and perplexed by his mother's anxiety. Daisy often commented about Eugene: "He listens to me attentively and respectfully—but has his own way." In this case, however, his affection for his mother proved dominant. He returned to Terre Haute and became a billing clerk at Hulman & Cox, the largest wholesale grocery company in the Midwest.

[4]

WHEN EUGENE DEBS left his job on the railroad, two main influences had shaped his nineteen-year-old mind: the humanitarianism of his family and the turbulent brutality of his frontier world. Saturated in Daniel's idealism, he had accepted the need for reflection, the belief in learning, the respect for human freedom and dignity. Debs' boyhood had spanned the Civil War and two depressions, catastrophes which had smashed all barriers between himself and his neighbors. He had heard about battle, known widows and orphans, seen crippled men stand alone on street corners. He had seen the unemployed shambling through the streets of St. Louis, and their children playing in the mud flats of the Mississippi River. Without knowing it, he had sunk his feet deep in the soil of the American Midwest.

Eugene Debs came to magnify the Midwestern virtues and to minimize the Midwestern faults, but even the faults he shared with others became a source of strength. Debs' influence with men and women was based on his similarity to them. He was able to understand their common mind because it was, in many ways, so exactly his mind. His generosity sometimes became mawkishness. His literary sense found satisfaction in both Goethe and ordinary doggerel. His delight in humor did not scruple at repeating Negro dialect jokes. He drank hard liquor because his fellows drank hard liquor. In his entire life, he never made an important decision on the basis of theoretical study. The facts of his own life kicked him into every step; often he required more than one kick. These faults, binding Eugene Debs to the men he knew and worked with, could scarcely be distinguished from his virtues.

Debs' mind often returned to the events of his early life. Although he had worked on the railroad less than five years, he had discovered the foundation for his entire career. "As a locomotive fireman," Debs wrote, "I learned of the hardships of the rail in snow, sleet and hail, of the ceaseless danger that lurks along the iron highway, the uncertainty of employment, scant wages and altogether trying lot of the workingman, so that from my very boyhood I was made to feel the wrongs of labor . . ."

CHAPTER 2

□

[*1*]

HERMAN HULMAN was glad to hire the son of his customer and good friend Daniel Debs. Hulman had been only twenty-two years old when he came to Terre Haute from Germany in 1854, and, with little capital, he had started a grocery store, then a wholesale grocery business. Next he installed a spice mill, and later he began roasting coffee. He worked hard, reinvested his profits, dabbled in real estate, kept his eye on the precious dollars. By 1874 his warehouse at Fifth Street and Wabash held one of the best concerns in the Midwest. Hulman thought he saw in Eugene Debs the same qualities which underlay his own success. Debs was honest and industrious, had modest needs. The boy's gaiety and kindness were so spontaneous that he would never be a trouble maker among the other employees.

Eugene Debs became a billing clerk. Every day tons of cartons, sacks, and bales moved through the warehouse, all cloaked in the heady odor of spices and dust. Debs had to keep track of every pound of it. The days became numbered boxes, one after another. He counted bags of coffee and made notations, then entered the notations in a ledger until his head ached. He hated the work. One afternoon Herman Hulman came to visit Daniel, and talked for hours about the limitless chances for a young man in the grocery business. But Eugene Debs was not impressed.

"There are too many things in business that I cannot tolerate," Debs wrote. "Business means grabbing for yourself." This attitude had already begun to take shape in 1874, but there were few outward signs. In his work he was efficient and cheerful, and he was soon on intimate terms with Herman Hulman, with the chief bookkeeper, Theodore Markle, and with the other employees. Debs smiled, joked, told stories, and did his job, but

20

the grocery house failed to enlist all of his abilities. His evenings and week ends were free of responsibilities; he used them to keep in touch with his old friends on the railroads.

He often walked down to the tracks in the evening to watch the engines back and switch, to see the repairmen fix broken couplings and the firemen throw wood into the roaring flames. The lanky figure of the billing clerk was often found in the saloons near the station, hunched over the bar to hear yarns that came from a dozen states. There one evening Debs heard that Joshua Leach, the Grand Master of the Brotherhood of Locomotive Firemen, was coming to Terre Haute to organize a union. Debs, although he knew nothing about unions, decided to go.

At the meeting, Leach told about the purposes of his organization, explaining that it tried to offer cheap insurance and a fraternal spirit to men who needed both. Debs felt drawn to Leach's "rugged honesty, simple manner, and homely speech." He leaned forward eagerly to hear this vivid plan. It brought to life a vision of firemen joining hands in a common cause. Here was the spirit of the French Revolution: Liberty, Equality, Fraternity. When the meeting ended, Debs went up to the front of the hall and asked to join Vigo Lodge.

Leach looked with surprise at this well-dressed youth who confessed that he no longer worked on a railroad. But he could not afford to be discriminating; in nearly two years of constant effort, he had organized only thirty-one lodges and six hundred members. He asked only one question: "If I admit you, do you think you can do your duty?" Debs had no precise idea what his duty would be, so he said simply, "Yes sir." Then he felt a hand slap his shoulder and heard a voice say, "My boy, you're a little young, but I believe you're in earnest and will make your mark in the Brotherhood."

His initiation into Vigo Lodge represented a continuation and a new beginning for Eugene Debs. Through his veins had flowed the needs and hopes of his ancestors, his family, his friends on the railroads, to find expression in the beliefs of his father. But Daniel's sentimental faith in human brotherhood had been a mere ideal; with Eugene it was to become a way of living. Yet

Debs joined Vigo Lodge for reasons that he could not have explained. The principal one, perhaps, was simply that he was an energetic young man who loved railroading and hated the grocery business.

Railroad expansion and combination during the 1850's had changed the local companies into nation-wide giants. The former paternalism became less common; wages were cut; the working day was lengthened. The first railroad craft to revolt against these changes was the most skilled, the locomotive engineers, who organized a Brotherhood in 1863. But strikes on the Chicago & Galena and on the Michigan Southern were broken by the combined power of the railroads, and the engineers decided to retreat. In 1867 they accepted a new theory: If we improve the efficiency of our members, the railroads will recognize our value and voluntarily increase wages. The only remaining incentives to join the Brotherhood were cheap insurance and the satisfaction of membership in a rather snobbish society. This same pattern was accepted by the Order of Railway Conductors, founded in 1868, and by the Brotherhood of Locomotive Firemen.

It was a pattern that suited Eugene Debs. He well knew the need of the firemen for cheap life insurance; the high accident rate on the railroads had forced his own retirement. The wages of firemen did not permit them to pay the premiums charged by private companies; so, if they were injured or killed, their families were forced to rely on charity. The sole escape from this impoverishment rested in a co-operative insurance order of the workers themselves, and the BLF, together with the other two Brotherhoods, aimed to meet this need.

Debs was elected first secretary of Vigo Lodge No. 16, a post that brought him into the closest touch with its affairs. He went to every meeting in order to keep the minutes, and often heard bitter protests against the low wages and speed-up conditions on the roads. This had little meaning for a man who spent his working day in a gray suit and stiff collar, solemnly entering figures and making out bills under the lax supervision of Hulman, more friend than employer. Firemen in the saloons sullenly muttered against the arrogance of their bosses, and Debs said nothing. All day he worked behind a desk at Hulman's; in the evening he worked behind a desk at home. He really understood only one thing about the BLF—its insurance system. Letters by the score went out from Debs to lodges all over the country, inquiries about accidents, descriptions of wrecks, claims for benefits. Each one began "Dear Brother" and ended "Fraternally yours."

The Order was so small that Leach knew every member, and he noticed the boundless activity of the secretary of Vigo Lodge. Soon he was boasting about Debs to a meeting in St. Louis: "I put a tow-headed boy in the brotherhood at Terre Haute not long ago, and some day he will be at the head of it." Leach was right; it was the kind of order in which a billing clerk would rise quickly, but most of the other members were dropping out. The firemen were not interested in insurance; they could not even afford to pay the premiums. They wanted an organization that would stop the wrecks, raise their wages, shorten their hours, take the boss off their necks. The BLF was concerned with one thing; the workers were concerned with quite different objectives. Debs watched in despair as the national membership fell rapidly. Several times he was the only person present at meetings of Vigo Lodge. He sat quietly until it was time to adjourn; then picked up his minute book and went home. Two weeks later he was back in the hall, waiting again.

It is difficult to say precisely why Debs did not desert the dying organization. His devotion was partly due to his belief in the purposes of the BLF, partly to mere obstinacy, partly to the absence of an alternative outlet for his energy. Although he was often discouraged, he continued his desperate efforts to rebuild Vigo Lodge. But he had not yet found the key to success.

When the railroad workers revolted against their conditions in July, 1877, the BLF was a bystander. Both the Pennsylvania and the Baltimore & Ohio had posted notices of wage cuts. The workers decided that the companies could go to hell. Engineers and firemen stepped down from their cabs. In West Virginia, Maryland, and Pennsylvania, crowds of strikers blocked the tracks to keep scabs from running the trains.

Pinkerton detectives and state militia began to move against the strikers. President Hayes sent Federal troops into West Virginia and Maryland in response to appeals from the governors. The revolt spread to Pittsburgh, where an enraged mob burned several Pennsylvania shops, a hundred locomotives, and five hundred freight cars. The local militia refused to fire on the rioters, but soldiers imported from Philadelphia killed twenty-six unarmed persons. The Locomotive Engineers and the Order of Railway Conductors furnished strikebreakers to the railroads. The strikers, thus faced by the railroads, state militia, Pinkertons, Federal troops, and hostile unions, were overwhelmed. More than a hundred workers were killed and several hundred others wounded. Two weeks after the strike began, railroaders were pleading for their old jobs. But the blacklist was still in good condition; the railroads were again cleared of the aggressive union men.

These developments confused and stunned Eugene Debs. The *Locomotive Firemen's Magazine*,* official journal of the BLF, charged that the railroads' "system of oppression" had caused the walkout. Although Debs, now a national officer of the order, agreed with *The Magazine*, he was more concerned about the violence that accompanied the strike. In a speech to the BLF national convention in Indianapolis soon after the end of the disturbances, Debs declared:

This continual reduction of the price of labor was the direct cause of the recent strikes which terrified the entire nation. A strike at the present time signifies anarchy and revolution, and the one of but a few days ago will never be blotted from the records of memory. The question has often been asked, Does the brotherhood encourage strikers? To this question we must emphatically answer, No, brothers. To disregard the laws which govern our land? To destroy the last vestige of order? To stain our hands with the crimson blood of our fellow beings? We again say, No, a thousand times No!

For this flaming bit of oratory, Debs was congratulated by Riley McKeen, his personal friend and the president of the Vandalia Railroad. Surely the young delegate deserved praise, if

* Hereafter called *The Magazine*.

not for the viewpoint he expressed, at least for the diligence
with which he had studied public speaking.

[2]

DEBS' ATTEMPTS to educate himself were one of the ruling
threads in his life. His first wages from Hulman's were used to
buy Appleton's *Encyclopedia*. For months he pondered over
Voltaire's *Philosophical Dictionary*, a gift from Daniel. He began to squander his money on books, buying his first dictionary
and a five-year subscription to Horace Greeley's New York
Tribune.

From Appleton's *Encyclopedia* Debs gained his first knowledge of American history. It was natural that the Revolution
of 1776 should be his main interest. From Daniel he had learned
the history of France, including the part that his own ancestors
had played during the uprising there in 1789. The stirring tale
of conflict between the thirteen colonies and the mother country furnished Eugene Debs with two new heroes, Thomas
Paine and Patrick Henry. "The revolutionary history of the
United States and France stirred me deeply and its heroes and
martyrs became my idols," he wrote. "Thomas Paine towered
above them all. A thousand times since then I have found inspiration and strength in the stirring words, 'These are the
times that try men's souls!' "

Never content to keep his knowledge as a personal trinket,
Debs now helped to found the Occidental Literary Club, a
weekly debating society. When his turn came to speak, Debs
chose to give Patrick Henry's famous oration. It roused him as
both philosophy and rhetoric; he was certain that it would also
rouse an audience. Struggling into his black suit, stiff collar,
and flowing tie, Debs gaily rehearsed his speech to himself.
The sight of the crowded hall made him even more jubilant.
Theodore was there, frankly proud of his big brother. Daisy
and Daniel had come, expecting the best. Every seat was filled;
people were standing at the sides and back.

But the time for the meeting arrived, and the other scheduled
speaker did not. The realization that he would have to give the

entire program proved disastrous for Debs. As he rose to speak, the faces in the audience seemed like the faces of hostile witnesses. Sweat ran down his stomach, his hands were cold. He forgot his lines, lost his voice, muffed his climax—it was dismal. When he had gasped, "I know not what course others may take; but as for me, give me liberty or give me death!" he bolted through the door and walked home through alleys so that he would not have to face his friends.

One disgrace was enough, thought Debs, and a multitude of compliments did not wipe out his shame. He could have forsworn oratory completely, but that solution he swiftly rejected. He began to practice at home, reciting to his family, rehearsing gestures before a mirror, polishing, drilling, perfecting. From French literature he had learned meter and climax; from constant effort he learned poise and platform technique. Gradually the tenseness passed, and that autumn he gave the keynote speech at the BLF convention in Indianapolis.

Early in 1878 the Occidental Literary Club decided to sponsor several lectures by prominent men. Robert G. Ingersoll, who had written the article that had awakened Debs' interest in Tom Paine, was chosen to begin the series. Ingersoll, powerful, handsome, magnificent of voice, was nearing the height of his reputation as an orator. A brilliant speech at the Republican convention of 1876 had placed his name in the headlines, and his attacks on religious dogma had kept it there. Ingersoll's manager merely repeated the public estimate in his advice to Debs: "Boldly announce him as the greatest orator in the world. *He is.*"

When Debs met his guest at the Terre Haute station, he was captured by Ingersoll's humanitarianism, and later that evening he was overwhelmed by the elaborate form of the lecture on "The Liberty of Man, Woman and Child." Every sentence was in rhythm; every line contained the right number of prose feet. The speech was studded with quotations and climaxed by a glittering peroration. The clamorous applause of that night's audience persuaded the Club to bring Ingersoll back a few months later to lecture about Robert Burns. An autumn downpour on the crucial night raised the threat of a small crowd and financial loss, but Ingersoll offered: "Boys, don't worry in the least. If the rain keeps people away I will charge you nothing for the lecture and pay my own expenses." As Debs, Ingersoll, and Daniel Voorhees, still Congressman from Terre Haute, boarded the streetcar for the Opera House, Voorhees predicted that there was no need to worry: "Colonel Ingersoll is the only man in America who can draw against the elements and fill the biggest house on the rainiest night." That prediction proved right—the hall was again jammed with wildly cheering spectators.

But the speaker's most avid admirer was Eugene Debs. Debs was so entranced that he walked to the station with Ingersoll. Even then he could not break away. He rode all the way to Cincinnati before he could force himself to return home.

Ingersoll's indictment of religion was soon followed by Wendell Phillips' scathing attack on monopoly power, growing so rapidly since the Civil War. Like Ingersoll, Phillips was too prominent to boycott; but Terre Haute revolted against an invitation to Susan B. Anthony, who shockingly advocated votes for women. Although the Occidental Club refused to sponsor Miss Anthony, Debs would not drop the project. He rented a hall himself, met the speaker at the station and escorted her to a hotel. As they walked down the street through the jeers and hostile glances of the townspeople, Miss Anthony bore herself with dignity and courage. "It would not have required any great amount of egging on," Debs later wrote, "to have excited the people to drive her from the community. Even my friends were disgusted with me for piloting such an 'undesirable citizen' into the community." The Terre Haute *Express* did not approve of woman suffrage, but it admitted that "Miss Anthony's lecture was . . . replete with well-stated facts in support of her arguments." And the meeting, although a failure, was beneficial to Debs. His rôle in the affair earned him the friendship of Mrs. Ida H. Harper, a neighbor and pioneer feminist. Also his first intimate contact with prejudice merely steeled Debs' belief that women were entitled to "any right or opportunity that man enjoyed."

Another experience emphasized the herd instinct in Terre

Haute. One evening Debs read in the newspaper an anonymous sketch of Hoosier childhood that captured his imagination. This sketch seemed so true to his own boyhood that he was instantly attracted to its author. When inquiries revealed that it had been written by James Whitcomb Riley, an unknown poet on the Indianapolis *Journal*, Debs caught a train to Indianapolis. Riley was in another city giving one of his dialect monologues, and Debs contented himself with scheduling an early performance in Terre Haute. Three times the Occidental Literary Club sponsored appearances by Riley, and each meeting was a failure. Although Debs was very fond of Riley's impersonations of the homespun farmer and the dandified schoolmaster teaching a country class, he seemed alone in his opinion. Then the well-known humorist Bill Nye invited Riley to give his act before an audience of celebrities at the Academy of Music in New York City. Literally overnight the Hoosier poet became a featured attraction. The next time he visited Terre Haute, the auditorium there was completely filled at a dollar a person. The entrance to the hall was littered with articles of wearing apparel that had been torn off and lost in the scramble to get inside.

[*3*]

THE DEPRESSION OF 1873 caused a powerful ground swell in the political reform movement. Farmers were trapped between the falling prices for their products and the combination of high mortgage rates, excessive prices for farm machinery, and extortionate rates set by the new railroad monopolies. Severe deflation created a demand for paper money and lent new frenzy to the Greenback movement. The working people, seeing their trade unions smashed by the gigantic power of the employers, also sought some relief through political channels.

Debs inevitably was captured by this flood. When he mounted the platform on August 30, 1878, for his first political speech, it was to champion the cause of the poor, the oppressed, the crucified, and the Democratic party. His youth was offset by his eloquence and his prestige with the workingmen. Almost immediately the local Democratic leaders offered him the nomination for Congress. Unwillingness to leave his family and the Brotherhood prompted Debs to decline. But the next year he was the Democratic nominee for City Clerk in Terre Haute, and easily won by an 1,100 majority. The entire Democratic slate was swept into office, including Ida Harper's husband Tom as the new City Attorney.

Debs, a naïve reformer, and Harper, a cynical one, were soon the centers of a vigorous battle. Terre Haute was then one of the most vice-ridden cities in America; the entire West End, colorfully known as the Tenderloin, was a sinful wilderness of gin-mills and whorehouses. A principal task of the City Clerk was to collect the fines levied against prostitutes who were picked up on the streets, but Debs refused to be strict with women who already had enough worries. He was told that it was his duty. He still refused, and Tom Harper supported him.

The failure of the police to bring in the pimps and vice-kings merely strengthened Harper's contempt for law-enforcement officers. Some years later, a popular policeman died suddenly and his friends decided to raise a fund for a large funeral. Harper, who gave freely to any cause, was approached for a contribution. When he heard the purpose of the fund, Harper was delighted to comply: "Did you say you want a dollar to help bury a policeman? Well, here are five—bury that many while you are at it."

In 1881 Debs ran for re-election. His job as City Clerk made him the trusted associate of politicians, businessmen, labor leaders; it was clearly preferable to working as a billing clerk at Hulman's. Two years earlier he had been pushed into office; he now was forced to fight for his job. He fought well. Although the Democratic ticket went down to defeat, Debs and one other member were kept in office. Debs received two more votes than in 1879.

His success was partly due to the political sagacity of Tom Harper, public support by Riley McKeen, president of the Vandalia Railroad and a prominent banker, and editorial tub-thumping by Colonel O. J. Smith of the *Gazette*. But the main cause was simply that men liked him. Debs knew every voter in town and called each one by his first name. He played with their children and carried groceries home for their wives. His leniency toward the prostitutes convinced some men that he was a dangerous idiot, but it persuaded many that he was a kindly saint. Debs often greeted his friends by kissing them on each cheek; the few people who did not like him still received a smile and a kind word. Men found it hard to vote against a person who ignored their rudeness and offered them friendship in return.

Even after his election as City Clerk, Debs worked each night on his duties in the Brotherhood. In 1878 he had been named assistant editor of *The Magazine;* and the editorial work, the advertising, and much of the copy depended on his efforts. Each dawn heralded sixteen hours of fierce, unrelenting toil at the City Hall and at home. When the Occidental Literary Club held a debate on the topic, "Hard Work versus Genius," Debs unhesitatingly championed "Hard Work" and was persuasive enough to convince the judges that "genius is a nonentity."

Then, early in 1880, Debs was given even heavier duties in the Brotherhood. The man who had been editor of *The Magazine* and secretary-treasurer of the order was expelled for drunkenness, and Grand Master Frank Arnold asked Debs to take both jobs. Debs refused. Three times Arnold and Grand Instructor Sam Stevens went to Debs and asked him to change his mind. Debs just didn't see how he could do it. He had a good chance for political advancement—Congress looked like the next step. He'd be a fool to give up his career to work for the bankrupt Brotherhood, which had only sixty lodges and a debt of six thousand dollars.

Probably the outcome of these discussions was decided as soon as S. M. Stevens said to Debs, "You can save the brotherhood." After the great strike of 1877, Debs had tried to save Vigo Lodge because of his belief in its purposes. Now he had an added reason. A portion of his life was bound up with the Brotherhood of Locomotive Firemen. To acknowledge defeat would be to acknowledge error, to admit that railroad workers did not need an organization. Debs could not do that. Having made many sacrifices, he was prompted to make even more and greater ones. So the BLF moved its national offices to Terre Haute, and Eugene Debs became the new secretary-treasurer and editor of *The Magazine*.

Debs' faith in the righteousness of his own decisions was a main source of his strength. He seldom hesitated to ask others to follow the road that he had chosen. Many persons agreed, more from faith in the spokesman than from faith in the cause. Debs now involved both family and friends in the task of reviving the Brotherhood. Theodore, his young brother, gave up a partnership in a local haberdashery to become the BLF bookkeeper at a salary of ten dollars a week. Emma Debs resigned a seventy-five-dollar a month job teaching school, and she and Eugenie became unpaid stenographers. Tom Harper became adviser, attorney, and theoretician of the revamped organization. A Woman's Department was established in *The Magazine* and turned over to Ida Harper, with instructions to get the railroaders' wives interested in the Brotherhood.

Several debts demanded immediate attention. A thousand dollars was needed to pay benefit claims to injured members. The firm that printed *The Magazine* held over-due bills for eighteen hundred dollars. Back salaries were due to all of the officers. When Debs took office, the Brotherhood's safe held $98.90 cash, a bank draft for twenty dollars, and $183.60 in postal money orders. But within a week, stopgap measures had been found. Debs gave his personal note to secure the debt to the printing firm and paid the insurance claims from his own pocket. All the officers and employees agreed that no salaries should be paid until the crisis had passed. As a final step, Debs persuaded several Terre Haute businessmen, including his father and Riley McKeen, to guarantee the Brotherhood's credit by posting a bond.

It seemed possible that all of these efforts would be wasted. When the national convention met in September, 1880, most of the delegates wanted to give up the struggle. But Eugene Debs had hypnotized himself into the belief that victory was certain. He went from room to room in the hotel where the delegates were staying, pleading with them to stick it out, promising that the Brotherhood would be a solvent organization within a year.

Man after man swung over to his side. They all knew that Gene Debs would give them the shirt off his back—he had done just that too often to leave room for dispute. When he wrapped his long arm around a man's shoulder and started to laugh, it wasn't likely that the man would say No. During the entire convention, not a single delegate moved to dissolve the BLF. Debs had won a year's grace. Now he had to make good his promises.

After the convention, Debs went back to his job as City Clerk of Terre Haute. The chief problem now was increasing the membership, and that was in the hands of S. M. Stevens and Frank Arnold. Debs made a few organizing trips around Indiana on weekends, but most of his leisure time was spent working on correspondence and the benefit claims. It was maddening to be tied down at the City Hall while his associates were fighting the good fight, but he was heartened by the knowledge that Stevens and Arnold were showing results. The membership rolls began to lengthen; dues payments began to increase. And in the Brotherhood's office in Terre Haute, Eugene Debs slouched in an armchair, laughed until the walls rocked and said that he thought they'd survive. Theodore, still only seventeen years old, grinned boyishly and buckled into his bookkeeping with renewed vigor.

While the BLF officers were desperately trying to save the Order, several railroad executives were planning new ways to destroy it. The 1877 strike had practically wiped out the railroad unions, and to finish the job the blacklist was revived, yellow-dog contracts became common. Mere suspicion of union membership was reason for discharge. Brotherhood officials who had formerly been given free passage over the railroads found this privilege was now revoked. Each day brought some new insult, and always Debs struck back with heedless fury.

One morning a minor BLF official came to Terre Haute, complaining that he had been thrown out of the office of a vice-president of the Pennsylvania Railroad. Debs picked up his hat, took a firm grip on the recent victim, and caught the next freight for Columbus and the offices of the Pennsylvania. When the two unionists walked into the vice-president's office, the executive set matters straight to start with: "Before we go any further, I want you to know, Debs, that I don't give a God damn for the Brotherhood of Locomotive Firemen." The answer was equally blunt: "And I want you to know that I don't give a God damn for the Pennsylvania Railroad. I'm not here to get your opinion. I'm here to get courteous treatment for our officials."

They were both big men, accustomed to shouting above the noise of a locomotive cab. Debs' astonished companion later said, "When they got going good you could hear them clear across Franklin County." The argument lasted for an hour, profane, bellicose, unyielding, abusive. Finally the executive paused, grinned, and offered Debs a job with the railroad. All he got was a curt refusal. Openly admiring, he next offered an annual pass on the Pennsylvania. Debs refused that also, but took a trip pass to get back to Terre Haute. He had his own ideas about gifts from corporation executives to union officials.

For a few months the union officials had little trouble with the Pennsylvania, but this incident had a more important result. All the way across the great plains, from the Alleghenies to the Rocky Mountains, men told how Debs had stood up to the vice-president. The story was repeated around the freightyards, above the clamor in the roundhouse, over beer in a thousand junction towns. Its hard-bitten dignity touched a dream that ran deep in men on the frontier. Debs' vigor and personal reputation began to draw men into the Brotherhood; Arnold and Stevens were working frantically; the temper of the railroaders was beginning to turn toward organization and resistance. By 1881 the membership had doubled; the next year it doubled again to reach five thousand. The debt had been wiped out. *The Magazine* was now read far beyond the ranks of the BLF.

Debs' contribution to this growth brought him new prestige; the union's 1882 convention at Terre Haute was largely a tribute to his efforts. When other men had wavered, he had stood firm as a rock. He had brought to the labor movement a determination and concentrated force which astonished his fellow officers. He worked with an urgency that affected his colleagues, and even his mother. Often Daisy went to her son's room long after midnight and found him asleep over a half-written letter.

With silent reproach, she turned out the lamp and left him slumped across the desk. The next morning he usually began working again before he had even finished breakfast. The problems of the firemen were Debs' whole life—yellow-dog contracts, the blacklist, poverty, accidents, corporate arrogance and corporate greed.

But Debs was still certain that labor disputes could be solved by reason and compromise. At the 1880 convention he told the delegates:

> In times gone by, laboring men who had been imposed on, formed themselves into a mob and with a recklessness that makes us shudder, began to burn and plunder the property of the corporations they were working for. . . .
> While we always sympathized with these deluded and miserable wretches, we have always felt that they were wrong in acting so violently. There is a different way of settling difficulties between employer and employee. Our organization believes in arbitration. . . .

Two years later, he took editorial notice of the fact that William H. Vanderbilt, "the great railroad president," had endorsed the principles of the BLF. "Not only have we met with these encouraging words from Mr. Vanderbilt," said the editorial, "but many other railroad officials have stood by us and given kindly words of sympathy."

Such statements quickly earned Debs recognition as a leading spokesman for conservative policies. His union had long been clasped to the bosom of the railroad corporations; he was now trying to snuggle closer.

CHAPTER 3

□

[*1*]

EUGENE DEBS would make a good husband. Terre Haute women with daughters of marrying age in 1882 all thought so, and their daughters sighed agreement. Dozens of young ladies gazed covetously after the handsome City Clerk as he glad-handed his way through the streets and public buildings. With his personal charm, Debs had prestige. At the age of twenty-six years, he was nationally known as a leader of the respectable Brotherhood of Locomotive Firemen, and he was powerful in local politics. He was even said to admit privately that he wanted to be President—no impossibility for a vigorous and eloquent young man. Debs filled every requirement of the eligible bachelor.

The resultant web of jealousy and intrigue always encountered the same obstacle—Debs. He had never been known to pay much attention to any girl. When he went for long tramps through the woods on bright spring mornings, Theodore tramped by his side. His social life consisted of occasional drinking sprees which carried him through every saloon in town, accompanied by his railroad friends or by Jamey Riley. He was never seen at dances or parties. With girls he was polite and cordial, never more than that. The local maidens began to think that there was little hope, and gradually the hunt turned to less desirable but more responsive game.

But Kate Metzel was long on staying power. Born twenty-five years earlier in Louisville, she knew poverty and hard work. Her father had died when she was a child, leaving a penniless wife to care for Kate and an older brother, Dan. After a desperate struggle to support her two children, the mother married John Jacob Baur, a widower with four children, and the family moved to Terre Haute, where four more children were born to the middle-aged couple. Baur, a shrewd, industrious Swiss immigrant, measured success solely in dollars; by 1880 his drug-store at Seventh and Wabash Avenue was the largest in town. He sent all of his sons to college or to Europe, but, in accordance with the tradition of both Switzerland and Indiana, his daughters were denied these advantages. Kate was tied to a daily routine of housework, caring for the younger children, washing and ironing dozens of shirts and collars for her brothers who went to college or worked in the store. The neighbors often saw her at night through the open windows, tall, proud, reserved, still busy with the chores. Her normal wishes for excitement and prestige, striking the barrier of reality, were exaggerated into abnormal ambition. Her hunger for jewelry and fine clothes was soon exceeded by her hunger for social standing.

Marie Heinl, Debs' oldest sister, was one of the few close friends of this singular girl. She, like Kate, knew the ruling hand of pride and dignity. At Marie's home, Kate Metzel often met Eugene Debs. Soon Kate became a regular visitor at the home of Daisy and Daniel, and the neighbors began to say that she was conducting a well-planned campaign. Certainly she was attracted to the gentle young City Clerk, who was able to understand the ways in which drudgery can disfigure dreams. Debs, for his part, might have seen in Kate Metzel the qualifications that his wife would need. Kate lacked the charm and kindliness that marked Eugene; she was ambitious and even self-centered; but she also had great strength within herself. She would never interfere with a man's decisions or try to control his life. She too recognized that Eugene Debs "has his own way," and that he alone would make the important decisions in his life.

Neither Kate nor Debs had the necessary temperament for a whirlwind romance. She often contrived to stay at the Debs' home until late at night, so that the chivalrous Eugene would feel obliged to take her home. Kate walked solemnly along at Eugene's side, listening to his personal plans, his plans for the welfare of workingmen. Although she failed to grasp many of his ideas, she was captivated by the fervor of his words. By May of 1882, Debs was definitely a suitor, but a very unorthodox one; as a present he gave Kate a bound volume of *The Magazine.*

[2]

EUGENE DEBS, in spite of his office in the BLF, was still unaware of the breadth of the labor movement. A business revival in 1880 had given new strength to the trade unions. The Knights of Labor, whose organizers had moved mysteriously through the railroad strikes of 1877, had now emerged from secrecy and was growing into a large movement. But the K of L was a reform organization rather than a trade union, admitting farmers, employers, everybody except lawyers and saloonkeepers. The trade unionists felt the need for a federation concerned solely with the welfare of the wage-workers; during the summer of 1881, nine men met in Terre Haute to discuss the formation of a national order of workingmen. Unable to take decisive action, they issued a call for a general conference in Pittsburgh that autumn.

The Federated Trades and Labor Council, which soon became the American Federation of Labor, was founded at the Pittsburgh meeting. The structure of the new federation was shaped in large measure by the ideas of Samuel Gompers. Only thirty-one years old, Gompers was already the chieftain of the New York cigarmakers. With severe handicaps—he was short, incredibly ugly, and a Jewish immigrant from the ghetto of London—he had become a leader by virtue of an iron will and a passionate belief in the labor movement. He had once been friendly with the radicals of New York City, but by 1881 he was concentrating solely on the economic organization of skilled workers.

From theoretical study and broken strikes, Gompers and the cigarmakers had fashioned a rigid creed: organize all workers; control working conditions in the shop; build the financial strength of the union. They charged high dues to finance unemployment and death benefits. By providing that no strike benefits would be paid unless the walkout had been approved by the national union, they guarded against spontaneous strikes, which usually ended in starvation and chaos. They found jobs for their members. They lobbied for legislation to enforce an eight-hour day, abolish child labor, and establish bureaus of labor statistics in all states. The pattern worked out by the cigarmakers was gradually adopted by most of the other unions connected with the new federation. The federation itself was intended to act as a court to settle jurisdictional disputes between unions, a center to organize new crafts, a source of support in strikes, and a legislative lobby to advance the cause of the workers.

Trade unionists from Indiana played a leading role in these developments. Mark Moore, who published a labor paper in Terre Haute, was secretary of the nine-man organizing committee. Samuel Leffingwell, an Indianapolis printer, presided at the Pittsburgh conference. Debs was either ignorant or indifferent to these developments until after the founding convention. But when P. J. McGuire, a genial and persuasive Irishman who headed the carpenters' union, visited Terre Haute, Debs quickly called together several of his acquaintances and helped McGuire to found a new local in the craft. Debs also organized the shop which printed *The Magazine*, wrote the constitution for a branch of the International Typographical Union, and cheerfully advanced money to meet its bills. *The Magazine* thus became the first official labor publication in the country to carry the union label, an honor about which Debs never tired of boasting.

A railroad brakeman who wanted to organize his craft came all the way from New York to get Debs' help. Debs drafted a constitution for the Brotherhood of Railroad Brakemen, drew up the Order's bankbooks and printed forms, gave his visitor some tips about unionism. He then took the man downtown and secured credit for him from every merchant with whom the BLF did business. When the brakeman was ready to leave Terre Haute, Debs asked a conductor to give him a trip pass. The conductor readily agreed, but when told the traveler's mission he derisively snorted: "Brotherhood of Railroad Brakemen! What next!" Ignoring the hostility of the Engineers and the Order of Railway Conductors, Debs wrote in *The Magazine* an open letter to all members of the BLF: "I want you to do me a personal favor; I want you to find a brakeman; I want you to hand him this letter, and ask him to get a few brakemen together and organize a lodge of the Brotherhood of Railroad Brakemen, because if there is any class of men in this country who need organization, it is the brakemen." The pocket of Eugene Debs became a general treasury for any trade union that needed money, and most of them did. Although he earned six thousand dollars in his four years as City Clerk and his Brotherhood salary was supposedly fifteen hundred a year, he had not saved a dollar by January, 1884, when his second term as City Clerk expired.

Now he really needed money. Freed from daily attendance at the City Hall, he grabbed the chance to set up new lodges all over the country. From coast to coast he followed the iron rails, riding in the cab if the crew was friendly, occasionally paying his fare, usually so broke that he caught a freight train, going wherever there were railroaders. Disappointments were frequent, hardships continuous, victories rare. In Elmira, New York, he was forced to jump from a moving train and fortunately fell in a snowdrift. One rainy night the police drove him out of a station yard and threatened to arrest him after he had waited for hours to see a fireman. When he arrived in Vicksburg, Mississippi, he was too poor to hire a hall, so he persuaded the fire chief to let him use a large room over the fire station for a meeting. Only three men came to the meeting; the others were afraid of losing their jobs. Leaving the three men behind, Debs went out on a tour through the saloons, and was overjoyed to find two other railroaders. When he got back to the hall with his two captives, the other three men had left.

It was slow, gruelling work, but he kept at it. He slept on the floor in cabooses, occasionally found a bunk in a junction house. He ate what he could find, wherever he happened to be. And everywhere he went he talked to the railroad workers—switchmen, section hands, Negro porters, firemen, the haughty engineers. The depression which had started in 1883 was again cutting living standards; the men all talked about low wages, piece rates, unsteady employment, the arrogance of the super-intendents. Now if ever, the workers needed unions. Besides building lodges of the BLF, Debs helped to form the Brother-hood of Railroad Car Men and to expand a local union in Chi-cago, the Switchmen's Mutual Aid Association, into a flourish-ing national organization.

He drove himself fiercely, desperately, until his strength failed or his need for advice and comfort carried him back to Terre Haute, to Daisy and Daniel, to Theodore, to Kate. Al-ways Kate was there, calm, sympathetic. They went for long walks along the towpath that bordered the old canal bed, while Debs talked vividly about the railroad towns, about the fear of the workers in Vicksburg, the callousness of company de-tectives, the poverty and bleak dread of his country and his people. He sometimes sounded listless, but when he spoke of what he had seen and what he hoped, burning words came from some hidden source. His supple hands moved in the air, making visions of the white-walled cities that men would some day build on earth. Although Kate would never have cared about the labor movement had it not been for the personality of the man who walked beside her, she felt strangely drawn by his candor and persuasiveness. Debs too felt the bonds that tied him to this woman, her independence and understanding. Life was too in-secure for a single person with no anchor, no foundation. One day he asked her to marry him. She accepted, but they were not married until more than a year later.

Debs would not stop his work, would not change his life. Even in Terre Haute he could not rest. Workers came to tell him their problems; he was asked to lend money and to officiate at fun-erals. He investigated every railroad accident that happened in the state, taking careful notes to be used in editorial demands for safety legislation. In Terre Haute the deaths were many— William Saunders, charter member of Vigo Lodge; Bill Morgan, veteran railroader and pioneer member of the Engineers. Ten years after Vigo Lodge was founded, only four of the twenty-one original members still answered the roll call. Some of the others had dropped out, but many had lost their lives. Debs had to make out all of the checks for death benefits; he knew how many there were. The list kept mounting—a thousand dollars to the widow, a thousand dollars to the widow, always the same, never different. He was thinking of names, places, when he solemnly said: "There are many homes that would be shadowed in gloom but for the Brotherhood."

The BLF continued to stand aloof from the more radical philosophy of Sam Gompers and the new federation. In 1879 the BLF convention had adopted a policy of "ignoring strikes," and that provision was rigidly enforced. The Brotherhood said that it was an insurance organization, denied that it was a trade union, carefully courted the favor of companies, but many railroads continued to be hostile. Debs fought vigorously against individual acts of repression—he said the blacklist was "dirty in its very conception and damnable in every feature"—but he had not changed his general views:

Some have gone so far as to say that there is a natural, a necessary conflict between labor and capital. These are very shallow thinkers, or else very great demagogues. Argument is of no use against these people, either they cannot or they will not see the falsity of their statement.

He still believed that a spirit of compromise and fair play could settle all labor difficulties without resort to strikes. But because he also thought that new laws were needed to protect the working people, he again agreed to run for office. At the national convention of the BLF in 1884, an amendment to the bylaws was introduced: "No salaried Grand Officer shall hold or accept a political office." On a voice vote the amendment was declared adopted. Debs then rose to state that the measure would force him to resign as Secretary-Treasurer, since he had accepted the Democratic nomination for the Indiana legislature. This office was largely nominal and required little time, he said, but it was nonetheless a political office. Only the earnest request of voters in his district had persuaded him to accept, but, having accepted he would not withdraw. After Debs' statement, the amendment was defeated by a vote of one hundred forty-nine Nays to fifty-seven Ayes.

"Grand Secretary and Treasurer, Brotherhood of Locomotive

Firemen, Candidate for the Legislature," read the campaign posters. Yellow handbills were thrown broadcast through the town. White ribbons proclaiming "Debs—Our Choice" appeared on velvet lapels, overalls, homespun shirts. A smooth voice and an eloquent forefinger harangued crowds of voters all over the district. In those frenzied autumn weeks Eugene Debs again proved that he owned the trademark of a true leader. The voters liked Debs because they recognized him as a local product. He could talk on equal terms with anybody in the district, simply because he was so commonplace. Debs wore his Sunday clothes to the political rallies and to all public gatherings, but he often wandered around his neighborhood dressed in overalls and a railroader's cap.

Typical, ordinary candidates often win elections, but they seldom arouse enthusiasm. Debs was more than typical; he was unusual. He had qualities which made him a part of the crowd; he also had qualities that made him stand out above the crowd. The Midwesterners respected kindliness, courage, and devotion, three traits which reached the extreme measure in Eugene Debs. So while the voters accepted Debs and felt at ease in his presence, they also recognized that his speeches, so ordinary in their florid phrasing, carried a sincerity and emotional impact that could never be manufactured by a political hack. The people believed in Debs, and sent him to Indianapolis to speak for them.

When Debs was sworn into the state House of Representatives on January 8, 1885, he had already drafted a bill which would require railroad companies to compensate their employees for injuries suffered on duty. Appointed to the Railway Committee, he maneuvered the bill through the lower chamber, and rejoiced when it was sent to the Senate. But his exultation was short-lived. When the bill reached the State Senate, the members of that body toyed with it for a few days, finally cut the guts out of it. Debs, convinced that he had failed the railroad workers, promptly withdrew the bill from consideration. Other measures in which Debs was deeply interested also went down to defeat. He bolted his party to vote with the Republicans on a bill to abolish all distinctions of race and color in the laws of

Indiana, but the bill lost by three votes. He voted for a bill to extend suffrage to women; again he was on the losing side.

By the time for adjournment, Debs had decided not to stand for re-election. He was ill-suited for the compromise and favoritism of political life, but his reaction was much too extreme. By the standards of the times, that legislative session in Indiana was a good one; it passed a resolution supporting a Federal eight-hour law for all trades but agriculture, and wrote into law an equal-rights act for all places of "public accommodation or amusements," a township tax of 1 per cent for the support of the libraries, a mechanics' lien law, coal-mine safety provisions, a prohibition on the importation of foreign contract-labor. But Eugene Debs felt that he had failed his electorate; when he reached home in March, he told Theodore that he would never again run for public office.

He went to see Kate Metzel, already preparing for their June wedding. Kate went to Louisville for her trousseau of fawn-colored cashmere with a brocaded front, collar and cuffs of crimson velvet, hat and gloves to match, all very proper for a ceremony in the Episcopal Church, of which she was a devout member. Town gossip and jokes revolved around the romance; when Ida Harper went south for a vacation she wrote to *The Magazine:* "Why is there no Brotherhood of Locomotive Firemen in Florida? . . . I would ask the Grand Secretary and Treasurer, but, with the Brotherhood, the Magazine, the Legislature and a sweetheart, all on hand at once, he has no time to answer questions."

Ida Harper failed to ask the most popular question: Why did Eugene Debs choose Kate Metzel? He was friendly and open-handed; Kate seemed frigid, aloof. This speculation ignored several factors. Debs was doubtless influenced by the happy marriage of his parents, in which Daniel was the man of affairs while Daisy usually remained at home, a retiring housewife. Although Eugene Debs did not believe in a subordinate position for women, he was subject to the power of example. Also Debs' career required frequent, extensive tours. His wife did not need to be a constantly charming companion; she did need to be stable, secure, self-reliant. Kate Metzel certainly had these characteristics. Debs was seeking a typical wife but an unusual marriage.

At 6:30 A.M. on June 9, 1885, the sun was pouring through the windows of St. Stephen's Church and splashing across the white drapes and fragrant flowers at the altar. Gifts had been arriving for weeks—silver, Persian rugs, furniture; the Brotherhood lodges in Chicago had sent a parlor set of mahogany, upholstered in blue, olive, and old-gold plush. The church was crowded with friends, sleepy, yawning, excited. Kate was quite handsome in her tailored traveling costume; the thirty-year-old bridegroom, wearing his inevitable gray suit, "looked exceedingly pale and thoughtful as he walked up the aisle," Ida Harper wrote, "as if he fully realized the important step."

The solemnity of the ceremony was forgotten on a luxurious spendthrift honeymoon in the East. After two weeks the young couple went home to a sentimental reception given by Vigo Lodge. Hundreds of people crowded into the hall to congratulate Debs, hear a mawkish speech by Frank Arnold, and vigorously applaud a recitation of "Katie Lee and Willie Gray." Debs felt uncomfortable at the thought of being alone with Kate in their housekeeping room; it would then be necessary to explain how they had spent a thousand dollars on a two-week trip. The inevitable moment came when he was seated at last on the ugly mahogany sofa, and Kate was facing him. Unable to tell the truth, unable to delay telling the truth, Debs chose a circular approach to the problem. He simply asked Kate if she had enjoyed their trip. When she enthusiastically said Yes, he relaxed into a broad grin and murmured, "That's good, because we're dead broke now."

[*3*]

FINANCIAL WORRIES, and they were not critical, quickly became Kate's problem; Debs was trying to understand and react to a growing revolt in the Brotherhood. Compelled by unemployment and bad conditions, the workers had begun a mighty counteroffensive. The Federated Trades and Labor Council, soon to become the American Federation of Labor, was spearheading a drive for an eight-hour day in all industries. This movement was to culminate in a nation-wide demonstration on May 1, 1886; the employers were fighting vigorously to stem the tide. The railroad workers, feeling the effects of the depression, began to rebel against the timorous no-strike policy of the Brotherhoods; a victorious strike by the Knights of Labor against the Gould system was a strong argument for aggressive action. When switchmen in East St. Louis struck for a pay raise the employers answered by importing thugs and gunmen from the South to guard their property and break the strike. These strikebreakers, deputized by the sheriff, fired into a crowd of strikers and several men were killed. The same tactic was used by the Pinkertons during a strike at the McCormick tractor plant in Chicago. In neither case were the gunmen indicted for the killings. There was bitter talk on both sides: Tom Scott of the Pennsylvania Railroad advised the "rifle diet" for all strikers, the Chicago *Times* argued the merits of hand grenades, several anarchists wrote about dynamite and the class struggle.

The delegates to the BLF convention of 1885 were tired of the blacklist, yellow-dog contracts, unemployment, and long hours. They were fed-up with meek submission. They thought the time had come for a fight. Their first act was to knock out the no-strike provision in their constitution. They did not want to strike, but by God they would if they had to; they proved this by providing a fifteen-thousand-dollar strike fund. Then the dissatisfied men went after their Grand officers. The previous December Grand Master Frank Arnold had written to the president of a railroad: "Labor always cripples and weakens itself whenever it antagonizes Capital. . . . So long as we keep it [the BLF] a benevolent organization, just that long will it thrive. . . ." The delegates resolved to "repudiate the said letter in all of its sentiments." They then deposed Arnold, electing Vice Grand Master Frank P. Sargent to head the order. They went straight down the list, throwing out every officer except Sargent and Debs. Debs tried to resign, but the resignation was turned down. He was unanimously returned to his job as Editor and Secretary-Treasurer.

The delegates also ordered Debs to attend the convention of

the Brotherhood of Locomotive Engineers the following month in New Orleans, and report that the BLF was "now a labor organization" and was "desirous of co-operating with them in all their grievances." There was obvious need for joint action by the two orders. Since the Engineers did not admit anybody who had not handled a locomotive for a year, many members of that craft still belonged to the BLF. When Debs presented a railroad with the demands of the engineers in his union, he was often confronted by a contradictory set of demands from the Brotherhood of Engineers. The resultant confusion defeated every move for a wage increase. Since 1877 the Firemen had tried to gain the co-operation of the Engineers, but every step in that direction had been blocked by P. M. Arthur, the conservative leader of the Engineers. Now that the Firemen had made provision for strikes, joint action had become doubly necessary, for no railroad walkout could succeed unless it stopped the trains, and no single craft could achieve that purpose.

The Engineers' convention in New Orleans started one of the most important battles in Debs' life. His proposal of friendship never reached the convention floor. P. M. Arthur, stodgy, well dressed, arrogant, solemnly proposed a motion to the machine-controlled delegates: "No engineer who belongs to the Brotherhood of Locomotive Firemen shall hereafter represent his division in the annual convention of the locomotive engineers." The delegates adopted the motion.

Eugene Debs, watching these events from the gallery, was scarcely able to believe the scene enacted before him. His violent indignation was heightened by the possibility that Arthur intended the motion as a personal affront. The next month he reported the New Orleans proceedings in an article that showed unusual restraint. Under a calm headline, "The Aristocracy of Labor," Debs declared that Arthur's motion "smacks of persecution. Its purpose is to embarrass our order." But the affair was not closed by the report in *The Magazine*. P. M. Arthur's arrogance started a chain of adjustments that revolutionized the labor movement on the railroads.

Debs now began a double-edged program: a criticism of all

tendencies toward exclusiveness, and a theoretical and practical demonstration of the virtues of joint action by the railroad unions. On January 6, 1886, his assistant editor, William Hynes, presided at a Denver conference of all BLF lodges on the Union Pacific. This conference pointed out that labor had suffered "due to the independent action of distinct organizations, attempting to adjust difficulties that involve the interests of many branches of industry." It then proposed a federation of all the Brotherhoods to settle disputes with the Union Pacific. This federation would act only if the individual union involved was unable to secure justice. Any desire to promote strikes was denied, but it was obvious beneath the doubletalk that strikes were considered preferable to further submission.

In spite of the opposition of P. M. Arthur, who believed that he could win greater gains by siding with the companies against the other Brotherhoods, the engineers and firemen worked together to score victories over the New York City Elevated Railways and the Ohio & Mississippi Railroad. Both disputes were settled peacefully. The New York Elevated contract won special acclaim, since it provided a pay increase, extra pay for overtime work, the nine-hour day, a half day's pay for reporting to work, strict seniority, and reinstatement of all men who had been fired during the dispute. Debs jubilantly wrote in *The Magazine:* "The incident supplies abundant proof that the two great Brotherhoods are necessary to each other . . ."

Some railroads counterattacked by trying to undermine the Brotherhoods. They set up compulsory insurance plans for all employees. The Pennsylvania thought of the idea, promoted it as a measure intended to help the workers. Debs, quick to realize the danger of the scheme, wrote a lengthy analysis for *The Magazine.* He claimed that the benefits were ridiculously low compared to the premiums, that the principle of compulsion was intended to wreck the workers' organizations, and that employees were required to sign away all claims against the company for damages in case of an accident. The Pennsylvania was forced to withdraw the proposal, but it was revived several times in the coming years.

Debs also struck a blow at this time against George M. Pull-

man, one of the most powerful industrialists in America. As a
young man, George Pullman had worked for his brother, a
cabinetmaker in Albion, New York. In 1855 he moved to Chicago, where he became a successful street contractor and worked
out the plans for building a railroad sleepingcar. The next nine
years were spent in perfecting the blueprint. Although the railroads showed little interest in the invention, Pullman gained
some practical experience by remodeling a few day coaches into
sleepingcars.

In 1864 Pullman and a partner began to build the first sleepingcar, concealing the upper berth in the wall and hinging the
seat cushion to form a lower berth. The inventor displayed great
skill; his basic design is still used. Pullman had refused to compromise in constructing The Pioneer, which was both higher
and wider than the locomotives and coaches. But the construction of the first transcontinental lines made the sleepingcar indispensable. Soon every railroad began to raise bridges and move
station platforms so that they could use Pullman cars. The Pullman Palace Car Company was established in 1867 at Palmyra,
New York, moved several times, and finally established its
main plant at Pullman, Illinois, in 1881.

George Pullman was certain that he alone knew how to build
sleepingcars. He was also certain that he alone knew how to
organize the lives of men. The town of Pullman, a Chicago
suburb, was widely advertised as a "model community," but
it was run like a feudal manor. Conductors on the Pullman cars
were treated like workers in the Pullman shops. They drew $75
per month wages, from which they paid $20 for meals and $4
for uniforms. They were subject to a system of fines which took
an average toll of $6 a month from each man. George Pullman
hired spies to ride in his cars and report the slightest infraction
of rules by any conductor. The conductor was fined for each
violation reported, and was given no chance to defend himself.

Debs collected these charges from such a variety of sources
that he could not doubt their truth, so he wrote a vigorous attack on Pullman's highhanded exploitation of his workers. This
incident, of minor importance at the time, became highly significant in 1894, when George M. Pullman and Eugene Debs were
the main actors in a drama that rocked the nation.

The complex struggle against the companies forced Debs to alter his notions of trade unionism. While keeping the insurance plans as a goal in themselves and as a means of stabilizing membership, he added new features. Written contracts with employers, to be won by strikes if necessary, were at the heart of his strategy. Such contracts were the main way to win better wages, hours, and working conditions, but he also advocated several new laws. His articles in support of eight-hour legislation, which carried the Federated Trades Council campaign into the Brotherhoods, emphasized that it would remedy unemployment and raise the level of public intelligence. To a large extent these ideas came from Debs' own experience, but they were influenced by the successful example of the unions in the AFL. The Cigarmakers, the Bakers, the Coal Miners, the building trades' unions, were all making huge gains in membership, proving the value of Samuel Gompers' theories.

Meanwhile, the Knights of Labor was falling to pieces. The Knights had long been divided into factions: the trade unionists who belonged to craft unions and regarded the K of L as a political supplement to the Federated Trades Council, and confused reformers who opposed the craft unions. The crisis had come in 1885, when the packinghouse workers completely shut down the Chicago stockyards. Conditions indicated that there was every chance of victory; then Terence Powderly, chief of the Knights, ordered the strikers to return to work. The strike was soon broken, and so was the K of L in Chicago. The next spring there was a bitter strike on the Gould railways in the Southwest, which ended in utter defeat. When the Knights' convention met in 1886, the antitrade unionists had a majority, and all members of the Knights were ordered to withdraw from the Cigarmakers' International Union. Most of them responded by withdrawing from the Knights of Labor. The once-proud organization, which had boasted an enrollment of more than a half million, began a precipitous decline. Debs followed these developments closely in *The Magazine,* wrote an article of protest against Powderly's actions, learned much from the history of the Knights.

The men who advocated the economic organization of the workers had won a clear victory over the champions of a multiclass reform organization, and Debs did not forget it. He was clearly lining up with the principles of the Federated Trades Council, but he lagged behind Gompers in two important respects: he denounced the boycott and the closed shop as infringements on liberty, and he sometimes acted hastily or carelessly, with little regard for the possible consequences of his action. His mistakes were usually of minor import, but one error, for which he was indirectly responsible, might have brought disaster to himself and the BLF.

[4]

LATE IN 1885, *The Magazine* carried an astonishing article about the use of dynamite in labor disputes:

Legitimate warfare in the future is to be in the interest of the weak, the oppressed, those who aspire to be free. Dynamite is to be a potent weapon in the contest.

Just seven months later came the Haymarket episode. Although Debs could truthfully have claimed that he did not endorse the use of violence, his argument would have been brushed aside during that frenzied affair. The phrases about dynamite as "a potent weapon" of "legitimate warfare" were sufficient provocation for the employers to move against the entire BLF.

Chicago, long known for the bitterness and violence of its labor struggles, was the national center of the eight-hour day campaign. The employers there were united in opposition to the shorter workday; the workers were equally determined to win their demand. On May Day, 1886, more than forty thousand workingmen put down their tools in the demonstration which climaxed the campaign. The entire city fearfully awaited the menacing outbreak. The wait was brief. On May 3 the police killed a striker at the McCormick reaper works, where fourteen hundred men had been locked out for months. The anarchists immediately called a meeting at Haymarket Square for the next evening to protest the killing. The meeting was entirely peaceful until a police captain led a large troop of his men to disperse the audience. As the patrol approached the crowd, a bomb was thrown into their ranks and seven policemen were killed or fatally wounded. Labor leaders and ordinary workers throughout the city were picked up by the police and finally eight anarchists and unionists, several of them leaders in the eight-hour movement, were indicted for the bombing.

Only two of the accused men had been anywhere near the meeting, and both of them were demonstrably innocent of throwing the bomb, but the judge presented a new theory in his charge to the jury: If the past language of the accused has been such as to incite violence, they are guilty of this crime, even if they knew nothing about it and were not present when it was committed. On a principle which violated the basic rules of American law, in a courtroom clotted with prejudice, the eight men were convicted of murder.

The public protest against this verdict was prompt and eloquent. Not merely labor leaders, but United States Senators and wealthy bankers, exclaimed that the judge was biased, that the jury was hand-picked, that the entire proceedings were highly improper. But Eugene Debs said absolutely nothing for more than five months. Debs, never famous for reticence, was truly in a dilemma. He had no sympathy for the anarchist doctrines of the accused men; he had often criticized the use of violence and had declared that the class struggle was only "the creation of diseased brains." His objection to the Haymarket trial was based on other factors: the irregular proceedings, a belief that the indictment was a punishment of free speech, a conviction that the employers were trying to frame eight labor leaders.

Only one theory seems to explain Debs' unusual silence. Any protest on his part might have called attention to the article about dynamite in *The Magazine,* with the result of dire punishment for the entire BLF. Perhaps Debs felt that he was forced to choose between treachery to his own union and treachery to the men convicted of murder. There is no evidence that Debs discussed this problem with anybody. For five months he wrestled with it in silence, and doubtless in torment.

Finally he could no longer remain silent. The higher courts had denied appeals for the convicted men. The last hope to save their lives lay in securing clemency from the governor of Illinois. Eugene Debs, in a fervent article in *The Magazine*, singled out the right of free speech as the major issue in the case. A free press and free speech he called "the twin glories of American government. . . . Let this verdict stand, let it become the practice of the courts, let it go unrevoked, and free speech is as dead in America as it is in Russia." The attack on freedom of expression was doomed to failure: "Ideas and opinions escape the death penalty, the halter, the faggot, and the wheel."

Debs spoke too late to help save the lives of the condemned men. One of them committed suicide, four were hanged, three were sent to prison. Eugene Debs never mentioned the rôle he had played in the defense campaign for the Haymarket martyrs. But for forty years he cherished the memory of these men. He wrote newspaper articles about them. He referred to them often in his speeches. He made frequent pilgrimages to Waldheim Cemetery in Chicago, where the executed men were buried. These eight men became, to Eugene Debs, "the first martyrs in the cause of industrial freedom." Eleven years after the execution, Debs sang to their memory: "aye, I would take them, if I could, from peaceful slumber in their martyr graves—I would place joint to joint in their dislocated necks—I would make the halter the symbol of redemption—I would restore the flesh to their skeleton bones—their eyes should again flash defiance to the enemies of humanity, and their tongues, again, more eloquent than all the heroes of oratory, should speak the truth to a gainsaying world. Alas, this cannot be done—but something can be done. The stigma fixed upon their names by an outrageous trial can be forever obliterated and their fame be made to shine with resplendent glory on the pages of history."

[5]

KATE DEBS, in 1886, was already learning the daily reality of marriage to an open-hearted labor leader. Debs was gone from Terre Haute for weeks at a time; when he came home he was often sick from fatigue or temporary discouragement. He told wearisome stories about meetings when nobody came, towns where the workers were frightened or indifferent. When he was in Terre Haute, he held long conferences with his brother Theodore, Frank Sargent, Tom Harper—then he left for another trip. Kate lived in housekeeping rooms because her husband acted as if his three-thousand-dollar-a-year salary was a fund for needy railroaders. Nobody ever asked Eugene Debs for money; he usually gave it to them before they asked. Debs often left on an organizing tour with two suitcases of clothes, and came back home with nothing but the shirt on his back. He just did not understand about health or money, squandering one as freely as he squandered the other.

So Kate Debs stayed in one or two rooms, learning to live a lonely and bitter existence. Since she took no interest in social life and had but few friends, she spent long hours by herself. She read books by the dozen, by the hundred. She also began to change slowly under the impact of her new isolation. Her home, always a matter of importance, now grew to exaggerated significance. She learned to clean the same room three times a day, and then to resent any disturbance, any untidiness. Always neat, she became too neat, unpleasant in her neatness. She also developed another habit which persisted for life. Kate Debs, caught between the example of her own family and the practice of her husband, attached her mind to the promise of financial security. She opened a private bank account, and often consulted her brothers about financial affairs. But Kate and her husband, with contradictory viewpoints, soon learned to ignore the conflict. Each of them went his own ways, in good-humored tolerance of the other.

Although Kate was not rich, did not have everything she wanted, she was comfortably situated and managed to save something. Worse than money problems was the attitude of some of the respectable element in town, who raised their eyebrows at the article about dynamite and gossiped some about Gene's drinking. Debs could not hold his liquor at all, but he drank because he was a genial man and his friends drank. When James Whitcomb Riley or some railroader offered to set them up, Debs could not refuse.

Kate was proud of Riley's poem about Terre Haute in which her husband was mentioned:

> Go search the earth from end to end
> And where's a better all-round friend
> Than Eugene Debs?—a man that stands
> And jest holds out in his two hands
> As warm a heart as ever beat
> Betwixt here and the Mercy Seat!

Besides being proud, Kate was truly fond of Riley, but she also dreaded his visits. His appearance was always the signal for a jovial, backslapping tour of the local saloons, with Kate standing at the window at home anxiously waiting for her husband's return. She was always greatly relieved when the two tipplers returned safely. On one occasion she waited for hours, pacing the floor, peering down the street, wringing her handkerchief. Finally the carriage came. Debs got out, shook hands, said good-by, then got back in with Riley and the carriage drove away.

Even in the Brotherhood his occasional intoxication caused Debs some embarrassment. The national convention of 1886 voted to expel any lodge that sold intoxicants at any entertainment. The next day Debs and Vice Grand Master John Hannahan were both accused of having been drunk at a meeting in Buffalo. "Debs admitted to having drunk to excess on the occasion referred to in the charges," said the report, but he was excused after he swore that it would never happen again. Then he was unanimously re-elected to both of his posts. and given a gold medal: "To Eugene V. Debs, by the B. of L. F.—an emblem of the unfailing esteem of his toiling fellow men."

[6]

IN HIS SPEECH to the 1886 convention, Debs emphasized that the BLF was "not engaged in any quarrel between capital and labor. There can be no such quarrel unless it is caused by deliberate piracy on one side and unreasonable demands on the other. . . . All we ask is an honest day's wages for an honest day's work, and we are willing to be considerate and just." But he carefully pointed out in *The Magazine* that preparedness was a wise policy:

For purposes of protection, the throttle and the scoop, the switch and the brake, must be in close alliance and equally firm and defiant, and when corporations see this federation accomplished, no strikes will occur, because a strike under such circumstances would mean an immediate cessation of railroad transportation on the line or system where it occurred.

Although there were occasional defeats, joint action by the BLF and the Engineers was bringing unprecedented gains. A wage increase was peacefully won from several lines in the East. Then followed a strike on the Brooklyn Elevated Railway to halt discriminatory firings of unionists. The first strike ever authorized by the BLF, it was broken within a week, but this defeat was more than offset by favorable contracts negotiated with the Louisville & Nashville, the Newport News & Mississippi Valley, the Wabash system. Debs used these victories to stress the need for continued co-operation:

Fraternal, brotherly unity is natural. . . . It does not mean federation but fraternity . . . it means that these Brotherhoods while one as the sea, one in the great fundamental purpose of improving conditions, in elevating character, are separate as the waves moving in grand procession toward separate and distinct goals. . . .

The BLF felt so prosperous that it moved into new offices in an elaborate building that Riley McKeen built on Wabash Avenue. But this expenditure was ill timed for the Brotherhood was soon embroiled in a costly strike. On February 27, 1888, the engineers and firemen called a joint walkout against the Chicago, Burlington & Quincy Railroad. The action had been brewing since 1886, when the workers accepted a very unsatisfactory contract. In 1888 they asked for wage increases, a minimum daily wage, acceptance of the double scale of twelve hours or a hundred miles as a standard day's work, seniority "when ability is equal," and a fair procedure for settling grievances. Negotiations proved fruitless; the company stalled and hedged, made offers and then withdrew them. Finally, at the demand of the rank and file the strike was called.

Trouble with other railroad unions began at once. The switchmen were so incensed at the past arrogance of P. M. Arthur
that they refused to quit work. The Knights of Labor were
openly filling the strikers' jobs in retaliation for strikebreaking
by the Engineers two months earlier during a K of L strike on
the Philadelphia & Reading. It was a delicate and critical situation. Sargent and Debs went first to see Joseph Buchanan, the
editor of a Chicago labor paper. Buchanan had been a labor
editor in Denver, member of the Executive Board of the Knights
of Labor, and had led the successful 1885 strike against the
Gould system. His influence might be strong enough to keep the
Knights off the engines. At first the editor was unwilling to
interfere. He reminded his visitors of the hostility that Arthur
had often shown to other unions.

But Debs turned loose his charm, and soon won his point.
"You are too true a friend of the cause of labor," he told Buchanan, "to allow another man's errors or your own personal
grievances to govern your course, Buchanan. No matter how
'leaders' may err, it is your duty and mine to exert what influence we may possess to prevent organized workingmen from
cutting each other's throats."

Buchanan was convinced for two reasons: "I liked Debs; he
was loyal and frank; besides, I saw the truth and good sense in
his remark." As the C.B. & Q. brought in the K of L strikebreakers from Pennsylvania, Buchanan assembled them in a
parlor of the Briggs House and urged them to respect the strike.
Most of them went back home.

Then the Brotherhood leaders made a passionate series of
appeals to the switchmen and coaxed them off the trains. No
other person, not even the leaders of their own union, was more
popular among the switchmen than Debs; man by man they
left their jobs. Debs strained every ability to make the walkout
a success, writing fiery articles for *The Magazine*, exhorting
groups of men on street corners or in the railroad yards. He
worked tirelessly, endlessly, not going home, not seeing Kate,
eating on the run, sleeping on desk tops and wooden benches.
He said the same thing at every meeting: the strikers had an

honest grievance, they had sought a peaceful settlement, every railroader had a personal stake in the outcome.

In spite of the determination and heroism of the workers, the tide began to run against them. By March 15, the company claimed to have a full working force on the job, but the men would not admit defeat. The walkout dragged on into the spring, with twenty-seven hundred strikers waiting for the company to surrender. Although train schedules were being met, the corporation was hard hit. Losses for the first six months of the year were nearly ten million dollars. The scab engineers and firemen were proving to be totally incompetent; wreck and damage losses alone exceeded a million dollars. Pinkerton detectives were hired to combat the strikers, but Debs confined his anger against the Pinkertons to an acrid blast in *The Magazine:*

They are distorted, deformed, hideous mentally and morally. Their trade is treason, their breath pollution and yet the officials of the C.B. & Q. formed a conspiracy with these professional liars, perjurers, cut-throats and murderers to overcome a strike, the result of a policy of flagrant injustice.

Debs knew that the detectives were spectacular but unimportant—the real enemies were hunger and a lack of unity. Strike relief was his personal responsibility and month after month he urged members of every Brotherhood to give three dollars to the strikers. He persuaded his own union to give more than two hundred and fifty thousand dollars by arguing that the C.B. & Q. would be forced to yield soon. He went to local unions and his friends with a plea for money. If they could only hold out they could win. And the money came, in dimes and dollars, poor men giving to those who were starving. But not enough of it came, so Debs borrowed twenty-nine thousand dollars for the strike fund, and insured the debt by his personal note. There was, thought Debs, still some hope. The men were standing together, absolutely peaceful, not giving the railroad any excuse to ask for the militia in a repetition of 1877.

Unable to defeat the rank and file, the corporation officials too became desperate. Finally they decided to go to court and ask for an injunction against the strike. Panic-stricken, P. M. Arthur consulted a lawyer, who advised that the strike leaders would be liable to jail sentences for contempt of court if the injunction were secured and they disobeyed it. That was enough for Arthur. He called together the joint strike committee and told them he intended to revoke the strike order: "Brothers, I am legally advised that unless this order is rescinded, I am liable to be sent to jail; I want to say here that I would not go to jail 24 hours for your whole Brotherhood." Debs was speechless. The injunction had not even been granted, might not be granted, and already Arthur was running for cover. But the Engineers were ordered back to work, and most of them went. The firemen were left to carry the battle alone, and the pressure was further increased when the Grand Chief of the Conductors issued a circular condemning the strike. This time Debs struck back in a furious article in *The Magazine*, but hope of winning the strike had become very slight.

The failure of the Engineers and Conductors to hold the strike reinforced Debs' conviction that his federation plan was necessary, and he pressed even more vigorously for "a union of Brotherhoods of certain railway employees for purposes of strength when union is required to secure a righteous settlement of controversies which relate to their welfare." Denying that such a plan was visionary, Debs claimed that the times demanded its immediate fulfillment. Just as individual workers had combined to protect their mutual interests, the Brotherhoods should combine on matters of common concern. A single union was helpless against a giant railroad, wrote Debs, but the Burlington strike could have been won in a day "if from the first there had been federation between engineer and firemen, switchmen and brakemen on the C.B. & Q." The firemen, who had rejected federation two years earlier, now accepted it completely. The convention of 1888 named Debs chairman of a three-man committee to set up a formal alliance with the other Brotherhoods.

In September and October of 1888 most of the strikers straggled back to work, and Debs turned his attention to the Presidential campaign. His personal disgust with the legislature had not blinded him to the need for political reform. Now he urged the workers to vote against the enemies of labor: "To wield the ballot intelligently and heroically is the workingmen's last resort, in fact, it is the remedy which commends itself to all right thinking men." To Debs the issues in this campaign seemed clear. The Republican Party, firmly controlled by the business interests, nominated Benjamin Harrison of Indiana, a corporation lawyer and Senator who had been exceedingly hostile to labor. On the other hand the Democratic incumbent, Grover Cleveland, was a man of great personal integrity, if little imagination. Cleveland had shown some respect for labor's rights and had been instrumental in setting up a board of voluntary arbitration for labor disputes on the railroads. So Debs agreed to share the platform with Senator Voorhees at a mammoth Democratic rally in Terre Haute. Most of Debs' speech was an attack on Harrison and the Republicans; only in the final sentence did he mention the Democratic nominee:

The immortal words of Grover Cleveland, "Tell the truth," have been inscribed upon the banners of the Democratic party and I believe that when the campaign will have closed the workingmen throughout the country will have dignified and glorified themselves and their cause by having shown to the people of the country that the man who volunteers to organize a company of soldiers to shoot down the workingmen when they are striking for their rights never can become President of this country.

In 1888 Debs applied these words to Cleveland's opponent. Six years later he applied them to Cleveland.

On January 3, 1889, the Brotherhood called off the Burlington walkout. It had actually ended months before, a complete defeat for the strikers. This labor struggle had been a crucial lesson for Eugene Debs. He had been educated in the only school he accepted—the fury of battle. He was still able to believe that the profit-sharing plans of John Wanamaker heralded a new era of labor peace. But he would never again be able to say, as he had said in 1877, that a strike "signifies anarchy and revolution." He had now signed his name to the opposite view:

The strike is the weapon of the oppressed, of men capable of appreciating justice and having the courage to resist wrong and contend for principle. The nation had for its cornerstone a strike, and while arrogant injustice throws down the gauntlet and challenges the right to the conflict, strikes will come, come by virtue of irrevocable laws, destined to have a wider sweep and greater power as men advance in intelligence and independence.

CHAPTER 4

◻

[1]

THEIR condemnation to a sterile marriage burned griev-
ously with Kate and Eugene Debs. They had fought
stubbornly against the realization of Kate's barrenness.
When they finally faced the problem, Kate proposed that she go
to Louisville for an operation. This plan was emphatically vetoed by her mother: "Now, Kate, you're not really sick. It's
better to let well enough alone." Forced to choose between his
desire for children and his concern for Kate's health, Debs
agreed with Mrs. Baur. Thus was blocked another potential
outlet for Debs' idealism. The consequences are uncertain. Perhaps normal family responsibilities, by emphasizing a whole
sphere of human problems, would have hurried his feet even
more rapidly along the path he ultimately chose. But as a
father, his love for his own children might have made him more
hesitant about decisions, more inclined to compromise.

The impact of childlessness on Kate Debs is more apparent.
She was unable to share completely the justification that Eugene
Debs found in his beliefs. For him the labor movement had
become thousands of brothers; for her it remained a faceless
mass. Through four long years she had lived a bleak and lonely
marriage. Only on those rare days when her husband was in
Terre Haute did she really have companionship. Owning few
friends, recoiling from women's clubs and civic activities, she
lived in self-imposed isolation from the warmth of social life.
Day after day she remained in her ugly housekeeping rooms,
reading novels, meticulously cleaning the furniture, resenting
her condition. Gradually there grew within her a fervent longing
for a home of her own, ornate, stately, imposing. By 1889 the
desire had become irresistible.

Kate and Eugene didn't really need a large house, but they
built one anyway. Kate had managed to save some money from

61

Debs' salary, and she inherited a sizeable amount from an aunt in Louisville. They spent four thousand dollars for a double lot in one of the wealthiest sections of town, North Eighth street, where Kate wanted to live. Debs himself drew up the plans for the house, which was disjointed, substantial, ugly, with gables that seemed to burgeon unbidden from other gables. The Debs' home, an architectural copy of the typical expensive house in the Midwest, quickly became a local showplace. Kate was delighted with its pretentious size and furnishings. Each room had a fireplace of blue tile—in the parlor and library the tile was carved and the mantles were San Domingo mahogany. Those two rooms were finished last because the mahogany was late in arriving. Kate promptly decreed that the parlor would be used only on special occasions, so the library became the living room. Debs had some shelves built into an upstairs bedroom and moved his books there.

James Whitcomb Riley was one of the first and most frequent guests in the new house. The friendship of Riley and Debs had ripened, and Riley had written a second poem, "Them Flowers," to Debs. Riley's presence in Terre Haute could be detected easily; the number of children around the Debs' house doubled. They wouldn't even wait until a proper hour, but crowded into the front bedroom—soon known as the Riley Room—long before Riley awakened in the morning.

Riley, on the rare occasions when he found himself alone, would wander into Debs' study and give private performances of his most cherished rôles. The two sentimental men would sit for hours, mocking, orating, laughing, crying, weaving from their lavender memories a blissful childhood without poverty, frozen ears, or pain. The friendship of Debs and Riley was due, perhaps, to their common ability to create a Utopia, and then believe in their creation. Riley actually lived in this dreamland, this Heavenly City of his poetry. Debs knew the sordid truth, but he forgot it in the company of the poet, and they wandered barefooted through the dusty paths down to the Ole Swimmin' Hole, where there were no insects and the water was clear as a mirror.

Often, when Riley was in Terre Haute, Daniel brought over a

bottle of wine from the store, causing Kate to fret at the realization that Riley occasionally missed his performance at the Opera House after these parties. A whimsical version of one celebration was set down in a letter from Riley to his friend and partner Bill Nye:

Have latterly returned from a brief visit to Debs, at Terre Haute, who wants me to remind you of him in a taking way. Mind, I say a brief visit—for, first dash out of box, he must drive out to that blessed little vineyard where they serve you, out under the trellis, with such tantalizing lunch, one must needs handcuff one's appetite, else plunge headlong into their seductive wines—made while you wait, by the gifted old man, who readily accomplishes his hellish purpose with one hand tied behind him. Need I dwell on the picture? I deem not by a dam sight. . . .

Riley, Ingersoll, a few personal friends and relatives in Terre Haute, formed Debs' only contact with the world outside the labor movement. He was a vivid conversationalist, but he shrank from formal society and had never learned to dance. His leisure evenings being few, he spent them with people he knew and liked. Every Sunday he went to his parents' home, where he and Daniel recited poetry and discussed Hugo's *Les Misérables*. Debs also studied Shakespeare, history, science, but many of his tastes were less discriminating—he reveled in mawkish doggerel, and Negro dialect jokes by the page found their way into *The Magazine*. The shelves in the second floor study held technical books on railroading, bulky reports on labor conditions by the state and Federal governments, French and German classics, together with the worst poetry being written in this country and newspaper clippings about circus freaks.

Eugene Debs was a very considerate husband—he never raised his voice in anger—but Kate tried to leave him alone when he was writing. Oratory came much easier to him; Debs' efforts to piece together an article always reminded him of Jamey Riley's remark: "Writing poetry is like giving birth to a rough-shod colt." Debs would fret and pace the floor trying to shape the ideas into a pattern; then he would sit down at his desk and write for hours.

Often an idea came to him after he had gone to bed. He tossed and turned until he put it into words, then he arose, lit the gas burner, and began to write. Kate usually awakened to gaze with pride and amusement at her husband, sitting at his desk scribbling frantically, gold eye-glasses pushed down on his nose, his nightgown billowing in the draught across the floor. Kate thought that "some of the things he has written that way in the middle of the night, have been the best and brightest of his works." When he had finished, he returned to bed and fell asleep at once.

[2]

DURING the early spring of 1889, Debs worked frantically to bring his federation plan to fruition. His own union had overwhelmingly endorsed his proposal, and he was confident that the rank and file in every Brotherhood favored joint action. But this enthusiasm could wane rapidly unless it were harnessed to a concrete program. The moment had arrived for decisive action —the result hung in the balance. And Debs was determined that his labor of three years would not be wasted. The proposed federation became the main theme in all of his speeches. He wrote countless editorials on the subject for *The Magazine.*

Debs proved, in his efforts to federate the railroad unions, that he was adept at the strategy of leading men. Not only did he muster every argument that might appeal to the railroaders, he also kept careful track of the developments in each Brotherhood and set the pace of the entire campaign. It seemed certain that the Switchmen and the Brakemen, two crafts that were relatively unskilled and recently organized, would promptly join any federation. But Debs, who had helped to found both of these unions, preferred not to leave their allegiance in doubt. He gladly accepted an invitation to speak at the national convention of the Brakemen in 1888 because it seemed an excellent chance to gain recruits for his program. The opening offered him was further improved by the remarks of Grand Master S. E. Wilkinson: "On my left sits our godfather, Eugene V. Debs. . . . He was our friend when we most needed a friend, and you and I in our life will never be able to repay him for what he has done for us and for the benefit of our Brotherhood." Debs, seeing the advantage that he held, quickly made his plea for common action:

Upon all hands and in all directions laboring men are organizing. Organizing for what? Organizing for mutual protection; organizing in order that they may demand and receive an honest day's wages for an honest day's work. . . . When . . . we come in contact with a narrow minded, bigoted and infamous railroad official, who will not accord us our common rights, then I am in favor of strikes. Why, my friends, there is not a star or a stripe in our national flag that does not tell of a strike; not one. From Lexington, from Concord, all along the track of gloom and of glory clear down to Yorktown, is one succession of strikes for liberty and independence. . . .

Debs then stressed the importance of "federation for mutual benefit. (Great applause) Not for the purpose of fostering or encouraging strikes, but to avert them. (More applause). . . . And if a strike should come, then I believe that out from the camp of the federated brotherhoods Perry's message will be sent. 'We have met the enemy and they are ours.' (Great cheering)"

The leaders of the Engineers and the Conductors were bitterly opposed to co-operation with the other unions, but they were faced by growing opposition within their crafts. Indignation at the no-strike policy and strikebreaking actions of the Order of Railway Conductors had prompted the formation of a dual union, or second organization in the craft, the Brotherhood of Railway Conductors. Debs hailed this event with "undisguised satisfaction": "It voices sentiments of harmony and unity, and strengthens faith that the day is not distant, when all the organizations of railway employes will be united in the bonds of federation to promote the welfare of each and all." George W. Howard, who resigned a supervisory job with the San Diego Street Car Company to become head of the Brotherhood of Conductors, was widely known among railroaders, having been at one time a Division Superintendent on the Ohio & Mississippi. He was flighty and unclear in his loyalties, but had a fine speaking voice, knowledge of the industry, and was known to favor federation.

Even among the Engineers the unity movement found powerful support. John A. Hill, editor of *The Locomotive Engineer*, had
supported the Burlington strike and advocated joint action
among the Brotherhoods. Hill also greatly admired Eugene
Debs, of whom he wrote: "His editorials are the ablest and more
widely read than those of any labor organ in America." The
efforts of Hill, Debs, and several others were convincing many
engineers of the need for federation. P. M. Arthur began to feel
rather insecure on his throne and was less outspoken in his contempt for other unions. Debs confidently predicted that the
Brotherhood of Engineers would soon join a federation. He also
thought that the Order of Conductors, meeting opposition
within its own ranks and losing members to Howard's dual organization, would be forced to repeal its no-strike clause and
co-operate with the other unions.

Important men in every Brotherhood were calling for federation, and they all looked to Debs for leadership. They had only
one question: Is the time ripe? Debs said Yes. Since 1885 he had
been working for this moment. Now it had come. Two or three
victories for the proposed federation and both the engineers and
the Conductors would be forced to join. On June 3, 1889, nine
men met in Chicago, the three top officers of the Firemen, the
Brakemen, and the Switchmen. A committee was chosen to draft
a constitution, including Debs for the BLF. Three days later the
plan was complete.

The new federation would be called the Supreme Council of
the United Orders of Railway Employees. Any grievance submitted for settlement had to be accepted by a unanimous vote
of the Supreme Council, which would then take all steps necessary to settle the dispute. In case a strike was required, all of the
affiliated crafts on the struck system would be ordered off the
job and would walk out together. The goal sounded simple:
"*MUTUAL JUSTICE.*"

The Supreme Council won every battle during its first year,
and it did not order a single strike. The railroads, confronted by
a united labor movement, now took a very conciliatory attitude,
which showed itself in every dispute. The Queen and Crescent
tried to discharge all union conductors. After a meeting with the

Supreme Council, the railroad's president agreed to reinstate the men who had been fired. An improved contract was negotiated for the switchmen in Pittsburgh. The Ohio & Mississippi granted seniority and a wage increase. The railroad workers had never won such gains in the past. Every grievance was settled to the satisfaction of the employees. United action was putting money in the workers' pockets. Debs jubilantly wrote of this record: "It inspires confidence; it silences doubts, and presages 'the good time coming' when strikes shall forever disappear, and a reign of good feeling exist between the railroad employer and employe."

Debs felt both satisfaction and pride in the developments of that year. An honest, likeable young Irishman named Sylvester Keliher took the lead in organizing the Brotherhood of Railway Car Men among the repair crews. A Brotherhood of Telegraphers was founded in opposition to the Order of Railway Telegraphers, a conservative, nonstriking order. L. W. Rogers, a consistent spokesman for unity, was elected editor of the Brakemen's *Journal*. George Howard's Brotherhood of Conductors joined the Supreme Council. The Order of Railway Conductors deposed its former Grand Chief and repealed its no-strike clause, prompting Debs to advocate an immediate merger of the two organizations of conductors. Even the Engineers began to retreat; they repealed their discriminatory clause against members of the BLF, and held a tumultuous debate before deciding to postpone entrance into the Supreme Council. And Debs constantly tried to force the issue: ". . . the B. of L.E., in case of trouble with a corporation, is not strong enough under all circumstances to 'go it alone,' and engineers know that such exigencies do sometimes arise when the united voice and strength of all are required to secure simple justice."

The continued isolation of the Engineers was not the only problem. A heated jurisdictional fight had started between the Switchmen's Mutual Aid Association and the Brotherhood of Brakemen, who had changed their name to the Brotherhood of Railroad Trainmen and begun to organize switchmen. At the meeting of the Supreme Council in June, 1890, Debs moved that each order be forced to limit its organizing to the craft over which it had jurisdiction. He hoped that soon all of the Brotherhoods would merge into a single organization, so he desperately tried to eliminate factional strife, but his motion was defeated.

The Supreme Council also had constant trouble because the Brotherhoods refused to admit Negro members. Many Southern railroads consistently pitted the Negro and white workers against each other, and the unions, instead of accepting the Negroes as equal members, satisfied their prejudices by trying to drive the Negro workers off their jobs. The Brotherhood of Trainmen even submitted a grievance to the Supreme Council regarding the employment of Negro switchmen on the Houston and Texas Central. The Council asked the railroad to discharge the Negroes, but met with a flat refusal.

Debs was not present when the Supreme Council considered this complaint, but he would have opposed their action. He was trying to bring together all of the railroad workers—Negroes, Catholics, Protestants, atheists, foreign-born. If a man worked on the railroad, he should be in a Brotherhood. Debs was sure, in January, 1891, that there would be a bitter fight with the corporations: "Workingmen . . . are now demanding in America . . . their fair share of the wealth they create. Do the capitalists hear the demand? Yes. Do they heed it? No. Hence the coming conflict. . . ." The railroad workers could win their rights, thought Debs, only if they stood together. Every movement to divide them should be vigorously fought. When an anti-Catholic organization, the American Protective Association, began to split lodges and create enmity on the basis of religion, Debs was furious. His mother had been a Catholic when she came to America, and Terre Haute at that time was dominated by another anti-Catholic society, the Know-Nothings. Although Daisy had not remained in the Church after she ceased to believe in its doctrines, she had gained an understanding and dislike of religious bigotry, and Daniel also had defended absolute freedom of belief. So now Eugene Debs wrote a forceful attack on the attempt to split the labor movement along religious lines:

The Brotherhood of Locomotive Firemen is not an organization of religious fanatics and bigots. It is not an organization which has a purpose of collecting fagots to burn heretics, to erect wheels to break their bones, or obtain thumb-screws to elicit recantations.

The Brotherhood of Locomotive Firemen tolerates, without question, all religious opinions, and the locomotive fireman, a member of the brotherhood, who, by word or deed, introduces creed questions in the lodge, or who uses the order in any way to promote religious dissension, is a deadly enemy of the order and should be forthwith expelled . . .

[*3*]

DEBS knew that there would always be problems, and he was confident that the workers would find the right solutions. He had joined an organization of two thousand members and seen it grow to twenty thousand. He had taken over a magazine with thirty-five hundred subscribers and was now printing thirty-three thousand copies each month. During his term in office the Brotherhood had established itself financially, had sought out the true principles of trade unionism. The movement for federation had grown from a sickly infant to an irresistible giant. Debs began to feel that his work in the Brotherhood was finished. The expansion of the organization had made it necessary for him to spend more and more time on routine work. Kate was dissatisfied because he spent so much time away from home and because he was wrecking his health. So Debs decided to quit.

He announced his retirement in the lead editorial of *The Magazine*, January, 1891. His term in office did not expire for another two years, but he wanted to give his Brothers ample time to choose a successor. The news created quite a stir in Terre Haute. The local *Gazette* immediately sent a reporter to interview Debs, who said that the drudgery of the job was becoming tiresome, and that he longed for larger fields. He expected to resign within a year. While admitting his intention of moving to New York City, where one of his sisters, Mrs. Emma Maillaux, now lived, he refused to tell his plans for fear that premature publication might injure his colleagues in the new venture. He did, however, clearly hint at the general nature of his intentions: "I think there is a field for a labor paper, covering the whole range of organized labor, not of one special trade or class, but in a broad sense taking in the whole of the labor world; something that will reach the masses."

Debs was clearly qualified to manage such a periodical. He even knew how to make it profitable. His decade on *The Magazine* had taught him advertising, circulation, printing, editing; and his experience extended beyond his work on *The Magazine*. In 1889 he had joined four other men to establish the Terre Haute *Daily News*, which intended to bring accurate news to his fellow townsmen; the pressure of other duties had soon forced him to quit the project. The American Press Association, which supplied syndicated material to small newspapers, had offered him a job as general manager at forty-five hundred dollars a year, but he refused.

But his real value was as an editorial writer, a field in which the other labor journalists freely acknowledged his superiority. He always seemed to know what the workers were thinking, what they were willing to read, what they wanted to hear. He had come straight from their ranks to his job in the Brotherhood, and, instead of losing contact with the rank and file, he had deepened and broadened his friendships among the railroaders. As an editor, he could carefully search out the flaw in the enemy's argument, then rip it apart with one well-placed, caustic comment. This was the method of the squirrel rifle; at other times his articles resembled a whole battery of shotguns. His wrath poured into deafening, unrestrained condemnation, which flattened the opposition and then destroyed the corpses.

Debs' partisanship was tempered, however, by reflection and by conscious purpose. His demands for the eight-hour day, higher wages, the abolition of convict labor and company stores, were bolstered by a careful use of statistics from government reports. He also brought to his task a deep understanding of the traps that awaited the labor movement. He was not a blind supporter of every trade union policy. His scorn for P. M. Arthur of the Engineers rivaled his attacks on such financiers as George M. Pullman and Jay Gould. Even within the BLF, Debs publicly criticized those theories and actions which he found distasteful. For instance, in 1891 a meeting of railroaders in Kansas City resolved against any reduction in freight or passenger rates on the railroads. Debs promptly denounced the resolution as an attempt "to form an alliance, offensive and defensive, with organized greed and capitalized fraud, in opposition to the people's demand for equity and justice." Throughout his life, Debs opposed every labor-management agreement to fleece the consumers.

[4]

ALTHOUGH Debs still clung to the standard of the Democratic Party, he carefully watched the growth of the political reform movement. Since the Civil War there had been frequent rumblings among the farmers of the West and South. In the early 1870's the Grangers had demanded and won railroad regulation in several states, while in 1878 the Greenback Party polled a million votes. The next decade witnessed the rise of the Farmers' Alliances, which elected two United States Senators and eight Congressmen in 1890. This farmers' revolt, through all of its ebbs and flows, had revolved around a few demands: free coinage of silver, the issuance of greenbacks, public regulation or even public ownership of the railroads and telegraph, a fair tax system, the abolition of privately owned national banks. In May, 1891, all of these planks were adopted by a convention of the reform elements in Cincinnati, and demands were added for the eight-hour day and universal suffrage. When this convention also took steps to found the People's Party, or Populists, Debs took an alert but neutral position in *The Magazine*. His article opposed government ownership of the railroads and criticized the free-silver panacea, but it also pointed out that the Populists might prove to be the party which would "discard . . . class legislation and inaugurate a reign of justice."

Debs' political views had been deeply affected by two contemporary books, Laurence Gronlund's *The Cooperative Commonwealth* and Edward Bellamy's *Looking Backward*. Gronlund's thesis was simple: A society based on co-operation should be substituted for a society based on competition. Believing that the co-operative commonwealth would be reached by a gradual extension of state activity, Gronlund wrote that such theories as Henry George's single-tax were "very far out on the road to Socialism." The perfect society would arrive as soon as all political offices were made elective and the recall, initiative, and referendum were made universal.

Gronlund had expressed his views in a tedious political treatise; Bellamy fashioned similar notions into a novel about Julian West, a young New Englander who fell asleep in 1887 and did not wake up until 2000 A.D. West found himself in a marvellous America. Poverty, strikes, war, every selfish sentiment and ugly sight, had disappeared, because the government had taken the country's factories out of private hands and was operating them for the good of the people. Public demand for *Looking Backward* was so great that the printer could not keep up with it. Bellamy's main plank, the nationalization of industry, stimulated a new political movement, the Nationalist clubs, which began in Boston and spread overnight across the country. Terence Powderly, Sam Gompers, and P. J. McGuire all announced their support. Volume I of a new magazine, *The Nationalist*, came off the press in 1889. Debs promptly subscribed for the magazine and wrote a lengthy review of the book: "*Looking Backward* . . . outlines a possibility, or rather many possibilities, some of which are to be accomplished facts a century in advance of 2000 A.D. Trusts will go, syndicates and monopolies will follow. Landgrabbers will be made to relax their grasp upon lands. Labor is organizing for such work, and those who relish good reading should read *Looking Backward*."

Debs' influence, already great, continued to climb. George Howard, in September, 1890, told the Brotherhood of Conductors: "The majority of our successes for the past year was brought about through Eugene V. Debs, . . . that fearless champion of the rights of organized labor under any and all circumstances." The *Railway Service Gazette* of Toledo, Ohio, suggested Debs as a candidate for President of the United States, saying that he was "absolutely above reproach." John A. Hill, hearing of Debs' proposed retirement, wrote in the *Locomotive Engineer* that Debs was "by far the ablest labor speaker and writer in America" and then added: "To the honesty, intelligence, ability and untiring energy of Eugene V.

Debs, the B. of L.F. owes its present prosperity, and probably its existence, and we do not doubt but that the members of the order give him full credit."

Personal praise was as gratifying to Debs as to other men, but he was even more pleased by the success of the federation plan. The Order of Conductors endorsed federation by the overwhelming vote of 293 to seven; it seemed a matter of weeks before a united organization of conductors would belong to the Supreme Council. The Order of Railway Telegraphers repealed its no-strike rule, and the two Orders of telegraphers immediately merged; they too were certain to apply for membership in the Supreme Council. The sole hold-out was the Brotherhood of Engineers, and the growing pressure would soon force them to comply. Eugene V. Debs was near victory.

[5]

THEN the Supreme Council collapsed. It had been founded on a basis of common interest. Eugene Debs, the chief architect, had believed that the railroad workers could improve their conditions by uniting against the companies. All of the Brotherhoods had won unprecedented gains. But these gains were not enough for some of the leaders, who thrust aside the common interest to promote their selfish advantage.

An insignificant fight between two men grew into a disastrous conflict within the federation. F. M. McNerney, a yardmaster on the Galena division of the Chicago & Northwestern, discharged a switchman named James E. Crowe for alleged insubordination and profanity. Complications arose because McNerney was a member of the Trainmen, and Crowe belonged to the Switchmen. For more than a year the jurisdictional quarrel between these two unions, both affiliated to the Supreme Council, had been dormant. Now it again flared into open conflict. The Switchmen asked the superintendent of the Galena Division to reinstate Crowe. When he refused, they called a local strike. This pressure forced the superintendent to reverse his previous decision. He now fired McNerney and made Crowe the new yardmaster.

The Trainmen immediately called a special session of the Supreme Council and submitted McNerney's discharge as a grievance. The Switchmen objected. The representatives of the Firemen and the Conductors, instead of trying to mediate the dispute, foolishly took sides. The meeting soon lost any judicial tone. Twelve opinionated, leather-throated men began to shriek at each other across the table. Words like "scab" were used with alarming frequency. And Eugene Debs, with a blithe indifference to the possible outcome of this quarreling, joined the fray with the others. Finally the Trainmen made the threats a reality—they moved the dissolution of the Supreme Council. Debs took the lead in defeating this motion, and the mere fact that it had been made was a sobering influence. The Trainmen agreed to withdraw the grievance, and the meeting adjourned in a chorus of apologies.

A month later, May 14, 1891, the Chicago & Northwestern Railroad discharged all of its employees who belonged to the Switchmen and replaced them with members of the Trainmen. Since the circumstances indicated a conspiracy between the officials of the railroad and the Trainmen, the Supreme Council was summoned to consider the offense. Debs insisted that the Switchmen should be restored to their jobs, but the Supreme Council was unable to settle the dispute. He had no doubt, even before an investigation, that the Trainmen were guilty of treachery. To attack their action would result in the disruption of the Supreme Council; to ignore it would equally disrupt the Supreme Council and also would be unjust to the Switchmen. In either case, a project on which he had lavished energy and devotion for six years was doomed to a severe setback. And Debs, if he were honest, must have realized that his own lack of foresight at the April meeting was responsible, to a slight degree, for the catastrophe.

In the June issue of *The Magazine*, Debs flatly charged that the Trainmen had conspired with the Chicago & Northwestern to destroy the Switchmen. It was a bitter hour for federation, said the article, as bitter an hour as Valley Forge had been for the American Revolution, but the annual meeting of the Supreme Council on June 15 would solve the dilemma. Although

Debs was reeling under this latest example of human selfishness and stupidity, he still voiced his confidence that the federation would be preserved: "If the bolts of corporation vengeance can be stayed, federation alone is equal to the requirement. I believe federation has come to stay, and believing that means will be devised to strengthen and perpetuate this bulwark of workingmen's rights, I close this communication."

The June 15 meeting opened in an atmosphere of extreme hostility. Again threats and profanity were exchanged during the brief session, which ended with the appointment of a trial committee to conduct hearings and present a report. The hearings of the trial committee established the facts beyond question. The head of the Trainmen, S. E. Wilkinson, had met with an executive of the Chicago & Northwestern, who said that he intended to rehire the yardmaster discharged in April. If the Switchmen struck, would the Trainmen furnish men? No, said Wilkinson, we won't scab. Then the railroad executive asked if the Trainmen would furnish replacements if he fired all members of the Switchmen. Wilkinson said nothing. On May 14, five hundred Switchmen were discharged. Wilkinson furnished replacements. It was also shown that, before May 14, an official of the Trainmen had toured the East, telling all unemployed switchmen in his union to report to Chicago.

The Supreme Council reconvened in Terre Haute on June 29 to consider the results of the investigation. Eugene Debs was determined upon two goals: to secure justice for the Switchmen, and to preserve and strengthen the federation. This program seemed feasible as the meeting opened. The twelve delegates united in their appreciation of the Supreme Council; even a representative of the Trainmen declared: "I would willingly make any sacrifice to preserve this Federation." The Trainmen's delegates, in a routine step, objected to the entire proceedings. But, they added, if the Supreme Council insisted on its authority in the matter, it should punish only the officers of the Trainmen and not the entire organization.

Eugene Debs clearly favored the punitive course recommended by the Trainmen. He claimed that the Supreme Council had power "to inquire into any case that touches the welfare

of the organizations here represented. And the crime of which
the Brotherhood of Railway Trainmen has been found guilty
deserves the severest condemnation of every laboring man. No
punishment could be too severe for such an act." On the other
hand, said Debs, "I confess that I am not ready to vote, for the
simple reason that I do not fully realize the effect of the vote,
not only on the B. of R.T., but on all labor organizations. Is it
right, is it just to place a stigma on twenty thousand men because of the action of five hundred of their number?" Debs
wanted to return the disputed jobs to the Switchmen, and to employ punitive action against the leaders of the Trainmen, but to
make certain that the Trainmen remained in the Supreme
Council.

This intention was repeatedly defeated by Frank Sargent,
president of the BLF, who was presiding at the session. Sargent,
on three occasions, ruled that the Supreme Council had no
power over individuals, and that it could only deal with the
Trainmen as an organization. Finally a motion was made to
accept the report of the trial committee, which harshly condemned the Trainmen. It was carried by the combined votes of
the Firemen, the Conductors, and the Switchmen, with the
Trainmen opposing it.

The full significance of Frank Sargent's earlier ruling now
became evident. The only punishment open to the Supreme
Council under Sargent's interpretation—the expulsion of the
Trainmen—was recommended by the Switchmen. This motion
was exactly what Debs had tried to avoid. The issue now was
the preservation of the Supreme Council, and on that issue
Debs was willing to use any argument or trick to carry his point.
He carefully began to delay the meeting, making the first in a
series of cool, reasoned pleas: "This is a grave matter and must
not be acted upon without due deliberation. I do not recede one
iota from my position as to the guilt of certain parties, but I do
not see how such extreme measures can be adopted without
doing a grave injustice to the many innocent members. If the
B. of R.T. is expelled, it will arouse a feeling that will go forward
to disintegration. We will only spread the fire that was kindled
on the Northwestern, and destruction is inevitable."

As man after man arose to speak his mind, it became clear that a majority favored the expulsion of the Trainmen. Even J. J. Hannahan, Debs' colleague in the BLF, and George Howard of the Conductors appeared to favor that course. It seems certain that Debs became increasingly desperate. Perhaps his mind journeyed over the entire history of the movement to federate the railroad unions, the beginning in 1885 when only a handful of radicals dared to advocate united action, the slow growth of favorable sentiment, the leap forward during the Burlington strike, the day in 1889 when the Supreme Council was founded. By 1890 the various Brotherhoods in several cities were holding joint meetings; an actual merger into one great organization seemed a distinct possibility.

During those six years, in spite of disappointments and the grinding labor, Eugene Debs had remained faithful to his goal. He had neglected his wife and parents, traveled a dozen times from coast to coast, pleaded and threatened and used trickery. He had helped to build a mighty structure of friendship and brotherhood. Now it was being destroyed by one sudden, overwhelming blow. The treachery of the Trainmen, followed by the recklessness of the other delegates to the Supreme Council, threatened disaster to every man who worked on the railroads.

So Debs again rose and made an oblique plea, with himself as the scapegoat: "The penalty is altogether too severe. When this came up I did not think too severe a penalty could be inflicted, but I can see now that the penalty proposed, expulsion, or even a great deal less than expulsion, would be too severe. The Switchmen on the Northwestern have been fully vindicated by the action of this Council, and the perpetrators of this crime have been condemned. The expulsion of the Trainmen would not assist the Switchmen on the Northwestern. I believe the penalty is too severe and should be voted down."

But there was no sentiment for compromise among the delegates. They were determined to carry the matter to its final, illogical conclusion. These hardfisted, headstrong men, who had been trained in the merciless battles against the corporations, were not amenable to control. The argument went on, rising to the crisis that Debs had feared. In a final, hopeless effort,

Debs made another speech and moved adjournment. Not a man in the meeting was willing to second his motion, and it died.

Next the motion to expel the Trainmen was put to a vote. Debs' arguments had persuaded J. J. Hannahan to change his position, and the result was tied. The three representatives each of the Firemen and the Trainmen voted against expulsion, the Switchmen and the Conductors voted for it. The Trainmen could not be expelled. Debs had no illusion of having won the battle. Such an issue, as Debs knew, could only be settled by agreement on a solution, not by a deadlock.

But even the relative victory that Debs had scored was immediately upset. The chairman of the meeting, according to the bylaws of the Supreme Council, had no right to vote except in case of a tie. Frank Sargent's vote was therefore invalid. The Trainmen were expelled by the margin of one doubtful vote. The spirit of strict justice, justice that became unjust, had prevailed in the meeting. All railroad workers would suffer because six men were determined to punish the leaders of the Trainmen.

Then followed another blow. The Order of Railway Conductors and the Order of Railway Telegraphers, both of which had applied for admission to the Supreme Council, withdrew their applications because of the action taken against the Trainmen.

Thus hit by a series of reversals, Eugene Debs again proved his dogged devotion to principle. He had real cause for grief and anger at the events of the previous six weeks, which had turned complete victory into a stunning setback. But, instead of yielding to barren resentment, he calmly prepared to regain the ground that had been lost. Convinced that the existence of the Council was now a barrier to a federation which would embrace all railroad unions, he moved that the Council dissolve. Hannahan seconded his motion. Exactly the same men who had voted to expel the Trainmen, by some perverse logic, spoke against the dissolution of the Council. Debs thought they were wrong—the Council now contained only three Brotherhoods and four refused to join—but he agreed to postpone any decision until all the railroad unions had held their autumn conventions.

The next issue of *The Magazine* carried a complete account by Debs of the Northwestern conspiracy, including a principle which had found new emphasis in the past few weeks: "We bank not on the common sense of officials, but of the rank and file."

Invited in September to address the convention of the Brotherhood of Railroad Conductors, Debs flatly told the delegates that there should not be two organizations of railroad men in the same craft. Both orders of conductors now had the same purposes, which could be better accomplished if they would merge. Then the convention, on George Howard's recommendation, elected a committee to negotiate with the Order of Conductors. Within a month, the two organizations had merged, and George Howard had retired from the labor movement. One of the terms of the merger was that the new ORC would work for a general federation of all railroad workers.

Debs was also heartened by other events. The telegraphers united into a single order. L. W. Rogers, editor of the *Railroad Trainmen's Journal*, wrote a two-page editorial condemning the rôle of his union in the Northwestern conspiracy. The call for the 1891 AFL convention, issued by Sam Gompers, contained a powerful demand for labor unity: "On every hand we find organization and combination on the part of those who own or control wealth, and using their possessions to crush out the liberties, to stifle the voice, and pervert the rights of the toiling masses. . . . These combinations can only be successfully met and coped with by a compact and thorough organization of the wage-working classes of our country."

But unity was not to be quickly achieved. When the Trainmen's convention met in October, the delegates accepted without question Wilkinson's denial of any conspiracy with the Chicago & Northwestern. L. W. Rogers immediately resigned his job as editor of the Trainmen's *Journal* to found the *Age of Labor*, an independent labor paper. George Howard became vice-president of a co-operative building and loan society in Chicago. Other advocates of federation were leaving the railroad unions. Federation had suffered greatly in the minds of the rank and file. Everybody still recognized the power of united action—

even the BRT, when it was forced to strike on the Canadian Pacific, ran to the other Brotherhoods for help and got it—but there was widespread cynicism and mutual distrust.

Realizing that the struggle for federation would be a long fight, Debs began to slacken his breakneck pace. He spent more time reading Ingersoll's orations, developed an interest in Walt Whitman, again invited Jamey Riley to visit Terre Haute. His main job now was writing editorials for *The Magazine*, so he lavished care on each. Most of them were about federation, but he also wrote a careful analysis of several compulsory arbitration laws. The supporters of these laws believed "that strikes do no good, that they are productive of evil," but, Debs said, "such persons know absolutely nothing of the history of organized labor in the United States or elsewhere." In eighty-five years the hours of labor had been reduced from fourteen hours a day to nine, and in each case the reduction had been won by a strike. Every advance in the wages of workers had been won by a strike. So the right to strike must not be infringed:

What is a strike? The answer is war. And what is war? Resistance to wrong. Such is the history of war in the United States. To say there have been unjust, unnecessary wars, begs the question. Who is the craven that would have the constitution of the United States so amended that congress should never declare war? And who but an enemy of organized labor would advocate the enactment of a law that so much as squints at depriving organized labor of the only weapon it possesses of maintaining its rights against those whose policy is oppression?

When the annual session of the Supreme Council was convened in Chicago, June 20, 1892, only the Firemen and the Switchmen were present. Debs immediately moved that the organization be dissolved to make way for a new and better federation. The motion carried, and Eugene Debs buried his first major dream, an apparent failure.

[6]

THE NEXT MONTH *The Magazine* carried a full-page advertisement for the E. V. Debs Publishing Company of Terre Haute. Several technical books about railroads were already being offered for sale by the new company. Debs was preparing to leave the BLF, but his resignation was meeting strong resistance. He had unanimous support in his own union, and the failure of the Supreme Council had damaged his prestige only in the Brotherhood of Trainmen. Sam Gompers had written asking him to remain in the labor movement: "Somewhere I read you contemplated starting a labor paper, and while I appreciate the great services rendered by self-sacrificing men in that field and can unPerstand what influence you would wield with your trenchant pen, still judging from the past and the experience of others I am inclined to the belief that your opportunity in and through the Bro'd is much better and more advantageous to all concerned." Debs had great respect for Gompers' judgment and that letter made him pause and reconsider.

Then came another strike which removed all hesitation from his mind. New York State had passed a law establishing the ten-hour day in all industries, but made no attempt to enforce it. The switchmen in Buffalo, still working twelve to fourteen hours a day, tried to negotiate a reduction of hours, but the employers refused to meet with the Switchmen. Hoping to compel the state to enforce its ten-hour law, five hundred switchmen called a strike. The governor, however, chose to send six thousand state troops to Buffalo to crush the walkout. The Switchmen immediately summoned the officers of the other Brotherhoods to Buffalo. P. M. Arthur refused to attend the meeting. The others went to Buffalo, and did nothing. Debs tried to persuade them to back up the strike, but they refused. So Debs sardonically wrote in *The Magazine:* "Some of the 'grand officers' responded. They came at his call like homing doves, each with the message under his wing that they 'had no grievance and wouldn't fight.' " The strike ended in utter defeat. It also finalized the rupture between Eugene Debs and the men who had been his associates for seventeen years.

Two weeks later Debs told the national BLF convention that he was resigning from all connection with the Brotherhood:

I do this because it pleases me, and there is nothing that I would not do, so far as human effort goes, to advance any movement to reach and rescue perishing humanity. I have a heart for others and that is why I am in this work. When I see suffering about me, I myself suffer, and so when I put forth my efforts to relieve others, I am simply helping myself. I do not consider that I have made any sacrifice whatever; no man does, unless he violates his conscience.

That speech, far from having the desired effect, strengthened the delegates' resolve to keep their Secretary-Treasurer.

Debs had shown that he was a constructive and brilliant organizer as well as an agitator. He had inaugurated the policy of bonding trade-union officials, in order to protect the organization against embezzlement. Under his direction, the benefit system had been firmly established and expanded. His skill in negotiations was unquestioned. His prowess as a strike leader, hinging on the ability to control large numbers of men and to anticipate the enemy's tactics, amounted to genius. The contents of *The Magazine*, in both scope and quality, had earned it first place among the labor journals. Debs' tenure as a unionist—seventeen years, including twelve as a top official—was exceeded on the railroads only by P. M. Arthur.

But Debs' popularity rested, not so much on spectacular achievements, as on constant service. This service was personal and intimate. Many men did the big things occasionally—he did the little things every day. When he was traveling with a companion, he carried the heaviest grips, slept in the upper berth, sat in the aisle seat. Men noticed that he never hurried a waitress or a bellboy, never complained about a hotel room. If there was not enough food to go around, Debs got the small portion. He was always willing to give a loan to a down-and-out railroader, and did not care whether it was repaid. Once he heard that the lack of a good watch was blocking the promotion of another fireman. That was easy enough to take care of, said Debs, and handed the man his own. He had proved a thousand times his willingness not merely to share sacrifice, but to exceed it. So an attitude had developed toward Eugene Debs, an attitude of complete faith and devotion.

No candidate had ever been nominated against Debs and no vote had ever been cast in opposition. Every year his popularity

had grown. Now the delegates steadfastly refused to accept his
resignation. They voted him a leave of absence and two thousand dollars for a trip to Europe. Debs refused. They came to
his hotel room in the middle of the night and begged him to run
for re-election. Debs refused. Finally he issued a statement
which emphasized his fundamental opposition to the Brotherhood's principle of craft unionism:

While I don't expect to disconnect myself from organized labor,
to continue in my present position would materially interfere
with my plans for the future. A life purpose of mine has been the
federation of railroad employees. To unify them into one great
body is my object, but I don't believe it can be done on the
present lines. Now the men are enrolled in classes [crafts] for
distinct departments. Class enrollment fosters class prejudices
and class selfishness, and instead of affiliating with each other,
there is a tendency to hold aloof from each other. Class organization is well enough, but they should be united when the time
comes for federation. With the present differences in organization and differences among Grand Officers, federation is imprac-
ticable and impossible.

It has been my life's desire to unify railroad employees and to
eliminate the aristocracy of labor, which unfortunately exists,
and organize them so all will be on an equality. To this I am
going to turn my attention. I have as yet no plans formulated,
but they will come later, after a needed rest. These are my reasons for declining re-election. To the firemen I have given my
best years, and naturally they will always be first in my thoughts
and always will have my best wishes for success in the future.

For another two days the delegates refused to accept his resignation, in spite of his unqualified attack on the principles of the
Brotherhood. Then a compromise was reached. Debs quit as
Secretary-Treasurer. He agreed to continue as editor of *The
Magazine* on three conditions: he would have nothing to do with
finances, he would not be an officer of the Brotherhood, he
would be paid only nine hundred dollars a year. The delegates
accepted the first two conditions, but insisted on a salary of
three thousand. It was fixed at one thousand.

Now Debs, with a clear mandate from the membership to
write anything he pleased, really unleashed his indignation.

The lead article in the December issue was headed "Farewell, 1892":

The old year bears away in its archives the switchmen's strike at Buffalo, where organized labor was *struck down* because organized labor was *deaf* to the appeals of organized labor for help. That is the humiliating record 1892 takes with him. Organized labor appealed to organized labor for support in a just cause and secured oceans of sympathetic drool. Like the man in the parable the switchmen asked for bread and were given only stones or peanut shells. Bayonets and bullets, scabs and capitalists won a victory, rode rough shod over a principle which must eventually triumph or labor's emancipation day will never dawn.

Part II.

The American Railway Union

A strike is a practical protest, or a revolt, frequently successful, against wrongs that may be unendurable.
It is resorted to only when rendered necessary
by the oppressive action of capital, exercised against the strikers or against
any portion of their brethren
with whom they have in-
terests or sympathies
in common.
JOHN SWINTON

CHAPTER 5

◻

[1]

THE PRESIDENTIAL CAMPAIGN OF 1892 offered little excitement in its early stages, when sparring revolved around the tariff issue. Neither Benjamin Harrison nor Grover Cleveland was a dynamic figure. During his Presidential tenure, Harrison had opened the pork barrel to the veterans, signed the protectionist McKinley Tariff Act, and kept the door ajar for the coinage of silver. Cleveland, although known to be politically fearless and honest, was hobbled by narrow understanding and no imagination. The trade unions adhered rigidly to their nonpartisan policy and ignored the political patty-cake of the campaign, until the two dramatic strikes of July.

A handful of giant corporations, grown to maturity during the decades since the Civil War, controlled state governments and had an influential voice in Washington by 1892. All major appointees were chosen from the business community. Court decisions and new legislation were bought and sold. In the United States Senate were men who had made fortunes in silver, oil, transportation, timber, all types of manufacturing. This political power had been freely used by the railroads during the 1877 strikes; now the silver kings and Henry Frick of the Carnegie Steel Company underscored the earlier lesson for labor.

The skilled workmen at the Homestead, Pennsylvania, works of Carnegie Steel had long been represented by the Amalgamated Association of Iron and Steel Workers, one of the strongest unions in America. In the spring of 1892, negotiations for a new contract deadlocked over the wage issue. The corporation, although it had persuaded Congress to raise the tariff on steel billets so that higher wages could be paid, insisted that wages should be cut. The workers soon saw that the company's primary purpose was to wipe out their organization. Even before

the old contract had expired, Henry Frick erected a high wooden
fence around the Homestead works, cut loopholes in it for rifles,
covered the top with barbed wire, and mounted searchlights on
several towers inside the grounds. On June 28, two days before
the contract expired, Frick locked out his men. He had already
hired three hundred Pinkerton agents to guard the entry of
blacklegs into his factory. These Pinkertons were moved by
special train from New York to Ashtabula, Ohio, thence to
Youngstown, where they were loaded in two armored barges,
outfitted like a regular army, and towed up the Monongahela
River to Homestead. Although they had hoped to disembark
secretly, they were met at the landing by a huge throng of
armed strikers. After a pitched battle which lasted the entire
day, the invaders surrendered and were quickly escorted out of
town; three Pinkertons and seven workers were killed. Henry
Frick then telegraphed the governor of Pennsylvania, and the
governor sent eight thousand state troops into Homestead.
Strikebreakers were brought into the plant under the protection
of the militia. The strike leaders were indicted for murder, aggravated riot, conspiracy, and treason; the character of the
evidence against them became clear when they were all acquitted of every charge, but they were kept out of Homestead
until the strike was smashed. The lockout proved effective—by
November the union no longer existed at Homestead. Henry
Frick had proved that a modern corporation could destroy
with one stroke the strongest craft union in America.

Corporate power was again demonstrated at Coeur d'Alene,
Idaho, where the silver miners struck in protest against a wage
cut and lockout by the mine operators. The very day the militia
arrived in Homestead, July 11, a pitched battle was fought at
Coeur d'Alene between the union miners and a large force of
strikebreakers. Although the miners drove out the blacklegs and
seized the mine, their victory was frustrated by the intervention
of the governor, who declared martial law and secured Federal
troops from President Harrison. The Army moved swiftly and
ruthlessly to smash the strike. All known union men were arrested. Several hundred strikers were imprisoned for months in a
barbed-wire concentration camp, or bull pen, where they were

starved and mistreated. Eighty-five miners were indicted for contempt of court, and twelve were convicted. These twelve men were actually fortunate for they were at least lodged in a regular jail, while their fellows were housed like animals in the bull pen. The Army took over the job of smashing the workers' organization, and even prohibited the mines from hiring unionists. At Coeur d'Alene, as at Homestead, an open shop was established, and the strikers were blacklisted throughout the industry.

The Democrats carefully used these incidents to attack Harrison's administration. Seizing upon the fact that Frick was a prominent Republican and that his firm had been a chief beneficiary under the McKinley Tariff, Cleveland called the Homestead massacre an example of "the tender mercy the workingman receives from those made selfish and sordid by unjust governmental favoritism." Debs, even more certain than in 1888 that Harrison was a tool of the corporations, again worked for a Democratic victory. He wrote dozens of letters to local unionists urging support of Cleveland, and on his organizing trips he seldom missed a chance to attack Harrison. In November, Grover Cleveland, with the active support of most union leaders, was again sent to the White House. Many workers' votes also went to the People's Party, which polled 8 per cent of the total. With more than a million votes in their first national effort, the Populists became a definite threat to the old parties.

The events at Homestead and Coeur d'Alene and the Buffalo switchmen's strike infuriated Debs. Month after month *The Magazine* ripped into Pinkerton treachery and corporate greed. After the Presidential election, Debs continued to call for vigilance by the unions, and at the year's end he wrote:

If the year 1892 taught the workingmen any lesson worthy of heed, it was that the capitalist class, like a devilfish, had grasped them with its tentacles and was dragging them down to fathomless depths of degradation. To escape the prehensile clutch of these monsters, constitutes a standing challenge to organized labor for 1893, and demands of workingmen an amount of sentinel duty which must be performed if victory is to perch upon their banners.

This sentinel duty must be done politically, said the article, at
the ballot box and in the legislatures: government must no
longer serve as the guardian of the open shop. Debs also called
upon the workers to cast off "the leadership of men who from
any base ambition hold their positions to promote selfish ends
and aims," and to "unify upon all questions where rights are
involved."

The trade union leaders were forced, in spite of their private
desires, to make several gestures toward labor unity. Top officials in the Knights of Labor, now shrunk to a parody of its
former lustiness, and of the AFL met in Philadelphia and again
in St. Louis to consider joint action by the two orders. But the
Knights insisted on maintenance of their unions and on the
endorsement of the People's Party. The AFL denied both conditions, and the project collapsed. In the railroad unions, popular insistence on harmony was strong enough to compel the
formation of a second alliance. The new plan, initiated by the
BLF, was a more cumbersome duplicate of the Supreme Council. At a conference in Cedar Rapids, Iowa, it was endorsed by
the Firemen, Conductors, Trainmen, Switchmen, and Telegraphers.

Although Debs gave editorial blessing to the Cedar Rapids
federation, he doubted its adequacy. More gradually than in
1873, but steadily, the country was sliding into another depression. Twenty-eight banks suspended payment between January and April, another fifty-four in May, a hundred and eighteen in June. The continued decline in the level of wholesale
prices, which had been falling almost constantly since 1865, in-
exorably squeezed the farmers and industrialists. Debs knew
what that meant for railroaders: irregular work, wage cuts,
mass unemployment. Against this menace, the new federation
was a frail barrier. The Engineers and the Railway Carmen had
not joined. Jurisdictional strife was still rampant between the
Engineers and Firemen. The Trainmen were systematically
raiding both the Conductors and the Switchmen. The officials
whose treachery and bad judgment had wrecked the Supreme
Council still ruled the unions. Worst of all, the combined mem-

bership of the Brotherhoods was less than a hundred thousand men, one-tenth of the railroad workers.

Debs had no plan to meet this crisis. From 1885 to 1892, he had been certain the correct policy was to bring craft unions into a federation, but that theory had been rudely smashed. Now he was unsure about basic strategy. In his search for a solution, Debs opened *The Magazine* to anybody with an idea, and to several writers who had no ideas at all. Single tax, tariff reform, free silver, Utopian socialism, civil service, the nationalization of railroads—they were all presented and destroyed and presented again. Words spawned more words. Every reformer in the country hastily took advantage of an editor searching for a cause. Joe Buchanan beat the drum for a one-sentence platform to unite all reformers: Government ownership and operation of the railroads and telegraph. The silverites said that Buchanan's platform was perfect, except that free silver should be added. The single-taxers stubbornly clung to their belief in the divinity of Henry George. The civil service crowd still wanted honest government, and they didn't care who owned the railroads. Sam Gompers and his allies sneered at the Populists. And meanwhile, the depression spread over America like a glacier. Factories closed. Families were evicted from their homes. Mothers plundered garbage cans in their search for food. Children were turned out to forage for themselves. Highways and city streets were clogged with wandering, homeless, barefoot men.

Desperate for an answer to this misery, Debs was studying as never before. He forgot about the plan for a labor newspaper, let Kate look after the slack affairs of the Debs Publishing Company, crammed his editorial work on *The Magazine* into a few days each month, and worked in his second-floor library from dawn until long after midnight. In a few months he organized into usable form the countless facts that he had collected in years of effort. Hundreds of newspaper clippings were kept in the attic, filed into large scrapbooks. Dozens of notebooks, filled with notations and incidents from his experience on the railroads, were now pulled out of their cardboard boxes in the drawers of his roll-top desk. Slowly, from letters, notebooks, labor and radical journals, government reports, economic textbooks, half-forgotten memories, he pieced together a daring plan. When Professor John R. Commons of Indiana University came to Terre Haute in the spring of 1893, the scheme was complete in Debs' mind. In the editor's "home and extensive library," wrote Commons, "he expounded to me his plan of the American Railway Union, modeled after the Constitution of the United States, which should include subordinate organizations of all railway employees as 'states' in the union."

The plan recognized the distinctive problems and needs of workers in the various crafts, and united workers of all crafts in matters of common concern. Similar types of organization were already followed by the brewery workers and the coal miners. In May, 1893, the metal miners furnished a third example. Lockouts, wage cuts, court orders, militia, and bullpens had left raw welts on the spirit of the Coeur d'Alene strikers. The strike leaders, while still in jail for contempt of court, had agreed to combine the unions in the metal mining industry. As soon as they were freed, they set up the Western Federation of Miners with headquarters at Butte, Montana.

Debs' chance to apply his plan came quickly. On June 20, 1893, fifty disgruntled and alarmed railroaders met in Chicago to launch a counterattack against the depression. In spite of the presence of job seekers and careerists, the gathering contained the militant leadership of railway labor, with Debs as the unchallenged spearhead. L. W. Rogers, who had resigned his job as editor of the *Railroad Trainman* after the dissolution of the Supreme Council, came down from Oshkosh, Wisconsin. Sylvester Keliher, secretary-treasurer of the Railway Carmen and editor of their magazine, was cheerful but tough-minded; George Howard supplied eloquence and a flighty temperament. Through the entire day the men wrangled and quarreled and compromised, until finally the disagreements were resolved.

That evening Debs announced in a press release the formation of the American Railway Union. Membership in the new organization was open to all "white" workers who served a railroad in any way, except managerial employees. Even coal

miners and longshoremen were eligible if they worked for a
railroad company. Dues were cheap—a dollar initiation fee,
a dollar a year to the national union, local dues to be decided by
each lodge. The purposes of the order were to protect pay scales
and hours of work, to lobby for legislation favorable to the workers, to publish a daily newspaper and a monthly magazine, to
provide cheap insurance.

The ban against Negroes, which was the one great error of the
ARU constitution, was never rescinded by any railroad union,
although both the Knights of Labor and the AFL had once
sought Negro members. When the Knights organized in 1869,
they agreed that no distinctions would be made on the basis of
color or nationality, and this declaration was rigorously followed. Negroes in large numbers were joining the order by
1885. Also the AFL had early followed a policy of equality, but
by 1893 its proclamations were being trimmed to suit local
prejudices. It now made little effort to organize Negroes, frequently shunting them into Jim Crow locals. All of the railroad
Brotherhoods denied membership to Negroes and tried constantly to drive them out of the railroad service. Within the
ARU there was strong opposition to the proposed ban, but the
proceedings of the founding convention were never published,
and fifteen months passed before the issue was publicly debated.

[2]

THE FORMATION of the ARU was a sensational development in
the labor world. The new organization boasted about its break
with tradition, and the caliber of its officers lent weight to the
boast. Rogers had been chosen editor, Keliher secretary, Howard
vice-president; and Debs, as president, had a national reputation. Even Frank Sargent grudgingly admitted later: "Eugene
V. Debs was better known to the rank and file of labor and in all
probability had more friends than any man who ever occupied
a like position." So the ARU expected wide publicity, but the
headlines were usurped by another event.

Six days after the ARU was launched, the surviving Hay-

market martyrs were pardoned by John Peter Altgeld, who had
become Democratic governor of Illinois early in 1893. The newspaper storm against the pardon of the three men was based, not
on the act itself, but on Altgeld's declaration of reasons. If the
governor had predicated his position simply on mercy, it would
have been received with mild applause. His actual course was
far different. Months of study had convinced him that the
original trial had scoffed at justice. His pardon message, by its
biting arraignment of the earlier proceedings, aroused passions
equal to those of 1886. The public press violently called attention to Altgeld's foreign birth, his full beard, his humble beginnings. He was denounced as a socialist, an anarchist, a
criminal. With the Chicago *Tribune* and *Harper's* in the lead,
the entire pack of journalistic bloodhounds chased Altgeld
through reams of imagined offenses against law and order.

Similar treatment, as Eugene Debs soon learned, awaited anybody who dared to support Altgeld's action. Debs' editorship of
The Magazine had often been criticized within the Brotherhood,
but his praise of the pardon message signaled a more furious
onslaught. Letters linked together the names of Altgeld, Debs,
and Alexander Berkman, an anarchist who had tried to as-
sassinate Henry Frick after the Homestead strike. One eloquent writer appealed to Debs not to "extend the hand of
cordiality to those red-fisted monsters of social depravity [the
Haymarket defendants]." But Debs again revealed that stubbornness which marked his entire career. The opposition to his
views, far from forcing him to retreat, merely drove him to a
new advance. He had read Altgeld's message, with its careful
review of the evidence, and its logic had underscored his conviction. Confident that he was right, he struck two blows for every
one from the dissenters. As it became apparent that a majority
of organized labor supported Altgeld, the verbal battle in *The
Magazine* slowly died away.

The Haymarket pardon, although it hindered the task of
publicizing the ARU, failed to divert Debs from that purpose.
He and his fellow officers were aware of the need to win labor
support and clarify their aims before beginning an organizing
drive. Dozens of conferences were held with local unionists,

friendly newspapermen, officials in the Brotherhoods and the AFL. The details of setting up the outfit were handled carefully but quickly. Headquarters were established in Chicago. Stationery was ordered. Credit was established. Every act pointed to the main goal: to stampede the railroaders into the ARU. The genius of an organizing drive lies in the creation of great enthusiasm for the venture and confidence in its leadership. The prime technique is to inflame a joyous headlong rush into the organization. The ARU, short of money, short of skilled leaders, had to compensate for these handicaps by its finesse and conviction. Debs was confident of success, so confident that he predicted at least three hundred lodges would be organized before the first convention in June, 1894. But his view found little support; the prediction was everywhere greeted by scornful disbelief.

The craft-union leaders were united in their opposition to the new movement. Resentment and fright were widespread among the Brotherhood officials. Their rosters were dropping rapidly, largely because of the inability of members to pay the high dues. The depression was cause enough for worry, and industrial unionism was added reason for alarm. Even Samuel Gompers, who had felt great respect and friendship for Debs, was openly hostile to the ARU. In a letter to Gompers, Debs had declared his attitude: "There is no purpose to antagonize existing organizations, but it is believed that on account of its [the ARU] superior advantages it will absorb some of them at least and that ultimately there will be one organization for railway employes." This candor failed to change Gompers' mind; the AFL leader regarded any dual union as treason to the labor movement.

Gompers implied in his autobiography, thirty years later, that Debs had been lured into the ARU by a desire for fame. When Gompers was on a trip to the West Coast in 1891, according to the autobiography, he was visited in Kansas City by George Howard. Howard stated that he had worked out a plan to bring all railroad workers into one organization, and he asked Gompers to launch the enterprise and be first president. Gompers refused because he "felt that it was better to let the brotherhoods correct their own mistakes rather than to foster a dual organization with the hope of bringing the railroad unions into the Federation." Howard then said that he would take the proposal to Debs. According to Gompers:

> I told Howard that if I knew anything about Debs he would repudiate the offer just as I had, and resent the proposal. . . . So when it was announced that Debs had accepted the position of leader and become president of the American Railway Union, I was truly shocked; though I bore Debs no ill will, I never could quite forgive him for his action and particularly for retaining the position of editor of the official magazine of the Brotherhood of Locomotive Firemen while undertaking to establish a rival organization which aimed for the disintegration and destruction of the brotherhoods, his own included.

In making such a statement, Gompers apparently was blinded by the accumulated quarrels of thirty years. Debs had continued as editor of *The Magazine*, over his repeated protests, at the unanimous insistence of the BLF convention. And, although perhaps George Howard fathered the idea for the ARU, Debs' philosophy was clearly moving toward industrial unionism. Debs joined the ARU in the belief that the Brotherhoods had failed to protect the interests of the railroad workers. His evidence for this belief was exaggerated but basically sound:

> I was now to organize, with half a dozen others, the American Railway Union, so that engine wiper and section man might come in for their share of consideration as well as the engineer and conductor.
> This is where I broke with the railway officials. They were perfectly willing that we should have a firemen's union, but they were not willing for us to have a union that would unite all employees in the service in the equal interest of all.

Although the corporation executives vigorously opposed the ARU, the organization was not without its partisan supporters. The news of its formation brought vigorous approval from Daniel DeLeon, leader of the Socialist Labor Party. DeLeon, a brilliant scholar who had lectured in international law at Columbia University from 1883 to 1889, had passed through several radical movements before joining the small Marxist party. In 1886 he supported the mayoralty campaign of Henry George in New York, when George ran a strong second to the Democratic victor and clearly bested the young Republican nominee, Theodore Roosevelt. Two years later DeLeon joined the Knights of Labor, then Edward Bellamy's Nationalist movement, and in 1890 the Socialist Labor Party. Completely devoted to the workers' cause, DeLeon was certain that he alone was competent to lead the workers. His intelligence, loyalty, and ruthlessness rapidly thrust him to the top of the SLP—he had become national lecturer of the organization in 1891 and editor of its weekly organ, *The People*, in January, 1892. He now used his editorship to hail the ARU's "deliberate or instinctive recognition of the identity of the class interests of all railroad employees." The new union, said DeLeon, was "a step in the direction of clasping hands with the whole working class in all other industries," and of posing for the labor movement "the question, the real question . . . —the abolition of the capitalist system of production, the establishment of the co-operative commonwealth."

But far more important than DeLeon's support was the enthusiasm of the railroaders after the first ARU lodge was formed on August 17. It seemed that every underpaid railroader in the country—and there were nearly a million of them—wanted to join the order. Debs and his cohorts had carefully plotted for a stampede, but they were not ready for the breakneck rush that greeted them. The officers were unable to pass out charters fast enough to keep pace with the applications. Entire lodges of the Railway Carmen and the Switchmen transferred to the ARU. Firemen, conductors, even engineers, joined the industrial union. But the great majority of recruits came from previously unorganized men who had been unable to meet the high monthly dues of the Brotherhoods. The unskilled workers had been unprotected, underpaid, exploited; now the dikes snapped and a reservoir of bitterness and hope drove men pell-mell into the American Railway Union.

Debs, always prodigal of his health, recklessly hurled his energy into an effort to sustain this gigantic upsurge. He followed the iron rails back and forth across the great plains, carrying his ideas and faith to the railroaders. Everywhere he spoke the same words: *organize; federate.* On his lips, Labor Unity became the war song of the new crusade. It even seemed that he would be too busy to accept an invitation from Henry Demarest Lloyd, the chairman of the Labor Auxiliary, to fill a lecture engagement at the Columbian Exposition in Chicago. But on August 30 Debs was in Chicago, calling on the workers to take the future into their own hands:

The time is coming, fortunately, when we are hearing less of that old paternal Pharisaism: "What can we do for labor?" It is the old, old query repeated all along the centuries, heard wherever a master wielded a whip above the bowed forms of the slaves. It is the language of the slave catcher, the slave pen, the slave block and the slave plantation. We hear it yet, occasionally, along lines of transportation, in mines and shops, but our ears are regaled by a more manly query, an interrogatory permeated with the spirit of liberty and independence, which is, "What can labor do for itself?" The answer is not difficult. Labor can organize, it can unify, it can consolidate its forces. This done, it can demand and command.

As soon as Debs had finished his speech, he left for another town to organize another lodge. Week after week, he rushed from one city to the next, speaking, conferring, sending an occasional letter or hurried telegram to Kate. It was a gruelling existence, but he knew that Howard and Keliher were working just as hard, accomplishing just as much. And they were winning. Never in the United States had an organizing drive met with like success. The officials did not have to coax or persuade; their main job was to sign cards and issue charters. By September 5, a scant twenty days after the first lodge was founded in Fort Madison, Iowa, thirty-four ARU locals had been established. With no money, with only three organizers in the field, the ARU was signing up two to four hundred members a day, day after day. Then Debs headed homeward to rest, lay the groundwork for a new spurt forward, and do some work on *The Magazine.*

[3]

THE BUSINESS CRISIS had continued to grow deeper and sharper, until *Bradstreet's* estimated that there were three million unem-

ployed in the United States. In Chicago, Debs had seen unbe-
lievable poverty. Thousands of transient workers had been en-
ticed there by the Columbian Exposition, only to be stranded
without jobs. Police stations all over the city sheltered from
sixty to a hundred men every night. Sprawling figures slept in
the corridors and on the stairways of the City Hall. Mayor
Carter Harrison stated that Chicago held two hundred thousand unemployed men, and a newspaper there estimated that
saloonkeepers were furnishing free meals for sixty thousand
men a day.

These conditions, paralleled throughout the country, stimulated a new growth of radical ideas in the labor movement. At
the AFL convention of 1890, Sam Gompers had flatly announced
his opposition to socialism and to political action by labor.
"The trade unions pure and simple," Gompers declared, "are
the natural organizations of the wageworkers to secure their
present material and practical improvement and to achieve
their final emancipation." But at the following convention, a
delegate from the machinists' union introduced a platform of
political demands which called for "the collective ownership
by the people of all the means of production and distribution."
This platform missed adoption by a narrow margin, and in a
subsequent referendum it was endorsed by a dozen large unions,
thus encouraging the socialist attack on "pure and simple trade
unions." The simultaneous growth of the People's Party gave
rise to a demand that the Federation discard its traditional nonpartisan policy, and either endorse the Populists or launch its
own political movement.

The new socialist agitation found a ready outlet in *The Magazine*. Debs' office was flooded by articles based on a loose and
confused Marxism. One contributor, in trying to criticize the
single-tax movement, managed to confuse himself, his readers,
and the theory of surplus value. Another article spoke with
respect of Karl Marx but argued that Marx's results could be
attained more simply by other means. Debs, without really attempting to understand these strange doctrines, used them to fill
the pages of *The Magazine*. He had no interest in theoretical
subtleties; his own energy was consumed in a pragmatic solu-

tion of daily problems. The idea of a social system other than capitalism had never seriously entered Debs' mind.

But although Debs still felt friendly toward Frank Sargent and John Hannahan, the issue of industrial unionism had imposed a definite strain upon their relations. The chief victim of Debs' heresy, however, was his brother Theodore. Since the ARU was unable to support a cashier and bookkeeper, Theodore had been forced to keep his old position with the Brotherhood. He felt more and more like an interloper, until finally he was able to tolerate it no longer. Early in 1894 he joined Eugene in the ARU. Never again did the two brothers work for competing interests.

Late in 1893, during one of Debs' visits in Terre Haute, Jamey Riley came there to give another lecture. Kate Debs made elaborate preparations for a family dinner to honor the poet, who was going to follow his usual custom of staying at her home. Small watercolor prints, brought all the way from Chicago, were used as placecards. All of the appointments were in yellow and white, according to the local society pages, and huge bowls of chrysanthemums were placed throughout the house. Much thought was lavished on the occasion, so that everything might be perfect. The dinner passed in gaiety and compliments, to Kate Debs' complete gratification. But the actual climax occurred in a press conference after dinner, when Riley proved that he, too, could meet the demands placed upon him. In his best stage voice, the poet molded a cornerstone for what came to be the Debs Legend: "God was feelin' mighty good when he made Gene Debs, and he didn't have anything else to do all day."

[4]

THE MIGHTY SURGE of the American Railway Union continued unchecked and undiminished. By November 15, charters had been issued to eighty-seven lodges, enabling the order to keep four organizers on the pay roll. At the year's end the Union Pacific, the Santa Fe, the Denver & Rio Grande, the Rio Grande

& Western, and several lesser roads were solidly organized. There were twenty-two ARU locals on the Northern Pacific and more than forty on the Southern Pacific. Debs was everywhere advising the workers to resist all wage cuts during the depression, because if wages were once cut it would take years to have them restored; but his advice was not needed. Never had he seen such a spirit among the railroaders. On one western railroad the auditing clerks wanted to organize, but the company stated that every clerk who joined the ARU would be discharged. A group of switchmen at once called on the manager and warned him not to threaten the clerks. During a grave depression, when unemployed men stood on every street corner, such action seemed suicidal, but the switchmen made it stick, and for the first time a railroad office was filled with union men.

The first number of the *Railway Times* appeared on January 1, 1894, and Rogers' trenchant arguments further accelerated the growth of the ARU. The union expanded so violently that it became chaotic and unwieldy. The top officials were experienced and capable unionists, but there was an alarming dearth of secondary leadership. Local unions of three to four hundred men were composed solely of raw recruits. The hat-waving, thigh-smacking youthfulness that gave the organization its vigor could also bring it to disaster. Debs knew that novices were poorly qualified to deal with corporation executives who were brilliant and adroit, men who held their cards close to their chests and played them with finesse.

But, by a peculiar twist of bad luck, the first challenge came from a Federal Judge. Early in March, receivers acting for a Federal District Court declared a wage cut for all workers on the Union Pacific, and Judge Elmer S. Dundy issued an injunction which forbade the workers to strike. This was not the first use of the injunction in labor disputes. In 1883 labor organizers in Baltimore and in Kent, Ohio, had been enjoined from attempts to induce workers under contract to leave their jobs. During the railroad strike of 1888, many state courts had issued restraining orders. A Federal court in Colorado, as early as 1885, granted an injunction during a labor dispute on a railroad which was being operated by the court, and six years later another District court intervened in a case that did not involve Federal receivership.

These judicial precedents meant nothing to Debs. Hurrying to Cheyenne, Wyoming, he condemned the injunction as a "death-blow to human liberty," since it prohibited any combination among the men to quit work. He also vigorously attacked the wage reduction. A few days later the senior judge on Dundy's court, Henry C. Caldwell, called a conference of the receivers and the employees for March 15 at Omaha. When this conference failed to reach agreement, Judges Caldwell, Dundy, and John A. Riner began hearings on both the wage cut and the injunction. The hearings completely vindicated the union's position. The decision of Caldwell and Riner ordered the former pay schedules restored. Equally important, it set aside the injunction on the grounds that no injunction could be issued requiring specific performance by the employees, and that workers have an indisputable right to combine in order to raise wages.

The ease with which the ARU won its first victory made its members cocky and also heightened the resistance of the railroads. When a dispute developed two weeks later on James J. Hill's Great Northern, neither the workers nor the company showed a willingness to compromise. Hill had often shown his unscrupulousness and financial shrewdness during his rise from Canadian obscurity to membership in the highest circles of railroad management. As clerk for a packetboat company at St. Paul and then as claim agent for the St. Paul & Pacific Railroad, he had acquired expert knowledge of transportation and storage. Realizing that coal would inevitably replace wood as train fuel, Hill began to buy coal lands; the wisdom of his prediction established him as an independent power in Minnesota finance. In 1878 he and three other men purchased the bankrupt St. Paul & Pacific, and for twelve years they carefully expanded their railroad holdings. The Great Northern, which was formed by combining the various roads in 1890, reached Puget Sound in 1893—the northernmost transcontinental line.

Hill, with a firm control over the entire system, did not pro-

pose to loosen his grasp. He was determined that he would retain the Great Northern, and that the Great Northern would
retain its profitable status. Wages on his line were slashed in
August, 1893, and again in January and March, 1894. After the
third cut, engineers and freight conductors were drawing eighty
dollars a month; truckmen, roundhouse workers, and section
hands a dollar per day; the average was less than forty dollars a
month. In April, the employees voted to strike unless Hill met
their representatives to set up a new pay scale. Hill refused to
answer an ARU letter informing him of his employees' decision.
His managers issued appeals to the workers to stay at their
jobs, promising promotions to those who were loyal to the company. But the men did not trust Hill, and the strike was called
at noon on April 13.

As the strike spread across the Northwest, James J. Hill instructed his superintendents to fire anybody known to be sympathetic to the union. In a further attempt to intimidate the
workers, huge cardboard signs were posted the entire length
of the Great Northern, carrying a declaration by the Assistant
Attorney-General that any interference with the Federal mails
could be punished by a ten-thousand-dollar fine and two years
in prison. But the trains were not halted by violence—they were
halted because nobody would work. On April 21 the mayor of
St. Cloud, Minnesota, wired to Hill: "Send no scabs here. Will
only tend to create a disturbance. R.R. property protected and
men orderly." That same day, as Debs' train rolled into St.
Paul, a stranger approached him with a request to attend a conference at Hill's home. Fearing a trap, Debs refused the invitation. He continued to St. Paul, where he, his brother Theodore,
and George Howard set up strike headquarters in the Sherman
House. The men who hurried into the hotel suite were all given
simple instructions: Nobody works. Nobody stops any trains.

When the chiefs of all the Brotherhoods either came out
against the strike or swore strict neutrality, L. W. Rogers opened
up with his heaviest sarcasm in the *Railway Times*. Frank
Sargent had told Hill: "If the firemen in your employ, who are
members of the brotherhood, have quit work in the present
strike, they have violated the rules of the organization and will

be expelled!" Rogers answered for Hill: "Thanks awfully." The Grand Chief Conductor announced: "Our members' duty is to comply strictly with our laws, to perform their regular and proper duties. If any participate in a strike they must abide the consequences, which are well known to all." And the *Times* replied: "Return and be forgiven. God bless you, my children; chip in the dues."

After his railroad had been closed down tight for more than a week, Hill summoned the ARU officials to a meeting, where he announced that he would arbitrate if the Brotherhoods were represented on the panel. Debs flatly refused on the grounds that the Brotherhoods were not a party to the dispute. If the Brotherhoods control your workers, why, asked Debs, can't they move your trains? He added that the strike would be settled on the union's terms, which had already been presented to the company. Debs knew that he was in a strong position. The nine thousand employees of the Great Northern were united in support of their strike. Every train was stopped except mail trains, which were moving on Debs' explicit orders. Instead of weakening the union, the strike was strengthening it. At one large meeting of railroaders in St. Paul, where Debs and Howard spoke, two hundred twenty-five men joined the ARU.

But James J. Hill was slippery. One day Debs was startled to find himself summoned to the office of Governor Knute Nelson. He was more startled when he arrived there. The governor, after studiously ignoring his caller for several minutes, began furiously to attack Debs as an "agitator," an "anarchist," a "foreigner," who was "stirring up strife among peaceful and contented workingmen." As Nelson talked his voice rose, his face became livid above his gray chin whiskers; his short body bounced around the room. But the strike leader quietly heard him out. Then Debs curtly told the governor about the conditions which had caused the walkout and ended by taking the offensive: "You can't bluff me. I can see clear through you and your game. You wear Jim Hill's collar. I don't. You are acting under his orders. I am here to fight him. I absolutely refuse to order the strikers back to work. . . . Moreover, I propose to place you and your attitude squarely before the workingmen of Minnesota and when you are next a candidate they will put you where you properly belong." By the end of the conference Nelson was begging Debs not to misunderstand him. The strike leader angrily replied: "No, governor, that is not the trouble; the trouble is that I do understand you."

Jim Hill now played his trump card. He arranged an invitation for Debs to address the St. Paul Chamber of Commerce, believing that contact with the strike leader would unite the business community in opposition to the ARU. Debs thought it would be fun to bait the bear in his own den, so he accepted. And this was truly the bear. As Debs entered the meeting, his audience was cold, hostile, rigid. These men had dealt in brains and ruthlessness to make fortunes on the frontier. Their depredations found virtue in a rigid philosophy: The earth belongs to the strong. A folk saying about them was more accusing: "They stole into the Territory. They stole the Territory. They stole out of the Territory." Trade unionism would find little support in this room. The air hung motionless and forbidding, much as it had when Debs and Susan B. Anthony walked through the streets of Terre Haute in 1879.

Debs began his talk calmly, taking his listeners along the railroads, telling them what it meant to be a section hand or a brakeman. His hands drew pictures of the small frame shacks behind the roundhouses and the freightyards. He explained the anguish and worry of rearing a family on a dollar a day. His lean body strode back and forward across the platform, the bald head bobbing like a Halloween apple. Most audiences in 1894 expected a speaker to furnish long words, Biblical constructions, wild bursts of oratory, and Debs had spent two decades copying this mode. But his ideas had begun to control his rhetoric; his speech was becoming more his own. He used fewer pointless images, fewer lush sentences. Now, as he stuck to living realities, minds began to move in rhythm with his high and melodious voice. The hostility in his audience collapsed, like a silent outpouring of swallowed breath. Man after man lost his animosity and began to feel friendly toward this hulking invader who talked so fervidly about his own people. When Debs had finished, the Chamber of Commerce demanded that the dispute be submitted to arbitration. Debs accepted. Hill was beaten.

Eighteen days after the strike began, the ARU leaders met the company in the anteroom of Hill's office to hear the decision of the arbitration board. As Charles Pillsbury, a flour milling magnate and chairman of the board, droned out the award, the jubilant unionists slapped their thighs and shook hands with each other. The strikers had won 97½ per cent of their demands, an aggregate wage increase of $146,000 a month. Debs and Hill arose in turn to announce that they were empowered to say that the award was satisfactory. Pillsbury proposed a lavish banquet to celebrate the settlement, but Debs made a counter-proposal: Spend your ten thousand dollars to buy calico for the wives of the section men. Jim Hill congratulated the strike leaders on their shrewd management of the walkout. Then the unionists hurried from the room to send wires to every point on the Great Northern, ordering the men back to work. Howard and Rogers left to travel over the system and make certain the wires were obeyed. In a brief press conference, Debs told of his joy and relief: "The one grand achievement of this strike is to prove to organized labor that there is nothing in violence. I do not think there will be any more big strikes for a long time. I hope not. . . . I feel as though a great load were taken off my shoulders. The strain was terrible, because there were so many interests to be considered. I want to go home for a while."

The train carrying Debs to Terre Haute moved slowly out of the yards in St. Paul. Both sides of the track were lined with railroaders, standing bareheaded to thank the man who had led them to victory. Debs never forgot a detail of the incident:

The greatest tribute that was ever paid to me was that of the section men after the Great Northern strike. As my train pulled out of St. Paul, those men with shovels in hand and happiness fairly radiating from their faces, yet with tears in their eyes— those section men stood at attention. That tribute was more precious to me than all of the banquets in the world.

The wonderful unity of the strikers had earned their triumph. Hill had not been able to set one Brotherhood against another, as the railroads had customarily done. From one end of the

Great Northern to the other, the men had peacefully left their jobs. Not a drop of blood had been shed, but not a wheel had turned, except those on mail trains. Peaceful and united action had proved the key to success. Debs afterwards wrote that the Great Northern strike was the only clear-cut victory of any consequence ever won by a railroad union in America.

This strike merely stiffened opposition to the ARU among the craft unionists. In his autobiography, Samuel Gompers wrote:

The A.R.U. made some progress during its first year. On the Great Northern there was a strike and for a moment circumstances were to their favor and they won an agreement. It was not due to the A.R.U. that they won; it was due to influences brought to bear other than the organization.

Unfortunately, Gompers did not name these "other influences," nor did he explain why they benefited the ARU but bypassed the other unions. During 1894 nearly seven hundred fifty thousand men took part in strikes, but the only important gains were won by the ARU. In one year Debs' union signed up a hundred fifty thousand railroaders, while the combined Brotherhoods could list only ninety thousand names and the AFL was hard driven to maintain its hundred seventy-five thousand members.

When Debs returned to Terre Haute, more than four thousand persons gathered to hear his account of the strike. Disdaining to attack Hill, Debs merely stated that "the reduction was without cause" and then stressed the heroism of the workers, the peacefulness of their conduct, and the mutual congratulations with which the strike had closed. The reaction of the Rev. Holmes Park of the First Baptist Church was true of many others: "I went to hear him that night with great prejudice. I remember that there was not an innuendo or a single fling at the men who had been his enemies. I said that he was a born leader, and I have never taken it back."

CHAPTER 6

◻

[*1*]

THE fierce, hard-fought Pullman boycott of 1894, named The Debs Rebellion by the commercial newspapers, began as a local dispute in the small Chicago suburb of Pullman, Illinois. During the previous year, more than sixteen thousand business firms had gone bankrupt, including fifty companies with a capital of more than a half million dollars each. Thousands of other firms were threatened with failure. The continued drop of wholesale prices made it increasingly difficult to produce goods at a profit. Companies, in a frantic attempt to cut their production costs and salvage their investments, repeatedly slashed the pay of their workers. These wage cuts and layoffs burst with a peculiar fury upon the residents of Pullman, where the Pullman Palace Car Company was the only employer and the only landlord. Since there was no competing demand for labor, and since most of the Pullman workers lacked the money to migrate elsewhere in search of better jobs, they were forced to submit or starve.

Even in prosperous years, wages at Pullman were below the union scale for similar work in Chicago, and this difference was accentuated during the depression. A Federal commission later estimated that Pullman slashed wage rates 25 per cent between 1893 and May, 1894. The Rev. William H. Carwardine, a minister in Pullman who later wrote a book about the labor dispute there, believed that the reductions were even greater: "The average cut in wages was 33⅓ per cent; in some cases it was as much as 40 per cent, and in many was fifty per cent." Iron machinists in the streetcar department at Pullman charged that their wages were reduced 70 to 85 per cent. Vice-President T. H. Wickes of the Company, contradicting these claims, said that the average daily rate of earnings had declined only 19 per cent, but he failed to point out that few men worked every day. The

108

size of the pay roll had declined drastically. In July, 1893, there were fifty-five hundred employees at Pullman, but the following May the total working force was only thirty-three hundred.

Just as wages were lower in Pullman, so rents were higher there. Jane Addams of Hull House, who investigated the town for the Civic Federation of Chicago, said that an eighteen-dollar-per-month cottage in Pullman could be rented for fifteen dollars in Chicago. In the words of the Federal commission: "If we exclude the aesthetic and sanitary features at Pullman, the rents there are from 20 to 25 per cent higher than rents in Chicago or surrounding towns for similar accommodations. The aesthetic features are admired by visitors, but have little money value to employees, especially when they lack bread." But the company refused to cut rents when it reduced wages, claiming that its rental of houses was a separate business from its manufacture of sleeping cars, and that there was no connection between the two enterprises.

Every foot of ground, every house, every church in the town was owned by the company, and they were run on a purely commercial basis. Even the sewage from the workers' homes was pumped to George M. Pullman's truck farm as fertilizer. Adults paid three dollars and children one dollar per year for the use of the town library, but the company said this charge was levied "not for profit, but to give the subscribers a sense of ownership."

The town was similar in many ways to a feudal manor, with George Pullman as absolute monarch. Since he believed that saloons and trade unions tended to inflame the workers, both were banned from the community. The eight-hour day was also banned, because Pullman thought that idleness would promote mischief. Professor Richard T. Ely and a Chicago judge both charged that the company hired spies to inform against the workers, and Mr. Carwardine wrote: "I am in a position to know that information of everything going on in the town of Pullman . . . is conveyed by letter every week to headquarters from the town proper." In order to maintain this absolute domination, the company freely interfered in local elections. Intimidation at the polls was common. The residents were advised how to vote, and the advice also held a poorly concealed threat. On one occasion a foreman was ordered to withdraw his name as a candidate for public office; when he refused he was fired.

Although most employees continued to live in Pullman because residents there were the last to be laid off and the first to be rehired, they deeply resented the destruction of their dignity. With grim humor one man declared: "We are born in a Pullman house, fed from the Pullman shop, taught in the Pullman school, catechized in the Pullman church, and when we die we shall be buried in the Pullman cemetery and go to the Pullman hell." Mr. Carwardine added that an awareness of George M. Pullman, not an awareness of God, ruled the community: "An unpleasant feature of the town is that you are made to feel at every turn the presence of the corporation. . . . This is a corporation-made and a corporation-governed town, and is utterly un-American in its tendencies." Four years later, the Supreme Court of Illinois agreed. Ordering the Palace Car Company to sell all property in the town of Pullman not needed for its manufacturing business, the Court declared that company towns were "opposed to good public policy and incompatible with the theory and spirit of our institutions."

The Pullman Company also exploited its monopoly position by charging exorbitant prices for its services, according to contemporary claims. Senator John Sherman, Republican of Ohio, who introduced a bill to bring the Pullman Company within the Sherman Antitrust Act of 1890, said to the Washington correspondent of the *Chicago Inter-Ocean:* "I regard the Pullman Company and the sugar trust as the most outrageous monopolies of the day. They make enormous profits, and give their patrons little or nothing in return." This attack aroused much comment, because George Pullman was a major source of campaign funds for Sherman's own party. Sherman exaggerated when he said that Pullman gave its customers "little or nothing in return," but he minimized when he said that it had made "enormous profits." Since its formation in 1867, the company had paid an annual dividend of 8 per cent, and during the depression dividends were increased while wages were being cut 25 per cent. For the year ending July 31, 1894, the corporation had an undivided surplus of $2,320,000, exceeding its total wage outlay for six months. Losses on the contracts received in 1894 were borne equally by the workers and the company, but, in the opinion of the Federal commission, "three-quarters of the loss for the company and the balance for labor would have more fairly equalized the division of loss on these contracts." Brushing aside the corporation's plea that, in addition to other losses, it had received no interest on its investment, the commission emphasized that much greater losses would have followed a complete shutdown.

As early as December, 1893, the Pullman Company was forced to issue a public statement denying the existence of extreme distress among its workers. The denial was easy to read, and easy to believe for men who had their own distress. Nobody cared much about poverty in Pullman except the residents of Pullman. During the harsh Illinois winter, want and suffering there became unbearable. Children lacked the money to buy school books, but that didn't matter—they also lacked the shoes and coats needed to go to school. In some homes they were kept in bed all day because there was no coal in the house; in others they were sent to bed early because there was no food for dinner. All joy passed from life. Sullen, tight-lipped women walked lead-footed through their worries. Men stood day after day by their windows and looked at the dirty black snow in the street—no work, no money, little hope. They erupted into violent rage, kicking the dog, swearing at the children, berating the wife for unmentionable evils. Nothing to do but stand at a window all day, looking at the dirty black snow and hearing a baby's whine from the next room.

Spring brought back hope, not much but a little. Men began to talk about striking one good blow against Pullman. During March and April, a majority of the employees joined the American Railway Union—they were eligible because the company operated a few miles of track near the factory. Finally on May 7, 1894, a committee of forty employees visited vice-president Wickes to present their complaints about wages and working conditions. Wickes told the committee to return two days later with their grievances down in writing; but on May 9 Wickes

again delayed, promising to personally investigate the shop
abuses. The men were not satisfied. Words were cheap, they
thought; you couldn't trust Wickes. The next night the grievance committee held an all-night session at the Turner Hall in
Kensington, an adjoining town, to discuss the advisability of a
strike. George Howard and Sylvester Keliher were both at the
meeting to urge delay until Wickes had completed his investigation. Howard had previously wired to Debs, who was in Terre
Haute, that a walkout might occur. Debs, knowing nothing of
conditions in Pullman, had advised caution until the union
could learn the facts. But Howard's oratory, Keliher's ebullient
charm, and Debs' influence all went for nothing. The workers
were mad. God Himself could not have stopped them. On the
third ballot they voted unanimously to strike.

At noon on May 11, three thousand workers left their jobs in
the Pullman shops, and the remaining three hundred men were
quickly laid off by the company. The walkout was calm, with
no hint of violence. The strikers posted guards around the plant
to make certain that vandals would have no chance to damage
corporation property. Driven to the end of the tether, these men
had snapped the chains and struck, but they struck without
much hope. Resigned desperation was the major key in a May 13
statement by Thomas Heathcote, the strike committee's chairman: "We do not expect the company to concede our demands.
We do not know what the outcome will be, and in fact we do
not care much. We do know that we are working for less wages
than will maintain ourselves and families in the necessaries of
life, and on that proposition we absolutely refuse to work any
longer."

Notified that the strike had begun, Debs at once hurried to
Pullman to investigate its causes. The ARU had neither called
nor authorized the walkout, but these men were members of the
union and Debs' clear responsibility was to ascertain the justice
of their action. Seven years earlier he had protested against
George Pullman's labor policies, but he was ill prepared for
what he found in 1894. The Pullman employees told incredible
but truthful stories of hardship. One skilled mechanic worked
ten hours a day for twelve days, and then received a pay check

for seven cents; his wages had been $9.07, but nine dollars rent for his company-owned house had been deducted in advance. A fireman worked "428 hours per month or about sixteen hours per day, and receives therefrom $40.00 per month pay," according to Mr. Carwardine. A blacksmith, paid forty-five cents for working six hours, declared that he was not willing to starve and wear out his clothes on Pullman's anvil at the same time. "I have a wife and four children," another employee said, "and it was for them that I struck, as I think that when a man is sober and steady, and has a saving wife, one who is willing to help along, and after working two and a half years for a company he finds himself in debt for a common living, something must be wrong."

Working conditions, almost as much as wages, had stimulated the revolt. There was a rigid hierarchy in the shops, no official daring to contradict his superiors. Foremen were free to curse and abuse their men, confident their authority would be always upheld. One worker explained how the company systematically used the speed-up system: "cabinet-makers were rated at seventeen to nineteen cents [per hour], and prices for piece work were supposed to be made to enable men to make that rate; wherever a man made over one or two cents per hour above day rate, that particular job was again pruned in price." There was no recognition of merit in the company's policies, and thirty years of loyal service were no guarantee against discharge without cause. One man was blacklisted for a trivial offense; forty employees were blacklisted in another case. There was no pension for laid-off or retired workers, many of them spending their last days in a poorhouse. Mr. Carwardine charged that the company did not pay disability damages "unless absolutely compelled to, to those who are injured or die in its service." All inventions by employees were simply appropriated by the corporation, the inventor receiving neither payment nor recognition.

On May 14, Eugene Debs spent the entire day wandering through the town of Pullman, inspecting the houses, talking with the women and children, noticing the size of pay checks, hearing complaints by the score, by the hundred. That night

Debs left for St. Paul, but four days later he was back in Pullman and spent most of the day and evening there. As one link clutched the next to form an ugly chain of greed and injustice, his hesitation disappeared. Finally he told a meeting of Pullman employees:

If it is a fact that after working for George M. Pullman for years you appear two weeks after your work stops, ragged and hungry, it only emphasizes the charge I made before this community, and Pullman stands before you a self-confessed robber . . . The paternalism of Pullman is the same as the self-interest of a slave-holder in his human chattels. You are striking to avert slavery and degradation.

[2]

WHEN the first national convention of the American Railway Union met in Chicago on June 12, 1894, the entire labor movement was in a critical situation. Layoffs and wage cuts had aroused fierce resistance, but strike after strike had been beaten down. The formula perfected at Homestead, Coeur d'Alene, and Buffalo, was even now being used against a hundred fifty thousand coal miners: strikebreakers, injunctions, Federal and state troops, starvation. The glorious promise of the unemployed march on Washington had ended a ludicrous shambles, with General Jacob S. Coxey arrested for walking on the Capitol lawn. Only the American Railway Union had managed to beat its way forward. Debs had been ridiculed ten months earlier when he predicted three hundred lodges within a year, but his estimate had been exceeded; the convention held more than four hundred delegates from four hundred sixty-five local unions.

Debs, in his opening speech, pointed a course that seemed well tailored to the organization's needs and strength. Recalling the aid received from coal miners and other railroad workers during the Great Northern strike, he applauded the growing unity of labor. The ARU did not wish to antagonize the Brotherhoods, but was trying to unite all railroaders, including those who had been "left out in the cold to endure the pitiless storms of corporate power." Just six weeks earlier in *The Magazine*, Debs had attacked government ownership of the railroads as a step that would increase "absolutism in government enterprises" and that would leave the employees defenseless, since the government would never tolerate strikes or boycotts against itself. Now he sharply reversed himself, urging government purchase in order to eliminate profits and thus insure lower rates to the public and higher wages to labor. Without recommending any specific action in regard to the strike at Pullman, he emphatically stated his opinion of the reasons for the walkout there: "It was work and poverty in Pullmantown, or Pullemdown, until, patience ceasing to be a virtue, and further forbearance becoming treason to life, liberty and the pursuit of happiness, the employees determined to strike to better their conditions."

John R. Commons, listening to Debs, "was thrilled by his eloquence and his sympathy for the factory employees." The delegates were overwhelmed. One passage in the address brought them to their feet screaming, whistling, cheering, throwing their hats and fans high into the air:

The forces of labor must unite. The dividing lines must grow dimmer day by day until they become imperceptible, and then labor's hosts, marshalled under one conquering banner, shall march together, vote together and fight together, until working men shall receive and enjoy all the fruits of their toil. . . . Such an army would be impregnable. No corporation would assail it. The reign of justice would be inaugurated. The strike would be remanded to the relic chamber of the past. An era of good will and peace would dawn.

Debs' militancy and fervor set the tone for the entire convention. Point by point, the young and enthusiastic delegates hammered out a program far in advance of the Brotherhoods. After an address by J. R. Sovereign, who had replaced Powderly as head of the K of L, the convention resolved to "tender to the Knights of Labor its hearty alliance in all movements brought about for the elevation and benefit of the laborer." Military intervention in strikes was condemned by a provision that no ARU member should join any state militia "until such time as they are used for a more righteous cause than at present." The People's Party was indirectly endorsed in vigorous language:

WHEREAS, It has been the common practice to ask candidates
for public office, their endorsement for the principles set forth
in the platform of labor organizations; and

WHEREAS, When office has been secured, the pledges have
been frequently broken and wholly ignored; therefore be it

RESOLVED, That it is the sense of this convention that to
secure perfect emancipation from the wrongs and inequalities
inflicted by our social system, that the laboring men must act
on independent political lines, and support men whom they
know to be in accord with their principles.

The delegates later approved a free-silver plank, one of the main
demands in the Populist platform.

Motion after motion was passed in this wave of solidarity.
Not even the boiling weather could ruffle tempers among the
delegates. Men from the great plains complained about Chicago
water—there was no alkali in it—but a soft-drink stand was set
up in the vestibule of Uhlich's Hall, and saloons rubbed elbows
for blocks along North Clark Street near the hall. The first
measure to arouse tension, as well as oratory, was an attempt to
wipe out racial discrimination in the order. Although the delegates had demanded an immediate ban on immigration of
"Chinese and similar classes," an amendment was offered to
strike out the words "born of white parents" from the membership requirements. Debate lasted a full day before the amendment was rejected by a vote of 112 to 100, and the delegates
offered their "sympathy and support" to any effort to organize
the Negro railroaders into a separate organization. "Sympathy
and support" has slight practical value, but even this evasive-
ness was an advance from the frankness with which the Brotherhoods demanded that all Negroes be barred from jobs on the
railroads.

On June 15 the convention began its consideration of the
Pullman dispute. Many of the delegates had already made in-
spection trips to the suburb and talked to the workers there.
They had returned to Chicago angry, resentful. Now a committee from the strikers presented a lengthy statement to prove
the greed and despotism of George M. Pullman. The statement
concluded with a passionate appeal for support from the convention:

We struck because we were without hope. We joined the American Railway Union because it gave us a glimmer of hope. . . . We will make you proud of us, brothers, if you will give us the hand we need. Help us make our country better and more wholesome. . . . Teach arrogant grinders of the faces of the poor that there is still a God of Israel, and if need be a Jehovah—a God of battles. . . .

Thus was the stage set for a moving statement by Jennie Curtis, a seamstress at Pullman, who lifted to reckless heights the growing excitement among the delegates. Miss Curtis, thin and tired, said that after her father died she had been forced to repay the sixty dollars back rent that he owed the company, even though her father had been a Pullman employee for thirteen years. The Rev. William Carwardine testified that the residents of Pullman were on the brink of starvation, but his plea was not needed. The story of Jennie Curtis was irresistible to the sentimental railroaders.

Debs now used every rein of control in the hands of a chairman. His shrewdness, his eloquence, his influence, were all thrown into battle against headstrong action, and, in the end, they all went for nothing. The entire hall was filled with muffled, bitter comments: George Pullman had gone too far. It was time to show the bloodsucker. The ARU should boycott all Pullman cars, not move a single sleeper until Pullman settled with his workers. By God, it wasn't right to rob a girl. No, by God. Finally one man spoke for dozens of men: A boycott against Pullman cars should be declared immediately. Debs, in his calmest voice, refused to entertain the motion. He suggested that a committee be appointed to confer with the Pullman Company. Committees from the convention had previously investigated charges of unfair labor practices against a certain corporation, of spying by an ARU member, of strikebreaking by a locomotive engineer—the delegates remembered that investigation had in some cases proved the charge untrue. So twelve men were chosen, including six strikers, to call on the company and propose arbitration.

Determined to settle the dispute peacefully, Debs fervently hoped that the company would agree to the proposal. Above everything else, he wanted to avoid a boycott on Pullman cars. Unemployed railroaders stood on every corner, just waiting for vacancies. The Brotherhoods were so unfriendly that they probably would not co-operate; some of them might even furnish strikebreakers. The General Managers Association, which united all railroads passing through Chicago, had efficiently forestalled a threatened strike by switchmen there in 1893, and it might interfere in a dispute between the ARU and Pullman. Injunctions, state militia, Federal troops might be used again as at Homestead and Coeur d'Alene. Most important of all, the ARU was not ready to tackle Pullman. The organization was big and growing rapidly, but it was inexperienced. The members were raw recruits to unionism, and most local union leaders were hayseeds in the labor movement. A conflict with Pullman might settle down into a long struggle, and the ARU had no strike funds at all. It was best to wait. The ARU had been lucky against the Great Northern; it might not be so lucky again.

But the Pullman Company refused to yield an inch. The company claimed that wages and working conditions should be decided by the management, with no interference by labor. George Pullman was in business for profit, and the decreased sale of his product made it necessary to cut wages. That was his position. And, from the company's viewpoint, it was undeniably true. On June 16, the mediation committee from the convention reported that the company refused to confer with any members of the American Railway Union. This news fairly exploded in Uhlich's Hall. Pullman's intransigeance infuriated the delegates, who were now ready for any action. Again a boycott was proposed, with overwhelming support. Again Debs blocked the move. At his suggestion a second committee, composed entirely of Pullman employees, was sent with a request for arbitration. Within a few hours the committee returned; vicepresident Wickes had said there was "nothing to arbitrate." The committee had then asked whether the company would consider restoring wages to the May, 1893, scale. The vicepresident's answer wiped out all hope for a peaceful settlement: "Mr. Wickes replied that we had no right to ask him that question, as he thought we stood in the same position as the man on the sidewalk."

Realizing that the dispute could not be settled promptly, the convention tried to alleviate the suffering at Pullman. Mayor John P. Hopkins of Chicago was thanked for his fifteen-hundred-dollar donation to the relief fund. The delegates also voted a two-thousand-dollar contribution to the strikers, and a weekly assessment of ten cents on every member at the discretion of the executive board. Then attention returned to the strategy to be used against the Pullman Company. The delegates wired to their local unions for instructions and the replies gave them blanket authority to use their own judgment. Finally a special committee was chosen to recommend a plan of action.

On June 22, this committee made its report: Unless the Pullman Company agreed to begin negotiations within four days, the Pullman shops at Ludlow, Kentucky, and at St. Louis, would be struck, and the ARU would refuse to handle Pullman cars. George Howard opposed this plan by arguing that mere cessation of work at Ludlow and St. Louis would force the company to yield. The delegates brushed aside this proposal. They knew that a major part of the company's revenue came from rental of its Palace Cars; it would surrender only if its income were completely cut off. Debs announced his readiness to accept the convention's verdict, but he again emphasized the need for caution. In no mood for caution, the delegates accepted the committee's report. The committee was then sent for a final conference with Mr. Wickes, who still refused to settle the dispute by peaceful means, so the convention unanimously voted the boycott, to begin at noon on June 26 unless the corporation changed its mind.

Debs' hesitation was now irrelevant. Every union leader must answer three questions when a strike is proposed: Do the workers have just and serious grievances? Have all peaceful avenues for settlement been exhausted? Can the workers win the strike? Debs could give affirmative answers to the first two questions. He was dubious about the chances for victory, but that decision had been taken out of his hands. He was the servant of the rank and file; it was now his job to move heaven and earth for victory. So he carefully outlined to the convention a plan for the boycott which would not, in his opinion, violate the Interstate Commerce Act. He was particularly anxious to avoid injunctions. Under his plan, the switchmen would refuse to switch sleeping cars. If they were discharged, every other ARU member on that railroad would quit work immediately. Then they could pray that nothing would go wrong.

Only one item now remained on the convention's agenda—the election of the nine-man executive board of the union. When Debs was nominated, he tried to decline for two reasons: "First, that he shared the belief of some that it would be to the best interests of labor if some of its leaders would step aside, and he desired to set the example, and he believed that he could be of more service, perhaps, to the laboring classes on the outside, than by remaining in active service with the American Railway Union"; and second, that his health would not allow him to continue the strenuous activities of an organizer. But the delegates quickly resolved that "the railroad men of the country could not afford to lose their honored leader, and his resignation should not be considered." The resolution was accepted without a dissenting vote. A motion was next made to raise the president's salary to four thousand dollars. Competitive bidding began; the stipend was jumped to five thousand, then to six thousand. But Debs refused to accept more than three thousand, so his salary was set at that figure. Then the delegates adjourned, realizing but imperfectly the battle that faced them.

CHAPTER 7

[1]

THE PULLMAN COMPANY did not retreat, nor did the workers. At noon on June 26, the deadline set by the convention, Debs ordered all sleeping cars cut from the trains and sidetracked. The railroads at once took an active rôle in the conflict; they refused to move any trains without Palace Cars on the grounds that their contracts with Pullman were inviolable. The General Managers Association,* which was the employers' general staff throughout the boycott, welcomed a showdown fight with the ARU. The railroads had consistently discriminated against ARU members, and they had refused to give Debs and his colleagues the free passes which they handed out to officials in the Brotherhoods. Thus the ARU came into immediate conflict with one of the strongest groups of employers in America; The Managers represented the twenty-four railroads terminating or centering in Chicago, which had a combined capital of eight hundred and eighteen million dollars, operated forty-one thousand miles of track, and had two hundred twenty-one thousand employees.

Foreseeing opposition from the railroads, Debs had already asked for assistance from the AFL and the Brotherhoods. A return wire from Samuel Gompers showed the reluctance in that sector: "Just received telegram signed your name. Verify same by letter giving full particulars." Only president John McBride of the Mine Workers promised full co-operation; the others replied evasively or negatively, and most of the Brotherhoods worked against the boycott. When four hundred engineers struck on the Wabash, P. M. Arthur denounced the act as a violation of the Engineers' rules. Under the circumstances, he said, unemployed engineers would be permitted to fill the vacancies left by the strikers. The chief of the Conductors took

* Hereafter called The Managers.

121

the same stand, replying that he had "neither authority nor inclination" to help the ARU. He later said that the craft jurisdiction of his organization made it hostile to the industrial union led by Debs, and that the boycott was wrong, "no matter what the conditions at Pullman were." The Brotherhood of Trainmen instructed its members to "perform their regular duties and no others, that is to say, they were not expected to leave their trains as conductors or brakemen and go into the yard where the switchmen had struck out of sympathy or otherwise." Since the Trainmen had itself organized switchmen, this provision had little practical meaning. The BLF was more cautious in its hostility; Frank Sargent later said:

The B. of L.F. could not take part in the strike because our Constitution prohibits it. The B. of L.F. must observe their agreements. B. of L.F. committees should immediately call upon railway officials and make arrangements so that they would not be called upon to fire engines vacated by strikers.

But Debs had no time to send Gompers "full particulars" or to negotiate with the Brotherhood leaders. The nerve center of the boycott was set up in Uhlich's Hall, the ARU offices, at 421 Ashland Block, being much too small. Co-ordination of five hundred local unions and thousands of men rested in the hands of Debs, Howard, Keliher, Rogers, a few organizers, and Theodore Debs, who was again working side by side with his brother. The boycott began slowly. In spite of the convention orders, each ARU lodge was constitutionally forced to hold its own vote to determine whether it would support the boycott. Every lodge voted to enforce the convention's decision. The boycott was not called solely from sympathy with the Pullman workers; the railroad employees were also suffering from blacklists, short hours, wage cuts, discrimination. Also the feeling was widespread that, if the corporations succeeded in conquering the unorganized workers, they would next move against the organized men. Even among skilled workers there was agreement with Debs' statement: "Every concession the railway companies have ever made, has been wrung from them by the power of organized effort." As lodge after lodge voted to quit work,

Debs sent them all the same instructions: Use no violence. Stop no trains. Elect a strike committee and send me the name of the chairman. In this way he hoped to keep control over the entire boycott.

By June 27 only five thousand men had left their jobs, but fifteen railroads were tied up. The Managers opened offices in Pittsburgh, Cleveland, Philadelphia, New York, and Buffalo, to recruit strikebreakers; they also opened a central publicity office in Chicago to furnish information to the newspapers. Soon the commercial press raised the cry of "Anarchy"; this charge was doubly effective because President Sadi Carnot of France had been assassinated by an anarchist just two days before the boycott began. The third day, more than forty thousand men had quit work. Traffic was stopped dead on all lines west of Chicago. In spite of Debs' orders to move mail trains, the Postal authorities reported that mails were obstructed at Chicago, St. Paul, and on the Southern Pacific in the Far West. United States Attorneys were instructed by the Justice Department to ask for warrants against all offenders.

One day later, nearly a hundred twenty-five thousand men had joined the boycott. Twenty roads were tied up. A crowd of a thousand strikers and sympathizers stopped a train on the Chicago & Erie at Hammond, Indiana, and forced the crew to detach two Pullmans. The head of the Switchmen warned that any member of his union supporting the strike would be subject to expulsion, and the Conductor's chief attacked the boycott in the public press.

But several unions rallied to the ARU. J. R. Sovereign pledged aid from the Knights of Labor. The Chicago Federation of Labor, with one hundred fifty thousand members, offered to call a city-wide general strike to enforce the boycott. In view of the probable effects on public opinion, Debs refused to sanction such an extreme measure at that stage. During the entire boycott he divided his attention between the need to maintain the strikers' morale and the equal need to win support among other trade unions and the general community. On one occasion he even relaxed the boycott in order to implement its ultimate chances. The Illinois Federation of Labor had called a conference to meet

in Springfield on July 1, to consider the political program of the
AFL and to organize "independent political action" by the
labor movement. In order to reach Springfield, the Chicago delegates would be forced to travel over a struck railroad. Finding
himself "at sea," president W. H. Madden of the state federation went to see Debs. The strike leader quickly grasped the
publicity value of the conference, which planned to use July
Fourth to "dedicate anew the common people to the principles
of the Declaration of Independence." So he willingly gave the
delegates permission to employ any service available to reach
Springfield.

Throughout the East, The Managers continued to hire strikebreakers, and the depression provided hordes of recruits. Intimate grudges also motivated many railroaders to become scabs.
One group in New York City told a reporter: "We are going to
settle an old account. We were strikers on the Gould roads
under Martin Irons [1886], and we haven't handled a switch
since then. The men who are striking now are the men who
helped to fill our places then. Now we are going west to take
their jobs." The Managers easily hired from one hundred to two
hundred fifty men daily; by the strike's end nearly twenty-five
hundred strikebreakers had been sent to Chicago.

On June 30, in spite of Debs' orders to the contrary, minor
violence again occurred. Crowds in Chicago temporarily halted
two express trains on the Illinois Central and Panhandle lines.
Union leaders were arrested in Indiana and Missouri. The first
demand for militia in Illinois came from the Illinois Central,
which claimed that its property in Cairo was endangered. Under
the laws of Illinois, the governor could call out state troops when
the legislature was not in session, but only at the request of the
mayor or sheriff. As soon as he had secured permission from
these local authorities, Governor Altgeld sent three companies
of militia to Cairo. Thomas Milchrist, the Federal district attorney in Chicago, telegraphed to Washington that strikers had
stopped mail trains in the suburbs the previous night. He also
reported that conditions in Chicago were so bad that special
deputies were needed, and recommended that the United States
marshal in Chicago be empowered to hire such deputies. This

wire by Milchrist exaggerated the actual situation. Five days after he sent the telegram, total strike damages were still less than six thousand dollars. There had been no major riots. The trains halted on the Chicago & Erie, Illinois Central, and Panhandle had soon been allowed to proceed. The telegram from Milchrist was contradicted by a simultaneous telegram from the Superintendent of Railway Mail Service in Chicago, telling the Postmaster General that no mail had accumulated in the city.

Most important of all, the local authorities were confident of their ability to handle the situation. Mayor Hopkins had not even applied to the governor for help, although Altgeld had shown both his willingness and efficiency in controlling labor violence. As recently as June 16, striking coal miners at Mount Olive, Illinois, had interfered with the movement of trains to prevent the shipment of nonunion coal. Mail trains were among those detained. The Federal court had issued an injunction against the rioters; and the United States marshal, believing that his forces were inadequate, had applied to the Attorney-General for advice. Attorney-General Richard Olney had immediately wired an answer:

Washington, June 16, 1894.

Allen, U.S. Judge, Springfield, Ill.:

Understand State of Illinois is willing to protect property against lawless violence with military force if necessary. Please advise receivers to take proper steps to procure protection by civil authorities of the State. If such protection proves inadequate, the governor should be applied to for military assistance.

Olney, Attorney General

Within one day after application was made to Altgeld, the state militia had arrived in Mount Olive and succeeded in moving all trains. Thus Richard Olney had established a procedure for such situations in which deputy marshals were not required; but Milchrist now asked for Federal marshals without first going to the Federal courts, the local authorities, or the governor of Illinois.

The newspaper campaign against the boycott was in full swing, with the Chicago *Tribune* leading the onslaught. On June

30 the *Tribune* let fly with both barrels. One headline read, "Mob Is In Control"; another charged, "Law Is Trampled On"; a third story began: "Through the lawless acts of Dictator Debs' strikers the lives of thousands of Chicago citizens were endangered yesterday." The Chicago *Herald* editorialized: "The necessity is on the railroads to defeat the strike. If they yield one point it will show fatal weakness. If the strike should be successful the owners of the railroad property . . . would have to surrender its future control to the class of labor agitators and strike conspirators who have formed the Debs Railway Union." There were recurrent charges in the press that Debs was a dictator, that he was personally profiting from the strike, that he had called the strike without consulting the union membership. It was widely, and falsely, reported that Debs had ridden in a Pullman car from Chicago to Terre Haute during the boycott.

Immediately after Milchrist sent his telegram to Washington, the General Managers Association met in closed session at the Rookery Building in Chicago. All newspaper reporters were excluded. At this meeting the railroads agreed that they would not rehire any of the strikers. They also sent a wire to Richard Olney, suggesting that he appoint Edwin Walker as special Federal attorney to handle the strike situation. Walker was, at that time, attorney in Illinois for the Chicago, Milwaukee & St. Paul Railroad, a job he had held since 1870. This railroad was involved in the strike, and was a member of the Managers Association. A few days earlier, Walker had been asked to handle all strike cases for the railroads. But within two hours, without even pausing to consult Milchrist, Olney had appointed Walker to represent the Federal government.

Eugene Debs, who had just tried to resign his job because of ill health, was being subjected to tremendous strain. He was working at top speed clear around the clock. Detailed instructions had to be sent to hundreds of railroad towns in order to bolster the weak spots. Constant warnings against violence and the obstruction of mail trains were necessary. Howard, Keliher, Rogers—they were burning up their lives with harried but jubilant abandon. Uhlich's Hall had become a delivery room for chaos. The executive board was in practically uninterrupted session, discussing this development, considering that possibility. The large hall was packed with excited men, screaming, yelling, shouting questions, singing. Exhausted men staggered out of executive board meetings in the small room, spoke briefly to the excited throng in the hall, went back to the board room. They hammered out press releases, sent appeals for help to labor unions from New York to San Diego. Couriers were constantly running back and forth to the Western Union—in three weeks the executive board sent more than nine thousand telegrams. And Debs moved from one room to another, talking, making decisions, always smiling, seeming strangely misplaced in an immaculate tweed suit and hard white collar. Even the reporters noticed that the calm assurance and control of the strike leader seemed indestructible. They always looked to him, watched him, wrote reams of copy about him, little realizing the expert organization that was working with him. Theodore was always at hand, the other ARU officers were indispensable.

Opposition to the boycott was gathering intensity. The railroads began deliberately to disrupt their schedules, hoping that the resultant inconvenience to the public would force government intervention. Pullmans were attached to trains that did not customarily carry them—freights, suburbans, and, most important of all, mail trains, trying to force the strikers to halt the mails. The Brotherhoods accelerated their campaign against the ARU. Conductors in Fort Wayne, Indiana, denounced the strike, declaring that they would not aid in any way. P. M. Arthur announced that he did not care whether the railroads employed union or nonunion engineers and firemen; any engineers who refused to work with strikebreakers could be fired without protest from the Brotherhood. Frank Sargent declared that any fireman who joined the strike would have to look to the ARU for help—he would get none from the BLF.

Never before had there been such a strike in the United States. More than a hundred thousand men had voluntarily quit work. Between Chicago and the Golden Gate, only the Great Northern was maintaining a semblance of its regular schedule.

Everybody in the country had taken sides in the dispute. Debs clearly stated the situation in a speech to the railroaders:

The struggle with the Pullman Company has developed into a contest between the producing classes and the money power of the country. . . . The fight was between the American Railway Union and the Pullman Company. . . . Then the railway corporations, through the General Managers' Association, came to the rescue, and in a series of whereases declared to the world that they would go into partnership with Pullman, so to speak, and stand by him in his devilish work of starving his employees to death.

On July 1, the union was firm at every point, and there was "no sign of violence or disorder," as Debs said. He later claimed that the railroads were losing a fortune daily: "Their immediate resources were exhausted, their properties were paralyzed, and they were unable to operate their trains." Although the ARU had few members in the East and South, it seemed that the boycott might spread to northern New York and perhaps to Pennsylvania. The Central Labor Union of New York City endorsed the boycott, and urged people not to ride in Pullmans until the company accepted arbitration. The Central Labor Union of Chicago took similar action. In spite of the massed billions of Pullman and the railroads, in spite of the newspaper barrage, in spite of strikebreaking by the Brotherhoods and inaction by the AFL, Eugene Debs saw the road to victory stretching bright and certain into the future.

[2]

DEBS' confidence reckoned without one possibility—Federal intervention. Throughout the critical period of the boycott, President Cleveland was occupied in a bitter fight with Congress over the Wilson Tariff Bill, and his only information about the strike came from Attorney-General Olney.

Richard Olney, from 1859 until his elevation to the cabinet in 1893, had been a corporation lawyer in Boston, representing mainly railroad interests and trust estates. He had also been a director of several railroads: the Eastern, the Boston & Maine, lesser New England lines, the Kansas City & Fort Scott, the Atchison. Since 1889 he had served on the board of the Burlington, which was involved in the Pullman dispute. His very appearance indicated his dominant characteristics—a narrow honesty, truculence, and stubbornness. He was tall, with open and quivering nostrils, a drooping mustache, dark brown hair just turning gray. His body tilted aggressively forward, he stalked swiftly in pursuit of Duty. Olney's violent and unpredictable temper had been illustrated by an incident several years earlier, when he forbade his daughter to enter his house following her marriage, even though he himself had approved the daughter's choice. The edict was still in effect.

Olney proposed to deal with the strikers much as he had dealt with his daughter. As soon as the Debs Rebellion started, the Attorney-General launched a series of maneuvers to defeat it. He thought that a nation-wide boycott was so essentially violent that Debs' order for peaceful conduct was a mere sham. In a memorandum about the Pullman affair, Olney later wrote: "The President might have used the United States Army to prevent interference with the mails and with interstate commerce on his own initiative—without waiting for action by the courts . . . But . . . it is doubtful . . . whether the President could be induced to move except in support of the judicial tribunals." So the Attorney-General decided to prod Cleveland by securing an injunction against the strike, and then use the Army to enforce the court order. This plan, as well as Olney's intention of smashing the boycott, was revealed in his telegram to Edwin Walker on June 30: "It has seemed to me that if the rights of the United States were vigorously asserted in Chicago, the origin and centre of the demonstration, the result would be to make it a failure everywhere else and to prevent its spread over the entire country. . . . I feel that the true way of dealing with the matter is by a force which is overwhelming and prevents any attempt at resistance."

Olney's attitude rested on three premises: (1) Any national railroad strike is automatically illegal; (2) The causes of the strike in Pullman were not relevant to the legality of the boycott; (3) The state and local officials could not be trusted to enforce the law. Altgeld, after all, had pardoned the Haymarket survivors, and Mayor Hopkins of Chicago had openly contributed to the relief fund at Pullman. Olney later claimed that Hopkins "even went so far as to openly wear the distinctive badge of the rioters" a white ribbon was the emblem of the strikers, and Olney thought all strikers were "rioters" in this instance.

In accord with this interpretation, the Attorney-General was trying to persuade the President that the Army should be used at Chicago, and the troops at Fort Sheridan, Illinois, were ordered to hold themselves in readiness. Meanwhile a constant demand for the maintenance of law and order was emanating from the pulpits and the commercial newspapers. On July 2 a headline on the Chicago *Tribune* screeched:

STRIKE IS NOW WAR

And the lead editorial had a shrewd caption:

> Six Days Shalt Thou Labor—BIBLE
> Not Unless I Say So   —DEBS

In New York the Reverend Robert S. MacArthur said that there were "more Anarchists today in Chicago than in St. Petersburg . . . Anarchists should be excluded from the United States." He added that all boycotts were "unmanly and un-American." The Reverend A. C. Dixon of Brooklyn also contributed to calm consideration of the matter: "the Anarchist is a savage in a civilized country who is trying to turn civilization into barbarism."

That same day, in a crushing blow, Judges Peter Grosscup and William A. Woods of the Federal Court in Chicago issued an omnibus injunction against the ARU leaders. The previous Decoration Day, Judge Grosscup had said in a speech: "The growth of labor organizations must be checked by law." It was later shown that Judge Woods had accepted such important favors from the railroads that his impartiality was doubtful. Their irregular procedure in this case is therefore not surprising: Milchrist and Walker had prepared the application for the injunction, and the two judges had helped them to revise it before court opened. The breadth of their order was astonishing.

Using the Sherman Antitrust Act of 1890 as authority, the injunction prohibited the strike leaders from any action to aid the boycott. They were forbidden to answer questions, to send telegrams. They were denied the right to urge men, by word of mouth, to join the boycott. Their constitutional rights to speak, write, and assemble freely, were ignored. They were, in short, completely shackled. Even Grover Cleveland was forced to admit that "a sweeping injunction had been granted against Eugene V. Debs."

Richard Olney, in a letter to Edwin Walker, September 24, 1894, justified the injunction under both the Sherman Antitrust Law and the powers of a court of equity "to enjoin a public nuisance when it threatens a public injury." Under his second thesis Olney made six points: (1) the obstruction of a public highway is a public nuisance; (2) railroads are public highways; (3) interstate railroads are Federal highways; (4) any obstruction of a Federal highway is enjoinable; (5) "the concerted, sudden, and simultaneous withdrawal from service of the trained corps of expert employees necessary to the operation" of railroads is an obstruction; (6) any act to promote a railroad strike can be enjoined. Olney's basic argument was used by scores of professors who defended the writ in law journals. Congressmen, without understanding the doctrine, spoke for days in its defense. Ministers solemnly identified the injunction with the voice of God.

The attack on the injunction was equally savage. The New York *Times*, while opposing the strikers, referred to the court order as "one of those peculiar instruments that punishes an individual for doing a certain thing, and is equally merciless if he does not do it, so it is difficult to understand how the strikers can maintain their present policy and at the same time evade its operation or escape its influence." The trade unions claimed that this injunction had taken from the railroaders the only weapon with which they could fight against corporate injustice, and that it gave the railroads unqualified power over all employees. Railroad workers still had the right to quit work individually, but where could they find other jobs during a depression? The unions objected to the absolute power of Judges

Grosscup and Woods to punish violations of an order they themselves issued. They protested against issuance of the injunction
without giving the ARU a chance to present its objections. They
vehemently exclaimed that the government had shown scant
knowledge and no respect for the rights and problems of the
workingmen.

As soon as the injunction was served, Debs called the ARU
executive board into session to decide their response. Violation
of the writ might result in jail sentences for the union officials,
and also have the effect of placing all strikers outside the law,
in active opposition to the Federal government. On the other
hand, obedience to the order would crush the strike, and would
end all hope of forcing compromise by the Pullman company.
Obedience would destroy the ARU and cause thousands of men
to lose their jobs, since the railroads had pledged themselves not
to rehire any striker. The job, already begun at Homestead,
Buffalo, and Coeur d'Alene, of crushing the morale of labor
would be completed; moreover, it would be a signal for the employers to move immediately against every trade union in
America. The executive board came to a decision—they would
ignore the injunction. Eugene Debs bitterly declared: "the crime
of the American Railway Union was the practical exhibition of
sympathy for the Pullman employees."

The ARU officials realized that they would surely be called
into court to answer for this decision. Legal advice had been
supplied, up to this point in the boycott, by the regular ARU
attorneys and by William Irwin, a well-known Minneapolis
lawyer; but Debs now resolved to hire an expert in equity and
constitutional law. His choice seemed rather strange on the
surface—he went to Clarence Darrow, attorney for the Chicago
& Northwestern Railroad, which was involved in the dispute.
Darrow had come to Chicago in 1887 from Ashtabula, Ohio, a
young, poorly trained, country lawyer. Having few clients,
Darrow was able to take an active part in Grover Cleveland's
campaign in 1888. He gave several speeches without attracting
any notice, but then he was invited to speak with Henry George
at a Free Trade Conference in the Central Music Hall. His address that evening was splashed all over the front pages; he

became a celebrity. In the audience had been DeWitt C. Cregier, who was elected Democratic mayor of Chicago a few weeks later. Judge John Peter Altgeld urged Cregier to give his friend Darrow a job. Cregier agreed. Darrow was named special assessment attorney of Chicago. Three months later a political shift forced the resignation of the Assistant Corporation Counsel, and Darrow was promoted. Soon after that, ill health caused the retirement of the Corporation Counsel, and Darrow, a resident of Chicago less than two years, became head of the city's legal department. In 1892 he left public office to become general attorney of the Chicago & Northwestern. The Northwestern Railroad thought that their new employee was rather eccentric —he sympathized with labor, was always speaking at meetings of radicals and free-thinkers, played a leading rôle in the amnesty campaign for the Haymarket survivors—but they knew that he was a brilliant lawyer. Debs' choice was not so strange after all.

This request by the ARU put Darrow in a ticklish position. He had previously been named by the Chicago & Northwestern as their representative on the committee that was conducting the strike for the railroads, and had refused the appointment on the grounds that his sympathies were with the union. But he was now being asked, in effect, to resign completely his job in order to take a series of cases that would involve little pay and gruelling work. The courts' preference for property rights over civil liberties would make it almost impossible to successfully defend his clients. It was a hard choice to make. Darrow's conviction, Debs' persuasiveness, and the arguments of several mutual friends, finally turned the trick. Darrow became special counsel for the ARU.

The situation was indeed becoming desperate. An increasing number of strikebreakers were being brought into Chicago. The ARU charged that the railroads were even trying to inflame religious divisions among the strikers. The governor of Michigan ordered out the militia, although the United Press stated from Battle Creek: "The company has no men here that it can use to pull the trains if there were 1,000,000 soldiers here, and it is esteemed unwarranted. Then again the men have done nothing to prevent the company from moving its trains. The strikers say they will furnish all the men wanted for mail trains."

Throughout the country the injunction was being used against the strikers. As sweeping as the court order had been, the interpretations of it were even more sweeping. George Howard later testified to the Federal investigating commission:

> Men have been arrested in Chicago because they refused to turn switches when told to; they were arrested when they refused to get on an engine and fire an engine; . . . in Albuquerque, New Mexico, they arrested a man and he was sentenced to fifteen days in jail because he refused to get on an engine and fire it when told; the fact that he did not get on the engine was considered contempt of court.

And then, on July 4, Grover Cleveland played the leading rôle in the last great act of the drama. The issuance of the injunction had severely increased the problems and anxieties of the strike leaders. Debs had slept only a few hours a night since the beginning of the boycott; with this added strain it was long after midnight when he and Theodore arrived at their room in the Leland Hotel for some brief and troubled rest. Early on the morning of Independence Day, they were awakened by the sound of bugles and voices right under their window. Thinking that it might be a parade, Debs sleepily walked to the window and gazed down at Jackson Street and Lake Michigan. The sight he saw caused instant consternation. Hundreds of Federal soldiers were encamped along the lake front.

Richard Olney, who furnished the guiding hand for Cleveland's act, could cite a precedent for the use of the Army in such cases. During the railroad strikes of 1877, United States troops had been sent into Maryland, Illinois, Pennsylvania, and West Virginia, at the request of the governors. Moreover, and this was of critical significance to Olney's plan, on that occasion the Army was used in Indiana and Missouri on application of Federal marshals, not of any state officials. Already during the Pullman boycott, the Army had been sent to Los Angeles, to Raton, New Mexico, and to Trinidad, Colorado. Although violence had occurred in these places, Governor Davis Waite of Colorado had violently objected to the Administration's action on the ground that the militia was competent to handle the small disturbance in his state.

When Olney first proposed sending troops to Chicago, Secretary of War Daniel S. Lamont and General Nelson A. Miles had both opposed the suggestion. But on July 3, Olney received from Judge Grosscup, Marshal J. W. Arnold, Walker, and Milchrist, a telegram that was misleading in five respects. This telegram stated that violence had occurred in Chicago, when it actually occurred in a suburb. The telegram failed to mention that the violence, which flared up briefly on July 2, had subsided by July 3. The wire also alleged, without proof, that no authority less than the Army could protect the mails, that the workers of Chicago would join a general strike "today, and in my opinion will be joining the mob tonight, and especially tomorrow . . ." Secretary Lamont and General Miles now approved Olney's plan.

President Cleveland promptly ordered the entire command at Fort Sheridan to Chicago for the following purposes:

1. To protect Federal property.
2. To prevent obstruction of the U.S. mails.
3. To prevent interference with interstate commerce.
4. To enforce the decrees of the Federal courts.

The facts were that no Federal property had been destroyed in Chicago, and there seemed to be no imminent danger. The Superintendent of Railway Mail Service had stated that no mail had accumulated there. Mail trains were still moving. Trains, including mail trains, had been detained in the suburbs, but this had not happened since July 2. The chief obstruction to interstate commerce lay in the workers' refusal to haul Pullman cars. If the ARU was right in its contention that the injunction was illegal, there was no court decree to be enforced.

Cleveland's action involved him in a heated dispute with Governor Altgeld. The President had relied for authority on two Civil War statutes, which had never been used in time of peace. The President has power, according to the United States Constitution, to send the Army into a state "on Application of the Legislature, or of the Executive (when the Legislature cannot be

convened)" in order to protect the state "against domestic
Violence." In a lengthy telegram to Cleveland, Altgeld protested that neither he nor the Legislature had applied for assistance. There were three regiments of militiamen in Chicago that
could have been mustered into service, but "nobody in Cook
county, whether official or private citizen," had asked for their
help. It was true that violence had occurred, but it was easily
handled by the local and state authorities. "At present some of
our railroads are paralyzed," wrote Altgeld, "not by reason of
obstruction, but because they cannot get men to operate their
trains. For some reason they are anxious to keep this fact from
the public, and for this purpose they are making an outcry about
the obstructions in order to divert public attention. . . . The
newspaper accounts have in many cases been pure fabrications,
and in others wild exaggerations." The Governor protested,
lastly, "that local self-government is a fundamental principle of
our Constitution. Each community shall govern itself so long as
it can and is ready and able to enforce the law . . ."

President Cleveland briefly replied that the postal authorities
had asked for the removal of obstructions to the mails, that
Judge Grosscup had asked for help in enforcing the injunction,
and that there was "competent proof that conspiracies existed
against commerce between the states." On any of these grounds,
wrote Cleveland, he could have ordered Federal troops into
Illinois.

Altgeld, however, was not to be put off so easily. In a second
long telegram he protested that Cleveland's action violated
state's rights, established military rule in Illinois, and indicated
a swollen and unconstitutional judgment of the powers of the
President. The conclusion of Altgeld's wire was plain enough:
". . . believing that the ordering out of the Federal troops was
unwarranted, I again ask their withdrawal." But Cleveland was
even more brusque: "While I am still persuaded that I have
neither transcended my authority nor duty in the emergency
that confronts us, it seems to me that in this hour of danger and
public distress, discussion may well give way to active efforts on
the part of all in authority to restore obedience to law and to
protect life and property."

Altgeld was forced to yield to the power of the Army, but similar protests were made by the governors of Kansas, Colorado, Texas, and Oregon. Neither Cleveland nor Olney had any doubts about the correctness of their action. When reporters called at Olney's office on July 4, they found him sending a wire to Milchrist instructing the immediate indictment of the strike leaders. He seemed pleased with developments, and told the reporters: "We have been brought to the ragged edge of anarchy, and it is time to see whether the law is sufficiently strong to prevent this condition of affairs. If not, the sooner we know it the better, that it may be changed." Cleveland had succinctly expressed his views to a friend: "If it takes every dollar in the Treasury and every soldier in the United States Army to deliver a postal card in Chicago, that postal card shall be delivered." A political colleague later said the President thought his action in the Pullman boycott was one of the best moves he made in either of his administrations.

Debs, like Altgeld, was unable to find any justification for the use of the Army. The militia were under arms in twenty states. In a few western states, the railroads were so unpopular that the state troops had refused to act against the strikers, but this was not true in Illinois. It seemed to the ARU officials that Cleveland and Olney had joined the railroads in a campaign to destroy their union, and this belief was heightened when The Managers announced that they would not confer with the municipal authorities or any other party to arbitrate or compromise the dispute. The Administration had exerted tremendous pressure on the strikers, but it had not said a single harsh word about George M. Pullman or the railroads. Debs had not objected to the use of state troops and local police, but he deeply resented the implication that the strikers were in rebellion against their government, and that the United States Army was needed to quell the riots. His protest to the President, made jointly with J. R. Sovereign, warned Grover Cleveland that his course would lead to rebellion. The two unionists contended that "a deep-seated conviction is fast becoming prevalent that this Government is soon to be declared a military despotism." The railroads themselves, who were accused of refusal to carry mail on trains to which Pullmans were not attached, were charged with full responsibility for the interruption of the United States mails.

Debs feared that the presence of Federal troops in Chicago would serve, not to keep the peace, but to inflame the populace, and he heatedly told a United Press reporter:

The first shots fired by the regular soldiers at the mobs here will be the signal for a civil war. I believe this as firmly as I believe in the ultimate success of our course. Bloodshed will follow, and ninety per cent of the people of the United States will be arrayed against the other ten per cent. And I would not care to be arrayed against the laboring people in the contest, or find myself out of the ranks of labor when the struggle ended.

This prediction proved all too true. Although there had been brief but serious outbreaks in the suburbs on June 30 and July 2, no violence had occurred in Chicago before July 5. On that day railroad tracks were blocked, a freight train was stalled, a signal house was burned. The regular soldiers made a bayonet charge against a crowd, and several people were injured. Strike damage in the city still totaled less than six thousand dollars, but Mayor Hopkins was sufficiently alarmed to issue a proclamation which forbade riotous assemblies.

At the suggestion of Governor Altgeld, Hopkins formally requested state troops on July 6. Railroad property valued at three hundred forty thousand dollars was destroyed in Chicago on that day alone, although on no other day did damage exceed four thousand dollars. The presence of the Army had indeed proved to be a "signal for civil war," as Debs said; but the hundreds of special Federal deputy marshals had an even worse effect. Since men with regular employment were unwilling to accept these temporary jobs, Marshal Arnold had deputized labor spies, professional strikebreakers, racketeers, petty gangsters, the flotsam and jetsam of the city. Several public officials fiercely attacked these special deputies. Governor Waite of Colorado called them "desperadoes" who had been hired "without any regard for their qualifications but simply for military purposes." On July 6 near Pullman, where a mob of hoodlums was overturning freight cars, one of these deputies deliberately killed an innocent spectator. Accidentally shot while standing nearly a hundred yards from the scene of the riot, the victim tried to rise, but the deputy advanced upon him and shot him again. The killer was never arrested, although his identity was well known. Police Chief John Brennan of Chicago later testified that, on one occasion, these deputies fired into a group of people when there was no disturbance and no reason for firing. "Innocent men and women were killed by these shots," he added. "Several of these officials were arrested during the strike for stealing property from railroad cars. In one instance, two of them were found under suspicious circumstances near a freight car which had just been set on fire. They were dangerous to the lives of the citizens on account of their careless use of pistols."

The union also claimed that the railroads had burned their own cars in order to discredit the strike and collect damages and insurance on obsolete equipment. According to Debs, the assistant fire chief of Chicago once caught several deputy marshals cutting fire hoses when some cars were burning. Some newspapers supported the union's claim. "The railroads had everything to gain by a little well advertised rioting which could be attributed to the strikers," said the New York *Morning Journal.* "The strikers had everything to lose by violence and they knew it." Although the maximum pay of Federal deputies was $2.50 per day plus $1.50 expense money, the government paid out three hundred seventy-five thousand dollars to deputies during the boycott. In Chicago alone, the cost to the Treasury was a hundred twenty-five thousand dollars, and many deputies were paid their salaries by the railroads.

It was charged that soldiers also deliberately tried to provoke violence. Brand Whitlock, Governor Altgeld's secretary, told about one colonel, drunk in a Chicago club, who wished that he might have an entire regiment to shoot the strikers, "each man to take aim at a dirty white ribbon." But several Army officers in Chicago, according to Mayor Hazen S. Pingree of Detroit, soon realized that the newspaper stories about the strike were biased. These officers, at a small meeting in a hotel, decided that the strikers had a just cause and that the Army had been called out solely to break the strike. Resolving to publicize their views, they scheduled a second meeting to draft a statement. Before

this second meeting could be held, news of the first gathering
leaked out. All of the participating officers were held for courts-
martial. This action was squelched by direct order of the President, said Pingree, "but the colonel was retired from active
service and the other officers cowed by pressure from Washington authorities." Pingree was convinced that the troops had
been used, "not so much to quell a riot as to crush labor unions."

Debs, continuing his efforts to stop the violence, repeated his
instructions to the strikers:

I appeal to you to be men, orderly and law-abiding. Our cause
is just, the great public is with us, and we have nothing to fear.

Let it be borne in mind that if the railroad companies can
secure men to handle their trains, they have that right. Our men
have the right to quit, but their right ends there. Other men
have the right to take their places, whatever the opinion of the
propriety of so doing may be.

Keep away from railroad yards, or right of way, or other
places where large crowds congregate. A safe plan is to remain
away entirely from places where there is any likelihood of an
outbreak.

The railroad managers have sought to make it appear that
their trains do not move because of the interference of the strikers. The statement is an unqualified falsehood, and no one knows
this better than the managers themselves. They make this falsehood serve their purpose of calling out the troops.

Respect the law, conduct yourselves as becomes men and our
cause shall be crowned with success.

The riots, the arson, the bloodshed, the deliberate provocations
to violence by soldiers and special deputies, had created new
worries for Debs. He was nearly always at ARU headquarters,
where the men had daily grown more serious, more intense,
wondering how the mad holocaust would end, whether it would
ever end. Only two days had passed since the Army entered
Chicago, but those forty-eight hours had bred a lifetime of
torture and anxiety. The ARU leaders were still united in their
determination to see the boycott through to the end. The future
of the entire labor movement rested with them; if they failed,
the workers would suffer for years to come. Clinging to this conviction, Debs sent a wire to all ARU lodges urging them to
stand fast:

Every true man must quit now and remain out until the fight is won. There can be no half way ground. Men must be for us or against us. Our cause is gaining ground daily and our success is only a question of a few days. Do not falter in this hour. Stand erect. Proclaim your manhood. Labor must win now or never. Our victory will be positive and complete. Whatever happens, do not give credence to rumors or newspaper reports.

The opposition was equally confident. Edwin Walker wired to Olney that he had gathered sufficient evidence of an ARU conspiracy to warrant presenting it to the grand jury, which was scheduled to meet July 10. This wire was a strange statement from a neutral official. Before anybody had been indicted, Walker wrote about the probable results of their trial: "I firmly believe that the result of these trials and the punishment of the leaders will be so serious that a general strike upon any railroad will not again occur for a series of years." The same day, the chief of the Brotherhood of Trainmen defended the actions of The Managers on the grounds that they had merely fulfilled their contracts with Pullman, while P. M. Arthur said of the boycott: "Inevitably it must fail. It is a question of but a short time. . . . The Engineers Brotherhood cannot take part in such an unwise movement. It informed Mr. Debs at the outset that we could give him no assistance. Engineers are employed to draw trains, not to build cars." In return, The Managers made it clear that they bore no ill feeling against the Brotherhoods, and Attorney-General Olney later intervened in behalf of the Trainmen in a legal case.

By July 7, the events in Chicago had captured the headlines of every metropolitan newspaper from coast to coast. Some of the headlines were truly terrifying. Destruction of railroad property had been widespread the previous day, with damages amounting to three hundred forty thousand dollars, but the press made it seem that the entire city had been despoiled. A headline in the Washington *Post* told its readers:

Fired By the Mob
Chicago at the Mercy of the Incendiary's Torch

and the New York *Sun* was on the same general track:

Wild Riot in Chicago
Hundreds of Freight Cars Burned by Strikers

The most extreme headlines came from the center of the dispute
—Chicago—where the *Inter-Ocean* might have been describing
the razing of Carthage:

Flames Make Havoc—Unparalleled Scenes of Riot,
Terror and Pillage

Anarchy is Rampant—Mobs at Pullman and Burnside
Apply the Torch

Two Chicago newspapers—the *Daily News* and the *Record*—remained neutral during the boycott, while the *Dispatch*, the *Mail*,
and the *Times* defended the strikers. Also individual writers on
other papers disagreed with the policy of their employers. The
Chicago *Tribune* was forced to fire one reporter who refused to
authenticate before the grand jury the printed version of his
interview with Debs. Finley Peter Dunne, through the words of
that shrewd Irish saloonkeeper Mr. Dooley, contradicted the
headlines of the Chicago *Evening Post*, which carried the Mr.
Dooley columns. The *Evening Post* on July 7 let its vocabulary
run wild:

THIRSTY FOR BLOOD
Frenzied Mob Still Bent on Death and Destruction
Violence on Every Hand

But, in the same issue, Mr. Dooley delivered some pointed gibes
at George M. Pullman, who had taken his family to their mansion at Elberon, New Jersey, early in the strike:

This here Pullman makes th' sleepin' ca-ars an' th' constitootion looks afther Pullman. He have a good time iv it. He
don't need to look afther himsilf. . . . He owns towns an'
min. . . . Whin he has throuble ivry wan on earth excipt
thim that rides in smokin' ca-ars whin they rides at all r-runs to
fight f'r him. He calls out George Wash'nton an' Abraham
Lincoln an' Gin'ral Miles an' Mike Brinnan an' ivry human
bein' that rayquires limons an' ice an' thin he puts on his hat
an' lams away. 'Gintlemin,' says he, 'I must be off,' he says.
'Go an' kill each other,' he says. 'Fight it out,' he says. 'Defind

the constitootion,' he says. 'Me own is not of the best,' he says, 'an' I think I'll help it be spindin' th' summer,' he says, 'piously,' he says, 'on th' shores iv th' Atlantic ocean.'

The most novel touch in this press war was provided by the Chicago newsboys. Most of them wore the strikers' white ribbon, and they dropped those journals which opposed the boycott into sewers.

Violence in Chicago, although abated somewhat from the previous day, was still serious on July 7, when two separate troops of militia were provoked into firing upon crowds of rioters who had taunted and stoned them. Four rioters were killed and forty wounded, some women among them. But at no time during the disorders in Chicago was an ARU member wounded by the police or troops. Debs had constantly argued that the rioting was being done by thugs and riffraff, not by the strikers, and he was determined to keep his men away from the riots. On July 7 he again said in a speech to the ARU men:

We have repeatedly declared that we will respect law and order, and our conduct must conform to our profession. A man who commits violence in any form, whether a member of our order or not, should be promptly arrested and punished and we should be the first to apprehend the miscreant and bring him to justice. We must triumph as law-abiding citizens or not at all. Those who engage in force and violence are our real enemies.

Debs was guided both by his dislike for violence and by the example of the Great Northern strike, in which peaceful tactics had won a great victory. Seeking to control the strikers, he and the other ARU leaders now moved rapidly from one open-air meeting to another. Each of them addressed from two to six meetings a day, everywhere urging the workers to stand fast and remain away from the railroad lines. During the entire disturbance, the union did not hold a single secret meeting. The leaders spoke on the public highways, near railroad yards or in districts where the railroad workers lived. They moved hastily to any scene of reported rioting and begged the crowds to return peacefully to their homes.

Support for the strike continued to mount among the trade unions. The Central Labor Union of New York City condemned the interference of the Federal government and referred contemptuously to the Brotherhoods as "the Benedict Arnolds of the labor movement." Grand Master Sovereign of the Knights of Labor wired an urgent appeal for fair play to the President. Sam Gompers sent a telegram to Debs: "Have protested Tuesday to President against base action judiciary and improper use of military." But the acts of military tyranny continued to multiply. Debs charged that one soldier had forced a switchman to work at the point of a bayonet. Governor Altgeld later described the arrest of George Lovejoy, a striking trainmaster at LaSalle, Illinois. Lovejoy was taken one hundred miles to Chicago, held for two days by the police, and then was told that they did not care to prosecute.

Debs, still trying to broaden his support, again wired on July 7 to several local labor bodies: "We ask your cooperation . . . we are making a great fight for labor, and deserve the support of all railroad employees. Capital has combined to enslave labor. We must all stand together or go down in hopeless defeat."

Events were moving swiftly. The deadlock could not last much longer. In Hammond, Indiana, one man was killed and several injured when the Army fired into a crowd of rioters. The man killed was a respected carpenter who had no connection with the boycott or the riots; he had gone to the railroad tracks in search of his young son who had wandered away from home. President Cleveland issued a proclamation which in effect declared martial law for the entire area. At that time, there were already six thousand state and Federal troops, five thousand extra deputy marshals, and thirty-one hundred policemen, in Chicago and vicinity.

The Chicago labor movement was infuriated by the events in Hammond and by Cleveland's proclamation. All locals in the city and the heads of seven national unions met at Uhlich's Hall, and demanded that Samuel Gompers call an immediate session of the AFL executive council in Chicago. This meeting also appointed a committee to request Pullman to arbitrate. If he refused, a city-wide general strike would be called. The three representatives from this meeting joined three aldermen in their visit to Pullman, but Vice-President Wickes told the delegation that "the Company was not able to consider the question of arbitration." Therefore the Trades and Labor Council called a general strike as planned, but not more than twenty-five thousand men left their jobs. Thousands of others had already quit work voluntarily in support of the strike, but the majority preferred to await the results of the AFL executive council session scheduled for July 12 in Chicago.

The propaganda campaign against Debs, the ARU, and Governor Altgeld daily outdid itself. A New York minister described Debs as the "son of a saloonkeeper, a man reared and educated upon the proceeds of human ruin." One of his Brooklyn colleagues piously declared: "The time has come when forbearance has ceased to be a virtue. There must be some shooting, men must be killed, and then there will be an end of this defiance of law and destruction of property. Violence must be met by violence. The soldiers must use their guns. They must shoot to kill." Dr. Lyman Abbott, one of the most prominent religious leaders in America, attacked Altgeld as the "crowned hero and worshiped deity of the Anarchists of the Northwest." The New York *Times* published sensational charges by Dr. Thomas S. Robertson, a local physician, who claimed to have treated Debs for dipsomania. Dr. Robertson claimed that Debs' memory and will power had both been impaired by frequent intoxication. "Those who knew Debs well when he was in this city," said the *Times*, "believe that his present conduct is in large measure, if not wholly, due to the disordered condition of his mind and body, brought about by the liquor habit . . ." The New York *World* gleefully inquired: "Is Eugene V. Debs responsible for his actions, or, indeed, is any man who once suffered from dipsomania a competent leader of his fellow men?"

The newspapers were not deterred by the revelation of a serious falsehood in this story. Dr. Robertson had claimed that Robert Ingersoll had sent him to Debs. When a reporter interviewed Ingersoll, he met with a flat denial: "I have known Mr. Debs for twelve years at least. I also know his parents. They are all excellent people, and I am their friend. Mr. Debs, I believe, is a perfectly sincere man, being enthusiastic in the cause of labor, and his sympathies are all with the workingmen. As to his drinking, I can say that I never met him when he appeared to be under the influence of stimulants. He was always in good health and in full possession of his faculties."

The end was in sight by July 10. Two more men were killed by soldiers at Spring Valley, Illinois. Another contingent of troops was sent to Chicago, locating there a total of 1,936 Federal soldiers. The House of Representatives approved a joint resolution "endorsing prompt and vigorous action of the military forces in suppressing interference with the mails and with interstate commerce." A Federal grand jury also met in Chicago to consider an indictment for conspiracy against the strike leaders. E. M. Mulford of the Western Union Company, the sole witness examined, produced copies of all telegrams sent from ARU headquarters during the strike. Only the most incriminating telegrams were submitted to the grand jury; not one counselled violence and many advised against it. But Debs, Howard, Keliher, and Rogers were indicted for conspiracy to interfere with interstate commerce. They were arrested at once.

When Debs was picked up, his books, personal papers, and private unopened correspondence were seized by the Federal marshal. This act was clearly unconstitutional, and Judge Grosscup ordered the items returned the following day. Richard Olney later pointed to the prompt restoration of Debs' property as an indication that the Administration had "done its best to hold an entirely even hand as between the striker on the one hand and capital on the other." The four accused men were released on bail of ten thousand dollars each, after they had been held only a few hours.

Only a miracle could now save the boycott. John M. Egan, Chairman of The Managers, had wired to the metropolitan newspapers: "The strike was broken Monday. All roads moved trains to-day, and to-morrow a general resumption of business will take place." Debs was very worried when he got back to his room in the Revere Hotel on North Clark Street—he had left the Leland soon after the Army camped under his window. The hotel clerk handed him a note in small, precise handwriting, "like fine steel print," Debs thought. Eugene Field, the famous poet who was then working for a Chicago newspaper, had sent a prediction and an offer: "You will soon need a friend; let me be that friend."

[*3*]

EUGENE DEBS had found time to write or wire to his parents every day since the boycott began, and Theodore Debs was with him in Chicago. But Daisy and Daniel, both quite elderly, had continued to worry, so on July 10 Debs' sister, Mrs. Emma Debs Maillaux, and Kate Debs arrived in Chicago to remain until the end of the boycott. Sensing a vital human-interest story, the reporters hurried to interview the strike leader's wife. They found their story. Kate Debs didn't believe in traipsing around the country in a cotton house dress, any more than her husband believed in wearing overalls to union meetings. She was boasting a gray skirt which matched her eyes and a dotted silk blouse with puffed sleeves. With diamond earrings, two diamond rings, a gold watch fastened to her belt, and a double gold necklace which reached to her waist, she was indeed a stately and imposing woman. Kate made a very favorable impression on the reporters by explaining that her husband was a quiet, studious man, who had never learned to dance and much preferred reading to social activities. When asked if she discussed economics and politics with her husband, Kate replied: "Oh, yes; that's all there is at our house, and I'm just as much interested in his ideas and works as though I was one of his men associates. I think Eugene is right and that the American people will sustain him in whatever he does." "And so do I," said Emma Maillaux quickly. "We are a very devoted family . . . and though we are scattered now, we are all just as much interested in each other's doings and plans and hopes as though we were back home and living together as in the old days." But Kate Debs, in spite of her cordiality, did not end the interview without protesting against press accounts of the boycott:

Some of the newspaper writers made me very indignant by charging that Eugene had organized this movement from mercenary motives. Now, that is perfectly absurd. He gets a paltry salary of $3,000 a year. I call it paltry—and it is paltry for a man of Mr. Debs' ability. The firemen offered him a salary of $20,000 a year to remain with them and he refused it. He was always a friend of the poor. His sympathies are always on the side of those that are oppressed. He is always on the side of the underdog in the fight.

While it is not certain that the Brotherhood had offered Debs a salary of twenty thousand dollars a year, it is certain that the ARU never paid him his salary of three thousand.

By July 11, trains were moving even in California, where the boycott had been most effective. When Mayors Pingree and Hopkins and Erskine Phelps called on Vice-President Wickes to again request arbitration, they met an emphatic refusal. "The issue at question, which was simply that of reopening the shops at Pullman, and carrying them on at a ruinous loss, was not a proper subject for arbitration," said Mr. Wickes. Meanwhile a committee from the Knights of Labor was conferring with the President. They left Cleveland with the clear understanding that a commission to investigate the dispute would be appointed within a few days.

The AFL executive council met in the Briggs House in Chicago on July 12, with the leaders of several other national unions present. Gompers had ignored the boycott for more than two weeks, and had called the conference only at the request of the Chicago unions. Thomas J. Morgan, a Chicago socialist, even charged that Gompers had said, "I'm going to the funeral of the ARU," when he boarded the train in Indianapolis, but Gompers flatly denied the charge. The first act of the executive council was to send a wire to Cleveland asking him to attend its meetings, and urging him to "lend your influence and give us your aid so that the present industrial crisis may be brought to an end," but not discussing the causes of the boycott. Cleveland did not bother to answer the telegram.

Then Debs appeared, with a request that Gompers carry to The Managers an offer to call off the boycott if all ARU members would be rehired. Gompers refused, believing that such

action would prejudice the interests of the AFL, but he offered
to accompany Debs on such a mission. The railroads would not
meet with Debs, and the ARU chief declined the offer. Becoming
angry, Debs asked the AFL to declare a sympathetic strike.
This request was very unreasonable, since the Army and the
courts would obviously crush any move to spread the strike. The
ARU was certain to be destroyed—nothing would be gained by
the added destruction of all other unions. Gompers, by his rigid
neutrality early in the boycott, had lost his chance to aid the
strikers. If, from June 26, the AFL had sought to keep the courts
and Federal government from entering the dispute, if it had
sought to counteract the misleading newspaper stories, if it had
tried to restrain the strikebreaking actions of the Brotherhoods,
it would have rendered great service to the strikers. By July 12,
the ship was already sinking. But Gompers' comment in his
autobiography revealed the motives for his inaction: "The
course pursued by the Federation was the biggest service that
could have been performed to maintain the integrity of the
Railroad Brotherhoods. Large numbers of their members had
left their organizations and joined the A.R.U. It meant, if not
disruption, weakening to a very serious extent."

After discussing the situation for a full day, the executive
council issued a statement on July 13:

> The public press, ever alive to the interests of corporate
> wealth, have, with few exceptions, so maliciously misrepresented
> matters that in the public mind the working classes are now
> arrayed in open hostility to Federal authority. This is a posi-
> tion we do not wish to be placed in, nor will we occupy it without
> a protest . . .
> We declare it to be the sense of this conference that a general
> strike at this time is inexpedient, unwise, and contrary to the
> best interests of the working people. We further recommend
> that all connected with the American Federation of Labor now
> out on sympathetic strike should return to work, and those who
> contemplate going out on sympathetic strike are advised to re-
> main at their usual vocations.

The statement concluded with an appeal for continued labor organization, and for the settlement of the issue at the ballot box
so that the workers could wrench the government "from the

hands of the plutocratic wreckers and place it in the hands of the common people."

The Chicago Building Trades Council at once called off its city-wide strike, and other unions followed suit. On July 14 the Chicago *Tribune* was pleased with these developments:

DEBS' STRIKE DEAD
It is Dealt Two Mortal Blows by Labor
Federation Hits First
Trades Council Follows with a Crusher

Mayor Hopkins carried to The Managers Debs' offer to call off the boycott if all ARU members were rehired; the offer was of course rejected. The merchants on Chicago's State Street were so hostile to the ARU that they began a boycott of the advertising columns of the Chicago *Times*, which had supported the strikers. In Chicago the disorders were at an end. The streets were clear, and flames no longer seared the evening skies. Train schedules were returning to normal. George M. Pullman, who had spent the strike in seclusion but had maintained direct contact with his general offices throughout the dispute, again showed his face to the country by issuing a statement to the press:

The public should not permit the real question which has been before it to be obscured. That question was as to the possibility of the creation and duration of a dictatorship which could make all the industries of the United States and the daily comfort of millions dependent upon them, hostages for the granting of the fantastic whim of such a dictator. Any submission to him [Debs] would have been a long step in that direction, and in the interest of every law-abiding citizen of the United States was not to be considered for a moment.

For ten years Pullman had protected his employees from liquor dealers and union organizers—he was now offering to extend the same courtesies to everybody in the country.

But the workers at Pullman were feeling distress which exceeded their want during the previous winter. Although Mayor John Hopkins of Chicago, owner of a large grocery, had donated twenty-five thousand pounds of flour and the same amount of meat to the relief fund in May, this food had been used in a few days. Most contributions came in small drops from other workers and local unions. Thomas Heathcote, on July 15, announced that the original strikers were being starved into submission, but the ARU refused to quit.

Fifteen meetings were held that day in Chicago, and Eugene Debs spoke to most of them. He bitterly jibed at his old enemy: "Grand Chief Arthur, of the engineers, is a jobber and he will go down in history as a traitor to organized labor. He instructs his men to work with non-unionists and tells them it is honorable. He is a tool in the hands of the general managers." The ARU was sending out organizers to encourage the strikers on several roads, and Debs still thought they would win in the Far West, where they were better organized: "Men there are loyal, fraternal and true. When they believe they are right, they all go out and stay out until the fight is over."

Eugene Debs, a lifelong Democrat who three times campaigned for Grover Cleveland, was deprived of faith in the major political parties by the actions of Cleveland and Olney. He could no longer advocate labor's adherence to parties which were firmly controlled by the large corporations. At the last strike meeting, Debs made a personal appeal to the workingmen: "I am a Populist, and I favor wiping out both old parties so they will never come into power again. I have been a Democrat all my life and I am ashamed to admit it. I want every one of you to go to the polls and vote the People's ticket."

On July 17, Debs and the other strike leaders were again arrested on a contempt of court charge for violating the July 2 injunction. This time they refused bail and were imprisoned. The railroads, quickly seizing this opportunity to deal the strike a last blow, sent agents to each town to tell the workers that the men in neighboring towns had returned to work. Doubtful of the truth of these reports, the locals wired to Debs for information; but he was in jail and unable to answer them. In this way the strikers were tricked into returning to their jobs.

Twenty-four hours after the ARU leaders were sent to jail, a large notice was posted on the gates at Pullman: "These gates will be opened as soon as the number of operatives is sufficient to make a working force in all departments." Two days later, the United States Army left Chicago. The Debs Rebellion was over.

CHAPTER 8

□

[*1*]

COOK COUNTY JAIL, standing at the corner of Austin Avenue and Dearborn Street in the heart of Chicago, was a huge granite structure set around a courtyard. Narrow windows, barred and begrimed by dirt and cobwebs, stared like blind eyes from high in the walls. The corridors leading to the cells were gloomy, the floors slippery with slime and tobacco spit. Eugene Debs, on July 17, 1894, was placed in a cell with five other men. Bunks stood three-high against the filthy walls. The straw mattresses had mildewed and were infested with vermin. The half-hundred women inmates of the jail moaned and sobbed so that it was impossible to sleep.

Day after day Debs watched his fellow inmates, squatting stripped to the waist on their bunks, scratch the vermin bites until blood ran down their bare chests. The prisoners never saw the sunlight. For twenty hours each day they were locked in their cell, without even a light to read by; for the other four hours they were permitted to walk through the damp corridors. Each night they heard the eerie symphony from the women's cell block. For recreation, a prisoner could scratch himself or watch the giant rats run across the floor. One day, when a deputy sheriff passed through the corridor with a fox terrier, Debs negotiated the loan of the dog so that it could kill the rats. But the first sight of one of the huge, vicious rodents threw the dog into a panic. It began to howl and whine, and the sheriff was forced to release his pet from the cell.

Not all officials were as friendly as the sheriff with the terrier. One guard gleefully showed Debs the death cells which had held the Haymarket martyrs. He then showed his prisoner the cell which had housed the assassin of Mayor Carter H. Harrison, and the rope with which this murderer had been hanged. Debs was horrified, but he soon found that this sadistic jailer was as

much an exception as the deputy sheriff. Neither consideration
nor deliberate cruelty was the dominant feature of Cook County
Jail. The cruelty was there, thought Debs, but it was blind, unthinking, callous, indifferent. The penal system was not immoral—it simply had never heard or thought about morality.

Preliminary hearings on the contempt of court charge were
begun before Judge William A. Woods, and the ARU leaders
spent the day hearing Edwin Walker denounce the Debs Rebellion. But Debs' confidence in the righteousness of his cause
remained unshaken. "Having only acted in this matter in
obedience to the dictates of our conscience and our judgment,"
he wrote to Henry Demarest Lloyd on July 24, "we shall accept
with philosophic composure any penalties, however severe, the
courts may see fit to impose. The one great result of this agitation has been to call the attention of the country to the flagrant
abuses of corporate power of which working people have so long
been the patient and uncomplaining victims. I am inclined to be
optimistic and do not hesitate to believe that all these things
are making for the emancipation and redemption of men from
the thraldom that has so long been theirs in slavery and degradation." The next day the hearings were set over until
September 5 due to the illness of Edwin Walker, and the prisoners were again released on bond.

Debs returned to Terre Haute, where he immediately became
ill and was forced to spend two weeks in bed. The strain and
unrelenting labor of the boycott, followed by his anguish for the
inmates of the jail, had bitten deep into his great strength. Nor
had the end of the strike ended his worries. The ARU leaders,
when they were first arrested on July 10, had been forced to
accept bond money from several politicians. They disliked being
under obligation to these men, and had immediately begun
efforts to raise bail from other sources. Although Henry Lloyd
and Florence Kelley had taken the lead in the campaign to
procure bail, many of the erstwhile liberals in Chicago had refused to help the strike leaders. The bulk of the ARU legal fund
finally came from the labor movement, including contributions
of nearly eight hundred dollars from the AFL. "In presenting
this to you," Gompers wrote, "we desire to convey more elo-

quently than I can find words to express our unqualified disapproval of the attempts on the part of government officials
and the courts in throwing the weight of their influence in favor
of corporate wealth and against the most necessary, useful and
liberty loving people of the country—the wageworkers. We
offer it to you as a protest against the exercise of class justice,
and as a further protest against the violation of rights guaranteed by the Constitution and the Declaration of Independence."

[2]

THE BOYCOTT had attracted too much attention to pass easily
from the headlines, now that it had been broken. The feudal
conditions which caused the initial strike, the nationwide tie-up
of the railroads, the intervention of the Federal government, the
dispute between Cleveland and Altgeld, the wild charges against
the strikers, had combined to make the Pullman boycott the
biggest news story of 1894. Thirty persons had been killed and
twice as many injured during the riots, according to John
Swinton. In Chicago alone, thirteen were killed and fifty-three
seriously injured. More than seven hundred men had been arrested. *Bradstreet's* estimated that the boycott had caused a total
loss to the country of eighty million dollars. The railroads had
lost nearly five million dollars in profits, and a hundred thousand railroad workers had suffered lost wages of one million,
four hundred thousand dollars. At the height of the outbreak,
there had been more than fourteen thousand law enforcement
officers in Chicago.

The press campaign against the strikers was undiminished.
Harper's Weekly, on July 21, featured a cover cartoon of a parade, led by Populist Senator William Peffer and Governors
Waite, Pennoyer, and Altgeld. King Debs rode on a litter borne
by the strikers, who also carried a skull, torch, dagger, and a
banner emblazoned, "Anarchy." The New York *Tribune*, following the viewpoint of George M. Pullman's statement of
July 14, again charged that Debs was a self-seeking dictator:
"One lesson of great importance should be learned from the
past few weeks. Working people should be able to see the danger

of surrendering their liberty and prosperity into the hands of a single individual."

Meanwhile at Pullman, the former employees were learning "the danger of surrendering their liberty and prosperity into the hands of a single individual." Every applicant for work was required to sign a yellow-dog contract, promising that he would not join a union. One veteran employee refused to yield up his ARU card—he said that would involve giving up his principles and "his rights as an American citizen." Fully 25 per cent of the men hired at Pullman were new employees. There was acute suffering among the residents, and, when the company refused to act in any way—to reduce rents or stagger work—Governor Altgeld issued a proclamation which called for a public relief fund. Even the Chicago *Tribune*, admitting the starvation at Pullman, cooperated in raising the fund. But Altgeld had not finished; he also stated that the Pullman Company had each year for several years defrauded the state of Illinois of more than six hundred thousand dollars in taxes.

President Cleveland, under a law which he had pushed through Congress in 1889 and in accord with his promise to the Knights of Labor, appointed a commission to investigate the boycott on two railroads, the Illinois Central and the Rock Island. This commission, composed of Carroll D. Wright, the United States Commissioner of Labor, and two other prominent men, began hearings in Chicago on August 15. Railroad executives, labor leaders, strikers, public officials, were all asked about their rôles in the boycott. The printed proceedings of the Commission took nearly a thousand pages.

In his testimony, Eugene Debs said that there would not be a single labor union in the world if employers had dealt honorably with their workers, but that unions would continue as long as injustice existed. In reply to the argument that the boycott should never have been called, Debs pointed out that men would have continued to work fourteen hours a day if they had not struck for their rights. A strike is always justified in opposition to tyranny, regardless of the consequences: "It seems to me that if it were not for resistance to degrading conditions, the tendency of our whole civilization would be downward; after a

while we would reach the point where there would be no resistance, and slavery would come." Contending that strikes
would occur until the government owned and operated the railroads "in the interest of the people instead of for private gain,"
Debs said that he believed in a co-operative commonwealth as
the solution to economic problems. He denied that he was a
socialist because his ideas had come from Laurence Gronlund
rather than Karl Marx; he also said that his mind was not
fixed and he was still studying the problem.

The commission's report, which was released in November,
was so favorable to the ARU that several railroads and newspapers intimated that it had been written by the union, a charge
Debs vehemently denied. But he had good reason to be pleased
with the conclusions of the commission. The ARU was criticized on two grounds: its constitution did not contain an explicit condemnation of violence, and it had admitted the Pullman employees, who were not railroad workers, to membership.
But the report denounced Pullman's refusal to arbitrate and
also exposed the railroads' conspiracy to reduce wages and
destroy the union. The blame for the boycott, said the commission, "rests with the people themselves and with the government for not adequately controlling monopolies and corporations, and for failing to reasonably protect the rights of labor
and redress its wrongs." Compulsory arbitration was recommended as insurance against future railroad strikes. Debs, while
he opposed this recommendation, was grateful that the facts of
the dispute had been clearly stated and gave the report his
"unqualified approval."

[*3*]

As SEPTEMBER 10 drew near, the date of the BLF convention in
Chicago, Debs thought with joy and regret about his twenty
years within its ranks. He had believed in it deeply and given it
his full power of body and mind during its rapid growth. Only
near the end had he begun to feel that the Brotherhood's nu-
merical strength concealed a shameful flabbiness of fiber. The
fault was not in the men, but in the principles of the organiza-

tion. Debs firmly believed in the labor movement as a means of education and battle, but he had seen meeting after meeting spent in initiation ceremonies, with the recruits wearing halters around their necks and performing silly ritual. Grieving at the difference between the possibility and the reality, Debs had gone home in disgust to read and to study. The Brotherhood, he thought, was high dues, broken strikes, and a missed opportunity. Its inner circle was too small; it knew too few men as brothers.

But Debs' sadness had never become bitterness. Even after he helped to organize the American Railway Union, he had continued to advise all firemen to join the Brotherhood. He had not used *The Magazine* to publicize the ARU—the Great Northern strike received one brief paragraph, and the Pullman boycott a single article. Even when the Brotherhood had actively worked against the ARU in these labor struggles, Debs had refrained from any attacks on its leaders. So when, on September 5, 1894, he wrote a letter resigning from *The Magazine*, its dominant notes were pride, nostalgia, and friendship. Without one word in criticism of the Brotherhood, Debs said simply that he had tried to resign two years earlier, but had been persuaded to continue "at no little sacrifice of a sense of duty." Now his obligation had expired, and he wished to be relieved as soon as his successor was elected and qualified. The memories of good times, of battles won and lost, the sense of a common cause, merged in Debs' avowal of deep fraternity: "In submitting my resignation I avail myself of the occasion of tendering to the delegates of the convention assurances that old time associations are not forgotten, and of wishing each and all the largest measures of prosperity attainable under labor's unfortunate environments."

The matter, as Debs learned, was not to be settled so easily. His friends at the convention soon notified him that he was being viciously attacked as selfish, as corrupt, as showing favoritism by hiring his sister Emma and his brother Theodore. It was charged that he had been dishonorable in keeping the editorship of *The Magazine* while he worked to destroy the Brotherhood. A delegate from Vigo Lodge, Debs' own local in

Terre Haute, was even reading clippings from the capitalist newspapers to prove that Debs was a dictator, a drunkard, and a racketeer. A campaign was afoot to refuse his resignation and then to discharge him under prejudice, yet he had not been asked to appear in his own defense. Without waiting for an invitation, Debs went to Chicago.

On the afternoon of September 13, it was announced to the convention that Eugene Debs was in the anteroom, and requested permission to speak. By order of Frank Sargent, he was admitted to the hall and escorted to the platform: "I address this body from a point of right and justice; I never go where I am not wanted and I will leave it to a majority here to decide if I am to be heard. . . . I came here to respond to all charges and innuendo affecting my character. I leave it to you whether I shall be heard in my own defense or not." When Sargent called for a vote, not a man in the room was willing to raise his hand in opposition, so Debs began his answer to the charges. "In all my life I have never directly, or indirectly, injured the Brotherhood of Locomotive Firemen." He had always urged the members to stay with the organization, and he had continued his efforts to win new adherents.

But he was unable to agree with many policies of the Brotherhood: "You can never succeed with the men divided in separate organizations. If engineers have a grievance the firemen will have none. An injury to one should be an injury to all. It is wrong to be separate. The corporations do not take this view of it; when a road becomes involved in a strike the other roads, the newspapers, the banks and all the rest come to the rescue. I wish that labor might follow the example set by capital. This is the only way you will ever support yourselves."

Debs bitterly attacked the claim that labor must wait for the slow movement of public opinion to support it: "I care nothing about public sentiment. Public sentiment hanged John Brown. I haven't forgotten that public sentiment supported slavery for years. If organized labor has a mission it is to make war on the public sentiment that makes these conditions possible. What are the brotherhoods going to do to relieve this calamity? What are any of these organizations going to do to relieve this calamity?

I do not believe that this brotherhood will move the country upward in one hundred years."

The lodge meetings of the Brotherhood were "a farce" when they should be a schoolroom to educate the firemen: "Intelligence is what is required; ceremonies give no returns." The beneficiary features of the union had caused it to expel three thousand men a year for nonpayment of dues. This was wrong, no man should be compelled to carry insurance if he couldn't afford it. The federation of the brotherhoods was founded on false principles, because a strike could be blocked by the vote of a single grand officer in any brotherhood. This placed despotic power in the hands of men like P. M. Arthur, "the worst enemy of labor today. He is the owner of a paper that fights labor, he is the director of a bank and the railways endorse him; and they say that I am the opposite. No man can be a friend of a corporation and a friend of labor. A railway official may be friendly with you personally, but he is subservient to those above him. I am one of those who believe that no railroad man gets too much wages, there are many not getting enough."

The Brotherhoods prided themselves on being craft unions, said Debs, but they were not. There were engine wipers who belonged to the Brotherhood of Locomotive Engineers. The Trainmen's union had organized five hundred firemen and thousands of switchmen. The Brotherhood of Locomotive Firemen held ten thousand engineers, five thousand hostlers and other crafts, and only nine thousand firemen. There were forty thousand firemen in the United States, but only ten thousand in the unions—"at that rate you will have the firemen organized in sixty years."

No brotherhood had ever won a strike. They had lost on the Burlington, the Ann Arbor, the Lehigh Valley, the New York elevated lines. And they never would win a strike until they amalgamated their unions into one solid organization. When the General Managers Association conspired to reduce wages, it was the ARU that blocked the plan. Wages were slashed on the Louisville & Nashville, the Big Four, the Union Pacific, the Northern Pacific. Then they tried the same trick on the Great Northern: "That's where we stopped them. . . . The General

Managers Association had books printed giving uniform wages so that they could say that they could pay no more than other lines. Then they would make more reductions until they had their men down to the level of slaves." Was it treason to oppose the suicidal policies of the Brotherhoods? In God's name, how long would they continue their disastrous retreat?

He had been called selfish and grasping. He could have earned far more money in other jobs. A career had been open in politics; a job had been offered as head of the American Press Association. But he had chosen to make sacrifices for the labor movement, and other members of his family had shared those sacrifices. Emma had resigned a seventy-five-dollar-a-month job teaching school to help him. Theodore had begun at ten dollars a week but not one cent had ever been defaulted in his accounts. Was this selfishness? Time after time the railroads had tried to bribe him. Time after time the Brotherhood had tried to raise his salary. But he had always refused. Then he resigned his four-thousand-dollar-a-year job to work for the ARU at seventy-five dollars a month. Was that selfish? He had tried in 1892 to resign from the Brotherhood, and in 1894 to resign from the ARU: "Has Mr. Arthur ever tendered his resignation? The railroad organizations would unite today but for the grand officers. I make you this proposition, I and my associates, my colleagues, will resign if the other grand officers will resign. Will Mr. Arthur, Mr. Wilkinson, or Mr. Clark accept this proposition? Yet they say I am selfish. I want you to unify; it doesn't matter how much you unify; you can wipe out the name A.R.U. but you must unify. . . . Railway corporations use one organization to defeat another. . . . In the late strike of the A.R.U. members of the brotherhoods took their places and in many instances took their own brothers' places. Who profited? The railway companies relied on the brotherhoods. I make the prediction that Mr. Arthur will never order another strike. He knows that for every man that would strike there are forty ready to take his job. I do not approve of this but it is a fact. . . . I am not criticizing you, I am only telling the truth."

Debs had joined the Brotherhood when he was only nineteen

years old. For two decades he had been a loyal member. He had
worked for its advancement, gone hungry for it, thought for it,
and battled for it. He had ridden in freight cars over thousands
of miles; he had been dropped off on the desert and into snow-
drifts. He had spent thousands of dollars of his own money to
organize the firemen. There had been no complaints, because it
was a righteous cause. And in all of the charges against him,
nobody had accused him of being on the side of the corporations.
He had spent eight days in Cook County Jail as a protest
against inhumanity. He was not sorry for that. He only wished
the labor organizations would unite to defend themselves: "I
will say to you individually and collectively, I wish you well.
. . . I assure you that you will always have my cordial support,
and if you will do what I believe should be done, you will unify
the railway labor of the country."

He had tried to do his duty as he understood it. For that he
had no apologies, and he would accept like a man any blame that
attached to his actions. He had no bitterness, no rancor, simply
a hope that the workers would understand each other better
than they had in the past. All differences should be discussed
honestly and with compassion. As for himself, he would always
be found at the side of the workingmen: "I have this for the
men who know me and believe in me, I hope my hand may be
paralyzed and my eyes blinded if ever I do aught against labor.
About the rest that my enemies have said about me I have
nothing to say. . . . From the depths of my heart I thank you
and wish you prosperity."

The speech had been a forceful and moving statement, but
there was nobody there to applaud—Debs' supporters had gone
down to defeat with the ARU. His message was received in
silence, and he sadly left the hall and returned to Terre Haute.

[4]

THE CONGRESSIONAL ELECTIONS OF 1894 were filled with meaning for the labor movement. Both of the major parties had
watched with folded hands the advent of the depression. They
had failed to reduce significantly the high tariff. They had failed

to increase the volume of money in circulation. They had failed to introduce a graduated income tax. In 1892 a Republican President, Benjamin Harrison, had used the United States Army to break the Coeur d'Alene strike. Two years later a Democratic President, Grover Cleveland, had used the Army to break the Pullman boycott. Many working men were persuaded that their sole hope for salvation lay in support of the Populists. Eugene Debs held this view. In his speech to the Firemen's convention, he had said: "You say labor organizations do not discuss politics. I would have labor to unify at the polls and vote for an independent people's party. Some say politics mean destruction to labor organizations, but the reverse is true. There are questions I would like to see labor interest themselves in. Their conditions are like a cancer, you can cover it with a poultice but the cancer continues to spread. You must apply the knife and root it out if you expect relief." Contending that the depression was premeditated and a bankers' panic, Debs had said, "If we could but destroy the money monopoly, land monopoly, and the rest of them, all would be different."

Quarrels about policy ran deep in the trade unions. Debs, for his part, regarded political action and collective bargaining as inseparable parts of the fight against the employers. Under present conditions, support of the People's Party seemed the most effective way of pressing that fight, but the trade unions should preserve their separate identity and not abandon the economic field, thought Debs. In every past depression, the American trade unions had tended to dissolve as working-class organizations in favor of political action, producers' co-operation, money reform, or some other panacea; this mistake was now being repeated by the Knights of Labor and several leaders of the ARU. The ruling circles in the Brotherhoods had largely abandoned both the economic and political fights in order to conciliate the employers, but many rank and file members would vote for the Populists. The position of the AFL was still undecided in August, 1894. Although several affiliated unions and state federations were working for the People's Party, Samuel Gompers and the other top leaders continued to equivocate.

It was in Illinois that a labor-Populist alliance had first been effected, and Illinois now supplied the tacticians to bring the entire AFL into the Populist column. These tacticians were not from the ranks of either labor or the farmers, but were professional men long sympathetic to both. The most important was Henry Demarest Lloyd, a millionaire journalist who had been financial editor and editorial writer for the Chicago *Tribune* from 1873 to 1885. After 1885 Lloyd devoted his great ability to writing and lecturing against the monopolies; in 1894 he published his *Wealth Against Commonwealth*, a documented and caustic attack on the Standard Oil Corporation, which was the pioneer muckraking volume and instantly became a classic of the reform movement.

Lloyd, recognizing the strategic position held by Gompers, had used both flattery and logic in his attempt to win over the AFL chieftain. His efforts proved fruitless. Gompers had declared, in a letter to Debs after the Pullman strike, that "the end of the struggle of the masses is not yet," but he disagreed with the strategy being followed by Debs and Lloyd. The Coeur d'Alene, Homestead, Buffalo, and Pullman disturbances had shown that labor could not win a strike against the power of the government. All previous political ventures by labor had weakened the trade unions, thought Gompers. So he now discouraged strikes and also used his great influence to keep the AFL from endorsing the Populists. By rejecting the People's Party, the AFL was forced to choose between the antilabor Democrats and the antilabor Republicans. In a misdirected blow at Grover Cleveland, it chose the Republicans.

Debs, Lloyd, Clarence Darrow, Lyman Trumbull, Joe Buchanan, and other prominent men spearheaded the drive to bring labor into the Populists' columns, centering their fire on the injunction and government favoritism toward corporations. Their efforts met with limited success. In the November election, the large Democratic majority in Congress was replaced by an even larger Republican majority. The Populists, although they received a half-million more votes than in 1892, saw their Congressional delegation drop from fourteen to ten. Henry Demarest Lloyd in Chicago and Joseph R. Buchanan in Newark were both defeated in their campaigns for Congress, making it clear that most workingmen did not regard the People's Party as their political champion.

[5]

AT THE TIME of the November election, the ARU leaders were all facing possible terms in prison. Judge William A. Woods had sentenced Debs to six months in jail and the others to three months for violating the July 2 injunction; they had immediately appealed to the United States Supreme Court for writs of habeas corpus to test the court order. Far more serious, however, were the possible consequences of the indictment for conspiracy to obstruct a mail train on the Rock Island Railroad. Judge Peter Grosscup had set over the trial on this charge from December until January 8, 1895, so that the defendants could spend the holidays with their families.

Eugene Debs failed to appear at Woodstock jail on January 7, the time and place set by the judge. He was not even abashed to be tardy. Although he explained that he had eaten too many cucumbers and become ill, the rumors gave intoxication as the true cause of his delinquency. Nor was that all. On the second day of his trial for conspiracy, Debs issued a press release about his conviction for contempt of court:

In going to jail for participation in the late strike, we have no apologies to make nor regrets to express. I would not change places with Judge Woods, and if it is expected that six months, or even six years, in jail will purge me of contempt, the punishment will fail of its purpose.

Candor compels me to characterize the whole proceeding as infamous. It is not calculated to revive the rapidly failing confidence of the American people in the Federal judiciary. There is not a scrap of testimony to show that one of us violated any law whatsoever. If we are guilty of conspiracy, why are we punished for contempt?

I would a thousand times rather be accountable for the strike than for the decision.

The defense attorneys were Clarence Darrow and S. S. Gregory, former city solicitor of Chicago and later president of the American Bar Association. The prosecution was conducted by

T. M. Milchrist, John C. Black, and Edwin Walker. As soon as a
jury had been sworn, Gregory began to indict the prosecution.
He objected to the presence of Edwin Walker for the government on the grounds that Walker was still in the employ of the
Chicago, Milwaukee & St. Paul Railroad. Judge Grosscup overruled the objection. Darrow took an even more accusing tone
in his opening remarks to the jury: "I believe Mr. Milchrist is a
humane man who believes in the law, and in the excuse of the
law as a means of working oppression. But Mr. Milchrist in this
case is simply a puppet in the hands of the great railway corporations in this persecution, not prosecution." The defense attorneys then pointed out that not a single man actually guilty
of obstructing the mail trains had been indicted, but the leaders
of the union had been brought into court under the catch-all
and tyrannical doctrine of conspiracy. There was absolutely no
evidence to support the charge, said Darrow; every session of
the ARU convention had been open to reporters except for one
executive committee meeting which was called to consider
finances. After the Pullman boycott began, the union held no
secret meetings. Throughout the disturbances it had warned its
members against violence. It had offered to move any mail
trains which might be tied up.

Every day for nearly a month the defendants were brought
the fifty miles from Woodstock, Illinois, where they were being
held, to the courtroom in Chicago. Woodstock was a clean, almost homelike jail, and Debs again became his natty self. Darrow, stoop-shouldered, slouchy, drawling, wore clothes which
looked as if he had slept in them, and often he had. But Debs
appeared in a well-tailored grey tweed suit, a hard white collar,
a fashionable black and white tie, and a boutonniere. When the
ARU chief took the stand to testify about his career on the railroads, he looked like a minister or a businessman. The jury was
impressed by his quiet recitation of the facts, but equally important were his benign manner, gold-rimmed eyeglasses, and
gentle face.

Darrow continued to carry the fight to the prosecution. He
had the advantage, and he pressed it vigorously. The union's
habit of operating in the public view contrasted sharply with

the railroad executives' lack of candor. The leaders of the General Managers Association were put on the stand, and they testified that they could "not remember" what had happened at their meetings. Debs charged them with perjury; they were not indicted. George M. Pullman refused to appear in court in answer to a subpoena; he was not punished. The prosecution was clearly losing the case when a juror became ill on February 8. Four days later Judge Grosscup discharged the jury and continued the case until May. As soon as he announced his decision, several jurymen crowded around the defendants and congratulated them on the outcome of the case. Clarence Darrow later claimed that the jury, when discharged, had stood eleven to one for acquittal. But Debs and Darrow were not pleased; they wanted to argue the case through on its merits. In spite of their repeated challenges to the prosecution to bring the defendants back into court, the trial was never reopened.

The final act in the legal drama was played in Washington, D.C. In January, the United States Supreme Court had denied a defense motion for a writ of error in the contempt of court conviction. Three months later the application for habeas corpus was argued before the court by Gregory, Darrow, and Lyman Trumbull. Trumbull, formerly on the Illinois Supreme Court and then a Federal Senator, had been a close friend and political associate of Lincoln. Originally a Democrat, he had become a Republican over the slavery issue and had returned to the Democrats because of his disgust at the corrupt ring surrounding President Grant. In his later years he had become steadily more radical, more friendly to labor. In 1894, when he was more than eighty years old, he campaigned for the Populists.

Trumbull's plea for habeas corpus followed a simple line of reasoning. His brief pointed out that it was legal to strike. Therefore, if the defendants had erred at all, their error must have been a criminal act. The Constitution guaranteed trial by jury in all criminal cases, but the ARU leaders were now being jailed without benefit of a jury trial. The same judge who issued the injunction had pronounced sentence for its violation. This procedure, argued Trumbull, was grossly unconstitutional. It set up the judges as virtual dictators over the lives of American citizens. If it were permitted to stand, liberty would be crushed by judicial despotism. The much-vaunted government by laws would become a government by men.

But he failed to convince the Supreme Court, which denied the petition for habeas corpus without even entering into the question of the scope of the Sherman Act, on which the injunction had been based. The Supreme Court also avoided any pronouncement on the specific terms of the injunction, but merely ruled that the equity powers of the Federal courts could be used to prevent obstruction of the mails and interference with interstate commerce. An injunction, regardless of the validity of its provisions, must be obeyed. Violation could be punished by a jail sentence. Eugene Debs and his fellows were now returned to Woodstock jail to serve their terms.

CHAPTER 9

◻

[*1*]

THE McHENRY COUNTY JAIL was merely a few cells in the home of Sheriff George Eckert. Eckert proved to be, if not sympathetic to Debs' manifesto, at least sympathetic toward his prisoners. A group of farmers from the surrounding area called at the jail to threaten lynching and to ask the sheriff to treat his prisoners rough, but Eckert said they would be treated like everybody else. The sheriff, believing the ARU leaders were in no sense criminals, gave them an incredible degree of freedom. The seven prisoners ate their meals with the sheriff's family, played football in the street behind the jail, and received all the liberty that the rules permitted. They were locked in their cells at night, but nobody took this formality very seriously. There were no uniforms—the prisoners wore their business suits and white linen. Each morning Debs placed a fresh carnation in his buttonhole.

The seven ARU chiefs wasted no time in demonstrating that they were born organizers. They elected officers for the duration of their terms, and named their new creation the Co-operative Colony of Liberty Jail. Each morning they rose at six o'clock and did an hour's military drill before breakfast. Sheriff Eckert kindly let them use his rifle for their exercises. At 7:30 they had a breakfast of a steak or chops, fried potatoes, and coffee in the Eckert's dining room. They then studied economics and history until noon from their library of two hundred volumes, which included the Utopian socialist writings of Gronlund, Bellamy, and Robert Blatchford. Debs read Victor Hugo and Eugène Sue, but he also glanced through several Fabian essays, the works of Henry George, and *Wealth Against Commonwealth*. Henry Demarest Lloyd, who had sent a complimentary copy of his classic to Debs the previous December, now did the same favor for the other prisoners.

From noon until one o'clock the prisoners exercised with dumbbells and chest weights. They had a beef roast for lunch, studied until 6 P.M., and again had military drill before their supper of cold meat, bread, and milk. From 8 until 10 every evening they debated under the direction of L. W. Rogers, who had taught school before he became a brakeman in 1880. This program worked quite well. There were few violations of the self-imposed rules, and the elected officers had power to punish the delinquents by locking them in their cells. The only disruptor was George Howard, who resigned from the ARU during his term in jail to become national secretary of the American Industrial Union. Howard was convinced that their attorneys had badly mishandled the legal defense; he had opposed making the appeal and had wanted simply to serve his term in the beginning.

Debs' part in the Pullman strike and his imprisonment had made him a national celebrity. He was forced to hire a secretary in order to keep abreast of the hundred letters which came each day from ARU members, cranks, panacea advocates, and some of the best thinkers in America. The post office at Woodstock was buried under a stack of mail for Debs, including dozens of socialist books and pamphlets. But he was kept so busy answering his correspondence and granting newspaper interviews that he seldom had time for serious study. Reporters came from the Chicago *Chronicle*, the New York *World*, the Cincinnati *Enquirer*, from papers large and small across the country. Debs often received these reporters in the sheriff's dining room, where there was a chair with wide arms on which the interviewer could rest his notebook. One journalist found Debs refereeing a football game among his fellow inmates. They had blocked off the street behind the jail and strung ropes between trees to serve as goal posts. Debs complained that he was unable to play because he had wrenched his foot the previous day trying to kick the ball.

Eugene Debs, while confined in McHenry County Jail, was more prominent in national affairs than he had ever been in his life. His opinion was sought on every conceivable subject. Debs said that he favored John Peter Altgeld for President, and predicted that the Pullman strike would "tremendously" increase the Populist vote in 1896. He then took his feet down from their resting place on the bars to emphasize the next point: "if that party's convention . . . formulate[s] a platform upon which the great mass of reformers, be they socialists, single taxers, trade unionists, or what not, can unite and harmonize, they will, in 1896, take at least second place, and in 1900 at the latest, sweep the country." He then said that he favored free silver, but thought it would benefit the people "to a limited extent and this only for an inconsequential period." Arbitration seemed to him a poor solution for labor disputes: "If it is compulsory, it is vicious in principle, and if it is voluntary it can't be enforced."

When Nellie Bly, the small and gentle woman reporter who had become famous by circling the world in seventy-two days, visited Woodstock, Debs had grown a sandy beard and his face looked much fuller than previously. Debs spoke softly and without rancor, telling Nellie Bly that his only hardship was the enforced separation from his parents. On July 18, the day after the boycott collapsed, Daisy and Daniel had sent a telegram to their son: "Stand by your principles, regardless of consequences." They had received no newspapers during the boycott, but they had been unable to shut out the cries of newsboys in the street. They had been driven frantic with worry and apprehension, but nothing could make them retreat from their place at Debs' side. This relation between parents and children had grown steadily, through a realization of common beliefs and sacrifices shared. Almost every Sunday night, Debs had contrived to be at his parents' home in Terre Haute, even though it often meant a trip of several hundred miles to fulfill the obligation. During the great boycott, he had wired or written to them each day. The devotion was mutual and steadfast.

So the weeks passed, with Debs frittering away in correspondence and interviews a period that he could have used for scrupulous study. He worked hard to collect, in his sentimental fashion, a complete scrapbook of all documents bearing on the Pullman boycott. He not only wrote for Altgeld's annual address to the Illinois legislature, in which the governor had caustically attacked the use of the injunction and the Army, he also wrote to Richard Olney in order to get a copy of Olney's arguments. Debs never resented the actions of the Attorney-General; in 1908 the secretary of the Interstate Commerce Commission said in a letter to Olney: "Eugene Debs was in the office a few days ago, and has repeated what he said before. 'He esteemed you as an absolutely honest man, and in sending him to prison you only did your duty as the laws existed.' " Certainly Debs, by this admission, weakened his fight against the injunction, but Olney did send him the requested briefs and report.

Debs drew great strength from the loyalty of the ARU members and his personal friends. James Whitcomb Riley, although he was indifferent to strikes and politics, had made an anonymous contribution to the legal defense fund merely because he was certain that Debs could never commit a crime. When Debs wrote to the poet for material to be used in the *Railway Times*, Riley denied the request because he was, "aside from magazine work, at labor on two separate books," but he sent Debs his best wishes and a volume of humor. Riley did not even mention in his letter that Debs was in jail. Another famous poet, Eugene Field, also remained true to the note he had sent Debs during the critical days of the boycott. Field had visited Terre Haute for a lecture in December, 1894, and had met Debs at the home of a mutual friend. Field, hearing children in an adjoining room, quietly disappeared from the reception in his honor. Soon joyous shouts came from behind the closed door. When Debs investigated, he found Field down on his hands and knees, minus his tuxedo jacket, in the middle of a group of screaming, excited children. After that Debs, too, was lost to adult company for the evening. Field had defended Debs in the days when the newspapers were heaping abuse on the strike leader's head, and had even attacked his fellow journalists:

The gentlemen who write so bitterly against Mr. E. V. Debs in our contemporaries are certainly unacquainted with him; we will not believe they would wittingly misrepresent so sincere, so loyal and so kindly a man. We do not question his sincerity because we know him personally . . . If ye be ill, or poor, or starving, or oppressed, or in grief, your chances for sympathy and for succor from E. V. Debs are 100 where your chances with G. M. Pullman would be the little end of nothing whittled down.

The brief acquaintance of Debs and Field had proved sufficient
for a deep friendship, and one morning Debs received a note
from Field: "You are now settled in your summer quarters, and
I'll soon be out to see you." But the promise was never kept;
two days later Debs read in the newspaper that the poet had
suddenly fallen dead.

On August 22, all of the ARU leaders except Debs completed
their three-month terms and were released. They intended to
return to their homes for brief vacations, and then to take up
once more the arduous task of rebuilding the wrecked union.
They had made several organizing trips during their brief periods of freedom between the boycott and the beginning of their
jail terms in March, 1895. These trips had shown that the organization was in a wretched condition. The railroads were
blatantly discriminating against ARU members. In some cases
railroad executives even boasted about their use of the blacklist; when the superintendent of the Southern Pacific was asked
if he would try to have the ex-strikers discharged from other
jobs they might find, he replied: "Yes. If I know that a man was
not true to his company, and if I find out that he has got a job
elsewhere, I will pursue him and use my best efforts to have him
discharged. Those fellows who killed our engines, destroyed our
cars and track and murdered our employes shall never earn
bread and butter in California if I can help it." Many railroaders
remained stanch advocates of the ARU, but most of them were
unable to pay dues. The union's income fell off so sharply that
it closed the Chicago offices and moved its headquarters to
Debs' home in Terre Haute. But the actual headquarters were
in Woodstock jail, where Debs edited the *Railway Times,* and
conducted his immense correspondence. The union's stationery
now bore the message: "This letter is written from McHenry
County Jail, Woodstock, Ill. Address all official correspondence
to Terre Haute, Indiana." And Sheriff Eckert did not interfere
with this humorous propaganda, although the stream of visitors was a genuine nuisance.

Debs had no complaints about his situation. In July he had
been notified that his application for a pardon was being considered by the Justice Department. He indignantly replied

that he had made no such application, that he was entitled to his freedom as a matter of justice and refused to accept it as a matter of mercy. As soon as Debs' colleagues were released, Kate Debs arrived in Woodstock. Kate was grateful that the McHenry County Jail was such an improvement over that in Chicago, where she had also visited her husband. She intended to remain in Woodstock until Debs had finished his sentence, and immediately set to work helping with his correspondence. Every afternoon Debs worked on his job of editing the *Railway Times*, which he had largely usurped from Rogers when they were imprisoned. He wrote to dozens of men for editorial contributions to the paper—Henry Lloyd, James Whitcomb Riley, President John McBride of the AFL, Clarence Darrow. When he received an article, Debs sat down at the heavy pine table in his cell and worked over the copy with his blue-pencil and scissors. The cell soon became a perfect replica of a newspaper office, even to the cockroaches which flitted across the table.

But Debs could no more work on the *Railway Times* than he could study. He was a celebrity, a key figure, and the socialists made strenuous efforts to convert him to their philosophy. In 1893 he had scarcely been conscious of the socialist movement; the next year he had occasionally read the radical publications; by 1895 he had subscribed to the *Coming Nation*, which was published by J. A. Wayland and then by A. S. Edwards at Ruskin, Tennessee. When he was sent to Woodstock, the heaviest guns in the socialist battery began to give him personal attention. Victor Berger, a stolid, learned German immigrant who published the *Milwaukee Vorwaerts*, visited Debs, talked for hours in his ponderous manner, and left behind him a copy of Marx's *Capital*. Debs tried to read it, but it seemed awfully dull; he was more attracted to the works of Karl Kautsky and the popularizers.

Berger was followed by Keir Hardie, an English trade unionist and socialist then lecturing in the United States, who was escorted by the Chicago socialist, Thomas J. Morgan. Morgan and Hardie found Debs, minus his suit coat, wearing a colored summer shirt and comfortably lounging in the yard of the jail. For the entire day, the three men talked about socialism and the need for an international organization to stimulate friendship among the workers. At the day's end, Morgan drafted a plan, based upon their conversation, for the International Bureau of Correspondence and Agitation. The object of the organization was "to bring into harmonious relations all organizations and persons favourable to the establishment of the Industrial Commonwealth founded upon collective ownership of the means of production and distribution." They all signed the document, but Debs was still not convinced; three months later he refused to permit Morgan to publicize it.

Debs could not learn much in jail; he could only learn by actively taking part in the battles of the outside world. When that form of activity was denied him, his entire method of educating himself came to pieces, and it was useless to give him books or to argue with him. From his conversation with Keir Hardie, Debs did not remember anything about Hardie's intellectual force, but a simple incident about Hardie's sentimentality. Debs wrote about it: "An advance agent of the locust brigade had been captured and was singing his lay in a bottle in which he had been placed. Hardie quietly disappeared and in a few minutes returned with a perforated cigar box, prepared with his penknife and half filled with grass, and carefully transferred the locust to his more comfortable quarters. . . . I conclude that a man who had solicitude about the comfort of an insect could be safely trusted not to wantonly injure his fellow men."

Debs, in his new rôle as guide for the American conscience, contributed an article each week to the Chicago *Evening Press* and freely granted interviews on every subject. To the Texas convention of the People's Party he sent a letter: "While I am committed unequivocally to 'free silver,' I regard the political shibboleth as of little consequence compared to that other battle cry, 'Free men' . . ." That was well enough, but his sincere and florid expression on some subjects looked rather strange in print. When asked to write for the Cleveland *Plain-Dealer* about "The New Woman, the Bicycle and Bloomers," Debs favored all three: "For myself, I confess to a liking for bloomers. They seem cool and comfortable and there is something about the air of the girl who wears them that reminds me of the Declaration of Independence."

Fortunately for Debs' reputation, he was soon able to set his hand to other activity. As the date for his release drew near, he learned that a huge reception in Chicago was being arranged by Lloyd, Trumbull, Florence Kelley, and the left-wing unionists. An effort was made to persuade the Chicago Trades & Labor Assembly to sponsor the reception, but it was objected that Debs no longer believed in trade unions as a solution for the workers' problems. Thomas J. Elderkin, the president of the trades assembly, was rash enough to write Debs for his views on the labor question. Elderkin's letter was written on October 30. The next day Debs wrote a lengthy, furious reply:

. . . . For twenty-nine years I have been defining my "position" in relation to trade unions, and on all proper occasions I have given full, free and unequivocal expression to my views, but I must respectfully decline to do so for a consideration, even though this consideration be in the form of a reception upon my release from a jail in which I have served a sentence of six months for my fealty to the principles of the very trade unions which now propose to interrogate me as to my "position" in relation to their interests.

The statement that I am or ever have been hostile to trade unions and that I am advocating or intend to advocate their "abolishment" is too palpably false and malicious to merit an instant's attention. There is, of course, a purpose in having this question raised at this time, but it is difficult for me to believe that it emanates from a trade and labor assembly. If it had its origin in the General Managers' association or some kindred body it would be in consonance with the fitness of things and I should readily understand it. . . .

The trades assembly decided that it would be wise to sponsor the reception, and did so.

[2]

THE STREETS AND LAWNS of Woodstock were blanketed by eight inches of snow on November 22, 1895, the day that Debs was released from jail. A special train from Chicago was scheduled to arrive in the early afternoon; it would immediately carry the labor leader back to the Lake city for the giant reception. During the morning Debs was eager and nervous, preparing for his departure. Theodore Debs, who had come from Terre Haute, borrowed a horse and cutter, and Kate and Eugene Debs spent hours visiting the townspeople who had opened their homes in generous hospitality. Kate had firmly established herself in the small community, due in large part to the friendly press notices that she received. When she first arrived in Woodstock, the Chicago *Chronicle* had printed a very warm description of the strike leader's wife: "She is a large, splendid looking woman, one of dignified manner and yet with a charming air which attracts a stranger at once. She has unbounded faith in her famous husband and thinks that he will be a notable figure in the future history of the country. As might be expected, Mrs. Debs is well read on the subjects in which her husband is so vitally interested and can hold her own remarkably well in a talk on economics."

Debs, having finished his round of visits, returned to the jail, where he packed his books in heavy boxes, put his clothes into suitcases, and donned a new black suit. The other inmates, none of whom had known him six months earlier, mourned Debs' release; four of them drew up a resolution which described their "heartfelt thanks and gratitude for the many acts of kindness and sympathy" which he had done for them. Sheriff Eckert genially discharged, with his own best wishes, the famous prisoner. Woodstock was already jammed with ten thousand persons when the special train, bearing a delegation of trade unionists, arrived from Chicago. When the passengers saw Debs, they "wept and cheered and laughed and cried as they stood there in the snow. They fell upon their hero and kissed him in the sight of thousands."

The jubilant throng continued to maul and pummel their idol all the way to Chicago, where a more hysterical scene was enacted by the hundred thousand people who crowded the station and the surrounding streets. When the train stopped in the city of his great defeat and triumph, Debs stood on the rear platform and waved to the crowd. The shouts of the throng beat like waves against the walls of the building. Men screamed and yelled and beat upon their neighbors; coats were ripped, noses bloodied, and nobody noticed or cared. Here before them was Eugene Debs, who had led his legions into battle against the massed power of the railroads, the newspapers, the Federal courts, and the United States Army, rather than turn his feet aside from the paths of conscience. That was what they thought, and they idolized him for it. Finally several admirers swung Debs to their shoulders and tried to leave the station, but they had not moved ten paces when the crowd closed in front of them. Twenty minutes were lost before the police and sweating unionists could force a slight break in the human barricade. Inch by inch, Debs' bearers fought their way through the mob, and the long swaying column moved toward Battery D Armory on Michigan Avenue. They tried to put Debs in a wagon, but he chose to march through the slush and rain with his fellows. "If the rest walk," he protested, "I shall walk, too. What is good enough for them is also good enough for me."

The Armory was filled to the walls with standing men and women. Messenger boys, arriving with congratulations for Debs, were passed over the heads of the audience so they could personally deliver the telegrams. The wild excitement continued while Henry Demarest Lloyd and Governor Davis H. Waite welcomed the guest of honor and fiercely attacked the use of the injunction, but the hall became silent when Debs moved to the front of the stage. His bitterness, stored through one hundred and eighty days of jail, flowed into a fiery demand that the conspiracy trial be reopened so that he could clear his name. In a caustic attack on "usurped and unconstitutional power," Debs declared that Judge Woods' contempt of court verdict was a threat to the freedom of every citizen. Americans were indeed fortunate "if when night lets down her sable curtains, they are out of prison, though still the wage-slaves of a plutocracy which, were it in the celestial city, would wreck every avenue leading up to the throne of the infinite by stealing the gold with which they are paved, and debauch heaven's supreme court to obtain a decision that the command 'thou shalt not steal' is unconstitutional." Liberty is never won or kept except through struggle, warned Debs; if men want to reclaim their country from the money power, they must recognize the enemy and fight back. The ballot is the best weapon known to mankind: "It can give to our civilization its crowning glory, the cooperative commonwealth," but men must use it wisely or it will bring them bondage instead of freedom. And when the main speaker left the hall, men rose to sing: "We'll hang Judge Woods to a sour apple tree, As we go marching on."

Debs had intended to return directly to Terre Haute, but he was forced to stop in Indianapolis to visit a doctor; he had shaken hands so many times that his wrist was twice its normal size and his entire arm was so badly wrenched that he could scarcely move it. There were also more serious problems. The ARU was on the skids, a fact that Debs had never admitted. In the autumn of 1894, he had told the New York *World:* "The union is booming." In March of 1895, while on an organizing tour in the West, he wrote to George Schilling: "We are having great success with our meetings and the trip will doubtless be fruitful of great good to our cause." These reports were greatly exaggerated; the meetings were immense, but the ARU did not grow. Men went to hear Debs' lectures, but they were afraid to join his union. On railroad after railroad the ARU members were blacklisted, driven from their jobs, hounded from city to city, until some of them finally became hoboes. Some anonymous vagabond wrote a song about his new vocation, complete with the jargon of his old:

> *Been on the hummer since ninety-four,*
> *Last job I had was on the Lake Shore,*
> *Lost my office in the A.R.U.*
> *And I won't get it back until nineteen-two*
> *And I'm still on the hog train flagging my meals,*
> *Ridin' the brake beams close to the wheels.*

Debs himself had hinted at the truth in his contribution to a Chicago *Tribune* symposium on the question: "What would you do if you had two hundred fifty million dollars?" Debs answered: "I would seek to provide employment for every member of the American Railway Union blacklisted by railroad corporations, and for all other idle workingmen."

The most pressing question was the union's debt of thirty thousand dollars for legal fees to its attorneys, and printing bills to the Terre Haute firm of Moore & Langen. One morning soon after his release from Woodstock, Debs strolled into the office of Thaddeus Moore and wordlessly flopped into a chair and tossed a piece of paper across the desk. When Moore glanced at it, he saw that it was a deed to Debs' home, the dream house on Eighth Street. Debs explained that it was meant as partial payment on the ARU debt. When Moore complained that the union leader had no personal liability, Debs insisted that the deed be locked into the Moore & Langen safe, so that it could be filed whenever his honesty was in question. He then wrote to the union's other creditors, taking full responsibility for all debts, and left on a lecture tour to raise the money and to rebuild the organization. At every step he was followed by railroad detectives, who watched his movements and attended all of his lectures. Any railroader who was caught at a Debs' meeting was fired. Debs continued to speak before large audiences, but there were noticeably few railroaders present. The ARU men had not turned against their leader, but they were eager to keep their jobs during the depression.

Debs worked out several shrewd techniques for beating the railroads. When it became obvious that any known ARU man would be fired, Debs asked all recruits to the union to mail their cards directly to Terre Haute; the membership would be kept secret until a system was completely organized. The plan was clever, but it did not work very well. Debs had only his wits; the railroads had men, money, jobs to hand out. The detectives also were alert. In Providence, Rhode Island, Debs held a meeting in his hotel room at midnight, the men entering the hotel one at a time from different directions. The next morning every one of them was fired. In North Decatur, Alabama, Debs secretly signed up a hundred and eleven men, not one of them knowing the name of any other. The company called in the eighteen leaders, read the names of the entire hundred and eleven, fired the eighteen, and gave the others ten days to leave the union. At Williams, Arizona, two thugs tried to break into Debs' hotel room, springing the bolt so badly that the lock had to be removed before he could open the door. His landlady, who hated the detectives, told Debs, "Watch out for the scoundrels or they'll get you yet." They had already gotten him. He was working on a hopeless job. When Christmas came, he was stranded in Des Moines without a dime. For the first time he had failed to spend the holidays with his parents.

The Brotherhoods as well as the railroads were intent on smashing the ARU. The *Engineers' Journal* attacked Debs so violently that he offered to debate the issues in Cleveland, P. M. Arthur's home town, with any leader from the Engineers. The Cleveland Central Labor Union agreed to sponsor the meeting, but Arthur would not accept. The *Locomotive Firemen's Magazine* said of the ARU leaders: ". . . henceforth the official publications will not hesitate to show to the world their villainy, treachery and dishontesty of purpose." According to Richard Olney, Chief S. E. Wilkinson of the Trainmen boasted that he had shaved off his beard and carried a rifle with the militia during the Pullman boycott. The Trainmen had lost at least nine thousand members during 1894, many of whom were expelled for their support of the boycott. Equivalent figures were true of the other Brotherhoods. The Brotherhood leaders hoped that, if they helped to wreck the ARU, they would wipe out a rival and also prove their own reliability to the corporations.

In spite of Debs' failure to revive the ARU, his personal prestige continued to grow. When he was speaking in a livery stable in Duluth, a man in the audience said something in a loud voice. Debs, not understanding the comment, asked the man to repeat it. The man did so: "I said you're all right." And some giant a few feet from the first speaker muttered, "By God, you'd better." In San Francisco, a little fireman in Debs' escort was horrified to find a spectator in the front row who was still wearing his hat. The fireman screamed in an outraged voice: "Take your hat off, you ——. Don't you know that Gene Debs is here." Later that evening, a switchman saw two detectives who had followed Debs into a hotel lobby, and hurled them out into the street. Debs could not possibly back down as long as he had such support. His speeches became more and more radical, until finally he was declaring that the wage system must be abolished. But he still would not permit Tommy Morgan to publish the agreement they had signed in Woodstock Jail.

The ARU leader spent May, 1896, in the South, June in the East, July in the West and Northwest, August in the Southwest, lecturing and organizing. From each city he sent checks to the ARU creditors. When he arrived in Los Angeles, General H. G. Otis' *Times* stated that Debs had come to stir up a new civil war. Debs replied by renting a hall which would seat five thousand persons, and flooding the city with handbills about the meeting. The hall was so crowded for the speech that Debs was forced to stand on a table to make himself heard. About the middle of the evening, he learned that General Otis and an antilabor judge were in the audience, and he immediately shifted his attack to them: "Judge Ross is just part of the rolling stock of the Southern Pacific. Look at his linen and you'll find it's marked 'S. P.' " The audience massed closely around Ross and Otis, so that they were unable to escape hearing the speaker: "If in what I now have to say I do not prove Otis a monumental liar, I'll give any charitable institution in California one thousand dollars," followed by a specific list of falsehoods printed in the *Times*.

Not even this flamboyant gesture could help Debs' cause. The judges and the publishers and the railroads had won. The ARU was a corpse, killed by one strike and the Federal government.

[*3*]

FEW EVENTS in American history have been so filled with meaning as the Pullman boycott and its attendant circumstances. The American Railway Union was destroyed, but its spectacular success publicized and proved the virtues of industrial unionism. Injunctions had been previously issued in labor disputes, but the court order of 1894 dramatically placed this practice before the great body of citizens. State and Federal governments had previously intervened in the struggles of the workingmen, but never with such disastrous consequences or obvious partisanship. Many outraged workers were convinced that they must control the government, or the government would control them. If they could not win major strikes, they must establish a society in which strikes would not occur. Many men now accepted, and Jack London later expressed, the view that there are two conditions when strikes do not happen: When capital absolutely owns labor, and when labor absolutely owns capital. Feeling that they were subject to the first, certain rebels chose to work toward the second.

From that day forward, the labor injunction, industrial unionism, and social reorganization became practical issues in the United States. With these demands as the touchstone, vast realignments occurred in both the labor movement and the political field. The most determined fighters had been driven off the railroads, and the Brotherhoods, which had suffered heavily during the depression, entered into a solemn marriage with the corporations. Samuel Gompers, re-elected president of the AFL in 1895, was thoroughly alarmed by the outcome of the strikes at Homestead, Coeur d'Alene, Buffalo, and Pullman. Gompers thought that economic action was unwise because the power of the state would be used against the workingmen, and that political action was unwise because it split the trade unions. Only one course was left open. The AFL followed the Brotherhoods into a conciliatory policy toward the employers. It began as a matter of tactics and ended as an unquestioned principle. The Federation, putting behind its radical days, began a long retreat in which it sacrificed both unskilled workers and consumers to win meager gains for its own members.

A great body of workers, refusing to accept this solution, continued the campaign for industrial unions and entered the People's Party. The minds of these native-born Americans were trending steadily toward the left. They felt that the corporations, who were their sworn enemies, controlled the Federal government. The result was a great social unrest, a gigantic nervousness in which men were casting about for a philosophy and a leader. For some of them the philosophy proved to be socialism.

In 1896, the only Marxist party in America was the Socialist Labor Party, dominated by the beliefs and personality of Daniel

DeLeon. DeLeon was honest; he was fearless; he was educated; but he was also arrogant and dogmatic. His uncompromising dictatorship caused one split after another in his party. The Socialist Labor Party had become a narrow sect, a religion which followed the Messiah DeLeon. Most of its members were foreign-born, who were divided by language differences from the great body of workers. When the German socialists refused on principle to learn English, this difference was made permanent. In 1895 the SLP isolation was accentuated by its own action; it called the radical workers out of the AFL and founded the Socialist Trades & Labor Alliance.

It was hopeless to expect any considerable number of American workers to join the SLP; but they would join a new Marxist party which avoided the mistakes of its predecessor, a party that was not superimposed from without but that emerged directly from the labor battles of the decade. Such a party could only be founded by a man recognized by the workingmen as a brother. Eugene Debs proved to be the man. He inspired a confidence and a devotion unequalled by any labor leader in the country. Already he had been shrouded in an aura of legend. When Debs spoke at Cooper Union in the autumn of 1894, there was in the audience John Swinton, sometime editorial director of the New York *Sun* and then the most prominent labor journalist in the United States. Swinton, as he listened to Debs, was reminded of another gaunt man from the West who had stood on the same platform in 1860: "Debs in Cooper Union reminded me of Lincoln there. As Lincoln, of Illinois, became an efficient agent for freedom, so, perchance might Debs, of Indiana, become in the impending conflict for the liberation of labor. Let us never forget Lincoln's great words, 'Liberty before property; the man before the dollar.' "

Part III.

American Socialism

The workers' flag is deepest red;
It shrouded oft our martyred dead.
But ere their limbs grew stiff and cold
Their life-blood died its every fold.

So raise our scarlet banner high;
Beneath its folds we'll live and die.
Though cowards flinch and traitors sneer,
We'll keep the red flag flying here.
　　　　—FROM AN OLD SOCIALIST SONG.

CHAPTER 10

◻

[*1*]

THE POLITICAL REVOLT which had been growing for three decades reached its climax in 1896. From Illinois to the Rocky Mountains, the prairies were aflame with discontent. The farmers were heeding the advice of that fiery Populist orator, Mrs. Mary Ellen Lease, to "raise less corn and more hell." The prices of farm products were lower than they had been since the Civil War, while drought and locusts had caused a succession of bad crop years. Urban workers likewise were suffering deeply. Total money wages were less than in 1892, and wage rates had fallen in most industries. Although the work week ranged from fifty-four to sixty-three hours, earnings in manufacturing averaged only $406 a year.

Special significance attached to the Democratic national convention, which met in Chicago in early July. For two years, John Peter Altgeld had been maneuvering an intra-party revolt against the policies of Grover Cleveland. The insurgents had rallied round the slogan of Free Silver, but Altgeld's aims ran far deeper than monetary reform. Free Silver, as Debs had said in his letter to the Texas Populists, was less important than free men. Debs, Altgeld, and hundreds of their colleagues wanted to deal a smashing hammer blow against corporation control of the government; and Grover Cleveland had become a political symbol for Wall Street. Altgeld, with consummate artistry, welded the various threads of revolt into an explicit condemnation of the Administration. For the first time in American history, a President was read out of his own party. The Democratic platform, bearing the unmistakable stamp of Altgeld's beliefs, declared for free silver, reduced tariffs, and strict control of monopolies. In a final, conclusive repudiation of President Cleveland, the platform denounced "government by injunction as a new and highly dangerous form of oppression." The President of the United States had lost his party to an ugly little "anarchist" from Illinois.

Although Altgeld had dictated the platform, he was unable to dictate the Presidential candidate. Ineligible because of his foreign birth, Altgeld tried to win the nomination for Senator Richard Bland of Missouri, a lifelong advocate of silver coinage. But a young ex-Congressman from Nebraska, William Jennings Bryan, with a rich, beautiful voice and a true orator's stance, upset the plans. Bryan's "Cross of Gold" speech voiced in unforgettable prose the inchoate thoughts of the delegates. When Bryan finished, the revolting workers and farmers went crazy with enthusiasm. They marched in snake dances about the hall, threw their hats high in the air, pummeled each other and screamed: "Bryan, Bryan, Cross of Gold." The Boy Orator of the Platte had just won a chance at the nation's top office. And John Peter Altgeld, realizing that he had lost, turned "his weary face and quizzical smile" to Clarence Darrow and said: "It takes more than speeches to win real victories. Applause lasts but a little while. The road to justice is not a path of glory; it is stony and long and lonely, filled with pain and martyrdom. I have been thinking over Bryan's speech. What did he say, anyhow?"

Eugene Debs, who had been on the Pacific Coast during the Democratic convention, was enjoying a brief rest in Terre Haute when the Populists met in St. Louis two weeks later. The People's Party was faced by a clear choice: it could name its own candidates and conduct an emphatic campaign against the trusts, or it could endorse Bryan and concentrate on the silver issue. Henry Demarest Lloyd had determined on the first, and he had chosen Debs as the Presidential nominee. Two years earlier, Lloyd had written to a friend: "My own preference for a ticket would be Coxey and Debs. Those are the two men who have done something, and have made the record that proves them indomitable and incorruptible." Victor Berger, the Milwaukee socialist who had visited Debs at Woodstock, also helped to line up convention votes for the ARU leader. And among the delegates at St. Louis, according to Henry Lloyd, were several "blacklisted members of the American Railway

Union," who had come "in the hope that they might have the opportunity to make their leader, Eugene V. Debs, a candidate for President." On the first day of the convention, an informal poll showed that a majority of the delegations of twenty-two states favored Debs, including the entire delegations from Ohio, Indiana, Illinois, Texas, Georgia, and Missouri. Lloyd, recognizing that his choice had a wide lead, wired to Debs in Terre Haute. He received an immediate reply: "Shall try my best to be with you tomorrow."

In 1894, and again in 1896, Debs had been mentioned as a possible Populist nominee for governor of Indiana. Feeling that acceptance would expose him to the charge that his labor activities had been directed toward election to office, Debs had refused. As early as April 26, 1896, Debs had been asked if he would accept the Populist designation for President. His reply had been unequivocal: "Well, I don't want the nomination. I have absolutely no political ambition whatever and most assuredly I should not accept the nomination even if it were tendered to me." But Eugene Debs, as he was to demonstrate repeatedly in the future, was usually subject to a draft. With complete sincerity, he considered himself the servant of the workers. If they wanted him to run, he usually ran. But in 1896 there was another consideration. Debs' mind was unsettled; his thinking was changing rapidly on basic questions of philosophy and strategy. He hesitated to identify himself completely with a capitalist reform party like the Populists.

On the second day of the convention, word came to Debs that he was still leading the field, and could probably have the nomination if he wanted it. The Ohio delegates at the convention were chanting:

> One, two, three,
> Who are we?
> We're for Debs, Eugene V!

Perhaps if Debs had been at the convention, this fervor would have swept him into the race. But in Terre Haute, he was guided by scruples rather than emotion. He thought it through, he talked it over with Kate, and then he decided: "Please do not permit use of my name for nomination. E. V. Debs." When Henry Demarest Lloyd read this telegram to the convention, the radical element collapsed. Left without a candidate, they simply floundered in the dark. Lloyd later wrote that his faction might still have won a majority if they had vigorously projected a program "demanding, for instance, the public ownership of all monopolies." But they did not. The convention made its own nomination for Vice-President, but it endorsed Bryan for President and accepted silver coinage as the dominant issue in the campaign. In one swift stroke, the People's Party cut its own throat.

Debs now began to base his lectures on the Presidential election. Although he had refused the nomination, he worked wholeheartedly to insure success for the People's Party. An article in the *Railway Times* after the St. Louis convention hopefully declared: "let it be understood that the Populist party has not surrendered its autonomy, and that its organization must not only be maintained but strengthened at every point." Debs and L. W. Rogers vigorously condemned the AFL admonition to keep politics out of the trade unions, but, as the campaign progressed, they made a vital concession on the silver issue. In September, the *Railway Times* claimed that the railroads were trying to center the battle on the currency question in order to divert attention from the real focus, government by injunction. Soon after that, however, Debs declared that the demand for free silver "afforded common ground upon which the common people could unite against the trusts."

For the remainder of the campaign, Debs wavered between these two positions. On October 2 he deserted his lecture tours and began to devote all his time to the election. George Schilling urged him to appear in Illinois, where Altgeld was having a bitter fight for re-election and Clarence Darrow was running for Congress. So Debs gave twenty speeches in Chicago, drawing thousands of people to every audience. While golden-voiced Bryan was haranguing huge crowds of farmers on the silver question, Debs was talking industrial unionism to equally large crowds of workers. Illinois became the center of the battle as the greatest Republican orators appeared to blast Altgeld— Carl Schurz, Chauncey Depew, Theodore Roosevelt, Albert J.

Beveridge, and Debs' intimate friend Robert G. Ingersoll. Theodore Roosevelt, who had yearned to lead his Dakota cowhands into battle against the Chicago rioters in 1886, offered an equally neat solution ten years later: "The sentiment now animating a large proportion of our people can only be suppressed . . . by taking ten or a dozen of their leaders out, standing . . . them against a wall and shooting them dead. I believe it will come to that."

If the election had been held in September, Bryan might have won; but sentiment shifted to the Republicans in the final weeks of the campaign. Bumper crops in the West deflated much of the agrarian discontent. The failure of the wheat crop in India opened a new market for American grain. The Republicans, having capitalized on the fear of revolution to bleed a huge slush fund out of the industrialists, now poured an endless supply of money into the battle. Representatives of the banks toured the rural districts, threatening to foreclose all mortgages if Bryan were elected. Several railroads forced their employees to join Sound Money Clubs. Factories posted large signs which told the workers that the plant would close if the Democrats won. Trying to fight back against this mighty tide, Debs again began to preach free silver as "the only solution to the problems now staring us in the face, as to how to open the mills and factories to the workingmen."

The effort was hopeless. Corruption, threats, and good luck brought a Republican landslide, making William McKinley the new President and Mark Hanna the new ruler. Bryan did not win a single state from Maine to Minnesota. He lost California and North Dakota; even Kentucky went to the Republicans. John Peter Altgeld, the foremost symbol for opposition to the trusts, lost the governorship of Illinois. Clarence Darrow lost his race for Congress in an overwhelmingly Democratic district. The election was a complete, utter defeat.

[2]

IF BRYAN had been elected President in 1896, Eugene Debs might never have become a socialist. Always moving under the impact of events, Debs never deserted a possible solution until he became convinced that it had failed. His childhood acquaintance with Voltaire, Victor Hugo, Thomas Paine, and Daniel Debs had taught him devotion to the cause of the common people. Every step he had taken was in obedience to this cause, but his education was dilatory and painful. In the labor movement he saw the workers' desire for higher wages conflict sharply with the employers' desire for higher profits. In the Indiana legislature he learned that economic and political power inevitably merge, that those who control the nation's industries will control the nation's government.

Finally concluding that the railroad workers needed a single organization, Debs helped to form the American Railway Union, only to see it destroyed by corporate power and government intervention. This was a crucial defeat for Debs. Cleveland's action seemed to prove that the government was not an impartial referee, towering austerely above the conflict, but was rather an active participant in the battle between the workers and the employers. As Debs himself wrote about the Pullman boycott: "I was to be baptized in Socialism in the roar of conflict . . . in the gleam of every bayonet and the flash of every rifle the class struggle was revealed . . . This was my first practical struggle in Socialism . . ."

Before July, 1894, Eugene Debs gave little attention to the Marxist philosophy. His creed reached as far as industrial unionism and no farther. But while in Woodstock Jail, he intensified his study of social problems and discussed socialism with Tommy Morgan, Keir Hardie, and Victor Berger. Debs still hesitated to declare war on the capitalist system; like most men, he would not adopt the revolutionary solution so long as reform seemed possible. In 1896 he campaigned for the Democratic-Populist fusion and Bryan. The steam-roller tactics of Mark Hanna showed Debs that he had underestimated the power of the corporations. Big Business not only had a firm grip on the government; it also had a firm grip on the American mind. The reform movement had run into a stone wall, which could not be scaled or breached, and could only be destroyed by means of a persistent, long-run battle to convert the common people to socialism. Resolving to take up this task, Debs pub-

lished his personal manifesto in the *Railway Times* on January 1,
1897:

The issue is Socialism versus Capitalism. I am for Socialism
because I am for humanity. We have been cursed with the reign
of gold long enough. Money constitutes no proper basis of
civilization. The time has come to regenerate society—we are
on the eve of a universal change.

Debs had moved slowly and backtracked often before deciding on this step. In September, 1895, he had signed a statement
favoring "collective ownership of the means of production and
distribution"; six months later he refused to allow Thomas J.
Morgan to publish the statement. During the summer of 1896
he signed the call for the convention which founded the Brotherhood of the Co-operative Commonwealth; he did not attend
the convention and he refused to be one of the officers. This organization intended to found a co-operative colony in some
Western state, not a very radical program. But Debs was hesitant. On December 12, 1896, he wrote an equivocal letter to
Henry Demarest Lloyd: "I desire to see you soon after the
New Year to advise with you in regard to the situation and the
outlook and plans for the future. I have a matter of importance
upon which I would like to have your views." Contrary to his
intentions, Debs was forced to publish the "matter of importance" without seeing Lloyd, because another responsibility
intervened.

A few days before Christmas there appeared in Terre Haute
the president of the Western Federation of Miners. Ed Boyce,
who had been through the 1892 Coeur d'Alene strike, was tall,
slender, bald, with good features and protruding teeth. He,
like Debs, had been a pioneer in the campaign for industrial
unions. His union was now in the seventh week of a strike at
Leadville and Cripple Creek, Colorado. Strikebreakers had
been sworn into the state militia and furnished with arms. Faced
with this situation, Boyce had attended the AFL convention
in Cincinnati to appeal for moral and financial help. The AFL
had endorsed the strike, but it had no money. So Boyce stopped
in Terre Haute to ask Debs for assistance. While Debs might

be reluctant to announce his belief in socialism, he had never failed to support an honest strike. He consented at once to go to Colorado, but he wanted to spend Christmas with his parents. Daniel, who had retired from his business in 1894, was seventy-six years old and nearly blind; Daisy was sixty-eight. Eugene Debs insisted that he must be in Terre Haute for the holidays, and it was agreed that he would get to Leadville as soon as possible.

When Debs arrived in the Colorado mining town, he was met at the station by a gang of thugs, who warned him not to give any speeches in the area. Debs answered calmly: "This will either be the beginning of organized labor in Colorado or the end of me." His meeting that night was one of the most successful he had ever held.

All of Colorado was in a state of hysteria. The Coronado mine in Leadville had just been attacked by the union miners, and many men had been killed and wounded on each side. The prevalent opinion held that all union organizers were murderers and anarchists, and this opinion covered Debs. One day as he stood in the street near his hotel, a companion pointed out a huge man standing a few feet away. This giant, according to the unionist, had been following Debs for days. Debs at once walked over to the suspected strikebreaker and asked why he was being followed. The big man gruffly replied that he was from Vincennes, Indiana, and knew that Debs was "on the level with the workmen"; so he had decided that anybody who touched his idol "would be carted out of this here region a corpse." Heartened by such support, Debs stayed in the strike zone more than two months. He gave dozens of speeches to encourage the miners. He tried to persuade the owners to agree to arbitration. But his work was futile. The strikers finally returned to work on the owners' terms.

Although Debs again refused the post of organizer for the Brotherhood of the Co-operative Commonwealth because of his duties to the ARU, he constantly defended the colonization plan. Daniel DeLeon's newspaper, *The People*, ridiculed colonization as "a mirage of false hopes" and "a thorny desert of utopianism." Victor Berger had already mentioned the possibility of "somewhat 'hazy' reformers pledging themselves to some sort of 'fad.' " Henry Demarest Lloyd, feeling that colonization could not succeed, had refused to become chairman of the organization. But these criticisms did not sway Debs, who emphasized that colonization was "the most popular feature of the plan, especially with the unemployed." Debs proposed to organize a mass migration to some Western state, where co-operative colonies would be formed. The radical immigrants would then nominate candidates for all state offices and capture the state government, thus providing a solid base from which the movement could spread in all directions. The plan was indeed, as Marx and Engels had said fifty years earlier, an attempt to establish "a pocket edition of the New Jerusalem."

The remaining skeleton of the American Railway Union met in Chicago on June 15, 1897. Just three years earlier, there had been more than four hundred enthusiastic delegates at the ARU convention. Now there were barely two dozen, most of them national officers. Realizing that the ARU had no immediate future as an industrial union, the convention voted to dissolve the old order and to found the Social Democracy of America. Debs, in his keynote speech, expressed the dominant view: "There is no hope for the toiling masses of my countrymen except by the pathways mapped out by the Socialists, the advocates of the co-operative commonwealth." The new party's emphasis was on the colonization plan, but it also adopted a political platform: public ownership of all monopolies and utilities, a shorter work day, public works for the unemployed. Every member of the party's executive board had been in Woodstock Jail; Debs was named chairman, James Hogan vice-chairman, Keliher secretary-treasurer, William Burns and R. M. Goodwin as organizers. The initiation fee was set at twenty-five cents and monthly dues at fifteen cents, including a subscription to the *Social Democrat*, as the *Railway Times* was now called.

The actions of the ARU convention brought forth a new storm of criticism by both radicals and conservatives. *The People* caustically spoke against the colonization scheme, while the

Detroit Free Press commented: "the most obvious intent of the new movement is the glorification of Debs." Isaac Hourwich, a Socialist attorney in New York, ironically said: "People cannot be kept enthusiastic in 44 states over the prospect of establishing a model commonwealth in the 45th on easy monthly payments." Henry Demarest Lloyd, in his reply to Hourwich, emphasized another weakness: "When I saw that all the offices, and power—and revenue—of the new body had been gobbled up by the 'old guard' of the A.R.U. I rejoiced that I was not involved in an organization which at the very inception wrecked itself by 'pure and simple' selfishness. Debs tried to prevent it— the merest instinct of self-preservation dictated that he should do so—but his hungry followers—poor fellows, they have suffered greatly—could not be restrained." Debs tried to defend the Social Democracy by describing colonization as "an incidental plan to relieve the present distress all about us as much as possible." In his first few speeches in Milwaukee and Chicago, he emphasized this viewpoint. Then his organizing tour was suddenly interrupted.

A bituminous coal strike had begun July 4 in West Virginia, and injunctions had been issued to prohibit the miners from holding public meetings on the highways. President M. D. Ratchford of the United Mine Workers summoned Debs to the strike zone, and Debs willingly went. The miners' leaders, Debs, J. R. Sovereign, and Samuel Gompers met in Wheeling on July 27 to consider the injunctions. They decided to ignore the court orders and continue the strike. For the next month Debs and the others toured the entire area, trying everywhere to rally the miners. Although the injunctions were never invoked, another circumstance removed Debs from the conflict. He suffered a severe sunstroke from speaking bareheaded on a hot day, and was forced to return to Terre Haute. The sunstroke caused persistent headaches, but when a group of labor leaders met in St. Louis two weeks later to consider the coal strike, Debs was among them. Once again he overtaxed his strength and went back to his sick bed. Finally word came to Terre Haute that the strike had been won. The coal companies signed a contract to cover the entire central competitive field, and an arbitration board awarded the miners a pay increase. Debs rejoiced in the victory, since it was the first major contract ever signed by the coal operators.

As soon as he had recovered slightly, Eugene Debs returned to the lecture platform and his organizing trips. He spoke for branches of the Young Men's Christian Association, for Chautauqua societies, for local trade unions and state federations of labor. Although he occasionally had trouble with the local authorities, usually he was warmly greeted. When he arrived in Topeka, Kansas, early in 1898, he was received at the Statehouse by the Governor and the Supreme Court judges. All of these officials sat on the speakers' platform to hear Debs praise socialism. A reporter present at the meeting wrote: "In all that vast audience, there was not a man who, when Debs had ceased speaking, would not of helped hang to 'a sour apple tree' any federal judge who had proposed to harm the leader of the A.R.U. strike." And a year later, Debs discussed the prison problem before the exclusive Nineteenth Century Club of New York City. Here, for the first time, Debs presented his theories about the cause of depressions. Business panics, he said, were due to the low wages of labor, which did not enable the workers to buy back the goods which they produced. During the resultant unemployment, men were driven to crime in order to support their families: "Industry has not been impoverished by prison labor, but prison labor is the result of impoverished industry." How, asked Debs, could any person support a society which forced men to steal?

When the Social Democracy was first founded, such leaders as James Hogan, Roy Goodwin, and William Burns had bitterly disapproved any mention of political action. They had wanted to concentrate on the colonization plan, and only Debs' personal influence had saved the political demands in the platform. By the second convention of the Social Democracy in June, 1898, a deep split existed around this question. Any attempt to continue the colonization plan was opposed by Victor Berger, Isaac Hourwich, G. A. Hoehn, and other ex-members of the Socialist Labor Party who had joined the Social Democracy. Debs, who had seen a year's campaign raise only twenty-five hundred dollars, was forced to agree that colonization was not feasible. A vindictive fight took place in the convention, with Debs playing a very inactive part. He had no interest in the sort of technical warfare, however principled, that marked the argument. Sylvester Keliher had refused to issue charters to eight new chapters in Chicago, on the grounds that the colonizers were trying to pack the convention. The national executive board ordered Keliher to issue the charters, and delegates from these new lodges were duly seated. After that the issue was settled, but the fight continued. James Hogan accused Keliher of misappropriating the funds of the colonization commission and using them to meet the general expenses of the organization. Charges and countercharges were exchanged for hours, with an occasional speech about the virtues or defects of colonization.

Debs watched in despair while his brother officers from the ARU endlessly reviled each other. He even went to lunch with Emma Goldman, the unofficial leader of the colonizers. This young, heavy, rather ugly philosophical anarchist, who had never joined the organization but now appeared as a key figure in its convention, found Debs "genial and charming as a human being." Debs expressed views which Emma Goldman found very much like her own. Finally she exclaimed, "Why, Mr. Debs, you're an anarchist!" Debs then clasped her hand and said, "Not Mister, but Comrade; won't you call me that?"

"I stressed the fact that political action is the death-knell of the economic struggle," Emma Goldman wrote. "Debs did not dispute me, agreeing that the revolutionary spirit must be kept alive notwithstanding any political objects, but he thought the latter a necessary and practical means of reaching the masses."

When the issue of colonization versus political action came to a vote, Eugene Debs was not present. He had been again stricken by a maddening headache, and was forced to remain in bed in his hotel room. The vote resulted in a clear victory for the utopians, 52 to 37, so Berger and Keliher at once led the political action group from the convention. The bolting delegates held their own meeting in a neighboring hall, and decided to found the Social Democratic Party. The new Party,

basing itself firmly on political methods, declared that it was "a
class-conscious, revolutionary, social organization." A leader of
the colonizers promptly replied: "Standing for all men, we condemn the class-conscious propaganda as a delusion and a snare,
as being not only ineffective but totally untrue."

With no hesitation, Debs announced his support of the Social
Democratic Party, thus reaffirming his belief in the existence of
a class struggle in America. The battle between workers and
employers had turned Debs against that society which caused
so much misery and pain for his fellows. He did not intend to
retreat now. When he was elected, together with Victor Berger,
Frederic Heath, Seymour Stedman, and Jesse Cox, to the Social
Democrats' executive board, Debs resigned all claim to the
fifteen hundred dollars owed him by the colonizers. But he had
no regrets. In an open letter to his colleagues, Debs declared:

The separation at the late convention was inevitable. It had to
come. The contemplation of division was painful, as those can
fully realize who were party to it. But painful as it was, the
operation had to be performed. And it was a success, for the
Social Democratic Party of America lives. All its members are
full fledged Socialists. They are in accord with the program of
International Socialism. There is not one in the number opposed
to independent political action; not one that asks or expects
anything from any old capitalistic party, by whatever name it
may be called.

On October 1, 1898, the Social Democrats opened their first
national office in the Old Opera House on Washington Street in
Chicago. Theodore Debs, the Party's treasurer, moved to
Chicago with his wife Gertrude, a Denver girl whom he had
married in 1894. There were fewer than fifteen Social Democrats
in the city, and at one time the Party's treasury held only two
dollars. Theodore was often forced to appeal to Seymour Stedman or Jesse Cox, both local lawyers and members of the executive committee, for ten dollars to pay the monthly rent on the
one-room office. If Stedman and Cox were unable to furnish the
money, Theodore pawned his watch, a transaction that he
customarily performed at a certain pawnship. Whenever the
proprietor saw Theodore's face in the doorway, he automatically

said to his cashier, "Give the Socialist gentleman forty dollars."
Gertrude Debs later remarked: "If Theodore had thrown that
watch out of the window on Sixty-sixth street, it would have
found its way straight to the hockshop in the Loop."

Meanwhile, Eugene Debs was again touring the country,
talking about socialism and selling subscriptions to the *Social
Democratic Herald*, which reached six thousand people weekly
in the autumn of 1898. In addition to the *Herald*, Victor Berger's Milwaukee *Vorwaerts*, the Jewish *Daily Forward* in New
York City, and Julius Wayland's *Appeal to Reason*, all supported
the Social Democrats. The most colorful and successful of these
organs was the *Appeal*. Julius Wayland, a native of rural
Indiana, had accumulated a modest fortune in job printing and
real estate speculation at Pueblo, Colorado. Just before the
panic of 1893, he sold his printing business, turned his real estate into cash, and returned to Greensburg, Indiana, where he
established a weekly newspaper, the *Coming Nation*. Wayland
had already lost his old Republican views and become interested
in the socialism of Edward Bellamy, William Morris, and John
Ruskin. So he established a socialist colony at Ruskin, Tennessee, and moved his newspaper there, but soon he became disgusted with the wrangling and fled to Kansas City, Missouri.

On August 30, 1895, Wayland published the first number of
the *Appeal to Reason*. This socialist paper suffered heavily during the Bryan craze of 1896, and it was temporarily suspended;
but Wayland made a fresh start in the small town of Girard in
southeastern Kansas. This time he succeeded. Except for brief
periods during the Spanish-American War and after McKinley's
assassination in 1901, the circulation of the *Appeal* rose steadily.
By 1899 it could boast a hundred thousand readers, and the
paper moved into a new building in Girard, a long, narrow, one-
story brick structure which resembled a prison.

Wayland, eminently a product of the moralistic, prohibitionist Bible Belt of the Midwest, spoke to his friends and neighbors
in words they both understood and believed. Wherever Eugene
Debs went, he found the farmers and workingmen delighted by
the epigrams and rambling anecdotes of the four-page weekly.
From Xenia, Ohio, June 6, 1899, he wrote a letter to Wayland

about the *Appeal:* "Its friendly face appears everywhere. It is literally honey-combing capitalism. Wherever the *Appeal* is at work, and that seems everywhere, socialism has at least a nucleus and the light is spreading. . . . More power to the *Appeal.*"

[*3*]

THE CLOSING YEARS of the century witnessed the development of a greater maturity and consistency in Debs' views. Throughout his life he believed his statement of 1897: "I make no attack upon the rich man. I do not deal with individuals. I realize that to a very large extent he is the product of his surroundings." But Debs never repeated his naïve error of June 19, 1897, when he asked John D. Rockefeller to help finance the colonization plan. "The purpose of the organization, briefly speaking," Debs wrote to Rockefeller, "is to establish in place of the present cruel, immoral and decadent system, a co-operative commonwealth, where millionaires and beggars . . . will completely disappear, and human brotherhood will be inaugurated to bless and make the world more beautiful. . . . In this movement there are no class distinctions: Rich and poor are equally welcome to help dethrone Gold and elevate humanity. Then the strong will help the weak, the weak will love the strong, and the Human Brotherhood will transform the days to come into a virtual Paradise. . . . Believing that you will find yourself in accord with your own feelings of social and patriotic obligations by your generous contributions to a worthy cause for freedom, I remain sincerely yours, Eugene V. Debs." If Debs had intended this letter as dramatic irony, it might have been called a stroke of genius, but he was completely sincere.

Rockefeller did not bother to reply, and Debs' illusions soon disappeared. He came to realize that, while wealthy individuals might support his cause, the responsibility for liberating the common people must rest with the common people. Only the workingmen had the power and determination to establish socialism. This conversion to the theory of class struggle soon led Debs to oppose all alliances with the capitalist parties. In

February, 1899, when the Union Reform party was being organized, Debs was invited to participate in its convention. He
emphatically declined: "being a Socialist . . . and being profoundly impressed with the conviction that only through Socialism is there relief from the ills of capitalism, I am not in favor
of such a party as is proposed, which, in the nature of things,
must be founded in compromise and cannot long survive the
internal dissensions which swept its predecessors from the field
and are bound to overwhelm and destroy the new party. It is
either Socialism or capitalism—complete freedom or total
slavery. I am a Socialist without a shadow of concession or
compromise."

Not even Debs' personal feelings could influence his political
course. Although Daniel DeLeon had repeatedly charged that
Debs was receiving free passes from the railroads, Debs advised
his followers in New York City to support the Socialist Labor
Party in the 1897 election, since the SLP was "the only anti-
capitalistic party in the field."

Debs' adherence to socialism was stabilized by the belief that
he was following in the path of the early American radicals. He
justified his own views by pointing to Thomas Paine, Patrick
Henry, John Brown, and the Haymarket martyrs. His scrapbook soon contained leaves which he had gathered at the grave
of Thomas Paine in New Rochelle, New York, and at the home
of John Greenleaf Whittier in Amesbury, Massachusetts. At
the founding convention of the Social Democratic Party, he
helped to draft a resolution in which the convention paid "tribute to the memory of Edward Bellamy, first to popularize the
ideas of Socialism among his countrymen and last to be forgotten by them." With these radical predecessors Debs shared
a common creed, a belief that human history means change,
that man must go forward or he will surely go backward. And
by 1900, Eugene Debs had arrived at the outlines of the program to which he devoted the next twenty-five years: industrial
unionism, a revolutionary socialist party, and stern opposition
to the capitalist system.

The outbreak of the Spanish-American War offered a clear
test of Debs' political views. By 1890, the American frontier

had practically disappeared as a field for investment and settlement. The large corporations sought raw materials and new markets in the Caribbean and the Pacific. When this program of expansion indirectly resulted in war with Spain, Debs publicly proclaimed:

There are thousands who are not swept from their feet by the war craze. They realize that war is national murder, that the poor furnish the victims and that whatever the outcome may be, the effect is always the same upon the toiling class.

In 1894 the press denounced us for the alleged reason that we were murderous and bloodthirsty, and now the same press opposes us because we are not.

We are opposed to war, but if it ever becomes necessary for us to enlist in the murderous business, it will be to wipe out capitalism, the common enemy of the oppressed and downtrodden of all nations.

And when the American Army began its campaign to conquer the Philippines, Debs told an audience of trade unionists in Indianapolis: "We are making a market over there in the Orient for the products of half-paid labor in this country; making the market by the force of arms and at the expense of the lives of a people whose only offense has been their love of freedom and self-control."

Those were Debs' views in 1898. When he said exactly the same thing twenty years later, he was sent to prison.

CHAPTER 11

□

[1]

EUGENE DEBS, when he deserted pure and simple trade unionism for a place in the socialist movement, found himself alienated from many of his former associates. For a dozen years he and Samuel Gompers had worked toward the same goal; this co-operation was now permanently disrupted. The leaders of the railroad Brotherhoods, in the years to come, did not try to conceal their hostility for the socialist champion. Even Debs' erstwhile colleagues in the American Railway Union broke with their old chief; George Howard moved steadily into the Gompers' camp; Hogan, Goodwin, and Burns remained with the short-lived colonization plan. Sylvester Keliher and L. W. Rogers joined the Social Democratic Party, with Rogers resigning his post as head of the Michigan Federation of Labor to manage Debs' lecture tours, but both of them soon dropped out of sight.

Even among Debs' relatives, his apostasy had considerable effect. His oldest sister Marie and her husband John Heinl, one of the prospering businessmen of Terre Haute, had never sympathized with Debs' activities in the labor movement. Another sister, Emma Debs Maillaux, was married to an electrical engineer of increasing wealth and conservative views. Several members of Kate Debs' family were already well on the road to becoming millionaires. These people, who were comfortable under capitalism, had no desire to see it changed. The Heinls, the Maillauxs, and Kate's family had for Eugene Debs an affectionate but questioning attitude. They felt that his sentimental nature was causing him to sacrifice a promising career in business or politics. He had an undoubted ability to make money and they wondered why he refused to do so.

This viewpoint was shared to some extent by Kate Debs. She was not certain that her husband should devote his life to the

radical movement, where the sacrifices were so real and the re-
wards so nebulous. New York socialists spread a rumor that
Kate had fainted when Eugene Debs first announced his conversion to socialism, but this rumor did not gain much currency
in Terre Haute. Kate Debs was not the fainting type. Even
those acquaintances who disliked her, who claimed that she
was frigid, prim, ambitious, and stingy, all credited her with
courage and devotion.

In 1922 Eugene Debs wrote a brief article on the topic: "How
My Wife Has Helped Me": "She shared what came in stormy
days without complaint, and when I returned after many weeks
of weary travel she had the home sweet and cozy and minis-
tered to me in all tenderness until I was rested and refreshed
for another journey. . . . For years she was our secretary of
state. She wrote all my letters in long hand before the days of
the type-writer, and I had a large correspondence. She trudged
through the snow to a cold office when I was out on the road,
lighted the fire, emptied the ashes, cleaned the office, answered
the mail, shipped bundles of literature to me and to others, and
then returned to cook her meals, set the house in order, and
attend to the wants of the home."

Exaggeration of the change in Debs' personal affairs after he
became a socialist would be easy. His parents and his brother
Theodore all clung with unyielding fidelity to the new banner he
raised. Arthur Baur, Kate's half-brother, served for years as un-
official banker to Eugene Debs, who had extended his boycott of
Pullman cars to include all banks. His habit was to stroll into
Arthur Baur's drugstore on Wabash street, drop a huge sheaf
of bills on the counter and ask: "Say, Art, will you keep this for
me?" Perhaps on his next visit to Terre Haute, Debs would ask
Baur to give him a thousand dollars. If Debs' account did not
hold that much money, the druggist merely drew it from his
own and handed it over. This arrangement continued for more
than two decades. Debs seldom knew how much money he had;
sometimes he was thousands of dollars in debt to Arthur Baur,
but Baur never mentioned that fact. To Debs the plan had
several virtues. It was no longer necessary for him to sully himself by entering a bank. He could always get any amount of

cash he wanted, and Kate never knew how much he had. Kate was not stingy, but she sometimes objected to the openhanded generosity of her husband. On one occasion—but unknown to Kate—Debs got three hundred dollars from Arthur Baur, gave it all away within a half hour, and then went back to the druggist for more.

Debs continued on intimate terms with several men who were nonpolitical, or even anti-socialist. Robert Ingersoll had been a leading Republican for more than twenty years, and had campaigned against Bryan and Atlgeld in 1896. But when Ingersoll died in 1899, the Socialist leader filled fifty-five pages of his scrapbook with clippings about his old friend. He always remembered the morning that he had been in Ingersoll's office in New York. The office was filled with people who had come to ask for loans or favors of some kind. Ingersoll, with tears in his eyes, had said to Debs: "I can hardly come to my office any more; I can't help them all and I haven't the heart to turn them away." Debs still had great affection for James Whitcomb Riley, and his friends in Terre Haute included several wealthy merchants—Ben Cox, Carl Stahl, Anton Hulman, Riley and Frank McKeen—but far more important was his meeting with another socialist, Stephen Reynolds.

Stephen Marion Reynolds and his gorgeous wife Jessica were considered rather peculiar by Terre Haute's respectable citizens. Jessica was descended from the McKinney family, which had been prominent in the early days of the Standard Oil Corporation, and Reynolds had come to Terre Haute in 1890 to promote several oil wells. When the wells failed to prosper, he returned to his original profession, the law. Although Jessie and Steve were recognized as eccentric intellectuals, their wealth gave them, at first, considerable standing in local society. They bought a large house at 1115 South Sixth Street, in one of the exclusive blocks in town, remodeled it and painted the exterior a bright red. Reynolds, however, did penance for this barbarism by vigorously campaigning for sound money and William McKinley in 1896.

Beginning with the Pullman boycott, there was a subtle change in Reynolds' views. He heard dozens of stories about

Eugene Debs, although they had never met, and his deep scholarship inevitably carried him into the socialist literature. Reynolds had long been in revolt against the society he knew, not because of its poverty and suffering, but because of its narrowness, its ignorance, its concentration on profit-making. In socialism he found an explanation and a solution for the things he hated. Jessie and Steve Reynolds fought their way through one radical book after another, reading them aloud, discussing them fully. Jessie progressed by means of intuition, Steve by means of logic, but they arrived at the same destination. In 1900 they joined the Social Democratic Party.

In many ways, Steve Reynolds was the exact antithesis of Eugene Debs. Debs, while he was determined to overthrow the basis of capitalism, accepted without question many of its incidental features. He always tended to underestimate theory, and concentrated his attention completely on practical activity. He lived in a conventional house, married a conventional local girl, and was known as one of the most sober and immaculate dressers in town. With Steve Reynolds it was different. Reynolds' defiance was leveled at the manifestations of capitalism. A tall, lean man with an ugly face, a leonine nose, and a deep scar near his eyes, he wore rumpled clothes, used profanity freely, and thumbed his nose at all critics. When he began to wear open-throated shirts and sandals while riding his bicycle around Terre Haute, the local legal profession was agog at the affront to its dignity. Jessie too, with her bright red hair tied in a small knot behind her neck, wore sandals and low-necked Grecian gowns while other women were wearing high, tight collars, many petticoats, and rigid corsets. Exceedingly dynamic, she was always talking, often in a loud voice, usually about important topics.

Largely cut off now from their former associates, the heretics found welcome companionship in Eugene Debs. And Debs joyfully returned their affection. He found constant delight in their three children, Jean, Ford, and Marian, who helped to fill a void in his life. He found at the Red House a broad grasp of culture which he had never acquired. He never did acquire it, because he always accepted work that seemed more important, but he liked to brush against the versatile mind of Steve Reynolds.

Perhaps most important, he found two people who shared his
faith in socialism, with whom he could talk freely, fully, and
passionately. Most aspects of Debs' personality found their
outlet on the lecture platform. The others were shared with his
wife Kate, his brother Theodore, and with Jessica and Stephen
Reynolds.

[2]

THE SOCIAL DEMOCRATIC PARTY scored several local successes
early in life. Although it received only twelve thousand votes in
the election of 1898, these votes were concentrated in Massachusetts, so that two socialists were sent to the state legislature
and a third was elected mayor of Haverhill. Independent socialist organizations in Iowa and Texas merged with the Social
Democrats. When the new party opened its first national convention in Indianapolis, March 6, 1900, it had 4536 members,
with 226 branches in twenty-five states. Debs played an important rôle in this expansion. In 1898, he had given dozens of
speeches to striking textile workers around Fall River, Massachusetts, and just before the election he spoke to twenty-seven
hundred people in Haverhill. The following May, while on a
lecture tour of the South, he had negotiated the merger with the
Socialist Party of Texas.

The Social Democrats also benefited from the dogmatism of
Daniel DeLeon; a large faction of the Socialist Labor Party, revolting against DeLeon's standards of purity, set up independent headquarters in Rochester, New York. The leaders of these
"Kangaroos," Morris Hillquit, Max Hayes, and Job Harriman,
appeared at the Social Democratic convention in 1900 and proposed co-operation in the coming election. The Social Democratic chiefs did not regard this offer as an unmixed blessing;
anybody so recently associated with Daniel DeLeon was considered tainted. The Rochester spokesmen explained that they
had nominated Harriman, a California lawyer, and Hayes, a
Cleveland printer and editor, as their Presidential slate, but
they offered to withdraw Harriman if they could name the Vice-
Presidential candidate on a joint ticket. They then quietly began

lining up votes to win the convention's endorsement for both
Harriman and Hayes, and had won over a majority of the delegates before the convention chiefs got wind of the move. The
session was hastily recessed and the Social Democratic leaders
converged on Debs' room in the Occidental Hotel. They told
Debs bluntly that he had to accept the Presidential nomination.
He refused. The previous autumn he had publicly announced
that he was not a candidate for public office; how would it look
if he changed his mind? For several hours Debs clung to his
position. He argued and pleaded, sat on the bed and then
bounced up to pace around the small room. Finally his colleagues told him that he alone could save the Party from the
DeLeonite scalawags, and Debs reluctantly agreed to run. The
following day he received the nomination.

Debs' hesitation was based on sound prophecy. Any labor
leader who runs for political office is subject to the charge of
insincerity. Debs was an easy target for this charge, since his
spontaneous affection and French traditions led him publicly to
kiss adults as well as babies. But the slightest acquaintance with
the socialist leader left most men completely charmed by his
affability. When he returned from the Indianapolis convention
to Terre Haute, a large crowd was waiting at the station to
celebrate his return. Many of them were friends and neighbors;
a few were socialists like Stephen Reynolds; others were skeptics
eager to see the Presidential nominee act like a pompous fool.
Debs appeared on the rear platform as the train slowed to a
halt. He took off his hat, waved it to the crowd, smiled and
shouted his thanks. Then he startled the onlookers by vaulting
the railing and dashing across the platform to embrace a Negro
porter whom he had not seen for years: "Why bless my heart,
Bob; it's good to see you!"

Three weeks after the Indianapolis convention, the Kangaroos
and the Social Democrats held a joint gathering in New York
City to complete the merger and work out a common electoral
program. The sole disputed point was a name for the new party;
the Rochester group preferred to call it the United Socialist
Party while the Social Democrats wanted to keep their former
name. It was finally agreed that the question would be sub-

mitted to a referendum of both parties. The rank and file thought that unity had been effected, but nothing of the sort had happened. In April, the national executive board of Debs' party issued a vicious denunciation of Harriman, Hayes, and Hillquit. Charging that these men had promised at Indianapolis to accept the name of the Social Democratic Party, Debs and his colleagues righteously declared: "A united Socialist Party cannot be built upon broken pledges."

This factionalism lasted throughout the summer. Debs warned that acceptance of the referendum results, which were unfavorable to his viewpoint, would result in the "swallowing up of the Social Democratic Party." Victor Berger referred to Morris Hillquit as "a thoroughly class conscious lawyer of New York" and called Job Harriman "a Tammany politican of the seventeenth degree." Hillquit answered with the charge that "the publication of the manifesto . . . was the most puerile and mischievous act any set of officers of a socialist party could make themselves guilty of."

There was considerable evidence to support Hillquit's statement. The real issue was not the name of the organization, but the distrust that Debs and his associates felt for any former friend of Daniel DeLeon. Victor Berger, now so busy attacking the Rochester leaders, had suggested a few months earlier that the Social Democrats should support the nominees of the Socialist Labor Party. Debs, when he heard about Berger's proposal, wrote an explosive letter to Fred Heath, another member of the Social Democratic executive board: "There are hundreds of perfectly straight 'Kangaroo' Socialists who will be disgusted and enraged by one of our leading papers supporting DeLeon. Nor do I agree with you that it would hurt the socialist movement to vote against such a black-hearted scoundrel as DeLeon. . . . I also disagree with you when you say you have nothing against DeLeon . . . Have we nothing against the arch-enemies of the socialist movement? Are you unconcerned about the slimy slander to your colleagues & yourself in this *official* capacity? I *have* something against DeLeon and every other enemy of my party . . ."

In the public discussion, Debs was considerably less candid;

and Victor Berger hastily forgot his former heresy. For months not a sensible word on the point at issue appeared in the press of either faction, but the fact of a common Presidential ticket worked strongly for unity. The socialists found widespread misunderstanding about their program, misunderstanding carefully promoted by the major newspapers. Debs was forced to explain that his party did not propose public ownership of white shirts or toothbrushes, but only of the capital goods of the country—the factories, the railroads, the banks. The growth of monopoly could never be checked by regulation, said the socialists; outright confiscation was the only cure for the problem.

Throughout the campaign, Debs emphasized that his party alone was loyal to the interests of the American people. He flayed both the American attack on the Filipinos and the British attack on the Boers, saying constantly that these wars would benefit only the corporate interests. He attacked the two major parties with complete impartiality; although the Republicans represented big business and the Democrats small business, they both represented the capitalist system, said Debs. Four years earlier the Populists had committed suicide by fusion with the Democrats, and now only the socialists could legitimately claim to fight for the welfare of labor and the poor farmers: "It is therefore a question, not of 'reform,' the mask of fraud, but of revolution. The capitalist system must be overthrown, class-rule abolished, and wage-slavery supplanted by co-operative industry."

The rival socialist factions, feeling that their common ticket was making huge gains, began to lessen their abuse of each other. The *Social Democratic Herald* finally repented enough to mention that Job Harriman was running for Vice-President. But this optimism was premature. The commercial newspapers, although they contradicted each other daily, united in their opposition to the Social Democrats. The *Chicago American,* a Democratic organ, gave currency to a rumor that the Republicans were furnishing large sums of money for the socialist campaign. A few days later, several Republican newspapers charged that Debs intended to withdraw in favor of William Jennings Bryan. Debs vigorously denounced this report: "It is a pure fabrication of the capitalistic press. . . . I am in the fight to the finish. All reports to the contrary are false and malicious." But his denials were not given the nation-wide publicity of the original charges. When the ballots were counted in November, Debs had polled 96,878 votes.

Soon after the election, Stephen Reynolds was summoned to his front door early one morning by a rather hesitant rapping. When Reynolds answered the door, he was greatly surprised to find Eugene Debs standing on the step. Debs was usually much too considerate to call before the family had finished breakfast, but on this occasion he seemed greatly disturbed. Accepting an invitation to join the family at the table, Debs began a halting account of a dream which had awakened him the previous night. In this dream, he was walking through a swamp when he saw a strange animal caught in the mire. The animal was struggling frantically to free itself, and Debs hurried to its aid. He tried for hours to extricate the beast, but his efforts were fruitless. Finally becoming convinced that a single man was inadequate for the job, he hurried to the nearby village and returned with another humanitarian, Stephen Reynolds. The two men toiled for the remainder of the day. Several times they had the animal on the very edge of the bog, but each time the beast made a false move and tumbled back. They even dragged brush to the bog and built a ramp to solid ground and tried to haul the animal up the ramp. But it persistently flopped back into the mire. At the day's end, the animal was exactly where it had been when Debs found it. Then Debs woke up.

This subconscious disillusionment was not shared by Debs' colleagues. The other leaders of both the Social Democrats and the Kangaroos were elated by the election results. Their joint ticket had, after all, polled ninety-six thousand votes while DeLeon's nominee received only thirty-four thousand. When another unity convention was held in Indianapolis the following July, the previous split between the Rochester faction and Debs' supporters was overshadowed by the emergence of a division into left and right wings. The left wing insisted that no important gains were possible until a socialist society had been established. These impossibilists, as they were called, would recognize only one demand—the unconditional abolition of capitalism. After a furious debate on the platform, the vote was eighty-two to thirty in favor of the inclusion of immediate demands. However, the delegates voted to drop all demands for farmers, because they did not consider farmers to be members of the working class. Having agreed upon the platform, the convention easily drew up a constitution, formed an executive committee with Leon Greenbaum as national secretary, and established national headquarters in St. Louis. The convention also agreed to call the new organization the Socialist Party, thus ending the battle on that score. But the Social Democratic faction, in order to protect itself against domination by the Kangaroos, insisted that each state organization should be autonomous in most respects.

Eugene Debs took no part in this convention. He had no stomach for intra-Party bickering, of which he had gotten his fill at the 1900 gathering. Even more important, Debs had a profound distrust of leaders and the principles of leadership. He felt that platforms should be settled, not by a handful of delegates, but by the great body of consumers in the political market place. The unity of the Party might be desirable, Debs thought, but it was not essential. When he disagreed with the policies of the organization, he made his own policies. Debs tried to convert the rank and file of the Party and depended on the rank and file to convert the leaders. In the next twenty-four years he appeared at only one Socialist national convention.

[*3*]

From the very beginning, the Socialist Party held conflicting, and even contradictory, groups. Membership was open to anybody who accepted, in the most general way, its principles, and who recognized the existence of a class struggle in the United States. These requirements were so vague that they covered a multitude of basic philosophies. Hundreds of Protestant ministers joined the Party in order to work for a truly religious society. Professional men and women joined in order to express their revolt against the narrowness and hypocrisy of American life. Small businessmen joined in order to strike a blow against their larger competitors. Politicians joined in order to gain public office. Labor leaders joined in order to win promotion in their unions.

All of these motives and theories exerted pressure on the policies of the Party. One faction offset another. Joint action by the organization was blunted or even paralyzed. And the Party was most divided on the precise question where unity was most important, a long-range strategy in the trade unions. Eugene Debs believed that, of all the groups in America, only the workingmen had both the need and the strength to lead the battle against capitalism. Since the trade unions carried on the daily guerrilla warfare of the workers, they were the logical agency to teach the connection between the short-run struggles and the ultimate socialist goal. Samuel Gompers and his colleagues, far from fulfilling this function, actually sabotaged the daily battles by their defense of craft unionism. That was Debs' theory, but it was not shared by the other leaders of the Socialist Party.

At the Social Democratic convention of March, 1900, this question held the center of attention. James F. Carey, a member of the Massachusetts legislature and a leader at the convention, offered a resolution against "coercing" trade unions to support the Party, since this would lose votes rather than win them. The resolution was attacked by Victor Berger and Fred Heath, who had succeeded in capturing the Central Labor Union of Milwaukee. For two days Eugene Debs remained in his chair, while the discussion grew louder and more venomous. Finally Debs declared that Carey's proposal was both ill-taken and unnecessary. His influence helped to table the resolution, but the narrow vote of 31 to 23 was ominous.

Debs' efforts to build a militant labor movement found strong support in the Western Federation of Miners. The battles of Coeur d'Alene, Telluride, Cripple Creek, and Leadville were fought out with a ferocity unequalled in the East. On one side were the employers, the state militia, private armies, strikebreakers, spies, court orders, damage suits, starvation. On the other side stood the miners, armed with rifles and dynamite. Between the two camps ran an unquestioned barrier. It was unnecessary to tell the western miners that the class struggle was a reality; they ridiculed any attempt to deny it. Many members of the union and its leaders, President Ed Boyce and secretary-treasurer Bill Haywood, joined the Socialist Party, and they invited Debs to address their Denver convention in 1901.

Bill Haywood recognized his great debt to Eugene Debs. Haywood, in the early spring of 1894, had been an unemployed miner and ranch hand in Nevada, who crossed the Western deserts with Kelly's army looking for work. The search was fruitless, and Haywood had rejoined his family in Winnemucca by the time of the Pullman boycott. The dramatic events of July, 1894, marked Haywood's introduction to trade unions: "Here, I felt, was a great power. It was not the fact that produce had been removed from the cars and the strikers were that much ahead. The big thing was that they could stop the trains." By 1900 Haywood was chosen secretary-treasurer of the WFM. Although he was only thirty-one years old and had spent less than five years in the mines, his lumbering frame and fighting spirit had already made him an idol of the mining towns.

Great enthusiasm greeted Debs' speech to the WFM convention; the delegates endorsed socialism and recommended that all miners join the Socialist Party. But Bill Haywood better remembered the night he and Debs got drunk at the Imperial Hotel. At a late hour Haywood and Thomas J. Hagerty, with two quarts of whiskey, knocked on the door of Debs' room. Debs, worn out from a long lecture trip, was already dressed for bed, but he willingly agreed to the interruption. The conversation was disorganized, noisy, and joyous, in a way that was shocking to the small family hotel. The three men discussed the eight-hour day campaign of the miners, in which Debs had taken an active interest for more than a decade. They discussed the series of socialist lectures that Debs and Hagerty were to give in the mining camps. But it proved difficult to stick to the point, and soon they began swapping anecdotes about their experiences in the labor movement.

Eugene Debs still found pleasure in the Negro dialect stories with which he had filled *The Magazine*, but now they always had a class-conscious twist when he told them. Some "impertinent cad," according to Debs, once tried to force Alexander Dumas to confess that his ancestors were Negroes. First he asked about Dumas' father, then about his mother, finally about his grandparents. Dumas finally replied: "My great grandparents were probably monkeys, my ancestors beginning where yours left off." And then Debs, without giving his audience a chance, told about a member of Parliament who pushed his way through a crowd with the cry: "Make way there! Don't you know that I'm a representative of the people!" But he did not overawe a coal-porter, who shouted back: "Hell, don't you know that we are the people!"

It was a remarkable group. This was one of the few occasions when Eugene Debs, who weighed a hundred eighty pounds and stood six feet two, found himself the smallest man in the room. Tom Hagerty, a former Catholic priest who had resigned to become a socialist, weighed more than two hundred pounds. Bill Haywood by any standards was a brawling giant. And each of them had a voice to match his size. They drank the whiskey and roared on while the hours passed, Hagerty pacing around the room; Haywood sprawled in a chair, his head turned slightly in an unconscious effort to conceal his blind eye; Debs sitting squarely in the middle of the bed, a glass in one hand and a pipe in his mouth, his legs crossed under him, bony ankles projecting from his pajamas.

Debs and Haywood, at the time of their meeting in Denver in May, 1901, were already aware that the National Civic Federation represented a grave threat to their plans. In 1893, a group of business and professional leaders in Chicago had organized a Civic Federation for the purpose of holding conferences about public issues, including the labor problem. This federation investigated the Pullman strike and issued a report generally favorable to the strikers. For the next half dozen years it limited its activities to occasional conferences and publicity for industrial peace, but in June, 1900, it changed its name to the National Civic Federation and prepared to play a more energetic rôle. The first major innovation was the establishment of an arbitration department, on which Samuel Gompers, President John Mitchell of the United Mine Workers, and President Dan J. Keefe of the longshoremen's union, all agreed to serve. In the summer of 1900, a serious strike threatened the anthracite coal fields. Senator Marcus Hanna of Ohio, Cleveland industrialist, President-maker to William McKinley, chairman of the Republican National Committee, feared that the strike would harm the chances of his party in the November elections. Therefore he persuaded the coal operators to sign a one-year contract which allowed a 10 per cent wage increase. The following year Hanna negotiated a one-year extension of the contract, and in December, 1901, he became chairman of the National Civic Federation.

The labor movement in 1900 had seemed to be prospering. The unions then had eight hundred sixty-eight thousand members; their enrollment had nearly doubled in four years. But this appearance of strength was deceitful, and Samuel Gompers knew it. No trade union could hope to win a strike against a major corporation, so Gompers thought it wise to continue the policy of conciliation adopted six years earlier. The AFL began, first as a matter of tactics, then as a matter of principle, to champion only the cause of skilled, white workers. Negroes had been used as strikebreakers in the Chicago stockyards, in the Western mining camps, in two towns in central Illinois; the question of accepting them into AFL locals had become critical. Since the Negroes were excluded from the unions, their only chance for factory jobs came during strikes. But Gompers urged organizing them into Jim Crow federal labor unions, and his suggestion was written into the AFL constitution. The craft unions also ignored the plight of the unskilled workers, making no effort to organize the mass-production industries. Most clothing factories, coal mines, and basic steel plants were free from the resistance of organized labor.

Thus the trade unions and the big employers came to an implicit agreement. The unions would make no effort to organize the unskilled and Negro workers; the corporations would make certain concessions to the trade unions. Many industrialists refused to concede anything at all. During the anthracite strike of 1902, President George F. Baer of the Philadelphia and Reading Coal and Iron Company piously declared: "The rights and

interests of the laboring man will be protected and cared for
. . . by the Christian men to whom God in his infinite wisdom
has given the control of the property interests of this country."
But the policy of conciliation was supported by John D. Rockefeller, August Belmont, J. Pierpont Morgan, C. M. Schwab of
United States Steel, Julius Kruttschnitt of the Southern Pacific,
Mark Hanna, and other key figures in the financial world. The
AFL, at its 1899 convention, had called upon the "trade unionists of the United States, and workingmen generally, to study
the development of trusts and monopolies with a view to na-
tionalizing the same"; this resolution was quickly forgotten in
the atmosphere created by the National Civic Federation.

The radical labor leaders were determined to counterattack,
but they pondered carefully about the time and the method.
They finally made their move at the convention, in May, 1902,
of the Western Labor Union. This rival federation to the AFL
had been founded by the Western Federation of Miners in 1898.
Gompers had tried to persuade the WFM to give up its plan
and return to the AFL. He had failed, but the AFL continued
its efforts to convert the metal miners; secretary-treasurer
Frank Morrison of the AFL came to Denver in 1902 to engineer
the dissolution of the Western Labor Union. Eugene Debs also
came, again as an invited speaker. It was so arranged that the
AFL chief spoke first. Morrison defended the policies of his
organization, and emphasized the need for unity in the labor
movement. He claimed that the miners, by their efforts to
organize dual unions, were harming the cause of labor; the existence of two unions in the same craft always resulted in chaos.

Then Debs launched a comprehensive attack on the craft
unions. When the AFL refused to organize Negroes and unskilled workers, when it refused to organize the mass-production industries, when it clung to the outmoded forms of craft
unionism, it was guilty of promoting the same disunity which
it now tried to condemn. But Debs' main attack was leveled
against the National Civic Federation. Gompers and John
Mitchell, by pretending that the workingmen had friends among
the industrialists, were undermining the very basis of the labor
movement. If the employers were willing to grant wage increases

and decent working conditions of their own free will, why were trade unions needed at all? Debs called upon the delegates to change their name to the American Labor Union, declare in favor of socialism, and begin a nation-wide campaign to organize industrial unions. Every one of these proposals was adopted by the convention in an outburst of fervent enthusiasm. Debs left Denver immediately to tour the entire Northwest in the interests of the American Labor Union and the Socialist Party.

This action by Debs and Haywood was severely rebuked by several leaders of the Party, who considered it a serious tactical error. Many socialists had already gained influential positions in the AFL. Fred Heath and Victor Berger were in firm control of the Central Labor Union of Milwaukee. Morris Hillquit had become attorney and adviser to several craft unions. J. Mahlon Barnes was a powerful figure in Gompers' own cigarmakers' union. The solid socialist base in the labor movement was demonstrated at the 1902 convention of the AFL, when the socialists introduced a resolution advising "the working people to organize their economic and political power to secure for labor the full equivalent of its toil and the overthrow of the wage system." This resolution was narrowly defeated by a vote of 7899 to 4171, and it received nearly unanimous support from the United Mine Workers, the carpenters, and the brewery workers.

Within three months after the formation of the American Labor Union, the wide split in the Party had become a public battle. The Party's constitution provided for the establishment of a Local Quorum in the city where national headquarters were located; and, between meetings of the Executive Committee, this Local Quorum could make policy and issue statements for the national organization. A semiannual report by the St. Louis Quorum in September, 1902, decried the autonomy of the state districts. Although the Socialist Party had pledged itself to the "unification of the trade unions," said the report, many comrades in the West were acting as organizers for the American Labor Union. By this action they were "misrepresenting the attitude of our party and compromising it in their attempts to build up a rival labor organization to the American Federation of Labor."

When this statement was published, Eugene Debs was furious. The report did not mention his name, but no great insight was needed to see that it applied to Haywood and himself. Debs wrote an immediate answer for publication in the *International Socialist Review*, already the organ of the Party's left wing. Debs argued that Gompers had wilfully refused to support the Leadville strike of 1896 and had constantly tried to destroy the Western Federation of Miners, while the metal miners had always supported their brothers in the East. The American Labor Union had organized four thousand members in September alone, and its existence was spurring the AFL to unprecedented organizing efforts. The Western miners had publicly declared for socialism; why should the Socialists attack them in favor of their conservative rivals? Debs answered his own question by charging that certain socialist politicians "were perhaps advised that it was wiser policy to curry favor with numbers than to stand by principles." The metal miners had "refused to be assimilated by Mark Hanna's Civic Federation," and Debs supported their refusal. He would be willing to support Samuel Gompers also "when the American Federation of Labor sheds its outworn pure and simple policy, when it declares against the capitalist system and for union, class-conscious action at the ballot box; when it relegates leaders to the rear who secure fat offices for themselves in reward for keeping the rank and file in political ignorance and industrial slavery, when it shall cease to rely upon cringing lobbying committees."

One misstatement of fact, and another serious disagreement, occur in this declaration by Debs. Little reason existed for referring to "Mark Hanna's Civic Federation." The National Civic Federation was a thriving national organization when Hanna became connected with it. The Cleveland industrialist served as president for less than eighteen months. Eugene Debs, however, in his search for evil personified, chose to present the Civic Federation as resulting from the diabolical tactics of one man. Second, Samuel Gompers vigorously denied that he had refused help to the Leadville strike of 1896. He even accused

Ed Boyce of the WFM of duplicity in attempting to wheedle financial support for the strike, when the AFL had no money for its own purposes.

But Debs was not finished. He promptly carried his battle into the Executive Committee of the Party, where he met bitter opposition. The pedantic, domineering Berger declared that Debs and Haywood were doing the Party immeasurable harm in the trade unions. Debs roared back that Berger's beloved trade unions had been seduced by Mark Hanna and were now unfit bedfellows for the socialists. The scholarly Hillquit tried to effect a compromise, but soon he too was engaged in a vindictive quarrel with Debs. Debs was vehement, accusatory, unyielding, and, in the end, he had his way. In January, 1903, the Executive Committee removed Leon Greenbaum as national secretary, replaced him with William Mailly, a young coal miner, and moved the national headquarters from St. Louis to Chicago.

The following autumn the socialists suffered an overwhelming defeat at the AFL convention. Their resolutions were beaten by a six to one margin, and their candidate for president of the Federation received only 1236 votes to 12,449 for Gompers. Debs wisely refrained from any comment on these results, but he probably did not rejoice in them. Although he criticized those socialists who compromised their principles to gain votes, he did not desert the men who continued to fight for socialist control of the craft unions. He thought that eventually the socialists in the American Labor Union and the socialists in the AFL would be able to unite the two organizations around a radical program.

Eugene Debs, in this quarrel about trade union strategy, emphasized the critical importance of the labor newspapers. In May, 1904, he wrote that the trade union journals should consistently give a radical analysis of society:

The editor of a labor paper is of far more importance to the union and the movement than the president or any other officer of the union. He ought to be chosen with special reference to his knowledge upon the labor question and his fitness to advocate and defend the economic interests of the class he represents.

The union journals could never be true to this purpose if they sought corporate advertising, said Debs, because such advertising could only be procured at the cost of editorial control. Although many advertisements for the Westinghouse Corporation and other companies had appeared in *The Magazine* when Debs was editor, he now wrote: "Capitalists do not, as a rule, advertise in labor papers that are loyal to working class interests."

CHAPTER XII

□

[1]

AFTER the Pullman boycott of 1894, Debs' only income came from his lecture fees and from his publishing firm in Terre Haute. The Debs Publishing Company was never a profitable venture; all of the ingenuity of Kate and Theodore, who alternated as manager, was needed to meet the expenses. When Debs accepted the socialist philosophy, the firm abandoned the field of railroad technology and became a propaganda outlet for the new gospel. And Eugene Debs, who had never understood the profit motive, usually gave away more books than he sold. He wrote hundreds of letters each month to friends and followers all over the country, and each letter contained a printed copy of one of his speeches, a leaflet containing Edward Bellamy's "Parable of the Water Tank," or some other jibe at capitalist selfishness.

Debs would have managed his lecture tours with the same indifference to finances, but fortunately L. W. Rogers, his colleague from the ARU, managed the tours in 1898, then a Lyceum Bureau in Chicago for several years, and finally Theodore and Kate from Terre Haute. The net income to Debs was normally about a hundred dollars a week, and he was well satisfied even though he was offered five times as much to speak on the Chautauqua circuit. Each week Debs gave seven speeches of two hours length, rode more than a thousand miles in stifling, filthy day coaches, slept in dirty country hotels, ate greasy food and lumpy potatoes, seldom saw his wife and parents, had few friends whom he met more than three or four times a year, gave up all of the usual comforts and luxuries of life. When Joseph A. Labadie, a philosophical anarchist in Detroit, inquired about the lecture business in 1905, Debs wrote in reply: "I can hardly find it in my heart to cheer you on. There is so much to contend with and to overcome in the present condition of things that the undertaking is fraught with all that is calculated to make a man think a second and a third time before engaging in it. If you were a quack revivalist, or sensationalist or fantastic humbug of some sort, starting out to pander to the ignorance of the people, it would be different."

Although Debs tried to discourage others from entering the lecture field, he personally enjoyed the routine for several reasons. He firmly believed in his message. He reveled in the honor and prestige which were justly his. He found in oratory the delight that any honest craftsman finds in his work. Lastly, he delighted in his contact with thousands of Americans, from the unknown to the great and the near-great. About 1903 when he spoke in Rochester, New York, a distinguished local citizen was in the audience. Nearly twenty-five years had passed since the first and only meeting of Eugene Debs and Susan B. Anthony. On that occasion Miss Anthony had been on the platform; in the audience was the callow, idealistic, twenty-three-year-old youth.

Now Debs had reached maturity, and Miss Anthony had passed her eightieth year. The orator instantly noticed that "the years of trial, persecution and incessant struggle had left their ruthless impress upon her noble features." After his speech Debs hurried to her side. She clasped his hands in both of hers and murmured: "You remember me?" Debs was shocked. "Remember you," he replied, "how could anyone ever forget Susan B. Anthony?" The veteran crusader for woman suffrage instantly pressed his hands and exclaimed: "How glad I am to see you after all these years!"

The two agitators argued briefly about the relative importance of their aims. "Give us suffrage," Miss Anthony said laughingly, "and we'll give you socialism." To which Debs blithely replied: "Give us socialism and we'll give you suffrage."

Miss Anthony, her face seamed, her eyes watering, her body infirm, was discouraged at the tedious progress of her life's cause. After fifty years of sustained effort, national suffrage for women was still far from achievement. She found it particularly painful to realize that she would die before victory had

crowned her banners. Not even the cheerful tenderness of the
Socialist leader could prevail against this pessimism.

[2]

WHENEVER EUGENE DEBS returned to Terre Haute, a large part
of the town soon knew it. The neighbors saw him swinging up
the alley from the railroad station, whistling loudly, and heard
him shout "Hello, Ducky" to Kate as soon as he entered his
block. The mailman noticed an interruption in the flow of letters which carried a crude picture of a duck and then the address, 451 North Eighth street. Debs' nieces and nephews and
all of their friends learned that their patron saint was back in
town. Daniel, who owned the building that housed the Debs
Publishing Company, once more became accustomed to early
morning visits from his older son.

Debs eagerly looked forward to the end of a lecture tour, when
he could return to the comfort and regularity of home. During
his days at the office and his evenings at home, he was always
surrounded by friends and members of his family. Both Kate
and Theodore helped with his correspondence, but in very different ways. Letters written by Theodore sounded exactly as if
they had been written by Eugene; the two brothers looked alike,
thought alike, wrote alike, using a common attitude and a common vocabulary. When Kate was taking dictation, she was more
than a stenographer; she was also an editor. Debs would be
striding up and down in the office, completely lost in the thread
of his oratory, when suddenly Kate's voice would break in:
"That is perfect nonsense. That is stupid." And Debs, reading
over what he had just said, usually decided that she was right.
He recognized that Kate had a restraint, a feeling for the literal
truth, that he lacked.

Kate's cool judgment made her a good critic. Although Debs
gave essentially the same few speeches for twenty years, he
never stopped trying to perfect them. He changed words, jug-
gled the rhythm of the sentences, carefully devised alternate
sections so that he could tailor every oration to fit the audience.

Many of these changes originated on public platforms, but the fluency of Debs' rhetoric depended in large measure on private sessions in his upstairs study, where Kate listened for hours to the high-pitched, mellow voice that poured through the open windows and brought the neighbors onto their front porches. Debs soon became aware that he was providing entertainment for the entire block, and he often closed the program by playing selections from "Thais" on his phonograph. Or, if the audience paid a personal visit, he would gladly recite Edwin Markham's "Man with the Hoe." When Debs first saw Markham's poem in some Eastern magazine, he became so excited that he jumped from his chair. He immediately read it aloud to Kate, and they both agreed, said Debs later, "that Markham had given voice to the soul of the revolutionary cause and the struggle for emancipation and human betterment."

This leisurely home-town life was enriched by frequent requests for Debs' services, both as an orator and as a trade unionist. Debs was rightfully regarded as the father of the Terre Haute labor movement, since he had helped to organize most of the local craft unions. He was always willing to help organize a factory or plan strategy for a strike. One afternoon a printer from Mackville, about a mile beyond the Wabash River, stopped at Debs' office to ask his aid in establishing a local union of coal miners there. Debs readily agreed, and that evening he, the printer, and two other men walked through deep, slushy mud to Mackville, appeared at the meeting, and then trudged back home. Debs made no complaint about the weather, but he talked all the way to Terre Haute about the marvelous spirit of the miners.

Debs' ventures into local affairs were sometimes less successful. During a bitter streetcar strike, a delegation of strikers came to him for advice when the company agreed to negotiate the grievances. Knowing that the strikers were all inexperienced in negotiations, he feared that they would be deceived by some clever official from the company. So he advised them to draw up in advance their list of demands, and then to "be firm" with the company. The union committee, with Debs' help, drew up a model contract and departed for the negotiating session.

Twenty minutes later, they sheepishly re-entered Debs' office. Startled that they had returned so quickly, Debs asked them for an account of the meeting. Not one of them would say a word about it. Growing impatient, he grabbed the most vocal man from the committee, sat down behind his desk, and said to the spokesman, "Now pretend that I'm the president of the company and that you're just entering my office. What did you do?" The recruit to unionism hesitated a moment, then whipped the model contract from his pocket, slammed it down on the desk, and shouted, "We want you to sign this, and be Goddamn quick about it!" The company president had promptly thrown them out.

Debs threw his head back and laughed until the tears rolled down his face. Although he regretted that he had not been more specific in his advice, he often told that story as one of the most amusing incidents in his career.

Debs normally spoke from the public platform in Terre Haute only during election campaigns, since he believed that no community wanted to hear him more than two or three times a year. But he often agreed, at the request of Steve Reynolds, to give informal talks before small groups. Although Reynolds had been largely ostracized from the business community after his conversion to socialism, he found it no hardship. His real estate furnished a comfortable income, and the decline of his law practice allowed him to set his hand to more congenial work. He immediately organized a series of classes for the young people of Terre Haute. This educational program, which was attended by five hundred persons in eight years, greatly influenced the life of the community. Reynolds taught countless young workingmen and farmers how to read and write. He gave a regular three-month course which described the formation of the earth, the beginnings of life, the origin of man, the evolution of society, the contradictions of capitalism and the need for socialism. Six or eight different groups, with pupils ranging from ten to thirty years of age, were always studying this program. The students were not well educated when they got their diplomas, but they could all read and write, they knew the general outlines of history, and they would never forget that knowledge

was a wonderful thing. Dozens of them, guided by the memories
of long evenings in Reynolds' Red House, where the bookcases
hemmed in the parlor, had an enduring passion for research
and learning.

An informal group known as the Co-operative Dinner Club
also found its locale and inspiration in the parlor of the Red
House. The personnel of this Dinner Club, although it was constantly shifting, was based upon the young professional men
of the immediate neighborhood and several other instructors
from Indiana State and Rose Polytechnic, the two local col-
leges. Anybody who was interested in new ideas was welcome
at the Sunday evening gatherings, where the discussions covered poetry, drama, socialism, the education of children, and
the current economic situation. Verbal exchanges were friendly
but emphatic; these were people who had their own notions and
knew how to talk about them. The conversation wandered
easily from the new drama of G. B. Shaw to the merits of modern architecture and then onward to Meredith's novels. Reynolds prompted a series of disputes about Upton Sinclair's
The Jungle. When several members who accepted its accuracy
were repelled by the brutality of the story, Reynolds bluntly
insisted that reality should be changed, not concealed or evaded,
but most of the members resisted his socialist views.

Steve Reynolds and the Co-operative Dinner Club were host
to dozens of guest lecturers who passed through Terre Haute.
Clarence Darrow explained his radical theories of law and
penology. Clarence White, a famous photographer, came to take
photographs of a family across the street, but when he discovered the Reynoldses, he deserted his employer and spent several weeks at the Red House. A man came to lecture about
Yogi, and made the entire group practice breathing exercises.
Another visitor presented a theory about changing the rotation
of the earth by causing explosions at the North Pole. Horace
Traubel, a prominent disciple of Walt Whitman, helped to
launch a Whitman cult at the Dinner Club. During a coal strike
in the adjacent mining area, Mother Jones was asked to explain
the cause of the strike, and the entire house was crowded by

"dirty, vile-mouthed, tobacco-chewing coal miners," according to one of the members. Anybody who had a new, vital idea, no matter how good or how bad, was welcome at the Red House.

Kate and Eugene Debs were neither frequent nor conspicuous guests at these meetings, but Debs was always grateful for a chance to be present. When he was in Terre Haute, Jessie Reynolds phoned the other members, always giving precisely the same message: "You must be certain to come Sunday. Mr. Debs is coming over." Then the meeting acquired a special dignity, since few of the members knew Debs well. Although Kate may have been upset by informality, her husband certainly did not request special attention, nor did he expect it. He usually sat in an easy chair at the corner of the sun porch, sprawled and smiling while Professor Guthrie talked about French classical drama, warming himself in the inquisitive, fun-loving atmosphere. But occasionally he broiled steaks and fixed asparagus with sauce vinaigrette for the entire group, and then proudly acknowledged the expressions of surprise and pleasure at his cooking.

At least once he gave a lengthy talk about his experiences in the trade unions and the radical movement. Even before this small audience, Debs paced the floor, gestured, crouched, and pointed, used every trick of his flawless rhetoric. He was no more successful than Steve Reynolds at gaining recruits for the Socialist Party, but members of the Dinner Club acquired from its meetings a breadth of vision, a new compassion for the problems of workingmen.

Eugene Debs reveled in his contact with friends who may have lacked discipline and discrimination, but who possessed mental agility and courage. Several of these men must have reminded Debs of his own father, whom he had never thought to call a dilettante. Daniel had bought volume after volume of the French and German classics; he always anticipated the day of his retirement from business, when he would again have time to read and to study. But when Daniel finally retired, he was nearly blind. He could not see his beloved paintings. He could not read his precious books. So Eugene Debs, on his rare visits to Terre Haute, spent much of his time reading aloud to his father, and he always sought out other men who were learned in literature.

[*3*]

THE SECOND NATIONAL CONVENTION of the Socialist Party met at Brand's Hall in Chicago, May 1, 1904. From thirty-six states and territories had come 183 delegates, seven of them women. The average age was thirty-nine years. Two-thirds of those present had been born in the United States. Although the main occupational groups were twenty editors, sixteen printers, and fifteen lawyers, seventy-eight delegates were members of trade unions. It was a young, native-born gathering of workingmen to whom Debs said: "Thomas Jefferson would scorn to enter a modern Democratic convention. He would have as little business there as Abraham Lincoln would have in a modern Republican convention. If they were living today, they would be delegates to this convention."

The platform was a perfect reflection of the view of Eugene Debs, who was present as a delegate from Indiana. The battle between wageworkers and their employers would continue, declared the convention, until a socialist society had been established in the United States. Every applicant for membership in the Party would be required to sign a statement in which he accepted the class struggle as the basic fact of capitalist society.

Eugene Debs was again the unanimous choice as Presidential nominee. He tried, as always, to decline the honor, but at last he yielded: "In the councils of the Socialist Party the collective will is supreme. Personally, I could have wished to remain in the ranks, to make my record, humble though it might be, fighting unnamed and unhonored, side by side with my comrades." The Vice-Presidential candidate, Ben Hanford, was entitled to make the same statement. Although Hanford had given his life to the socialist movement, his reputation rested on a single act—he created the mythical Jimmie Higgins, the "unnamed and unhonored" rank and file worker, the man who swept out the meeting halls, passed out leaflets, was blacklisted from his job and beaten over the head by nightsticks on a thousand picket lines. When two hundred fifty thousand people read J. A. Wayland's epigrams in the *Appeal to Reason*, Jimmie Higgins sold the subscriptions. When ten thousand people came to a lecture by Eugene Debs, Jimmie Higgins sold the tickets. Debs, in spite of his great prestige, was merely a fraction of a devoted, energetic army. The fortunes of the Socialist Party rested, not on a few famous leaders, but on Jimmie Higgins.

Debs always attacked the egotistical pretensions of some of his associates. In 1902 a wealthy Socialist editor tried to garner exclusive credit for the growth of the Party in Wisconsin. Debs urged his friend Fred Heath, then editor of the *Social Democratic Herald*, to expose the "bragging, bluster, misrepresentation and downright lying" of their colleague. The point was driven home by an anecdote that Debs thought pertinent: "A fly sat on the horn of an ox who pulled a heavy load up a steep hill. When the top was reached the fly spread his wings and exclaimed, 'I had a hell of a pull but I got here just the same.' "

The growth of monopolies furnished the major issue of the 1904 campaign. Since 1897, consolidations had taken place at a frantic rate, until by 1904 the three hundred largest corporations controlled more than two-fifths of the industrial capital of the country. The United States Steel Corporation, the sugar trust, Standard Oil, International Harvester, the American Smelting and Refining Company, the tobacco trust, United Shoe Machinery had all arisen in seven years to plague the workingmen, farmers, and small businessmen. Debs ridiculed the trust-busting ideas of Theodore Roosevelt, and scoffed at the belief that mere government ownership would solve the problem:

Every hint at public ownership is now called Socialism, without reference to the fact that there can be no Socialism, and that public ownership means practically nothing, so long as the capitalist class is in control of the national government. Government ownership of public utilities means nothing for labor under capitalist ownership of government.

The other Presidential candidates, who knew Debs only as a fierce opponent, might have wondered at two events of that campaign, had the events become public. When Debs spoke in

Camden, New Jersey, he and Steve Reynolds made a pilgrim-
age to the home of Walt Whitman. Debs gathered five elm
leaves, which he pasted on a sheet of paper and packed in his
suitcase. The leaves finally made their way into Kate Debs'
scrapbook, where they were preserved for more than forty
years. And Eugene Debs, marveling at Whitman's vision of
American democracy, cried without shame as he stood on the
ground where his idol lay buried.

A few days later, the weary middle-aged Socialist stopped in
the Pittsburgh hotel where he had spent his wedding night, more
than nineteen years earlier. From this hotel he wrote a letter to
his wife in Terre Haute: "You have grown more beautiful and
more precious to me with each passing year. It is many years
ago since we came under the roof of this old hotel as bride and
groom and it seems to me that from that day to this we have
enjoyed together an unbroken honeymoon. Where I took you
as my wife I did not lose you as my friend and comrade, and
the years that trail behind us have borne beautiful testimony
of the sweetness and sanctity of our love."

The Chicago *Chronicle* said of this man: "Debs is opposed to
government, to society, to all political parties and to all labor
organizations. . . . What he and other revolutionists desire is a
state of affairs that will be intolerable and, therefore, a direct
incentive to revolt." These newspaper attacks seldom ruffled
the Socialist nominee, but he was infuriated by an obvious conspiracy between the California railroads and the Los Angeles
Times. Debs had not ridden in a Pullman since the boycott of
1894. But, as he was going south from San Francisco, the conductor announced that every coach on the train would be sidetracked at Bakersfield. Debs was thus forced to abandon his
boycott of Pullman, or to arrive in Los Angeles too late for his
scheduled meeting. He did the former. When his train pulled
into Los Angeles, newsboys were already hawking the local
Times: "All about Debs riding into Los Angeles in a Pullman."
General H. G. Otis, owner of the *Times*, obviously remembered
the tongue-lashing that Debs had administered in 1896.

Throughout that campaign, the Socialist machine worked in
high gear. The Party had collected a small campaign fund **for**

the first time, each member having donated a half-day's pay. These contributions, which totaled about thirty-three thousand dollars, permitted twenty-two organizers to remain in the field. Jimmie Higgins worked day and night, ringing doorbells, selling newspapers, talking with his shopmates and neighbors, speaking from soapboxes and the courthouse steps, painting large banners "Workers of the World Unite!", marching jubilantly beside the bass drummer. Eugene Debs spoke to two hundred fifty thousand people from Maine to Oregon. And in November, the Socialists received four hundred twenty thousand votes. In four years they had quadrupled their electorate.

CHAPTER XIII

□

[1]

THE SOCIALIST PARTY had been unified in 1900 by its slight gains in the Presidential election; no such happy result followed the much larger gains of the 1904 campaign. The advocates of revolutionary, industrial unionism continued to clash violently with the supporters of the AFL. By July of 1904, the schism within the Party had grown so deep that Robert Rives LaMonte urged official neutrality on the trade-union question, thus permitting each faction to follow its own program. Algernon Lee replied that no Socialist should be indifferent to the problems of union organization. Lee also charged that the Party held "certain non-proletarian and even possibly reactionary elements," who had become members to further their own careers.

Eugene Debs worried about this problem throughout the 1904 campaign. It seemed to him that the issue could not and should not be compromised. His strenuous speaking tour left him exhausted, and he was barely able to drag his weary body back to Terre Haute. Once there, he simply collapsed. For a week he ate, slept, listened to the phonograph, and did little else. Then he overruled Kate's emphatic objections and began to write *Unionism and Socialism*, a vivid and concise diagnosis of trade unionism. This pamphlet, which was intended primarily as an explanation of the current situation, became a major contribution to the theory of American socialism.

The pamphlet began with an analysis of the development of trade unions. In the childhood of capitalism, wrote Debs, the workers lost ownership of their tools, which passed into the hands of a separate owning class. Technological change increased both the size of the factory and the strength of the corporations. The workers, helpless as individuals, established craft unions in each community to protect their living standards. When these isolated local unions proved incapable of reaching their goal, they merged to form national craft unions.

The early employers tried to crush these infant organizations, but violent opposition often fostered trade unionism. Seeing the futility of force, some industrialists abandoned their private armies and Pinkerton detectives in favor of the National Civic Federation, which professed friendship for labor in order to "take it by the hand and guide it into harmless channels." These owners gave relatively high wages to the skilled workers, thus buying off any attempts by the craft unions to organize the unskilled trades. They also became allied with the Federal and state courts, and used the injunction to solve every crisis in their labor relations.

Debs declared that the craft unions should merge into industrial unions, but he added that this amalgamation would not halt the subtle corruption of the labor movement. The workers not only must unite, wrote Debs, they must become revolutionary. They must realize that the true objective of the workingmen is not merely to raise wages, but to overthrow the wage system. The wageworkers must fight on both the economic and the political battlefields. Trade unions protect the daily economic interests of labor, and the Socialist Party protects its political interests. There is great need for a revolutionary industrial union, which will be "uncompromising" in its attempts to advance the cause of socialism, since the AFL has deserted this task. But this is not enough, said the pamphlet: A man who votes for a capitalist party is little better than a scab, because the Socialist Party is the "political movement of the working class, clearly defined and uncompromising, which aims at the overthrow of the prevailing capitalist system."

You can judge a tree by its fruits and a social system by its people, said Debs. Capitalism, which daily produces "vagrants, tramps, outcasts, paupers, thieves, gamblers, pickpockets, suicides, confidence men, fallen women, consumptives, idiots, dwarfed children," no longer deserves to live. It is dying. Socialism is being born. The supreme need is to make the workingmen "conscious of the power of their class," so that they will take their places in the struggle for a new society.

The earth for all the people. That is the demand.

The machinery of production and distribution for all the people. That is the demand.

The collective ownership and control of industry and its democratic management in the interest of all the people. That is the demand.

The elimination of rent, interest and profit and the production of wealth to satisfy the wants of all the people. That is the demand.

Co-operative industry in which all shall work together in harmony as the basis of a new social order, a higher civilization, a real republic. That is the demand.

The end of class struggles and class rule, of master and slave, of ignorance and vice, of poverty and shame, of cruelty and crime—the birth of freedom, the dawn of brotherhood, the beginning of MAN. That is the demand.

This is socialism.

For all its eloquence, Debs' pamphlet failed in its immediate purpose. At the AFL convention of 1904, Max Hayes, a leader in both the AFL and the Party, stated that the Socialists would no longer try to capture the official machinery of the unions, but would be content to agitate for Socialist votes. Debs thought this statement was nonsense. He failed to see how the Socialists could educate the membership so long as Samuel Gompers and his colleagues controlled the trade-union publications, the conventions, and the leading positions in the unions. Debs feared that certain men in the Party would trim their principles to conform to the views of the conservative craft unionists. He had concluded that the AFL could not be transformed into a revolutionary union. A new labor federation was absolutely necessary, both to organize the unskilled workers and to protect the integrity of the Socialist Party.

Debs was not alone in this view. The American Labor Union had been mildly successful since its formation in 1902. Its leaders were convinced that a more vigorous enterprise along the same lines would win overwhelming victories. They won endorsement at the 1904 convention of the Western Federation of Miners, which instructed the executive board to make plans for uniting the entire working class into a single organization.

Charles Moyer and Bill Haywood met in Denver with President Dan McDonald of the American Labor Union and with George Estes of the United Railway Workers. Their plans were complete by late 1904.

Late in December, 1904, Thomas J. Hagerty, the former Catholic priest with whom Debs had toured the West in 1902, and William E. Trautmann, who edited the official journal of the Brewery Workers, arrived in Terre Haute. They talked to Debs for several hours. While they were presenting their plan, Debs slumped in his armchair, smoked his pipe, and gazed intently at the picture of Karl Marx above his desk. He frequently broke into their discourse with questions and elaborations. A light began to kindle in his eyes. When Trautmann and Hagerty had finished, Debs leaped from his chair and strode about the study, exclaiming, "I see it! I see it all very clearly!"

Eugene Debs was one of the six men who signed a secret letter, mailed from Chicago on December 22, 1904, to the thirty radical leaders of the country. The recipients were invited to meet in Chicago on January 2, 1905, "to discuss ways and means of uniting the working people of America on correct revolutionary principles." Debs, still confined to his home by exhaustion and illness, doubted that he would be well enough to attend the conference. The effects of prolonged overwork had left their mark on the fifty-year-old Socialist leader and he was recovering slowly.

The meeting on January 2, 1905, was another step toward formation of the new dual union, a rival organization to the AFL. When the conference opened, there were thirty-two delegates representing nearly fifty-five thousand workers. Big Bill Haywood and Vincent St. John were present as spokesmen for the Western Federation of Miners, the largest supporting union. Trautmann and Hagerty both played leading rôles. Mother Mary Jones, the fearless seventy-five-year-old organizer of the miners, was one of the best known participants. Charles O. Sherman represented the United Metal Workers, a group which had seceded from the AFL. This group of radical unionists drafted a manifesto which demanded the formation of a new, revolutionary, industrial union. They also called a conference for June 27, 1905, at Brand's Hall in Chicago formally to launch the organization.

More than two hundred delegates and scores of spectators crowded into Brand's Hall on June 27. Debs, Mother Jones, and Bill Haywood were on the speakers' platform; the delegates included Trautmann, Sherman, Moyer, Father Hagerty. Lucy Parsons, widow of one of the Haymarket martyrs, became the second woman to join the order. Daniel DeLeon led a group from the Socialist Trades and Labor Alliance, which he had founded ten years earlier. Debs, Haywood, Ernest Untermann, and A. M. Simons, editor of the *International Socialist Review*, represented the left-wing faction of the Socialist Party. Several members of the right wing, including Victor Berger and Max Hayes, had been invited. Berger had not even bothered to answer the invitation. Hayes had replied that he thought there was a good chance to capture the AFL and depose the bureaucrats, so he intended to agitate for socialism within the craft unions.

Exactly at 10 A.M., Bill Haywood lumbered to the front of the platform, picked up a loose piece of board, and rapped on the table for order. Haywood had puzzled over the proper way of addressing the delegates. He could not call them "Comrades" —many were not socialists. Use of the phrase "Brothers and Sisters" was absolutely banned because it would imply some concession to the hated AFL. But the problem had been resolved. This burly giant turned his head to the side, beat furiously on the table with his piece of lumber, and shouted down the last whispers in the audience:

Fellow workers! . . . The aims and objects of this organization should be to put the working class in possession of the economic power, the means of life, in control of the machinery of production and distribution, without regard to capitalist masters.

This spirit dominated the discussions. The delegates urged the working class to unite in order to seize control of the country. The new organization, which was named the Industrial Workers of the World, decided to admit only wageworkers to membership, but any person who held a union card in any foreign country would be accepted without question. This feeling of international friendship was shown by two other resolutions. The convention heartily welcomed the revolution which was then taking place in Russia. It also adopted May Day, which had originated in the AFL's campaign for the eight-hour day in 1886, as the international holiday of the workingmen.

Eugene Debs, obviously ill at ease in a convention, spoke only once, on the afternoon of the third day. His brief speech was a plea for unity in the organization. There was ample cause for apprehension on this count. The convention held every shade of radical opinion: Debs' socialism, Lucy Parsons' anarchism, Mother Jones' trade unionism, Bill Haywood's developing syndicalism. Individual differences, jealousy, and fights for position, were certain among these strong-willed men. DeLeon had never learned to co-operate with anybody. Charles Sherman and several other leaders were considered as mere pie-card artists, men who wanted easy jobs for themselves. Big Bill Haywood as he listened to Debs' speech, was already conscious of one source of friction:

Debs was the workingman who had laid down his shovel on the locomotive when he took up the work of organizing the firemen. Debs' ideas, while not clearly developed, were built upon his contact with the workers in their struggle. DeLeon's only contact with the workers was through the ideas with which he wished to "indoctrinate" them, to use his own word.

At the conclusion of his speech, Debs was approached by reporters from the Chicago newspapers, who asked for a statement about the objectives of the Industrial Workers of the World. Each of them was furnished with copies of the constitution, excerpts from several addresses, and the plans of the IWW. Not a word of this material was ever printed. The same sequence of events occurred two days later. The newspapers filled column after column with attacks on the radical union, but they were unwilling to publicize its announced aims.

Even the Socialist press took a hostile position. Max Hayes' Cleveland *Citizen*, the New York *Forward* of Morris Hillquit and Abe Cahan, the *Social Democratic Herald* of Victor Berger and Fred Heath, all attacked the IWW. A few days after the founding convention, Debs met Victor Berger in Racine, Wisconsin. Debs predicted that the IWW would soon have a strong following in Milwaukee. Berger laughed at him. The next issue of the *Social Democratic Herald* conceded that Eugene Debs was an excellent fellow, but it also implied that he was a bigot and a fool. Debs found this "a fine combination that I suppose I should be proud of." The *Herald* charged that Debs and his colleagues were guilty of splitting the trade unions, and advised them to return to the labor movement and the Socialist Party.

This was more than Debs could tolerate. With the jeering face of Victor Berger before his eyes, he wrote an indignant letter to one of the editors of the *Herald*. "Since when," he asked, "has the S. D. Herald become the official organ and special champion of the A.F. of L.? And since when is it a condition of membership in the Socialist Party that one must belong to the A.F. of L.? . . . The Chicago dailies are all, like the S. D. Herald, the champions of the A.F. of L., guard it and defend it, and if this is not significant, then nothing is. They understand the rottenness of the old trade union movement . . . , but it is good enough for them, in fact just what they want, for a rotten labor movement is their salvation and that is why they lied about the Industrial convention and why they hold up the A.F. of L. as the one organization for workingmen to tie to."

In this letter, Debs denied every charge that had been made against the IWW. He denied that he had deserted his former faith: "I have simply joined a labor union that suits me. That's all." He denied that Berger and Heath could make the AFL into "a clean industrial union": "The Brotherhood of Engineers is where it was thirty years ago and there it will remain forever so far as any change from within is concerned." He denied that the IWW would split the labor movement: "Just take a glance at Chicago today and in the presence of such a situation the talk of splitting the trade union movement is nothing less than idiotic." Debs thought that the AFL was already divided by a factional struggle for power; he wanted to divide it according to principles.

Debs, when he wrote this letter, was so incensed that he made several extreme statements. He declared that the June 27 convention "was in many respects the most representative proletarian gathering I have ever seen. . . . I saw not one who was ambitious for personal laurels, not one who wanted office, not one who in any sense was a self-seeker and I am proud and shall always be of being a delegate, whatever the outcome may be." Debs also charged that "Berger and Heath probably never worked for wages a day in their lives, have no trade, never had on a pair of overalls and really have no excuse to be in a trade union at all, and yet they appear in leading trade union rôles and tell me to what particular union I must belong under penalty of being visited with their displeasure." The entire tone of Debs' letter was bitter, vitriolic, but, typically, he softened it at the end: "In closing allow me to say that I am deeply sensible of all your personal words. For you and the Milwaukee comrades I would do anything but violate my conscience. That I will not do and that you will not expect."

Fred Heath, in a prompt reply, pointed out several misstatements in Debs' letter. Both he and Berger, in point of fact, had been wage earners for much longer than Eugene Debs. Debs had largely forgotten that he had worked on the railroads less than five years. Heath declared that every trade union had a certain number of crooks. The ARU had included "such skates as Hogan, Howard, Bill Burns, and Goodwin"; the IWW also had its share of these men. When Debs joined the IWW, he deserted his former comrades and allied himself with Daniel DeLeon, who was "an enemy of Socialism and a prevaricator and slanderer," with anarchists like Lucy Parsons and Father Hagerty, and with countless "industrial fakirs," according to Heath.

Heath also claimed that the AFL could be captured by the Socialists: "What we have done in Milwaukee can be done everywhere else, if you fellows have the gumption to do it. And its the only right way to go about it." It was not true, said Heath, that Debs had a monopoly on virtue; he himself was "moved by a sense of duty to the cause." It was to be hoped that Debs would reconsider his rash action in joining the IWW:

"This is not saying that you are not a free agent, it is reminding you that Eugene V. Debs, leader in the Socialist party, should shrink from identifying himself with a movement calculated to do injury to the party—if it were to succeed at all. . . . As ever—your pal."

This exchange of angry letters merely served to widen the gap. Debs admitted, in the *International Socialist Review*, that the delegates to the June 27 convention had disagreed about details, but they had agreed perfectly on the need for a new industrial union. In all of his speeches and pamphlets Debs defended the IWW and attacked the AFL. Referring to the National Civic Federation, he claimed that every beast of prey told its victims: "Our interests are one"; then the victim was eaten. The employers, said Debs, will never consent to a fair scale of wages. But if the workers realize their combined power, they can easily overthrow the entire wage system:

As individual wage-slaves you are helpless and your condition hopeless. As a class, you are the greatest power between the earth and the stars. As a class, your chains turn to spider-webs and in your presence capitalists shrivel up and blow away.

The individual wage-slave must recognize the power of class unity and do all he can to bring it about.

This conviction of brotherhood and solidarity, which formed the recurring theme in Debs' public expressions, was equally prominent in his conversation and personal letters. Writing to Joseph A. Labadie, the Detroit anarchist, in December, 1905, Debs said: "In all these relations we poor, petty individuals, as such, amount to little, . . . but as we come in real touch with each other and draw upon each other for strength and size, and feel the essential unity of the race, we grow tall as gods, and our heads are among the stars."

At this time Debs was lecturing in the East to rally support for the Socialist Party and the IWW. He had often demonstrated his willingness to set aside personal quarrels and minor disputes in order to gain agreement on fundamentals. This willingness was strikingly demonstrated by his relations with Daniel DeLeon. Debs had often referred to DeLeon as a "scoundrel" but he now brushed aside the accumulated rancor and defended the leader of the Socialist Labor Party. In the autumn of 1905, he wrote for the *Miners' Magazine:* "DeLeon is sound on the question of trade unionism, and to that extent, whether I like him or not personally, I am with him." But, in spite of this hint about Debs' attitude, his Socialist colleagues were astonished by later developments.

On December 10, 1905, Debs gave a speech about the IWW at Grand Central Palace in New York City. Before the meeting, Daniel DeLeon went backstage with his wife and his son Solon, then a young man. Solon DeLeon, who was but little more than five feet in height, had the impression of Debs "coming down out of the sky to me." Then Debs was shaking his hands warmly and saying, "Why, Comrade DeLeon has a son almost as big as he is." Solon, quite flustered by this comment, seemed even smaller as he replied, "But not as big as Comrade Debs."

Daniel DeLeon was puzzled, throughout Debs' address, because Debs consistently faced the side of the hall where the DeLeons were sitting. Finally the SLP leader noticed that the other side of the hall was a solid mass of German socialists, all active in the AFL, who were completely opposed to the IWW. Not even Debs' oratory could sway them. But Daniel DeLeon remarked Debs' hold on the remainder of his audience. DeLeon always refrained from emotional appeals in his speeches, preferring to be deliberate and logical. Later, in discussing Debs' speech with his colleagues in the SLP, DeLeon commented, "What Debs can do, I can't do, and what I can do, Debs can't do."

Members of the Socialist Party and the Socialist Labor Party were equally confused by the depth of co-operation between Debs and DeLeon. Their confusion was greatly magnified when DeLeon republished, as an SLP pamphlet, Debs' address at Grand Central Palace. And the following summer Debs again struck at his colleagues in his own party: "The fact is that most of the violent opposition of Socialist party members to the I.W.W. is centered upon the head of DeLeon and has a purely personal animus."

The right wing of the Socialist Party had already taken steps to discipline the dissidents. Debs' weekly column in the *Social*

Democratic Herald, which had appeared continuously for more than two years, was dropped in October, 1905. Big Bill Haywood and Debs were now regarded as outcasts by Berger, Morris Hillquit, and J. Mahlon Barnes, the national secretary of the Party. But Debs, always indifferent to the official policies of the Party, was not dismayed by the attacks of a few leaders. He had repeatedly said that he had no ambitions for place and power; his classic formulation of this attitude was made in a speech at Turner Hall in Detroit, January 11, 1906: "But I am no labor leader. I don't want you to follow me, or anyone else. If you are looking for a Moses to lead you out of this capitalist wilderness, you will stay right where you are. I would not lead you into the promised land if I could, because if I could lead you in someone else could lead you out. You must use your heads as well as your hands and get yourselves out of your present condition."

There was reason to doubt, at that moment, if labor would ever reach "the promised land." The IWW had divided both the labor movement and the Party into warring camps. It separated men who had been friends for years, and united men who had always been enemies. Samuel Gompers referred to the IWW as "Father Hagerty's Wheel of Fortune," but this jest was mere bravado. Gompers was actually frightened by the new competitor. The AFL, which had been quiescent for more than a year, was racked with ferment by the beginning of 1906. Various cliques within the craft unions were fighting each other, and they were all fighting the industrial unions. The supporters of each group in the Socialist Party were waging a vitriolic battle in the newspapers and in local meetings. The anarchists were attacking the socialists, and the socialists were attacking the labor fakers. It was impossible to conceive any issue on which there could be agreement. But such an issue occurred. Bill Haywood, Charles Moyer, and a Denver businessman named George Pettibone were indicted for murder.

[2]

ON DECEMBER 30, 1905, former Governor Frank Steunenberg of Idaho was killed by a bomb as he opened the gate to his home at Caldwell, Idaho. A certain Harry Orchard, a member of the Western Federation of Miners, was arrested on suspicion. Two weeks later, Orchard dictated a full confession to the manager of the Pinkerton Detective Agency in Denver, claiming that Haywood, Moyer, and Pettibone had hired him to kill Steunenberg. Their alleged motive was a desire for revenge against the former governor, who had called out the militia during the Coeur d'Alene disturbance of 1899.

A secret complaint against the accused men, all of whom lived in Denver, was filed in Canyon County, Idaho, a month after Orchard's confession. The governor of Colorado secretly signed extradition papers. One Saturday night, when the courts were closed so that the defendants could not secure a legal stay of the extradition, the three men were arrested. They were escorted directly to a special train, on which they were the only passengers. This train was given absolute right of way to Idaho, proving that there had been careful arrangements between two governors and the railroad. Moyer, Haywood and Pettibone were jointly indicted for the murder on March 6, 1906.

The commercial newspapers were immediately in full cry for justice, and their notion of justice was dramatically revealed by a headline in the Chicago *Tribune:*

Arrests Thwart
Vast Murder Plot

Moyer and Haywood of Western Miners' Federation
Suspected of Fiend-
ish Conspiracy

James McParlan, the Pinkerton detective who had extracted the confession from Harry Orchard, told a *Tribune* reporter that the accused men "will never leave Idaho alive." McParland also stated that Moyer and Haywood had planned to "destroy the train" on which they were to be taken to Idaho, so he had insisted on a special train. Even if the accused were acquitted in Idaho, said McParlan, he had "information and proof of their connection with a dozen atrocious murders in Colorado."

Debs believed that this newspaper hysteria was designed to

immobilize every cry for a fair trial. Perhaps he remembered his own equivocal rôle in the Haymarket defense campaign, and was determined that such a frame-up would not occur again. He did not doubt that the current indictments were a frame-up. Pettibone seemed to be merely an incidental victim, window-dressing to conceal the true aim of the indictments. The entire proceedings, thought Debs, were an attempt to dispose of two leaders of the IWW, Bill Haywood and Charles Moyer. Within twenty-four hours after he heard about the indictments, Eugene Debs had mailed his comment on the case to the *Appeal to Reason*.

Debs was shrewd to choose the *Appeal* as the outlet for his article. By the autumn of 1905, J. A. Wayland's weekly was sent from Girard, Kansas, to a quarter-million enthusiastic subscribers. Its circulation was evenly divided between the cities and the rural areas; it was read in the steel mills of Pittsburgh and the country stores of Oklahoma. There was a second reason why Debs favored the *Appeal*. Wayland and Fred Warren operated their newspaper with sublime disregard of libel laws. They had engaged in continuous battle with the postal authorities in Washington, and had won at every turn. These experiences had taught Fred Warren, editor of the *Appeal*, that he should never print an item he could not prove. But if there was proof, Warren never hesitated to print the article and take his chance in court.

Debs' comments about the Moyer-Haywood indictments, however, were so inflammatory that even Fred Warren hesitated to authorize publication. When the article arrived in Girard, Warren read it through several times, shook his head, and took it to J. A. Wayland. Wayland read it carefully, and then paced up and down the room. Finally he dropped it on Warren's desk and said calmly, "Fred, you have been doing most of it lately, and I guess you'll have to do as you please about this." Warren then asked if Wayland realized that publication of the article might lead to "the suppression of the *Appeal* and the arrest for feloniously inciting to armed rebellion of every one of us." Wayland was still calm: "Yes, and the only question I want you to settle in your mind before acting

is, Will it work to the best interests of Socialism." Warren decided to print the article.

The headline on the *Appeal* of March 10 roared at its readers:

AROUSE, YE SLAVES!

The center of the front page contained Debs' answer to the
statement that the indicted men "will never leave Idaho alive."
"Well, by the gods, if they do not," wrote Debs, "the governors
of Idaho and Colorado and the masters from Wall Street, New
York, to the Rocky Mountains had better prepare to follow
them."

Nearly twenty years ago the capitalist tyrants put some innocent men to death for standing up for labor.

They are now going to try it again. Let them dare! There
have been twenty years of revolutionary education, agitation,
and organization since the Haymarket tragedy, and if an attempt is made to repeat it, there will be a revolution and I will
do all in my power to precipitate it. The crisis has come and we
have to meet it. . . .

If they attempt to murder Moyer, Haywood and their
brothers, a million revolutionists at least will meet them with
guns.

Debs' threats did not paralyze or coerce the prosecution. The
Idaho Supreme Court, on March 12, denied a petition for a writ
of habeas corpus, and the Federal District Court also denied
the petition ten days later. The decision was immediately appealed to the Supreme Court of the United States, and Debs
intensified his efforts to arouse the trade unions. His activities
met with striking success. Ten barrels of ink, six carloads of
newsprint, three thousand mailbags, and ten United States
mail cars were needed to print and mail a single edition of the
Appeal to Reason. Debs again charged that the prosecution
was trying to lynch the defendants. "The fight is on," he declared. "It has been forced upon us. We are not responsible
for it. We are not favoring violence but resisting it. We are seeking not to commit, but to prevent murder. Beware the wrath of
an outraged and avenging people."

In addition to his weekly articles in the *Appeal*, Debs gave
hundreds of speeches from coast to coast in defense of Moyer

and Haywood. He found that the labor movement was gradually beginning to grasp the significance of the case. The defense campaign was by no means a one-man show. Even the craft unions were protesting. The leaders of the AFL entered the fight, hesitantly at first, then more emphatically. Both factions of the Socialist Party were trying to mobilize support for the defendants. The radical newspapers headlined every development and printed countless editorials on the corruption of the capitalist courts. Throughout the country, Jimmie Higgins, the mythical rank and filer, was talking to his neighbors, passing out leaflets, offering resolutions in meetings.

Debs spent several months in the West and Northwest, where Moyer and Haywood were already celebrities in the trade unions. In Denver, where the newspaper hysteria was at its peak, Debs discovered a surprising amount of support for the defendants. He was even invited to address the Press Club there, and the president gave him a very cordial introduction: "Gene Debs may be a Socialist, but there are a few democrats in these western diggin's who love him for the good he has done." Although Debs had never admitted, even to himself, the possibility that Moyer and Haywood might hang, he was doubtless encouraged by the breadth and determination of the defense campaign. Everything seemed to be going well, when suddenly tragedy struck at his family.

Daisy Debs died in the spring of 1906, at the age of seventy-eight. Thus separated from his wife, largely blind, eighty-six years old, Daniel lost all will to live. In the autumn he too died, quietly, willingly. This gigantic blow at Eugene Debs was further complicated by the death of Kate's only brother, Daniel Metzel. A weaker man than Debs might have been completely prostrated. He had constantly looked to his parents for advice and encouragement. They had never failed him. In the fifty years of Debs' life, no incident had occurred to mar his respect for Daisy and Daniel. Many years later, when he was himself an old man, he told a reporter: "I never knew my mother until she died. We never know anyone until they are dead. Then we understand their work and we love them for it, whether or not they succeeded."

Now Eugene Debs, who had been totally absorbed in the tangible problems of food and shelter, marched blindly into the greatest puzzle of them all. In his agony he pondered the inscrutability of life, the swooping breathlessness of death, the finite line between existence and its cessation. After the manner of the healthy and the optimistic, he had always assumed that life is eternal. This view was shattered. On January 10, 1907, six weeks after the death of his father, he wrote his own will and testament. The entire text was less than thirty words: "I, Eugene V. Debs, of Terre Haute, Vigo County, Indiana, hereby will and bequeath all my property, real and personal, to my beloved wife, Katherine M. Debs."

The anguish promoted by the triple tragedy in his family aggravated a number of bodily ills, originally caused by his furious activity for Haywood and Moyer. Recurrent attacks of rheumatism forced him back to Terre Haute. His throat, irritated by a dozen speeches each day, felt as if he had been eating glass, and he visited a throat specialist in Cincinnati. But he refused to be diverted from his main purpose. Early in January of 1907, he wrote to J. A. Wayland that he intended to "come to Girard . . . and take a hand at helping you on the *Appeal*." Debs said that only the force of public opinion could possibly save Moyer and Haywood: "If we cannot arouse the people sufficiently to threaten revolt on a large scale they are gone. Nothing else can save them."

By the end of January, 1907, Debs had arrived in Girard. When he walked into the office of the *Appeal*, his first words closed the deal: "I want to do something in this crisis. It must be something far-reaching. Only through the columns of the *Appeal* can I express myself as I will, and reach the audience that I must." Fred Warren, known among the prairie socialists as The Fighting Editor, was receptive to this offer. Debs was promptly hired at a salary of a hundred dollars a week as a contributing editor.

Thus began one of the happiest partnerships in the history of the radical movement. Wayland, who was a few years older than Debs, had masterfully combined sound business management of the paper with its socialist purpose. When Wayland stepped aside in 1904, Warren continued and perfected these practices. The *Appeal*, by the time Debs joined its staff, employed more than a hundred men and women. Its mailing costs and payroll each amounted to more than twelve hundred dollars each week. Here, indeed, was a socialist organ that could furnish Debs with an extensive audience. And the *Appeal*, for its part, was certain to benefit from Debs' weekly articles and his lectures in its behalf.

As soon as he had worked out his arrangements with Fred Warren, Debs left Girard for another tour of the mining areas of the West. The Supreme Court of the United States, in December, 1906, had denied a Moyer-Haywood-Pettibone petition for a writ of habeas corpus, and thus had remanded the case to a trial court in Boise. The sole hope for saving the three defendants now lay in a favorable verdict by the jury. But the commercial press had convicted the labor leaders before their trial even began. Debs thought it necessary to take steps to counteract this publicity campaign, so he interrupted his tour and went to Washington, D. C. After two weeks of intensive lobbying, he persuaded Senator Carmack of Tennessee to enter all records of the case into the *Congressional Record*. Well satisfied with this result, which was widely publicized, Debs again returned to the lecture platform in Colorado.

Personal sorrow at the death of his parents, bad health, and prolonged exertion had left their mark on Debs. Frank O'Hare, a young Socialist organizer who was also mobilizing support for Moyer and Haywood, encountered him one day on a train in Colorado. Debs, sound asleep and dead drunk, was curled up in a chair in the smoker. When O'Hare tapped him on the shoulder, he jumped up, blinked, and shouted in a loud voice, "Hello, Frank, you old son of a gun, how are you?" And then he continued his maudlin monologue, "You know, Frank, I've been out lecturing for Haywood for two months, and three days ago I passed through Terre Haute and I couldn't even get off the train for an hour to see Ducky."

O'Hare was not easily embarrassed, but he felt rather uncomfortable with this lanky frame draped around his neck and slobbering on his collar. He kept saying in soothing tones, "I know, Gene. Sit down, Gene." Finally he succeeded in pushing Debs back into the chair and putting him back to sleep. When the train arrived in Pueblo at 6 o'clock, Debs was still unable to walk or to talk coherently. He was slated to speak at 8:30, and O'Hare was determined that the audience would not be disappointed.

The local committee which met Debs was astonished to find him drunk; they had considered him a god, not at all like other men. But O'Hare rallied the committee, formed a flying wedge, and hustled Debs through the waiting crowd into a cab. At the hotel they registered Debs in one room, then took him to another to avoid his admirers. O'Hare rolled the Socialist leader into bed, stationed two guards in the room and a third in the corridor, and gave them exact instructions: Wake him up at 8 o'clock; give him a bowl of soup and a cup of coffee; and bring him directly to the meeting. Then O'Hare grabbed a hasty meal and rushed to the hall to stall the audience until 8:30.

Precisely on time, Debs stepped onto the stage. He acknowledged O'Hare's brief introduction and began his speech. As usual, he charmed the audience. They were spellbound. And O'Hare grinned knowingly at the three young miners who had rolled a drunk man into bed just two hours earlier.

On the very eve of the trial in Boise, when tension had become unbearable, Eugene Debs crossed swords with a worthy opponent. Theodore Roosevelt also was accomplished, in his spectacular Rough Rider way, at the art of capturing headlines. A year earlier he had made his first pronouncement on the Moyer-Haywood case. The occasion was the laying of the cornerstone of the new House of Representatives building in Washington. While the entire nation listened, the President compared certain industrialists to "the so-called labor leader who clamorously strives to excite a foul class feeling on behalf of some other labor leader who is implicated in murder." On April 2, 1907, Roosevelt again turned to the events in Idaho. His conduct would have been brash in a private citizen, but when cloaked with the prestige of the Presidency it seemed like gross treachery. At a press conference, he made public a letter in which he stated that a particular railroad magnate was "at least as undesirable a citizen as Debs, or Moyer, or Haywood."

Eugene Debs would certainly have resented the reference to his own character, but he boiled over at the notion that the President was trying to convict Moyer and Haywood. He publicly accused Roosevelt of improper action, and charged that the President was conniving at the legal murder of two labor leaders. Nor was Debs alone in this opinion. Many commercial newspapers and conservative politicians, while believing merely that Roosevelt had made a mistake, nevertheless agreed that it was a serious mistake. The President issued another statement denying that he had implied that Moyer and Haywood were guilty of murder, but Debs was not to be appeased so easily. In an article that was printed by several major newspapers, Debs said that the President was lying when he denied his earlier statement: "He thus stands pilloried before the American people. If he attempts to deny the charge, I shall convict him with the proof." Debs also claimed that the public outcry had forced Roosevelt to retract his original letter: "The 'explanation' of President Roosevelt is the first decisive victory for organized labor in the kidnapping battle of the class war in the United States."

Although Roosevelt backed down on his statement about Moyer and Haywood, he continued to attack Debs, and he called the *Appeal to Reason* a "vituperative organ of pornography, anarchy and bloodshed." Debs promptly replied that the President was both a coward and a hypocrite. He asked why Roosevelt had never denounced his own friends who had said "To hell with the constitution" and "To hell with habeas corpus; we'll give 'em postmortems." And then came the cruelest cut of all:

Does the President remember one John P. Altgeld?

And one Theodore Roosevelt who in the same year of 1896 said that said Altgeld and one Debs should be lined up against a dead wall and shot?

Which said Roosevelt never denied until four years later, when he became candidate for Vice President?

Is this the "temperate" language of a perfectly "desirable" citizen?

The rancorous dispute between Debs and Roosevelt helped to fasten the country's attention on the courtroom in Boise, Idaho, where Bill Haywood was already being tried. It also gave added impetus to the defense campaign. The entire labor movement had rallied to the cause of the defendants. Protest parades were held in every major city during the spring months. In San Francisco an unprecedented crowd heard several speakers impugn the motives of the prosecution. Fifty thousand men marched through the streets of Boston, chanting in unison:

If Moyer and Haywood die; if Moyer and Haywood die;
Twenty million workingmen will know the reason why.

On May 4 two long files of men and women estimated at twenty thousand persons, began to parade uptown from the lower East Side of New York City. The two files merged into one at 40th Street and Lexington Avenue and continued their parade to Grand Central Palace, where a frenzied throng heard John Chase, Morris Hillquit, and Joshua Wanhope denounce the proceedings in Idaho.

While these protest parades were being duplicated throughout the country, Eugene Debs continued to needle Theodore Roosevelt: "Patrick Henry was denounced by King George and William Haywood by President Theodore." On May 23, when Haywood's trial was in its sixth week, Debs finished his preparations to leave for Boise as a special correspondent for the *Appeal*. Then his trip was cancelled at the request of the defense attorneys, Clarence Darrow and E. F. Richardson. Debs was undoubtedly disappointed, and he probably resented Darrow's blunt suggestion that he stay out of Boise, but he yielded to the judgment of the attorneys. Bill Haywood, in his autobiography, later charged that Darrow was motivated by his desire to save the center of the stage for himself, but this interpretation probably missed the real point. Darrow, in spite of his cynicism, continued to believe that the capitalist courts dispensed justice. He thought that Debs' presence in Boise would prejudice the jury against the defendants. Both Debs and Haywood vigorously dissented from this view, and argued that only an aroused citizenry could guarantee a fair trial.

The headlong, hectic defense campaign grew in vigor through the three long, breathless months of Haywood's trial. On June 29, when the trial was in its seventh week, the *Appeal* predicted an acquittal, but there was no diminution of the public protests against the prosecution. Debs called the trial "the greatest legal battle in American history." This comment approached the truth. Trade unionists and socialists had contributed more than sixty thousand dollars to fight the case. Literally hundreds of protest meetings were held. Not since the Dred Scott case in 1857 had such militant action been conducted to protest a court's decision.

In Boise the trial swept to a dramatic climax. The case was given to the jury about 10 o'clock one Saturday evening. All night the streets were filled with groups of men awaiting the verdict. At 7 A.M. Sunday word was sent that the jury had agreed, and the verdict was read to a jammed, silent courtroom one hour later. As soon as the decision was known, the crowd rushed into the streets, reporters ran for the telegraph office, the streets filled with a boisterous, raucous crowd, some men hilarious in their joy, others surly in their disappointment.

On August 3, the *Appeal to Reason* trumpeted victory. Haywood had been acquitted. The socialist weekly printed an ordinary front page, then superimposed over it in gigantic red letters:

NOT
GUILTY

After the acquittal of Haywood, it was mere formality to win the trials of Pettibone and Moyer. The labor movement had won. It had saved its leaders.

When the battle was finished, many men asked the same question: What would Debs have done if Haywood had been convicted? Would he have marched to Idaho at the head of "a million revolutionists with guns," as he had threatened? It seems likely that Debs himself did not fully resolve this question. Soon after his flaming articles in the *Appeal*, he left Stephen Reynolds' home one day in the company of a friend who was a respected professional man in Terre Haute. The friend commented, "Gene, sometimes I just can't take some of these wild things you write in the *Appeal to Reason*." According to the friend, Debs replied, "Well, you have to give the workingmen something vigorous if you want to wake them up."

Since it was not necessary for Debs to reach a decision, any answer is speculative, but a hint is given by the Socialist leader's adulation of Old John Brown, that violent revolutionary who led twenty-one armed men into the death trap at Harper's Ferry. Debs was neither a terrorist nor a doctrinaire pacifist. He had never raised his hand in anger against a fellow being, either as boy or man. He believed that only the most extreme provocation could ever justify the use of violence. On the other hand, he believed that this degree of provocation existed in certain situations. On March 16, 1907, he wrote in the New York *Worker:* "It is not that we object to the lawful punishment of crime; not at all. The precise contrary is true. We are opposed to the commission of crime, *especially in the name and under the forms of law*." * And there can be little doubt that Debs was in deadly earnest about the proceedings in Boise. There was no bravado in his comment to several friends: "If they hang Haywood and Moyer, they'll have to hang me."

[*3*]

DEBS had reason to be proud of his part in the defense of Moyer and Haywood, which compensated in some measure for his rôle in the Haymarket campaign. But the legal battle of 1906 and 1907 had not been wholly a triumph, since it almost destroyed the Industrial Workers of the World.

The membership of the IWW was centered in the western states, where many workingmen scorned the established principles of trade unionism. This tendency had been held in check by the influence of the Western Federation of Miners, which founded stable local unions, signed contracts with employers, and fought for control of working conditions in the factories and workshops. The imprisonment of Haywood for fifteen months, and the involvement of his supporters in his defense campaign, permitted his enemies to capture the Western Federation of Miners. They promptly withdrew it from the IWW. Having

* The italics are the author's.

lost its membership among those workers with stable employment, the IWW ceased to function as a trade union. Its ranks
held a select corps of organizers and strike leaders but not a
single business agent. It became an organization which was
geared to meet crises but which did not offer guidance to the
workers on a stable, day-to-day basis.

This new trend was simply nonsense to Eugene Debs, who
well understood the value of collective bargaining. But Debs'
main quarrel with the IWW pivoted on another issue. The
Moyer-Haywood trial, even more than the Pullman boycott,
turned the radical leaders against the government itself. Socialist politics and capitalist politics became equally bad. Elections
were a lot of bunk. The trade unions themselves should run the
country. This viewpoint, the philosophy of anarcho-syndicalism,
dominated the IWW by 1908. That spring the IWW convention
dropped the last mention of political action from the preamble
to the order's constitution.

It was inevitable that Eugene Debs, who insisted on both industrial unions and the Socialist Party as the cornerstones of
sound policy, would resign from the IWW. His traditional
practice demanded a public statement of the reasons for his
resignation. He had issued such statements when he left the
Brotherhood of Locomotive Firemen and the Social Democracy
of America. In 1900 he had publicized the sources of his disagreement with Daniel DeLeon. But he could not bring himself to
attack the IWW. The organization was led by men with whom
he had co-operated for years. Bill Haywood, one of the main
spokesmen for the erroneous policies of the IWW, was still a
leader in the Socialist Party. And the IWW, with its militant
spirit and unyielding honesty, could still be of service to the
American workingmen. So Eugene Debs, in a case that stands
without parallel in his entire career, simply permitted his dues
to lapse and his membership in the IWW to expire.

[4]

WHEN EUGENE DEBS helped to establish the Industrial Workers
of the World in 1905, he selected a method that defeated his own

purpose. Debs and his colleagues conceived of the IWW as a powerful instrument in the campaign for industrial unions. They confidently expected that the IWW would soon demonstrate its superiority over the craft unions, and that the majority of craft unionists would rally to the standard of the New Unionism. This failed to happen for several reasons: the employers made concessions to the AFL, but fought viciously against the IWW. Many workers had a financial stake in the insurance funds of the established unions, and they were unwilling to sacrifice these benefits. The workers' own sense of labor solidarity drove them into the largest federation, the AFL, and mere habit tended to keep them there. The AFL knew the importance of stable locals, signed contracts, and control of working conditions.

Thus the formation of the IWW tended to delay rather than to promote the campaign for industrial unions and socialism. Eugene Debs always argued that the labor movement should strive for the complete destruction of the wage system. But in 1905, by his own action, he isolated himself from the great majority of the organized workers, who still clung to the AFL. The leaders of the AFL denied everything that Debs affirmed. Samuel Gompers was not merely a craft unionist; he also bitterly opposed the theory that the labor movement should fight for socialism or any other ultimate goal. His program was based on the improvement of living standards within the capitalist framework: More; Here; Now. Inadvertently, Debs had delivered the basic organizations of the workingmen, the trade unions, into the grip of Gompers' philosophy.

The example of his own American Railway Union doubtless inclined Eugene Debs toward the IWW, but the two cases were not the same. Only tortured reasoning could call the ARU a dual union. The ARU came into being because the established Brotherhoods had failed to organize many railroaders who were eager for organization. It was led by a group of men who already had immense prestige on the railroads. From its very origin, it scored overwhelming victories. By working among the unskilled and neglected crafts—the switchmen, section hands, the carmen —it achieved a membership greater than the combined strength of the Brotherhoods. It was able to extract signed contracts from two of the strongest corporations in the country, the Union Pacific and the Great Northern. If Debs and his colleagues had not founded the American Railway Union, the workingmen themselves would have established local organizations in hundreds of railroad towns.

The real reason behind Debs' infatuation with dual unionism was not related to the ARU. Eugene Debs considered every question in terms of the working class against the capitalist class, and he absolutely refused to compromise with his chosen enemy. When he became convinced that the AFL was simply an auxiliary of "Mark Hanna's Civic Federation," he became a bitter opponent of the AFL. But even so, this opposition was qualified. Debs did not try to destroy the AFL, and he always supported its strikes. He merely refused to join it, refused to try to change it from within, refused to dirty his hands by contact with Samuel Gompers' federation. As he commented in his letter to the *Social Democratic Herald:* "I have simply joined a trade union that suits me. That's all."

In several other instances, Debs chose a method that defeated his goal. Each of these mistakes stemmed from his habit of regarding every question as a "purely class question." Thus, even though the Party could have gained members and spread its doctrines by participation in several reform movements, Debs always refused to co-operate with any reform party to achieve a limited objective. In June, 1903, Henry Demarest Lloyd tried to enlist Debs' support for a municipal ownership campaign in Chicago. Debs replied that he did not believe "that single taxers, socialists and anti-socialist trade unionists can successfully harmonize upon any question whatsoever. . . . Experience has satisfied me of the futility of such an undertaking, however promising the prospect might seem. I have long since determined to stick to the main issue and stay on the main track, no matter how alluring some of the byways may appear." Debs' attitude was fully supported by the Socialist Party, which had an unqualified rule against any alliance with nonsocialist political parties. This policy caused the Party to miss many opportunities to educate workingmen outside its ranks, but the

Party's attitude toward the Negro people was even more short-sighted.

Many leaders of the Socialist Party, either consciously or unconsciously, had ill-concealed prejudice toward Negroes. Thus, in the *Social Democratic Herald* for May, 1902, Victor Berger wrote: "There can be no doubt that the negroes and mulattoes constitute a lower race—that the Caucasians and indeed even the Mongolians have the start on them in civilization by many thousand years—so that negroes will find it difficult ever to overtake them." Berger's indictment of the "barbarous behavior of the American whites toward the negroes" would scarcely have made his article palatable either to Negroes or scientists.

Eugene Debs' attitude on this question was quite different. His numerous organizing trips through the South had convinced him that white workingmen would be exploited so long as the Negroes were held in an inferior position. As early as January, 1898, Debs ironically wrote from Montgomery, Alabama: "It is no longer the pauper labor of Europe, but of the United States that we need to be 'protected' against. Congress should promptly erect a tariff barrier along Mason and Dixon's line." On his lecture tours of the Southern states, many of which were sponsored by branches of the AFL or of the YMCA, Debs always refused to speak before segregated audiences. In several cases he threatened to cancel engagements rather than yield to local prejudice.

Debs' firm stand against racial prejudice was not solely due to general good will. He was convinced that any racial or religious division was harmful to the entire labor movement. A statement he made in 1903 helps to illuminate this attitude: "The convention of the American Railway Union which resulted in the great railroad strike of 1894, after a fierce and protracted debate, turned down the Negro and this was one of the factors in our defeat. The leaders of the opposition, as I remember them, proved subsequently to have been traitors to the union, sent to the convention, doubtless, at the instigation of the corporations to defeat the unity of the working class."

When he did encounter discrimination against Negroes, Debs'

wrath fairly boiled over. One day when he was carrying his two heavy grips away from the railroad station in a small Southern town, he passed a group of local loafers sitting along a rail fence. A voice from the fence said, "There's a nigger that'll carry your grips," and an accompanying hand pointed across the street. A second fence-sitter observed, "That's what he's here for," and a third, "That's right, by God." Debs described these philosophers in the *International Socialist Review:* "They were ignorant, lazy, unclean, totally void of ambition, themselves the foul products of the capitalist system and held in the lowest contempt by the master class, yet esteeming themselves immeasurably above the cleanest, most intelligent and self-respecting negro, having by reflex absorbed the 'nigger' hatred of their masters."

Debs soon received, in answer to his article, an anonymous letter, which predicted that the Socialists would "lose more votes than you think" if they insisted on equality for the Negroes. The letter was signed, "A stanch member of the Socialist Party." Debs printed this advice in the *International Socialist Review*, and furiously replied that the Party "would be false to its historic mission, violate the fundamental principles of Socialism, deny its philosophy and repudiate its own teachings if, on account of race considerations, it sought to exclude any human being from political and economic freedom."

But Debs refused to concede that poor Negroes were in a worse position than poor white people. When the Party convention of 1903 resolved to make a special fight for the rights of Negroes, Debs opposed the action. He expressed his "hope that the convention may repeal the resolution on the Negro question. The Negro does not need them and they serve to increase rather than diminish the necessity for explanation." Debs then argued: "We have nothing special to offer the Negro, and we cannot make separate appeals to all the races. The Socialist party is the party of the whole working class, regardless of color —the whole working class of the whole world."

So the Socialist Party, immobilized by Berger's prejudice and Debs' oversimplified analysis, failed to adopt a specialized program for the Negro people. When race prejudice was thrust at

Debs, he always publicly repudiated it. He always insisted on absolute equality. But he failed to accept the view that special measures were sometimes needed to achieve this equality. After Debs had decided that the main problem was the emancipation of the workingmen, he refused to be concerned with lesser problems, although he himself had argued that white workers would never be free so long as Negroes were oppressed.

Debs' beliefs on dual unionism, co-operation with reform parties, and the problems of the Negro people, all flowed from a common source. He was determined to hew to a revolutionary program and not be diverted by reform movements. If his mind failed to grasp a direct connection between a proposed reform and socialism, he refused to waste time with the reform. Then argument became futile; he could not be swayed. His basic convictions had been set in a steel mold by the teachings of his father and Victor Hugo, and Debs never doubted them. This gave rise to an almost mystical faith in the dictates of his inner self. Always willing to concede his fallibility on minor issues, he went his own way on basic policy. In each case he sought justification in that most private of all places, his conscience. Debs had supported his resignation from office in the Brotherhood of Locomotive Firemen by saying: "I do not consider that I have made any sacrifice whatever; no man does, unless he violates his conscience." In the quarrel about his affiliation to the IWW, he again said, "I would do anything but violate my conscience. That I will not do and that you will not ask." His conscience was the Great Umpire, and Debs was the only spectator near enough to hear the umpire's decisions.

CHAPTER XIV

◻

[1]

FOR sheer novelty and drama, the political show staged by the Socialists in 1908 has few equals. The Party managers proved that they had originality, a quality rare in American politics. Scorning ambiguity and caution, the Socialists candidly stated their beliefs and still remained two steps ahead of the opposition. The resulting campaign was rich with humor, with confident abandon, and, ultimately, with a touch of tragedy. Much of the interest arose from Eugene Debs' marathon performance. He spoke from five to twenty times a day for sixty-five consecutive days. This in itself was not a record—William Jennings Bryan made six hundred speeches during his campaign in 1896. But Debs in 1908 was fifty-two years old, subject to rheumatism, lumbago, and chronic headaches, and was widely rumored to be half dead. Also, Debs began his campaign immediately after having finished an exhausting lecture tour.

The campaign started ominously for the Socialists. It was apparent that Bryan, the Boy Orator of the Platte, would be the Democratic nominee. William Howard Taft was draped with the personal endorsement and trust-busting mantle of Theodore Roosevelt. Against these candidates, the Socialists could not hope for many votes from the reformers. And the Socialists could not agree among themselves about either platform or candidates. Behind the Party's debonair face, two factions were jockeying for place and power.

The top offices in the Party were largely held by professional men. Morris Hillquit, Seymour Stedman, and Job Harriman were lawyers. Victor Berger, Max Hayes, A. M. Simons, John Spargo, Fred Heath, and John Work were all editors or writers. These men wanted to base the Party on the craft unions and the reform vote. But the Party's left wing, as represented by

Debs and Haywood, emphasized the problems of the unskilled, unorganized workingmen and the poor farmers.

This basic cleavage about policy dominated the Socialist national convention, which opened in Chicago on May 10, 1908. After brief and covert sparring, the convention adopted a platform which bore the imprint of the left wing. The tone of the entire document followed from its Marxist opening: "Human life depends upon food, clothing and shelter. Only with these assured are freedom, culture and higher human development possible." Eugene Debs, working at his desk in Girard, Kansas, must have been gratified when the 1908 convention largely copied the platform he had written in 1904.

The radical leaders did not relax after this initial victory. Frank O'Hare, the young Socialist organizer who had worked with Debs in the Moyer-Haywood defense campaign, heard rumors that an attempt would be made to brush Debs aside as the Presidential nominee. According to the rumor, Hillquit, Berger, and J. Mahlon Barnes had perfected a detailed strategy to accomplish this purpose. Although this charge seems improbable, certainly Debs' flirtation with the IWW had convinced many leaders that he was unreliable. Also, both Berger and Barnes had an egocentric approach to the Socialist Party. No Socialist lecturer could enter Wisconsin until he had been approved by the state committee of the Party, on which Berger was the leading member. Barnes had been frequently accused of expelling on trumped-up charges all dissident members of the Pennsylvania organization. Whether these accusations were true or not, they had earned the Triumvirate—Barnes, Berger, and Hillquit—a reputation as petty conspirators.

The left wing promptly devised its own conspiracy to insure Debs' nomination. One of their men was chosen as chairman of the nominating session. He immediately recognized Phil Callery of Missouri, who made a fiery, tub-thumping speech for Eugene Debs. Then Seymour Stedman, the Socialist veteran from Chicago, spoke for several minutes about the uncertain state of Debs' health. He questioned that Debs could stand the rigors of an energetic campaign. He pointed out that Debs had recently undergone a throat operation. Finally he nominated A. M.

Simons, who had just been deposed as editor of the *International Socialist Review*. After Frank O'Hare had seconded Debs' nomination, the floor was given to Ben Hanford, Debs' running mate in 1904.

If there actually was a conspiracy to defeat Debs, Hanford destroyed completely its chances for success. A few days earlier Hanford had received a letter from Debs, and he now read this letter to the convention: "My health is about all that could be desired. So far as strength is concerned, I never had more to my credit, if as much. . . . I have never refused to do, so far as I was able, anything the party commanded me to do, and never shall. I have taken the nomination under protest, but I have no desire to run for office and a positive prejudice against the very thought of holding office. . . . My whole ambition—and I have a goodly stock of it—is to make myself as big and as useful as I can, as much opposed to the enemy and as much loved by our comrades as any man in the ranks. You need have no fear that I shall shirk my part in the coming campaign. I shall be in condition, and I hope there will be no good ground for complaint when the fight is over."

A tremendous roar of support rose from the delegates as soon as Hanford finished reading. A word from Debs had silenced all fears about his health. Questioning eyes had turned toward Stedman while Hanford was reading. When Hanford revealed that Stedman had seen the letter at the beginning of the convention, the questioning look changed to hostility. The rank and file delegate was convinced that a handful of insiders, guided by the Triumvirate, were trying to pull a fast one. Several other names were offered in nomination, and Victor Berger rightfully warned against forming a "one-man party," but the result was already determined. Debs received 90 per cent of the votes on the first ballot. Then Ben Hanford, the hero of the convention, was again nominated for Vice-President.

The convention had chosen the right man to head its ticket. Few people bothered to distinguish between Eugene Debs and the Socialist Party. Even the Terre Haute *Tribune*, a commercial newspaper, called it "an honor" to the city that the Socialists had nominated Debs, who was deemed outstanding for the "genuineness of his convictions, for his honesty, for his ability, and for his charming personality." The *Appeal to Reason* printed a poem in which Debs appeared as a modern Messiah:

> *I'll vote for Debs, for the Faith I have*
> *That we'll reach the promised land;*
> *A joyous vote and a splendid vote, and*
> *A clasp of a comrade's hand!*
>
> *I'll vote for Debs for the Hope I have*
> *That shall flood the world with its light!*
> *And I must answer the call I hear*
> *That the working class unite!*

[2]

MEANWHILE Eugene Debs was in Girard, furiously grinding out copy for the *Appeal*. In his letter to Hanford, he had said: "In the coming campaign, however, I would prefer, if I had my choice, to see what I could do with my pen and give my tongue a rest. I feel as if I can write a campaign and make some of the enemy take notice that there are Socialists in the field." Debs' resolution on this score proved vain; he could not stay in the office. One day Fred Warren walked up to his desk and suggested that they stroll down to the town square of Girard, where a street carnival was being held. Debs readily agreed; county fairs were always a favorite with him. Although a huge crowd had gathered around the town square, there was no carnival. The attraction was a speech, with Debs as the featured speaker.

In his earlier years, Eugene Debs might have been thrown off balance by a request for an impromptu speech. Julius Wayland had written in 1898: "Mr. Debs is not an orator, nor can he be said to be graceful, but I never saw an audience to follow a talker with greater interest. He got the attention of the audience and they remained as if spellbound." Art Young, the famous cartoonist, was more critical of a speech about 1900 at the Academy of Music in New York City: "I was disappointed that night— not by what he said, but by his manner. I thought him too much like a school-boy elocutionist." Incessant practice had its effect on Debs' rhetoric and by 1908 he was generally recognized as one of the great American orators. The content of his speeches had captured control over the form, so that he could shuttle easily from royal indignation to irony to a gentle humor.

On May 23, 1908, there on the town square of Girard, Debs shouted to the farmers and small merchants that the rulers had always ground the workingmen beneath an iron heel. Crucifixion was the invariable reward of men who were generous and saw a higher vision: "He who has dared to voice the protest of the oppressed and downtrodden, has had to pay the penalty, all the way from Jesus Christ to Fred Warren . . . I am in revolt against capitalism because I love my fellow men, and if I am opposing you it is for what I believe to be your good, and though you spat upon me with contempt I would still oppose you to the extent of my power."

Debs made a bitter, slashing, angry attack on the Goulds and the Rockefellers, because these men stood as a barrier against the glorious vision he had seen. He pleaded with his audience to stand with him on the mountain peak and gaze down into the future: "When we are in partnership and have stopped clutching each other's throats, when we have stopped enslaving each other, we will stand together, hands clasped, and be friends. We will be comrades, we will be brothers, and we will begin the march to the grandest civilization the human race has ever known."

With those words, Eugene Debs hurled himself into the Presidential campaign. His desire to rest his tongue was hastily forgotten; by the first of June he was speaking three or four times a day in New York City. Before the major parties had even nominated their candidates, Debs was striving to fulfill his injunction to the Socialist convention: "The working class of the United States must be aroused this year and made to feel the quickening pulse, the throbbing hope and the stern resolve of the social revolution. . . . Duty to the cause transcends all else, and touching elbows, and hearts keeping time to the quick steps of the revolution, we march beneath the banner (no compromise) to certain victory."

Debs' speeches in New York inspired scenes of exultation. At one meeting a woman in the audience leaped to her feet and screamed, "There he is. There he is. Gene Debs. Not the missing link, but the living link between God and man." Such an incident was unusual but not unique; every speech by Debs tended to become a catharsis for his listeners. He unconsciously created an emotional tension that was bound to burgeon into ecstasy. He hurled his lean body back and forth across the platform until his shirt was a sodden rag plastered to his body. He crouched on the very edge of the platform, extended a gaunt forefinger at the audience, and literally drew them into the orbit of his mind. Each listener felt that Debs was talking to him personally, that the two of them were simply having a private and friendly talk. The atmosphere carried sincerity like an electric charge; few men were able to doubt the strength and the honesty of his sympathy for them. Even when the speech was over, dozens of people followed Debs to his hotel room, crowding the corridor in the hope that they could shake hands or exchange greetings. These men were personal admirers, not the job-seekers who customarily torment a Presidential candidate. But, just as the job-seekers almost killed Lincoln, so the admirers almost killed Debs. Seldom able to turn them away, Debs carelessly sacrificed both sleep and regular meals. His only complaint was made in a five-word note to Fred Warren: "My Dear Warren: Strenuous? Whew!"

Debs' reputation rested in considerable measure upon his own personality and his unquestioned contribution to the cause of the workingmen. But there was also a Debs Legend, which the Socialist propagandists had been cultivating for several years. Radical ministers, journalists, and poets turned out literally hundreds of pamphlets and articles about Eugene Debs. A few of these efforts had real literary merit; some were confined to the presentation of facts; but most of them were eulogies about the greatness of Debs' soul. These incongruous mixtures of religion and psychology found a sympathetic audience in the America of 1908. Every time a writer claimed that Debs "has a great soul," "is the greatest lover of us all," or "is a true disciple of Jesus Christ," the Socialist vote spurted upward.

These eulogists may be justly accused of mysticism, but they cannot be called insincere. Almost everybody who met Eugene

Debs had the same reaction. Scores of businessmen, who had no sympathy with Debs' socialism, still observed: "He's a great man," or "I love him." Heywood Broun later recorded a comment on this subject by a "hard-bitten Socialist": "Gene Debs is the only one who can get away with the sentimental flummery that's been tied onto Socialism in this country. Pretty nearly always it gives me a swift pain to go around to meetings and have people call me 'comrade.' That's a lot of bunk. But the funny part of it is that when Debs says 'comrade' it's all right. He means it. That old man with the burning eyes actually believes that there can be such a thing as the brotherhood of man. And that's not the funniest part of it. As long as he's around I believe it myself."

Debs' reputation was not the sole beneficiary from the influx of professional men after 1905. In that year the Intercollegiate Socialist Society was founded, with Jack London as chairman, to spread radicalism in the college communities. The Christian Socialist Fellowship supplied a second gospel to hundreds of pulpits. Socialist publications, with dozens of skilled journalists competing for jobs, took a leap forward. The New York *Call* began publication in May, 1908, with money that had been partially raised at Debs' lectures that month. Charles H. Kerr, publisher of the left-wing *International Socialist Review*, fired A. M. Simons and assumed the editorship himself, with an announcement that his journal aimed to please workers rather than college professors.

The Socialist election machinery was moving into high gear by early June. Then Mahlon Barnes, the campaign manager, invented a new piece of machinery. Barnes walked into a meeting of the National Committee and sheepishly said that he had an idea. He knew it sounded silly, but it might work. When he finished presenting the plan, his colleagues thought he was crazy. They were, in fact, a little apprehensive about Barnes' equilibrium; maybe he was getting to be as unreliable as Gene Debs. But Barnes continued his argument, and finally the committee agreed to give the plan a trial. Barnes proposed that the Party rent a locomotive and a sleeping car, load them with literature, and let them carry Eugene Debs across the country on a speaking tour. The train was immediately dubbed The Red Special.

The obstacle which had halted Barnes and the National Committee was the estimated expense—twenty thousand dollars. The Socialist press and a corps of speakers began efforts to raise this money by voluntary contributions, but Bill Haywood and Eugene Debs acted as if the problem had to be solved by them alone. Haywood had been frequently suggested as the Presidential nominee, but he had feared a split in the radical contingent to the Chicago convention and had withdrawn in favor of Debs. He now held a series of mammoth meetings in Ohio, Pennsylvania, Connecticut and New York; contributions poured in from each meeting. Barnes' idea had instantly seized the imagination of the Socialist rank and file. When Haywood shouted at an audience: "Well, Comrades, do you want to see Gene Debs and the Red Special," Jimmie Higgins was actually glad to empty the frayed pockets of his shiny black suit.

Eugene Debs, meanwhile, was visiting the Socialist encampments of the Southwestern states. Frank O'Hare, Oscar Ameringer, and Otto Branstetter, all natives of the region, had devised an institution that was perfectly suited to their purpose. The poor farmers of the Southwest, living miles from their closest neighbor, walled off by continuous drudgery and the difficulties of travel, were starved for any sort of recreation. O'Hare conceived the notion of annual encampments, sponsored by the Socialist Party, which would be a combined square-dance fest, socialist school, and revival meeting. Then Ameringer persuaded local merchants to finance the encampments by saying that it would bring them new business. The Socialist encampments aroused the same wild enthusiasm that had been aroused by the announcement of the Red Special. By 1908, scores of thousands of farmers were spending their annual vacations at these temporary tent colonies.

Debs spoke at several of these camps during early July. In every case the scene was precisely the same. One evening there were two or three organizers alone in a grove of trees near a small creek. The next morning a steady stream of wagons came into view across the prairie, a red flag waving from each whipsocket. Debs thought this was one of the greatest sights in the world—uneducated, poverty-stricken men who had brought their families fifty or a hundred miles in search of good talk and a little company. These men deserved the best he could give, and Debs spoke for hours while the sweat streamed down across his face. On July 4, he spoke at the picnic grounds in Coalgate, Oklahoma, to five thousand people. That night he wrote to Fred Warren: "thousands and thousands—woods full of 'em, all blazing with zeal for socialism." The next day he was in Oklahoma City, talking to three thousand spectators: "What can we promise you? Ostracism and persecution. We can promise you more. We can promise you victory in the interest of the human race." Men threw their dirty hats in the air, repeated phrases to themselves, threw their small coins into the blanket. One of them wrote in to the *Appeal:* "With the exception of the great Lincoln, where can we find the like of this man?"

Sometimes an elderly farmer would come out of the crowd yelling, "Gene, Gene, don't you remember me any more?" Many of these farmers were old-time members of the ARU who had been blacklisted and driven off the railways after the Pullman boycott. Debs always remembered them, "threw his long arms around them, pressed them to his heart until their eyes moistened in love and gratitude to the leader who had lost them their strike, their job and their home," as Oscar Ameringer wrote. Eugene Debs always felt a special kinship to the ARU veterans. One morning Dan Hogan, the chairman of the Party in Arkansas, paid Debs the usual fee of a hundred dollars for speaking at an encampment and then went with him to the railroad station. A woman was waiting for Debs on the platform. When she explained that she was the widow of an ARU striker, Debs guided her away from Hogan. Debs talked with the woman for several minutes, then bade her good-by and walked back to Hogan with the request: "Dan, will you lend me five bucks to pay my fare to Girard?"

By July 12 Debs was in Milwaukee, speaking to twenty-five thousand persons who paid admission to a Socialist picnic. Mingling with the audience was the celebrated journalist, Lincoln Steffens, who was writing a series of articles about the

Presidential candidates. Steffens was deeply impressed by the way that Debs crouched when he was speaking, the way his hands reached out and the sweat dripped from his chin and forehead, the way the speech was "smooth, correct and truly eloquent." But Steffens, like other reporters, became mystical in trying to explain the source of Debs' appeal: "It wasn't art that kept that Milwaukee crowd steaming out there in the sun and, at the close, drew it crushing down upon the orator. And it wasn't what he said, either; too much of the gratitude was expressed in foreign tongues. It was the feeling he conveys that he feels for his fellow men, as he does, desperately."

When Eugene Debs had finally escaped from his admirers, he was interviewed by Steffens at Victor Berger's home. The startling similarities and contrasts among these three men all emerged in the course of the interview. Steffens' amused eyes and devilish Van Dyke gave the precise impression of what lay inside his mind—a detailed acquaintance with corruption and violence had never shaken his faith that all men were really good men. Debs, gaunt, volatile, apostolic, expressed himself passionately on every point that Steffens raised. Berger was cautious, ponderous, scholarly, with carefully prepared opinions on every issue. It was appropriate that Steffens should ask the questions; the other two men had absolute faith in their own answers.

Steffens, with his usual bluntness, observed that Debs seemed ill-fitted to be President. Debs admitted it freely: "When Socialism is on the verge of success, the party will nominate an able executive and a clear-headed administrator; not—not Debs." The three-time candidate then explained that the Party had no hope of winning in 1908. It was in the race purely to educate the workingmen, and it did not want a single vote that was not a vote for socialism. Berger listened passively to these preliminaries; the real fun began when Steffens started asking about the Socialist program. Debs and Berger gave different answers. When Steffens asked how the Socialists would confiscate the trusts if they came to power, Debs replied tersely, "Take them." This statement brought Berger protesting from his chair: "No. No, you wouldn't. Not if I was there. And you shall not say it for the party. It is my party as much as it is your party, and I answer that we would offer to pay."

Before the day ended, Steffens had raised most of the objections usually made to socialism: It is visionary; it won't really solve anything; the workingmen will become lazy. And, in spite of Berger's attempts at censorship, Debs answered them all freely. The journalist must have been satisfied; his article in *Everybody's Magazine* was friendly to Debs. Just before the election, Steffens publicly announced his support of the Socialist nominee. His reasons were explained in his letter to Brand Whitlock, the mayor of Toledo: "And Brand, vote for Debs. Don't try to decide the election; don't choose between the two evils. Vote for that sweet, good, passionate lover of mankind who offers hope and service, and leave the rest to God and the rest of us." Steffens wrote to his sister that he would vote for Debs "as a protest and as an encouragement to the third party idea. I couldn't vote for either of the other parties; their candidates are good men, but blind."

Early in August, Debs was back at his desk in Girard, writing fervent appeals for contributions to the campaign fund. Three weeks later, six thousand dollars had been raised for the proposed trip, and J. Mahlon Barnes signed a contract with the railroad for the first half of the tour. The Red Special would leave Chicago on August 31, proceed to southern California, make its way up the coast to Washington, and return to Chicago on September 25. Every night a meeting would be held in a large city, and the train would stop briefly at small towns along the route.

The major parties were first astonished, then worried, by the success of the Socialist plans. Theodore Roosevelt, more than three years earlier, had written to a friend: "The growth of the socialistic party . . . [is] far more ominous than any populist or similar movement in times past." The fund raised by the Socialists in 1908 was even more "ominous"; it really seemed that radicalism was taking root in America. Desperation, largely unwarranted, crept into the campaign to "Stop Debs." Supporters of Taft and Bryan aimed blow after blow at the Socialists, but the Party managers were difficult men to hit. A good referee would have awarded them every round.

The first anti-Socialist broadside was fired by Samuel Gompers, who charged that the Republican Party was secretly financing the Red Special. J. Mahlon Barnes immediately made public every contribution to the Socialist treasury. There were few donations larger than ten dollars; the largest was two hundred. Debs added that he was opposed to all capitalists, whether Republican or Democratic, and that the Socialists got their money from men who believed in socialism. Perhaps by this time Gompers regretted having opened his mouth, but the *Social Democratic Herald* fired an even more pointed jibe on September 19: "Sam Gompers is trying to line up the labor fakirs for Bryan. But their enthusiasm does not last longer than the effect of the whiskey which produces it." The laugh was now on Gompers, whose appreciation of good bourbon was no secret in the labor movement.

Before the flurry against Gompers had subsided, several newspapers charged that the Socialist Party was a "foreign" organization. Barnes again answered by opening his books. He replied that more than 70 per cent of the forty thousand Socialists had been born in the United States, and another 20 per cent were immigrants from western Europe. The Socialist Party based its views on the writings of Karl Marx, who was German. But Marxism was a scientific analysis which applied to any capitalist society, said the socialists. Was mathematics a purely "American" science? they asked.

Although the Socialists continued to do a creditable job of refuting the charges made against them, their answers had little effect. The enemy's attacks were front-page news in the metropolitan dailies; the Socialist replies were often suppressed or buried on an inside page. The parties that controlled the newspapers could, to a great extent, control public opinion, and the Socialists were ill-equipped to compete with their opponents. Several major newspapers printed articles that were fair or even partial to Debs; but for the most part the Socialists were forced to rely on their own press, leaflets, and stump speakers.

This obvious handicap did not discourage Eugene Debs. On a brief tour through the corn states in late August, Debs found the same enthusiasm that he had noted six weeks earlier in the Southwest. His elation at this discovery is apparent from his let-

ter to a colleague: "The meetings out here are big as all out-
doors and red hot with enthusiasm. Ye Gods! But these are
pregnant days! The hosts pour in from all directions—men,
women, children and babies, and all of them, including the
babies, are up in arms against the capitalist system. The farmers
out here, thousands of them, are revolutionary to the core and
ripe and ready for action. Socialists are nearly as thick out here,
and quite as strictly strenuous, as the grasshoppers used to be.
The plutes will need a doctor and the preacher when the votes
are counted. The 'Red Special' is trump. The people are wild
about it and the road will be lined with the cheering hosts of
the proletarian revolution."

[3]

DEBS went to Chicago on August 30 and boarded the Red
Special for the first lap of his campaign. The sleeping car contained berths for Debs and his brother Theodore, for Stephen
Reynolds, and for Harry Parker, who had charge of the train.
Reynolds had just finished his campaign biography of the Socialist candidate, and his reward was a bunk on the Red Special.
The walls of the coach were lined with huge stacks of literature,
crowned by cardboard cartons of the bright red Socialist buttons. Other pamphlets and buttons, together with hundreds of
the huge "Debs and Hanford" posters, had been shipped ahead
to points along the route. Arrangements had been made to pick
up the local Party leaders in every state, so that they could
introduce Debs in their home localities. Every detail had been
worked out carefully. Painfully aware that they were spending a
hard-earned twenty thousand dollars, the Socialist managers
wanted to make every cent of it pay.

This worried planning contrasted strongly with the mood of
Jimmie Higgins. The huge crowd which gathered in Chicago's
station on August 30 was shouting, laughing, gaily waving red
flags at the standard-bearer. The atmosphere was alive with
hope; even the conservative Berger had predicted one and a
half million votes for Debs and Hanford. This jubilation was
shared by the occupants of the train. They all flaunted their

red lapel buttons, and Steve Reynolds even pinned his button to his pajamas every night. If he should die in his sleep, he explained, he wanted everybody to know that he "wasn't a Republican." The Red Special, moving with the jaunty air of a playboy, left Chicago that evening and headed west.

The Socialist candidate quickly revealed the tactics of his campaign. Two days later in Des Moines, he charged that the Republicans were tied hand and foot to Wall Street. William Howard Taft, said Debs, had been issuing antilabor injunctions for fifteen years. As for Bryan, his claim to represent both workers and employers was held up to ridicule. Such a feat, joked Debs, was just as impossible as it would be "to ride two horses at the same time, going in opposite directions."

A woman reporter from the Des Moines *News* boarded the train early the next morning to interview Debs. He received her in the best of spirits, even though he had not yet dressed for the day. Sitting on the arm of a seat, in his shirt-sleeves and without a collar, he answered all questions about the trip. Finally the reporter asked when the Socialists would elect a President, and Debs promptly replied that "in ten years they will at least be crowding the capitalists."

Eugene Debs was having the time of his life as the train moved across the prairies. Every day he met some old friend whom he had not seen for years. In Muscatine, Iowa, he was hailed by a man with whom he had worked on the Vandalia railroad thirty-five years earlier. Debs immediately threw his arms around his former companion, and the train was delayed while they exchanged gossip and good will. Dozens of ARU veterans presented themselves at the platform of the Red Special; one of them produced his membership card in the dead organization and commented that he "would rather have that than a king's ransom." The events held humor as well as devotion. In Corning, Iowa, a woman snorted derisively "Did you take one of them things?" to a man who held a Socialist pamphlet. The man shuffled his feet self-consciously, crammed the pamphlet hastily into a pocket of his overalls, then glared back at his tormenter.

In Omaha the train was decorated with red bunting by the

local Socialists. Red streamers floated from the roof, from the wheels, from the rear platform. As the Red Special hurtled across the prairies toward the West Coast, oncoming trains could identify it for miles. Flags and bandannas were waved from coach windows as the trains passed. Sympathetic engineers blew long, shrill blasts on their locomotive whistles. The tracks were lined with buggies which had come for miles; often the spectators crowded forward and forced the train to halt. Then Steve Reynolds and Theodore would circle through the crowd selling literature while Debs gave a brief talk from the observation platform. When the train moved on, it left old grizzled farmers gazing after it, scratching their heads and muttering, "By God, he's right."

The meetings in Colorado were large—five thousand in Denver and two thousand at an open-air gathering in Leadville— but these were dwarfed by the crowds in California. When the Red Special arrived in Santa Barbara at four o'clock in the morning, a huge throng of Socialists waited in the railroad yards. Debs genially rolled out of his berth and went out on the platform in his nightshirt to give a brief talk. In San Diego, fifteen thousand persons paid their way into an open-air speech, and Spring Stadium in Los Angeles was jammed on September 9.

The crowd was never disappointed; Debs was first-rate, whether he gave a prepared speech or had a rough-and-tumble scrap with hecklers in the audience. His meetings were often graced by several disrupters, but he was never flustered. One night a man in the front of the hall shouted that anybody who voted for socialism was throwing his vote away, and Debs flared back: "You argue that you are throwing your vote away. That's right. Don't vote for freedom—you might not get it. Vote for slavery—you have a cinch on that." Or there was the prosperous gentleman who angrily accused Debs of demagogy, and the speaker softly inquired: "If there are no classes, how can I array them against one another?"

When Debs arrived in Spokane, three thousand persons were waiting at the station, and an even larger number paid from fifteen to twenty-five cents to hear his speech. The crowd was entranced by his vigor and his spirit, but Eugene Debs was scarcely his normal self. He had given thirty long orations and more than a hundred brief ones in the previous two weeks. As far back as Kansas City, he had begun locking himself on the train and refusing to see anybody; then the appearance of some old friend always shattered the resolution. Theodore and Reynolds often tried to eliminate the need for a short speech by playing the *Marseillaise* to a crowd of farmers along the track. But the strains of the French anthem only made the farmers more determined to hear Debs, so the practice was quickly abandoned.

From that time on, Debs had spoken to every crowd that wanted to hear a speech. He was now so weary that he could hardly crawl out of his berth, and the sound of his voice had scarcely died out before he was back in bed. His throat felt raw and tired; a metal band seemed to be tightening across his forehead. Day after endless day, Debs drove himself out on the rear platform to smile and wave at the adoring hundreds, to tell them that man could be better than he was. But the time finally arrived when he just could not stand the pace. It became obvious that Debs would never finish the trip unless he conserved his energy. So Reynolds and Theodore worked out a trick. Theodore was almost a dead ringer for his brother, except that he was nine years younger. When a crowd in a station yard at night began to shout for Debs, Theodore turned up his coat collar, pulled down his hat brim, and stepped onto the back platform. Reynolds hastily announced that "Comrade Debs is quite tired; we are now behind schedule; we have a very important meeting in the next town; Comrade Debs will not speak." Then Theodore quickly stepped back into the coach.

A few days of this favored treatment gave Debs a chance to partially regain his strength. The accustomed fire came back into Debs' voice as he repeated, in town after town, the speech he had given four months earlier in Girard. At Billings, Montana, he ate a tremendous steak dinner, then strode through the clear autumn air to the public library and addressed three thousand from the steps: "Our conduct is largely determined by our economic relations. If you and I must fight each other to exist, we will not love each other very hard." And in St. Paul he jestingly told another six thousand people: "Competition was natural and constructive once, but do you think you are competing today? Many of you think you are. Against whom? Against Rockefeller? About as I would if I had a wheelbarrow and competed with the Sante Fe from here to Kansas City."

The Socialist candidate was still leaning heavily upon Theodore. Acting as stand-in for his brother was the smallest part of Theodore's job. He arranged for hotel rooms, fended off the adoring Socialists, saw that Debs did nothing but let words come from his tiring throat. Even more important, Theodore took the main responsibility for answering the heavy flow of correspondence. Most of the letters moved through Theodore's typewriter, Debs himself did not even see many of them. Eugene had never learned to use a typewriter because, as he said, "A machine is too cold"; but he occasionally wrote a brief note in his forceful handwriting.

As his train rolled across Minnesota, Debs finally read Lincoln Steffens' article in *Everybody's Magazine:* "Eugene V. Debs on What the Matter Is and What to Do about It." He excitedly read portions of it aloud to his companions, and his face flushed with pleasure at the tone with which Steffens reported their interview. Debs admired Steffens' writing as much as Steffens had admired Debs' oratory. When he had finished the article, Debs wrote a brief note to the author: "You have written from and been inspired by a social brain, a social heart and a social conscience and if you are not a socialist I do not know one."

The arrangements for the trip had been amazingly thorough. With the foresight born of practice, the Party managers had accurately estimated the literature sales, so that a steady stream of leaflets had been delivered to the Red Special for sale to the workingmen and farmers. Thousands of copies of Reynolds' biography of Debs, with a rising sun printed in gold on the red cover, had been sold since the train left Chicago. But the very success of the literature sales and collection speeches had created an unexpected problem. The Red Special was now carrying twenty-one hundred dollars in small change. In Duluth this money was loaded in cloth sacks and carried into the city for deposit in a bank. Two men spent the entire day carrying those

sacks of money from bank to bank, but not a single commercial
house in Duluth was willing to accept a deposit by the Socialist
Party. So the two men carried their sacks of money back to the
train. They were completely exhausted. The sacks held nineteen
thousand different coins, and weighed more than two hundred
pounds. When they told the sad story of their adventure, Debs
laughed until the tears ran down his cheeks.

That night a group of ARU veterans from Two Harbors
journeyed the forty miles to Duluth to hear their old leader
Gene Debs. After the speech they held an all-night celebration
in Debs' hotel room. Tired as he was, the Socialist candidate
was the most hilarious member of the party.

When the Red Special passed through Chicago on September
25, ending its western tour, it had travelled nine thousand miles
and made a hundred and ninety stops. Debs had spoken to two
hundred and seventy-five thousand persons in less than a
month.

The metropolitan newspapers were still laying down a relentless barrage against the Socialists. The opposing parties had accused Debs of belittling the national flag, and he flared back
that "the national flag has been polluted by the plutocracy who
have used it to shield themselves in their evil doing. It is not
at present the flag of the patriot but has become the flag of
predatory wealth, in its exploitation of the working class and its
ravages upon the people generally. This is the only objection
the Socialists have ever urged against the colors of the United
States, and in this position they have the indorsement of every
true patriot in the land."

The attacks on Debs' patriotism were soon dwarfed by the
attacks on his honesty. When his train reached Detroit, the local
Free Press ran a screaming headline:

Debs, in Luxury,
Ignores Crowd
Sleeps in Magnificent Palace Car
While Followers Wait
in Vain
Flunkies Guard Leader
From the Common Herd

Several trade-union papers tried to counteract the stories in the commercial press. The *Journal* of the Railroad Switchmen, saying that Debs was "loved by his fellowmen because of his honesty, for his many sacrifices to the cause of humanity," called upon all switchmen to "Cast a UNION ballot for UNION men" by voting for Debs and Hanford. The *Miners' Magazine*, published by the Western Federation of Miners, commented on Stanford University's act in closing its chapel to a speech by Debs: "It is doubtful if Christ returned to earth and preached the same doctrines that He proclaimed nineteen hundred years ago that He would have been admitted to the chapel of Stanford University." But these articles in the labor and radical press were like a small boy blowing into the face of a mighty wind. The enemy carried the power.

The Socialist meetings were characterized by a long line of children, waiting to present Debs with bouquets of red roses and each received a kiss in return. Debs always delayed his speech in order to have a private talk with the junior Socialists. In one small town, a group of school children had long planned to be down at the tracks when the Red Special passed, but the train was running ahead of schedule and threatened to pass through their town before they were dismissed from school. When Debs heard of this from local Socialists on the train, he insisted that they should stop and wait. At last the children came running headlong down to the tracks, and Debs sat on the back platform and talked to them. He explained that some children in the big cities had never seen a blade of grass or a cow. He told about children in the coal and textile towns who were sent to work at the age of nine or ten years. The men on the Red Special, he said, wanted to win a new chance for all children.

The gigantic wave of the Socialist campaign drew thousands of men into torchlight parades, open-air meetings, screaming, hysterical receptions for the Red Special. When Debs marched through Toledo, Mayor Brand Whitlock strode by his side; and that evening Congressman Isaac R. Sherwood applauded Debs' attack on the capitalist system. Five thousand people crowded Convention Hall in Rochester to hear Debs say: "The capitalist refers to you as mill hands, farm hands, factory hands, machine hands—hands, hands! . . . A capitalist would feel insulted if you called him a hand. He's a head. The trouble is he owns his head and your hands."

New York City furnished the grand climax of the campaign. When the Red Special pulled into Grand Central Station, the crowd jammed the platform trying to get a glimpse of the Socialist candidate. People were knocked down, trampled underfoot, a few were injured. Debs came out on the observation platform and vainly tried to calm the shouting, cheering mass. Realizing that it was hopeless, he left the station by a rear door and made a wide detour to reach his room at the Grand Union Hotel. The next day he spoke twice, at the American Theatre and at the Hippodrome. Ten days in advance the ten thousand tickets to the Hippodrome were sold out, and that evening they were being sold for five dollars each on the sidewalk in front of the hall. When Debs appeared on the stage, the audience cheered for fifteen minutes, weeping, laughing, filling the air with red flags. The New York *Times* called it the greatest political meeting ever held in the city. But the final word was left for Joshua Wanhope, the Socialist leader and ex-sailor. Wanhope looked at the crowd, then drily commented, "If Roosevelt were here I believe he would remark, with amazement, upon the astonishing increase of 'undesirable citizens!'"

The following day Debs invaded the tenement district on the lower East Side of Manhattan, where Morris Hillquit was locked in a bitter campaign for Congress. The district had been filled for months with hordes of young Socialists, who passed out literature and gave hundreds of street-corner speeches. But Debs' appearance marked the "red-letter day of the campaign," according to Hillquit. Ernest Poole, the novelist, left his own record of Debs' laborious progress through the tenement section: "I stood near him for hours one night on a truck that slowly plowed its way through a roaring ocean of people as far as the eye could see, all up and down dark tenement streets. No loudspeakers, no brass bands. The truck stopped and Debs leaned out with both arms raised, smiling over the roaring crowd. Stillness came. And then only his voice was heard—a voice that could do with a crowd what it willed, not because of the mind behind it but because of the great warm heart which the crowd felt speaking there. . . . I listened to him, tingling deep. What could I myself do for the cause?"

On Sunday afternoon, October 11, Debs addressed two meetings in Philadelphia, and that night a third in Camden. When he finished the Camden address he was exhausted and cold with sweat. But he was immediately hurried into an open car and driven to the ferry for the forty-minute trip back to Philadelphia. During the night he was seized by a violent chill, which developed into the grippe. Debs missed his Monday speech in Newark, but no more than that. None of his other audiences guessed that he had been ill. He certainly seemed well to a Pittsburgh reporter, who went to a meeting intending to ridicule the Socialist candidate. The city editor deleted the sections most favorable to the speaker, but the remainder still read: "With his bursts of oratorical splendor and flowery panegyric, Debs lifted his hearers out of themselves and was compelled to stop for minutes at a time because of the rounds of deafening applause."

The Red Special halted in Harper's Ferry so that Debs could visit the memorial to John Brown. After he had spent several minutes gazing at this monument to his idol, Debs issued a statement to the press: "The Socialist Party is carrying on the work begun by John Brown."

As his train rolled back into the Midwest, huge crowds gathered to hear his speeches. William Howard Taft had barely filled the Music Hall in his own city of Cincinnati, but Debs' meeting in the same hall was forced to turn people away. When Taft spoke, admission was free; it cost a dime minimum to hear Debs. The two candidates spoke on the same night in Evansville, and again more persons paid to hear the Socialist than went free to hear the Republican. Debs' managers, giddy with success, decided to press their advantage. They offered to let Taft address the Socialist rally for twenty minutes if Debs were accorded similar rights at the Republican rally. The offer was rejected.

On October 23, Debs gave seventeen speeches as he went across Illinois. One of them seemed like a triumphant homecoming. In Woodstock, Illinois, the Socialist spoke to five hundred people from the steps of the jail. Then he had a long chat with George Eckert, the sheriff who had once been his jailer, and showed his companions the cell in which he had been confined for six months.

When Debs gave his last Red Special speech at the University of Wisconsin, the St. Louis *Mirror* predicted that he would get one and a half million votes and that the 1912 election would be a clear-cut contest between capitalism and socialism. The five hundred thousand people to whom Debs had spoken had provided fifty thousand new subscribers for the *Appeal to Reason.*

Bill Haywood joined the Red Special in Chicago, where he and Debs, on November 3, marched at the head of a parade of fourteen thousand workingmen. The long, swaying file extended more than two miles. An estimated sixteen thousand spectators heard Debs' address in the Seventh Regiment Armory. Not since 1895, when Debs was released from Woodstock, had the Windy City seen such a political meeting. Every hand seemed to be holding the red-and-gold jacket of *Eugene V. Debs: His Life, Writings, and Speeches*, by Stephen M. Reynolds. The air was alive with jerking flags, hats, canes, and fierce optimism. Debs, his body racked with fatigue, scraped together the energy for a fiery speech.

At that point, Debs had been moving on sheer determination for two months. Since Camden he had been suffering from the grippe. He had kept laughing and talking, refusing to let himself quit. But the day had arrived when determination was no longer enough. As Debs spoke in Terre Haute on the last day of the campaign, his voice was so weak that he could scarcely be heard. The president of the local district of the United Mine Workers, who had a huge, booming voice, easily overshadowed Debs' performance at that final rally. But the Socialist enthusiasm was unshaken in Terre Haute. Debs' appearance at his polling place, the Friendly Inn, was the signal for several men to crowd around him and grip his hand.

Debs sat quietly at home with Kate and Theodore to wait for the results. When the count was complete, it proved very disappointing to the Socialists. Their vote was 420,973; it had

not changed since 1904. Bryan's attacks on monopoly had won
the reform vote. The upswing from the depression of 1907 had
given the Republicans a chance to pose as the party of prosperity. The AFL leaders had influenced a large portion of the
labor movement, and the big newspapers had influenced everybody. It was more difficult to win an election than the Socialists
had thought.

A strange occurrence in Terre Haute also cast light on the
reasons for the disappointing Socialist vote. Debs did not get a
single vote in his own precinct, although he knew of several
supporters, including himself, who had voted there. He hastily
said that the error probably was caused by defects in the voting
machines, which had been used for the first time. Debs' explanation of the local results may have been accurate, but it
seems likely that several metropolitan cliques had deliberately
miscounted the Socialist vote.

The *Appeal to Reason* refused to be staggered by the outcome.
Its headline comment was: "Taft is elected; Bryan defeated;
Debs victorious." Katherine Debs had reason to think otherwise—her husband was dreadfully ill for a month after the
election. By the year's end, the *Appeal* itself might have doubted
its brazen assertion; its paid subscription list had again fallen
to the normal three hundred and ten thousand readers a week.

Probably the man least discouraged was the Socialist candidate. Before the votes had even been counted, he issued a press
statement: "The campaign is ended, and my very first thought
is of the kindness shown me and the loyal support given me in
every part of the country. While at times the exactions were
trying, I was sustained every hour by the loving care and unflagging support of comrades. To me this was the most beautiful
and satisfying feature of the campaign. It expressed the true
spirit of Socialist comradeship, which is the making of our
movement, and which will sustain it through every ordeal until
it is finally triumphant."

CHAPTER XV

◻

[1]

AT THE END of the Red Special campaign, Eugene Debs was exhausted. Rheumatism and lumbago plagued him as old and serious afflictions. Vicious headaches had recurred continually since the sunstroke ten years earlier in West Virginia. Recognizing that her husband could no longer shrug off these complaints, Kate urged him to take a long rest. Debs, with rare exercise of common sense, actually avoided the lecture platform for nearly a year, but he made numerous short trips and wrote three or four articles each week for the *Appeal to Reason*.

Early in 1907, when Debs first joined the staff of the *Appeal*, Wayland and Warren asked him to move to Girard, Kansas, where the weekly was located. Debs refused because, as he said: "I can't make up my mind to leave Terre Haute. It has always been my home. I was born here and my father and mother are both buried here. No, I shall never leave Terre Haute. It shall always be home to me, even if my work will not permit staying at home as much as I should like to."

Debs did, however, maintain a room in a Girard hotel, and he spent much of his time in the small Kansas town. Although his only intimates there were the employees of the *Appeal*, he was soon well known to the local citizens. In Girard as in Terre Haute, Debs quickly gained a following among the children. When he tired of working at his desk or in his hotel room, he strolled down to the public square to sit in the sun. Inevitably, a crowd of young children soon gathered around him. One day Fred Warren found him there, acting as sponsor and judge of a jumping contest. Debs had offered a quarter to the best broad jumper, and the competition was keen. Warren was forced to wait until the prize had been awarded; then he and Debs walked over to Debs' room at the Osborn House. Their conversation was soon interrupted by a timid knock. The intruder was a young boy, who had arrived at the public square immediately after the close of Debs' competition. Not wanting to miss a second chance, the boy anxiously inquired: "Mr. Debs, when are you going to have another jumping contest?"

Debs soon became almost a member of the family to most of the *Appeal's* staff. One evening at dinnertime he walked into the Warren's kitchen with a huge package under his arm. Ordering Mrs. Warren into the living room, he prepared a dinner of beefsteak and biscuits. The three Warren boys howled with laughter when Debs brought the meal into the dining room. He was still wearing his gray trousers and vest, but he had removed his coat, rolled up his sleeves, and was wearing one of their mother's dainty aprons. After dinner Debs spent more than an hour telling stories and playing jokes, with himself as the usual scapegoat. These tactics quickly established him as a prime favorite in the house. Fred Warren once returned from the office to find his son Carl, then eight years old, sitting quietly and gazing into space. When Warren asked the cause of this unusual preoccupation, Carl replied that he was wishing Mr. Debs was his father. Warren was not upset; he could understand Carl's wish.

When he was with his friends in Girard, Debs often joked about the unfortunate plight of the people who lived in cities. Decades of travel had not lessened his dislike for urban life; they had, in fact, strengthened it. Chicago, for Eugene Debs, was "that great madhouse I escaped from." He said that his only happy time in the Windy City "was when they locked me up." And he made at least one cruel jest about the wretchedness of city dwellers: "They are strangers, not because they don't know each other, but because they do."

The Socialist leader slipped naturally into the folkways of Girard, where even the cobblestones seemed curved to fit his feet. Southeastern Kansas, the center of the Bible Belt and the prohibition movement, proved congenial ground to a man who scorned religion and charged the prohibitionist "fanatics" with spreading a "gospel of gloom." There was actually nothing strange in this apparent contradiction. Debs' attitudes toward both religion and prohibition stemmed from one conviction:

each man should be free to go his own way. Nor was Debs vitally interested in either of these issues. As in the case of municipal ownership or the problems of Negroes, he tended to regard them as secondary problems overshadowed by the campaign for socialism.

In spite of his dislike for the organized church, Debs was never a militant atheist. His few references to religion were usually concerned with the political activities of specific ministers and priests, or with sectarian divisions in the trade unions. On the Great Plains he was among a deeply religious folk. But they had not enrolled in the legions of Christian pacifism. Far from it. They had enrolled Jesus in the legions of social justice. This view was accepted completely by Eugene Debs, who seldom troubled to seek out the original source. He had learned about Marxism from the popularizers of Karl Marx. Similarly he learned about Christianity from the tent preachers of the Midwest.

In March, 1914, on the very eve of the European war, Debs referred to Jesus of Nazareth as "the master proletarian revolutionist and sower of the social whirlwind." He denied the divinity of Jesus, but lauded Him as "the grandest and loftiest of human souls—as real, as palpitant, and as pervasive as a historic character as John Brown, Abraham Lincoln, and Karl Marx." The Prince of Peace, in Debs' opinion, "was of the working class and loyal to it in every drop of his hot blood to the very hour of his death. He hated and denounced the rich and cruel exploiter as passionately as he loved and sympathized with his poor and suffering victims."

This interpretation of Christianity was heartily endorsed by the Socialists of the Southwest. Regarding liquor as well, Debs' viewpoint was not unpopular. His reputation as a heavy drinker was based on a few isolated cases, which had been blown into a spectacular portion of the Debs Legend. He had learned to use wine because of his French ancestry, and whiskey because most trade unions met in saloons during the early days. But liquor had never become either a necessity or a habit. During the six years that Debs worked for the *Appeal*, Fred Warren never saw him take a drink.

Basically, the Socialist movement on the Great Plains was a perfect foil for the personality of Eugene Debs. Among the immigrant workingmen of the Eastern slums, Socialism was often regarded with deep piety. It was the object of fierce, unrelenting effort, which forbade all jesting. But a man starving, dying of tuberculosis, his children in rags, cannot wait forever, so the Eastern socialists seized any chance to make a small gain, to escape from the ravages of poverty.

Both of these attitudes were reversed in the Southwest, where the present was tolerable but socialism held the promise of a golden future. Many prairie farmers sneered at immediate demands and insisted upon a clear-cut fight for the ultimate goal. These impossibilists, as they were called, were unable to preserve a serious attitude toward any desire. They commonly fought their heads off to win a point, and then jeered at the effort they had made. This pose had become second nature to the Westerners, the dauntless hero laughing as he pulls the beard of God. Prairie radicals, while they paid grudging respect to shrewd, tight-fisted businessmen, also admired generosity, courage, and rebelliousness, three qualities exaggerated to enormous power in Eugene Debs.

To most American Socialists, Debs had a status near to divinity. He was adored, almost worshipped, but he was also mocked by the men who knew him best. The Debs Legend held two sets of anecdotes about the Socialist leader: those which emphasized his unusual aspects, and those designed to prove that he was, after all, just an ordinary person. The second category is typified by a story about Debs' speech at a Labor Day picnic in Terre Haute. These picnics were always gay, rollicking affairs, with the beer getting more attention than the orator. But this day Debs was in fine fettle, holding his audience spellbound for more than two hours. Such a long speech in hot weather left him very thirsty, and he was glad to share several schooners of beer with the men around the barrel. As usual, he was unable to hold his liquor, so he soon lay down under a tree on the brink of the bluff. Some of his friends, also rather drunk, quickly took advantage of their chance and rolled him over the low cliff into the river. They then stood on the bank and slapped their thighs as he emerged from the river, water dripping from his clothing and slushing in his shoes.

This story was true, but its popularity did not rest on its truth. The plain fact was that these men enjoyed the humiliation of their chosen hero. Another anecdote persisted in spite of its dubious accuracy and doubtful parentage. One night in Debs' youth, according to the story, his mother was awakened by the sound of footsteps climbing to the attic. It was long after the family curfew, so she went to investigate. The attic held only her two sons. Since both of the boys seemed to be sleeping soundly, Daisy relied on her intuition. She made Theodore climb out of bed for a strapping. Shivering from cold, sleep, and bewilderment, the younger son merely tightened his jaw and said nothing. Eugene Debs, the actual culprit, let his brother take the whipping. Theodore was justly angry for several days, but even this treachery was not enough to shake his adoration of his brother. And Eugene Debs, so the story ends, became so ashamed of his rôle in the affair that he never mentioned it again.

[2]

DURING the spring and summer of 1909, Debs must have felt like a man on vacation. Although he did his share of work for the *Appeal*, it was a novelty for him to eat regularly and to sleep in a bed rather than a coach seat. His health mended rapidly in the leisurely atmosphere of Girard and Terre Haute. Debs' love of the public platform, his fondness for a more strenuous life, would inevitably have whirled him out of this office routine. But his return to the lecture circuit was doubtless hastened by an action of the Federal courts.

The Postal authorities had taken exception to two articles in the *Appeal to Reason* of January 5, 1907, at the height of the defense campaign for Moyer, Haywood, and Pettibone. The *Appeal's* protest in this case was based on a contention that the defendants' extradition was illegal, that they were actually kidnapped. When the Supreme Court refused to grant habeas corpus, Debs termed their decision "the blackest chapter in the history of that tribunal." He further charged that the verdict meant that "the workingman has no right the capitalist is bound to respect."

Fred Warren, in the second disputed article, had gone much further. A former governor, Taylor of Kentucky, was wanted in his native state for questioning in connection with the murder of a political rival. Taylor had fled to Indiana, and the governor refused to extradite him. Warren decided that this case was analogous to the situation of Haywood, except that Haywood was a labor leader and Taylor was a capitalist politician. In order to prove his point, Warren offered a thousand-dollar reward to anybody who seized Taylor and turned him over to the Kentucky authorities.

These articles by Debs and Warren had stimulated two separate indictments for sending "scurrilous, defamatory and threatening" literature through the mails. The case against Warren, after being postponed for more than two years, was finally decided in the spring of 1909. The editor of the *Appeal* was sentenced to six months in jail and a fine of five thousand dollars. If this verdict were permitted to stand, separate indictments on the same charge could be brought against the other responsible editors of the newspaper. The *Appeal to Reason* would be put out of business. So the decision was immediately appealed to a higher court, and plans were made to enlist public sympathy on this issue.

Like the Moyer-Haywood campaign, the Warren defense was based on joint action by the *Appeal to Reason* and Eugene Debs. Several conferences were held in Girard to perfect the arrangements. Finally terms were announced for the lecture tour by Debs, under the national auspices of the *Appeal:* The local sponsor in each city agreed to sell a thousand tickets at twenty-five cents each, of which fifteen cents went to the *Appeal*, and each lecture ticket carried a forty-week subscription to the Girard weekly. Thus every speech by Debs would gain a thousand readers for the *Appeal*.

The tour began in November at Fred Warren's home town of Rich Hill, Missouri. Debs was profoundly convinced that there was no basis for the indictment; the entire case against Warren seemed a frame-up to the Socialist orator. His voice had new zest as he tried to make the people of Rich Hill understand the greatness of their local son. Fred Warren, said Debs, was one of the modern apostles of freedom: "All great movements are organized by the few and in their inception are unpopular, their principles are misrepresented and their leaders are compelled to pay the penalties which have always attached to those who have paved the way to better conditions for the human race." This idea was featured in every Debs speech for twenty years; his expression in Rich Hill was simply a rephrased version of his speech in Girard, May, 1908. His listeners long remembered his main point: that the Socialists were the forerunners of a new society, much as the early Christians had been forerunners, and the Socialists too were being crucified for their ideas.

As the tour went on, Debs became more and more outspoken in his criticism of the courts. He constantly repeated his earlier epigram: "Under capitalist misrule the judicial nets are so adjusted as to catch the minnows and let the whales slip through." Enormous crowds turned out to hear Debs lambast the Supreme Court. The circulation of the *Appeal* which was 368,791 when the tour began, averaged more than five hundred thousand for the year. The Postal authorities tried to halt this rise by ruling that all subscriptions given with tickets to Debs' lectures counted as free copies and could not be mailed second class. But Fred Warren simply ignored the ruling, and it became a dead letter.

Shortly before Christmas, Debs returned to Terre Haute to spend the holidays with Kate. Jubilant over the growing support for Warren, he was sparkling with stories about his travels. In October, while on a short swing through the East, he had spent an evening with two close friends whom he seldom met, Horace Traubel and William F. Gable. He was greatly amused by Gable, who owned a large department store in Altoona, Pennsylvania, and still contributed generously to radical causes. Debs later described the full extent of his friend's schizophrenia: "Gable never let his right hand know what his left hand did, because that hand was nearer his heart. Gable always gave money in cash. He never kept any record or any account of his contributions to the causes in which he believed."

Horace Traubel, in his own way, was just as peculiar as Gable. Traubel was one of the leading disciples of Walt Whitman, having been one of Whitman's literary executors. His entire life was spent in an effort to realize his idol's dream of a New Democracy. For thirty-eight years he published in Philadelphia a small newspaper, the *Conservator*, which he wrote, edited, and printed himself. Although Traubel was not a Socialist, his fervid humanitarianism attracted him to Debs, and he wrote one of the better poems about the Socialist leader. Debs responded by a glittering eulogy to Traubel: "In his fearless search for truth and his passionate demand for justice there is nothing too sacred for this brilliant iconoclast to attack and nothing too humble for him to love." In fact Debs, with literary taste much weaker than his father's, even asserted that Traubel "goes beyond his revered master." As in most instances, Debs was more concerned with a man's intentions than his accomplishments.

Debs was scheduled to open his winter tour on January 23, 1910, in Chicago. Just as he was preparing to leave Terre Haute, he was again stricken by the grippe. Kate urged him to cancel his first engagements, but Debs refused to hear of it. After all, the Chicago comrades had distributed thirty thousand copies of the *Appeal* to advertise his meeting. So a feverish Debs caught a train for Chicago and drove himself through a long oration. In the next eight days he gave fourteen lectures in Ohio, during February another twenty in Pennsylvania. The weather was extremely bitter in both states; there was a blizzard in Pennsylvania, but Debs acted as if he had never been ill a day in his life.

Not content with carrying his message to the large cities, Debs left the main road to venture up a gully, which held a dingy row of miners' shacks. When he left the highway, he had two hundred dollars in his pockets. When he emerged from the gully, he was forced to walk to the next town where he borrowed enough change to wire Girard for more money. He had given his expense money to the miners' wives.

Tramping through waist-deep snow and giving away his money were not the limits of Debs' impetuosity. Ella Reeve

Bloor, a middle-aged mother and Socialist organizer, was on the committee which arranged his meetings in Philadelphia. He was coming from Wilkes-Barre, and Mother Bloor met his train at the station. He seemed very tired, so his hostess charged, "I'll bet you have been staying up every night talking to the miners."

"Yes, I have," Debs admitted. "Aren't they great fellows? Last night they were talking to me until pretty nearly morning and then when I was going to bed, a fellow timidly knocked on my door. 'I thought,' he said, 'since you have to get up at five anyway, we might as well spend the rest of the night talking.' " The miner's logic seemed perfect, so they did.

After he had described the incident, Debs exclaimed, "Now, aren't they wonderful fellows? Ella, I know you do the very same thing." As he said this, Mother Bloor thought that "his tired face [was] alight with warmth and love." She also recorded that her children were so taken by Debs that they insisted on going with him to the railroad station.

Debs was justly proud of the political results of his tour, which he described as "in all regards the most successful of my experience." But his personal elation was marred the very day the tour began by news of the accidental death of the eldest Reynolds daughter. Even after Jean Reynolds died, Debs could see her running up the stairs of the Reynolds' home, her red hair floating in a long stream. He remembered her gay laughter as she played the grand piano in the living room. The day after his Chicago speech, his body still racked by fever, Debs wrote to the grief-stricken parents: "My Dearest Comrades—Never have I felt so near as now, in the deeps of your greatest sorrow. Dear, sweet, beautiful Jean has been before me all these hours, and my tears have mingled with yours, and I have been with you, my dearest comrades, in every moment of your agony. . . . Jean was as sweet and pure as the soul of an angel and Katherine and I loved her as if she had been our own child. . . . She is not gone from you, this divine daughter of your dream, this perfect daughter of your love—she is with you still and her hallowed presence will sweeten your lives and be to you a bow of promise and a perpetual benediction."

When Debs got back to Girard late in February to prepare for a spring tour of the Great Lakes region, he found Julius Wayland waiting for him. Several stories about "generous Gene Debs" had reached Wayland's ear. Louis Kopelin, later a reporter for the *Appeal*, claimed that he had met Debs on Park Row in New York City. Although the day was bitterly cold, Debs was not wearing an overcoat. He finally admitted that he had given his coat to a tramp at the entrance to Brooklyn Bridge. Frank Roderus of Terre Haute told a similar yarn. He had run into the Socialist leader a few blocks from the Dearborn Street station in Chicago. Debs had immediately hailed his fellow townsman and borrowed twenty dollars, explaining that he had given all of his money to an elderly woman he met on the street.

Incidents of this sort, which formed a major part of the Debs Legend, disgusted Julius Wayland. He had often lectured Debs about the stupidity of wasting time on the individual victims of capitalism, many of whom could never be restored to happiness. This time Wayland was so annoyed that he scarcely waited until Debs got inside the office before he began: "Every minute you waste on an individual is at the expense of the greater good you could be doing for all of society. Cut it out and devote your time to the larger movement. Fight the system and let its victims go to the devil."

Debs conceded the theory, but he balked at any attempt to practice it: "I know, J. A., that you are philosophically correct, but for me to follow any other course than I do would be impossible. We are not constituted alike." Wayland turned on his heel and left the office. He later said that "Debs has the soul of a poet," as if that explained everything.

[*3*]

DEBS soon left Girard on another leg of the Warren defense campaign. While on tour he was forced to pay some attention to the factional fight in the Socialist Party. Year after year this fight had grown in bitterness, but Debs had consistently tried to stay out of it. There were several reasons for Debs' attitude. He thought that Jimmie Higgins, the real authority in the party, should hear all positions and choose among them. One Sunday in Girard he discussed the factional quarrel with Allen W. Ricker, a reporter for the *Appeal*. Debs repeated to Ricker something that he had often said: "It is my greatest concern that I use no personal power which I may possess. The masses have ever been betrayed by the ambition and selfishness of leaders." This position was fully supported by Warren's weekly, which urged the workingmen to "trust no man as a leader."

Another reason why Debs tried to stay out of the factional fight was the identification of certain policies with certain individuals. It was impossible to attack anarcho-syndicalism without attacking Bill Haywood, who had earned Debs' deep respect by his part in the Western Federation of Miners and the IWW. It was impossible to attack the reform elements in the Party without naming Morris Hillquit, Victor Berger, Seymour Stedman, J. Mahlon Barnes, and Max Hayes. All of these men had been charter members of the Socialist Party. Victor Berger's visit to Woodstock had helped convert Debs to radicalism, and, as Debs said, "I have loved him ever since." The reform wing of the Party also held several journalists who had written glowing eulogies of Debs and thus earned his enduring affection. The Socialist leader set too high a value on personal friendship to denounce his old acquaintances.

This identification of policies and individuals complicated the situation in yet another way. Haywood did not believe in political action, was a dual-unionist, and had departed from several basic tenets of unionism; but he believed in the Socialist goal and industrial unionism, and was a marvelous fighter. The right wing had abandoned the campaign for industrial unions, was compromising with the labor bureaucracy, had lost sight of socialism; but it believed in political action, secured many valuable reforms, and its adherents were sincere. Debs, unable to join either of these factions, was forced to hold an anomalous center position and fire blasts at both sides. He hoped for the impossible—that the two factions would neutralize each other without immobilizing the Party. Then the rank and file could march straight ahead down the path charted by Eugene Debs. Actually, the factionalism did immobilize the Party, and it also caused thousands of members to resign in disgust.

Although Debs usually ignored the internal politics of the Party, he did intervene in several situations after 1908. The first crisis recognized by Debs occurred in the autumn of 1909. The National Executive Committee was elected annually by a direct vote of all members. The rank and file in each state usually voted for local favorite sons, splitting their vote in fifty directions. Only the writers and lawyers could command a national following, so they were consistently re-elected with 5 or 10 per cent of the total vote. Many workingmen revolted against this method of election which tended to perpetuate control by the intellectuals. In August, 1909, a Socialist local in Denver withdrew from the Party, charging that the leaders were "faddists, careerists and notoriety-seekers." Similar action was taken by other locals. Debs was so alarmed by this exodus of the workingmen that he briefly entered the fight in December with a letter to William English Walling, a Socialist writer. The letter was immediately published by the *International Socialist Review:*

. . . I have been watching the situation closely and especially the tendencies to reaction to which we are so unalterably opposed. The Socialist Party has already CATERED FAR TOO MUCH to the American Federation of Labor and there is no doubt that A HALT WILL HAVE TO BE CALLED.

The REVOLUTIONARY character of our party and our movement MUST be preserved in all its integrity AT ALL COST, for if that be compromised, it had better cease to exist.

I have no fear that any great number will be deflected when it comes to a show-down. . . . I am more than gratified with your uncompromising spirit and attitude. If the trimmers had their way, we should degenerate into bourgeois reform. But THEY WILL NOT HAVE THEIR WAY.

Debs had clearly stated his position, but he neglected to name the "trimmers." He also neglected to follow up the fight he had begun. Six months passed before he issued another statement on Party policy.

In May, 1910, a biennial policy convention of the Socialist Party was meeting in Chicago. This convention resulted in a clear victory for the "tendencies to reaction" that Debs feared, and he was again forced to take up the cudgel against the right wing. In an obvious bid for support from the AFL, which had long sought restrictions on immigration, the Committee on Immigration advocated the exclusion of all Orientals from the United States. Debs promptly sent the convention a forceful denunciation of this proposal, calling it "unsocialistic, reactionary and in truth outrageous." Such a suggestion, he roared, would be "entirely consistent in a convention of self-seekers." If socialism does not "stand staunchly, unflinchingly, and uncompromisingly for the working class and for the exploited and oppressed masses of all lands, then it stands for none and its claim is a false pretense and its profession a delusion and a snare." This letter arrived too late to be read at the convention, and was printed later in the *International Socialist Review*. The issue was finally settled, not by Debs, but by the Party's genius at compromise, Morris Hillquit. Hillquit's substitute resolution opposed "the exclusion of immigrants on account of their race or nationality," but favored exclusion in order to limit the number of wage earners competing for jobs. Actually no compromise at all, the Socialist position was perfectly acceptable to Samuel Gompers.

Even more important was the convention's discussion of trade unionism. The quarrel between radicals and conservatives again flared into open conflict. This question had been argued for years, and only one new argument was presented: A southern delegate maintained that industrial unionism was the only way to reach the Negro workers and win them for socialism. But the controversy was already decided. The right wing had a majority and did not hesitate to use it. In another concession to the AFL, the delegates refused to take any position on unionism, declaring that they would not interfere with the policies or structure of the trade unions. The left wing minority promptly termed this action a "betrayal of the cause of the working class."

Debs' viewpoint was published in the *International Socialist Review*. Again he simply stated his attitude, without denouncing the leaders of the opposition. He called for a campaign to enlist every American workingman in unions organized on an industrial or plant-wide basis: Such unions must be immediately founded in the mass production industries, which operate on an open-shop basis. But he did not favor "organizing dual unions in any case where the old union substantially holds the field." In any honest struggle against the employers, the craft unions are entitled to the full support of all labor, said Debs; but we must simultaneously strive to dislodge the "labor fakers" and convert the craft unions into class-conscious, industrial unions. Once more Debs had taken a middle position in the Party; he had attacked dual unionism, an avowed left-wing policy, and craft unionism, a tacit right-wing policy. He was not alone in his views, but his support was scattered and unorganized. The article had no immediate results, and Debs again turned his back on the entire problem of Party policy.

[4]

EXCITING problems, personal problems, controlled Debs' heart and mind as he headed toward Terre Haute in June, 1910. For thirty years he had wanted a child of his own. Now, in his middle age, he had a foster son. Oscar Baur, Jr., a ten-year-old, was the son of Kate's stepbrother. The boy's mother had died two years earlier, and he had come to live with Kate and Gene Debs. Kate Debs was severely strained by her new position. Having grown to maturity in a home that had no children, she was ill-equipped to cope with the situation. Long years of solitude had converted her into a prim housekeeper, whose life centered on her home. She was more than neat; she was fastidious. Years of habit made her resentful of muddy footprints on the rugs and of clothing and toys scattered through the house. Her morbid concern about the health of children prompted her to give them a single piece of candy, then put the box away and refuse to give another. Ten-year-old boys do not take kindly to such treatment.

Eugene Debs did not make these mistakes. He did not care if Oscar tore the house down; in fact, he was willing to aid the process. He bought the boy a fox terrier, Buster, and accompanied the two of them on long tramps over the surrounding hills. He delighted in throwing a stick several yards and sending the dog to retrieve it; as they prowled through the meadows and tramped along the Tow Path by the old canal bed, Debs doubtless remembered the countless mornings, forty years earlier, when he had come this way with his father. Debs also revived a pastime nearly forgotten, one which had caused the German residents to call Daniel a "crazy Frenchman." After a heavy spring rain, Debs and Oscar would go away in the back country; the next day the entire attic of the Debs' home would be festooned with drying mushrooms.

These new relations had a catalytic effect on the household. When George Bicknell, a friend of Steve Reynolds, was preparing an article about Debs, he decided to interview Kate. In reply to a question, she said: "Indeed I am a Socialist. We are all Socialists around here." Then came the astounding disclosure. Oscar Baur, Jr. had been reared in comparative luxury, the son of a wealthy man. But a few years with Debs had changed his childish convictions. According to Kate, "My little nephew, Oscar Baur, Jr., who lives with us, says he is a Socialist, too. He was not sure at first, but finally decided to follow in Mr. Debs' footsteps."

In her interview with George Bicknell, Kate said, "I think the solution of all the great economic problems will be made by the Socialist party, following the lines of Socialist theories." This statement is rather misleading; Kate often doubted the wisdom of socialism. Her contribution to the Socialist cause had been both indirect and simple; she had contrived to keep her husband out of the poorhouse and the cemetery. But in the summer of 1910 she made a more spirited venture into the field of politics. "The Right of Women to Vote," by Katherine M. Debs, appeared in the Terre Haute *Post* and was reprinted by several radical journals. This well-written article was based on the situation of five million working women in the United States. These women were forced to compete with men for jobs, and many of them supported large families; but they were shoved consistently into poor jobs at little pay. Their lack of suffrage deprived them of that small measure of protection which men possessed. Kate also met head-on two of the main arguments against woman suffrage, by stating that "woman has all the essential qualities of man, not excepting mentality and initiative" and "the kind of politics that will degrade a woman will also degrade a man."

One portion of the article clearly shows the hand of Eugene Debs: "Thirty years ago Susan B. Anthony, the noble champion of woman suffrage in the early days of the movement, was treated with almost brutal contempt by the 'better element' of society, in the city of Terre Haute; today her name is honored throughout the civilized world." Debs had never forgotten the jeers and catcalls of his friends as he escorted Miss Anthony through the local streets, that day in 1879. In April, 1910, just three months before Kate wrote her article, Debs spoke in Susan B. Anthony's home town of Rochester, N. Y. The following morning, even though it was raining, he placed a large bouquet on the grave of the champion of woman suffrage.

That summer in Terre Haute really seemed like another vacation to Eugene Debs. He wrote his weekly articles for the *Appeal* and stayed abreast of his extensive correspondence, but he was not working under the customary pressure. So he genially agreed to co-operate with the young Terre Haute philosopher and poet, Max Ehrmann, who intended to write his biography. When Ehrmann first made the proposal in February, 1910, Debs was in Pennsylvania lecturing for Fred Warren. He was not very excited by the idea of a second biography of himself. Reynolds' effort had been part of the campaign literature in 1908; Ehrmann's proposal did not have a similar justification. Debs tried to discourage the project: "The suggestion you make in reference to my biography interests me although I can hardly persuade myself that it is worth the while. I believe with Ingersoll that a life should be lived before it is written. When mine is over there may not be enough in it to claim biographical attention."

But, at Ehrmann's insistence, Debs finally agreed to furnish him with some recollections. The writer spent several mornings at Debs' office on Wabash Street, listening to Eugene and Theodore talk about old times. Debs even revealed that he had once wanted to be a song-and-dance man, and told how he had cried when his class graduated from high school without him. His main emphasis, however, was upon his early experiences in the labor movement, which Debs considered the focal point in his life. He and Theodore had a wonderful time trying to piece together the story of Debs' first job on the Vandalia, the organization of the BLF, the mighty struggle against the Great Northern. One of them would begin to talk; the other one would interrupt; soon they were both laughing together. Unfortunately, these conversations were fragmentary and contained little usable information. The project gradually died. Both Debs and Ehrmann became busy with other things; the book was never written.

During the last twenty years of his life, Debs spoke often about his early manhood, mainly because he thought his own experience might be helpful to others. The Socialist leader recognized that he was, in many ways, a typical American workingman. His own intellectual progress had been uncertain and painful; events had always kicked him into the next step forward. In several cases, repeated kicks had been needed before he would move. Eugene Debs, in his entire life, had never based an important decision on words written by somebody else. But certain writers—Victor Hugo, Thomas Paine, Edward Bellamy, Karl Kautsky—had clarified and strengthened the results of his own observation. Debs hoped that the story of his life could perform this same function for the men who came after him.

Another factor prompted Debs to co-operate with his would-be biographers. He felt a personal obligation to encourage writers with a humanitarian outlook. He warmly praised dozens of journalists and poets; he unofficially sponsored several men of letters. One of these protégés was Max Ehrmann. Thinking that Ehrmann's work expressed the idealism of the Socialist cause, Debs once sent a sample to Edwin Markham. He hoped that Markham would encourage the Terre Haute author. Within a few days the package was returned, unopened. Markham said that he was too busy to bother with it. Debs was furious. Markham had been an unknown California schoolteacher when Debs praised "Man with the Hoe." To make matters worse, Markham now claimed to be a Socialist. That was more than Debs could tolerate. In the middle of an election campaign, the Socialist leader wrote a reproachful letter to the famous poet. Successful men, Debs said, had an obligation to help their younger colleagues. The condemnation was so unqualified that Markham reconsidered his previous decision. He also sent Debs an autographed copy of "Man with the Hoe," which was promptly framed and placed on the wall of the upstairs study.

One August morning in 1910, when Debs was in the office giving dictation to his brother, a carpenter came to see Theodore about some hardware needed on the new home Theodore was building. The problem was quickly settled, and Debs strolled up Wabash Street with the carpenter. At Eleventh Street there were several men at work repairing the pavement. The events which followed made a deep impression on the carpenter; thirty years later he wrote an illiterate but moving account of the incident:

Gene asked the foreman when the men would get off for noon he said as he had no watch the foreman a big "rough neck" answered him very roodly "when it was 12 o'clock" Gene then said it is awful hot for men to have to work out there in that terrible heat. The forman said if they had taken care of their money they might not have to work in the hot sun and walked away Gene turned to me and asked the time it was just 2 minutes until 12 o'clock we waited the forman blue a little whistle the men stoped work and went after their lunch buckets Gene called to them saying men who have been working out there in that awful hot sun please step over here we walked across 11th St. to a restaurant and he asked them all to come in who had been working out in the browling hot sun on the pavement he then asked the proprietor of the restaurant if he had any good cold butter-milk to let these men have a big glass then he ordered a meal for each one of the workers and an extry glass of butter-milk the men took up about all the available chairs and tables in the restaurant. I heard one man ask another who is that who is that man that is treating us to this lunch the other man said I do not know it may be Eugene Debs they say he does things like this to working men I managed to see what money he handed the proprietor it was a $10.00 bill and he received 15 cents in change back, and we walked on down the street Debs said to me that cold butter-milk will do them good after working in that awful hot sun.

[5]

IN JULY, 1910, Debs went to the hospital for another throat operation; but a month later he wrote to Julius Wayland: "I'm getting all right and am champing at the bit for action." This note was mere bluster; he was still recuperating in November when a Federal Circuit Court upheld the sentence against Fred Warren. Unable to restrain himself any longer, Debs dispatched a telegram to the offending court: "Capitalist class supremacy and working class slavery are triumphantly vindicated in your post-election decision in the Warren case. All things come to those who own the earth and the courts thereof—even the social revolution." Then he began another lecture tour. By the year's end, the *Appeal to Reason* had 472,255 paid subscribers. Debs had given more than two hundred speeches for the weekly during 1910; 90 per cent of them made a profit for their local sponsor.

When Debs crossed North Dakota and Minnesota on the Great Northern railroad, he found every conductor wearing a red button. Most of them were selling Debs' lecture tickets to the passengers. Debs, delighted at this sign of rebellion against one of his oldest rivals, asked if they were not afraid of losing their jobs. One conductor replied: "When Jim Hill starts to firing men on the Great Northern for being Socialists he won't have enough slaves left to people his hand cars."

Since the Pullman strike of 1894, Debs had despised the federal courts, and all of his rancor poured into the campaign to prevent Fred Warren's imprisonment. He regarded the judiciary as the most concentrated expression of modern inequality. Every exposure of legal injustice, to his mind, was a blow for socialism: "The capitalist court is an infallible index to the capitalist system. To know the court is to understand the system. The court cannot be abolished or reformed while the system remains."

Debs insisted that Fred Warren was a legitimate heir to the principles of John Peter Zenger, who had been tried a hundred and seventy years earlier for defying the British censorship in America. Warren, too, was being tried for his ideas: "When the federal court sent Warren to jail it was not to punish crime, but to strangle free speech and stifle the voice of protest against crime. . . . Let the shibboleth of the American people ring from ocean to ocean and resound throughout the land: FREE SPEECH, A FREE PRESS, AND A FREE PEOPLE!" And, once again, Debs was on the winning side.

On February 2, 1911, President Taft decided to exercise his executive clemency. For unstated reasons, he struck the six months' imprisonment from Warren's sentence and reduced the fine to a hundred dollars. An official pardon was duly delivered to Fred Warren in Girard. The pardon did not bear a union label. Elated at this oversight, Warren hastily seized his chance to jeer at the President. Pasting on the document a huge sticker: "Demand the Label on All Your Printing," he returned it to Taft. The next issue of the *Appeal* carried a reproduction of the pardon. Beneath the picture, Warren declared that he would not "pay the $100 fine otherwise than in the form of *Appeal* sub cards." But Taft, more cautious than Roosevelt, refused to engage in a public discussion with the Girard weekly. Warren never did pay the fine.

Before Fred Warren was pardoned, Debs was embroiled in an even more momentous court battle. On October 1, 1910, during a strike of metal workers in southern California, the Los Angeles *Times* building was destroyed by dynamite. Twenty persons were killed and seventeen injured. General Harrison Gray Otis, the *Times'* publisher and a long-time advocate of the open shop, held the entire labor movement responsible for the crime. All union men, said Otis, were murderers at heart.

Debs at once renewed his enmity with General Otis. Every victim of the *Times'* explosion was a worker, said Debs' article in the *Appeal;* the publisher had conveniently arranged to be miles away. This was a clear charge, with no available proof, that General Otis had prior knowledge of the dynamiting. The *Times* and its coterie of antilabor industrialists were deemed to be "themselves the instigators, if not the actual perpetrators" of the crime. But a vigorous investigation yielded no clue to the identity of the culprits, and Debs thought that the case was closed. He was mistaken.

Two officials of the AFL Structural Iron Workers, John J. McNamara and his brother James B., were indicted for the bombing in March, 1911. At the time of his arrest, John McNamara was attending an executive board meeting of his union in Indianapolis. The other men present were held incommunicado while he was secretly extradited by a justice of the peace who had no jurisdiction. The events were, in their essentials, a repetition of the Moyer-Haywood arrest five years earlier.

Eugene Debs was again one of the first men to rise to the defense. His articles in the *Appeal* carried the fiery tone of his articles for Moyer and Haywood: "Sound the alarm to the working class! . . . Arouse, ye hosts of labor, and swear that the villainous plot shall not be consummated." Throughout the spring and summer, Debs toured the country in defense of the McNamaras. His position was once more based on the belief that the trial was a frame-up of innocent labor leaders. He demanded that the case should be decided in a court of law, not in the newspaper headlines. In New York City he told his audience: "We have a better right to presume these men innocent before they are tried than the corporations and their hirelings have to presume them guilty."

This case involved far more than the lives of the McNamara brothers. Many newspapers were using it to prove that all trade unionists and socialists believed in sabotage. The Los Angeles *Times* charged that "anarchist paper," the *Appeal to Reason*, with "appealing to the prejudices and the lurking criminality and the ignorance of its readers." These charges had united the entire labor movement in defense of the McNamaras. Even the AFL Executive Council had published an appeal to the workingmen in behalf of the defendants. Yet another consideration motivated the Socialists; one of their leaders, Job Harriman, was the foremost contender in a bitter campaign for mayor of Los Angeles. His chances were widely understood to hinge on the outcome of the McNamara case.

The defense campaign had reckoned without the defendants. Two of Debs' close friends, Lincoln Steffens and Clarence Darrow, reached a secret understanding with the prosecution. On December 1, 1911, the McNamara brothers confessed their guilt to the Los Angeles jury. John McNamara had agreed to plead guilty on the promise of clemency to his younger brother; otherwise, they might both have been hanged. But the confession was a terrific blow to the labor movement, which had worked its way out to the end of the limb. Trade unionists and Socialists issued hasty disavowals of their previous statements. Five days later, Harriman polled only fifty thousand votes against eighty-seven thousand for his opponent.

Eugene Debs was one of the few men who refused to be routed. His article in the *Appeal* began a retreat by stating that the McNamaras had been Catholics, not Socialists, but he quickly resumed the offensive. General Otis and his friends, said Debs, were indirectly responsible for the bombing: "Jim McNamara may have placed, and very likely did place, the dynamite, but who placed Jim McNamara?" The McNamaras had seen twenty members of the Lake Seamen's Union shot down by agents of the United States Steel Corporation, the article stated. They had seen their own union wrecked and nearly destroyed by company violence. They had seen each session of Congress refuse to pass an anti-injunction bill. They had seen the courts legalize the kidnaping of Bill Haywood and Charles Moyer. Daily for years they had risked their lives on the high-altitude scaffolding where they worked. Their entire background had turned their faces to violence. Debs declared that he had no apologies to make for either the McNamaras or himself. But their violent act, if they were indeed guilty, had been a horrible error; it had harmed the labor movement and given the corporations cause to rejoice.

With that analysis of the McNamara episode, Debs simply put the whole matter out of his mind. There was a Presidential campaign to be handled. As early as March 14, 1912, Debs wrote to a friend: "I think the outlook is positively inspiring. There is some fierce fighting ahead without a doubt but the gods are all with us and things are shaping rapidly for the undoing of the powers that are grinding the faces of the people." Once again, his spontaneous optimism was speaking instead of his knowledge. Actually the factional fight in the Party was heading for a showdown, and Debs fired a blast at both groupings.

The Socialist Party had scored several electoral victories in 1910, electing mayors in Schenectady and Milwaukee, winning numerous positions in state legislatures, and finally electing its first Congressman, Victor Berger. But Debs was far from elated by these seeming victories. In each case, he thought, the candidates had won because they had deserted their principles. They had been elected by reform votes, not by Socialist votes. In the winter of 1911, Debs again charged that the Party held "not a few members who regard vote-getting as of supreme importance, no matter by what method the votes are secured, and this leads them to hold out inducements and make representations which are not at all compatible with the stern and uncompromising spirit of a revolutionary party." It was treason, he continued, to regard the Socialist platform "as a bait for votes rather than as a means of education."

The basis for this reformism was discovered in the leadership of the Party. The Socialists elected to public office were mainly ministers, lawyers, and editors. The top officials of the Party were chosen from the same occupations. Debs declared this wrong. The Socialist Party, as the party of the American workingmen, should be guided and led by workingmen. Its policies should be decided by workingmen. The better-educated members can serve in other ways, said Debs—as writers, editors, lecturers, cartoonists—but control of the organization should not remain in their hands.

The left-wing tendencies in the Party were subjected to equally pointed criticism. Debs gave a detailed analysis of the IWW tactics, which called upon the individual worker to revolt against his employer by stalling on the job and deliberately wrecking machinery. He stated that he had no respect for capitalist laws and would not have "the least scruple about violating them," but such violations were foolhardy. Most American workingmen were law-abiding and completely rejected violent tactics. Violence actually played into the hands of the employers, who welcomed it because it assured them of public support. Moreover, individual action was the method of an anarchist, not a socialist, because it did not promote but destroyed the solidarity of labor. The conclusion was clear enough: "I am opposed to any tactics which involve stealth, secrecy, intrigue, and necessitate acts of individual violence for their execution."

Having publicly expressed his opinions, Debs again withdrew from the discussion. He refused to wield his personal influence to win support for his policies; he even refused to be a delegate to the Socialist national convention in Indianapolis in May, 1912. Although he knew that this convention would decide the basic questions before the Party, Debs preferred to continue his lecture tour. He had said everything he had to say; the rank and file had elected delegates; now the delegates could decide without any pressure from him. Since the results of the convention were partially due to Debs' refusal to take part in its deliberations, he had no just cause for complaint when it was over. But he did complain at the top of his voice less than three months after the convention adjourned.

In the battle for representation at Indianapolis, a decided advantage was held by the conservative leaders. They had controlled most of the Party machinery and Party press for more than a decade. They had usually set the policies, so that large numbers of reform voters had joined the organization and large numbers of radical workingmen had left it. Eugene Debs, in assuming that two factions of roughly equal strength would neutralize each other, had neglected this factor. But Bill Haywood noticed its effects. Haywood later expressed his contempt for the 294 delegates who met in Indianapolis on May 12: "The class struggle meant nothing to many who were there supposedly representing the working class." This contempt was mutual; a right-wing leader said that Haywood's election to the National Executive Committee had been "a grave misfortune."

The convention immediately split, as had every Socialist gathering for twelve years, over the trade-union question. The majority of the Resolutions Committee favored an endorsement of the AFL, the minority an endorsement of industrial unionism but no specific organization. After a long and complex discussion, the minority gained enough converts to carry its position, and a unanimous endorsement of industrial unionism was sent to the floor, where it was passed. On the next day, the radical delegates again scored a victory by electing one of their number as chairman of the convention.

The conservative leaders recognized the necessity of halting this trend, and they cleverly seized the issue on which the radicals were most vulnerable. A secret caucus of the Hillquit-Berger adherents drafted an amendment to the Party constitution, which was introduced by the Rev. W. R. Gaylord, a state senator in Wisconsin:

Article 2, Section 6. Any member of the party who opposes political action or advocates crime, sabotage or other methods of violence as a weapon of the working class to aid in its emancipation shall be expelled from membership in the party.

The heated debate led to the inevitable result. The amendment was adopted by a vote of 191 to 90.

Having regained the initiative, the conservative leaders decided to deny the Presidential nomination to Eugene Debs. They had made a similar effort, with little success, in 1908; and their determination had increased since that time. During the 1910 convention, when Debs attacked the Immigration Committee's proposal to exclude Orientals, Ernest Untermann had replied for the right wing: "Comrade Debs is no doubt a great orator and a fiery revolutionist, but he is also one of the poorest generals and tacticians that our movement has . . . he has shown himself utterly unreliable in the meeting of the practical problems of the day and the selection of his advisers. Nearly all of his advisers in the labor movement have turned out to be crooked."

If the entire right wing at the convention had united on a single candidate, they could have made a strong showing against Debs. But the Milwaukee and Chicago groups nominated Emil Seidel, the mayor of Milwaukee, and the New York caucus put up Charles Edward Russell, a magazine writer who had joined the Party only four years earlier. Debs won three-fifths of the votes on the first ballot, and Seidel was nominated as his running mate.

Eugene Debs, meanwhile, had made an abortive effort to promote Fred Warren for the Presidential nomination. During his lectures in defense of Warren, he had constantly praised the *Appeal's* editor as "the real champion of the working class, the true leader of the people." Partly as a result of Debs' agitation, many Socialists had sent letters to the *Appeal* suggesting Warren for President. Once when Warren was away from Girard, Debs and Julius Wayland set a whole edition of the newspaper which featured these letters. But Warren returned before the issue had gone to press and insisted that it be changed. The entire staff of the *Appeal* worked all day Sunday to undo what Debs and Wayland had done. Whether he desired it or not, Debs was again the candidate of the Socialist Party.

When he was nominated, Debs decided to rest during the hot summer months and save his strength for the home stretch. This decision was quickly broken; he began his campaign on June 29 at St. Louis. There were factors working both for and against the Socialists in the coming campaign. Theodore Roosevelt had broken with the Republicans and was running on the Bull Moose ticket. He and William Howard Taft were busily calling each other names, thus providing ammunition for the Socialists. On the other hand, both Roosevelt and Woodrow Wilson had adopted several planks from the Socialist platform and were certain to get the reform vote. Every ballot cast for Debs would be a ballot for socialism.

The Socialists had a large and efficient election machine ready to take the field, but there was again dissension within the Party. At the convention, Morris Hillquit had managed to effect the choice of J. Mahlon Barnes as campaign manager, even though Barnes had been forced to resign as national secretary because of gossip about his personal life. The Christian Socialist Fellowship now renewed its attack on Barnes. The left wing, hot for revenge because of the "sabotage" amendment, gleefully joined the onslaught.

At a meeting of the National Executive Committee to consider Barnes' position, Debs read several letters from comrades who threatened to work against the ticket if Barnes remained as manager. Debs was angry about the whole affair. He did not like Barnes' morals, nor did he like Barnes' politics. Barnes should be removed. Then John Spargo charged that the attacks on Barnes were merely a cowardly attempt to blackmail the Hillquit supporters; those who refused to work with Barnes should leave the Party. Berger and Hillquit said exactly the same thing—Get out. Now Debs was so furious that he was literally screaming. With his long body leaning across the table, he waggled his finger under Hillquit's nose and shouted that the objections to Barnes had come from Socialists "just as good as you, Comrade Hillquit." But the National Executive Committee decided that Barnes should stay. Barnes stayed.

Victor Berger's newspaper in Washington, D. C. commented about the affair: "Many intelligent Socialists have long known that Gene suffers from an unduly exaggerated ego." John Spargo added that "Comrade Debs should be recalled" if he persisted in his dictatorial complex. Spargo and Berger, whatever their motives, were justified in their comments on this occasion. Since Debs had refused to participate in the convention which chose Barnes, he had no legitimate grounds for complaint about the results.

The "exaggerated ego" of Eugene Debs did not interfere with his campaign. He made a headlong tour of the country, giving even more speeches than in 1908. His meetings were colorful and dynamic. Late in September, eighteen thousand persons crowded into Philadelphia's Convention Hall. Even the anarchists left their usual hangouts south of Pine Street. Several professional politicians were present, perhaps to learn how to use the propaganda their own parties had stolen from the Socialists. Girls wearing white dresses and red sashes moved among the audience, selling leaflets and red flags for "only a nickel." The box office receipts alone were twenty seven hundred dollars.

At Madison Square Garden in New York City, thirteen thousand persons paid from twenty-five cents to a dollar each to hear Debs. His appearance on the stage set off ten minutes of deafening applause. Two hundred girls, in the traditional red and white costume, acted as ushers. Art Young was present to report the meeting for *The Masses*, a rollicking left-wing monthly. Ten years earlier, Young had called Debs "a school-boy elocutionist." He now found the Socialist leader "an inspiring man, because he was himself inspired. He was emotional, and used the logic of understanding born of long experience with the workers. When one heard him voice a natural sympathy for the enslaved, one felt that here was a champion who would go to the stake rather than sacrifice his own beliefs." This speech was not without results; the New York *World* estimated that ten thousand dollars was collected at the meeting.

In 1908 several attempts had been made to discredit Debs, but these were far surpassed in 1912. In one city Debs checked into a strange hotel late at night. When he opened the door of his room he noticed assorted pieces of women's lingerie strewn around the furniture. The author of this plot underestimated his intended victim. Debs returned to the lobby, took witnesses up to see the room, and insisted that all of the clothing be removed before he would enter it. If any photographers were lying in ambush, they were never discovered.

The reform platforms of Roosevelt and Wilson probably hurt Debs badly, but he still amassed a record vote for the Socialist Party. The final count showed that nearly nine hundred thousand ballots had been marked for Debs and Seidel, almost 6 per cent of the total. The Party vote had more than doubled since 1908. There were several striking angles to the results. The Party membership had declined throughout the campaign, largely because of the "sabotage" amendment. The best showing, both in total vote and in percentage, had been made in Ohio. At the May convention, the Ohio delegates had voted nineteen to two against the "sabotage" proposal; it had been the only large state controlled by the left wing.

Immediately after the election the Republican administration again opened its prosecution of the *Appeal to Reason*. Indictments were issued against Debs, Julius Wayland, and Fred Warren in connection with a series of muckraking articles about Leavenworth prison. Debs had to go to the Federal Commissioner's office in Terre Haute and post bond guaranteeing his appearance in a Kansas court. Accompanied by his brother-in-law and private banker, Arthur Baur, Debs strolled into the office one morning and presented the bond. The Federal Commissioner, an old friend, felt rather sheepish about his part in the matter, but Debs quickly threw an arm around his shoulder and laughingly said, "That's all right. This is just perfect. When I get out there, I'll strip their goddam hides off." This pleasure was denied him; the case never came to trial. It did, however, almost wreck the *Appeal to Reason.*

The indictments for violation of the postal regulations had scarcely been served when a rumor reached the *Appeal* office. A girl who had once been employed by the weekly charged that Julius Wayland had taken her to Joplin, Missouri, for immoral purposes. This charge was ridiculous on the mere face of it. Wayland was fifty-eight years old. It was less than a year since his wife had been killed in an auto crash, and he was very broken up about that. He was much too shrewd to be caught in so obvious a trap. Finally, and conclusively, Wayland was so moralistic that he was often unpleasant about it.

But the truth of the charge, actually, was irrelevant. The Federal District Attorney was ready to issue an indictment against Wayland under the Mann Act. Wayland's name would be smeared in half of the country's newspapers. The *Appeal to Reason* would be destroyed. The case would drag on for years, furnishing steady copy to the metropolitan dailies. The Socialist movement would suffer even more than it had suffered during the McNamara trial. And all of this would happen whether Wayland was innocent or guilty.

An obvious solution presented itself, and Wayland took it. One evening he placed a brief note in his copy of *Looking Backward,* then blew his brains out with a revolver. The note read: "The struggle under the capitalist system isn't worth the effort. Let it pass." One of the most colorful and capable figures in the American Socialist movement had given up the fight.

Eugene Debs, already exhausted by his work in the campaign, was completely prostrated by this newest tragedy. He and Julius Wayland had been friends, almost partners, for fifteen years. They had been business associates for more than five years. And, in spite of their vigorous disagreement about individual charity, they understood and loved each other. They were both Midwestern radicals, born of the same society, dedicated to the same principles. Debs felt for Wayland the respect that comes from long association in the same battle.

The most fitting epitaph was pronounced, not by Eugene Debs, but by Kate Richards O'Hare, who soon replaced Julius Wayland as Debs' business colleague. Kate O'Hare sent a brief telegram to Wayland's son: "We shed no tears of grief; grief is for the naked lives of those who have made the world no better."

Part IV.

World Socialism

"And, in heaven's name, who are the public
enemies?" exclaimed Dr. Leete. "Are they
France, England, Germany, or hunger, cold, and nakedness?"

EDWARD BELLAMY

Debs' character,
tendency for the
dramatic

CHAPTER XVI

◻

[*1*]

EUGENE DEBS was growing old; in that winter of 1912 he passed his fifty-seventh birthday. The signs were in his face. Even during speeches now, he sometimes wore his gold-rimmed spectacles. The gashes across his forehead had deepened. The crow's feet near his eyes met furrows rising from the corners of his mouth. His cheeks were concave. His jaw had come to resemble a giant bone pendulum, attached as an after-thought to a previously finished face.

The signs were also in his mind and manner. He had been a very sentimental young man, given to florid utterances that tended toward ambiguity. During his middle years, from 1885 to 1908, a note of factual precision had crept into his speeches and writings. There was a new, harsh tone. His articles in *The Magazine* were buttressed by the statistics derived from government reports. As his life swung past the apex, the trend was in the other direction. Once more he tended to be carried away by his own rhetoric. All too often he was careful about the flourishes and careless about the core. In his search for the spiritual essence, he sometimes showed little regard for the exact truth. The question is one of degree; both elements were always present, but the change in degree was noticeable.

Even in his halcyon days, Debs was in no sense a scholar. He was both uneducated and uncultured. But he usually recognized these limitations and tried to overcome them. He freely admitted his extravagances. In 1910 during the Fred Warren defense campaign, a friend in Cleveland protested against one of Debs' speeches. Debs' reply showed a commendable amount of humility: "Your criticism of my speech is right and I heartily approve it. My wife, had she been present, would have thanked you for your candor. She has often said just what you have told me and I know she is right and you are right but there are times

317

when it seems impossible to keep within the bounds of calmness and discreet expression. In discussing such corrupt judges as Grosscup and Pollock it vexes one sorely to find decent words with which to characterize them. And yet you are right in regard to the effect upon the audience and I am glad you have written just as you have."

That was in 1910. But as the years passed, Debs became more contemptuous of careful scholarship. He came to believe that knowledge could be acquired quickly from the condensed versions of literary and scientific classics. His oratorical style had become automatic, and he tended to use it even in personal conversation. The reaction of the younger intellectuals to this characteristic is apparent in the comment of Floyd Dell, an editor of *The Masses* in 1916: "I did not like Eugene V. Debs to talk to; he orated blandly in private conversations, taking no particular note of whether he was talking to Tom, Dick or Harry." Two years later, in 1918, Debs made a particularly sweeping comment in a discussion with a young Socialist attorney. The attorney quickly interrupted him: "You don't really believe that, do you? Who do you think you're talking to, a crowd of 500 under-fed, under-educated workingmen?" Debs became very angry and said that he was deeply hurt by the attorney's insinuations, thus shifting the entire argument away from the accuracy of the original statement.

As long as he was "in general correct," Debs did not much care if he was wrong in the specific instance. This occasionally led to ludicrous actions. There was in Terre Haute, for instance, a very small, chivalrous Southern gentleman who edited a Socialist newspaper. One day Debs asked the editor to stop by his office. A friend went along with the editor. As soon as they entered Debs' office, the giant Socialist leader began to talk about seeing the editor on the street, one cold day the previous week, without any overcoat. This was, said Debs, very unhealthy for a middle-aged man, and he wanted the editor to have his overcoat. The editor tried to explain that he had an overcoat already and that he did not need another one. His protests were vain. When the editor left that office, he was wearing Debs' overcoat. It dragged on the floor as he walked. That did not matter to

Debs, who was elated to know that he had been spiritually correct.

This was purely a process of self-hypnotism, of pulling the wool over his own eyes. But there was an even more astonishing example. Debs remained largely unconscious of what was happening within his own family. There had long been ill will between his wife and his brother. Although Kate had never been completely persuaded of the wisdom of her husband's views, she had been of enormous assistance. She had helped with his correspondence, managed the Debs Publishing Company, entertained his friends, nursed him time and again back to health. She had never publicly complained. But the years passed, and the millennium did not arrive. Her husband continued to drive himself without mercy, and she continued to worry about his health. Then many Socialist leaders joined the metropolitan newspapers in saying unpleasant things about Eugene Debs. Kate gradually began to rebel under the strain.

Her rebellion was shown in two ways. She sometimes remarked to small groups of Socialists that her husband was killing himself for people who did not appreciate it. She began to be cold and formal to Socialists who called at her home. She wanted Eugene to be more a husband and less a Socialist, to pay some attention to his health and the family income. She also wanted him to stop supporting his lazy brother Theodore.

Many years later, Debs' sister Emma Maillaux said: "Theodore and Gene were of one flesh. They fairly breathed through one another. Theodore was Gene's foundation. Without him Gene's career could never have been." This was undoubtedly true. Theodore had served his brother for three decades by 1912, without glory or wealth. He had been adviser, private secretary, valet, stand-in. But Kate did not appreciate the truth. She thought that Theodore had been sponging off her husband. She did not like the relationship whereby a third or even half of Eugene's salary went to his brother. This animosity was fed by her family and by several of her friends, all wealthy women in Terre Haute. One day soon after the completion of Theodore's new home on Ohio Street, Kate passed by in an automobile with Mr. and Mrs. Carl Stahl. Mr. Stahl, who owned a prosperous garment factory, ironically pointed to Theodore's house and commented: "There lives a great man. He has a fine home and doesn't work." That was Kate's attitude too.

Theodore, for his part, heartily reciprocated this dislike. In 1897, when he was in Chicago trying to support a wife, a baby, and the Socialist Party on a shoestring, Kate was living in *her* fine home in Terre Haute. Even more than that, thought Theodore, she was a drag on his brother. She was the discordant partner, the rebel who rocked the boat of the rebels. She was, in short, a throwback. That was Theodore's notion, but he exaggerated. Kate was a peculiar woman, who varied between belief and disbelief in her husband's cause. Ignoring her contributions, Theodore considered her more a handicap than a help. He occasionally commented to his friends that Eugene should have married somebody else.

Eugene Debs was actually the cause of this bitter enmity between Kate and Theodore. Also, since they were the two persons closest to him, he was caught squarely in the middle of it. His reaction was typical—he ignored it. There was no diminution of his regard for either his wife or his brother. Theodore continued as his secretary, and Kate continued as his domestic companion. If rumors reached Debs of Theodore's angry mutterings, he gave no sign. When Kate complained publicly about her husband's wasted career, Debs used his great diplomatic talent to guide the discussion into other channels. A witness to one of these scenes later commented that Kate's cutting remark "just disappeared" during Debs' conjuring act.

Debs refused to pay attention to personal animosities, no matter who was involved. Also he had more important things on his mind in May, 1913. A coal strike in the Cabin Creek district of West Virginia was following the long-established pattern of antilabor violence. Even Mother Jones, the almost legendary eighty-year-old organizer for the United Mine Workers, had been seized and thrown into a bull pen without benefit of trial. All segments of the labor movement protested against this wanton viciousness. The Socialist Party sent an investigating committee to the strike zone, and Debs agreed to serve with Victor Berger and Adolph Germer. Debs spent several weeks hurling himself around West Virginia, exhorting the miners to stand firm. When the fight was on, Debs' haziness always disappeared. He urged the craft unions in the strike area to call a general strike. If this proved ineffective, said Debs, they should make "an appeal to force of arms." But these measures proved unnecessary. By the middle of June every union man had been released from jail. Debs, in his customary state of exhaustion, returned to Terre Haute.

The Cabin Creek episode was paled, less than a month later, by a national storm arising from Debs' defiance of social convention. On July 10, 1913, newspaper readers throughout the country thrilled to essentially the same headline in every metropolitan daily:

DEBS GIVES GIRL OUTCAST A HOME

Five days earlier, Debs had learned that the daughter of an old friend in Terre Haute had been arrested for immorality and taken to the city jail. He promptly put on his hat and went after her. Debs thought that the girl was merely unhappy due to her recent divorce. She had lost her moorings; she was not evil. And even if she truly had been a prostitute, it would not have mattered to Debs. Hadn't he refused, as City Clerk, to levy fines against any streetwalker? So he persuaded the authorities to appoint him as temporary probation officer, and he then took the girl back to his home.

Eugene Debs was so angry that he was boiling over. The police had told the girl that she must keep off the streets or go to the proper section of town. Debs, in a public statement, vigorously attacked this attitude: "Do the police mean to get recruits for the red light district? . . . It is time for this pitiless cruelty to stop. Why not war on the immoral people in high life instead of persecuting this penniless girl?" All of his friends, said Debs, must accept the girl as a member of his own family. The Milwaukee *Leader* significantly added: "Mrs. Debs, in accordance with her invariable custom, refused to talk for publication. It is known, however, that the girl was taken into the Debs' home with Mrs. Debs' full accord."

Debs may have been surprised by the public acclaim that

greeted his action. This was not revolution; this was charity; several newspapers believed in charity. Scores of editors who had been excoriating Debs for years now found occasion to say a kind word. Typical was the headline in the Houston *Chronicle:* "Debs Challenges Christianity." When it came to a verbal defense of Christianity, the *Chronicle* was not found wanting. But the task of supporting the girl and re-orienting her life was left to Debs. He was not found wanting either.

After he had secured a new job for the girl in a strange city, Debs felt the need of a long vacation. He decided to go to Estes Park, Colorado, and he remained there for more than two months. While on vacation he made an important decision. He would retire. He was still writing two or three articles each week for the *Appeal to Reason,* but it wasn't the same now that Wayland was dead. He had just finished paying off the twenty-two-thousand-dollar debt of the American Railway Union—it had taken eighteen years—so he was freed from that self-imposed financial pressure. And Kate wanted him to give up the lecture platform and stay in Terre Haute. The idea was reasonable; they were coming into the twilight of their lives. Debs could still sell all of his articles to the Socialist newspapers; money would be no problem. He wrote a letter of resignation to Fred Warren, ending a frolicsome and fruitful partnership in socialism.

By Christmas Debs was back in Terre Haute. He was in a mellow mood, and so was Kate. When a woman reporter from the Terre Haute *Post* appeared for an interview, she was graciously admitted by Kate into a scene of domestic happiness. Looking back over his career, Debs thought an injustice had been done. "She has always been my inspiration," he said of Kate. "If I have done the least thing toward the betterment of the world, it has been due to her. She has always kept in the background and it isn't fair. I say it isn't fair."

But Kate would not have it so: "I have always told him that it was enough for him to be in the front. I prefer it that way."

Debs would not be diverted from his main point: "She has been a loyal companion through thick and thin. She has never faltered for a moment and God knows we have had some strug-

gles in the past twenty years. We have been hounded and persecuted and she has stood for the right through it all. . . ."

Then Debs began to drag out the family heirlooms. He
proudly exhibited a meerschaum pipe which had belonged to his
father (he smoked it only on Daniel's birthday each year). A
cup and saucer, both monogrammed in gold, had belonged to
Nathaniel Hawthorne; they had been presented by Hawthorne's
granddaughter after she heard Debs make a speech. But Debs'
favorite possession was a battered tin candlestick which had
lighted John Brown's last hours in Harper's Ferry. In speaking
of John Brown, Debs was always moved to oratory: "He used
this in his cabin that terrible night he was captured. Imagine
the flickering candle glow over that terrible scene. One of John
Brown's sons dead on the floor, while the father with one hand
on the pulse of another dying, clutched a gun in his other."

Just one political note crept into that entire interview, in-
serted, surprisingly, by Kate: ". . . some people say that Socialism will break up the home. Why, one divorce is granted now
where two marriage licenses are given. When our economic conditions are made what they should be and women cease marrying
to be provided for because their wages do not enable them to
live as human beings should, then will the divorce question be
solved. Marriage then will be founded on its only *true* basis,
love."

What did Mr. Debs believe to be the major question before
the American people? Mr. Debs did not say. What did Mr. Debs
think of the chances of war? Mr. Debs did not say. The readers
of the Terre Haute *Post* were left completely unenlightened for
another six weeks. When Debs did break through the veil of
silence that shrouded his mind, he chose an unusual subject.
On February 24, 1914, he wrote for the *Post* a long article on
municipal corruption and efficiency. Still angry about the attitude of the police toward prostitutes, Debs asked why the authorities did not get after the big lawbreakers. He found his
answer, not in the natural depravity of mankind, but in the
workings of the capitalist system: "Men are naturally honest
and the worst of them will be straight instead of crooked, and
clean instead of corrupt, when it is as easy and pays as well to

be straight and clean, as it now does'to be crooked and corrupt."

As Debs issued his statements about Nathaniel Hawthorne's teacup and municipal reform, the impression grew that he was about finished. Some of his Socialist colleagues had long thought that his mind was going soft; they now began to think that he was growing soft all over. The word got around that old Gene Debs didn't have a good fight left in him. The word, as it turned out, was wrong.

[2]

THE PRESIDENTIAL ELECTION of 1912 had been remarkable in many ways: all four candidates had wrapped themselves in the mantle of liberalism; the Bull Moose nominee had polled more votes than the Republican incumbent; the Socialist electorate had approached the million mark. But most remarkable of all had been the indifference shown to the overwhelming issue, the threat of war. Foreign policy had scarcely been discussed in the entire campaign. Not even Eugene Debs had been aware of the imminence of conflict.

This was, on Debs' part, a serious but temporary lapse. As early as 1907, the International Socialist Congress in Stuttgart had called on the workers of all nations to stand firm against the war drive and "to take advantage of the opportunities offered by the economic and political crises brought about by the war by arousing public sentiment to hasten the overthrow of capitalist class rule." The last suggestion was added at the initiative of Nikolai Lenin, who headed the delegation of Russian Bolsheviks. At the International Socialist Congress of 1910, Debs' old friend Keir Hardie had proposed an international general strike if actual fighting began.

The American socialists paid sporadic attention to these resolutions. The Denver *Post*, in 1909, charged that the socialists were circulating "seditious documents" in the Army and Navy. Two years later the assistant secretary of war asked for legislation in every state to provide military training in the high schools. At this point Debs entered the discussion. War, declared the Socialist leader, was "the supreme crime of twentieth century civilization." He urged the Socialist Party to make a frontal assault "against war and all that makes for war." He then neglected his own advice for nearly three years.

In February, 1914, Debs abandoned his plan to retire. His retirement had lasted the usual two months. This change of front was inevitable; he just was not adapted to a leisurely life. His friends did not believe that he really wanted to sit around Terre Haute and write an occasional blast at the local politicans. Among these friends were Kate Richards O'Hare and her husband, Frank P. O'Hare. Kate O'Hare had long been the most prominent and most effective woman Socialist in the country. Her success and prominence were due in large part to the behind-the-scenes activity of her husband, a brilliant organizer who had worked with Debs during the Moyer-Haywood campaign. In 1912 Kate O'Hare had become a lecturer for the *National Rip-Saw*, a Socialist monthly in St. Louis. Her husband Frank was named editor. In order to round out his staff, Phil Wagner, the publisher, offered Eugene Debs a job lecturing and writing editorials for the publication. Much to his wife's chagrin, Debs agreed.

Debs had returned to active duty just in time. War in Europe seemed so near that the National Committee of the Party issued a manifesto declaring their "opposition to this and all other wars." But when war actually threatened the United States, the chosen enemy was not Germany but Mexico. Just a few days after the Party manifesto, some American soldiers were arrested in Tampico. This minor incident nearly precipitated an open conflict with Mexico, where the unsettled political situation had been publicized as a standing menace to American lives and property. President Wilson demanded an apology to repair the damage to our national honor. To enforce this demand, and to forestall the rumored arrival of a German ship bearing arms for the Mexican government, Wilson sent the marines ashore at Vera Cruz. We had invaded Mexico.

Eugene Debs leaped into print in the *Rip-Saw*. Our soldiers should never have been in Mexico in the first place, he declared; they were there for the sole purpose of protecting the ill-gotten property of the Standard Oil Company. Instead of sending more marines to crush the peons "into hopeless slavery and degradation," Wilson should immediately withdraw all troops from Mexico. American citizens who chose to live and invest their money in foreign countries should do so at their own risk, not at the risk of our soldiers' lives.

Thus did Eugene Debs begin his crusade against war. Superficially, he seemed badly qualified to lead such a campaign. He had never set foot on any soil beyond the continent of North America. He was unable to read a single foreign language; thirty years earlier he had been competent in French and German but he had forgotten both. He was in no sense a careful student of international affairs. Actually, however, these considerations were irrelevant. Debs' basic attitude hinged, not on diplomatic subtleties, but on broad socialist principles. He thought that our foreign military adventures were being undertaken in the interests of the same capitalist clique that ruled America. That was all he needed to know. His attitude toward the developing war depended on happenings in the United States.

This emphasis was apparent from the very beginning. At the same time that our troops landed in Mexico, there were two dramatic strikes in the United States. During a hard-fought battle in the Michigan copper country late in 1913, the strikers gave a Christmas party for their children in a schoolhouse at Calumet. When the hall was filled with hundreds of holiday revellers, an unknown person shouted "Fire." Panic swept through the hall. Everybody bolted for the door. But the doors had been barricaded by the same unknown person. Wave after wave of hysterical children and adults beat against the barred doors. Seventy-two lives were lost. The copper miners refused all offers of help, and marched cold-faced to bury their children in a common grave.

The tragedy at Ludlow, Colorado, was even more deliberate and wanton. A strike by the Western Federation of Miners became an armed battle. When militia were sent in to escort strikebreakers through the picket lines, the miners protested by deserting the town of Ludlow. They set up their own tent colony in a neighboring meadow. On April 20, 1914, the militia raked the colony with machine-gun fire. They then burned the tents to the ground. No warning had been given. This brutality had tragic results. Two women and eleven children were burned to death.

Here, indisputably, was a situation in which Eugene Debs believed in violence. His article in the *International Socialist Review* urged the miners to raise a Gunmen Defense Fund, "sufficient to provide each member with the latest high-power rifle, the same as used by corporation gunmen, and 500 rounds of cartridges." If the government was unable or unwilling to provide protection, the miners had a solemn duty to protect themselves. The company guards, said Debs, were "hired assassins" and "professional man-killers": "You should have no more compunction in killing them than if they were so many maddogs or rattlesnakes that menaced your homes and your community." His suggestion of counterviolence was made "advisedly" and he held himself responsible for "every word of it," a declaration that was sustained by the gravity of his closing words:

It remains only to be said that we stand for peace, and that we are unalterably opposed to violence and bloodshed if by any possible means, short of absolute degradation and self-abasement, these can be prevented. We believe in law, the law that applies equally to all and is impartially administered, and we prefer reason infinitely to brute force.

But when the law fails, and in fact, becomes the bulwark of crime and oppression, then an appeal to force is not only morally justified, but becomes a patriotic duty.

The miners in Colorado were employed by a corporation of which John D. Rockefeller was the directing force. The financier's son had neither apologies nor regrets about the destruction of the tent colony. As he told a Congressional committee: "If I had failed in my duty, I would resign, but my conscience utterly acquits me." Although he may have questioned the morals of John D., Jr., President Wilson sent Federal troops into Colorado to protect the property of John D., Sr. It so happened that Rockefeller also had a large interest in the oil fields that our marines were protecting in Mexico. In the eyes of Eugene Debs, the American government was little else than an armed guard for capitalist investments. He did not hesitate to say so.

It is one thing, ye uniformed slaves, to fight for your country and another thing to fight for Rockefeller's oil derricks.

You never had a country to fight for and never will have so much as an inch of one as long as you are fool enough to make a target of your bodies for the profit and glory of your masters.

Let the capitalists do their own fighting and furnish their own corpses and there will never be another war on the face of the earth.

That same month, August of 1914, the dispute with Mexico was paled by the beginning of the war in Europe. Debs advocated complete neutrality, in fact as well as name. In his opinion the bloody conflict was the outcome of fifty years of commercial competition among the capitalist nations. The ruling class in each country had the same goal: "to extend the domination of their exploitation, to increase their capacity for robbery, and to multiply their ill-gotten riches." With all of the colonial countries divided up among the imperialist powers, any attempt at re-division must result in war. The workers of the world, Debs concluded, had no interest in the bloody conflict. Since the war was an inevitable result of capitalism, the great task of the Socialists was to explain its causes and so prepare the workingmen for "the impending social revolution."

Through the summer and autumn of 1914, through the winter and spring of 1915, Debs continued his tireless activity in behalf of the peace movement. He made a broad sweep across the Midwest. He appeared at the Socialist encampments of Oklahoma and Texas, inspiring many men to bring their families a hundred miles in a wagon to hear his fiery message. He stormed his way down the West Coast. Week after week, he wrote trenchant, biting editorials in the *National Rip-Saw*.

And, all the while, the United States was moving toward armed intervention. A flood of war orders from the Allies had lifted America out of the depression which had gripped its industries for more than two years. American citizens continued to cross the Atlantic on British ships, and a momentary crisis followed the sinking of the Lusitania in May, 1915. President Wilson placed the National Guard on a war footing in the interests of "national security." The first Allied War Loan in the autumn of 1915 effected a practical merger of the American and British economies. Step by step, foot by foot, Debs tried to stem this steady drift toward involvement in the European conflict. Every move toward American preparedness brought forth from Debs the caustic comment: "Any nation that today PRE-PARES for war INCITES war and slaughter."

Debs did not draw any fine distinctions between the different groups supporting the war. Capitalist or socialist, instigators or perpetuators, he struck viciously at all of them. The entire war could have been prevented, he wrote in the *Rip-Saw*, if the socialists in every country had stood by their principles. The Bolsheviks of Russia, alone in the belligerent countries, had waged a firm struggle to halt the bloody massacre. Of the hundred socialist deputies in the German Reichstag, only Karl Liebknecht had voted against war credits for the government. In France, in England, in Italy, the former socialists had be-become nationalists and had followed their rulers into war. This insane nationalism had to be stopped, had to be rolled back, wrote Eugene Debs in November, 1914:

We socialists are not wanting in genuine patriotism but we are deadly hostile to the fraudulent species which is "the last refuge of the scoundrel" and which prompts every crook and grafter and every blood-sucking vampire to wrap his reeking carcass in the folds of the national flag that he may carry on his piracy and plunder in the name of "patriotism. . . ."

Patriotism, like brotherhood, must be international and all-embracing TO BE AT ALL.

Even within the Socialist Party there was considerable opposition to Debs' attitude. At the time of the Lusitania crisis the National Committee issued a flaming proclamation: "We call upon the workers of America to oppose war and all agitation for war by the exercise of all the power in their command." But this antiwar position was seriously compromised by the failure of the National Committee to denounce the war-socialists of Europe. As late as May, 1915, the Socialist leaders in America piously declared: "With every power at their command the socialists of all nations have worked to prevent it." This statement, as Eugene Debs well knew, had no relevance to the actions of the prowar socialists of Germany, France, and England.

Nor was this all. In December of 1915 Charles Edward Russell, whom the Hillquit forces had tried to nominate for President in 1912, declared himself in favor of preparedness. There was, said Russell, imminent danger of invasion by Germany and Japan, the leaders of world despotism. Somewhat similar views were held by Upton Sinclair, the Socialist novelist, who had been horrified by German militarism. Sinclair, like Russell, believed that the urgent necessity was the defeat of Germany. He incorporated this attitude in a statement which he mailed to Debs, hoping that it would be endorsed by the Socialist leader.

On the contrary, it met with a summary rejection. "Dear Comrade Sinclair," Debs replied, "I regret not being able to sign the document as requested, for the reason that I do not coincide with the views therein set forth. . . . Any kind of an army that may be organized . . . under the present government will be controlled by the ruling class, and its chief function will be to keep the working class in slavery. I have not the least fear of invasion or attack from without. The invasion and attack I want the workers to prepare to resist and put an end to comes from within, from our own predatory plutocracy right here at home."

"I do not know of any foreign buccaneers," wrote Debs in memory of the Ludlow massacre, "that could come nearer skinning the American workers to the bone than is now being done by the Rockefellers and their pirate pals. The workers have no country to fight for. It belongs to the capitalists and plutocrats. Let them worry over its defence, and when they declare wars as they and they alone do, let them also go out and slaughter one another on the battlefields."

As Germany continued her submarine attacks on Allied shipping, an increasing number of Socialists began to support the preparedness campaign in the United States. But these conversions had little effect on Eugene Debs. Even if he had been completely alone in his views, it seems certain that he would have remained "true to himself." His conscience had guided his hand in 1892 when he left the Brotherhood of Locomotive Firemen; it had ruled in 1905 when he joined the Industrial Workers of the World; it was still dominant in 1915. So Debs persisted in his peace crusade, under the aegis of Thomas Paine, Wendell Phillips, Charles Sumner, Abraham Lincoln, and John Peter Altgeld, all of whom had opposed the unjust wars of their own times. When asked whether he was opposed to all wars, Debs gave an answer that foreswore evasion: "I am not a capitalist soldier; I am a proletarian revolutionist. . . . I am opposed to every war but one; I am for that war with heart and soul, and that is the world-wide war of the social revolution. In that war I am prepared to fight in any way the ruling class may make necessary, even to the barricades. That is where I stand and where I believe the Socialist Party stands, or ought to stand, on the question of war."

Debs envisioned a three-fold program to make his attitude effective: unity of the American Marxists, reconstitution of the Socialist International, formation of a powerful and class-conscious labor movement in the United States. There had been abortive moves, for more than a decade, to unite the Socialist Party and the Socialist Labor Party. Debs now set himself to this task in earnest. He wrote a lengthy laudation of Daniel DeLeon for the SLP journal. He tirelessly emphasized the absolute necessity for joint action against the war danger. Finally, in 1916, this agitation bore fruit; committees from the rival parties began negotiations for a merger.

The Socialist International, thought Debs, must spearhead the campaign for friendship among the peoples of all countries. He was painfully conscious that the International had failed in the hour of crisis. A new International, he wrote in July, 1915, must "utterly outlaw war and declare against the abomination under any and all circumstances." Thus far he was in perfect accord with the leaders of his Party. But he broke sharply with the supporters of Hillquit and Berger in his additional statement: "those so-called socialists who prefer nationalism to internationalism must never be given another chance to betray and

destroy the movement." That was Debs' program in 1915, a
purge of the war-socialists of Europe from positions of power in
the Socialist International.

Debs' third suggestion, and the one which received most of his
personal attention, was the complete rebuilding of the labor
movement. He recognized that this task could never be accomplished by the IWW, or the Wobblies as Daniel DeLeon had
called them. Although he admired the militant spirit of the
IWW and its leadership of the strikes at Paterson and Lawrence,
Debs had become increasingly impatient with their tactics.
Finally, in 1914, a group of Wobblies dynamited the Western
Federation of Miners' hall in Butte, Montana. That was going
too far. For the first time, Debs issued a bitter, unqualified blast
at Bill Haywood and his associates: "It is vain to talk about the
IWW . . . Let all who oppose political action and favor sab-
otage and the program of anarchism join that faction."

The IWW could not rejuvenate the labor movement. Samuel
Gompers and his colleagues in the AFL, who had supported each
step of the preparedness campaign, obviously would not do it.
How then was it to be done? Debs' projected answer was a new
labor federation, based on the WFM and the United Mine
Workers, which would promptly begin organizing drives in the
rapidly expanding war industries. He also advocated a determined attempt within the local craft unions to wrest control of
the AFL from the hands of Gompers. As early as August, 1910,
Debs had expressed this same program: "we must bore from
within and without, the industrial unionists within the old
unions working together in perfect harmony with the industrial
unionists upon the outside engaged in laying the foundation
. . . of the new revolutionary economic organization . . ."

Through the summer and autumn of 1915, through the winter
and spring of 1916, Eugene Debs was one of the handful of
prominent men who opposed the preparedness torrent. Although
William Jennings Bryan, Jane Addams, Senators LaFollette and
Norris, continued to battle for true neutrality, their voices
seemed weak indeed compared to the anti-German barrage in
the newspapers. And yet Debs found a surprising amount of
support all over the country. On June 11, 1915, he wrote to

Frank O'Hare from Garrison, North Dakota: "If you could only be here and see this demonstration! . . . The old warehouse was packed as soon as the doors were open and hundreds couldn't get in. . . . The farmers and their families have come from a hundred miles around—and they are red to the core." More than seven thousand people came to the meeting in Chisholm, Minnesota. A hundred men joined the Party in Williston, North Dakota, when Debs spoke there. The Socialist leader had "a wonderful meeting" at Ann Arbor, Michigan, the home of the state university. "It was extremely cold, below zero," he wrote to Max Ehrmann, "and yet the Auditorium was packed and overflowing and many had to be turned away."

In the early spring of 1916, soon after Debs' speech in Ann Arbor, attention was again diverted from the European war. Pancho Villa, the Mexican bandit, crossed the border with a hundred men and raided the little town of Columbus, New Mexico. President Wilson despatched the American Army into Mexico in pursuit of Villa. Once more there was danger of war on the American continent. When the news reached Debs, he was traveling from Pittsburgh to Cleveland on a lecture tour for the *Rip-Saw*. His comment appeared in the Akron *Times:* "I want the people of America to understand that if we have war with Mexico, our boys will not be fighting for their country. They'll be fighting for the Wall Street interests that own four billion dollars' worth of property in Mexico for which they paid not one hundredth part. That's all there is to this Mexican trouble."

These outspoken pronouncements by Debs met with extreme disapproval among the Socialist leaders. Even Debs failed to recognize the growing breach until February, 1916, when the leaders of a strike in New Jersey were sent to jail for contempt of court. Debs wrote one of his unbridled attacks on the judiciary and, as a matter of course, mailed it to the New York *Call* for publication. The editor returned it, saying that it might involve the paper in a libel suit. Debs had seldom been as disgusted as he was on this occasion. Hadn't he helped to raise money to launch the *Call* in 1908? Was this an attempt by Morris Hillquit to punish the Party's mavericks? Was the *Call* afraid of trouble with the government? "There are times," Debs said contemptuously, "when a libel suit, or the threat of one against a revolutionary paper is the very thing that it needs." The article finally appeared, not in the *Call*, but in the *Appeal to Reason*.

The right-wing Socialists had tried in 1908, and again in 1912, to deny the Presidential nomination to Debs. Perhaps they could have done so in 1916, but they were unexpectedly relieved of the problem. Debs rejected all attempts to draft him for the job. Doubtless Kate's wishes, his own ill health and his desire to step aside for a younger man, all played a part in this decision. The nominations went to a pair of journalists, Allen L. Benson and George R. Kirkpatrick, who were chosen by a referendum vote of the membership. For the first time since the formation of the Socialist Party, Eugene Debs was not to be the standard-bearer in a national campaign.

[*3*]

DEBS' HOPES to shirk an official designation by the Party were quickly frustrated. In spite of his plea of ill health, the Socialists of Terre Haute nominated him for Congress in April, 1916. Debs was completely trapped. His statement after the 1912 election had proudly predicted: "It is entirely possible that in four years more the Socialist party may sweep the nation." That day had arrived, and he had refused responsibility for the national campaign. Could he similarly betray the confidence of his local comrades? Those were the terms in which the problem appeared to Debs, who had repeatedly sworn that he would carry out any task the Party assigned him. No choice was involved; Debs felt honor-bound to make the race.

First, however, the national platform had to be settled. Since the Party had held no convention, policy questions were in the hands of the National Committee, which had shown a definite tendency to straddle certain problems. Debs set himself the task of bringing both clarity and determination to the Party's campaign. "The issue," he wrote in August, "is socialism against capitalism, imperialism and militarism. The hordes of hell are all against us, but the hosts of justice are on our side. We can win and must. Comrades, I am counting on you, each of you, as if our very lives were at stake—and they are." To emphasize his uncompromising position, Debs again lashed out at the right-wing leaders:

There has been a tendency in our party for some years, and it has been quite marked, to obscure the class character of our party to make it the more acceptable to the middle class, and on this account many . . . working-class revolutionists . . . have deserted the party.

Another and perhaps the principle cause of defection and desertion from the party ranks has been the weak, evasive, if not cowardly attitude of the party toward economic organization. There has been and is now in certain quarters mortal fear that the party may by some act or utterance give offense to the Gompers A.F. of L. machine. . . .

I am not foolish enough to contend for an instant that the Socialist party should meddle in the management of union affairs but I am quite sure that the party . . . can only maintain its own integrity by standing staunchly and uncompromisingly . . . for the industrial organization of the workers [and] against the principles of craft unionism . . .

With the urgency born of desperation, Debs brought this program to the voters of the Fifth Congressional District. He worked in constant awareness that the American people were knocking on the door to the charnel-house in Europe. Constantly there flickered in his mind the vision of shell-torn fields, of wrecked cities and tortured hearts, of maimed men and starving babies, of the wanton brutality that is war. At the end of this insane horror, Debs could see no shining future. The public enemy, in all truth, was not Germany, but hunger, cold, and nakedness.

Never had a Debs' campaign risen to greater emotional intensity. He worked as if the fate of the world rested in his two hands. During the first two weeks of September he gave fifty-five speeches, moving over the rutted roads in a Model T touring car. In each community this Ford drove up to the town plaza and Debs clambered out on the sidewalk to give his speech. With his arms waving frantically above the audience, he vowed stern opposition to the agents of capitalism and war. As the crowd grew larger, he jumped up on the hood of the car and continued his stirring indictment of the munition-makers. Coal miners, housewives, merchants—many of them yielded to this fervent plea for peace and socialism.

Debs was receiving a great concentration of support. The eyes of socialists throughout the world were focussed on the Congressional campaign in Indiana, where the issues were so clearly drawn. Each day brought unsolicited contributions from New Zealand, from Alaska, from the Orient. Several speakers from foreign countries, including James Larkin of Ireland and Madame Kollontai of Russia, appeared in the district. In every small town the Socialists sold huge red feathers bearing the tag: "Feather your nest. Vote for Debs." One of Debs' close friends, the Rev. J. H. Hollingsworth, edited a booklet, *Eugene V. Debs: What His Neighbors Say of Him*, which was distributed by the thousands of copies. By election day, one and a half million pieces of Socialist literature had been spread broadcast throughout western Indiana.

Nor was the opposition idle. Both the Republicans and Democrats poured money and orators into the fight. Then, as the campaign neared its climax, the Democrats made a desperate move. With the open co-operation of the AFL they sent Mother Mary Jones on a tour of the mining towns in the area. Mother Jones had devoted her life to the struggles of the coal miners. Debs had always considered her as one of the heroes of the American labor movement. "No other soldier in the revolutionary cause," he had written in 1907, "has a better right to recognition . . . than has Mother Jones." In 1913, when the fearless woman was imprisoned for her activities in the Cabin Creek strike, Debs had hurried to her side. Now, a scant three years later, she was advising her beloved miners to vote against the Socialist Party. Whatever Debs may have thought, he said absolutely nothing.

While this battle was raging in the lecture halls and town squares, a truly gripping drama, about which Debs knew nothing, was being enacted in his own home. Kate Debs had heard recurrent gossip that she did not love her husband enough to go to meetings with him. To some extent this was true. But one day when Debs was giving a speech in the street, a spectator was startled at the sight of Kate Debs, standing on a bank and waving her hands to attract her husband's attention. Such incidents were either unknown to or ignored by the gossip club. The ugly rumors went on, until Kate Debs broke down under the strain. A neighbor found her one afternoon crying in her anguish. Then Kate took her stand publicly.

In the final Socialist parade, held the Saturday night before the election, Kate and Eugene Debs marched arm in arm at the head of the column. The boisterous files stretched for fifteen blocks through the streets of Terre Haute. The air was filled with red flags and the smoke from countless torches. Gigantic signs called on the voters to speak out against the war. The parade swept hilariously onward to the Grand Opera House, which proved far too small to hold the crowd. Debs hastened through his address, then he and Kate hurried on to other meetings at the Armory and the Coliseum. These buildings also were filled with throngs of cheering, ecstatic admirers. Deb's hopes soared high as he witnessed the popular enthusiasm of the closing days of his campaign.

Four days later they fell sharply. Far from sweeping the nation, as Debs had predicted, the Socialist vote had dropped more than three hundred thousand since 1912. Since the vote for Benson and Kirkpatrick was artificially swollen by many pacifist and pro-German ballots, the result could only be termed a severe setback. In Terre Haute Debs, by more than trebling the Party's vote of 1914, had run ahead of the Democratic incumbent, but the Republican won an easy victory. Confident that he had been "true to himself," Debs was not upset by his failure. Probably he had realized from the beginning that victory was impossible. He now had only one comment: "Blessed are they who expect nothing, for they shall not be disappointed."

In that crucial campaign of 1916, Debs again found sanction in his early beliefs. When he gazed at the huge picture of Karl Marx above his desk he actually saw the face of Victor Hugo. When he read the novels of Hugo he thought about the doctrines of Marx. One night at a meeting in Parke County Debs

furiously attacked the capitalist warmakers. But he talked
softly to his campaign manager during the long trip back to
Terre Haute. As he puffed contentedly at his pipe, Debs medi-
tated about the meaning of *Les Misérables*, with its message of
redemption through brotherhood.

[4]

THROUGHOUT the winter of 1916, as the country rushed toward
war, Eugene Debs was held inactive by recurrent attacks of the
grippe. From his home in Terre Haute he watched the final
disintegration of his plans for peace. The negotiations for a
merger of the Socialist Party and the Socialist Labor Party
ended in extreme bitterness. The Socialist International could
not be reconstituted during the war: the Bolsheviks of Russia
were in prison or exile; the leader of the antiwar socialists of
France had been assassinated; the antiwar socialists of both
England and Germany were in prison. Most American workingmen had fully accepted the preparedness program of the AFL.

The economy of the United States had become inextricably
tied to the war effort of the Allies. Skilled workmen were drawing large salaries from the munitions plants. The prices of wheat
and cotton were booming on the world market. Corporation
profits soared to unprecedented heights. Wall Street had engi-
neered gigantic war loans to the English and French governments. Step by step, month by month, American neutrality had
been converted into a mere word. Then, on February 1, 1917,
Germany announced unrestricted submarine warfare against all
shipping, and President Wilson promptly broke off all diplomatic relations.

At the very moment that the German ambassador was being
handed his passport, both Kate and Eugene Debs were suffering
from serious cases of the grippe. Before Debs had recovered,
word arrived from Helena, Montana, that one of Kate's sisters
had died and her body was being shipped to Terre Haute for
burial. So that month of February hurtled onward; war with
Germany became ever closer; and Eugene Debs was bound in a
straitjacket of sickness and personal sorrow. When he became

able to leave Terre Haute, Debs' first action showed a startling detachment from the growing crisis. Frank Harris, an English socialist who had just become editor of *Pearson's Magazine*, hired Debs as a regular monthly contributor. While the imminent promise of war hung over the face of the land, Debs submitted lengthy accounts of his friendships with Robert Ingersoll and James Whitcomb Riley.

This mood, however, soon passed. In early March Debs began a tour of the Eastern states. Recognizing that the United States was truly poised on the brink of the European crater, he fiercely attacked Wilson's pleas for national unity. "There is much talk at the present time," he said, "of standing by the president. I am willing to stand by the president if he stands for the things I want, but when I look at the gang that stands behind the president, I know it isn't my crowd." This was not a war for national defense, screamed Debs, but a war for capitalist profits. The working men had no true interest in the murderous business.

As Debs swept eastward into New York City, he was invading the very center of the preparedness sentiment. Yet two thousand persons crowded into Cooper Union to hear his speech, and police were needed to disperse another two thousand who milled in the streets after the doors were closed. Debs did not disappoint his audience. In his most fiery tones, he proposed a nationwide general strike if Congress declared war. This idea was far from new. Jack London had used it in his novel, *The Iron Heel*, as far back as 1908. A similar proposal had been complacently adopted by the International Socialist Congress of 1910. But, as the war began, Jack London and most socialists of Europe had become jingo nationalists. Debs had removed their suggestion from the realm of theory and offered it as a concrete program.

The program, as Debs well knew, had no chance of success. Just six days after he spoke at Cooper Union, a joint conference of the AFL and the Railway Brotherhoods issued a solemn declaration: "Despite all our endeavors and hopes, should our country be drawn into the maelstrom of the European conflict, we . . . offer our services to our country in every field of activity . . . and call upon our fellow workers and fellow citizens

. . . to give like service." It made little difference that Daniel Tobin, president of the Teamsters, charged that Samuel Gompers had controlled this conference so tightly that the other delegates were "not allowed to change a word." The leaders of labor had approved the program of Wall Street and the Administration.

For Eugene Debs, there was nothing more to be done to block a declaration of war. The scene shifted to Washington, where a handful of Senators were filibustering the armed-ships bill. These dissenters were ostracized by their colleagues, denounced as traitors in the newspapers, flayed by President Wilson. This is not strange; Senator George W. Norris was voicing the convictions of Eugene Debs when he declared: "We are going into war upon the command of gold. . . . I feel that we are about to put a dollar sign on the American flag." The words went unheard.

CHAPTER XVII

◻

[*1*]

ON APRIL 7, 1917, the day after the declaration of war, the Socialist Party met in emergency convention at St. Louis, Missouri. Planter's Hotel was filled with 193 Socialists who had come to decide the Party's position on the war. Through four heated days the Committee on War and Militarism wrangled about a resolution. On the fifth day they appeared before the convention and Morris Hillquit began to read the majority report:

The Socialist Party of the United States in the present grave crisis reaffirms its allegiance to the principle of internationalism and working class solidarity the world over, and proclaims its unalterable opposition to the war just declared by the government of the United States. . . .

The mad orgy of death which is now convulsing unfortunate Europe was caused by the conflict of capitalist interests in the European countries.

In each of these countries the workers were oppressed and exploited. They produced enormous wealth, but the bulk of it was withheld from them by the owners of the industries. . . .

The capitalist class of each country was forced to look for foreign markets to dispose of the accumulated "surplus" wealth. . . .

The efforts of the capitalists of all leading nations were, therefore, centered upon the domination of the world markets. Imperialism became the dominant note in the politics of Europe. . . . This led to the mad rivalry of armament . . . The ghastly war in Europe was not caused by an accidental event, nor by the policy or institutions of any single nation. It was the logical outcome of the competitive capitalist system. . . .

Our entrance into the European war was instigated by the predatory capitalists of the United States who boast of the enormous profits of seven billion dollars from the manufacture and sale of munitions and war supplies and from the exportation of American foodstuffs and other necessaries. . . . We brand the declaration of war by our government as a crime against the people of the United States and against the nations of the world.

341

A more subdued antiwar report received only thirty-one votes; a prowar report only five votes; the majority report read by Hillquit was supported by 80 per cent of the delegates. When the majority report was submitted to a national referendum of the membership, it received an even more overwhelming vote. The Socialist Party had taken its stand.

But the appearance of monolithic unity was deceptive. A number of warring groups had agreed to the majority report: the Christian pacifists who opposed all force and violence, possibly a few pro-German delegates, the reform elements led by Morris Hillquit, and the revolutionary left wing. This left wing had no relation to that which had existed during the first decade of the century. Bill Haywood had been recalled from the National Executive Committee in 1913 for violation of the "sabotage" amendment adopted the previous year, and he had soon led the anarcho-syndicalists out of the Party. The new revolutionary faction had developed since 1914 on the basis of opposition to the war and adherence to working-class internationalism. The dominance of the war issue had stimulated a rapid growth of the Party's foreign-language federations, and the Russian democratic revolution of March, 1917, further accelerated this trend. These groups, together with the state organizations of Ohio, Michigan, and Washington, now held a majority of the left-wingers.

At the St. Louis convention the left wing recognized that the majority report was subject to a variety of interpretations. Determined to destroy forever the influence of Morris Hillquit and Victor Berger, whom they completely distrusted, they tried to enlist the support of Eugene Debs. Their spokesman, Charles E. Ruthenberg of Ohio, telephoned Debs in Terre Haute and urged him to come to St. Louis. Debs refused; not even the war crisis could persuade him to attend a convention. But Ruthenberg was not satisfied. One night he loaded two cars with delegates and drove the hundred and fifty miles to Terre Haute. The trip was made in vain. Debs absolutely refused to take part in the St. Louis deliberations. He had already stated his attitude; now it was a matter for the delegates to decide.

The next twelve months, for Eugene Debs, were a time of restraint, and hesitation, and endless suffering. The party to which he had devoted his life proved to be indeed a frail barrier to the war hysteria. At the first critical test in its history, three important groups had deserted the American radical movement. Dozens of capable publicists, who had controlled the Party since its formation, now became war patriots. John Spargo, A. M. Simons, Phelps Stokes and his wife Rose Pastor Stokes, Charles Edward Russell, Harry Slobodin, William English Walling—these had all been important names in the history of the Socialist Party. By their mass secession they disrupted and wrecked the Party organization.

Second, those trade-union leaders who were Socialists hastily complied with the war program advocated by Samuel Gompers. In several major unions which were indispensable to military production—the coal miners, the machinists, the needle-trades, some building-trades—the Socialists had formed an important part of the leadership. Almost without exception these men now left the Party. They attacked every strike during the war, no matter what the cause, and they failed to launch organizing drives in the mass-production industries.

Finally, it became apparent that the radical newspapers existed only on sufferance from the Federal authorities. One journal after another was suppressed or deprived of its second-class mailing permit. The New York *Forward* began to give qualified support to the war. *The Masses*, after a brief suppression, reappeared as *The Liberator* and carefully stayed within the law. Even the *Appeal to Reason*, which had once thundered at Roosevelt and scoffed at Taft, changed its name and endorsed the policies of President Wilson.

In view of these important defections the protest movement showed a surprising strength. Huge demonstrations were staged in New York, Chicago, San Francisco. Even in small cities like Moline and Rock Island, Illinois, anticonscription meetings overflowed from the hall into the street. The *International Socialist Review* reported that eighteen thousand men had failed to register for the draft in the Twin Cities. The largest May Day parade in the history of Cleveland marched through the central area in 1917, with the marchers bearing banners that denounced

the war and the capitalist class. After three years of preparedness agitation, a sizeable segment of the population still did not
believe in the war.

No government can afford to tolerate open dissent in wartime.
Woodrow Wilson had sadly recognized this truth just before he
asked for the declaration of hostilities. According to Frank I.
Cobb, editor of the Democratic *New York World*, the President
had said to him on the early morning of April 2: "Once lead
this people into war, and they'll forget there ever was such a
thing as tolerance. To fight you must be ruthless and brutal, and
the spirit of ruthless brutality will enter into the very fiber of
our national life, infecting Congress, the courts, the policeman
on the beat, the man in the street." The same note had been
sounded by the Socialist convention in St. Louis: "Our entrance
into the European conflict at this time . . . will give the powers
of reaction in this country the pretext for an attempt to throttle
our rights and to crush our democratic institutions . . ."

These predictions proved only too true. The Espionage Law,
passed by Congress to guard the country against sedition, served
as a potent weapon against the nonconformists. The act was
construed loosely and applied without remorse. In Grand
Rapids, Detroit, Kansas City, Minneapolis, St. Paul, Boston,
Seattle, all over the United States, those who opposed the war
were imprisoned. The three leaders of the Socialist Party in
Ohio—Alfred Wagenknecht, Charles E. Ruthenberg, and
Charles Baker—were charged with advocating resistance to the
conscription law. Debs' close friend and colleague, Kate Richards O'Hare, was indicted because of an antiwar speech she
gave in July, 1917. Twelve radical publications were banned
from the mails in August. On September 7, 1917, Federal
agents made simultaneous raids on IWW and Socialist headquarters across the country. And the Terre Haute *Tribune*,
which had always been friendly to Eugene Debs, counselled
much harsher treatment, "the firing squad."

These developments were clothed with the formalities of the
law. Far more frightening was the extralegal campaign against
the peace movement. A wave of insane hysteria swept through
the "man in the street," even as the President had predicted.

Police officials turned their backs while mobs of servicemen and civilians terrorized Socialists and pacifists, wrecking their halls and stoning their homes. A typical incident occurred in Tulsa, Oklahoma, where a crowd of hooded men took seventeen Wobblies away from the local police, slashed them with whips, then covered them with tar and feathers. A United Press dispatch from Tulsa stated that similar treatment was contemplated for every IWW in the oil fields. The real cause of action in many cases lay, not in the antiwar activities of the radicals, but in their efforts to organize trade unions in open-shop areas. During a mine strike at Bisbee, Arizona, more than eleven hundred men were forced into cattle cars and carried far into the desert, where they were dropped off without food or water. They were told never to return to the town where they lived and worked.

Month after month in the *Social Revolution,* as the *Rip-Saw* had been renamed, Eugene Debs wrote outraged protests against these atrocities. Late in October one of his acquaintances, a pacifist clergyman in Ohio, was seized by a mob as he was about to enter a hall in Newport, Kentucky. The clergyman was thrown into an automobile and driven miles away to a forest where he was stripped and lashed with a blacksnake whip. His attackers even soaked his hair with gasoline, as if in preparation to set him afire, but they were frightened away before the plan was carried out. As these incidents multiplied, Debs became ever more caustic, more accusing, more rebellious. Not even the Germans had ever been charged with worse cruelty than this. Then thirty Negroes were killed in a race riot at East St. Louis, only a few hours drive from Terre Haute. In bitter anguish Debs called the murders "a foul blot upon the American labor movement." "Had the labor unions ever opened the door to the Negro," Debs continued, "instead of barring him . . . and forcing him in spite of himself to be a scab, the atrocious crime at East St. Louis would never have blackened the pages of American history."

Yet, in spite of his anger about the destruction of civil liberties, Eugene Debs was following an equivocal policy. His lecture tours had been largely discontinued with the declaration of war, and the few surviving Socialist periodicals furnished the sole outlet for his opinions. He had continued to excoriate the capitalist class; he had furiously denounced the vigilantes; but there he had stopped. The conscription act, the Liberty Loan drives, the mounting subsidies to England and France had all been inaugurated without opposition from Eugene Debs. He was trying to escape the results of war without attacking the measures that made possible the continuation of the war itself.

Nor had he ever denounced those Socialists who had left the Party. Some of these persons, like Rose Pastor Stokes, had been both respected colleagues and cherished friends. As recently as July, 1916, Debs had written a warmhearted birthday note to Rose Stokes. "Dear, dear Comrade Gene!" had been the reply, "One forgets birthdays these terrible times—remembering days of world-wide death and the moaning of the women, who have lost. But sometimes, perhaps, it is well to remember—and remembering the struggle to which we were born—and dedicate, vow anew our allegiance to the cause of the People. Great leader of that cause, loving greetings to you." Eugene Debs' whole spirit prevented him from turning against these men and women who had been his comrades. Knowing Rose Stokes' sincerity and her unflagging devotion to the workers' welfare, he realized that her support of the war sprang from her belief that it was, in all truth, a war for democracy. While vigorously dissenting from this view, he was unable to denounce those friends who held it.

Even when Charles Edward Russell publicly referred to his former associates as "dirty traitors" who should "be driven out of the country," Debs was not moved to vehemence. He replied in compassionate and mournful terms: "No one attacked Elihu Root more fiercely as a Wall Street tool and a public enemy than Charles Edward Russell, but now Mr. Russell receives him with open arms, and jointly and severally these twin darlings denounce those who are for peace, and want them driven out of the country. . . . Poor Russell! He will pay dearly enough before he gets through." This note of detachment, of passiveness, was struck repeatedly during the final months of 1917. "It is good indeed," he wrote to a friend, "to feel now and then the heartening comrade-touch across the spaces. If only the world, the whole of it, had your fine spirit and your tender regard for all that is flesh."

Debs was indeed hesitant and floundering, for reasons that now can only be guessed. He was in ill-health; he was old; probably Kate tried to deter him; he may have thought that protest against the war was hopeless. Some Socialists in Terre Haute even believed that his brother Theodore was urging him to refrain from any statement that might be termed criminal. Whatever the cause, Debs was certainly groping in the dark. He still believed in friendship among the workers of the world; he still believed that the war had been inspired by the capitalist pirates; he still longed for peace; but he had no program. He was lost. Month after month he shouted his mighty protests, and they turned out to be frail bleats in an indifferent country. He was not of this world at all. America had become a strange land, in which Eugene Debs was a bewildered and unnoticed vagabond.

The newspapers paid almost no heed to his tour of Ohio in the autumn of 1917. For several weeks he traveled around the state, holding small and ineffectual meetings in the homes of Socialist friends. His headquarters were established at the home of Mrs. Marguerite Prevey in Akron, as was his custom whenever he visited Ohio. Mrs. Prevey, vivacious, matronly, a pioneer Socialist, had clung to her radical convictions in spite of a modest fortune made from local real estate. Her own example had persuaded her that the wage earners had no monopoly on radicalism, and she brought into the Party dozens of prominent and wealthy citizens. Her latest recruits were Mr. and Mrs. William M. Brown of Galion, Ohio. Brown had been a bishop in an organized church. Mrs. Prevey was determined that they should be welcomed into the fold by the high priest of American Socialism, Eugene Debs. Every time Debs' travels carried him near Galion, Mrs. Prevey asked him to visit the Browns. Something always seemed to interfere. Finally Mrs. Prevey insisted that he comply with her request. In justification of his negligence, Debs protested that ministers never amounted to anything in the Socialist movement. But at length he yielded, and he was completely charmed by the bishop and his wife. His general opinion of ministers, however, remained unchanged.

The one memorable incident of Debs' tour in Ohio, his meeting with Bishop Brown, was completely unrelated to the war. Then, beginning late in 1917, the daily happenings beat upon his mind with the fury of a clenched fist. Increasing numbers of American troops moved into the European conflict, to mingle their blood and bodies impartially with the others. The vision of violent death, of the unseen hand of war cruelly striking across gutted fields, moved with maddening effect before the eyes of Eugene Debs. The news from Europe further inflamed the festering nakedness of his anguish. He carried within himself the inchoate strains of primitive religion, the deep yearnings toward brotherhood, the tender suffering from universal pain. As he visualized the agonies of Europe he fell victim to a wistful and haunting melancholy which moaned for an end to the international crime. "I abhor war," said Debs in 1918. "I would oppose the war if I stood alone. When I think of a cold, glittering steel bayonet being plunged into the white, quivering flesh of a human being, I recoil with horror. I have often wondered if I could take the life of my fellow man, even to save my own." This was the reality of 1917, a reality from which Debs was desperate to escape.

In November the Bolsheviks of Russia seemed to point the road to peace. News of the Russian Revolution sent a tremor of hope through the American radical movement. After long years of struggle without reward, at the very moment when the entire world seemed insane, the Marxian theory had demonstrated its strength. Foundation of the first socialist government thrilled and inspired the socialists of every country; the peasants and workers of Russia had proved that they had both the will and the strength to take power. They soon proved that they knew how to use it by signing a peace treaty with Germany and taking their country out of the war. But before the treaty, came another German invasion of Russia. The Terre Haute *Tribune*, which had so recently hinted at "the firing squad" for dissenters, asked Debs to comment on the invasion. He pointed a stern finger at the war socialists of Germany: "In standing for this crime, they cap the climax of their betrayal and disgrace of the Socialist movement. In standing for this, the majority Socialists of Germany prove finally that they will stand for anything except Socialism and democracy."

Rumors promptly began to the effect that Debs was ready to announce his support of the Allied cause, and these rumors were accelerated by the opening paragraphs of his article in the *Social Revolution* for January, 1918. The quickest way to end the war, Debs declared, was to encourage the workers of Germany and Austria to overthrow their emperors. The end of this same article, however, proved that his views had not changed: "The ruling classes of all nations engaged in the conflict, including our own profiteering plutocracy, must also be overthrown and this is the great work that confronts us on the threshold of the new year."

The November Revolution and Russia's retirement from the war, while inspiring the American socialists, alarmed the pro-war forces in the United States. Inevitably there came another wave of arrests, raids, indictments. The editors of *The Masses* were summoned into court. Victor Berger and four other Party leaders were charged with violation of the Espionage Act. During the opening months of 1918, more than two thousand Wobblies were arrested. It was reported that a thousand indictments and two hundred convictions had already been secured under the Espionage Law. The hysteria and fear ruling the country were clearly illustrated by the experience of John Reed, one of the best and most popular war correspondents. In April, Reed returned from Russia with the biggest story on earth. He had been in St. Petersburg in November; he had seen the revolution. But none of the magazines would print his account because they knew he favored the Bolsheviks. *Collier's* accepted one article, had it set in type, then returned it to the author. Oswald Garrison Villard was warned by the Federal authorities that the *Nation* would be suppressed if it printed any of Reed's stories.

This vigorous censorship, coupled with the President's declaration of war aims, wrought considerable change in the views of many prominent Socialists. Morris Hillquit, in the autumn of 1917, had made a gallant race for mayor of New York on a qualified antiwar platform. But the seven Socialist aldermen who had been elected in that campaign now declared themselves in favor of a Liberty Loan drive. Meyer London, the only Socialist Congressman, announced that the President's declared objectives coincided with the Party's views. Victor Berger said that he wanted to win the war "for democracy." These statements were a sharp reversal of the majority report adopted at St. Louis the previous year. At that time the Party had termed the war "the logical outcome of the competitive capitalist system"; many Socialists now hoped to halt the war without disturbing the capitalist system. Woodrow Wilson, who had been a "tool of Wall Street," was hailed as the "champion of democracy."

Eugene Debs found himself in violent disagreement with this trend in the Party, which amounted to following the war-socialists of Europe in their nationalistic program. He was also shocked and repelled by the swollen casualty lists, by the bestiality of "a cold, glittering steel bayonet being plunged into the white, quivering flesh of a human being." Daily his mind became more tortured, more tormented, as he realized that the labyrinth of cruelty and pain retraced itself to end at the beginning. Ferocious drums of suffering began to throb within him. His anguish became a spasm, but the spasm did not move his legs or his lips. He had been a changed man since the war began, more restrained, seemingly older, unhappier. No longer was Eugene Debs the rollicking radical who had coined witticisms and used them freely. His articles had no incisiveness and no irony; they were mere protests, shrilly uttered but dying into a whisper.

And then, with the rapid swish of destiny, he was thrown back into the battle. Eugene Debs had not gone in search of the dark core of national life; it came to him as man after man was sucked into the whirling torrent. Day by day, incident by incident, the pressure rose and his personal explosion grew more imminent. The previous December, when Kate O'Hare was convicted of violating the Espionage Act, Debs had been incredulous. "I cannot yet believe," he had written to Kate O'Hare, "that they will ever dare to send you to prison for exercising your constitutional rights of free speech, but if they do . . . I shall feel guilty to be at large." Two months later Frank P.

O'Hare began the organization of a defense campaign for his wife and the other political prisoners, and Debs' program began to take shape. A new spirit of determination appeared in Debs' letter to Frank O'Hare on March 2: "You can be no more anxious, even as the husband of your beloved Kate, than I am as her comrade, to see her defense made complete in every particular, as well as the defense of all other persecuted comrades who have been arrested and made to suffer for our sake. It is our fight, and we have got to put our hearts into it if we are worthy of the sacrifices these splendid comrades have made in our behalf."

This trenchant tone had already reappeared in Debs' defense of the 105 Wobblies who were on trial in Chicago. Wall Street interests, said his article in the *International Socialist Review,* were directly responsible for the propaganda attacks on the IWW, which was being blamed for every grass fire, shortage of rain, and crop failure in the United States. These attacks occurred, not because the Wobblies were unpatriotic, but because they were a "growing menace to capitalist autocracy and misrule." And, most significant of all, Debs called for a national campaign to insure the civil rights of all men charged with political crimes.

The mob lawlessness which had appeared at Bisbee, at East St. Louis, at Tulsa, relentlessly swept into Debs' home town of Terre Haute. A schoolteacher of German parentage was summoned before the Vigo County Council for Defense, then was summarily discharged for disloyalty. Her crime: she belonged to the Socialist Party and had told her pupils to remain seated while singing *The Star-Spangled Banner.* Two brothers who owned a small store were invaded by a mob of vigilantes, roughed up, their stock despoiled, their store boycotted. For the next several months they received frequent orders from Kate Debs, who previously had traded elsewhere.

The self-appointed loyalty agents never molested 451 North Eighth Street, but they struck on every side of Eugene Debs. A capable professor at Indiana State College was forced to resign because of alleged pro-German views. Books in the German language were publicly burned in the streets; the vigilantes gathered this kindling by checking the libraries of private citizens. One of Theodore Debs' neighbors, a German grocer, was beaten up by a banker while a policeman held the grocer's arms. A Socialist coal miner in a near-by town was nearly lynched because he refused to buy a Liberty Bond. Cruelty, deceit, arrogance, fear spread their paralyzing tentacles over the whole of local life. The accusing finger and the strident voice became the true marks of the patriot. And Eugene Debs became ever more angry, more resentful, more determined. Feeling confined by the prejudices of his countrymen, he resolved to break out of this prison created by popular hysteria.

For the first time in thirteen months Eugene Debs had his say about Socialist policy in May, 1918. In a personal statement issued through the national office of the Party, he proposed another convention because the St. Louis Manifesto contained "certain propositions . . . which are now impossible." Many leaders claimed that a new national convention might split the organization, but Debs declared that a split was preferable to "confusion and chaos within the Party." He also repeated his unqualified opposition to the entire war: "I have condemned the German majority socialists, and I am not now going to imitate their perfidy, much as the capitalist press may abuse me for not doing so." The statement closed with an impassioned defense of the men and women who had violated the Espionage Act: "The party leaders and many other comrades have been indicted and are now in prison or out on bail pending trial for being true to our cause. They are charged with being pro-Germans, disloyalists and traitors, and if they are guilty so am I. But they are not guilty and their alleged disloyalty is to the real traitors of this nation and will be written to their everlasting honor."

Several newspapers immediately seized upon Debs' convention proposal as proof that he intended to repudiate his antiwar views. Actually he wanted to work out a program to make these views effective, and he thought that elected delegates were the proper persons to take such a step: "Let the rank and file be heard and we shall make no mistake." The gossip about his pending renegacy so infuriated Debs that he issued another curt, conclusive statement:

Years ago I declared that there was only one war in which I would enlist and that was the war of the workers of the world against the exploiters of the world. I declared moreover that the working class had no interest in the wars declared and waged by the ruling classes of the various countries upon one another for conquest and spoils. That is my position today.

When a member of the Party's National Committee visited Terre Haute early in June, he found Debs seething with resentment against the President's pretensions of democracy, while Kate O'Hare and all the others were being sent to prison. Noble C. Wilson, Debs' campaign manager in 1916, dropped into Debs' office a few days later. The Socialist leader, sprawling idly in a chair behind his desk, seemed more animated than he had been for months. He laughed and joked as he told Wilson his plans. The hour had finally come, said Debs, for him to speak out against the war and accept the consequences. He had no doubt what the result would be. With the words bubbling through his clear, vigorous chuckle, he concluded, "Of course, I'll take about two jumps and they'll nail me, but that's all right." The next day, Eugene Debs caught the train going east from Terre Haute.

[2]

THE ONLY AVENUE of expression still open to Debs was the public platform. The Socialist press had been practically wiped out. Paper after paper had been suppressed or stripped of its second-class mailing permit—the *American Socialist,* the New York *Call, The Masses,* finally the *International Socialist Review* and Frank O'Hare's *Social Revolution.* But Debs knew that he would have no trouble securing lecture engagements. He deliberately framed his indictment of the war in extreme terms; such an approach jibed with both of his objectives. He wanted to arouse resentment and opposition to the war; he also wanted to taunt the Federal authorities into placing him on trial. Debs had been completely serious in his statement to Kate O'Hare that, if she went to prison, he would "feel guilty to be at large." Well, she was about to go to prison. So were hundreds of others. Rose Pastor Stokes had re-entered the Party and publicly expressed antiwar views, for which she had already received a ten-year sentence. Debs was determined either to open the prison gates or to swing them shut behind himself.

But his hope was frustrated. During the first two weeks of June, he gave his antiwar speech a dozen times in Indiana and Illinois. It was greeted with enthusiastic approval—and the Federal government took no steps against him. Debs became increasingly angry. After fifteen months of inactivity he was finally free. Although he persistently baited the district attorneys and vehemently denounced the President, nothing happened. Half of his beautiful plan was being spoiled by the callous indifference of the law-enforcement officials. This was the final insult.

As he took the train eastward into Ohio, Debs was happier than he had been for what seemed eternity. His own move would encourage similar action by other Socialists. At last he had resumed his customary post, at the head of the radical offensive. His love of a hard fight in a good cause was being satisfied to the utmost. If only the Federal government would take some notice of him, everything would be perfect, just perfect. And in Ohio the fight would be even more exultant. For a decade Ohio had been the center of the Party's left wing. It had been the only state to vote against the "sabotage" amendment in 1912. The Socialists there had waged a forthright struggle against every measure for the prosecution of the war. The leading Socialists of Ohio—Alfred Wagenknecht, Charles E. Ruthenberg, and Charles Baker—were all serving terms at the Stark County Workhouse in Canton for their opposition to the draft act. And Eugene Debs was in Canton on June 16, 1918, to speak at the Ohio convention of the Socialist Party.

Early in the afternoon, the local reception committee picked Debs up at the Courtland Hotel to drive him to Nimisilla Park, where he was to give his speech. As the small group of Socialists passed through the hotel lobby, Debs was intercepted by Clyde

R. Miller, a reporter for the Cleveland *Plain-Dealer*. Debs agreed to answer a few questions, so Miller asked if he still supported the St. Louis Manifesto. "I approved of the adoption of the platform in form and substance at the time it was created," said Debs, "but in the light of the Russian situation I think we should put forth a restatement of the aims of the Socialist Party." When asked to amplify this statement, Debs continued "that the Bolsheviki of Russia were the inspiration of the world and that he hoped their ideas would come to prevail in America." Miller also recalled that Debs "pointed out that the success of the Bolshevik movement in Russia was something on which to model and base the ideals for this country—the ideals espoused by the Socialists."

Eugene Debs did not go directly to the meeting at Nimisilla Park. He insisted that he must first stop at the Stark County Workhouse, which was almost across the street from the park. From his brief interview with the three Socialist prisoners, Debs acquired a new fury, a new determination. When the three men first were imprisoned, Wagenknecht and Ruthenberg were assigned to work in the laundry. This, they thought, was clearly discrimination against their political views, so they thanked the warden but felt compelled to refuse. For the next two days they hung by their wrists from a rafter. Charles Baker managed to smuggle this news out of the jail, and a fierce public uproar resulted in a compromise between the inmates and the warden. In spite of this experience the three men made no complaints to Debs. They felt confident that they were standing on the proper side of the battle.

A few minutes after Debs left the jail Alfred Wagenknecht, crowding up to the bars of his cell, saw him walking through the crowd in the Park. Not even the scorching heat had forced the Socialist leader to discard his tweed jacket or to unbutton his vest. As he made his way through the crowd, a Socialist on the platform opened the meeting by reading the Declaration of Independence. Then Mrs. Marguerite Prevey, Debs' hostess of preceding years, began to introduce the main speaker. Her remarks were brief, and they centered upon the widespread newspaper reports that Debs had repudiated his antiwar statements.

Mrs. Prevey thought this was quite amusing, and the gales of laughter seemed to prove that the audience agreed.

Finally Eugene Debs, calm, smiling, moved to the front of the platform, a plain wooden bandstand undecorated by the American flag. That seemed strange at a public meeting on June 16, 1918. But even more strange was Debs' speech. There was not much in it that he had not said many times in the past. But that speech became a byword, a flaming document in the Socialist movement, because this was war, and men did not say the things they might say in time of peace. Thousands of Socialists warmed themselves on bleak, cold days with the memory of Eugene Debs standing on the platform at Canton, speaking his mind.

Alfred Wagenknecht, although he pressed hard against the bars of his cell, could not hear the speaker in Nimisilla Park. It was too bad, because Debs was talking about Wagenknecht and the others: "I have just returned," said Debs, "from a visit over yonder, where three of our most loyal comrades are paying the penalty for their devotion to the cause of the working class. They have come to realize, as many of us have, that it is extremely dangerous to exercise the constitutional right of free speech in a country fighting to make democracy safe in the world. I realize that, in speaking to you this afternoon, there are certain limitations placed on the right of free speech. I must be exceedingly careful, prudent, as to what I say, and even more careful and prudent as to how I say it. (Laughter) I may not be able to say all I think; (Laughter and Applause) but I am not going to say anything that I do not think. I would a thousand times rather be a free soul in jail than to be a sycophant and coward in the streets. They may put those boys in jail—and some of the rest of us in jail—but they can not put the Socialist movement in jail."

And Debs swept irresistibly onward, defying the very injunction that he had laid down in his opening words. "There is but one thing you have to be concerned about, and that is that you keep four-square with the principles of the international Socialist movement. It is only when you begin to compromise that trouble begins. So far as I am.concerned, it does not matter what others may say, or think, or do, as long as I am sure that I

am right with myself and the cause." Now for the first time
Debs struck out at those Socialists who had deserted the Party:
"They lack the fiber for the revolutionary test; they fall away;
they disappear as if they had never been. On the other hand,
they who are animated by the unconquerable spirit of the social
revolution; they who have the moral courage to stand erect
and assert their convictions; stand by them; fight for them; go to
jail or to hell for them, if need be—they are writing their names,
in this crucial hour—they are writing their names in fadeless
letters in the history of mankind."

The crowd of twelve hundred persons was pressing forward
excitedly toward the platform. They laughed, shouted, applauded, clapped their hands, and waved their hats. And all
the while the Department of Justice agents and American Protective League volunteers moved through the audience, checking draft cards. Sweat ran down Debs' face as he moved back
and forth across the stage, then turned to lean far over the rail
and stretch his lean hands toward the men before him. "It
felt," said one man, "exactly as if that forefinger was hitting you
on the nose." The words, however, struck elsewhere: "They tell
us that we live in a great free republic; that our institutions are
democratic; that we are a free and self-governing people.
(Laughter) This is too much; even for a joke. (Laughter) But
it is not a subject for levity; it is an exceedingly serious matter."

The levity failed to disappear. As Debs continued his detailed
indictment of American society, he often remembered that
laughter is a potent weapon. The Supreme Court came in for
special treatment: "Why, the other day, by a vote of five to
four—a kind of craps game—come seven, come 'leven—they
declared the child labor law unconstitutional . . . and this in
our so-called Democracy, so that we may continue to grind the
flesh and blood and bones of puny litle children into profits for
the junkers of Wall Street . . . The history of this country is
being written in the blood of the childhood the industrial lords
have murdered."

During the next two hours, Debs passionately defended the
men who were being called murderers, and German agents, and
hoodlums. He spoke for Tom Mooney, who had been convicted

of throwing a bomb at a San Francisco preparedness parade in 1916. He spoke for Bill Haywood and the other Wobblies, who were even then on trial in a Chicago courtroom. He spoke for the Bolsheviks of Russia, who were being reviled and denounced in Congress, in the headlines, in the pulpits. What right had the profiteers, shouted Debs, to parade as superpatriots? The rulers of Wall Street, now vehemently denouncing the German junkers, had consorted with the junkers for years, traded with them, played golf with them, married their daughters to them. What right had Theodore Roosevelt, who had been so fond of Kaiser Wilhelm, to appear on the stage as the great enemy of German autocracy? While Theodore Roosevelt and the Kaiser were vacationing together at Potsdam in 1907, there were German socialists rotting in German prisons for their opposition to that same Kaiser. Who, in the name of truth, who was the real foe of German autocracy?

Only once in the entire speech did Debs speak about war, and even then he did not speak specifically about the World War. But his statement clearly was meant to cover the World War: "The master class has always declared the wars; the subject class has always fought the battles. The master class has had all to gain and nothing to lose, while the subject class has had nothing to gain and all to lose—especially their lives."

A government stenographer was frantically writing each word as Debs went into his stirring climax: "Yes, in good time we are going to sweep into power in this nation and throughout the world. . . . The world is changing daily before our eyes. The sun of capitalism is setting; the sun of Socialism is rising. . . . In due time the hour will strike and this great cause triumphant —the greatest in history—will proclaim the emancipation of the working class and the brotherhood of all mankind." As he walked down from the platform, roar after roar of applause and cheers broke from the audience. Each man felt surging within him a new devotion, a new strength, a strength that he had never realized in the past. Throughout the entire world socialists looked toward Eugene Debs and smiled.

But there were also frowns, and hostility, and anger. The government stenographer turned in his report of the speech, and the Federal Attorney's office in Cleveland read it carefully. The Espionage Act had just been amended to include several non-military offenses, such as uttering "profane, scurrilous and abusive language" about the government. Just thirteen days after the Canton speech, a Federal grand jury in Cleveland indicted Eugene Debs. Perhaps they thought it was "abusive" to call the Supreme Court "a kind of craps game," as he had done. They decided, at any rate, that Debs' speech at Canton had violated the new Sedition Act on ten different counts.

Debs was arrested on June 30, 1918, as he was about to enter the Bohemian Gardens in Cleveland to address a Socialist picnic. Taken to the Federal Building in Cleveland, he rode up in the elevator with Clyde R. Miller, the *Plain-Dealer* reporter who had interviewed him two weeks earlier in Canton. Miller again asked if Debs wanted to repudiate the St. Louis Manifesto. "I do not," replied Debs, "and, if necessary, I shall die for those principles." A few minutes later in the marshal's office, Debs told the reporters about his rôle in the formation of the American Railway Union and his indictment during the Pullman boycott.

Since it was Sunday, most of the offices were closed, and the authorities refused to make arrangements for Debs to post bail. So Eugene Debs, for the first time in twenty-three years, was compelled to sleep in a cell. A jailer awakened him the next morning with the news that he had been nominated for Congress by the Socialists of Terre Haute. Mrs. Marguerite Prevey and a Cleveland comrade, A. W. Moskowitz, soon provided the ten-thousand-dollar bond, and Debs was released.

When the Socialist leader returned to Terre Haute he spoke at a large meeting at the baseball park on Wabash Avenue. Although the audience was honeycombed with members of the local Defense League, Debs gave a two-hour presentation of his reason for opposing the war. Many of his fellow townsmen had become proficient at book burning, the detection of subversive schoolteachers, the destruction of German-owned grocery stores, threats to lynch Socialist miners, and other types of secret-service work. But when Debs finished his speech the audience rose to applaud.

CHAPTER XVIII

□

[1]

EUGENE DEBS was neither surprised nor alarmed by his arrest. In discussing the indictment with friends, he said simply: "I had a hunch that speech was likely to settle the matter."

But the rest of the country did not exhibit this same equanimity. Nothing during the entire war had shocked the American people in quite the same way as Debs' arrest. Most citizens had shown little concern about the suppression of the Socialist press, the mass arrests, the Bisbee atrocity, the long sentences and harsh treatment meted out to dissenters. But it was particularly revealing to hear Eugene Debs called a traitor and a German agent. Thousands of men who felt no sympathy for the Socialist cause were acquainted with Debs. Letters of support and applause arrived from every part of the land, and Debs replied by advising firm devotion to the principles of socialism.

Just a few days after he returned to Terre Haute from Canton, Debs was stricken by a severe attack of lumbago. Art Young and John Reed, covering the trial of the 105 Wobblies in Chicago for *The Liberator*, took advantage of the July Fourth recess to visit Debs. The door to 451 North Eighth Street was opened by Kate Debs, who explained that her husband had "not been well—not for a whole year." But she invited them to come in, and Debs, hearing about his visitors, insisted that he should dress and come downstairs. His descent reminded Art Young of "a human motor with wings." Debs shook hands with both of his guests at once, and Young noticed that "the old fire" was back in his eyes.

As the three men sat talking in the parlor, the sounds of the July Fourth parade came floating through the windows. In his report of the interview, John Reed mentioned the men who passed the house and looked at it "with expressions compounded

360

half of eager malice, and half of a sort of fear. 'That's where Gene Debs lives,' you could see them saying, as one would say, 'The House of the Traitor.' "

Finally Debs got up and said suddenly, "Come on, let's go out and sit on the front porch and give 'em a good show, if they want to see me." So they all moved out to the porch and sat there in their shirt sleeves, laughing among themselves at the passers-by. Whenever Debs was able to catch the eye of a man going down the sidewalk, the man "bowed over-cordially," according to Reed. The others "only looked furtively our way, and whispered." Reed asked Debs if he wasn't afraid of being lynched, and the Socialist leader confessed that the notion hadn't even entered his mind. "I guess I'm physically protected, anyway," he said. "I know that so long as I keep my eye on them, they won't dare to do anything. As a rule they're cowardly curs anyway."

Debs was inspired by the continuation of the antiwar movement in spite of the efforts of the government and the newspapers to destroy and silence the opposition. Speaking of his comrades, he said, "If this can't break them, why then I know nothing can. Socialism's on the way. They can't stop it, no matter what they do." Art Young drew a sketch of Debs' "lean, expressive hands" and another of his profile as he leaned against a porch box full of petunias. Finally the two men got up to leave, the youthful, sparkling John Reed who left the world one immortal piece of reportage, and the brilliant cartoonist, whose bald head and paunch gave him the appearance of a genial small-town politician. As they walked down the steps, Debs clasped their hands and slapped their shoulders, and told them not to break faith with the cause. "Now you tell all the boys everywhere who are making the fight, Gene Debs says he's with you, all the way, straight through, without a flicker."

But Debs had a premonition that he would not be a free agent very long; he refused to run for Congress in his home district. There was nominated in his stead Shubert Sebree, a young glassworker who had learned his Marxism under the tutelage of Stephen Reynolds. Here, thought Debs, was a living example of that heroism that gave him so much confidence in the final triumph of Socialism. "Please accept hearty congratulations from Theodore and myself upon your nomination for congress," Eugene Debs wrote to Sebree. "A better selection could not have been made. I need not say to you that you will have all the support we can possibly give you. You are a true representative of the class and the cause which the Socialist party represents and your nomination is alike creditable to yourself and the party."

Although Debs' lumbago lingered throughout the summer, he found the strength to make several speeches for Sebree's campaign. In August he attended a meeting in Chicago of all state secretaries of the Party, where he helped to defeat a move to repudiate the St. Louis Manifesto. On Labor Day he gave an antiwar speech in Akron. He was in Rochester on September 5, urging continued opposition to the war and a strong campaign to free the political prisoners. Kate O'Hare was now in a Missouri prison. Rose Pastor Stokes had just been convicted of violating the Sedition Act, but she was free on bail pending her appeal. And for Eugene Debs the doors of prison seemed a short step ahead.

In the last few days before his trial, which was scheduled for September 9 in the Federal District Court in Cleveland, Debs had several conferences with his attorneys. He had ignored Clarence Darrow's offer of help because of Darrow's prowar views, and Morris Hillquit was confined to a sanitarium with tuberculosis, but he was represented by a full battery of Socialist attorneys—Seymour Stedman and William A. Cunnea of Chicago, Joseph W. Sharts of Dayton, Morris H. Wolf of Cleveland. This array of legal talent found itself with almost nothing to do. Both Debs and his lawyers were agreed that they would not take advantage of any technicalities to secure an acquittal. They were prepared to admit that Debs had given the Canton speech, but they denied that his speech was criminal. They had filed a demurrer to the indictment, but it was overruled. Their sole argument was that the Sedition Act violated the First Amendment, and that question could scarcely be decided by a trial court. At a conference the night before the trial the four lawyers and Debs all felt that he was certain to be convicted. But the defendant had no regrets. "I have nothing to take back," he contended. "All I said I believe to be true."

The attorneys realized that the best weapons available were the personality and philosophy of Eugene Debs. Morris Wolf suggested several times that Kate Debs should be present in the courtroom, so that the jurors would regard Debs as a normal citizen rather than as a monster. The other attorneys tended to agree with Wolf. But each time this was mentioned to Debs he gave an evasive reply, saying that it might not be good for Kate's health. At no time, according to Wolf, did he say that he did not want Kate in the courtroom. Later, however, Debs told the reporters that Kate had remained in Terre Haute at his request.

For several hours before court convened on September 9 Debs was holding open house for his friends at the Hollenden Hotel and the Gillsy House. He was in perfect spirits and seemed quite unaware that there was anything unusual about that particular morning. To one comrade who was concerned about the outcome he said, "This is but another milepost along the pathway of progress. We shall not tarry here very long." When at length he went to the Federal Building he found the corridors of that huge and forbidding stone edifice packed with friends and sympathizers, all hoping for a seat to witness the trial. Most of them had removed their Party buttons from their coat lapels, but one man was wearing a bright red necktie. As the spectators passed into the courtroom they ran a gauntlet of FBI men and members of the American Protective League, who searched all pockets and purses for revolvers or bombs.

The courtroom itself was oak and marble, with a ceiling of gilt and tall windows. The judge's bench was long and imposing. On the wall above it hung an enormous painting of angels with swords of fire, guarding stone tablets on which were engraved the Ten Commandments. The judge seemed one with the bench, as immovable as the oak panels or the avenging angels. Judge D. C. Westenhaver was perhaps a typical judge. He had once been law partner to Secretary of War Newton D. Baker in Martinsburg, West Virginia; to that relation he possibly owed his appointment to the Federal bench. The Ohio Bar respected

him as a learned and industrious jurist. He was so rigidly honest
that he had resigned from the Union League Club when he became a judge. On the other hand, while a member of the Cleveland School Board, he had upheld the discharge of several
teachers who dared to organize a trade union. A man of narrow
sympathies, still he conducted the trial fairly, according to his
lights. Morris Wolf, of Debs' counsel, believed that the judge
was annoyed because the defendant held the center of the stage.
Certainly Judge Westenhaver was determined to uphold the
dignity of the bench. With heavy jowls, his lips drawn tightly
at the corners, he presided sternly over the proceedings.

The jury, equally with the judge, had a predisposition against
the defendant. Jury panels in the Federal District Court of
Cleveland were not chosen at random from the list of property
holders or voters. The method used was far more selective.
County judges in that Federal District recommended to the
Clerk of the District Court those men in their counties whom
they would consider qualified for jury duty. The jury was then
chosen from this panel. Thus the entire venire of one hundred
men, from which Debs' jury was chosen, had an average age of
seventy years, and came from the wealthy and respectable
class of citizens.

Several times during the questioning of the venire the ludicrous nature of the proceedings became obvious to the spectators. One talesman testified that he had no occupation. When
Seymour Stedman continued to question him, he finally said:
"Well, I'm president of an insurance company and director of a
bank, if you call that an occupation." He was not dismissed
until he was challenged by Stedman. Although the defense exhausted all of its peremptory challenges, the jury had been sworn
by 2:25 that afternoon. The twelve jurors were about seventy-
two years old, were worth from fifty to sixty thousand dollars
each, and were "retired from business, from pleasure, and from
responsibility for all troubles arising outside of their own families," according to Max Eastman who reported the trial for
The Liberator. Seven of them were former merchants or farmers.
All of them said that they believed in the Constitution and had
no prejudice against Socialists.

The case for the prosecution was opened by the assistant district attorney, F. B. Kavanagh, who pointed toward the defendant and said: "This man is the palpitating pulse of the sedition crusade." His speech lasted nearly an hour. When he had finished, Debs cordially leaned across the table and congratulated Kavanagh for his oratory.

In his opening statement for the defense Seymour Stedman took his cue from a remark by Kavanagh, who had said: "by his words shall he be judged, and by his words shall he be condemned." Stedman spoke at length about the career of Eugene Debs, concluding: "We ask you to judge Eugene V. Debs by his life, his deeds and his works. If you will do that we shall abide by your verdict." At this statement there was a flurry of clapping in the courtroom. The judge instantly shouted, "Arrest that man, and that woman! Arrest everybody you saw clapping their hands!" One of the offenders was Rose Pastor Stokes, who was attending Debs' trial while waiting for the decision on her appeal. It now seemed likely that she would be sent to jail for contempt of court. But William Cunnea, one of the defense lawyers, said quietly to Judge Westenhaver: "I don't like to see you sit up there and play God to your fellow men." The judge was so startled by this impertinence that he adjourned court for the day.

The following morning a few of the culprits were fined and the incident was forgotten; the brash Irishman William Cunnea had scored his point. Then began the procession of witnesses for the government. Clyde R. Miller, the reporter for the *Plain-Dealer*, testified about his interview with Debs in the Hotel Courtland before the Canton speech. Miller, regarding his rôle with obvious distaste, seemed personally friendly to the defendant. As he left the stand Debs walked over to him and said quietly: "Mr. Miller, all that you said about me is true. You quoted me straight and accurate. I don't want you to ever feel that you have done me an injury by testifying against me. You had to do it, and you did it like a gentleman. We all do what we cannot possibly help doing, and no blame or stigma attaches to any of us for doing that."

The second witness was Virgil Steiner, a twenty-year-old

youth who read his version of Debs' speech at Canton. When he was hired by the Department of Justice to go to Nimisilla Park, Steiner was regularly employed by a motor concern in Canton. His shorthand was hopelessly inadequate and he had abandoned all effort to follow the speaker, simply writing until he became tired, pausing to rest, then catching a few more sentences. Another version of the Canton speech was read by Edward R. Sterling, a Canton attorney who had been hired by the Socialist Party as a stenographic reporter for the meeting on June 16. Whenever Sterling read a passage that struck him as particularly damning, he glanced at the jury to make certain they understood its true significance. These two reports of Debs' speech, one of them 25 per cent shorter than the other, were printed side by side in parallel columns. They formed the main evidence for the prosecution.

The entire trial had developed a festive atmosphere. Dozens of Socialists had come to Cleveland for the proceedings and each noon they held a gay luncheon at the Hotel Hollenden, where most of them were staying. The bills for the entire party were being paid by William Bross Lloyd, the millionaire son of Henry Demarest Lloyd, who had provided bail for Bill Haywood, Kate O'Hare and other Socialists. But Eugene Debs graciously denied Lloyd's hospitality. He insisted on staying at a more modest hotel, the Gillsy House on Ninth Street, where he had always stopped in Cleveland. He was even less concerned about the trial than were the spectators and attorneys. In his opinion he was already convicted and the trial was a mere formality. He had spent an entire day listening to staccato versions of his speech, and his beautiful prose had been mutilated. This was so upsetting that he began to pass the time by doing some rather heavy drinking. Each day at noon he tried to sneak away from his companions at the Hotel Hollenden and go to a small saloon around the corner. Finally Morris Wolf, one of his attorneys, was detailed by the others to keep Debs sober. Actually there was not much else for the lawyers to do.

On the morning of September 11, the third day, the court was so densely packed that the doors could not be closed. The spectators, once inside, found it impossible to leave the room. Between the audience and the participants there stretched a thin line of secret service agents. The first witness was Charles E. Ruthenberg, who was called to identify the St. Louis Manifesto. "His coming there from the prison cell," wrote Max Eastman, "was designed to impress the jury, I suppose, with an idea that all Socialists ought to be in jail. His quietness, his gracious demeanor, his thin, keen, agile face—he is like a smiling hawk— seemed to testify to the absurdity of sending any of them to jail."

Ruthenberg was followed by a few witnesses who had attended the meeting at Nimisilla Park, and whose estimates of the crowd varied from two hundred to fifteen hundred persons. But they did establish that Debs had given a speech, and that the audience had contained several men of draft age. Then Clyde R. Miller returned to the stand to testify about his conversation with Debs in the Federal Building after the Socialist leader was arrested on June 30. Every five or ten minutes Seymour Stedman rose to his feet, as he had been doing throughout the trial, to take exception to a question. Several times Stedman seemed to be trying to conceal or qualify Debs' views, a tactic that the defense had specifically rejected in advance. But his objections were almost always overruled by Judge Westenhaver, so it made little difference.

The final witness for the prosecution was Joseph Triner, an officer attached to Naval Intelligence in Chicago. Triner, in the course of his investigation of a mysterious explosion in the Federal Building in Chicago, had attended the August 11 meeting of the state secretaries of the Socialist Party. The witness was extremely vague as to the facts: he did not know whether there had been ten men or fifty present in Imperial Hall; he did not know what had been said either before or after Debs' speech. But he did know that Eugene Debs, during a ten-minute statement to the Socialist leaders, had said: "A working man has no place in a capitalist's war such as this. The only war in which I have any interest is that of the workers against the capitalists. They may call me a disloyalist and brand me a traitor, but I shall stick to my principles. The master class is pretending to wage this war for democracy, but by persecuting us they have branded this pretension a lie. I earnestly hope that there may be no one present here today that will want to change the party's attitude toward the war."

When the Federal attorney announced that there would be no more government witnesses, there was a pause. Debs glanced at Stedman. Stedman glanced at the prosecutor. Then Stedman said, "Let's see, you rest. We rest." Max Eastman thought that "a kind of numb surprise" went through the courtroom. But this step was easily predictable. The defense had no witnesses. They were prepared to admit all the facts which the government, to the intense disgust of Eugene Debs, had just spent two days proving. The judge declared a recess of ten minutes, and Morris Wolf, the only Cleveland attorney on Debs' staff, headed for His Honor's chambers. Wolf pleaded that Debs should be allowed to speak in his own way. Judge Westenhaver agreed to accord him that privilege.

When the court reconvened, Seymour Stedman announced that Debs would make his own plea to the jury. At once the atmosphere became concentrated in the courtroom. The badly diluted drama of the previous two days abruptly changed. A dull and ponderous proceeding acquired a tension that was immediately felt. An expectant air permeated the spectators, the prosecutors, and the judge. It was two o'clock on the afternoon of September 11, 1918. Thunderclouds had shut out the sun. Somber shadows sprawled through the vacant windows and splashed upon the floor. The avenging angels above the bench were scarcely visible in the failing light. Debs' friends had seen him the previous evening, sitting near an open window in the Gillsy House, clad in pajamas, calmly smoking a cigar and writing on a pad propped against his knees. He now rose, scraped a few sheets into a single pile, and carried the papers in his left hand as he walked toward the jury box.

All memory of the 1895 conspiracy trial faded from his mind as he began to speak: "For the first time in my life I appear before a jury in a court of law to answer for a crime. . . . Standing before you, charged as I am with crime, I can yet look the Court in the face, . . . for in my conscience, in my soul, there is festering no accusation of guilt." His worn gray suit hanging

from his shoulders, his left arm limp at his side, his right hand
extended to punctuate his remarks, Debs spoke in a quiet but
firm voice: "Permit me to say in the first place that I am entirely satisfied with the Court's ruling. I have no fault to find
with the district attorney or with the counsel for the prosecution."

"I wish to admit the truth of all that has been testified to in
this proceeding. I have no disposition to deny anything that is
true. . . . I admit being opposed to the present form of government. I admit being opposed to the present social system. I am
doing what little I can, and have been for many years, to bring
about a change that shall do away with the rule of the great
body of people by a relatively small class and establish in this
country an industrial and social democracy."

When Debs began to explain why he was sympathetic to the
Russian Bolsheviks, the Federal attorney objected that his remarks were not relevant "to the evidence in the case." But
Judge Westenhaver, faithful to his agreement with Morris
Wolf, replied that he would "permit the defendant to proceed
in his own way." Debs went on: "It may be that the much-
despised Bolsheviki may fail at last, but let me say to you that
they have written a chapter of glorious history. It will stand to
their eternal credit." Lenin and Stalin and Trotzky were being
denounced as "criminals and outlaws." But the vituperation
against George Washington and Samuel Adams and Patrick
Henry had not halted the American Revolution. The murder
of Elijah Lovejoy had merely hastened the abolition of slavery.
Thus the minority of today became the majority of tomorrow,
and found its vindication in universal acclaim.

Debs contended that he himself was charged with crime because he believed "as the revolutionary fathers did in their
time, that a change was due in the interests of the people, that
the time has come for a better form of government, an improved
system, a higher social order, a nobler humanity and a grander
civilization." The ruling class was helpless against "the rise of
the toiling and producing masses," said Debs: "You may hasten
the change; you may retard it; you can no more prevent it than
you can prevent the coming of the sunrise on the morrow."

Such intensity is normally reserved for love scenes, when one person speaks to another of those visions that hold his every wish. The spectators were hushed and frozen; the jurymen were leaning forward as if to hear the next sentence before it was uttered; the Federal attorney and the judge rested in their seats of power. Gone now were the technicalities and the haggling; gone was the ludicrous tone, as men clambered above the trivial facts to reach a more concentrated atmosphere.

It was mere prattle to speak of brotherhood, Debs protested, so long as men tolerated a social system "in which we are a mass of warring units, in which millions of workers have to fight one another for jobs, and millions of business and professional men have to fight one another for trade, for practice—in which we have individual interests and each is striving to care for himself alone without reference to his fellow men." This commercial conflict led directly to armed conflict, and no amount of talk could hide the truth. American workers had been paid so little that they could not purchase the goods they produced. American businessmen, in their search for profits, had been forced to battle for foreign markets. They had been opposed by the owning classes of Germany, Austria, even of England and France. The war had resulted from exploitation in every capitalist country. Exploitation always led to militarism, as Eugene Debs had seen even in time of peace—the Pullman boycott, the bull pens at Cripple Creek, the Ludlow Massacre.

Debs asked the court for permission to present statistics on profiteering during the war, so that this point would be established beyond dispute. But Judge Westenhaver refused the permission, saying that there would be "no consensus of opinion or agreement" on the matter. Thus Debs lost the chance to say the one thing that, above all others, he truly wanted to say.

But Debs made his point in other ways. He defended his right to oppose a war that he thought was unjust: "The Mexican war was bitterly condemned by Abraham Lincoln, by Charles Sumner, by Daniel Webster and by Henry Clay." He defended all those who had exercised this right during the World War— Rose Pastor Stokes, Kate O'Hare, Big Bill Haywood, and the Wobblies. He defended the St. Louis Manifesto because "I believed then, as I believe now, that the statement correctly defined the attitude of the Socialist Party toward war. That statement, bear in mind, did not apply to the people of this country alone, but to the people of the world. It said, in effect, to the people, especially to the workers, of all countries, 'Quit going to war. Stop murdering one another for the profit and glory of the ruling classes. Cultivate the arts of peace. Humanize humanity. Civilize civilization.' That is the essential spirit and the appeal of the much-hated, condemned St. Louis platform."

Eugene Debs had been talking for nearly two hours. The shadows had completely blotted out the former streak of light across the floor. His voice became muffled: "I do not know, I cannot tell, what your verdict may be; nor does it matter much, so far as I am concerned. Gentlemen, I am the smallest part of this trial. I have lived long enough to appreciate my own personal insignificance in relation to a great issue that involves the welfare of the whole people. What you may choose to do to me will be of small consequence after all. I am not on trial here. There is an infinitely greater issue that is being tried in this court, though you may not be conscious of it. American institutions are on trial here before a court of American citizens. The future will tell."

As Debs returned slowly to his seat, Morris Wolf noticed that several of the jurymen were crying. A Department of Justice agent said to a reporter at the press table: "You've got to hand it to the old man. He came through clean."

Edwin S. Wertz, the Federal attorney, used the remainder of the afternoon to sum up for the prosecution. He reviewed all of the testimony that had been given, and attributed to Debs the willful obstruction of the draft act. Eugene Victor Debs, said the prosecutor, was "an old ewe" who was trying to lead his flock of innocent followers into prison. Debs' professions of international friendship were held up to ridicule. "I'll tell you what internationalism is," exclaimed Mr. Wertz. "Pitch all the nations into one pot with the Socialists on top and you've got internationalism." At these words the Socialists in the courtroom flushed; Judge Westenhaver looked restive; the Federal attorney seemed pleased. Hadn't Debs said that he was as guilty as Rose Stokes, and hadn't Rose Stokes been convicted by a jury in Kansas City? The conclusion was too apparent to require emphasis, but the prosecutor drew four heavy black lines under it to enlighten the jury.

Court adjourned for the day at the end of Wertz's summation. As Eugene Debs emerged from the courtroom into the corridor a young girl handed him a huge bouquet of red roses, and then fainted at his feet.

Debs spent the evening at the Gillsy House, writing letters and chatting with his friends. Max Eastman had asked him one day if the trial was an emotional strain. "No," Debs had replied, "it doesn't rest on my mind much. You see, if I'm sent to jail it can't be for a very long time, whereas if you go it may be an important part of your life. That's why my heart has been with you boys all these months."

The next morning Judge Westenhaver gave his final charge to the jury, and it was eminently fair. He instructed the jury to find the defendant Not Guilty on those counts dealing with ridicule of the Federal government. The counts remaining in the indictment charged that Debs had willfully and knowingly tried to obstruct the operation of the conscription act. Then the jurymen struggled to their feet and hobbled out of the courtroom, carrying copies of the speech and the indictment. They remained absent for six hours, while the defendant regaled his friends with dozens of anecdotes about Abraham Lincoln.

Eugene Debs was fascinated by the Civil War President. The comparison between Lincoln and himself, drawn in 1894 by John Swinton, had proved irresistible, until even Debs sometimes thought in those terms. Certainly there was a superficial resemblance. Both men owned that peculiar mixture of crudeness and gallantry so common to the dirt farmers of the Corn Belt. Long before 1900 Debs had revealed Lincoln's gift for the homespun epigram, as in his comment that a trade-union opponent sounded like the wind wailing around the corner of a silo, or his more famous remark: "Corporate capital has reduced labor to a fluttering rag—a walking hunger-pang." But Debs showed small understanding in his attempts to remake Lincoln in his own image. His stock of Lincoln lore included a

story about Lincoln's visit to New Orleans in 1828. Seeing a
Negro girl auctioned from the block, Lincoln had firmly resolved: "If I ever get a chance I'll hit at the very foundations
of chattel slavery, and I'll hit it hard." That was the way Debs
told the story. Unfortunately it was not true at all. The leading
rôle in the drama was tailored for Eugene Debs, not for Abraham Lincoln. But Debs' scholarship was not always so faulty.
One paragraph of his plea to the jury was faithfully, and perhaps
unconsciously, molded from John Brown's Final Address to the
Court.

Shortly before five o'clock the jurymen filed back into the
courtroom. The youngest among them, Cyrus H. Stoner, aged
fifty-eight years, rose to read the verdict. The inevitable words
were droned out. On three separate counts: "Guilty as charged
in the indictment." Judge Westenhaver fixed Saturday morning, September 14, as the time for passing sentence, and Debs
left the courtroom facing a possible prison term of sixty years.
Walking up the corridor, he said of the jury: "There is something
pathetic about dressed up faces—smug bodies. If they had been
dressed in rags it would have been all right. What a contrast
to turn toward the back of the court-room and find a little
group of beautiful Socialists, with stars for eyes—you can always tell them!"

Court being recessed on Friday, Debs spent the day in Akron
at the home of Mrs. Marguerite Prevey. His lawyers insisted
that he should take advantage of his right to make another
speech before sentence was passed. Debs, tired of the whole proceeding, adamantly refused. A heated wrangle followed, and
finally Debs yielded. He ventured forth on a brief errand, and
then retired to a small room at the head of the stairs to write his
speech. When Morris Wolf went up to see Debs a few hours
later, the nature of the errand became obvious. A pint bottle of
bourbon, now sorely emaciated, was on the corner of the table.

Debs was angry at the Federal attorney. Mr. Wertz, in his
final summary, had referred scornfully to both Rose Pastor
Stokes and Kate O'Hare. Debs was now writing a bitter attack
on the prosecutor. Wolf objected that such a descent to personalities would obscure the real issues and make the entire trial

a burlesque. Debs glared at Wolf: "He isn't a friend of yours, is he?" Wolf tried to explain that he could do more for his client if he did not alienate the Federal officials. Men like Wertz, said the attorney, were mere hired hands who had no responsibility for the proceedings, they were just trying to make a living. Debs was not convinced, and there was another long argument. Finally Wolf, close to despair, summoned Marguerite Prevey to the room. She prevailed where Wolf had met with failure and Debs agreed to delete all references to Wertz.

Then Debs had to write a new beginning for his speech. Back in January, 1913, he had crowded his entire philosophy into a single sentence that appeared in *The Masses*. He had used the same phrases, changing but a single word, on the title page of *Labor and Freedom*, a collection of his writings and speeches published in 1916. He now returned to the original version and began to write: "While there is a lower class . . ."

When court opened on Saturday, the Federal attorney moved for the imposition of sentence. The clerk asked if the defendant would like to make a final statement. Eugene Debs again rose from his chair and began talking as he moved toward the bench. There were no notes to be gathered up, no papers to guide him, but all that an honest man can learn in sixty years was contained in his opening remark: "Your Honor, years ago I recognized my kinship with all living things, and I made up my mind that I was not one bit better than the meanest of the earth. I said then, I say now, that while there is a lower class, I am in it; while there is a criminal element, I am of it; while there is a soul in prison, I am not free."

Eugene Debs had already forgotten his promise to Morris Wolf and to Marguerite Prevey: "Everything in connection with this case has been conducted upon a dignified plane, and in a respectful and decent spirit—with just one exception. Your Honor, my sainted mother inspired me with a reverence for womanhood that amounts to worship. I can think with disrespect of no woman, and I can think with respect of no man who can. I resent the manner in which the names of two noble women were bandied in this court. The levity and the wanton-

ness in this instance was absolutely inexcusable. When I think of
what was said in this connection, I feel that when I pass a
woman, even though it be a sister of the street, I should take off
my hat and apologize for being a man."

Debs' friends had long noticed that liquor made him even
more eloquent, more sensitive, more gentle—and it was true.
"In the struggle," he continued, "the unceasing struggle—between the toilers and producers and their exploiters, I have
tried . . . to serve those among whom I was born, with whom
I expect to share my lot until the end of my days."

"I am thinking this morning of the men in the mills and factories; I am thinking of the women who, for a paltry wage, are
compelled to work out their lives; of the little children who, in
this system, are robbed of their childhood, and in their early,
tender years, are seized in the remorseless grasp of Mammon,
and forced into the industrial dungeons, there to feed the machines while they themselves are being starved body and soul.
I can see them dwarfed, diseased, stunted, their little lives
broken, and their hopes blasted, because in this high noon of our
twentieth century civilization money is still so much more important than human life. Gold is god and rules in the affairs of
men. . . ."

"I never more clearly comprehended than now the great
struggle between the powers of greed on the one hand and upon
the other the rising hosts of freedom. I can see the dawn of a
better day of humanity. The people are awakening. In due
course of time they will come into their own. . . ."

When the end came, Judge Westenhaver still sat, unshaken
and severe. The judge declared that he was second to no man in
his sympathy for the poor and suffering. But he was amazed by
the "remarkable self-delusion and self-deception of Mr. Debs
who assumes that he is serving humanity and the downtrodden." Those who violate the law must suffer the penalties.
This applied with double force to those persons "within our
borders who would strike the sword from the hand of this nation while she is engaged in defending herself against a foreign
and brutal power." Declaring himself "a conserver of the peace

and a defender of the Constitution of the United States," Judge Westenhaver imposed a sentence of ten years in prison upon the Socialist leader.

Many spectators scarcely heard the sentence. They had been transported into a cleaner, better land by the speech of Eugene Debs, which caused many a strangled gasp in the courtroom. He had appeared as a gigantic bridge, a man who stood with one foot firmly anchored in the present, the other in the future, while the multitude walked across his shoulders. A portion of humanity felt purified in the sacremental vision of Eugene Victor Debs:

> Let the people take heart and hope everywhere,
> for the cross is bending,
> the midnight is passing,
> and joy cometh with the morning.

CHAPTER XIX

◻

[1]

WITH the exception of the Pullman boycott, no incident in Debs' career aroused so much comment as the Canton speech and the subsequent trial. Thousands of people who neither knew nor cared about his Socialist beliefs vaguely understood that he was sent to prison because he opposed the World War. Some men adopted the romantic viewpoint that it was a transmuted Eugene Debs who faced the jury in a Cleveland courtroom. So gradually, over a number of years, the events of 1918 came to form an important part of the Debs Legend. Typical are the comments of Heywood Broun: "Debs . . . was never the brains of his party. I never met him, but I read many of his speeches, and most of them seemed to be second-rate utterances. But when his great moment came a miracle occurred. Debs made a speech to the judge and jury at Columbus after his conviction, and to me it seems one of the most beautiful and moving passages in the English language. He was for that one afternoon touched with inspiration. If anybody told me that tongues of fire danced upon his shoulders as he spoke, I would believe it."

This statement by Broun probably missed the main point. Debs' speech in Cleveland was a culmination, not an explosive miracle. Given his early convictions, given his intimate acquaintance with the workingmen of America, given his two decades in the Socialist movement, he inevitably faced his accusers in a Federal courtroom. Arrived there, he said nothing that he had not said in the past. Even his phrases, his images, had been accumulated during countless appearances on the lecture platform. The importance of Eugene Debs derives from the road he followed to reach that courtroom in Cleveland, not from a single afternoon when "tongues of fire danced upon his shoulders as he spoke."

Equally popular was Broun's belief that Debs "was never the brains of his party." This description was endorsed by most Socialist leaders, whether radical or reformist. Although they acknowledged Debs' "spiritual" leadership, they steadfastly contended that he was no thinker or theoretician. This too became an unquestioned segment of the Debs Legend, but it seems just as mistaken as Broun's other concept about Debs. Certainly Eugene Debs was untutored in both literature and science, lacked the will for serious scholarship, was unable to reach decisions by theoretical study. Sometimes he reacted to new conditions with astonishing tardiness. His flirtation with the IWW badly retarded the growth of industrial unionism. His opposition to reform parties hindered the development of a working-class political movement. He misjudged the plight of the Negro people. His failure to insist on a united Socialist movement had tragic consequences in 1917.

But in spite of these faults Eugene Debs deserves to be known as the political leader of American socialism. He clung with stubborn insistence to the basic principles of Marxian socialism. He showed an uncanny ability to foresee issues and to devise remedies. He first raised the standard against the prosecution of Bill Haywood and Fred Warren and the McNamaras; against intervention in Mexico; against participation in the World War. He played a part in hundreds of hard-fought strikes. He hurled his waning energies into the struggle for American recognition of Soviet Russia. Debs' sole purpose was to inspire a working-class revolt against the capitalist system, and his success was truly remarkable. He kindled the fires of a newer hope for millions of his fellow citizens.

And through all of these temporary battles, Debs held to the twin objectives that he had announced before 1900, industrial unionism and revolutionary politics. No other prominent radical was entitled to the same boast. The right wing of the Party had become enamored with reform platforms and machine methods; the left wing had sought the illusory success of anarcho-syndicalism; Debs had stanchly opposed both trends. He had consistently been among the first to capitalize on immediate issues, and he had never forgotten his ultimate goal of socialism.

Debs' career is startling, not because he made mistakes, but because he made so few of them.

The attacks on Eugene Debs were directed against his associates as well as his principles. In 1910, for instance, Ernest Untermann said of Debs: "Nearly all of his advisers in the labor movement have turned out to be crooked." Certainly the facts lend weight to the charge that Debs was both naïve and sentimental in his estimates of other people. His cordiality toward the prowar Socialists, even after they had deserted the Party, is illustrative of the value he placed on personal friendship and the former records of his associates.

A second explanation, however, is needed to complete the story. Eugene Debs was neither a purist nor a moralist, but a trade-union leader and a Socialist. He firmly believed that basic changes in human behavior would follow rather than precede the establishment of socialism. So he took help where he could find it, balancing the risks against the benefits. These colleagues inevitably acquired a measure of power, and some of them used it to their personal advantage. In the Socialist Party this policy led to chaos; in the American Railway Union it led to success. No criticism of Debs is involved in the splotchy records of such men as George Howard; actually it is a tribute that Debs was able to use Howard's abilities for a constructive purpose.

[2]

AFTER JUDGE WESTENHAVER imposed sentence on Eugene Debs, the defense attorneys announced their intention of challenging the Espionage Act and the conviction of Debs in the Supreme Court. As Debs stepped into the corridor, he was approached by Clyde R. Miller, the *Plain-Dealer* reporter who had testified for the prosecution. "Mr. Debs," Miller began, "you got exactly the sentence you deserve, but I am sorry it had to be you. You are such a decent guy."

Debs smiled and placed his hand on Miller's shoulder: "Listen, son, I want to say something to you. First, I want to thank you for your testimony. It was straightforward, clear and accurate. . . . Because I hold my opinion I am going to Atlanta for twenty years. Because you hold your opinion you are going to France. I don't know that I shall ever live out my sentence. You don't know that you will ever get back from France. But if you do get back, and if I get out of prison and we should meet, what do you say we agree now to sit down together and tell each other which one of us was most nearly right or wrong about this war."

"That seemed fair," Miller recalled, "and I said so. We shook hands. He left for Atlanta and I for France."

Actually, however, Debs returned from Cleveland to await the results of his appeal to the Supreme Court. Under the terms imposed by Judge Westenhaver he was forbidden to venture beyond Terre Haute and the Northern District of Ohio. The Socialist Party of Ohio arranged more than twenty meetings for him in the northeastern part of the state. Debs was eagerly preparing to leave Terre Haute when the outbreak of a serious influenza epidemic made it necessary to cancel all of the engagements. This untoward event frustrated Debs' thirst for activity; it also threatened financial calamity. His income had practically ended fifteen months earlier at the outbreak of the war; but he and Theodore had continued to maintain their office in Terre Haute, handle their voluminous correspondence, mail out thousands of free pamphlets. By the autumn of 1918 Debs was more than a thousand dollars in debt, with no change in sight.

But he accepted his situation and settled down to a quiet life at home. He had been in Terre Haute only a few days when he read in *Upton Sinclair's Magazine* the first installment of Sinclair's new novel, *Jimmie Higgins*. In this novel Debs, who appears as The Candidate, finds new strength and devotion from his brief contact with the mythical rank-and-file Socialist invented by Ben Hanford, and now cleverly elaborated by Sinclair. Debs was delighted by this fictional likeness of the men who personified the socialist movement. "JIMMIE HIGGINS," Debs wrote to the author, "is the chap who is always on the job; who does all the needed work that no one else will do; who never grumbles, never finds fault, and is never discouraged. All he asks is the privilege of doing his best for the cause where it is most needed. . . . The pure joy it gives him to serve the cause is his only reward. . . . Almost anyone can be THE CANDIDATE, and almost anyone will do for a speaker, but it takes the rarest of qualities to produce a JIMMIE HIGGINS. These qualities are developed in the 'lower class' only. They are denied those who know not the trials and privations, the bitter struggle, the heartache and despair of the victims of man's inhumanity to his less fortunate fellow-man."

Even as Debs was writing this letter, its calm assurance was being fulfilled in Terre Haute. The home of Noble C. Wilson, who had managed Debs' campaign in 1916, was raided by Federal agents. They confiscated large quantities of literature and several letters from Debs; this material was never returned. They carefully inspected a box of charcoal tablets in the belief that they might have found dynamite. Wilson warned them to be careful; they might blow their noses off.

Shubert Sebree, the Terre Haute glass worker who had been nominated for Congress when Debs refused to run in 1918, was visited by the foreseen reprisals. Less than a month after he accepted the nomination, he was discharged from his job, deserted by his union, and blacklisted by the employers of Terre Haute. He was forced to move to Danville, Illinois, taking with him his wife, a young son, and a dependent mother. Eugene Debs was not alone in his willingness to make sacrifices for his convictions, and he well knew it. "I am more than sorry but not a bit surprised," he wrote to Sebree, "that you have been hounded out of town. It is the fate of such true souls as you and I know you can bear it. You were too good and real a union man to last among these miserable pretenders. But your day will come as sure as truth prevails. I know how gladly you would serve my sentence and my heart goes to you in love and gratitude."

It was true of Eugene Debs, as it was true of Jimmie Higgins, that "the pure joy it gives him to serve the cause is his only reward." After nearly twenty years as The Candidate, Debs still regarded himself as merely a small part of a mighty movement. He had never built a personal machine in the Socialist Party; nor had he ever sought honors or power for himself. But the praise of his comrades, the confidence given him by men of like

mind, always warmed his soul and inspired him to greater
efforts. Thus he gained considerable satisfaction from John
Reed's report of their meeting on July Fourth in Terre Haute.
"I have read and been deeply moved by your fine article in the
September *Liberator*," Debs wrote to Reed. "You write differ-
ently than anyone else and your style is most appealing to me.
There is a living something that breathes and throbs in all you
say."

Eugene Debs and John Reed found common cause in their
belief in the Bolshevik Revolution. During the autumn and
winter of 1918, these two men did all in their power to halt the
American intervention in Russia. Reed published his account
of the events in St. Petersburg, *Ten Days That Shook the World*,
and gave dozens of speeches based on his eyewitness knowledge
of the revolution. Eugene Debs, speaking "as a Socialist, as a
revolutionist, and as a Bolshevist, if you please," issued a
series of stirring appeals for support to the Soviet government.
In November of 1918, when the American armies had invaded
Russia, Debs publicly pledged his aid to the Communist country:

> Comrades of the Russian Soviet and the Bolshevik Republic,
> we salute and honor you on this first anniversary of your great
> revolutionary triumph, the greatest in point of historic signifi-
> cance and far-reaching influence in the annals of the race. . . .
> The chief glory of your revolutionary triumph is that you
> have preserved inviolate the fundamental principles of inter-
> national Socialism and refused to compromise. . . .
> You . . . are resolved that . . . the working-class . . .
> shall not allow itself to be used . . . to install some intermediate
> class into power and perpetuate its own slavery and degrada-
> tion. . . .
> We pledge you . . . to strive with all our energy to emulate
> your inspiring example by abolishing our imperialistic capital-
> ism, driving our plutocratic exploiters and oppressors from
> power and establishing the working class republic, the Common-
> wealth of Comrades.

Nikolai Lenin, it soon became known, fully reciprocated
Debs' respect and admiration. In December, 1918, the *Class
Struggle*, an organ of the new left wing in the Socialist Party,

published Lenin's "Letter to American Workers," which had
been written the previous August. "I also recall," Lenin had
written, "the words of one of the most beloved leaders of the
American proletariat, Eugene Debs, who wrote . . . that he,
Debs, would rather be shot than vote for loans for the present
criminal and reactionary imperialist war; that he, Debs, knew
of only one holy and, from the standpoint of the proletariat,
legal war, namely: the war against the capitalists, the war for
the liberation of mankind from wage slavery!"

Meanwhile the war had ended. A gigantic strike wave was
sweeping the United States. The split between the left and right
wings of the Socialist Party was daily growing deeper and
sharper, based primarily on a difference in attitudes toward the
Bolshevik Revolution. Peace negotiations were being conducted
at Versailles. And Eugene Debs was denied an active rôle in
these titanic events because he had suffered another nervous
and physical breakdown. He was held to his home in Terre
Haute, issuing an occasional blast at the meetings in Versailles,
pleading for American recognition of the Soviet government.
Early in December he recovered sufficiently to make a few
speeches in Ohio, but both his health and his financial plight
were continuous cause for concern. Debs was scarcely aware
of these problems; a New Year's card to a friend said: "I love
and salute you at the dawn of the New Year and the New Era."

During the early months of 1919 Debs continued to give occasional speeches in northeastern Ohio and to write articles for
the Socialist press. Then, on March 10, 1919, his conviction was
upheld by the United States Supreme Court in a remarkable
opinion. Mr. Justice Oliver Wendell Holmes, one week earlier,
had declared that free speech could be abridged only in case of
"a clear and present danger" to the public safety. But Mr.
Justice Holmes, in writing the majority opinion in the Debs
case, did not even mention the doctrine that he himself had
invented. Nor did the Justice have much sympathy with those
who criticized his apparent inconsistency. "I am beginning,"
he wrote to a friend on April 5, "to get stupid letters of protest
against a decision that Debs, a noted agitator, was rightly convicted of obstructing the recruiting service so far as the law is

concerned. . . . There was a lot of jaw about free speech, which I dealt with somewhat summarily in an earlier case . . ."

Unless the President chose to exercise clemency, Eugene Debs was now certain to go to prison. Debs, however, was singularly unmoved by his impending fate. The day after the Supreme Court decision was announced, he issued a broadside to the newspapers:

The decision is perfectly consistent with the character of the Supreme Court as a ruling class tribunal. It could not have been otherwise. So far as I am personally concerned, the decision is of small consequence. . . .

Great issues are not decided by courts, but by the people. I have no concern in what the coterie of begowned corporation lawyers in Washington may decide in my case. The court of final resort is the people, and that court will be heard from in due time. . . .

As the harsh Indiana winter began to give way to a mild spring, a Terre Haute barber casually commented to a customer: "Well, it's coming along to Easter time, and we're getting ready for another crucifixion." And on April 12, 1919, Eugene Debs received a phone call from the Federal attorney in Cleveland, ordering him to report at once for delivery to prison.

[2]

THE MOMENT had arrived. The telephone call came at eleven o'clock in the morning, and Debs intended to catch an overnight train to Cleveland. He passed the day calmly making preparations for an extended absence. Hundreds of telegrams and special letters wished him good fortune, and he answered as many of them as possible. He walked around Terre Haute saying good-by to old friends. It seemed pleasant to stroll through the warm, clean air of the Indiana springtime.

David Karsner, a young reporter for the New York *Call*, had arranged to spend the day with Debs and accompany him to prison. Karsner asked if Debs had thought about the possibility of a pardon. "I don't know anything about one," Debs replied. "I have asked for none, nor shall I. I stand on the threshold of going to prison with malice toward none, and with perfect faith in the rectitude of my course and an absolute confidence in the justice and ultimate triumph of the cause to which I have gladly given my services. To ask a pardon would be to confess guilt."

"During my incarceration," Debs added, "my comrades will be true and my enemies will be satisfied, and therefore, as far as I am concerned, all will be well with the world."

At nine o'clock that evening, Debs was sitting in a large rocking chair in his parlor, quietly telling jokes and smoking a cigar. Gathered around him were Kate, Theodore and his family, Kate's mother Mrs. Baur, who had lived with Kate and Eugene for several years, and Arthur Baur the druggist. A vase on the table held a gigantic bouquet of American Beauty roses, which had been sent by an elderly Irish neighbor. "She is a Roman Catholic," Debs said musingly, "and every morning for many years she has prayed for me." Karsner noticed that Debs "blew a ring of blue smoke and smiled sadly."

"Well, Eugene," Kate broke in, "we had better start." Theodore went to get his brother's coat, and Debs noticed that Mrs. Baur was weeping. He went over to pat her cheek and whisper, "It is all right, mother; it will come out all right in the end."

Debs had vetoed the proposal of the Socialist Party and the Central Labor Union to hold a demonstration as his train left Terre Haute, but more than two hundred of his friends had gathered at the station. A coal miner emerged from the crowd and grabbed Debs' arm: "We're with you, Gene—by God, we're with you to the last man." Debs kissed the man's cheek and murmured, "I know it. Until the last drop we'll stand together, all of us. Only by standing together can we hope for victory. You boys take care of the outside and I'll take care of the inside."

As the train left the station Debs threw a kiss to his wife. Karsner later asked how Kate was bearing up under the strain. "She has stood shoulder to shoulder with me through every storm that has beat upon us," Debs replied, "and she is standing firm now."

Debs, Karsner, and Arthur Baur prepared to spend the night on the train, but Debs was unable to sleep. Until nearly four o'clock he smoked cigars and talked to Karsner. He seemed in the best of spirits; his manner was even jovial. Karsner chanced to mention that his imprisonment would accelerate the movement to nominate him for the Presidency again, and Debs waved it aside. He still had no desire to be a leader. "Very often," he explained, "a leader is, in fact, a misleader. It is the workers, the men and women who do all the hard work in every line of trade and profession—in building up their own Socialist branches and their unions, to whom all the credit, homage, honor and glory is due."

At five o'clock on Palm Sunday, April 13, Debs was already awake and fully dressed. He had slept only an hour. As his train crawled into the railroad yards in Cleveland, he dictated to David Karsner a statement "for my comrades throughout the United States." Although his arrest had been announced only eighteen hours earlier, the streets of Cleveland were already covered with dodgers printed in scarlet ink, announcing that Eugene Debs would speak at a protest meeting that afternoon. The meeting was held as scheduled—fifteen thousand workers stood in Free Speech Park and sang the Marseillaise—but Debs was not present. He was already halfway to Wheeling, West Virginia.

Debs had been met at the depot in Cleveland by Mrs. Marguerite Prevey and her husband, and they enjoyed a gala breakfast. Then the party moved to the Gillsy House, where it was joined by Alfred Wagenknecht and J. Louis Engdahl. Debs was writing a note to his wife when two United States deputy marshals arrived to escort him to the Federal building. The government authorities, in order to forestall any demonstrations along the route, conducted the job in the utmost secrecy. Debs, his Socialist companions, and the Federal marshal, drove to a suburban station before catching a train to Youngstown. From Youngstown the entire journey was made by interurban over a circuitous route.

Just before they arrived in Youngstown, Debs commented that interurbans were a rather slow means of transport. "Well," the marshal smiled, "we can make an all-day job of it."

"Oh, yes," Debs quipped back, "we have ten years in which to get there." As the prisoner reminisced with his companions, his eye chanced to land on the union button in his conductor's lapel. He slumped back in his seat and commented: "Were I to engage in satire, I would say how ironical it seems that I, who have been forty years in the service of organized labor, am now being taken to prison by union men." Every scene represented a memory, as when the sight of the Palm Sunday picnics caused Debs to remark: "What a beautiful day it is. I have been all over this part of the country and have talked to thousands of these miners."

A long day hopping on and off trolleys exhausted the sixty-four-year-old Debs, and he was asleep in his seat when the group arrived at Moundsville, West Virginia. The Federal prisons were filled to overflowing, and it was here in the state prison that Debs would be incarcerated. Eugene Debs dictated his final statement to his Socialist escort: "I enter the prison doors a flaming revolutionist—my head erect, my spirit untamed and my soul unconquerable." He then picked up his heavy suitcase, which he had refused to turn over to his companions, threw his arm around the shoulder of the Federal marshal, and passed under the giant turrets.

On his first day in prison Eugene Debs received a message from his brother Theodore: "They have your body behind prison walls but your unconquerable spirit, radiant as a sunburst, scars humanity's luminous heights a million miles beyond the foul touch of filthy hypocrites and their prostituted mercenaries. Your unwavering fidelity to principle, your unfaltering love and devotion to the cause of the crushed and oppressed will be an unceasing inspiration. I was never so proud of you. My arms are about you, old pal, and will be through time and eternity."

Warden Joseph Z. Terrell was quick to appreciate the unusual qualities of his new inmate. The prison rules allowed only one visitor and two letters a month, but Debs was permitted an unlimited number of visitors, and he could write as many letters as he wished. He was also allowed to receive the Socialist newspapers after he promised that he would not distribute them to the other prisoners. Although he was assigned to a light job in the prison hospital, the assignment was merely on the records; actually he was free to do as he pleased. The door to his cell was never locked, and he wandered at will through the prison yard.

Eugene Debs felt so guilty about these extra privileges that he asked to be put to work at manual labor. "I want to earn my board here, at any rate," he laughingly said. This is probably the only request from Debs that Warden Terrell ever denied.

Most of Debs' time was passed in reading, talking with his guests, chatting with the other inmates. He found great pleasure in several books by Upton Sinclair, and David Karsner one day found him engrossed in *Ten Days That Shook the World*, John Reed's account of the Bolshevik revolution. Debs was perfectly reconciled to his situation. "I'm here for a purpose," he wrote to Horace Traubel, "and I know how to be patient. The lessons I am learning here are of inestimable value to me and I am not sorry that my lot is cast for a time among 'Les Misérables.' . . . Yours until the stars go out, Gene."

Within the prison Debs quickly found ways to help the other men. Almost immediately he became father-confessor and un-official chaplain to the prisoners, writing letters for them, giving them advice and encouragement. He enjoyed and believed in his new rôle, which actually was not different from the old. To a visitor he commented:

The very lowest and most degenerate of criminals is not a whit worse than I. The difference between us is against me, not him. All my life I have been the favored one, the creature of fortune. We both did the best we could, and the worst we knew how, and I am the beneficiary of that society of which he is the victim. . . . I belong in prison. I belong where men are made to suffer for the wrongs committed against them by a brutalizing sys-tem. . . . The roots of the social system are here. They are nowhere else.

One day A. W. Moskowitz, Debs' bondsman, and Alfred Bosch, a Cleveland history teacher, called at Moundsville. They were immediately shown into the warden's office, where a guard was instructed to take them to Debs. They walked through much of the prison and finally emerged into a courtyard which held a small cottage. This cottage had been used by the prison doctor, but it was now occupied by the newly appointed soul-doctor. Eugene Debs was standing in front of his private mansion, deep in conversation with another prisoner. At the sight of his friends he hastily finished his business, swooped across the courtyard and threw his arms around Moskowitz and Bosch. Debs reached down into his pocket for the key to the cottage and invited his guests to enter. He then chanced to see the guard, who had remained at a respectful distance. "Won't you come in too?" he smilingly said to his keeper, then unlocked the door and the four men entered the cottage. Throughout an extended conversation, the guard kept a discreet silence.

As the two guests left by way of the warden's office, the warden said to them: "He's a great man, isn't he?"

Eugene Debs learned that other persons than the American Socialists still remembered him. Soon after his imprisonment, the Bolshevik government had tried to win his release in exchange for an American citizen held for sabotage in Russia, but the negotiations failed.

The idyllic life at Moundsville ended quickly. On the morning of June 13, 1919, just two months after he arrived, he was told that he was being transferred to the Federal prison in Atlanta, Georgia. This transfer was widely regarded as a malicious act by the Administration in Washington, but the actual explanation seems to be otherwise. Any institution holding Federal prisoners was required to have a certain ratio of guards. The state of West Virginia protested that they were not paid enough to make it possible to hire these added guards. The Federal authorities chose to withdraw their prisoners rather than pay the added board bills required by the state. Certainly the warden at Moundsville tried to ease the hardships of the transfer. In a letter to the warden at Atlanta, Joseph Z. Terrell said of Debs: "I never in my life met a kinder man. He is forever thinking of others, trying to serve them, and never thinking of himself."

CHAPTER XX

▣

[1]

LIFE in prison has its own mood, its own tempo. It resembles a giant calliope in the twilight, moving without end on a course without meaning. Wrenched from the normalities of home and family, the inmates are confined by a distorted and hideous pattern. Some few contrive to keep a sense of purpose. The others find themselves on a flat and deathly expanse. The need for decision and conscious purpose are forgotten. All beauty and significance disappear. Pain also disappears, save only the dull throbbing of the continuation of existence. Yesterday is today, and tomorrow shall be no different. All days are one, all the same. This lack of novelty, reaching its most exaggerated form in the prison, makes men sensitive to the smallest change, thirsty for it. Thus the prison grapevine.

While Debs was in quarantine during his first week in Atlanta, the grapevine was fairly singing with news of his arrival. The other prisoners were not only eager to meet Debs; they also thought his presence would tend to secure better treatment for all of them. In the words of one inmate, Eugene Debs in a prison was "like putting perfume in a stall." Finally the disinherited had a spokesman.

Nor were they disappointed. Within a few weeks after his arrival in Atlanta, Debs had forced a concession from the authorities. One of the prison rules prescribed attendance at chapel for every prisoner. Eugene Debs attended the services only once; he was repelled by the sight of guards walking around the chapel with their clubs swinging. Reminded of his childhood visit to a Terre Haute cathedral, Debs declared that he would not observe the rule. The prison authorities, thus meeting an attitude of rigid defiance, announced that attendance would no longer be compulsory. Attuned to a fine sensitivity, the other inmates also noticed that the guards now tried to modulate their voices and were less free with their nightsticks.

Eugene Debs could have had almost the same privileges in Atlanta that he had enjoyed in Moundsville. His correspondence was severely limited, but he was permitted to receive the radical newspapers and an abnormal number of visitors. In compliance with the letter from Warden Terrell, Warden Fred G. Zerbst offered Debs a clerical job in the hospital. Debs turned down the offer and was assigned to the clothing warehouse. He also refused to wear ordinary blue jeans and insisted that he wear prison stripes like the other inmates.

The benign figure of Number 9653, ambling around with his hands thrust deep in his hip pockets, became a familiar sight in the prison yard. He was usually surrounded by a cluster of other prisoners, all of them struggling to present their problems. A seat next to Eugene Debs became the place of honor at the Sunday baseball games. For one thing, Debs always had extra tobacco. He received a great many packages from friends and sympathizers, and the contents were freely distributed among the other prisoners. When this supply proved inadequate, Debs himself stopped smoking so that he could give away his tobacco ration. When he had been in the prison less than a month the other inmates began calling him Little Jesus.

Debs' personal prestige worked to the advantage of the eight other political prisoners. The inmates observed a very rigid caste system, in which the bank robbers refused to associate with sneak thieves; the thieves snubbed the counterfeiters; and the "bolshies," as all political prisoners were called, ranked at the absolute bottom of the hierarchy. This division between the political prisoners and the other inmates was based on two factors: the criminals understood that anybody caught talking to a radical would lose favor with the authorities, and the radicals understood that anybody who informed against themselves would gain favor with the authorities. This mutual distrust tended to be obliterated by the presence of Debs. He belonged to all factions and all cliques. He avoided only the sexual perverts, whom he sadly described as "sick men." His protective feeling extended to everybody, but two men became his personal favorites.

A Wobblie from Ohio was christened by Debs as Duke the

Beak, due to his formal manner and prominent nose. This man had been sent to Atlanta merely because of his membership in the IWW. Duke, after several months in the prison tailor shop, managed to be transferred to the prison orchestra, where he played violin. This transfer earned him much derisive treatment from Debs, who jokingly commented on the propriety of a radical scheming for his own promotion. Soon after this incident another Ohioan who had held up a post office, became furious at the Duke. He was almost angry enough to start a fight. "If you weren't a bolshie," screamed the stick-up man, "I'd kick the hell out of you."

Debs' other favorite was a Mexican general who had fought with the revolutionary Zapatistas. General Nicholas was confined in the tent colony which held the tubercular inmates. Although Debs hesitated to take advantage of the comparative freedom offered him, he seized every chance to walk down to the tents and discuss the international revolution with his Mexican colleague. The General, who had been captured on one of his many attempts to smuggle ammunition into Mexico, was very bitter about his confinement in Atlanta; presumably he would have preferred a jail in his native country. But he had great respect for Debs, whom he called "goodness itself." Debs was always interested in the Mexican revolution, which he had tried to aid in many ways, and he delighted in the General's descriptions of the beautiful new Mexico which they had tried to build. All of the political prisoners traded their tobacco for chocolate bars, and Debs carried this chocolate down to the tubercular patient.

It was not long, however, before Debs himself was in wretched health. The food was so unpalatable that two weeks passed before he could force himself to eat, in spite of his hard labor in the prison warehouse. For fifteen hours each day he was confined with five other men in a small cell, which was stifling in the fierce heat of the Southern summer. Alexander Berkman, the anarchist, reported in October upon his release from Atlanta that Debs was very near to death, due to a combination of lumbago, heart trouble, blinding headaches, and kidney trouble caused by the prison food. No hint of these difficulties ever came from Debs. His letters to Theodore were always cheerful and optimistic, and he never complained to his visitors.

But Warden Zerbst was determined that his most famous prisoner would not die while in his custody. He abruptly removed Debs from the clothing warehouse and transferred him to a light job in the hospital, where he was given a private room. The prison grapevine reported that Number 9653 was receiving a certain amount of whiskey for reasons of health. It became known that Debs was entertaining visitors in the private office of the warden, and even that he made occasional trips to Atlanta in an automobile.

Surprisingly, these favors were not resented by the other inmates, who were deeply disturbed by the possibility that Debs might die. One elderly Italian grieved: "Mista Debs was justa like God. He try to show me how to speak English, but I didn't like it. Now I'm sorry." A political prisoner roared that the imprisonment of Debs was a bigger crime than the American invasion of Russia. The radicals warned the other inmates not to bother Debs all the time; that did a little good. Under the influence of all this coddling, Debs gradually regained his strength. Finally it became apparent that the grave danger had passed, but the Socialist leader was still a very sick man.

The extreme solicitude for Debs' health was not entirely unselfish. The prison administration feared the public commotion that might result from his death, and the other inmates were anxious to preserve his wholesome influence on the authorities. The radicals, for their part, were trying to maintain their chief contact with the outside world. Debs managed to slip surreptitiously to the other political prisoners some of the radical newspapers that he received. His stream of visitors brought a week-by-week account of political and trade-union developments, which were moving at a rapid clip during the years after the war.

[2]

FOR EUGENE DEBS, the most fateful of these developments was the final disintegration of the Socialist Party. The right-wing leaders, who still controlled the official policies, hurriedly dissociated themselves from the Russian Bolsheviks during 1918, and many of them shifted to a tacit support of the war effort. That year the most radical demand in the Socialist Congressional platform called for the nationalization of public utilities and basic industry "as speedily as is consistent with public order and security, and allowing the utmost possible degree of local autonomy." The left wing found three critical flaws in this program: It did not call for the transfer of political power to the workers; It seemed to attach more importance to "public order and security" than to socialism; The provision for local autonomy hinted at a protest against central economic planning—a major socialist device.

In 1918 the left wing had begun to organize as an independent force within the Party, holding its own conventions and starting its own newspapers. Two months before Debs went to Moundsville, a meeting in New York issued the Left-Wing Manifesto, which demanded that all reform planks be dropped from the Party platform: "The party must teach, propagate and agitate exclusively for the overthrow of capitalism and the establishment of socialism through proletarian dictatorship." The left wing also demanded Socialist participation in the Third Communist International, which was founded in March of 1919. But the right-wing leaders, led by Morris Hillquit and Victor Berger, ridiculed the left-wing emphasis on the inevitable use of violence by the capitalists against the revolutionaries. The destruction of their newspapers, the jailing of their leaders, and the suppression of free speech and assembly had not shaken the belief of these leaders that the change to socialism would be gradual and peaceful.

The showdown fight between the two factions came in the national referendum to elect the Party officials. The left wing won twelve of the fifteen seats on the National Executive Committee; John Reed was elected international delegate over Berger, and Kate O'Hare international secretary over Hillquit. But the existing National Committee, controlled by the reformers, declared the election void and refused to yield office. In order to make this policy effective, the National Committee then expelled all of the left-wing groups—the foreign language federations, and the entire state organizations of Ohio, Michigan, and Massachusetts.

Half of the expelled members, including the language federations, the Michigan organization, and most of the Ohio organization, favored the immediate formation of a Communist party. But the other thirty thousand expelled Socialists, led by John Reed, Alfred Wagenknecht, and Ben Gitlow, advocated an attempt to capture the Socialist Party for the left-wing program. So they presented themselves at the Socialist national convention, which met in Chicago on August 31, 1919. When they were denied admission there, they immediately formed the Communist Labor Party. On the same day the extreme left wing founded the Communist Party, led by Charles E. Ruthenberg of Ohio. On August 31 there was only one organization; the following day there were three, which at once began to war among themselves. The Communist Party charged that the Communist Labor Party still held the reformist notions of the right wing; the Communist Labor Party held that the Communists were sectarian and dogmatic.

This wrangling and confusion prevented the radical parties from taking an effective part in the popular battles that followed the war. The AFL in 1918 had adopted a plan, introduced by William Z. Foster, to organize the steel industry. The campaign was greeted with startling enthusiasm by the steel workers and with last-ditch resistance by the employers. In September of 1919 the organizing committed ordered an industry-wide strike vote. Samuel Gompers urged Woodrow Wilson to arbitrate the dispute, but the President was unable to persuade the corporations even to confer with the union. Gompers then tried to halt the strike vote, but he failed. On September 22, 1919, more than three hundred sixty-five thousand workers walked out of the steel mills.

Six weeks later a half million coal miners went on strike. When a Federal court enjoined the United Mine Workers from paying any strike benefits or aiding the strike by "messages of encouragement or exhortation," President John L. Lewis ordered the miners back to work. Eugene Debs was disgusted when he read this news in Atlanta. Debs later said that Lewis' compliance with the injunction was "a cowardly act. . . . That was the time when Lewis should have shown his real leadership of the miners." The steel strike also was called off on January 8, 1920. Its defeat was mainly caused by the jealousies and inaction of the AFL officials, by the return to work of the skilled members of craft unions, and by the importation of thirty thousand Negro strikebreakers, who still were not allowed to join most trade unions.

The open-shop war by the employers flared on a thousand fronts, with the Great Steel Strike serving as the stimulus for a fierce antiradical hysteria. On January 2, 1920, the Department of Justice raided meetings throughout the country, arresting 2,758 men and women, holding 556 aliens for deportation. In Massachusetts the Sacco-Vanzetti case aroused the indignation of all fair-minded Americans. By the end of January nearly ten thousand persons had been arrested for alleged radicalism, and they were treated with extreme brutality. A revived Ku Klux Klan tortured and murdered throughout the South and Midwest, with no interference by the police. During 1920 more than sixty Negroes were lynched. Twenty striking miners, peacefully and legally picketing on the public highway near Butte, Montana, were shot down by Anaconda Copper Company guards, and two of them died.

A newspaper reporter who visited Atlanta Prison found Eugene Debs furious about these events. The Socialist leader immediately pointed out that force and violence were being employed by the ruling classes, not by the radicals. He thought these instances in the United States were relevant to the dictatorship in Russia. "All along the track of the ages," Debs declared, "wherever a government has been overthrown by force and violence, that government had been maintained by force and violence."

Debs tried to orient himself in relation to the split in the Socialist Party, but he was at a serious disadvantage. His policies had always grown out of detailed, first-hand knowledge of the needs and thoughts of the American people. Perhaps more than any other man, he had maintained intimate personal contact with scores of thousands of workingmen and farmers. His reactions were usually based on his sensitivity to popular moods rather than on theoretical analysis. But this approach was now denied him. His only information came from the newspapers and the comparative handful of socialists who visited him in Atlanta prison. He found it impossible, however, to ignore the divisions in the radical movement. Writing to his brother Theodore, Debs reflected on these divisions with deep sorrow: "It has been the fate of our movement from the beginning, especially in this country, to split. About the time we get in shape to do something we have to split up and waste our energy in factional strife. We preach unity everlastingly, but we ourselves keep splitting apart." At the same time Debs sent an appeal for unity to the New York *Call* and other radical journals. "I do not believe," he stated, "that there is any real difference among the rank and file of socialists; the real contentions very likely lie in the leadership of the different groups. The socialist movement must rise to the occasion this year and unite the industrial and political wings."

Debs himself was chosen to lead this effort. For the first time in American history, a man in prison was selected to run for President. The Socialist national convention, which nominated Debs for President in May of 1920, sent Seymour Stedman, James Oneal, and Julius Gerber to notify Debs of the nomination. The committee met the Socialist leader in the office of Warden Zerbst in Atlanta. Although Debs cheerfully agreed to accept this new honor and responsibility, he freely criticized the Socialist Party. The campaign platform, according to the candidate, "could have been made much more effective if it had stressed the class struggle more prominently and if more emphasis had been placed on industrial organization. . . . There is a tendency in the party to become a party of politicians instead of a party of workers. That policy must be checked, not encouraged. We are in politics not to get votes, but to develop the power to emancipate the working class."

Debs went on to decry the Socialist criticism of the Communists. The two Communist parties had maintained their emphasis on industrial unionism and the class struggle, as Debs requested, but they also tended to scorn parliamentary action and to overestimate the imminence of revolution in the United States. However, reflecting on the presence in the Communist parties of such friends as Marguerite Prevey, Rose Pastor Stokes, Charles E. Ruthenberg, Alfred Wagenknecht, John Reed, and Ella Reeve Bloor, Debs was confident that they would correct their errors. So he told the Socialist committee: "I was sorry to read a speech of Berger's the other day attacking the Communists. I have known many comrades in all these parties. I have high regard for them. They are as honest as we are."

On another point also, the Presidential nominee disagreed with his party. The so-called "dictatorship of the proletariat" inspired one of the main disputes between the Socialists and the Communists. This theory, as it had been elaborated by Nikolai Lenin, was in no way intended to imply a dictatorship by one man or a small clique or a political party. But the success of every revolution required the suppression of the previous rulers —in the American Revolution the Tories, in the French and English Revolutions the nobility. So Lenin concluded that it was necessary to deny civil liberties to the capitalist class of Russia. This viewpoint was supported by Eugene Debs, who again reproached his Socialist colleagues: "During the transition period the revolution must protect itself. . . . I heartily support the Russian Revolution without reservation."

The Presidential campaign, unlike past years, brought no great change to Debs' life. He had been asked by the Socialist notification committee how he would conduct his campaign. "I will be a candidate at home in seclusion," he laughingly replied. "It will be much less tiresome and my managers and opponents can always locate me." Although he began to write occasional articles for publication, the major part of his time was still spent talking to the other prisoners or reading the books which were sent to him. *The Brass Check*, Upton Sinclair's study of the unseen censorship in America, was described by Debs as "his bravest, and, in many respects, his best book." The same author's *Mammonart*, a discussion of the effects of capitalism upon American culture, received even higher praise from the Socialist leader. "It is a wonderful book," he wrote to Sinclair, "and must be an eye-opening one to many of the artists, writers and others who serve the leisure class in everything they do but indignantly resent the idea that there is any propaganda in their work. . . . I would like an inscribed copy of 'Mammonart' simply your name in it with your hand for my little collection of the immortals."

One book which fell into Debs' hands, however, met with an indignant repudiation. Reading the entire *Bible* for the first time in his life, he was shocked by the "monstrous" God of revenge presented there. Debs' conception of Christianity is revealed in his description of an interview with a minister who visited his cell in Atlanta prison. "I told my friend of the cloth," he recalled, "that I did not believe Christ was meek and lowly, but a real, living, vital agitator who went into the Temple with a lash and a knout and whipped the oppressors of the poor, routed them out of doors and spilled their blood-got silver on the floor. . . . He denounced the profiteers, and it was for this that they nailed his quivering body to the cross and spiked it to the gates of Jerusalem, not because he told men to love one another. That was a harmless doctrine. But when he touched their profits and denounced them before their own people he was marked for crucifixion."

The minister was glad to escape and never returned, but the Catholic chaplain of the prison remained one of Debs' closest friends. Throughout his imprisonment Debs kept a large portrait of Jesus of Nazareth on the wall of his room. His repudiation of the *Bible* and the organized church in no way lessened Debs' homage to the Prince of Peace, whom he had described twenty years earlier as "the great Divine Tramp who never had a dollar, but who understood and loved the common folk, the ordinary ruck of men, with an absorbing and abiding affection."

This same absorbing affection for the common folk was the chief characteristic of Eugene Debs. Since it had always been transmuted into active concern it had never found expression in words. Here the confinement of prison wrought a change. Debs was powerless to interfere in the struggles beyond the walls. He began to brood and worry, until finally he became persuaded that his was a melancholy nature. In writing to his brother

Theodore of this mood, he again found a comparison with Abraham Lincoln: "I think Lincoln must have known something of this when he said that if there was anyone in purgatory who suffered more than he did he pitied him. During these periods of moral pregnancy and travail, for such they are, it seems to me that my heart is the very heart and centre of all the sadness and sorrow, all the pain and misery, and all the suffering and agony in the world. I don't know why it is so. I only know that deep melancholy is so completely a part of me, and I have so often been under its chastening influence, that it has become sacred to me, and costly as it is, I should not wish it taken out of my life."

This self-analysis by Debs was never revealed to the Socialists, who were exclusively concerned with the Presidential race. Debs' nomination was a strong stimulus for the amnesty campaign, which had begun even before he was confined. The arguments for a general pardon for all political prisoners were reinforced on September 5, 1919, when President Wilson declared in a speech: "Is there any man here or woman—let me say is there any child—who does not know that the seed of war in the modern world is industrial and commercial rivalry? . . . This was a commercial and industrial war." Soon after that speech the Chicago Federation of Labor, with two hundred fifty thousand members, petitioned for immediate freedom for Eugene Debs. The United Mine Workers of Indiana asked both the release of Debs and the removal of Postmaster-General Albert S. Burleson, who was still zealously suppressing the radical newspapers. "We try to be fair to both sides," observed one miner. "Debs and Burleson should both be let out."

An amnesty committee of trade-union officials visited Debs on April 15, 1920, and Warden Zerbst permitted his famous prisoner to leave the prison in their custody. Riding for several hours through the city and suburbs of Atlanta, Debs suddenly became conscious of the oppressive influence of walls and bars. "How good it is," he exclaimed, "to see the sky in all its bigness and splendor." But this brief taste of freedom did not stimulate any overwhelming desires for a pardon. When Clarence Darrow, who had become a leader of the amnesty campaign, visited Debs

later that summer, the Socialist leader declined to ask any favors
of the Administration in Washington. Darrow recorded that he,
Debs, and Warden Zerbst had spent the entire morning in the
warden's office, discussing "all sorts of subjects, from Socialism
and Anarchism to prisons and punishments, and every other
social question." No train was leaving for Washington until late
that night, so Darrow asked permission to spend the afternoon
with Debs in his cell. The warden readily granted the request,
and then decided to accompany Darrow. The six cell mates,
Darrow, and Zerbst sat around on boxes, the few chairs, and the
bunks, chatting about their "experiences, hopes and visions,"
Darrow said. A beautiful flower garden was just outside the
cell. "Really," Debs commented, "this place is not so bad. I
look at that garden of flowers. There are bars in front, I know—
but I never see the bars." During his brief visit, Darrow remarked the extent to which Debs was "loved and idealized by
all the inmates."

The Federal authorities granted Eugene Debs permission to
issue one bulletin a week to the United Press for the final months
of the campaign. Neither the Republican nominee, Senator
Warren G. Harding, nor the Democratic candidate, James M.
Cox, received much attention from Debs, who directed a series
of broadsides against the incumbent President. The Socialist
leader entertained a bitter hatred of Woodrow Wilson. In view
of the President's admission that the World War had been a
"commercial and industrial war," Debs failed to see how he
could honestly deny pardons to the men who had been jailed for
saying the same thing. Wilson had spoken fine phrases about the
need "to make the world safe for democracy," Debs declared,
and he was now using the same propaganda about the League of
Nations, which Debs called the "new capitalist international."
Debs also held the President responsible for the American invasion of Russia. In a conversation with another prisoner, he
stated that all the foreign armies in Russia should be "cleaned
out like mice." This condemnation of Wilson was only exceeded
by Debs' scorn for the White Russian General Kolchak. "Every
country has its traitors," Debs said of Kolchak. "We had our
Benedict Arnold." And in the same conversation, he denounced

Woodrow Wilson as "pro-British and a tool of Wall Street . . . a college professor who isn't fit to be President because he doesn't know the lives of the people."

During an interview with Charles Wood of the New York *World*, Debs repeated that he was "heart and soul with the Russian Revolution," although the violence in Russia made his "heart ache to think of it." He also gave a clear statement of his general attitude toward revolutionary violence:

> As a student of history, . . . I know that these great movements for human emancipation do not come without bloodshed; and although I would not kill a man in self-defense, I am in favor of shedding as much blood as is absolutely necessary in order to emancipate the people. But not one drop more. Moreover, if bloodshed is necessary, I shall not follow the course of some of America's superpatriots, who insisted on others going into battle while they stayed home and piled up profits.

The excitement of the campaign proved to be good for Debs' health. When the Socialist campaign committee visited him in October, they found him lean, tanned, clad in blue denims and canvas sneakers. He was eager to get out of prison and take an active part in the election fight. He had also decided that, when he was released, he would make a mammoth organizing tour to build up the socialist movement.

In fact, Debs could doubtless have organized several Socialist locals within the prison itself. The Federal prison at Leavenworth, Kansas, where most of the political prisoners were incarcerated, boasted a newspaper named *The Can-Opener* and weekly study classes in Marxism, but Debs lacked the temperament to defy the prison authorities. His influence was expressed in his social case work. From the very beginning, he had consciously sought out the worst prisoners. Many of them became model inmates due to his application of the philosophy of *Les Misérables*.

Warden Zerbst, realizing Debs' immense popularity, was always careful not to interfere with his activities. A colorful anecdote, of uncertain validity, illustrates the warden's attitude toward his famous prisoner. The story describes Debs strolling about in the prison yard, hunched forward, his elbows sticking out behind his back. A hand waved to him from the solitary confinement block, and he immediately waved back. Since the rules forbade any communication with the so-called dungeons, a guard promptly put Debs in the cell next to the man who had waved to him. News of this action threw Warden Zerbst into a panic: "My God, take him out, take him out. Don't you know that if the men heard that Debs was in the hole they would tear down the walls of this prison, brick by brick, to get him out?"

His dynamic charm was only one reason for the popularity which Debs enjoyed among his fellow inmates. Many of them firmly believed that he would be elected President, and then he could pardon all of them. He was often asked if he intended to pardon himself. The prison grapevine stoutly contended that Number 9653 would be the next Chief Executive, and that neither Harding nor Cox would receive a single electoral vote from Atlanta prison.

In the final stages of the campaign, Debs was forced to repudiate statements by both his enemies and his friends. Upton Sinclair wrote to inquire about press reports that Debs had tried deliberately to obstruct the draft act. Replying through his brother Theodore, Debs wrote: "Tell him (Comrade Sinclair) that the statement in the Christian Science Monitor editorial that I had declared my determination to obstruct the draft is an absolute falsehood. I never mentioned the draft in my speech, nor made any reference to it."

The Socialist newspapers, in order to counteract some of the adverse publicity, began referring to their candidate as "the grand old man." This appellation proved very annoying to its subject. "I am anything but 'a grand old man,' " he snorted in a public statement. "A grand man is not old and an old man is not grand. I am not an old man and do not intend to be. I have no time to get old. The spirit within me and the soul of me, the spirit and soul of socialism, are a sure guarantee against 'old age.' I need not seek the gurgling spring of eternal youth. I have found it."

The day of the election arrived, and the votes were counted, and the Socialist hopes were destroyed. Although the adoption of the Woman Suffrage Amendment had vastly increased the electorate, Debs' total vote barely exceeded that of 1912. He had been campaigning for this amendment for more than forty years. Now it had been adopted, but he had derived scant immediate benefit. The vote for Eugene Debs was particularly disappointing since it did not represent votes for socialism. Thousands upon thousands had cast their votes for the prisoner in order to protest the infringements of civil liberties. The election finally established what everybody had known: the Socialist Party had almost disappeared as an organized movement.

The size of the Socialist vote was not, however, wholly discouraging. It demonstrated that many citizens had rejected the newspaper headlines about The Red Menace. The antiradical hysteria of 1920 had exceeded the repression of the war period. The year had begun with the Palmer Raids, which flared up periodically throughout the campaign. Both major parties had joined the attacks on all radicals. Five legally elected Socialists had been denied their seats in the legislature of New York. The Communists had been confused and disorganized by their practical illegality. But still an inmate of Atlanta Prison had polled nearly a million votes.

Debs' comment on the results had been published even before the votes were cast. In his "Last Call to the Voters in 1920," he had written: "There is one thing I know on the eve of this election. I shall not be disappointed. The result will be as it should be. The people will vote for what they think they want, to the extent that they think at all, and they, too, will not be disappointed."

"In my maturer years I no longer permit myself to be either disappointed or discouraged. I hope for everything and expect nothing. The people can have anything they want. The trouble is they do not want anything. At least they vote that way on election day."

[*3*]

ALTHOUGH Theodore Debs' hopes for a prompt pardon for his brother were crushed by the election results, many Socialists took the opposite view. The overwhelming vote for the Republicans seemed to express disapproval of the policies of Woodrow Wilson, including his attitude toward political prisoners. A new surge of optimism swept the amnesty campaign two weeks after the election, when the President pardoned a German spy. This spy had been convicted in February, 1918, of conspiracy to sabotage the food and munitions ships of the Allies. Surely, thought the Socialists, their leader had not committed a crime that compared with this.

On January 31, 1921, Attorney General A. Mitchell Palmer recommended to the President that Debs' sentence be commuted to expire on Lincoln's birthday, February 12, 1921. The recommendation pointed out that Debs was in poor health, sixty-five years old, and that his friends feared he might die in prison. Unless executive action were taken he would not be eligible for parole until August 11, 1921. Completion of his sentence, allowing time for good behavior, would not come until December 28, 1925.

Woodrow Wilson, when he received the recommendation, wrote across it the single word: "Denied."

The reasons for Wilson's action were later explained by his private secretary, Joseph P. Tumulty, who was with the President when the recommendation arrived from the Attorney-General. The President, after carefully reading the recommendation, burst out: "I will never consent to the pardon of this man. While the flower of American youth was pouring out its blood to vindicate the cause of civilization, this man, Debs, stood behind the lines, sniping, attacking, and denouncing them. Before the war he had a perfect right to exercise his freedom of speech and to express his own opinion, but once the Congress of the United States declared war, silence on his part would have been the proper course to pursue. I know there will be a great deal of denunciation of me for refusing this pardon. They will say I am cold-blooded and indifferent, but it will make no impression on me. This man was a traitor to his country and he will never be pardoned during my administration."

On February 1, 1921, the day the President's action was made public, Debs discussed the matter with a visitor. The Socialist leader was particularly indignant because it looked as if he had

applied for a pardon. This course he had consistently rejected as
a tacit admission of guilt. Debs' wrath became so intense that
he gave his visitor a public statement, which appeared in the
New York *Times* the following day:

I understand perfectly the feelings of Wilson. When he reviews what he has done, when he realizes the suffering he has
brought about, then he is being punished. It is he, not I, who
needs a pardon. If I had it in my power I would give him the
pardon which would set him free.

Woodrow Wilson is an exile from the hearts of his people. The
betrayal of his ideals makes him the most pathetic figure in the
world. No man in public life in American history ever retired so
thoroughly discredited, so scathingly rebuked, so overwhelmingly impeached and repudiated as Woodrow Wilson. . . .

The appearance of this statement caused the Department of
Justice to withdraw all of Debs' visiting and writing privileges,
and he was placed incommunicado for an indefinite period. But
the damage had been done. The government's reprisal was interpreted as an act of personal spite, and the protest was enormous. The day before Wilson's retirement the order was partially
revoked.

After that the amnesty movement grew daily, but it received
little help from the radical parties. The Communists, now united
into one illegal party, were so preoccupied with internal problems that they gave little aid to the political prisoners. Also they
had reached an impasse in their negotiations with Eugene Debs.
The previous summer a Communist committee had visited Debs
in Atlanta and offered their support to his Presidential campaign if he would repudiate such right-wing leaders as Morris
Hillquit and Victor Berger. Although Debs disagreed with
Berger and Hillquit about the Russian Revolution and industrial unionism, he regarded the Communist ultimatum as an
attempt to dictate his beliefs and he repudiated it with char-
acteristically strong language. There the matter rested, and
neither Debs nor the Communists made the first move toward
a reconciliation.

Nor was the Socialist Party of much practical help. On January 17, 1921, Otto Branstetter, now National Secretary, had

written derisively to Debs about "the handful of disgruntled comrades who have left the Party." But his admission to Debs on April 4, 1921, came much closer to the truth:

The Party is in a weaker and more disorganized condition than at any time in its history. We are entirely without courage or self-reliance. We are doubtful of ourselves and our own ability. We are seeking help and assistance from every possible source and are depending entirely on other people and other organizations to do the work which we ought to be doing ourselves. . . .

New factors, however, were operating in favor of Debs' release. Doubtless the most important was the fact that the White House had evicted a Puritan moralist and replaced him with an easy-living Midwestern politician. Warren G. Harding, whatever his faults, was more receptive to the amnesty committees than Woodrow Wilson had ever been. During the 1920 campaign the Farmer-Labor nominee for President, Parley P. Christenson, had asked the other candidates to join him in petitioning for the release of Debs. They refused to join such a petition at that time, but Harding wired to Christenson that he favored a general amnesty for political prisoners. Scores of prominent citizens and large sections of the labor movement now insisted that Harding make good on this promise.

Accordingly, one of the first acts of the new Chief Executive was to instruct Attorney-General Harry M. Daugherty to review the Debs' case. On March 24, 1921, Eugene Debs, alone and unguarded, took the train to Washington for a three-hour interview with the Attorney-General. Neither Debs nor Daugherty would comment on the interview at that time, but the Attorney-General later told Clarence Darrow about the affair: "He spent a large part of the day in my office, and I never met a man I liked better."

Debs made a notable impression on everyone he met in Washington. The most notorious member of the Harding administration was Jesse Smith, who held no public office but was the actual director of the graft, corruption, and bribery by which America signaled the return to normalcy. Any favor at all—a seat on the Federal bench, a pardon for a public enemy, ambassadorships and contracts—could be obtained from Jesse Smith, and the prices were always reasonable. This same Jesse Smith met Eugene Debs at the station in Washington, escorted him to Daugherty's office, and returned him to the train. Smith too was a victim of Debs' charm. On the return trip to the station he asked Debs if he could be of any assistance. The Socialist leader opined that he had always been very fond of quill toothpicks, but he hadn't seen a single one since he went to Atlanta. Smith ordered the driver to stop the car, ran into a store, and returned with a huge bundle of quill toothpicks.

After Debs' trip to Washington, the amnesty campaign really went into high gear. The Socialist Party, with its weakened organization of about five thousand members, secured three hundred thousand signatures on an amnesty petition, as well as the endorsement of seven hundred organizations with a combined membership of more than three million. A petition in Terre Haute alone received twenty-one thousand signatures. The growing disillusionment about the war, the League of Nations, and the Treaty of Versailles, also worked to Debs' advantage. Even Clyde R. Miller, the reporter for the Cleveland *Plain-Dealer* whose testimony had helped to convict the Socialist leader, had begun to doubt his earlier actions and made a personal appeal to Harding, then still a Senator. Upton Sinclair, Clarence Darrow, Lincoln Steffens, and other early participants in the amnesty movement now redoubled their efforts.

Harding had told Miller that, if he were elected President, he might pardon Debs by July Fourth. Steps were actually made toward this end, but they were dropped due to the opposition of the American Legion and other groups. The matter dragged on into the summer, and the Socialist hopes began to drop. Late in August the White House announced that no decision would be made in the Debs' case until the Senate had ratified a peace treaty with Germany.

But the stream of visitors to the prison all brought encouraging news. Norman Hapgood, former ambassador to Denmark, told Debs that the President would soon act favorably on his case. Even Samuel Gompers, in Atlanta for the AFL national convention, called to see Debs. The meeting of these two men set up a flickering spectrum of memories and reversals. Thirty-five years earlier Gompers had been the more radical of the two young trade unionists. But he had grown steadily more conservative while Debs moved the other way. Their paths split sharply after the Pullman boycott. The Socialist leader had found his place with the unskilled workingmen, the unorganized farmers, the disinherited convicts, at the bottom of the social heap. Gompers had consciously chosen to speak for the skilled craft unionists. Now they met again: the squat and well-tailored confidant of industrialists and statesmen; the gaunt intimate of criminals, wearing his shabby prison stripes.

Debs broke the silence with a curt greeting: "How do you do, Mr. Gompers."

"How do you do, Gene," Gompers replied. Then, stung by the formality of Debs' words, he hurried on: "Many years ago you called me Sam. Can't we get back on those terms again?"

Frigid and unforgiving, the prisoner replied: "Perhaps some day we can." The two men spoke of generalities for a few minutes; then Debs returned to his duties in the hospital.

Some of Debs' contacts with the outside world must have been even more painful than his brief conversation with Samuel Gompers. On May 5, 1921, he received a letter from Portland, Oregon, crudely written in pencil on the back of an envelope. The letter, for some unknown reason, had been passed on to him by the prison censor. "Dear Gene," it began. "We working people of Oregon hope that the guards throw the whips into you every day. You aren't a toiler. You never produced anything. You tried to prolong the war so that 1000000's of the US boys would be slaughtered. We hope you'll never come out of the jug alive. You are a parasyte We hope the guards will lash you on the *bareback*." The letter was signed "A. Producer." Fifteen years later this document was still preserved among the papers of Kate Debs.

[4]

IN 1916 the gossip in Terre Haute lingered over the failure of Kate Debs to attend her husband's speeches. Two years later it pointed out that she had not attended his trial. But the most severe criticism centered on her failure to visit him a single time during his entire term in Moundsville and Atlanta prisons. Certainly this seeming neglect is hard to understand, and even harder to justify. Although the chivalrous nature of Eugene Debs may have protested against the thought of any woman visiting a prison, his guests in Atlanta included Kate Richards O'Hare, Dr. Madge Patton Stephens, and Marguerite Prevey. Mrs. Mabel D. Curry, the Socialist wife of a professor in Terre Haute, worked side by side with Theodore Debs during the entire period when Eugene was in prison, but Kate Debs never appeared in her husband's office.

Difficult to explain as these facts are, they are only part of the story. Kate Debs never tried to escape from responsibility for her husband's actions, and she gave both sympathy and support to other victims of the anti-Socialist feeling. Her brother, Arthur Baur, supplied bail money for dozens of victims of the Palmer Raids. And the depth of Kate's attachment to her husband is apparent in the message which she wrote on her Christmas card in 1919:

To that Old Sweetheart of Mine
Greetings and good wishes

> I think of you lovingly and devotedly each passing hour of the day; at night I lay my hand reverently on your dear pillow and say "good night" and in the morning I step in and say "good morning dear" and kiss your pillow. *Love, Love, how wonderful it is!* And *mine* is true and enduring through all time.

Your devoted wife

K.

Several explanations for Kate Debs' failure to visit Atlanta, and a wholly charming facet to her personality, appear in her correspondence with Kate O'Hare late in 1921. The prison term of Mrs. O'Hare had ended with a Presidential pardon in 1920; and in October of that year she and her husband, Frank O'Hare, had revived the *National Rip-Saw*. A year later they proposed to do an article about Kate Debs. The subject evinced every desire to co-operate, but she was more concerned that proper credit should be given to her brother Arthur, "who has been such a comfort to me and who went clear to the prison doors with Gene." In order to prove that Arthur Baur was a wonderful person, Kate Debs pointed out that her husband thought so.

Kate Debs was also puzzled about the attention that was being directed toward her. "I have often wondered," she wrote to Mrs. O'Hare, "what you could write that would be interesting, just about 'me.' The wives of great men always suffer by comparison, and people expect them to be as great as their husbands, when they know, that as a rule, great men marry inferior women."

When the article appeared in the *Rip-Saw*, it included an appeal for funds for Kate Debs. This was a perfectly natural course for Kate and Frank O'Hare to follow, since they regarded the gifts as a "love token" for Eugene Debs and his wife. But Kate Debs' self-reliance rebelled at the idea of charity. She forced the return of every dollar which was collected in her behalf. "My wants are few," she wrote to Mrs. O'Hare, "and are amply provided for without such an effort on the part of the comrades." The original plan had been for Kate Debs to autograph receipts which would be sent to all of the donors, and she enumerated the reasons which made this impossible: "In the first place, I am not well and it would simply be a physical impossibility; there are home duties, the care of mother, and the daily demands to meet and under these conditions you can readily understand that my hands are already full to overflowing." These same reasons partially explain Kate Debs' neglect of her husband: her own ill health, the care of her aged mother, who had lived with her for many years, and the care of her home in Terre Haute.

The editors of the *Rip-Saw*, however, were not to be so easily dissuaded. Kate and Frank O'Hare made separate visits to Terre Haute in order to plead with Kate Debs. They were completely unsuccessful; she insisted that the money be returned to the donors. Finally, in complete despair, they suggested that they buy her an electric car. Her reply came on December 7, 1921; "This morning I had Gene's usual weekly letter . . . In

commenting on the edition he says, 'Kate O'Hare wrote beauti-
fully and brilliantly. She made a great story. . . . you and I
in particular may well be proud and grateful for it. . . . But
you *must not* let them get an electric car.' "

"So hear what the Great Mogul says," continued Kate Debs
irreverently, "and don't dare send me a car. I never took that
seriously, I thought you said it jokingly. But I could not accept
a car. Trust you and the children and your dear mate are all
well."

[5]

AFTER the Senate ratified the peace treaty with Germany it became obvious that the amnesty campaign was nearing a successful close. President Harding signed the official proclamation
of peace on November 14, 1921. The following day a large group
of ex-servicemen staged an amnesty demonstration at the World
Disarmament Conference in Washington. Each day seemed to
bring the pardon closer. When Kate Debs wrote to Kate O'Hare
on December 7, she was elated over a visit from Otto Branstetter, the National Secretary of the Socialist Party, who had
just visited Washington. "His reports were all very favorable,"
wrote Kate Debs, "and I was so pleased to have them."

A leading rôle in the final negotiations was played by Lincoln
Steffens, who had idolized Eugene Debs since the 1908 interview
in Milwaukee. The journalist had consistently urged the President to wipe out the atmosphere of hatred and repression by
issuing a general pardon to all political prisoners. The Administration, on the other hand, wanted to release a few prisoners at
a time. Attorney-General Daugherty even drafted a statement
that Debs was to sign before his release, in which he would
promise to abstain from attacks on the government. Steffens
persuaded Harding to throw the pledge in the wastebasket.

Steffens then went on to Atlanta to talk with Debs. He had
just returned from a trip to Russia with an official mission, and
he wished to present his observations to the Socialist leader.
Debs too was eager to talk about Russia. He was greatly disturbed by the stories which had reached him about Bolshevik

activities—the violence, the denials of free speech, the civil war and the executions. Debs contended that it was not a socialist revolution, and then he vividly repeated the stories which the Socialist leaders had told him. Having heard him out, the journalist quietly observed: "True, 'Gene. That's all true that you say. A revolution is no gentleman."

Debs jumped to his feet and exclaimed, "Of course, I forgot." As a token of his good faith, he swore that he would never again repeat any accusation against the Russian Bolsheviks until he had discussed it with Steffens.

This account of the visit, recalled by Steffens for his *Autobiography*, is supplemented by a letter from the journalist to his sister, December 16, 1921:

The interview with Debs was good. The Warden left me two hours alone with him, and I spent it trying to get Debs to understand (and not to judge) Russia. He saw it all. He said so; he showed it in his questions; and he was delighted. He agreed that the thing for him to do was to go out with or after me to plead for bread for Russia—to be sent to the Soviet Government direct. He hadn't been clear on the dictatorship, minority rule, the red terror, etc. I just told him the story, showing how some things happen that we don't expect.

He's a Man—

Finally Warren G. Harding decided that public opinion would react favorably toward some affirmative action. On December 23, 1921, the White House announced that Eugene Debs and twenty-three other political prisoners would be released on Christmas Day. For Debs this was only a partial victory. He had kept his resolve never to ask for a pardon. On the other hand, no general amnesty had been granted. Even the favored men were not fully pardoned and their civil rights were not restored; their sentences were simply commuted to the time already served. But Debs decided that he could do more for the amnesty campaign as a free man than as a prisoner, so he accepted the commutation.

The news of his impending release did not reach Debs until the day before Christmas. He was immeasurably saddened by the realization that he was deserting the other inmates of the prison. "These men need me," he said to a friend, "they trust me and depend on me, and I hate to leave them." But he was also cheered by the thought of rejoining his wife. "My darling Kate," said his telegram on Christmas Day, "Greetings of love to you and Dear sweet Mother. The day has come and our blessed communion is near. A necessary trip to Washington and then home to you, my beloved. With an overflowing heart I embrace you and God bless you."

When the nation's foremost political prisoner became a free man that afternoon, the warden suspended all rules, and twenty-three hundred convicts crowded against the front wall of the huge prison building. Each chest became a sounding board. The ivied walls trembled with the vibrations from a shouted farewell. Eugene Debs turned and paused for a moment, facing his friends, tears streaming down his cheeks, his hat held immobile high above his head.

CHAPTER XXI

◻

[*1*]

EUGENE DEBS had hoped to return from Atlanta directly to Terre Haute, but the President of the United States asked him to call at the White House. Refusal was a patent impossibility. Debs caught the train to Washington. When he stepped into the President's office on the morning of December 26, a free man, he murmured simply, "Good morning, Mr. President." Warren G. Harding, jovial, handsome, friendly, bounded out of his chair and walked toward the convict. "Well," said the President, "I have heard so damned much about you, Mr. Debs, that I am now very glad to meet you personally."

Scores of reporters waylaid Debs when he emerged from his interview with the Chief Executive. They asked him how he liked the White House and the President. "Mr. Harding appears to me," said the gaunt Socialist leader, "to be a kind gentleman, one whom I believe possesses humane impulses. We understand each other perfectly. As for the White House—well, gentlemen, my personal preference is to live privately as an humble citizen in my cottage at Terre Haute."

One of the reporters abruptly pointed out that Debs could not live as a citizen in Terre Haute or anywhere else, because his commutation of sentence had not restored his civil rights. "That is a matter of no import to me," Debs stated curtly. "The sovereignty of my citizenship resulted in my imprisonment. The government has made me a citizen of the world."

Debs spent the entire day in Washington, receiving a number of distinguished callers. One of them was the mysterious Urbain Ledoux, who had achieved fame by his sensational efforts in behalf of the unemployed of New York and Boston. Ledoux, a modern Diogenes, had haunted the Government offices and the

Washington Disarmament Conference, carrying a lamp in his search for an honest man. He left the lamp with Debs.

Samuel Gompers and Frank Morrison of the AFL also brought their congratulations to Debs. A few months later, Gompers recorded this meeting in his autobiography. "After peace was declared, I assisted a movement to release him [Debs] and did everything within my power to accomplish that purpose. . . . I saw him again when he came to Washington after his release from Atlanta. He was gentle and genial and seemed greatly touched at what I had done for him. He allowed the message to be brought to me that he had completely changed his point of view. However, it was only a short time before he avowed anew his pre-War and during-the-War attitude. To have done otherwise would have been to invite oblivion."

Like other parts of Gompers' memoirs, this commentary is misleading. The AFL chieftain was notably a latecomer to the amnesty campaign, running several paces behind Warren G. Harding and even more behind important parts of the labor movement. Both during and after his prison term Debs was unrelenting in his dislike of Gompers, and there is no reason to believe that he had "completely changed his point of view," as Gompers claimed. According to Lincoln Steffens, Debs had agreed to devote his energies to appeals for Russian relief rather than acrid attacks on the government, but this is far different from Gompers' contention. Lastly, it was far afield to call Debs a publicity seeker. In the golden age of the American salesman he had the needed qualities to be one of the greatest salesmen of them all. He could have been a leading figure in the Democratic Party if fame had been his chief concern. Probably he could have made a fortune in business had his inclinations been in that direction. He enjoyed public acclaim as much as other men, perhaps more than most, but to say that is not to explain his motives.

On December 27, Debs wired to his wife that he would leave Washington at 6:20 P.M. and arrive in Terre Haute at 3:40 P.M. the following day. This news threw the reception committee into a panic. Debs' injunction delivered to James H. Maurer the previous August, against any demonstrations at the time of his release, had been largely unheeded. The very suddenness of the event had precluded any meeting at Atlanta, but this oversight was being corrected at Terre Haute, where a local committee had been planning for weeks toward this day. Kate and Frank O'Hare had arrived from St. Louis to make their contribution to the welcome of Eugene Debs. Charles W. Ervin, the editor of the New York *Call*, was reporting the occasion and also helping to organize it. Thus three different groups, each largely unbeknownst to the others, were arranging a reception for Debs in his home town.

Originally Debs was expected to arrive on Christmas Day, and the local committee waited at Phil Reinbold's home until late in the afternoon for advance notice of his approach. Finally Otto Branstetter, with the Socialist leader in Washington, sent word that they would not arrive until December 28. The excitement had to be kept at a fever pitch for two extra days, a task that was difficult if not impossible. But Kate O'Hare and Ervin spoke at a mass meeting on the evening of Monday, December 26, and furnished front-page copy for the local press. The next day Ervin took the visiting newspapermen on a tour of the town, where they interviewed countless citizens about Debs' anticipated return. That kept the event alive for the second day. Debs himself would take care of the third day.

Meanwhile the three groups had continued with their arrangements for a reception on the evening of December 28. Phil Reinbold and Will Schuhardt of Terre Haute called on the stationmaster to discuss Debs' arrival. When they said that they expected at least twenty thousand people at the station, the official hooted derisively. They also asked permission to run a truck up to the door of his coach so that he would not have to fight his way through the crowd; the stationmaster denied the request because he feared that the crowd and the truck might break through the wooden platform under the train sheds.

Neither Charles Ervin nor the O'Hares had been idle. Frank O'Hare, with a keen eye for audience participation, ordered from a printer fifty thousand small cards on which red letters bore the legend: "Welcome Home—Gene Debs." He then combed the local shops for every inch of red ribbon, so that the cards could be fastened to hats, to wrists, to coat lapels. Dissatisfied with the quantity of ribbon available in Terre Haute, he sent to Indianapolis for more.

Charles Ervin led a delegation to see the mayor, who agreed that all fire bells should ring to greet Debs' arrival. He also chanced to speak with an old resident who remembered that Debs had ridden on a large wagon, drawn by dozens of his neighbors, from the station to his home on his return from Woodstock in 1895. Ervin, quick to detect the angle involved, led a fevered search for the identical carriage. It was finally found in the livery stable yard of an undertaker, and it was drawn up on Ninth Street near the station.

The scene had been carefully set. For nearly a week the local newspapers had been filled with news of Debs' release. The Terre Haute *Tribune*, so recently in hot pursuit of the disloyal elements, reflected the change of public opinion in its unctuous declaration: "Terre Haute citizens count Debs as an esteemed friend, no matter how reservedly they view his economic theories." Way out in Kansas, William Allen White wrote in the *Emporia Gazette:* "Pardons, like kissing, go by favors. Debs was pardoned for the same reason he was jailed: Because he was a man of charm and eloquence whom it was dangerous to have out fighting the war when we were in war, and also whom it is dangerous to have in jail now when we are at peace."

This broadside of publicity ensured a gigantic demonstration for the evening of December 28. Workingmen from all over Indiana would congregate in Terre Haute. A stonemason from Dayton, Ohio, had already been waiting three days on the back steps of Debs' house. But the telegram from Debs, announcing that he would arrive at 3:40 in the afternoon, threatened to disrupt the entire plan. The postwar recession was in full swing, and it was manifestly unfair to ask the coal miners and factory workers to leave their jobs in order to attend the meeting. Charles Ervin immediately wired that Debs would have to stop over in Indianapolis for four hours in order to arrive in Terre Haute at 8 P.M. Phil Reinbold met Debs in Indianapolis to ensure that there would be no mistake. So Eugene Debs, who had not seen his wife in nearly three years, was allowed to set one foot on the front porch, then was ordered to pause and wait for four hours.

Excitement gripped the entire city when the expected train pulled into the station. Fire bells and chimes pealed. Dozens of torches swung through the cold darkness. More than twenty-five thousand people shouted and screamed up and down on the platform under the train sheds. Eugene Debs was roughly seized by adoring hands, hoisted far above the crowd, and carried to the wagon waiting on Ninth Street. Dozens of eager men seized the ropes to drag the wagon through the streets to his home. As the hysterical throng moved toward its destination, a Negro band played "Swing Low, Sweet Chariot."

[2]

EUGENE DEBS—had he come home only to die? His health had broken completely. Prison food had completely wrecked his stomach and his kidneys. The recurrent headaches were malevolent torture. Rheumatism and lumbago twisted and perplexed his muscles. He found it impossible to rest, and rest he desperately needed. Every night he lay taut and sensitized, waiting for the sleep that never came. His heart jerked so gaspingly that noise from the rattling bed struck the walls of the room.

The previous August Debs had told a leading Socialist that he did not want to be bothered for at least a month after his release. This request was never observed. Political warfare between the Socialists and Communists had become ever more bitter, and each side now attempted to enlist the convictions and services of Eugene Debs. In the resulting struggle, however, the Socialists showed by far the greater persistence. The Communists sent an occasional emissary to Terre Haute; the Socialists maintained an unbroken stream of visitors, letters, telegrams, requests.

Even if Debs had been completely well, the choice before him would have been fraught with difficulties. He had serious disagreements with both of the contending factions. The Socialists, for their part, were furiously attacking the Russian Bolsheviks, the American Communists, and the Third Communist International. They had in effect abandoned the campaign for industrial unionism in favor of a working agreement with the Gompers grouping in the AFL. Their political program had been reduced to the effort to stimulate a broad reform party, based on the craft unions, in which they could recoup their waning fortunes. The theory of the class struggle had disappeared from the Socialist philosophy, and the Party was following the same program of right-wing opportunism which Debs had so heartily condemned in the past.

The Communists had drifted to the other extreme. Their practical illegality had stimulated in some members a glorification of underground activity, a juvenile posturing in place of decisive action. Their sectarian tendencies, reminiscent in some ways of Daniel DeLeon, had alienated large groups of revolutionary workers. Several of Debs' close friends, among them Marguerite Prevey, had left the Communist Party because of these errors. Finally, Eugene Debs had been personally affected by the Communist failures. Their abandonment of the campaign for amnesty had doubtless lengthened his prison term. Their rejection of his candidacy in 1920 had the same ultimate effect. Many Communists, angered by his refusal to break with Hillquit and Berger, had already denounced him as a traitor to the workers.

Finding himself unable to make a decision easily, Debs refused to decide at all. He maintained his membership and paid his dues in the Socialist Party. More than that he would not do. He refused to appear at meetings, to accept speaking engagements, or to issue a public avowal of his loyalty. In December, 1921, when the Communists formed a legal organization called the Workers Party, Debs had asked Theodore to send "his cordial greetings and best wishes" to their convention. The following April he conveyed his "cordial greetings" to the Socialist convention, and added "that the state of my health alone prevents my being in attendance." So the issue was held in abeyance, with both parties frustrated but hopeful.

A continuous stream of visitors appeared at the door of 451 North Eighth Street. Many persons sternly refused to be turned away. One woman knocked at the door repeatedly, even after

Kate Debs had stated that her husband was too tired and ill to see anybody. The woman spent the entire night on the front porch in quest of an interview. Recalling the incident later, Debs said that he became "so hopping mad that I told her under my breath to go to hell."

This nagging, relentless attention, although motivated by sympathy and devotion to the Socialist leader, actually became a severe drain on his strength. The telephone rang twenty-four hours a day. Each mail delivery brought a huge mound of letters asking for articles on every subject, endorsements for organizations and products, and even four offers to appear in vaudeville. A man who had built a large amphitheatre in Toledo offered Debs two thousand dollars to walk across the stage on opening night.

Kate Debs revived several harsh measures to meet this threat. All callers were curtly told that Debs was not receiving anybody. This rejection was meted out one morning to Powers Hapgood, a young, rugged Harvard graduate who chose to make his living as a coal miner. Hapgood turned away and strolled up the street. Suddenly he met a man whom he recognized as Eugene Debs. He hailed the Socialist leader, who seemed to be healthy enough. Debs tarried for a fifteen-minute chat about socialism and the United Mine Workers and conditions in the coal industry.

Hapgood was not the only caller, nor was he the first, to complain that Kate Debs was a gruff and frigid doorkeeper. The same charge had been made as far back as 1897 by James Oneal, a Terre Haute steelworker who became a Socialist leader. The popular interpretation was simply that Kate Debs did not like her husband's working-class and Socialist friends. But dozens of these same friends remember the extreme cordiality with which they were welcomed by Mrs. Debs. A better explanation is found in Kate Debs' desire to protect her husband's health. This version is advanced by Eugene Debs himself in an article written later in 1922: "How My Wife Has Helped Me." Debs recorded his wife's talents as a homemaker, her services as secretary in the early days, "her loving ministrations during days of trial and adversity."

"My wife," Debs wrote, "has been with me heart to heart, in unvarying loyalty and devotion, in every hour of trial and every moment of adversity. She has stood by my side without flinching when I was vilified, condemned and socially scorned and exiled; when I went to prison with the world's execration in my ears and my own soul erect and unafraid. . . . During my prison days she awaited my return with a patience as sublime as the devotion that inspired it and the courage that sustained it, without ever uttering a disheartening word."

Finally, in a particularly revealing and pertinent passage, the Socialist leader concluded: "But it must be confessed that my wife has not always been truthful when inquiry has been made as to my whereabouts when I was tired and worn and she had me tucked away for needed rest . . . I should be a far better man than I am if I had been as good a husband to my wife as she has been a wife to me."

The early months of 1922 were a constant strain to Kate Debs. Her mother, Mrs. Baur, then far into her eighties, required even more attention than Eugene Debs. The front porch on the house, which had been neglected throughout Debs' term in Atlanta, was being repaired, and Kate lived in mortal dread that her mother would be injured by falling into one of the gaping holes in the porch floor. At length she could stand it no longer, and Mrs. Baur was dispatched to the home of her son Arthur. A few weeks later she died. Kate Debs' health now broke, and she was confined to bed with influenza. Recovering from this illness, she was forced to make several trips to a nerve specialist in Indianapolis.

Meanwhile Eugene Debs, his own life in a shuddering collapse, was trying to fulfill an obligation to his recent associates. He had been sensitive to prison conditions since his childhood, when he first read Les Misérables. His own terms in the Cook County Jail, Woodstock, Moundsville, and Atlanta had imparted detailed knowledge and intimate loathing. The qualities which Eugene Debs most hated were summarized by the crude, petty, furtive, brutal methods of the penal system. During his confinement he was content to meliorate the conditions of the other inmates. But on his release he again became a radical, determined to uproot a lust for vengeance which he considered medieval and hateful.

Scarcely had Debs returned to Terre Haute in 1921 when he contracted to write a series of twelve articles about Atlanta for the Bell Syndicate, which was to publish them in commercial newspapers throughout the country. Debs lacked the strength to carry through this task alone. The ghost writer chosen to help him was young David Karsner, the Sunday editor of the New York *Call*. Karsner had reported the 1918 trial and Debs' trip to Moundville, had frequently interviewed the Socialist leader, and had written a brief biography of Debs in 1919. The two men knew each other's methods, liked and respected one another.

Karsner arrived in Terre Haute on March 10, 1922, and Debs immediately began work on the articles. His appearance startled the reporter. His lips were almost colorless, the skin tight around his mouth, his eyes "too bright," Karsner thought. But each morning he strode up and down his study, his voice flaming as in the old days, and dictated painful memories of the prisons he had known. Although he tried to restrain his tone so that the articles would be printed, the final result was shocking, bitter, agonized. Recalling a life in shadow and despair, Debs' mind knew stormy autumn nights when compassion flashed like lightning across the clouded skies. The enormous effort of calling forth these visions could not be maintained. After a few minutes, an hour or two, Debs would signal a close, and the two men would wander forth in search of friendship and entertainment.

Several times Debs escorted Karsner to Western movies, which called to mind his own experiences in Colorado organizing the Brotherhood of Firemen and the Western Federation of Miners. He kept up a running commentary all through the films. When a scene took place in a brawling saloon, Debs exclaimed in delight: "I've seen places like that a thousand times."

Debs decided one morning to visit another local citizen who had been with him in Atlanta prison, but an automobile was needed. Debs had never owned either a carriage or a car; his only vehicle was a bicycle on which he ambled sedately through the streets of Terre Haute. A bicycle was scarcely suitable to carry Debs and Karsner several miles to the friend's home. So Debs decided to enlist Phil Reinbold as chauffeur, and he strolled into Reinbold's bakery. The proprietor immediately fell upon Debs with both hands, leaving two white and sticky handprints on the tails of his coat. Reinbold agreed to take the afternoon off and drive Debs out to the friend's place in the country. It was decided that they would start at 12:30, and Debs spent the remainder of the morning acquainting Karsner with the man they intended to visit.

Buster Clark, once king of the red-light district in Terre Haute, had a reputation of being as honest as anybody in his business. Legend reported that he drove all the panders out of town, and that no prostitute without previous experience could operate in his area. Among vice kings, this was exceptional morality. Doubtless deserving to serve time on a hundred legitimate charges, Clark was finally sent to prison on a frame-up by his associates. Although he and Eugene Debs had lived in the same town all their lives, they first met in Atlanta. Close acquaintance taught Debs that the vice lord was kindly and generous in his relations with other prisoners, and the Socialist leader concluded that Clark, like everybody else, was merely a victim of his surroundings.

When Debs, Karsner, and Reinbold arrived at the ramshackle farm near Fort Harrison, Clark was sitting in a chair on the lawn. He was a huge fat man, weighing nearly two hundred fifty pounds, with sweat running down his red neck and his sticky black hair parted in the middle. His handshake was weak, his jaw flabby, his lips heavy, his ears gnarled and colorless. A derby hat was tilted over one eye. Diamond rings shone from his fingers, and another stone "as big as a dime" from his flashy necktie. He greeted Debs enthusiastically and introduced the three visitors to his wife, who seemed perfectly healthy but was slowly dying of paresis.

As the former convicts philosophized about their past, Debs contended that each man followed a predestined course. His own place he had found among the "scorned and shunned outcasts." Then he continued: "Well, I would rather a thousand times stagger to the judgment bar of God Almighty with the habitués of the Red Light district than to appear before St. Peter among the swaggering elements of the Country Club."

"The trouble with you, Gene," Buster Clark protested, "is that you were born 2,000,000 years ahead of your time. The world ain't cut out for men like you. Human beings are rotten, corrupt, and that's all there is to it. You believe that people are corrupt through circumstances over which they have little say. I don't. I made my life and I fought for it at every step and I'd fight for it now all over again, maybe not just the same way, maybe I wouldn't open a house again, but I guess it wouldn't take on a much different color at that."

So there sat Buster Clark, with nothing in the world but a few diamonds, a small farm, two dozen chickens, a wife dying of paresis—surrounded by a waste land and musing that it had all been played the right way.

David Karsner and Debs spent many hours discussing the current American writers and the future of literature. They shared an acute admiration of Walt Whitman and Horace Traubel—Karsner had named his daughter for the first and written a brief biography of the second. Although Debs was in no sense a judicious critic, some of his comments were peculiarly penetrating. Of H. L. Mencken he said: "His style is incisive, quick, sure, and he has a good bit to say. But it is all so very negative, so hopeless, so pessimistic, that when you get through reading him you wonder what life is all about and whether there is any sense in anything."

Among the poets Debs preferred his friend Horace Traubel, and among prose writers the Englishman Frank Harris, who was also a personal friend. But he protested that Harris' biography of Oscar Wilde was "so brutally frank and so cruel . . . there should be a line drawn somewhere between that part of a man's life that is peculiarly personal to him and his, and that part which belongs to the public. I would not want Frank Harris to be my biographer," he added to the amusement of his wife and Karsner.

Two Socialist novelists, Upton Sinclair and Jack London, were enduring favorites of Eugene Debs. London and John Peter

Altgeld were the two men whom Debs always admired but never met. After London's death in 1916 the Socialist leader had written a eulogistic epitaph for the *Rip-Saw*. He now elaborated his views in a conversation with David Karsner: "I think London wrote some mighty fine books, and I specially liked his *Call of the Wild*, *The Iron Heel*, and *The Sea Wolf*. London was unquestionably a genius, an artist of the first water. There was nothing surprising to me in the fact that Jack endorsed the war. His was a romantic mind, an adventuresome spirit, and that combination cannot be expected to sink itself into the grooves of logic and practicability."

When the discussions between Debs and Karsner ventured into trade unionism, the Socialist leader praised William Z. Foster, the leader of the 1919 Great Steel Strike who had recently joined the Communists. Debs was sitting in his favorite leather armchair, a gift thirty-five years earlier from the Brotherhood of Locomotive Firemen. His gaunt hands seemed to caress the wide leather arms as he spoke: "Foster has the right idea of a labor organization, but the pity of it is that he will not be able to make any headway with industrial unionism as long as Gompers and his crowd hold labor by the throat."

This led Debs into a diatribe against the AFL chieftain. His analysis was far from reliable. Speaking of the Pullman boycott, Debs declared: "Gompers did everything he could to break the strike. He was then, as now, hand in glove with the employers so far as any actual freedom of the workers was concerned." This is a strained interpretation of the AFL actions. Gompers had issued numerous protests against Federal interference; he had announced his support of the strikers; he had appealed for contributions for the legal defense fund after the ARU leaders were arrested. His actions were tardy and halfhearted, but they cast doubt on the contention that he was "hand in glove with the employers" in 1894.

The conversation meandered onward to the subject of Jesus of Nazareth, which always intrigued Debs. Karsner idly mentioned his doubts about the celibacy of Jesus. Debs found this a very interesting notion, and he himself had speculated on the topic. Pressed by Karsner, he explained his belief "that Jesus had an intense passionate love for Mary Magdalene. I believe that if the real story were known it would prove to be one of the most beautiful love episodes in history." He was refreshed by the thought of a romance between the Son of God and a woman accused of prostitution. "If there did exist warm human love between Jesus and Mary of Magda, how beautiful it must have been and what an inspiration it would be to those who are horrified by the thought of such a union, to know of it."

When with David Karsner and his brother Theodore, Debs again revealed his playful, lusty spirit. Chivalrous to the extent of prudery in the company of women, he could still be coarse and vulgar with his friends. About 1914 George D. Brewer, formerly one of his colleagues on the *Appeal to Reason*, was publishing the *Worker's Chronicle* in Pittsburg, Kansas. Brewer vividly described the murder of a Mexican revolutionary in a Paris cafe. Three assassins crept furtively to a window, fired five fatal shots into the body of the Mexican radical, and then made their escape. When this issue of the *Chronicle* arrived in Terre Haute, the ferret eyes of Eugene Debs discovered a typographical error in the word "shots." His hilarious letter to Brewer maliciously suggested that the Mexican revolutionary had been sent out on a foul. All revolutionaries, he commented, were entitled to better treatment from editors.

This cajolery was a common pastime for Eugene and Theodore Debs. Having read hundreds of mawkish poems in praise of his brother, Theodore vowed to shoot any poet on sight. Karsner promptly reported this statement to Debs, with his own endorsement. Debs laughed heartily and continued puffing at his pipe. Finally he broke off smoking to roar at the journalist: "I have told Theodore that if he didn't behave himself and treat me with proper respect I would feed his hide to the wolves, which are still prowling around Indiana prairies. As for you, well——"

Karsner endured this nonsense, but Theodore had his revenge. A few months later Eugene Debs was confined in a sanitarium. Theodore, on one of his frequent visits, managed to steal all of his brother's underwear.

On his last day in Terre Haute Karsner was invited to lunch at the Debs' home. Debs, jaded by the incessant requests for lecture dates, complained that he wanted to be left alone until he had recovered his health. His wife softly commented: "Well, dearie, suppose no one paid any attention to you at all. Suppose when you came out of prison they all had let you severely alone and had not asked for a speech or a letter. You'd feel mighty blue about that indifference to you, now wouldn't you?"

Perhaps Debs felt somewhat ashamed of this snivelling about his own condition, in which he had never indulged until the very twilight of his life. At any rate, he hastily corrected himself: "I am not ungrateful. I am only tired, very tired."

Those early months of 1922 were brightened by occasional golden moments. Debs and Karsner one morning visited a local grammar school. All of the children, mostly from mining families, were eating lunch. But they leaped to their feet when they saw Debs and clustered around to talk with him. Another day the Children's Crusade for Amnesty visited Terre Haute to call on Debs. This modern crusade, conceived and organized by Kate and Frank O'Hare, was composed of the wives and children of the political prisoners still in jail. They were on their way to Washington to make a personal appeal to the President. His brief contact with these women and children, who had suffered so bravely for so long a time, brought new zeal and determination to Debs' preparation of the prison articles.

These glimmerings of joy, however, were all too brief. The general pattern of 1922 was woven from constant annoyances and deepening gloom. On every hand Debs seemed to meet duplicity, frustration, and sorrow. Soon after his release he received a congratulatory telegram from Father Michael J. Byrne, the prison chaplain who had become his friend. The next day Father Byrne died. Three months later the Socialist leader wrote to J. O. Bentall, a political prisoner at Leavenworth. His letter was returned with a curt note from the prison officials: "Inmates of this institution are not permitted to correspond with inmates or former inmates of this or any other penal institution, except by special permission from the warden. . . ."

In March, Irwin St. John Tucker arrived in Terre Haute. While Debs was in prison, Tucker had established the *Debs*

Freedom Monthly to aid in the amnesty campaign, listing the Socialist leader as chief contributor. Debs had warm respect for Tucker, and even considered asking him to help with the prison articles if Karsner felt unable to spare the time. But Tucker returned to Chicago after a brief talk with Eugene and Theodore Debs, wrote up the interview and published it over their names, making it appear that they had written it. Debs had always suffered from the exercise of this license by Socialist editors, and his wonted reaction was to complain bitterly. But he was now so weary that his only mention of the affair was in a private conversation with David Karsner.

Then the prison articles began to appear. The first one carried an evasive heading: "(The views expressed in this article and in others of this series are those of Eugene V. Debs and not of the Bell Syndicate, Inc. Mr. Debs has agreed not to insert any political propaganda into the article.)" Debs was completely unable to abide by the agreement. The restriction was impossible. The articles placed responsibility for the penal system on the larger capitalist system of which it formed a part. In his first column, Debs had written: "A total of almost four years of my life has been spent behind the bars as a common prisoner; but an experience of such a nature cannot be measured in point of years. It is measured by the capacity to see, to feel and to comprehend the social significance and the human import of the prison in its relation to society."

The commercial newspapers, although they were eager to publish sensational exposés of the Federal prisons, were unwilling to consider "the prison in its relation to society." Debs' first nine articles were edited before they appeared. The final three were not printed at all. In large measure, the excruciating labor of preparing the material had gone for nothing. Not until after Debs' death were the original articles published in their entirety. And, ironically, his doctor had warned that Debs was committing suicide by his stubborn insistence on writing the articles immediately after his release.

Late in March, only a fortnight after the death of Mrs. Baur, another letter from Otto Branstetter urged Debs to announce publicly his support of the Socialist Party. Kate Debs was ill from anguish and worry. Debs himself had spent the previous night pacing the floor, unable to sleep, unable to stop thinking. He had repeatedly said that he wanted to be left alone to decide his affiliation in his own good time. Now his disgust and self-pity flowed into a molten accusation to Branstetter:

You cannot seem to understand that I am sick and worn and that I have not had the ghost of a chance to rest since I got out of the penitentiary. . . . But this probably does not mean anything to you for I doubt if you can understand it. You may be sure it is not to my liking to write to you in this way. I have made it a life-long rule to keep my troubles to myself. But your persistency must be my excuse. You and those you speak for insist that I must declare myself and of course declare myself your way. It seems to me that you would not care what became of me so I did what you wanted me to do. . . . I have given all but my life and I would like to keep that for a little while yet. Perhaps I may and perhaps not.

Debs added that a public statement by him would merely serve as additional fuel for a factional fight which was "utterly disgusting in some of its phases." He absolutely refused to take part: "I have never engaged in that sort of thing, having always considered it beneath me, and I shall not do so now." He thought that his continued membership in the Socialist Party should be enough to satisfy everybody. He planned to go away "to a retreat in the mountains where I may have a chance to get into condition to do something."

Four days later a letter from Branstetter stated that "a personal controversy" was "entirely foreign to" his intentions. Repenting, Debs wrote a conciliatory reply: "No, our controversy cannot become personal in any unpleasant sense. I know you are actuated by the best of motives and I give you full credit though I may not at all agree with you. I am glad to have this candid expression of your views."

But Debs also underscored his partial disagreement with the Socialist leaders. In a special article to the *Appeal to Reason*, he stated that the three immediate problems were aid to the Bolshevik government of Russia, a general amnesty for political prisoners, and unity of the radical parties. Any leaders who op-

posed such unity, Debs bluntly declared, should be thrust aside
by the rank and file.

[*3*]

As THE SUMMER approached Debs' health went into a long decline. Drastic action became imperative. Yielding at last to the
remonstrances of his doctor, he agreed to seek out a "retreat
in the mountains." The doctor, however, may have disapproved
of his choice. Joseph W. Sharts, one of Debs' attorneys in the
1918 trial, had interested his client in so-called nature cures.
Accordingly, Debs now resolved to go to Lindlahr Sanitarium,
a nature-cure resort in the Chicago suburb of Elmhurst, Illinois. As he left for Lindlahr in mid-July, he predicted that two
or three months of rest would completely restore his health.

The medical staff at the sanitarium took a more serious view
of the situation. They ordered Debs to halt all correspondence,
to restrict the number of visitors, and to follow a leisurely schedule. These orders were practically impossible of fulfillment. A
flood of visitors from Chicago and surrounding towns descended
upon Eugene Debs, and they proved most obstinate in their
determination to talk with their idol. Otto Branstetter continued
his requests for speaking engagements, personal appearances,
and press releases. The metropolitan newspapers either ignored
the Socialist leader or published dispatches that made him
scream with anger. He had scarcely reached Lindlahr when the
Christian Science Monitor published an unsigned account of a
conversation which Debs had held with Rose Pastor Stokes just
before leaving Terre Haute. The article quoted Debs in a number of extreme statements: "I am unqualifiedly opposed to communism. It has not a single constructive plank in its entire
platform. . . . I am in deepest sympathy with Russia and her
people in their efforts to work out a government in which
czarism has no part. But I am opposed and strongly opposed to
dictatorship, regardless of the class by which it is prac-
ticed. . . ."

Otto Branstetter sent a clipping of the story to Debs, asking
whether it was true. Debs was highly mystified by the origin

of the dispatch. He and Mrs. Stokes had been the only participants in the conversation. It was unreasonable to believe that
Mrs. Stokes, herself a Communist, would publicize such an anti-
Communist and distorted account of the discussion. Debs preferred to let the incident end quietly, and he refused to authorize
its use by Branstetter or to issue a denial. Thus a newspaper
story, of which Debs wrote that "some of the interview is true
and some is not," was publicly offered as his position on the
Bolshevik Revolution.

Some of the story was doubtless true, because it was authen-
ticated a few days later. During his interview with the Socialist
notification committee in 1920, Debs had upheld the Communist theory of a workers' dictatorship by stating: "During
the transition period the revolution must protect itself." Just
before his release from Atlanta, he convinced Lincoln Steffens
that he understood the denial of civil liberties in Russia. "And
he promised me then and there," the journalist recalled, "never
again to denounce the Russian Revolution on any charge without first hearing my answer to it." Debs now forgot both of
these earlier statements. He received a telegram from Russia on
July 24, 1922, asking him to request clemency for twenty-two
Russian Social Revolutionaries on trial for treason. Two days
later he dispatched a wire to Nikolai Lenin: "I protest with all
civilized people of our common humanity against the execution
of any of the Social Revolutionaries or the unjust denial of their
liberty. Soviet Russia can set an example by refusing to follow
the practices of world-wide czardom and should uphold the
higher standards we seek to erect and profess to observe."

This telegram set off a tremendous stir in the radical ranks.
Lincoln Steffens promptly wrote a letter of protest, but he was
not favored with an answer. Perhaps Steffens' letter did not
even reach the Socialist leader, since at this time all of his mail
was being received and answered by other members of his family. The two men never saw each other again. Many Communists
interpreted Debs' action as a sign that he was becoming senile
or even insane; this was not true at all. Many Socialists rejoiced that Debs had completely broken with all Communists;
this was not true either.

Eugene Debs was still a contributing editor of the *Liberator*, which was increasingly shifting toward the Communist philosophy. And less than a month after his telegram to Lenin, Debs rushed to the defense of one of the Communist leaders, William Z. Foster. In August Foster visited Denver to fill a speaking engagement. He was arrested at his hotel before the lecture, driven across the state line into Wyoming, and dumped out in the desert, with orders never to return to that area.

News of this incident roused Eugene Debs to high fury. He immediately wrote a warm and fraternal letter to the victim:

Dear Comrade Foster: If I were not confined in a sanitarium under treatment I would be at once with you and tender my services in any way in my power. . . .

You are to be congratulated, after all, upon the infamous outrages perpetrated upon you in the name of capitalist law and justice, for in these outrages . . . is revealed the fear of their thieving and brutal masters, and this is the highest compliment they could possibly pay you . . . all I have to say is that when I have recovered my strength sufficiently to take up my work again I shall be with you shoulder to shoulder in your stand for the working class and industrial freedom.

By August 26, 1922, when he wrote this letter to William Z. Foster, Debs' strength and optimism had begun their recovery. It was already clear that his series of prison articles would yield little money and less reform. Most papers were unwilling to print them. One publisher even stated that he would not carry them if full advertising rates were paid for the space. Debs did not show very great concern. Not even a rumor that the Terre Haute newspapers had been forbidden to mention his name in any way could interfere with the surge of new vigor. His only comment was half in jest: "I shall pry them open in due time, when the necessity arises."

As Debs began to recover he found scant satisfaction in the nature-cure diet of grain and fresh fruit. It proved to be easy to slip away from the crowded, bustling corridors of the sanitarium. He spent less and less time on the grounds where he was supposedly confined. August Claessens, who went to visit him one evening, was startled to find that he was not in his room. An orderly laughingly revealed that an ex-railroad buddy, now the proprietor of a restaurant on Ashland Avenue in Chicago, often took Debs for a walk in the evening. Immediately divining the truth, Claessens rushed his small body and giant cigar to the restaurant. There sat the convalescent, gazing hopelessly at a steak that drooped over the plate onto the table. Two waiters and the proprietor hovered anxiously about the table. When the proprietor noticed the arrival of the other Socialist, he burst out angrily: "Goddammit, Mr. Claessens, they're starving him; those bastards are starving him." Claessens and Debs burst into hilarious laughter, Debs rocking back and forth in his chair, the cigar rocking up and down in Claessens' mouth.

By September Debs was well enough to search actively for amusement. He ran foot races with a young tuberculosis patient. He spent many pleasant evenings with Mrs. Ralph Chaplin and Mr. and Mrs. Carl Haessler, all of whom lived near Lindlahr. Haessler, formerly an instructor of philosophy at the University of Illinois, had just been released from prison after a term for anti-war activity. Ralph Chaplin, convicted with the 105 Wobblies in the Chicago trial, was still in Leavenworth, and Debs repeatedly assured Mrs. Chaplin that her husband would soon be free. The Socialist leader found great pleasure in these brave, cultured people, and he played for long hours with their young children.

The outlaw strike by the railroad shopmen, which took place in the summer of 1922, was of particular interest to Debs because it was broken by means of injunctions, Negro strikebreakers, the National Guard, and the treachery of the railway Brotherhoods. Pointing out the parallel to the Pullman boycott, Debs warned that the existing open-shop drive could only be defeated by a maximum degree of labor unity. This unity, he said, must be achieved in spite of the opposition of the craft union leaders. Talking with Carl Haessler during the strike, the Socialist leader reflected upon the fact that union railroaders had carried him to prison.

In September the conservative policies of the Brotherhoods were further emphasized for Eugene Debs. His own former union, the Brotherhood of Locomotive Firemen, voted down a convention proposal to invite him to speak. He noted this action in a long and reminiscent press release: "I did not start out expecting gratitude and I have never been disappointed. . . . My heart has been, is and will be with the working class, and even though they deny me and reject me and turn me from their ranks, they can never turn themselves from my heart."

A sure token of Debs' mental state always appeared in his recurrent musings about death. The stunning demise of his parents in 1906 had revealed to him, for the first time, the transitory character of human life. He had promptly registered a will at the Vigo County Courthouse. Seven years later the *Medical Review of Reviews* asked him to contribute to a symposium on euthanasia. Debs replied that he favored mercy killing "upon the voluntary request of the already doomed sufferer, or, if he has already passed to the stage of mental irresponsibility, of those responsible for him." In obvious good humor, he continued: "It ought to be the privilege of every human being to cross the River Styx in the boat of his own choosing . . ."

Death seemed a vague and distant unknown in 1913. It was twined around his heart in 1922, when he burst forth to Otto Branstetter: "I have given all but my life and I would like to keep that for a little while yet. Perhaps I may and perhaps not." By the autumn he again had a poised, objective view of the matter. In discussing the newspaper business with a friend, he took occasion to philosophize on the imminence of death: "The newspaper men have to keep pace with modern times. There is a rush about news gathering that we never had before. For example, I appreciate my own unimportance, but when the report was sent out that I was ill, the Associated Press sent a representative to find out my exact condition. I suppose they have my obituary written but I'm going to prevent its publication as long as possible."

The final days of Debs' confinement at Lindlahr were more vacation than convalescence. Sheriff George Eckert and his daughter drove to Elmhurst from Woodstock, Illinois, where Eckert had been Debs' jailer in 1895. The sheriff had become quite friendly with Kate and Eugene Debs, and each Christmas for twenty-six years he had sent them a reminder of the old

days. As Debs talked with Eckert, who was eighty-one years
old and had fought in the Civil War, he felt more sanguine
about the chances of living a few more years.

One stroke of fortune which fell to Debs during those weeks
was a chance to renew his friendship with Carl Sandburg. The
reporter, poet, and biographer had been casually acquainted
with Debs in 1910, when he served as secretary to the Socialist
mayor of Milwaukee. Now working on the Chicago *Daily News*,
Sandburg lived only three blocks from the sanitarium. He and
Debs frequently traded visits in order to discuss the Socialist
movement and Sandburg's biography of Abraham Lincoln,
which was shaping up after years of research. It was a delight
for Debs, who had accepted every discredited legend about the
Civil War President, to chat about Lincoln with somebody who
knew the facts and seized the spirit of a mystical career.

Sinclair Lewis arrived at Lindlahr in August for a brief rest,
and he was quickly recruited for the discussions held by Debs
and Sandburg. One Saturday night Sandburg even brought his
guitar to the sanitarium and gave the patients "a most charming
entertainment in folk lore, etc. It was a complete conquest,"
Debs wrote to David Karsner, "and they all love him. Lewis will
also entertain them and the patients here feel big with importance. No 'Main Streeters' here."

Late in November Debs realized that he had no legitimate
excuse to prolong his stay at Lindlahr, and so he returned to
Terre Haute. A few days later he received a brief note from
Carl Sandburg: "You will always be close to us. The only way
we can decently remember you and what you left with us here
will be a certain way of living it, maybe dying it.

"And some day I hope to get the strong truth about those
hands of yours into a poem. It's only a hope but I'll try for it
and learn something. . . .

"With you it isn't really a good-by because you are still here."

[4]

ON OCTOBER 8, 1922, six weeks before he left Lindlahr, Eugene
Debs' declaration of his political views appeared in the New

York *Call*. He had resolved to keep his membership in the Socialist Party. This decision cannot be explained wholly on the basis of his principles. Debs had serious disagreements with the Communists about the imminence of revolution in the United States, about the need for a workers' dictatorship, about the Third International. He felt that the Communists had failed him and the workers in the 1920 election and in the amnesty campaign. But he also seriously differed from the Socialists about the Russian Revolution, industrial unionism, and class-conscious politics.

The personal nature of Debs' reasoning appeared in his statement in the *Call*. He was unable to admit failure and make a fresh start by resigning from the Socialist Party. As he declared: "I have spent the better part of my active life in its service and why should I now turn upon it and rend it? . . . I admit the party has made some mistakes and that it is not today what I should like to see it, but the same would be true of any other party I might join."

Having tried for twenty-five years to build a revolutionary organization, Debs did not see how any other party, working with "the same material, the same comrades, the same ultimate aims," could succeed if the Socialist Party had failed. He clung to his intention of uniting all American radicals in one great revolutionary party. So he again praised the Communist Workers Party and John Keracher's Proletarian Party, which had split from the Communists in 1920: "I know many of the members of the Workers Party and of the Proletarian Party and I know that in taking the position they have they are actuated by the best of motives and that they are as honest as we are in their efforts to build up a party to serve the working class in the revolutionary struggle."

CHAPTER XXII

[*1*]

EUGENE DEBS returned to Terre Haute in November of 1922. He was supposedly cured and healthy. But by Christmas he was again confined to his bed with lumbago, unable to receive visitors, unable to answer correspondence. In his earlier years a fortnight of convalescence had customarily followed six months of rending toil. This was radically changed. A major part of his time for the next five years was to be devoted to caring for his own health. Preparation for a lecture tour now involved at least three months of rest. A few weeks of strenuous activity exhausted him completely, forcing another retreat to the ministrations of his wife or of Lindlahr Sanitarium.

The revised methods necessitated by his broken health help to explain many of the abortive starts and the equivocal positions held by Eugene Debs during the final years of his life. He had never been able to sit down in his study with a pile of books and think his way to a conclusion. His understanding was a product, not of scholarly research, but of participation in the problems and the struggles of the common people. He himself distrusted the decisions he made on the basis of facts gathered by other men. However emphatically they were expressed, they were subject to prompt change and even to contradiction.

Thus, in October of 1922, he announced his continued adherence to the Socialist Party. But his actions of the following months showed that, on many issues, he was more in accord with the Communists than with his own party. He remained a contributing editor of *The Liberator*, which was rapidly becoming an unofficial spokesman for the Communist Workers Party. In December of 1922, a brief four months after he had sent his telegram of protest to Nikolai Lenin, Debs wrote for this journal an article in praise of the Russian Bolsheviks:

For five years they have stood with more than Spartan courage against the foul assaults of the whole criminal capitalist world.

They have waded through hell in their own blood to banish hell from the earth and bring peace to the world.

They have fought in rags to clothe the naked, they have starved themselves to feed the race, and they have died in fetters to free the world.

The Russian Republic stands triumphant, gloriously triumphant on its fifth anniversary, a beacon light of hope and promise to all mankind!

The greatest division between Debs and his party, however, arose from the issue of industrial unionism. A few important unions, notably the needle-trades unions of New York, were still led by Socialist officers. Each of these unions contained a strong Communist minority. The Socialist officials, in order to resist the growing influence of the Communists, had reached a working agreement with the Gompers' grouping in the AFL. A major plank in the agreement was complete abandonment by the Socialists of the drive for industrial unions. Leadership in this campaign was firmly held by the Trade Union Educational League, in which the main figure was the Communist William Z. Foster.

Eugene Debs balked at even tacit endorsement of the policies of Samuel Gompers. In September, 1922, his article for the Socialist Press Service bluntly declared: "There is but one labor organization absolutely free from capitalist domination in the United States and that is the I.W.W., and its headquarters are in the penitentiary." This sentence was struck out by Otto Branstetter, who then wrote Debs asking approval of the deletion. Debs' reply was hesitant: "I would rather the alteration had not been made but perhaps you are right, and I am satisfied."

He was not, however, satisfied. His first public appearance in 1923, after he recovered from the lumbago which marred his release from Lindlahr, was made in Chicago. He seized the chance to visit the offices of the Trade Union Educational League. His unannounced visit was a great surprise to Earl Browder, alone in the office at the time. Debs remembered

Browder's imprisonment for anti-war activity in Kansas City in 1918. They talked at length about the need to work within existing unions in order to convert the labor movement to industrial unionism. Debs seemed eager to use the Trade Union Educational League as an organization which could unite the Socialists and Communists for a common program. Before saying good-by to Browder, he promised to contribute to the League's magazine, *The Labor Herald*. His first article, which appeared in April, 1923, was an eloquent plea for amalgamation of the craft unions.

From Chicago Debs journeyed eastward to New York. He was slated to give a few speeches, but his compelling interest was an intended conference with Morris Hillquit. The commutation of Debs' sentence in 1921 had not included a full pardon, and he believed that he had forfeited his citizenship. On behalf of himself and thousands of other ex-convicts, Debs was determined to crusade for a full restoration of all civil rights. Immediately after his release from Atlanta, he had set Morris Hillquit to work checking the legal aspects of the matter. He now intended to get together with Hillquit and plan the entire campaign. It promised to be a worthy battle, just like the old days.

Entering his office one morning, Hillquit found Debs already there, slumped in a chair and waiting impatiently. Debs was joyous in his anticipation of the coming fight. He immediately launched into a fervent presentation of the plans for his crusade. Listening, Hillquit was uneasy. The task before him was not a pleasant one. His research had uncovered some recalcitrant facts. Finally he broke in hesitantly: "The weakness of your case lies in the fact that you have not forfeited your citizenship at all. You are still a citizen of the United States."

"What do you mean, I am still a citizen?" Debs stormed back. "All newspapers assert that I have lost my citizenship and the United States Attorney General has confirmed the statement."

Hillquit passed to his client an array of legal citations in support of his position. Debs frowned as he read the memorandum. At length he passed it back. He seemed heartbroken. Conscious of his guilt, Hillquit haltingly suggested: "If you feel like testing your rights, Gene, you might offer to register and vote in the next election; and if the local election board interferes with you, we will take the case into the courts."

"Oh, they will not question my right to vote in Terre Haute," Debs muttered in disgust.

The Socialist leader never visited New York without paying a special visit to the homeless inhabitants of Union Square to discuss their problems, cheer them up, distribute money among them. There had always been thousands of these outcasts. But in the pre-War era they were the backwater, divorced from the confident optimism which typified that period. One day before the World War, Art Young had found Debs in Union Square and escorted him to the office of *The Masses*. Young later recalled that Debs had "talked to a group of artists and writers with enthusiasm for our work, and hopefulness for the future— over all his towering form as if looking down from his own Heaven." A vast disillusionment followed the Treaty of Versailles and the postwar economic slump. Only the radicals now dared to be hopeful. The mood of Union Square was engulfing the city and the nation.

A few weeks after his visit to New York Debs spoke at the University of Wisconsin in Madison, which was also the state capital. The lower house of the General Assembly formally resolved "that the legislature in as far as possible go in a body to listen to his lecture on socialism and freedom in the University gymnasium this evening." Eugene Debs had "proved to be an outstanding American," said the legislators, "in that he had the courage during the hysteria and war madness to stand up and defend the ideals and splendid traditions of this republic regarding equality of opportunity and the rights of freedom of religion, free press, free speech and peaceable assemblage, the keystone and guarantee of free institutions."

This reception, however, was in no sense typical. Hostility and denunciation were the common reactions to Debs' lecture tour in 1923. Just two months after the cordiality of Madison, he encountered the strident resentment of several patriotic societies in Ohio. Protests by Kiwanis Clubs, posts of the American Legion, Army and Navy Unions, and the commercial newspapers vastly increased the difficulties of booking halls for his lectures. For the first time in his career, Eugene Debs found the prominent auditoriums were beyond his reach. But in each city he ultimately gave his speech, and in each city a capacity crowd turned out to hear him.

[2]

THE EXCITEMENT of this transcontinental tour, which carried him as far as Seattle in September, again wiped out his fragile strength. While traveling he completely ignored his correspondence and refused to see visitors, but these precautions proved vain. An attack of nervous exhaustion forced a limping retirement to Terre Haute. Through the long autumn of 1923 he clung to life with feeble hands. His home was converted into a hospital. Theodore closed the office in order to spend all of his time with his adored brother. Kate, herself far from well, hovered attentively nearby. Debs delayed his recovery by his own exaggerated prejudices against all types of medicine. Theodore reluctantly admitted that Eugene had only an even chance to survive, but the patient stubbornly rejected all heart stimulants. Time after time Theodore was practically required to use force before Debs would submit to the medical prescriptions.

By March of 1924 it was apparent that Debs would recover. Although nobody was certain of the reasons, Theodore ascribed the recovery to his brother's dogged determination and the skill of the doctor. Even Debs recognized that the end was drawing near. While he was still confined to bed, he donated most of his library to the Rand School of Social Science, a Socialist Party school in New York. Into the boxes were packed complete files of every publication for which he had written. Nearly twenty volumes of the *Locomotive Firemen's Magazine*—the leather decayed, the memories ripe and intimate—including the volume which he had given to Kate three years before their marriage; the minute books of the Supreme Council of the United Orders of Railway Employes; the *Railway Times* and the *Social Democratic Herald*—they represented half a lifetime. The rest of the story was in the *Appeal to Reason*, from the golden years of the Socialist Party; in the *National Rip-Saw* and the *In-*

ternational Socialist Review; in the *Nationalist* and the *Challenge* and the *Comrade.*

A true indication of Debs' perspectives is given by the thoroughness with which he uprooted his possessions. He yielded up books which had been presented to him by David Karsner, Horace Traubel, Frank P. Walsh, A. M. Simons, Elbert Hubbard, Morris Hillquit, Henry Demarest Lloyd. He wrenched from his home the scrapbooks which had been compiled with so much care and precision. They held more than four thousand pages of newspaper clippings, doggerel, reports of his speeches, articles about Robert Ingersoll and the 1905 revolution in Russia, popularized accounts of American and French history. When Eugene Debs dispatched those boxes to the Rand School, he parted with the defeats and triumphs, the joy and sorrows of six decades. It was an eloquent recognition of the end.

He kept only his belief in the final victory of socialism. That never left him. In June of 1924 an article in *Current History Magazine* contended that socialism had begun in Woodstock jail and died in Atlanta prison. The author was David Karsner. For nearly six years Karsner had been the most intimate friend of the Socialist leader. He had reported the Cleveland trial, journeyed with Debs to Moundsville, frequently visited Atlanta. He had helped to write the series of articles about the penal system. He and Debs had discussed Western movies, contemporary fiction, Jesus of Nazareth, Russia and the Communists.

Always loyal to personal friends, Debs felt no bitterness toward the young journalist. But he refused to admit the failure of his own convictions. When asked about Karsner's article, he smiled sadly across his wrinkled face. "I am sorry that David did that," Debs murmured, "because he will regret it and be unhappy over it some day. He is supersensitive and very young. He has had some trying experiences, had trouble with his colleagues and has acted unwisely. If I had been with him, he would have done otherwise. . . . No, no, Socialism will never die. It is inevitable. We may retard or impede its progress through our political organization. But the inevitable cannot die."

By early summer Debs was strong enough to travel to Lindlahr, where he underwent another series of nature-cure treatments. He soon returned to his earlier routine at the sanitarium: visits with Carl Sandburg in Elmhurst or at the office of the Chicago *Daily News*, huge steak dinners at the restaurant on Ashland Avenue owned by the former railroader, leisurely conversations with other Socialists. Although constantly ugly weather deprived him of sunshine and fresh air, his health continued to mend.

Responsibility for Eugene Debs was a severe trial to the doctors at Lindlahr. He persistently wandered away from the sanitarium. He gave little heed to the rules about rest and sleep. He refused to sacrifice the pleasures of foot racing for so trivial a reason as a weak heart. His room was usually filled with visitors. But the real crisis in the relations of patient and doctor was precipitated by the Chicago locals of the bakers' union. In order to show their affection for the Socialist leader, they baked a cake three feet in diameter and at least that high. The physicians at the sanitarium, dedicated to strict dietary rules, were astounded when this cake was presented to Debs. It was borne through the corridors by four men, each of whom held a corner of a large board. They were surrounded by a gleeful, jabbering committee from the local. One of the doctors, extremely agitated, crowded into Debs' room immediately behind the committee. Turning to August Claessens, a chance visitor at the time, he feverishly protested: "Mr. Claessens, this does not conform to our methods of treatment." Claessens laughingly took the doctor away and told him not to worry. The entire cake was presented to an orphans' home in Chicago.

One day in the late summer Debs journeyed to Lombard, Illinois, only two miles from Elmhurst, for a visit with Ralph Chaplin and Carl Sandburg at Chaplin's home. It was a gorgeous warm day, and soon Debs was comfortably established in a large wicker chair under an elm which the Chaplins had named for him. He seemed vigorous and alert, but Chaplin noticed that his hands "rested strangely stiff and unresponsive" on the arms of the chair. Since both Debs and Chaplin had been imprisoned for their opposition to the war, they inevitably began to reminisce about life in prison. Debs' voice trembled as he recalled the inhumanity of it. Seeking some interruption, Chaplin hastily cut a rosebud and handed it to Debs, saying, "Maybe this will help you to forget."

"It's almost like murder to cut the stem of a beautiful thing like that!" Debs protested. "Why didn't you let it live?" Small wonder that so many of his acquaintances contended that he "wouldn't kill a fly."

As the afternoon wore on Chaplin presented the Socialist leader with a small watercolor portrait of John Brown which he had just copied from a biography of the abolitionist. Almost ecstatic, Debs exclaimed that John Brown had been a true prophet. Carl Sandburg interposed his own opinion that Brown had been more like a brigand. That set the two men into a fierce argument, and Debs eloquently expounded the entire story of his foremost idol. Like most arguments, this one was never resolved.

That autumn at Lindlahr also marked the first unqualified attack by Debs against the Communists. Although several public disputes had occurred since 1919, one overwhelming factor had prevented a complete rupture. Debs and the Communists shared an unflinching opposition to the capitalist system. The Communist departure from the Socialist Party had been stimulated by their desire to repudiate the pro-war socialists of all countries and to support the Russian Bolsheviks. Both of these positions had been supported by Eugene Debs before his imprisonment. Similarly, after his release from Atlanta, he had agreed with the Communist campaigns for Russian relief, for industrial unionism, and for defense of all political prisoners.

But other factors were working to separate Eugene Debs and the Communists. Debs' resentment about the 1920 election and the campaign for his own pardon played a large part, as did his inability to leave an organization in which he had spent his mature years. Even more important, however, were the differing emphases of Debs and the Communists. Each was strongest where the other was weakest. Eugene Debs was bone and fiber of the American people. His sensitivity to the popular mind of the workingmen and farmers was almost uncanny. His ideas, his language, his very personality, were all native to the Midwest. This quality the Communists lacked. Many of their members were from factory towns where the recent immigrants had been drawn in their search for work, and the mass repression after the war had further separated them from the rest of the community. The deportation statutes and the criminal syndicalist laws had been swung like a club at their heads. Forced underground, they had succumbed to several romantic and sectarian ideas, and the imprisonment of their leaders had further disrupted their organization.

Faced with this power which seemed overwhelming, the Communists insisted upon the importance of discipline and Marxist theory. They claimed that they could ill afford to tolerate divisions within their ranks, but Eugene Debs was not convinced. He had always ignored the official policies of his party, making his own policies as he went along. Nor had he ever paid much attention to Marxist theory. Again a typical Midwesterner, he had focussed his attention on the immediate facts and the practical issues that he saw around him. An experimentalist, he had only one general principle—the achievement of socialism. Beyond that he improvised. His contempt for technical haggling and theoretical arguments had always prompted him to refuse to serve as a convention delegate or as an official in the Socialist Party.

Always, that is, until 1923. Alarmed by the disintegration of the organization which he had helped to found, Debs in that year agreed to serve as national chairman of the Socialist Party. Thus he conclusively indicated his basic affiliation. However much he might co-operate with other groups, his basic loyalty was to the Socialists. This new responsibility, added to the disagreements on other points, finally prompted his cleavage with the Communists during the Presidential campaign of 1924. The Socialists endorsed the Progressive candidate, Senator Robert M. LaFollette. This action was supported by Eugene Debs and denounced by William Z. Foster, the Communist candidate for President. Foster described the Progressive movement as a one-man show, the voice of the middle-class reformers. His demand for the immediate formation of a farmer-labor party stated that Debs' endorsement of LaFollette would shock thousands of workers.

Debs flared back that this was a peculiar attitude for Foster to take. The Communists themselves, said Debs, would have endorsed LaFollette, "had not LaFollette, knowing the record of the Communists and understanding their game, denounced them and positively refused their endorsement." While admitting that the Progressives were not a workers' party, Debs claimed that many of their policies would benefit the common people.

The Socialists soon learned that they had walked into a trap. The results of the election almost completed the destruction of their party. After his defeat Senator LaFollette withdrew from the Progressive Party. The railroad Brotherhoods and most AFL unions joined the exodus. The entire third party collapsed, and it dragged the Socialist Party down with it. Having led their members into a much stronger organization, the Socialist officials now found it difficult to hold them together. The smallest convention in the history of the Socialist Party met in Chicago on February 23, 1925. There were forty-five delegates, all of them veterans. Morris Hillquit called them the die-hards.

Eugene Debs witnessed this collapse with anguish and wistfulness, but without despair. Writing to his friend Joseph A. Labadie soon after the election, he voiced a requiem on their common lives: "I well know, dear Jo, how abnormally big you are in the cardiac region and how you would if you could give your all and give it freely to the last drop of your blood to see your fellow beings free and happy. But it can't be done in any other than its own tragically slow and painful way. You and I can do our little utmost and then drop away to make room for others to do the same, and all the reward, all the honor, all the satisfaction we ever want is the knowledge that we have given all and done our best without expecting anything in return. One of these good days we shall clasp hands again and sit heart to heart in 'the dear love of comrades.'"

This mood of calm reflection had disappeared by the time of the Socialist convention in Chicago. As chairman of the Party, Eugene Debs delivered the principal address. Although he had advocated endorsement of LaFollette to bring the Socialists "into contact with the great body of workers," he had felt very uncomfortable during the alliance. Now he was glad to be free again. "I seem to have been delivered from a nightmare," he laughingly told the convention. "While we were in the so-called Progressive movement I felt as if I had lost my wings. I felt like an octogenarian snail just crawling along. Now I feel as if I could leap from crag to crag like a Rocky Mountain goat."

The following day, while Debs was presiding over the convention, John Work was astonished to see Stephen Reynolds enter the hall. Reynolds had dropped out of the Party soon after he left Terre Haute in 1910. Nobody had seen him for years. Work concluded that he must have come to talk with Debs. Reynolds walked to the front of the small hall and sat down immediately in front of the speakers' stand, in full view of the chairman. Debs didn't smile, didn't wave, didn't blink an eye. When he left the stand, to the further amazement of John Work, he walked straight past Reynolds without even nodding to him.

The effect of the 1924 campaign on the Socialist Party was a powerful argument for the independent policy advocated by William Z. Foster. But there was no reconciliation between Debs and the Communists. Debs was infuriated by the persistent reports that he had in effect broken with the Socialist Party. Finally he yielded to the urging of his colleagues and issued a harsh disclaimer of these statements: "some unscrupulous communist propagandists are using my connection with the Labor Defense Council as a means of discrediting the socialist party by spreading the report in a surreptitious way, in accordance with 'underground' methods, that I am really with the communists and a socialist in name only. . . . Now if hereafter any communist whispers it into your ear that I am with the communists in anything except their right to free speech and other civil rights, just answer by turning your back upon him and leaving the vulgar falsifier to himself."

[*3*]

"WHEN I GO, I shall be going, not stopping. I shall welcome my new adventure with open arms, shall take old Father Time by the arm with a smile and make a socialist out of him."

Thus spoke Eugene Debs in 1925 to a reporter for the Terre Haute *Tribune*. Much of his time now was spent looking forward to death or backward to the dead. Each week or month some event called forth a soothing flood of mellow recollections. When Waldo R. Browne's biography of Altgeld was published, Debs received a gift copy from Clarence Darrow and George Schilling. His letter of thanks contained candid expressions about two leaders of his age. Although both were lifelong Democrats, Debs could find no resemblance between them. William Jennings Bryan was found to be "petty, mean and contemptible, . . . this shallow-minded mouther of empty phrases, this pious, canting mountebank, this prophet of the stone age." Still the Great Commoner "was popularized almost to idolatry and glorified by press and pulpit as an apostle of truth and an evangel of religion." On the other hand John Peter Altgeld, "supremely great . . . in heart and brain, in soul and conscience," had been "rewarded with contumely, malice, hatred and almost oblivion." The Socialist leader was confident that in time these errors would be corrected, "and in that day John P. Altgeld the hero and martyr, the apostle and saviour of his age will be known and loved of all men and his memory honored and revered throughout the world."

Another sign of advanced age appeared at the close of Debs' letter to Darrow and Schilling. It was signed: "Yours to the last turning of the road." But that last turn lay somewhere ahead. In May Debs toured Ohio to rebuild the local branches of the Socialist Party. In July he and Theodore made a hectic trip to California on the same mission, and he spoke in the Hollywood Bowl with Upton Sinclair as chairman. He also gave an address in the Los Angeles zoo, while lions roared accompaniment in the background. A few days later Debs spoke in Los Angeles and then headed for home.

Well-earned recognition by the workingmen of his own community finally came to Eugene Debs on August 27, 1925. He was justly known as the father of the labor movement in Terre Haute. Fully half of the local unions in the area had been launched as a direct result of his efforts, and the others had all benefited indirectly from his activities. His experience, his savings, his magnificent voice and deep compassion had been lavished freely on the cause of his neighbors. After his release from Atlanta prison, he threw his great prestige into the campaign for the erection of a new AFL Temple in Terre Haute. These efforts were successful, and the 1925 convention of the Indiana Federation of Labor showed its appreciation of his services. One session of the convention placed at the entrance to the Labor Temple a large bronze tablet which bore the portrait of the Socialist leader. The inscription was plain but memorable:

In Honor
of
Eugene V. Debs
April 1, 1925.

On this occasion Debs gave one of the last major speeches of his career. The tribute given him had not blunted his hostility or softened his rhetoric. The huge audience, which stood in a burning sun throughout the two-hour address, heard little except criticism of their trade-union policies. Stomping back and forward as of old, Debs roared his indictment of pure-and-simple unionism. His arm and forefinger slashing the air like a scimitar, he hurled crashing epigrams into the crowd before him: "The capitalist politician tells you how intelligent you are to keep you ignorant. I tell you how ignorant you are to make you desire to be intelligent."

The kernel of this speech offered a telling measure of the foresight of Eugene Debs. "This world respects as it is compelled to respect," he declared. "Develop your own capacity for clear thinking. Unorganized, you are helpless, you are held in contempt. Power comes through unity. Organization or stagnation, which will you take? The labor movement must either go for-

ward or backward. Merge your craft unions!" Although this
exhortation had remained unchanged since the Pullman boycott, it was perfectly appropriate in 1925. The craft unions
were still divided by narrow policies and jurisdictional disputes.
Injunctions and military intervention were still being used to
break strikes. The mass production industries had never been
organized. The postwar depression had given way to an economic boom, and the trade unions uneasily succumbed to a
belief in constant prosperity. Schemes based on the co-operation
of workers and employers were adopted in scores of industries.
In opposition to these plans for class conciliation, the Socialist
leader offered industrial unionism and stalwart battle against
the employers.

However modern Debs' ideas, his mannerisms bore the imprint of an earlier age. The United States had entered the epoch
of speakeasies, of short skirts, of cynicism and sexual excesses,
of naturalism in the novel and optimism in the stock exchange.
But in language, in dress, in artistic judgment and human val-
ues, Eugene Debs was yet the chivalrous Victorian. A jesting
but considered estimate of the elderly Debs was given in 1946
by a Michigan newspaperman: "St. Eugene Victor was of
another world, untainted by the jagged crassness of the era
that followed World War I and continued to sour and fester
until pregnant women must stand in buses and no man has a
friend. *He did kiss babies.* Honest tears rolled down his face when
he talked of Little Nell. With his head he never understood
Marx, but with his heart he instinctively felt the answers that
the Great Karl pondered and labored and buried in verbiage
and statistics."

Soon after his speech to the Indiana Federation of Labor Debs
began a lecture tour of the East. The tour carried him to Boston,
the national center of the campaign to win a new trial for Sacco
and Vanzetti. The defense committee had found it difficult to
break into the metropolitan newspapers, and they viewed the
arrival of Eugene Debs as a certain solution to this problem.
They proposed that Debs visit Vanzetti in Charlestown prison,
only a few miles from Boston. The resulting story, warm with
parallels and human interest, would bid for front pages from

coast to coast. Although Debs was eager to comply, his lecture managers flatly rejected the proposal. They contended that he was touring for the Socialist Party and his health required special care. So the projected visit was abandoned. But Debs told the Sacco-Vanzetti Defense Committee to issue any statement at all over his signature, the more emphatic the better.

In New York City Debs finally broke through the restrictions placed upon him by his managers. His main speech was scheduled for Hunt's Point Palace in the Bronx. August Claessens, in charge of the meeting, was worried by the memory of Debs' occasional drinking sprees. To guard against this problem he appointed two reliable teetotalers to keep watch over the featured speaker. As soon as Claessens departed from the three men, Debs turned on all of his eloquence. With masterful candor he stated the predicament: "Now look, comrades, there's an old Indiana miner who runs a tavern up on 125th Street. He's there all alone, just phoned me that he won't be able to get down for the meeting, and asked me to come up and see him. We've enough time before the meeting, so why don't we all go up there just for a little while?" The two watchdogs were reluctant. But they were confident of their ability to control Debs, so they agreed.

August Claessens, later that evening, presided over the meeting at Hunt's Point Palace. The hour arrived for the main speech, but Debs was not present. For forty-five minutes Claessens stood on the speaker's stand and told stories. He peered expectantly toward the entrance. He fussed and fidgeted and held whispered consultations with ushers. The audience became increasingly restive. Feet began to stamp in different parts of the hall. Hands started to clap. Somebody shouted for Debs and the cry spread. Claessens, excitable, agitated, became desperate.

Suddenly there was a tremendous uproar in the rear of the hall. Through a rift in the crowd Claessens could see Debs and the escort. The lanky Socialist leader and one of the watchdogs were dragging between them the limp body of the second, whose feet trailed loosely across the floor. He was completely drunk. Debs was not entirely sober. Claessens hurried down to the scene of the disturbance, blasted his small body through the crowd, and found several ushers to carry the culprits to the platform. Debs, even more affectionate at such moments, took a half-hour to reach the stage. Claessens thought that he would stop to kiss each member of the audience. But at length they reached the stage, and two cups of black coffee had some effect.

Debs opened his speech with a florid discussion of the glories of autumn, the delightful life of the birds and the bees, the pure pleasure of belonging to the human race. The audience loved it. Most witnesses did not even notice one of the most ludicrous errors he ever made. His speeches were customarily organized into several sections, so that the length and meaning could be adjusted by inserting and deleting sections. On this memorable night, Eugene Debs repeated one entire section. His ability to escape detection in such a blunder proved to Algernon Lee that the crowd actually was hypnotized.

A few days later the Socialist Party in New York gave a banquet for Debs on his seventieth birthday. Dozens of men who had rejected the Party and all its activities felt themselves drawn to the banquet by their respect and affection for the guest of honor. Bitter enemies sat elbow to elbow in apparent friendship and good cheer. The banquet hall was aflame with gossip and speculation at the sight of so many forgotten faces. After the festivities Louis Boudin, an attorney who had resigned in 1919, was cornered in a cloakroom by Victor Berger. The portly Berger edged over to the slight frame of Boudin. "Well," he inquired, "are you coming back to the Party?" Boudin was greatly amused. "No, I just came to see Debs," he laughingly replied.

Apart from the general reorganization of the Socialist Party, Debs' lectures in 1925 aimed to promote funds and enthusiasm for a new weekly newspaper. The first number of the *American Appeal* was released on January 2, 1926. Eugene V. Debs, as editor in chief and regular columnist, wrote a fiery appeal for the striking anthracite miners, a plea for Sacco and Vanzetti. His vaunted militance was revived in his attacks on the Treaty of Versailles: "The word of the imperial masters is not good. Their treaties are worthless. They lie to each other and they lie to the world to perpetuate their own vicious and debasing misrule. Down with capitalism, imperialism and militarism."

Each day seemed to bring new justification for his opposition to the World War. When the Disabled American Veterans charged that soldiers who died in the Federal hospitals were buried without so much as a headstone to mark their graves, Debs commented that he had long known "the postwar value of human cannon fodder." Taft and Coolidge he denounced as pious hypocrites who plundered the Unknown Soldier during his life and honored him after his death. The measure of their sincerity, he declared, lay in their fawning upon the bloody dictatorships of Admiral Horthy and Benito Mussolini concurrently with the denial of recognition to "the working class government established by Soviet Russia."

The career of Eugene Debs was ending where it had begun, in the editorial office of a labor publication. He was again back in the fray, doing battle for his chosen cause. His biting pronouncements carried the joy of conviction, the pure love of combat. But this frenzied activity was doomed to short life. The health of Kate Debs had suffered a serious relapse. She too was growing old and worn. The years of her husband's exile in Atlanta had been a prolonged trial. In Christmas week of 1925 one of her sisters was killed by a bus in Terre Haute, with shattering effects on Kate's nerves. Late in March Debs abandoned his work on the *American Appeal* so that his wife could convalesce in Bermuda.

In his entire life the Socialist leader had never journeyed beyond the continent of North America. He had contemplated a trip to Europe in 1900 to study economic conditions and the socialist movement, but the Presidential campaign of that year had disrupted the plan. Again in 1907 he had spoken of following socialism "around the world, spending at least a year in foreign countries," only to rediscover that the United States afforded ample thrills, fights, and novelty. Now his maiden voyage was made under trying conditions. He was unable to secure a passport because his citizenship was open to doubt, and it seemed possible that he would be denied entrance on his return to Ellis Island. Aliens usually gained readmittance by swearing fidelity to the Federal Constitution, but Debs considered this pledge a confession that he had erred in 1918. He had resolved never to humble himself in this way.

These worries about Kate's health and his own citizenship were complicated by the Federal officials and the newspapermen. Although the reasons for the trip were common knowledge, Debs was subjected to constant intrusions upon his privacy. On the ship in New York harbor he was interviewed by a horde of reporters and photographed by four different cameramen. Arrived in Bermuda, he was promptly questioned by the immigration inspector and the chief of police, who asked about his past occupation and future intentions. They departed after solemnly reading aloud the laws providing for the deportation of undesirable aliens. In spite of these annoyances the journey was effective. Five weeks of rest and tropical sunshine proved an effective healing agent, and they left for New York much improved in health. Debs gave only one brief statement about the trip: "Bermuda is a fine place, but I'm glad to be back in America."

The salutary results of the vacation were largely offset by the return voyage, when a rough sea caused extreme seasickness. Now illness followed illness. Death lurked in every twilight. The end was drawing ever more near. When Kate and Eugene Debs arrived in Terre Haute they found both Theodore and his wife were seriously ill, their home in the care of a doctor. Faced with this added worry, Debs himself became sick. His strength fell rapidly. He had hoped to attend the Socialist national convention in Pittsburgh on May 1, but he was unable to leave his home. When the Indiana convention of the Party began in late May he was confined to his bed. The other three convalescents soon recovered, but Debs' vitality continued to wane. Writing to a friend on July 7, Theodore said of his brother: "He has had a prolonged siege and has suffered all the tortures of the damned. It would seem as if all the devils in and out of hell had conspired, by the most refined process, to torture the last breath out of his already weakened body." But even in this miserable condition Debs played an active rôle in the campaign to save Sacco and Vanzetti, "these two honest, clean-hearted brothers of ours." His appeal for the two Italian immigrants was written for the Labor Defense Council that had provided the basis for his denunciation of the Communists fifteen months earlier, indicating that the denunciation was far from conclusive.

Debs also summoned up the energy to make one final venture through the streets of Terre Haute. Friends who knew of his critical illness were astonished to see him enter the City Hall. He had known five years of torture because of the doubts about his citizenship. The yearning toward his rootholds ran too deep to allow a casual acceptance of this alienation from the only land he had ever known. He finally had resolved to bring the test case suggested by Morris Hillquit. His errand at the City Hall was easily performed; he merely registered to vote in the November election.

Never again was the gaunt, tidy figure of Eugene Debs seen strolling about his home community. On September 20 he was taken to Lindlahr Sanitarium for another nature cure. It was a beautiful autumn in northern Illinois. The geese passed overhead in solid formation, etched sharply against the curtain of blue that fell behind the horizon. The air seemed washed and purified. In this weather Debs again became cheerful and hearty. The danger had passed. On October 6 he was bundled up and taken for a short drive in an automobile. That night he suffered a painful attack of rheumatism, which lasted four days. It drained his last shallow reservoir of strength.

Nothing, however, seemed able to break his spirit. One day he recited to a fellow patient William Ernest Henley's "Invictus." The friend promptly asked him for a copy. Turning to his wife Kate, Debs asked for paper and pencil. The pad was propped against his knees as he scrawled in a shaky hand:

> *It matters not how straight the gate,*
> *How charged with punishment the scroll,*
> *I am the master of my fate,*
> *I am the captain of my soul.*

Less than a week later, on October 15, 1926, he lapsed into a coma following a heart attack. For the next five days Kate and

Theodore Debs kept unbroken vigil by his bedside. Not once did he open his eyes, speak, smile. There was no sign of life save the muted sound of his breathing. Then there was no sign of life at all.

[4]

THE WIDOW received hundreds of letters of condolence from personal friends and prominent men. "I never knew a man whom I loved more than I did him," wrote Clarence Darrow. "No better kindlier man ever lived than Gene. I shall miss him as I have missed few others." It was generally agreed that Eugene Debs would not be forgotten. Edgar Lee Masters honored him as "one of those Americans—too few—who by the purity and strength of his character, add to the real virtues of the nation as living influences, and as memory for posterity to contemplate." Sinclair Lewis struck the same note: "There is scarce a day when I do not speak of him . . . To talk of 'how great a loss he is' is vain, because he is not lost, but eternally here, a beacon in a world where we might otherwise be lost in darkness."

But these individual letters were insignificant beside the popular outpouring of grief. Memorial meetings were held in every large city and in a thousand hamlets. Eight thousand persons crowded into Chicago's Ashland Auditorium, and the local Joint Board of the Amalgamated Clothing Workers issued black lapel ribbons:

In Memoriam
Our Friend
and Comrade
Eugene V. Debs

In New York massed battalions of mourners paraded through a chill October rain. The *Record* in distant Los Angeles spoke its simple homage: "All that was mortal of lovable Gene Debs slips back this week into the quiet, cool earth for its long rest. And in the homes of thousands of the world's common folk there is sorrow."

In Terre Haute the president of the Central Labor Union

called upon Theodore Debs. His statement was above challenge: "You will have to give him to us for a while, Theodore. You know he belongs to us." For two days the body lay in state at the Labor Temple. The funeral was held on Saturday, October 23, on the front lawn of the family home. At 6:30 P.M., when the warm day had become a dark and somber evening, the coffin was sent to Indianapolis, where the doors of the mortuary stood open for an hour. At the Labor Temple, at the funeral, in Indianapolis, the patterns of grief were tinted by the hues of dedication. Delegations arrived from New York, from Chicago, from Pittsburgh and Omaha, from countless villages once visited by Eugene Debs. Men walked past the coffin with lowered heads and fever-brightened eyes, in sanctification of the past and tribute to the future.

Few Americans stood apart from the national sorrow at the death of Eugene Debs. The audience at his funeral included famous writers, wealthy attorneys and businessmen, ordinary men with the grease of a lifetime ground into their thumbnails. Each of these mourners created an idol in his own image. Some found in Eugene Debs a misguided zealot who nonetheless was sincere and charitable. Others admired the Socialist leader because of his pioneer work for woman suffrage, social security legislation, industrial unionism, the extension of civil liberties.

So it became fashionable to minimize his radical beliefs in favor of his purity of character. On this count he was deemed above reproach. But much of the acclaim was viewed with suspicion by certain critics. Was it possible, after all, to sever each connection between a person's motives and his policies? The very universality of the applause drew an acid comment from Heywood Broun: "Eugene V. Debs is dead and everybody says he was a good man. He was no better and no worse when he served a sentence at Atlanta."

Surely Debs deserved little credit for whatever was worthy about his motives. He never doubted his moral responsibility for the welfare of his brother, having absorbed as a child his unqualified answer. The identification of his brothers, the quest for policies which would promote their common welfare—these were the critical problems for Eugene Debs. From his observations of American life he arrived at a specific solution. His conclusion held that the common people were being crucified by an outmoded economic system. On the accuracy of that belief must rest the ultimate worth of his career. The admonition to love one another, which dominated his early thinking, he characterized in 1919 as "a harmless doctrine." He had come to believe that devotion to the oppressed must be shown by resistance to the oppressors. This contention that modern society holds two social classes, two conflicting interests, lay at the root of his entire program.

The process of change from Christian to Marxist was never completed by Eugene Debs, and it cast up grave inconsistencies in his temperament. While some of his talents flourished, others were static, still others atrophied. His gifts as an agitator and his feeling for social realities were matched by a gross ignorance of science, literature, all fields of scholarship. His activities were rife with contradictions, with petty foibles, with mistakes both minor and serious. But it is difficult to speak with confidence of the faults of Eugene Debs. His popularity was much beholden to the periodic drinking sprees, to the coarse and indiscriminate humor, the unthinking chivalry where women were involved, the devotion to friends who became political enemies. In all of these qualities he was more Midwestern than a worn and rotting plow-handle buried deep in the soil of a Kansas farm.

Hence the story of Eugene Debs becomes the story of a whole generation of wage earners and dirt farmers. While these people learned something from the Socialist leader, he learned even more from them. His awesome strength in time of crisis was made possible by his confidence in his fellows. At such moments his finite self seemed to merge with the agonized wanderings of the nameless multitude. Out of these popular yearnings and struggles the mind of Eugene Debs fashioned a supreme maxim: Human happiness is never found by a solitary search. No man rises far above the ranks.

SELECTED CHAPTER SOURCES

It is neither expected nor intended that the following notes should serve as a substitute for footnotes, which are reluctantly omitted for reasons of space and readability. The procedure here has been to give the general source or sources for each chapter; no further citation is given for material located in the contemporary issues of these periodicals. Specific citations are given for quotations or important facts taken from other sources. Short titles only have been used in this section; the long titles are given in the Bibliography.

CHAPTER I

Material for this chapter was furnished by Oscar Baur, Fred Heinl, Martin E. O'Connell, and two confidential sources.

The available data on Debs' childhood is both sparse and unreliable. The best sources are the earlier biographies by Stephen M. Reynolds, 4–6, 58–59, 73–74, and by McAlister Coleman, 1–28; *Talks With Debs in Terre Haute*, by David Karsner, 70–83, 141–42; the Memorial Volume for the Golden Wedding Anniversary of Marguerite and Jean Daniel Debs (Fairbanks), and the Notes by Max Ehrmann.

Debs' article, "My First Job," is in the *Appeal to Reason*, October 1, 1910. The Terre Haute *Express*, September 14, 1899, and the St. Louis *Chronicle*, September 1, 1900, contain some history of the family, as does John Reed's article in *The Liberator*, September 1918. The quotation about John Brown is in the *Appeal to Reason*, November 23, 1907. For an illustration of the impact of *Les Misérables* on Eugene Debs, see his article, "Fantine in Our Day," *International Socialist Review*, March 1916.

The incident in St. Louis involving Debs and the locomotive engineer is from Arthur M. Lewis, *The Art of Lecturing*, 20. The status of education in Debs' outlook is illustrated by his articles in *Locomotive Firemen's Magazine*, October 1884, 614–15, and May 1890, 389; see also *Talks With Debs*, 88. His superficial technical knowledge is revealed in his article, "The Education of Locomotive Engine-men," *Locomotive Engineering*, January 1892, 12, and in the popular engineering works issued by the Debs Publishing Company during the 1890's.

For background material on Terre Haute I have consulted the Terre Haute business directories, the standard histories of Indiana and Vigo County; Kenworthy's biography of Daniel W. Voorhees; Foulke's biography of Oliver Morton; a series of articles by A. R. Markle, "When Terre Haute Was Young," (Ind Div); Charles Roll, *Colonel Dick Thompson;* Lyman Abbott, *Reminiscences;* John J. Schlicher, "Terre Haute in 1850," *Indiana Magazine of History,* 16: 245–70; Carl F. Brand, "History of the Know-Nothing Party in Indiana," *Indiana Magazine of History,* 18: 187–201. The contemporary Terre Haute newspapers are rich in background material but extremely arid in relation to the Debs family.

The final quotation in the chapter is from Debs' article in the New York *Comrade,* June 1904.

CHAPTER II

For information used in this chapter I am indebted to Oscar Baur, Fred Heinl, A. R. Markle, Martin E. O'Connell, Peter Witt, and the same two confidential informants (chapter I, above).

The indispensable sources for the entire period 1875–1894, chapters II–VIII in this work, are the files of *The Magazine* and the *Proceedings* of the BLF conventions (Rand). Useful material on the entire period will also be found in Debs' speech to the BLF convention in 1894.

The story of Herman Hulman is in Beckwith's *History of Vigo County,* 245–246; see also the speech by Debs, "Hulman & Co.," Terre Haute *Gazette,* September 29, 1893. Debs' reactions to his job as billing clerk are told in the Notes by Max Ehrmann; his subsequent statement about business is from an interview with Floy R. Painter, August 28, 1924, quoted in *That Man Debs,* by Painter, 10.

Debs' recollections of his early experiences in the BLF are told in *American Railroader,* September 1885; New York *Comrade,* April 1902, (Reynolds, *Debs,* 79–84), and June 1904; *National Rip-Saw,* April 1914; the speech to the BLF convention of 1894 mentioned above; and his letter to the *Locomotive Firemen's and Enginemen's Magazine,* January 1912, 117. These reminiscences by Debs, in common with most material of this sort, contain numerous errors and must be used with caution.

Volume II of *The History of Labor in the United States,* by John R. Commons and Associates, is still the best survey of the labor movement from 1880 to 1894. The generalizations of the Commons group of historians are expertly presented in *The Theory of the Labor Movement,* by Selig Perlman. Philip S. Foner is now at work on the second volume of his *History of the Labor Movement,* which will begin with the formation of the AFL in 1881. An excellent account of the railroad strike of 1877 is in Samuel Yellen's *American Labor Struggles,* chapter 1; its effects on the BLF are told in Debs' pamphlet, *The American Movement* (Reynolds, *Debs*, 103–105).

For Debs' memory of the Patrick Henry speech see Debs Scrapbooks, VI, 255 (Rand). Another version, by Phil K. Reinbold, is in Debs *Mss* (Fairbanks). Debs wrote about Susan B. Anthony in the *Socialist Woman*, January 1909, and in *Pearson's*, July 1917; about Robert G. Ingersoll in *American Journal of Politics*, 2:198–202, *Pearson's*, March 1917, and Karsner, *Talks With Debs*, 98–101; about James Whitcomb Riley in *Pearson's*, April 1917, and *National Magazine*, January 1914; about Wendell Phillips in *Pearson's*, May 1917.

Debs discusses Tom Harper in Karsner, *Talks With Debs*, 130–1; his leniency toward prostitutes is described by Tom Hickey, Debs Scrapbooks, IX, 256 (Rand). The clash with the Pennsylvania Railroad official is told in Coleman, *Debs*, 63–66; a slightly different account was told to me by Peter Witt.

The statement by Marguerite Debs about her oldest son is in the reminiscences of Theodore Debs, Chicago *Sun*, January 24, 1943.

CHAPTER III

In this chapter I have used material furnished by Oscar Baur, Mrs. Carabelle G. Dickey, Ed Evinger, Martin E. O'Connell, Mrs. Raymond P. Harris, Helen Ross, and the same two confidential informants (chapter I, above).

The biography of John J. Baur is in Beckwith, *History of Vigo County*, 317. Most of the other information about the Baur family and Kate Metzel was furnished by the persons listed above, but a few facts were taken from newspaper and magazine articles which will be listed in the sources for subsequent chapters. The volume of *The Magazine* inscribed by Eugene Debs to Kate Metzel is in Debs Collection (Rand).

Lewis Lorwin's history of the American Federation of Labor and Commons' *History*, II, should be consulted, but the best source of information on the AFL in this period is Samuel Gompers' autobiography, *Seventy Years of Life and Labor*. Debs' failure to attend the 1881 conference in Terre Haute was revealed to me by Ed Evinger, a Terre Haute printer who was present at this meeting. The debt of the local trade unions to Eugene Debs in these early days was told to me by Mr. Evinger; see also the statements by Phil K. Reinbold and J. P. McDonagh in *Eugene V. Debs: What His Neighbors Say About Him*. Debs recalls his relations with the other Brotherhoods in the *Switchmen's Journal*, August, September, 1906; in the *Appeal to Reason*, February 3, 1906; and in a press release written in 1922 (Ind Div).

Some campaign material from the 1885 election is in Debs Collection (Shannon). The official record of the Indiana legislature is Drapier's *Legislative Reports*, 1885. Debs' comment to Theodore on his return from Indianapolis after the session adjourned is in Coleman, *Debs*, 85. The wedding is described in the Terre Haute *Gazette*, June 9, 1885; and in *The Magazine*, July 1885. The reception following the honeymoon is reported in *The Magazine*, August 1885. Debs' comment to Kate on their financial status was reported to me by Helen Ross, while I am indebted to Mrs. Raymond P. Harris for the version of the incident involving Kate Debs, her errant husband, and James Whitcomb Riley.

The strife between the Knights of Labor and the AFL is best followed in Gompers' autobiography; Terence V. Powderly, *The Path I Trod;* and Joseph R. Buchanan, *The Story of a Labor Agitator*. Several dozen letters casting light on the subject are in Joseph A. Labadie's correspondence (Labadie). There is no adequate history of the Knights of Labor; a useful account is Carroll D. Wright, "Historical Sketch of the Knights of Labor," *Quarterly Journal of Economics*, January 1887, 137–68.

The Haymarket affair is described fully in Henry David's work on the subject; the best brief account is Yellen's *American Labor Struggles*, chapter 2. Harry Barnard's biography of Altgeld, *Eagle Forgotten*, contains a careful analysis of the bombing and the trial. The theory here given about the reasons for Debs' silence is original with me; while it seems to fit the available facts, it must be counted as speculation. Debs' subsequent article about the Haymarket martyrs is in *The New Time*, February 1898 (Reynolds, *Debs*, 263–267).

The conversation between Debs and Joseph R. Buchanan during the Burlington strike is taken from Buchanan, *Story*, 306–10. P. M. Arthur's fear of an injunction is criticized by Debs in *The American Movement* and in the *Social Democratic Herald*, August 29, 1903.

The speech by Debs in behalf of Grover Cleveland is reported in the Terre Haute *Weekly Gazette*, November 1, 1888.

CHAPTER IV

Material for this chapter was furnished by Mrs. Carabelle G. Dickey, Mrs. Raymond P. Harris, Helen Ross, and Dr. and Mrs. John R. Shannon.

The sterility of Mrs. Kate Debs was revealed to me by Mrs. Raymond P. Harris and Helen Ross, both of whom heard the story from Mrs. Arthur Baur.

Dr. and Mrs. John R. Shannon, the owners of the former Debs' home at 451 North Eighth Street, Terre Haute, showed me through the house and told me its history. The abstract of the lot and several bills from the original construction are in their possession. Newspaper clippings about the house are in Debs Scrapbooks, I, 225 (Rand).

The anecdotes about James Whitcomb Riley are in *National Magazine*, January 1914. Riley's letter to Edgar Wilson Nye is taken from *The Letters of James Whitcomb Riley*, edited by William Lyon Phelps, 104. The other facts about Debs' personal life at this time are gleaned from Kate Debs Scrapbooks (Shannon); Debs Scrapbooks and his library (Rand); Kate Debs' interview with the Chicago reporters on July 12, 1894 (clippings in Debs Scrapbooks, I, 127–8, Rand); Karsner, *Talks With Debs*, 20.

The story of the federation movement and the Supreme Council has never before been told, either by labor historians or by the previous biographers of Eugene Debs. It has been reconstructed from the files of *The Magazine;* the *Proceedings* of the BLF conventions of 1890 and 1892; and the minutes of the sessions of the Supreme Council, which are contained in a single bound volume in Debs Collection (Rand).

The clipping from Terre Haute *Gazette* about Debs' proposed resignation from the BLF is in Kate Debs Scrapbook (Shannon); Debs' statement is in *The Magazine*, January 1891.

Debs referred to Gronlund's *The Cooperative Commonwealth* on numerous occasions; see for instance his testimony to the United States Strike Commission of 1894, *Report*, 170, and Reynolds, *Debs*, 83. The review of *Looking Backward* is in *The Magazine*, February 1890.

The quoted letter from Gompers to Debs, November 20, 1891, is in Samuel Gompers Copy-Book No. 6, 460–2. Debs' respect for Gompers at this time appears in numerous articles in *The Magazine;* see, for instance, December 1891, 1102.

That the disruption of the Supreme Council in 1891 was a critical incident for Eugene Debs is apparent, not merely from his actions at the time, but from his later references to the event; see, for instance, his testimony to the United States Strike Commission of 1894; his speech to the BLF convention of 1894; and his articles in *Switchmen's Journal*, August, September, 1906.

CHAPTER V

The best secondary source on the Homestead strike is Samuel Yellen, *American Labor Struggles*, chapter 3; see also Allan Nevins, *Grover Cleveland*, 499–502; Commons, *History*, II, 495–7. For the Coeur d'Alene strike see Commons, II, 497–8, and IV, 170–3. For the 1892 Presidential campaign see any standard history; Nevins, *Grover Cleveland*, 498–502; Matthew Josephson, *The Politicos, 1865–1896*.

The exact sequence of events in the formation of the ARU is far from clear. The account given here has been pieced together from clippings in Debs Scrapbooks, I, 59 (Rand); John R. Commons, *Myself*, 149–50; *The Magazine;* Coleman, *Debs*, 103–6; United States Strike Commission, *Report*, 52–7.

An excellent account of the pardon of the Haymarket survivors is given by Harry Barnard in *Eagle Forgotten;* see also Henry David, *History of the Haymarket Affair*.

The history of the ARU from its formation until the end of 1893 has been taken from scattered sources: U. S. Strike Commission, *Report*, 11–13, 33, 142, 209–10, *passim; Railway Times*, January 1, 1894; Samuel Gompers, *Seventy Years*, I, 404–7; Nathan Fine, *Labor and Farmer Parties in the United States, 1828–1928*, 187; the *National Rip-Saw*, November 1921, and Debs' pamphlet, *You Railroad Men*. After the establishment of the *Railway Times* on January 1, 1894, the story can be followed easily.

The visit of James Whitcomb Riley to Terre Haute is taken from the Terre Haute newspapers, November 13–15, 1893. The speech by Eugene Debs at the Labor Congress in Chicago, August 30, 1894, is reprinted in *The Magazine*, October 1893, 875–9; Debs' preliminary correspondence with Lloyd is in Lloyd *Mss.*

The dispute on the Union Pacific can be followed in *The Magazine* and *Railway Times;* see also *Record in Oliver Ames, Second, et. al. v. Union Pacific Railroad Company, et al.* (Rand). For the Great Northern strike, in addition to the current issues of *Railway Times* and the Minneapolis and St. Paul newspapers, the following sources are helpful: posters in Kate Debs Collection (Shannon); Reynolds, *Debs*, 7–12; *Appeal to Reason*, September 29, 1900, and July 9, 1910. See also Debs' speech to the BLF convention of 1894, and the Notes by Max Ehrmann.

CHAPTER VI

The best primary sources on the causes of the original dispute in the town of Pullman are the testimony before the U. S. Strike Commission, the conclusions of the Commission, and William H. Carwardine, *The Pullman Strike;* the sole account of this phase of the dispute which does not condemn the company is George M. Pullman, *The Strike at Pullman* (the statements of George M. Pullman and T. H. Wickes before the U. S. Strike Commission). The quotation about Pullman houses and Pullman hells is taken from John Lee, *Industrial Organization*, 20. Debs' first speech to the strikers in Pullman is from W. T. Stead, *Chicago Today*, 177–8. The exhaustive secondary source is Almont Lindsey, *The Pullman Strike*.

For the ARU convention see the *Proceedings* (Crerar Library, Chicago), which unfortunately is not a verbatim transcript; *Railway Times*, June 15 and June 22, 1894; Commons, *Myself*, 150; the contemporary Chicago newspapers; and the testimony of the ARU officials, Thomas Heathcote, Jennie Curtis, and William H. Carwardine before the U. S. Strike Commission.

CHAPTER VII

There is an enormous body of literature on the Pullman boycott. For the most part the account given here has been taken from the following primary sources: U. S. Strike Commission, *Report; Railway Times;* the contemporary Chicago, New York, Washington, D. C., and Los Angeles newspapers; several magazines, including *Harper's Weekly, Leslie's, Public Opinion, The Nation;* Samuel Gompers Copy-Book No. 11; Henry Demarest Lloyd *Mss;* Grover Cleveland *Mss;* Richard Olney *Mss;* Walter Q. Gresham *Mss;* John Peter Altgeld, *Live Questions*, 652–683, 922–937; Hazen S. Pingree, *Facts and Opinions*, 5–13; Samuel Gompers, *Seventy Years*, I, 409–10, 414. *Striking for Life*, by John Swinton, a pro-ARU account of the boycott, includes several documents as well as articles by Debs, Gompers, and John Hayes.

The comprehensive secondary source on the boycott is Almont Lindsey, *The Pullman Strike*. Much material of value will be found in the biographies of three leading participants: Allan Nevins, *Grover Cleveland;* Harry Barnard, *Eagle Forgotten* (of Altgeld); Henry James, *The Life and Public Service of Richard Olney*. Nevins, while writing fairly about the entire dispute, has centered his attention on the actions and motives of the Administration; the analyses here given of the July 3 telegram from T. M. Milchrist to Richard Olney and the letter from Olney to Edwin Walker, September 24, 1894, are his work. Barnard gives an excellent analysis of the Cleveland-Altgeld dispute. In addition to publishing several important documents, James describes Olney's indifference to the causes of the strike and his single-minded determination to restore order. My total debt to these earlier historians is immense.

Grover Cleveland's subsequent justification of his course during the Pullman boycott, given in a speech at Princeton University in 1904, will be found in his *The Government in the Chicago Strike of 1894*. The criticism of this speech by Eugene Debs is printed in Reynolds, *Debs*, 181–206.

The incident involving Eugene Field is told by Debs in *National Magazine*, January 1914.

CHAPTER VIII

Debs' memories of Cook County Jail are told in his posthumous *Walls and Bars*, 27–29. The letter from Debs to Henry Demarest Lloyd, July 24, 1894, is in Lloyd *Mss;* Samuel Gompers to Eugene Debs, August 16, 1894, is in Samuel Gompers Copy-Book No. 11, 263.

The letter from Debs to the BLF convention, September 5, 1894, is in the *Proceedings*, 473–4; his speech is also in the *Proceedings*, 499–505. This speech is a review of his entire career in the BLF and discusses at length his disagreements with the organization. In my opinion it is much more significant than his oft-quoted speech of resignation to the 1892 convention.

American Radicalism, 1865–1901, by Chester McA. Destler, contains provocative analysis of the labor-Populist alliance in Illinois. Mr. Destler is now at work on a biography of Henry Demarest Lloyd. Other useful material on the Congressional election of 1894 will be found in Clarence Darrow, *The Story of My Life;* Joseph R. Buchanan, *The Story of a Labor Agitator;* Solon J. Buck, *The Agrarian Crusade;* John D. Hicks, *The Populist Revolt;* and the works by Barnard and Nevins cited above.

Debs' manifesto of January 9, 1895, appears in Reynolds, *Debs*, 41. For the 1894 injunction see *United States v. Debs et al.* (64 Fed. 724); for the appeals see *In re Debs* (159 US 251) and *In re Debs* (158 US 564). On the appeal to the Supreme Court see also James, *Olney*, 57–8. For the appeal on the conspiracy trial see *Debs v. United States* (73 Fed. 1021). The conspiracy trial is best followed in the Chicago newspapers; a large body of material on the trial is brought together in Reynolds, *Debs*, 23–40.

CHAPTER IX

From May until November, 1895, *Railway Times* and all the Chicago newspapers contain frequent articles about the prisoners in Woodstock Jail; see especially Chicago *Journal*, July 29, 1895; Chicago *Times*, August 22, 1895; Chicago *Chronicle*, November 23, 1895. Large collections of newspaper clippings are in Debs Scrapbooks, I, 192–3,

197, 206, 239, 288 (Rand); Eugene V. Debs *Mss* (Labadie); Kate Debs Collection (Shannon). Debs describes Sheriff George Eckert in *Talks With Debs*, 216.

For Debs' correspondence during his incarceration see *The Letters of James Whitcomb Riley*, 200–1; Peter Witt *Mss;* Henry Demarest Lloyd *Mss;* Samuel Gompers Copy-Book No. 12, 291; George A. Schilling *Mss.* The material about Eugene Field is again taken from *National Magazine*, January 1914. Field's testimonial for Eugene Debs is taken from a clipping in Debs Scrapbooks, IV, 215 (Rand).

The visit of Keir Hardie to Woodstock is described by Debs in *Railway Times*, September 15, 1895, and in a letter from Thomas J. Morgan to Henry Demarest Lloyd, September 6, 1895, Lloyd *Mss.* For Debs' description of the visit by Victor L. Berger see Reynolds, *Debs*, 84.

The ARU song is taken from Carl Sandburg, *American Songbag*, 190. The conversation between Debs and Thaddeus Moore was told to me by A. G. Slemons. The tribulations of Eugene Debs after his release from Woodstock can be followed in *Railway Times;* Coleman, *Debs*, 176–8; and New York *Comrade*, June 1904.

The estimate here given of the significance of the Pullman strike is original with me, at least as to its emphases and formulations. The final quotation is taken from a pamphlet by John Swinton, *1860–Lincoln; Debs–1895.*

CHAPTER X

Mr. and Mrs. Frederic Heath, Louis Lazarus, Mrs. Seymour Stedman, and Harry F. Ward furnished material for this chapter.

For the Populist convention of 1896 see Henry Demarest Lloyd's article in *Review of Reviews*, September 1896; Caro Lloyd, *Henry Demarest Lloyd*, 259; Debs Scrapbooks, II, 30, 37, 52–4 (Rand); Eugene V. Debs to Henry Demarest Lloyd, July 21, July 25, 1896, Lloyd *Mss.* Debs' activities in the campaign have been followed in *Railway Times;* see also Thomas I. Kidd to Henry D. Lloyd, April 9, 1896, Lloyd *Mss;* Painter, *Debs*, 80 ff; Karsner, *Debs*, 68.

For the story of the campaign I have leaned heavily on the cited works by Nevins and Barnard; Paxton Hibben's biography of William Jennings Bryan; James Peterson, "The Trade Unions and the Populist Party," *Science and Society*, Spring 1944. Useful material is in Robert G. Ingersoll *Mss*, and George A. Schilling *Mss.*

Debs describes his conversion to socialism in New York *Comrade*, April 1902, but this article gives the false impression that he became a socialist during the Pullman boycott, or at the very latest by the time of his release from Woodstock. For the story of Debs' equivocation during 1895 and 1896, see Thomas J. Morgan to Henry Demarest Lloyd, July 18, 1901, Lloyd *Mss;* this letter is very important for its critical view of Debs' activities from 1895 to 1900. Debs himself gives a more accurate account of his conversion to socialism, *Appeal to Reason,* September 5, 1903.

For Samuel Gompers' version of the Leadville strike, see *Seventy Years,* I, 421–2; Debs gives a conflicting account in the New York *Comrade,* November 1903, and in Karsner, *Debs,* 69–70.

The founding convention of the Social Democracy has been reconstructed from the *Social Democrat* and the Chicago newspapers. For the expressions of opinion about the Brotherhood of the Cooperative Commonwealth and the Social Democracy, see *Railway Times;* Debs Scrapbooks, II, 106 (Rand); Detroit *Free Press,* June 20, 1897; Barney Berlyn to Daniel DeLeon, January 1, January 6, 1897, DeLeon *Mss;* Victor L. Berger to Henry D. Lloyd, January 11, 1897; Isaac Hourwich to Henry D. Lloyd, June 23, 1897; Lloyd to Hourwich, July 21, 1897, all in Lloyd *Mss.*

The best source on Debs' rôle in the bituminous coal strike of 1897 is the collection of clippings in Debs Scrapbooks, II, 121–29 (Rand).

The *Social Democrat* is the title of the *Railway Times* after June 1897. A year later the title was again changed to the *Social Democratic Herald.* This organ and the *Appeal to Reason* carry extensive reports of Debs' activities during the final years of the century. Debs' speech to the Nineteenth Century Club, March 21, 1899, is reprinted in *Walls and Bars,* 194–212.

The convention of the Social Democracy, June 1898, can be followed in the Chicago newspapers; the *Social Democratic Herald;* Emma Goldman, *Living My Life,* I, 220–1; Debs Scrapbooks, II, 251–5 (Rand). The early trials of the Social Democrats are told by Coleman, *Debs,* 201 ff, and were further told to me by Mrs. Seymour Stedman and Mr. and Mrs. Frederic Heath. The letter from Debs to Julius A. Wayland is reprinted by Wayland, *Leaves of Life,* 38.

The closing examples of Debs' political views are taken from the *Appeal;* the *Herald;* Debs Scrapbooks, II, 251, and III, 233 (Rand); Kate Debs Scrapbooks (Shannon). The letter from Debs to John D. Rockefeller, June 19, 1897, was discovered by Louis Lazarus in a Yiddish translation in Dr. I. A. Hourwich, *Selected Writings,* IV, 101–3 (Yiddish). I am also indebted to Mr. Lazarus for rendering this Yiddish version into the English form given here. The letter is explicitly mentioned in *Bill Haywood's Book*, 95, and it seems typical of Debs' general thinking at this time.

CHAPTER XI

Material for this chapter was furnished by Oscar Baur, Robert F. Baur, Mrs. Annette Baur Calder, August Claessens, Mrs. Carabelle G. Dickey, Mrs. Edith L. Drake, Mr. and Mrs. Frederic Heath, Fred Heinl, G. A. Hoehn, Algernon Lee, Mrs. Cecelia Baur Martin, James Oneal, John Panzner, John C. Prechtel, Helen Ross, Mrs. Clarence Royse, Mrs. Seymour Stedman, Mrs. Frank Casper Wagner, John M. Work, Dr. and Mrs. J. Rudolph Yung.

The political views of Debs' relatives at this time were described for me by Oscar Baur, Robert F. Baur, Mrs. Carabelle G. Dickey, and Fred Heinl. The rumor that Kate Debs fainted when her husband announced his conversion to socialism was reported to me by August Claessens and James Oneal, but it is seriously questioned by several relatives and other residents of Terre Haute: One relative for instance, who is quite critical of Kate Debs, told me that Kate was "not the fainting type." Debs' dislike for banks and his private arrangement with Arthur Baur were reported to me by Robert F. Baur and Helen Ross. Several friends of Jessica and Stephen Reynolds furnished me with information about their personalities and the Co-operative Dinner Club—Mrs. Carabelle G. Dickey, Mrs. Edith L. Drake, Helen Ross, Mrs. Clarence Royse, Mrs. Frank Casper Wagner, Dr. and Mrs. J. Rudolph Yung. For Debs' correspondence during this period see Henry Demarest Lloyd *Mss;* Frederic Heath *Mss;* James Whitcomb Riley *Mss;* Debs *Mss* (Yale); Debs *Mss* (Shannon); Robert G. Ingersoll *Mss.*

The early history of the Social Democratic Party may be followed in *Social Democratic Herald; Appeal to Reason;* and Cleveland *Citizen.* I also discussed this period with Frederic Heath, G. A. Hoehn, Algernon Lee, and John M. Work. There is no official transcript of the proceedings of the Social Democratic convention of 1900; a useful collection of clippings is in Debs Scrapbooks, IV, 234–40 (Rand). The best secondary sources are Nathan Fine, *Labor and Farmer Parties*, chapter 7; and Howard H. Quint's survey of the socialist movement up to the Unity Convention of 1901 (Unpublished Ph.D. thesis, Johns Hopkins, 1947). I am indebted to Mr. Quint and to Chester McA. Destler for their generous co-operation in connection with this section of my manuscript.

A biography of Daniel DeLeon is now being prepared by Louis Lazarus. Debs' vehement attack on DeLeon is contained in a letter to Frederic Heath, December 26, 1899, Heath *Mss.* The post-election dream of Eugene Debs in 1900 was told to me by Mrs. Edith L. Drake, who lived with the Reynoldses at that time.

Bill Haywood's reaction to the Pullman boycott is described in his autobiography, 53. For the party at the Imperial Hotel see the same source, 95; some of the details were supplied to me by Covington Hall. The anecdotes told by Debs appear in the *Social Democratic Herald,* September 12, 1903. Samuel Gompers' account of the WFM convention in 1902 appears in *Seventy Years,* I, 424.

For Mark Hanna's connection with the National Civic Federation see Herbert Croly, *Hanna,* 386–410; for Gompers' view of the organization see *Seventy Years,* I, 399. The dispute within the Socialist Party about the formation of the American Labor Union is presented in the *International Socialist Review,* October, November, 1902. Until its suppression in 1918, this left-wing organ carried most of the theoretical, as distinguished from agitational, articles written by Debs.

Debs' article on the labor press appeared in the *Metal Worker,* May 1904 (Reynolds, *Debs,* 239–42).

CHAPTER XII

Information for this chapter was supplied by Mrs. Carabelle G. Dickey, Ed Evinger, Mrs. Raymond P. Harris, Frederic Heath, Algernon Lee, Martin E. O'Connell, Winifred O'Connell, Shubert Sebree, A. G. Slemons, and John M. Work.

Debs' letter to Joseph A. Labadie about the lecture business was written December 12, 1905, Labadie *Mss.* The meeting with Susan B. Anthony is told by Debs in *Pearson's,* July 1917.

The material about Debs' personal life at this time was told to me by the persons listed above; I have also taken a few statements from Karsner, *Talks With Debs,* 40, 105.

The organization of the local union of coal miners in Mackville was told to me by A. G. Slemons. The part played by Debs in the Terre Haute streetcar strike was related to me by Ed Evinger and Algernon Lee. Coleman, *Debs,* 72–73, gives a somewhat different version of this story, and he places the incident about 1882. Conversations with Ed Evinger and A. G. Slemons, both leaders in the Terre Haute trade unions at that time, convinced me that the incident really took place during the winter of 1901–1902, when there was a hard-fought streetcar strike in Terre Haute. An article by Eugene Debs about this strike appears in the Terre Haute *Toiler*, February 7, 1902 (see clippings in Debs Scrapbooks, V, 278–81, Rand).

For the sources of information about S. M. Reynolds and the Co-operative Dinner Club see the sources for chapter XI. The classes conducted by Reynolds were described for me by Shubert Sebree. The portrait given here of Daniel Debs is taken from an article by George Bicknell, *Twentieth Century*, August 1910; Terre Haute *Tribune*, December 25, 1910 (see clipping in Debs Scrapbooks, IX, 127, Rand).

The best source on the Socialist campaign of 1904 is *Appeal to Reason*. On Benjamin Hanford see the tribute paid to him by Eugene Debs, *Appeal to Reason*, February 5, 1910. I also discussed Hanford with Frederic Heath, Algernon Lee, and John M. Work. The attack on the wealthy Socialist editor is made in a letter from Debs to Frederic Heath, January 3, 1903, Heath *Mss*. The letter from Debs to his wife is printed by Karsner, *Talks With Debs*, 113–14. Debs' boycott of Pullman cars, and its untimely end, are described in *National Rip-Saw*, March 1915.

CHAPTER XIII

Frank Bohn, Louis B. Boudin, George D. Brewer, Solon DeLeon, Elizabeth Gurley Flynn, Frederic Heath, Algernon Lee, Frank P. O'Hare, Dr. John R. Shannon, Fred D. Warren, John M. Work, and Dr. J. Rudolph Yung contributed material to this chapter.

The pamphlet, *Unionism and Socialism*, is reprinted in Reynolds, *Debs*, 119–42. The turbulent situation in the labor and socialist movements from 1904 to 1907 and the Moyer-Haywood campaign are best followed in the *American Federationist; Appeal to Reason; International Socialist Review;* and *Social Democratic Herald*. The visit to Terre Haute by Thomas J. Hagerty and William E. Trautmann was described for me by Frank Bohn. For the developments culminating in the formation of the IWW in June 1905, see *Proceedings of the First Convention of the Industrial Workers of the World*. Bill Haywood's commentary on Debs and DeLeon is in *Bill Haywood's Book*, 183–84. For the heated exchange between Debs and Fred Heath, see Eugene Debs to Miss Elizabeth Thomas, July 19, 1905, and a draft of a letter from Heath to Debs, July 1905, no day, both in Heath *Mss*.

For the expressions of class solidarity by Debs, see *You Railroad Men* (Reynolds, *Debs*, 207–26), and Debs to Joseph A. Labadie, December 12, 1905, Labadie *Mss*. The meeting in Grand Central Palace, December 10, 1905, and Daniel DeLeon's subsequent comment about Debs, were told to me by Solon DeLeon. Debs' defense of DeLeon is in the New York *Worker*, July 28, 1906, and his speech at Detroit's Turner Hall is in the Detroit *Times*, January 12, 1906. I have also discussed the IWW of this period with Louis B. Boudin, Elizabeth Gurley Flynn, Frederic Heath, Algernon Lee, and John M. Work.

The quotations from the Chicago *Tribune* appear on February 20, 1906. The events following the arrival in Girard of Debs' article, "Arouse, Ye Slaves!" are described by George Milburn, "The Appeal to Reason," *American Mercury*, July 1937, 365–6. Milburn's account was corroborated by Fred D. Warren in a conversation with Ann Fagan Ginger. Also see the pamphlet by Debs, *An Inside View of the Appeal to Reason*.

Obituaries of Daniel Debs appear in the Terre Haute papers and the Indianapolis *News*, about November 28, 1906. The statement by Debs about his mother is taken from a clipping in Debs *Mss* (Labadie). Debs' last testament appears in the Terre Haute *Star*, November 6, 1926.

For Debs' accession to the staff of the *Appeal*, see the contemporary files of that paper and also Louis Kopelin, *Life of Debs*, 44. In addition to the article by Milburn cited above, there are three brief discussions of the *Appeal to Reason:* Stewart Holbrook, *Lost Men of American History*, 313–7; W. J. Ghent, "The Appeal and Its Influence," *Survey*, 26:24–8 (1911); and an unpublished essay by David A. Shannon, "The Appeal to Reason." The articles by Milburn and Holbrook tend toward sensationalism and are not entirely reliable; Ghent briefly presents the important facts and a usually sound interpretation; Shannon has done a scholarly and often exciting job.

The incident involving Debs and Frank P. O'Hare was told to me by Mr. O'Hare. Theodore Roosevelt's attacks on Debs are taken from the Washington, D. C., *Post*, April 15, 1906, and Henry F. Pringle, *Theodore Roosevelt*, 452. Debs' replies are in Reynolds, *Debs*, 247–52, 257–61; and New York *World*, April 25, 1907. Clarence Darrow describes his rôle in the Moyer-Haywood trial in *The Story of My Life*, 127–56.

The statement by Debs in justification of his inflammatory articles was told to me by Dr. J. Rudolph Yung, and his comment, "If they hang Haywood and Moyer, they'll have to hang me" appears in Walter Hurt, *Eugene V. Debs*, 33.

Since Debs did not issue any public statement on his departure from the IWW, it is impossible to know with certainty either the exact time or the reasons. As to the time, Dr. John R. Shannon saw Debs' dues card in the IWW for 1907, and his dues had been paid for that year. Debs had not written for the IWW journals or agitated for the organization since 1906, when the syndicalist trend first became apparent. My statement of the reasons for Debs' resignation is based on my general understanding of his thought rather than on direct evidence, but my general view was corroborated by Frank Bohn, George D. Brewer, and Algernon Lee.

The best criticisms of dual-unionism by conservative unionists appear in the contemporary issues of the *American Federationist*. The outstanding criticism by a radical unionist was made by William Z. Foster in *The Agitator* (Home, Washington), April 15 to July 1, 1912. A subsequent and more extensive discussion by Foster will be found in *The Bankruptcy of the American Labor Movement*.

For Debs' views on reform movements and parties see his letter to Henry Demarest Lloyd, June 22, 1903, Lloyd *Mss;* the *Social Democratic Herald*, February 25, 1899; Los Angeles *Social Democrat*, July 31, 1915 (Debs Scrapbooks, IX, 306, Rand).

The quotations given to illustrate Debs' views on the Negro problem are taken from *Social Democrat*, January 20, 1898; Indianapolis *World*, June 20, 1903; *International Socialist Review*, November 1903, January 1904. See also his letter to J. Milton Waldron of the Negroes' National League, June 30, 1908, printed in Karsner, *Debs*, 192–4; and his letter of protest against the motion picture, "The Birth of a Nation," Terre Haute *Post*, January 6, 1916.

CHAPTER XIV

Material for this chapter was contributed by William B. Bohn, Frederic Heath, Frank P. O'Hare, Will Schuhardt, Dr. John R. Shannon, Alfred Wagenknecht, and John M. Work.

The best source for the Socialist campaign of 1908 is the *Appeal to Reason*. That journal, on August 8, 1908, carries a schedule of the principal Debs' meetings, and I have checked the accounts of many speeches in the local newspapers of the various cities. Several clippings are collected in Debs Scrapbooks, VIII, 168 ff. (Rand) and Kate Debs Scrapbooks (Shannon). See also Karsner, *Debs*, 183–206; Painter, *Debs*, 98; Coleman, *Debs*, 243–8. The excerpts from speeches to the Socialist national convention are taken from the official *Proceedings;* the letter from Debs to Hanford is printed 151–2. The left-wing's fear of a conspiracy against the nomination of Debs was told to me by Frank P. O'Hare; but three other participants in the convention—Frederic

Heath, Alfred Wagenknecht, and John M. Work—all say that they know nothing about any plots toward this end.

Julius Wayland's estimate of Debs' oratory in 1898 appears in the *Appeal to Reason*, February 19, 1898; the statement by Art Young appears in *Art Young: His Life and Times*, 216. One of the best estimates of Debs' rhetoric was told to me by William E. Bohn. For the speech in Girard, May 23, 1908, see Reynolds, *Debs*, 473–91.

Most of the earlier writing about Debs falls in the category here described as the Debs Legend; consult the Bibliography. Several "Appreciations" of Debs are collected in Reynolds, *Debs*, 495–515. Heywood Broun's column about Debs is reprinted in *It Seems to Me, 1925–1935*.

The meeting of the Socialist National Committee at which J. Mahlon Barnes proposed the Red Special was described for me by John M. Work. The origin and methods of the Socialist encampments in the Southwest were explained to me by Frank P. O'Hare; and several of these meetings are reported in the *Appeal to Reason*. See also Oscar Ameringer, *If You Don't Weaken*, especially 267–8.

Steffens' article appears in *Everybody's*, October 1908; his private expressions of opinion are taken from *The Letters of Lincoln Steffens*, I, 209–11; for Debs' letter to Steffens see *ibid.*, 203. The excerpt from the letter by Theodore Roosevelt is in Pringle, *op. cit.*, 413. For examples of the charges made against the Socialists, see the contemporary *American Federationist;* Chicago *Record-Herald*, August 30, 1908; Detroit *Free Press*, September 28, 1908.

Theodore Debs disclosed his impostures during this campaign to Dr. John R. Shannon, who passed them on to me. Debs' aversion to typewriters is told by Louis Kopelin, *Debs*, 98. Descriptions of Debs' tour of the East Side of New York appear in Morris Hillquit, *Loose Leaves*, 114–6; and Ernest Poole, *The Bridge*, 196. The anecdote about the Pittsburgh reporter is taken from a clipping, Debs *Mss* (Labadie). The final rally in Terre Haute was described for me by Will Schuhardt.

CHAPTER XV

George D. Brewer, Mrs. Carabelle G. Dickey, Elizabeth Gurley Flynn, Mrs. Raymond P. Harris, Algernon Lee, Frank P. O'Hare, Helen Ross, Shubert Sebree, Fred D. Warren, and Noble C. Wilson were interviewed in connection with this chapter.

The agitational articles by Debs in this period are taken from the *Appeal to Reason;* his statements about the policy dispute within the Party appear in the *International Socialist Review*.

Debs' explanation of his refusal to leave Terre Haute is taken from a clipping in Kate Debs Scrapbooks (Shannon). Most of the anecdotes about his habits in Girard were told to Ann Fagan Ginger by Fred D. Warren. The scrapbooks kept by Debs in Girard (Rand) and Henry Vincent Scrapbooks (Labadie) are also valuable. The critical remarks about Chicago are taken from an informal speech by Debs, reprinted as *An Evening in Girard*. For his views on prohibition see Terre Haute *Tribune*, March 1, 1908; and his letter to Charles R. Jones, May 24, 1912 (Shannon). The quoted article about Jesus was reprinted in Debs, *Labor and Freedom*, 22–9; see also *Christian Socialist*, December 18, 1915. The anecdote about the Labor Day picnic in Terre Haute was told to me by Algernon Lee; the childhood incident involving Eugene and Theodore Debs is taken from a clipping in Debs *Mss* (Labadie).

For Debs' friendship with Horace Traubel and William F. Gable, see their correspondence in Debs *Mss* (Yale); Debs' library (Rand), which includes several books inscribed by Traubel and Gable; *Talks With Debs*, 24, 42–3. Debs' eulogy of Traubel appears in Karsner, *Traubel*, 100–1.

The chief source on the Fred Warren defense campaign is of course the *Appeal to Reason*. Debs' costly hike up the Pennsylvania gully is described in John Haynes Holmes, *Debs*, 12. The incident involving Ella Reeve Bloor is taken from her autobiography, *We Are Many*, 52. The eulogy of Jean Reynolds is contained in Eugene Debs to S. M. Reynolds, January 24, 1910 (Shannon). For the incident near Brooklyn Bridge, see Kopelin, *Debs*, 39; that involving Frank Roderus is taken from a clipping in Debs *Mss* (Labadie). The argument between Debs and Wayland is described in the *Appeal to Reason*, May 24, 1913.

For information about Kate Debs and Debs' home life in this period, see George Bicknell, "Eugene V. Debs at Home," *Twentieth Century*, August 1910; *Socialist Woman*, October 1908; Chicago *Daily Socialist*, May 13, 1912. I also received several facts from Mrs. Carabelle G. Dickey, Mrs. Raymond P. Harris, and Helen Ross. The article on woman suffrage by Kate Debs appears in the Terre Haute *Post*, May 21, 1910; *Appeal to Reason*, June 11, 1910; *Progressive Woman*, July 1910. For the biography proposed by Max Ehrmann, see Eugene Debs to Ehrmann, February 15, 1910, Ehrmann *Mss*, and the Notes by Max Ehrmann. The anecdote involving Edwin Markham is taken from *Talks With Debs*, 107; the autographed copy of "Man with the Hoe" is now owned by David A. Shannon. The stirring incident recounted by the carpenter is taken from Esau Carnes to Dr. John R. Shannon, February 1940, no day (Shannon).

Fred Warren's return of the pardon is told by George Milburn in the cited article; it was verified by Mr. Warren in a conversation with Ann Fagan Ginger. The best source on the McNamara case is the *Appeal to Reason;* see also Coleman, *Debs,* 252. The quoted letter of March 14, 1912, is Eugene Debs to Joseph A. Labadie, Labadie *Mss.*

For the Socialist campaign of 1912 and the factional fight, see the convention *Proceedings; Bill Haywood's Book,* 257; *International Socialist Review;* New York *Call;* Tom Hickey's article in *The Rebel,* May 1, 1915; *Appeal to Reason; Wilshire's,* September 1912. The quotation by Art Young is taken from *Art Young,* 216. The story involving the feminine dainties and Eugene Debs was told to me by Shubert Sebree, who heard it from Theodore Debs.

Debs' visit to the Federal Commissioner in Terre Haute was described for me by Noble C. Wilson. The basic facts about the threatened indictment of J. A. Wayland on a morals charge were told to Ann Fagan Ginger by Fred D. Warren; see also Upton Sinclair, *American Outpost,* 209. Wayland's suicide note is printed in Coleman, *Debs,* 266. The epitaph by Kate O'Hare is taken from the *Appeal to Reason,* November 16, 1912.

CHAPTER XVI

I am indebted to Delbert Earley, Mrs. Raymond P. Harris, John Keracher, Winifred O'Connell, Frank P. O'Hare, Will Schuhardt, Shubert Sebree, Phil Wagner, Noble C. Wilson, Peter Witt, and Morris H. Wolf for material used in this chapter.

The 1910 self-criticism by Debs is taken from his letter to Peter Witt, February 15, 1910, Witt *Mss.* For the comment by Floyd Dell, see his autobiography, *Homecoming,* 267. The 1918 incident was told to me by Morris H. Wolf. The anecdote involving the Socialist editor in Terre Haute was related to me by Noble C. Wilson.

At least twenty-five persons told me about the quarrel between Kate Debs and Theodore, and I feel satisfied that the attitudes here ascribed to both of them are fairly accurate. The incident involving Carl Stahl was told to me by Helen Ross; Morris H. Wolf described for me Debs' diplomacy when Kate publicly complained about her husband's sacrifices. The portrait of Kate Debs in this book is based on more than a dozen newspaper interviews with her between 1894 and 1921, on testimonials by her husband, and on my own interviews with more than two dozen persons who knew her. Many of these persons were quite critical, and I have tried to include their criticisms and to explain them in terms of Kate's character. It is my belief, for reasons indicated in the text, that her supporters have a sounder position than her opponents.

While there is room for differing opinions of Kate Debs, one recent allegation cannot go unchallenged. More than ten years after her death, it was charged that she had harbored German agents before American entry into World War I and had then hypocritically sold Liberty Bonds after the declaration of hostilities by Congress. I investigated this contention thoroughly and found the following: The charge was never made publicly before 1947. Nobody in Terre Haute can offer any evidence to support it, and the two dozen persons whom I questioned there unanimously said that it was new to them. Of all the Socialists interviewed by me, only James Oneal believed that the charge was correct, and he offered no evidence beyond the statement that the charge originated with Theodore Debs. Although the Terre Haute newspapers, all vigorously prowar, would unquestionably have printed any facts which discredited Eugene Debs, a search of their columns reveals no evidence to support the claim.

The Cabin Creek strike in West Virginia can be followed in the *Appeal to Reason*. A large collection of clippings relating to Debs and the so-called girl outcast is in Debs Scrapbooks, IX, 268–72 (Rand); see also Robert D. Heinl to Eugene Debs, July 7, 1913 (Shannon). The vacation at Estes Park, the retirement of the ARU debt, and Debs' retirement are related in Debs Scrapbooks, IX, 273 (Rand); and a clipping in Debs *Mss* (Ind Div). The interview in the Terre Haute *Post* appears January 13, 1914.

For the Socialist antiwar campaign prior to 1914, see Hillquit, *Loose Leaves*, 148; Denver *Post*, October 2, 1909; *Appeal to Reason*, August 5, 1911. After February 1914, Debs' articles and accounts of his activities appear in the *National Rip-Saw, International Socialist Review*, and *American Socialist*. Information about Debs' connection with the *Rip-Saw* was given me by Phil Wagner and Frank P. O'Hare. I am also indebted to an excellent essay by David A. Shannon, *Antiwar Thought and Activity of Eugene V. Debs, 1914–1921*.

For the Calumet strike see Perlman and Taft, *History of Labor*, IV, 248–252; Debs' activities in this strike were told to me by Will Schuhardt. The best secondary source on the Ludlow Massacre is Yellen, *American Labor Struggles*, chapter 7. The statement by John D. Rockefeller, Jr., to a Congressional committee is given by Granville Hicks, *John Reed*, 141.

The quoted letter from Debs to Upton Sinclair was written January 12, 1916, Sinclair *Mss*. The article by Debs beginning "I am opposed to every war but one" is taken from the *Appeal to Reason*, September 11, 1915. His epitaph for Daniel DeLeon appears in the New York *People*, July 11, 1914. For his attack on the IWW, see *Miners' Magazine*, May 7, 1914. The letter to Max Ehrmann about the Ann Arbor meeting was written January 21, 1916, Ehrmann *Mss.* The letter attacking the New York *Call* was written to Louis Kopelin, February 16, 1916, and is quoted by Painter, *Debs*, 113.

For the 1916 Congressional campaign in Terre Haute, the stories in the Socialist press and the local newspapers were supplemented by interviews with three members of Debs' campaign committee—Will Schuhardt, Shubert Sebree, and Noble C. Wilson. Mrs. Raymond P. Harris told me about a friend who saw Kate Debs waving to her husband at a street-meeting; and Winifred O'Connell told me how she found Kate in tears over the local gossip. That Kate marched in the final parade was confirmed by Mr. Sebree and Mr. Wilson, and Debs' monologue about *Les Misérables* was told to me by Mr. Wilson.

As background material on American entry into the war I have used chiefly Walter Millis, *The Road to War;* Charles Seymour, *American Neutrality, 1914–1917;* C. C. Tansill, *America Goes to War.* The classic Marxian statement is Nikolai Lenin's *Imperialism*, which lucidly analyzes the changes in world capitalism since 1890. The AFL conference in March 1917 is described by Lorwin, *American Federation of Labor*, 144–5.

CHAPTER XVII

Material for this chapter was furnished by Frederic Heath, John Keracher, Frank P. O'Hare, Helen Ross, Lena Schuhardt, Oswald Schuhardt, Will Schuhardt, Shubert Sebree, Maurice Sugar, Norman Thomas, Alfred Wagenknecht, and Noble C. Wilson.

The best source for this period is the *National Rip-Saw* (renamed *Social Revolution*). The background material was taken from a score of Socialist periodicals and autobiographies by Socialists, all of which are listed in the Bibliography.

The St. Louis Declaration was printed in all of the Socialist journals; it is reprinted in full by Fine, *op. cit.*, 310–4. The contemporary journalistic accounts of the St. Louis Emergency Convention were supplemented by interviews with several participants—Frederic Heath, John Keracher, Frank P. O'Hare, Maurice Sugar, and Alfred Wagenknecht. Charles E. Ruthenberg's negotiations with Debs were told to me by Mr. Wagenknecht.

The statement attributed to Woodrow Wilson by Frank I. Cobb is reprinted by Walter Millis, *Road to War*, 430. All of Debs' protests against the infringements on civil liberties appear in *Social Revolution* except his article on the race riot in East St. Louis, which will be found in *Intercollegiate Socialist*, December–January 1918. The letter from Rose Pastor Stokes to Eugene Debs was written July 22, 1916 (Shannon). The reference to "the heartening comrade-touch" occurs in Eugene Debs to Joseph A. Labadie, January 4, 1918, Labadie *Mss*. The rumor that Theodore Debs was restraining his brother during this period was reported to me by Noble C. Wilson. The incident involving Bishop William M. Brown is described in his letter to Charles Baker, May 23, 1925, printed in *Marguerite Prevey—In Memoriam*, 49–51. Debs' 1918 statement, "I abhor war," is taken from his plea to the jury, *US v. Eugene V. Debs*, Criminal No. 4057, Federal Court for the Northern District of Ohio, September 1918. For the cold reception furnished John Reed by the journalistic world in April 1918, see Hicks, *John Reed*, 307.

The letter from Eugene Debs to Kate O'Hare appears in Painter, *Debs*, 117. The correspondence of Debs and Frank P. O'Hare, O'Hare *Mss*, is also very helpful for the light it casts on Debs' state of mind. Debs' article about the IWW is taken from *International Socialist Review*, February 1918.

The anti-Socialist campaign in Terre Haute is based on the local newspapers; Debs' article, "The Reward of Paytriotism" (Ind Div); my interviews with Helen Ross, Lena Schuhardt, Oswald Schuhardt, Will Schuhardt, Shubert Sebree, and Noble C. Wilson; and Coleman, *Debs*, 279–80. For Debs' statement on Socialist policy in May 1918, see a mimeographed press release, Debs *Mss* (Ind Div). The member of the Socialist National Committee who visited Terre Haute was James Oneal; see Coleman, *Debs*, 283–4.

Norman Thomas told me that Debs had given the same speech more than a dozen times before his indictment by the Federal government. Two different versions of the Canton speech are printed in *US v. Debs* (1918), and the interviews with Clyde R. Miller were reported by Mr. Miller during his testimony in this case. Debs' visit to the Stark County Workhouse was reported to me by Alfred Wagenknecht. See also Cleveland *Plain-Dealer*, June 17, 1918. The meeting on Debs' return to Terre Haute was described for me by Noble C. Wilson.

CHAPTER XVIII

Mrs. Yetta Land, Shubert Sebree, Peter Witt, and Morris H. Wolf furnished material for this chapter.

The complete transcript of the proceedings will be found in *US v. Eugene V. Debs*, Criminal No. 4057, Federal Court for the Northern District of Ohio (September 1918). All quotations from the official record have been taken from this source.

For the visit of John Reed and Art Young to Terre Haute, see John Reed, "With Gene Debs on the Fourth," *Liberator*, September 1918; *Art Young: His Life and Times*, 347–9; Art Young, *On My Way*, 168; Granville Hicks, *John Reed*, 309. The letter from Eugene Debs to Shubert Sebree was written August 27, 1918, Sebree *Mss.* According to Ralph Chaplin, *Wobbly*, 210, Debs visited the IWW trial while he was in Chicago in August. For Clarence Darrow's offer of help, see his letter to Eugene Debs, July 20, 1918 (Shannon). The pre-trial conferences between Debs and his attorneys were described for me by Morris H. Wolf; see also Scott Nearing, *The Debs Decision*, 15.

Those features of the trial which are not included in the official record are taken from Max Eastman, "The Trial of Eugene Debs," *Liberator*, November 1918 (reprinted as a pamphlet and in Max Eastman, *Heroes I Have Known*); David Karsner, *Debs*, chapter 2; the contemporary Cleveland *Plain-Dealer* and New York *Times;* report of a speech by Rose Pastor Stokes, New York *Times*, September 23, 1918; interviews with Mrs. Yetta Land, Peter Witt, and Morris H. Wolf.

The portrait of Judge D. C. Westenhaver is based on Max Eastman's description and my conversations with three members of the Cleveland Bar. The hospitality of William Bross Lloyd, the difficulty in keeping the defendant sober, and the incident at the home of Mrs. Marguerite Prevey, were all described for me by Morris H. Wolf. On Eugene Debs' stock of Lincoln legends, see Karsner, *Debs*, 9; and Max Eastman, *The Trial of Eugene Debs* (pamphlet reprint), 22.

CHAPTER XIX

Material for this chapter was contributed by Alfred Bosch, John Keracher, Shubert Sebree, Alfred Wagenknecht, and Noble C. Wilson.

The comments by Heywood Broun are taken from his newspaper column, "The Dream of Debs," as reprinted in *It Seems To Me, 1925–1935*. The analysis here given of Debs' career is original with me, at least as to its emphases and interpretation. I also believe this is the first time it has been pointed out that Debs' plea to the jury was an edited version of hundreds of his previous speeches, with a paragraph largely borrowed from John Brown.

The incident involving Clyde R. Miller is taken from Miller, *The Process of Persuasion*, 75–6. The information about Debs' personal and

financial affairs is contained in Theodore Debs to Upton Sinclair, No
vember 6, 1918, Sinclair *Mss.* The letter from Eugene Debs to Sinclair
about *Jimmie Higgins* was written September 19, 1918. The incidents
involving Shubert Sebree and Noble C. Wilson were told to me by Mr.
Sebree and Mr. Wilson, respectively, and the letter from Eugene Debs
to Sebree is dated September 20, 1918, Sebree *Mss.* For Debs' letter to
John Reed, see Granville Hicks, *John Reed,* 314. For Debs' tour of
northern Ohio, see Detroit *News,* April 1, 1919; *New Solidarity* (Chicago), March 30, 1919. Debs' pledge of support to Soviet Russia,
November 1918, is reprinted in Alexander Trachtenberg, *Eugene V.
Debs,* 67–70. The quotation from the New Year's card is taken from
Eugene Debs to Joseph A. Labadie, marked by Labadie "1–4–1919,"
Labadie *Mss.*

For the decision of the United States Supreme Court on Debs' appeal, see *Eugene V. Debs v. U. S.,* 249 US 211 (March 1919). The letter
from Oliver Wendell Holmes is printed in *Holmes–Pollock Letters,* II, 7.
For Debs' statement on the decision, see *Liberator,* April 1919.

Practically all of the material about the trip to Moundsville is taken
from a pamphlet by David Karsner, *Debs Goes to Prison* (reprinted as
chapter 3 of David Karsner, *Debs*). Alfred Wagenknecht gave me his
memories of the trip, and John Keracher described for me the protest
meeting in Cleveland. See also New York *Times,* April 12, 1919.

For Debs' two months at Moundsville see Karsner, *Debs,* chapter 4.
The message from Theodore Debs to Eugene is taken from a typewritten draft, April 14, 1919, Debs *Mss* (Shannon). The letter to Horace
Traubel is in Karsner, *Debs,* 99. Alfred Bosch described for me his visit
to Moundsville. The information about the Soviet attempt to win
Debs' release is given in Detroit *News,* October 21, 1926. In December,
1926, the *Labor Defender* printed a letter from an inmate of Moundsville prison describing the impression that Eugene Debs had made on
his contemporaries there.

CHAPTER XX

Two persons who were prisoners at Atlanta during Debs' stay and
who furnished me with much information shall remain unnamed here.
The best source for this period is the series of newspaper columns by
Eugene Debs, published after his death as *Walls and Bars.* Debs'
transfer from Moundsville is described by David Karsner, *Debs,* chapter 5. For a different version of the motives behind his transfer, see
Liberator, September 1919. Frequent reports by Debs' visitors appear

in *Appeal to Reason, Chicago Socialist, Liberator,* and New York *Call,* throughout the term of his imprisonment.

The split in the Socialist Party is best followed in those radical journals representing the various factions. See also Ella Reeve Bloor, *We Are Many;* William Z. Foster, *From Bryan to Stalin; Bill Haywood's Book;* Morris Hillquit, *Loose Leaves From a Busy Life;* James Oneal, *American Communism.* The most helpful secondary source is Granville Hicks, *John Reed;* see particularly the chronological chart, 420–1. For Debs' attitude toward the various factions in this period see Karsner, *Talks With Debs,* 155–61; Coleman, *Debs,* 315–6; and particularly his interview with the Socialist notification committee, New York *Times,* May 15, 1920.

For the statement by Debs about John L. Lewis see Karsner, *Talks With Debs,* 95; about "force and violence" see a clipping, Debs *Mss* (Labadie). His views on *The Brass Check* are contained in Mable D. Curry to Upton Sinclair, June 10, 1920; on *Mammonart* in Eugene Debs to Upton Sinclair, October 26, 1920; both in Sinclair *Mss.* For Debs' account of the minister's visit, see Karsner, *Debs,* 10–11. The introspective letter from Eugene Debs to Theodore is printed by Coleman, *Debs,* 320–1.

For Clarence Darrow's visit, see *The Story of My Life,* 71–2; Debs, *Walls and Bars,* 95–6. The interview with Charles Wood appears in *Literary Digest,* October 23, 1920. The anecdote which depicts the warden's hysteria when Debs is punished is taken from John Haynes Holmes, *Debs—Lover of Men,* 13. The letter to Upton Sinclair about the editorial in the *Christian Science Monitor* was written by Theodore Debs, October 26, 1920, Sinclair *Mss.* Debs' objections to being called a "grand old man" are emphatically stated in his leaflet, *The Fight for Liberty,* 4.

Theodore Debs seems to despair of any hope for his brother's prompt pardon in a letter to Frank P. O'Hare, November 23, 1920, O'Hare *Mss.* For the recommendation by A. Mitchell Palmer, see New York *Times,* February 1, 1921. Woodrow Wilson's statement is taken from Joseph P. Tumulty, *Woodrow Wilson As I Know Him,* 505.

The attitude of the Communists toward the amnesty campaign and Debs' candidacy in 1920 was reported to me by Alexander Trachtenberg, Alfred Wagenknecht, and William Weinstone, all of whom expressed the belief that it had been a grave mistake. See also the articles by Alexander Bittelman, Earl Browder, and William Z. Foster, *The Communist,* September 1939. The invaluable correspondence of Eugene

Debs and Otto Branstetter during 1921–1922 will be found in Debs *Mss* (Ind Div).

Much of the information on the amnesty campaign is taken from David A. Shannon, *Anti-war Thought and Activity of Eugene V. Debs, 1914–1921*. Debs' trip to Washington is reported in New York *Times*, March 25, 1921; the purchase of the quill toothpicks by Jesse Smith was told to me by Peter Witt. For Daugherty's statement about Debs, see Clarence Darrow, *op. cit.*, 73. For Clyde R. Miller's conversations with Newton D. Baker and Warren G. Harding, see Miller, *op. cit.*, 76–7. For Norman Hapgood's visit see Debs, *Walls and Bars*, 97; for the visit of Samuel Gompers see *ibid.*, 96, and Karsner, *Talks With Debs*, 59–60. The letter from A. Producer to Eugene Debs, May 5, 1921, is in Debs *Mss* (Shannon).

Arthur Baur's activity in connection with the Palmer Raids was told to me by Noble C. Wilson. The Christmas card, 1919, from Kate Debs to Eugene is in Debs *Mss* (Shannon). The remainder of the section is based on the correspondence of Kate Debs and Kate O'Hare, O'Hare *Mss*; this is the largest collection of letters written by Kate Debs.

The activities of Lincoln Steffens during the final month of 1921 are told in Steffens, *Autobiography*, 843–4; *The Letters of Lincoln Steffens*, I, 580–1; Debs, *Walls and Bars*, 98. The announcement of the commutation by the White House is reported in New York *Times*, December 24, 1921. For the statement by Debs, "These men need me . . . ," see Bloor, *We Are Many*, 148–9. The telegram from Debs to his wife is in Debs *Mss* (Shannon). Debs describes his departure from Atlanta in *Walls and Bars*, 122–6.

CHAPTER XXI

George D. Brewer, Charles W. Ervin, Powers Hapgood, Frank P. O'Hare, Will Schuhardt, Shubert Sebree, Phil Wagner, and Noble C. Wilson contributed material for this chapter.

More than half the material in this entire chapter is taken from Karsner, *Talks With Debs*, where the statements can easily be found. The other indispensable source is the correspondence of Eugene Debs and Otto Branstetter, Debs *Mss* (Ind Div).

The selection from the Emporia *Gazette* is taken from William Allen White, *The Editor and His People*, 208. For the incident involving Urbain Ledoux, see New York *Times*, December 28, 1921. The statement by Samuel Gompers is taken from *Seventy Years*, I, 416. The description of the reception in Terre Haute was pieced together from

Kate Debs Scrapbooks (Shannon); James H. Maurer, *It Can Be Done*, 250–2; the contemporary Terre Haute newspapers; and interviews with Charles W. Ervin, Frank P. O'Hare, Will Schuhardt, Shubert Sebree, Phil Wagner, and Noble C. Wilson. All of the incidents during Karsner's stay in Terre Haute are taken from *Talks With Debs*.

I was unable to find any evidence that Debs and Altgeld had ever met, and there is also some positive confirmation. According to Harry Barnard, he heard from George A. Schilling that Debs and Altgeld exchanged autographed photographs, but never met personally.

The incident involving George D. Brewer was told to me by Mr. Brewer; see also the unsigned review of Irving Stone's *Adversary in the House*, *American Freeman*, February 1948. The letter from Eugene Debs to J. O. Bentall, April 3, 1922, is in Debs *Mss* (Ind Div). For the information about Debs' prison articles, see *Walls and Bars*, 21, 22, 25. Debs' statement of the three immediate problems appears in *Appeal to Reason*, April 15, 1922.

For Debs' telegram to Lenin, see *Talks With Debs*, 171–3; see also Steffens, *Autobiography*, 844; Mary Heaton Vorse, *Footnote to Folly*, 380. The letter from Debs to William Z. Foster, August 26, 1922, is in *Talks With Debs*, 96–7.

The incident involving August Claessens was told to me by Mr. Claessens; Debs' participation in foot races at the sanitarium was told to me by Sol Klapman. Carl Haessler described for me his visits with Debs in Elmhurst. For Debs' comments on the railroad strike of 1922, see his article, "What You Fought for in the War," Debs *Mss* (Ind Div); his statement after he was rejected by the BLF convention is contained in a press release, Debs *Mss* (Ind Div). The three statements by Debs about death are taken from these sources: *Medical Review of Reviews*, February 1914; letter to Otto Branstetter, March 25, 1922, Debs *Mss* (Ind Div); Detroit *News*, October 21, 1926. The letter from Carl Sandburg to Debs is dated November 26, 1922 (Shannon). All other information about Debs' convalescence at Lindlahr is taken from *Talks With Debs*, 187–221.

Debs' declaration of principles appears in New York *Call*, October 8, 1922 (reprinted in part by Karsner, *Talks With Debs*, 32–3).

CHAPTER XXII

For material in this chapter, I am indebted to Louis B. Boudin, Earl Browder, August Claessens, Peter Fagan, Carl Haessler, Mrs. Powers Hapgood, Algernon Lee, Frank Pfister, John C. Prechtel, Mr. and Mrs. Shubert Sebree, Norman Thomas, and John M. Work. During the final years of his life Debs did not contribute regularly to any specific periodicals, but several of his statements appear in the New York *Call* and the *New Leader*.

For the bitter strife between Socialists and Communists in the trade unions, see *American Federationist*, May 1922; *Labor Herald*, June 1922; *Liberator*, June 1922; James Oneal, *American Communism*; William Z. Foster, *From Bryan to Stalin*. For Debs' hesitation about policy, see Otto Branstetter to Eugene Debs, September 22, 1922, and Debs to Branstetter, September 23, 1922, Debs *Mss* (Ind Div). Debs' visit to the Chicago offices of the TUEL was reported to me by Earl Browder.

The conversation with Morris Hillquit is described by Hillquit, *Loose Leaves*, 49–50. For Debs' habit of visiting Union Square, see Art Young, *On My Way*, 160–2. The resolution by the General Assembly of Wisconsin is quoted in Painter, *Debs*, 155. A large collection of clippings about the Ohio tour of 1923 will be found in Debs *Mss* (Ind Div).

Debs' acute illness during the winter of 1923–1924 is reported in Theodore Debs to Joseph A. Labadie, December 12, 1923, March 6, June 10, 1924, Labadie *Mss*; and Theodore Debs to George A. Schilling, April 17, 1924, Schilling *Mss*. Debs' library is still located in the Rand School. His comments about the article by Karsner are taken from his interview with Floy Ruth Painter, August 28, 1924, quoted by Painter, *Debs*, 188. For his relations with Carl Sandburg in 1924, see Sandburg to Debs, October 18, 1924 (Shannon). The incident involving the Chicago local of the Bakers Union was told to me by August Claessens. Debs' visit to the home of Ralph Chaplin is described by Chaplin, *Wobbly*, 340–3.

For the dispute between Debs and Foster during the 1924 Presidential campaign, see James Oneal, *American Communism*, 208–9. The letter to Joseph A. Labadie was written January 5, 1925, Labadie *Mss*. Debs' address to the Socialist national convention of 1925 is contained in a clipping from the *Socialist World*, Debs *Mss* (Ind Div). Carl Haessler told me his memories of this convention. The incident involving S. M. Reynolds was told to me by John M. Work. Debs' statement about the Labor Defense Council is contained in a clipping from the *Socialist World*, Debs *Mss* (Ind Div).

Debs' jovial approach to death is taken from a clipping in Kate Debs Scrapbooks (Shannon). For the expressions about Bryan and Altgeld, see Eugene Debs to Clarence Darrow, June 4, 1925, Schilling *Mss*. For the trip to California in 1925, see Theodore Debs to Upton Sinclair,

July 31, 1925, Sinclair *Mss*. Mr. Sinclair described for me one of his conversations with Eugene Debs.

For Debs' speech at the 1925 convention of the Indiana Federation of Labor, see Terre Haute newspapers, August 28, 1925. John C. Prechtel gave me his memories of this occasion. The description of "St. Eugene Victor" is contained in a letter from Peter Fagan to me, July 30, 1946. The negotiations with the Sacco-Vanzetti Defense Committee during Debs' trip to Boston were told to me by Mrs. Powers Hapgood. The speech at Hunt's Point Palace was described for me by August Claessens and Algernon Lee. The banquet for Debs was related to me by Louis B. Boudin.

From January until March, 1926, Debs' weekly editorials appear in *American Appeal*, which is also the source for most of the information about the trip to Bermuda. For Debs' earlier plans to travel, see *Social Democratic Herald*, August 5, 1899; Debs Scrapbooks, VIII, 65 (Rand).

Debs' final plea for Sacco and Vanzetti is contained in *American Appeal*, June 29; 1926; his pamphlet on this subject for the Labor Defense Council is in Debs *Mss* (Fairbanks). For Debs' illness in May and June, 1926, see Theodore Debs to Joseph A. Labadie, July 7, 1926, Labadie *Mss*. His final trip to the City Hall in Terre Haute and the events leading up to his death at Lindlahr are all taken from clippings in Debs *Mss* (Labadie).

The quoted expressions of condolence are taken from Clarence Darrow to Kate Debs, November 5, 1926; Edgar Lee Masters to Kate Debs, November 13, 1926; Sinclair Lewis to Kate Debs and Theodore Debs, April 30, 1927 (Shannon). The mourning is described in all of the Socialist journals and many metropolitan newspapers. For descriptions of the funeral, see all of the Terre Haute and Indianapolis newspapers; see also M. Haldeman-Julius, "The Funeral of Eugene Debs," *Haldeman-Julius Monthly*, December 1926. Norman Thomas gave me his memories of the funeral. The comment by Heywood Broun is taken from his article cited above.

BIBLIOGRAPHY

Primary Sources

I. UNPUBLISHED MANUSCRIPTS

Grover Cleveland *Mss*, Library of Congress. Valuable for Pullman boycott.

Clarence S. Darrow *Mss*, Library of Congress.

Eugene V. Debs Collection, Fairbanks Library, Terre Haute, Ind.

Eugene V. Debs *Mss*, Indiana Historical Society, Indianapolis. Three unimportant letters from Eugene Debs to various correspondents, 1907–1908.

Eugene V. Debs *Mss*, Indiana Division, Indiana State Library, Indianapolis. Exceedingly valuable correspondence of Eugene Debs and Otto Branstetter, 1921–1922. Also drafts by Eugene Debs of several articles for the Socialist Press Service, 1922; a large collection of correspondence relating to the amnesty movement; and many published items by Eugene Debs.

Eugene V. Debs Collection, Joseph A. Labadie Archives, University of Michigan, Ann Arbor. Few manuscripts, but an excellent collection of newspaper clippings, published material and Socialist periodicals.

Eugene V. Debs Collection, Rand School of Social Science, New York City. No manuscripts, but still the best single source of material on Eugene Debs. Complete files for the relevant periods of the *Locomotive Firemen's Magazine; Proceedings* of the BLF national conventions; minutes of sessions of the Supreme Council of the United Orders of Railway Employees; *Railway Times; Social Democrat; Appeal to Reason;* plus broken files of many other radical journals. Of particular value are nine volumes (300 pages per volume) of clippings kept by Debs, 1894–1918; a separate series of clippings (about 600 pages) that he kept in Girard; and 150 volumes from his personal library.

Eugene V. Debs *Mss*, possession of David A. Shannon, Pittsburgh, Pa. Several notes from Eugene Debs to Mrs. Kate Debs; about three dozen letters to Debs from various correspondents, 1898–1926; three valuable scrapbooks kept by Kate Debs; a large collection of clippings and photographs.

Eugene V. Debs *Mss*, Yale University Library, New Haven, Conn. Eleven letters from Eugene and Theodore Debs to William F. Gable,

Horace Traubel, and an unnamed person, 1909–1918. Also an unmarked carbon copy of the typewritten Ms. for Debs' book, *Walls and Bars*.

Daniel DeLeon *Mss*, Wisconsin Historical Society, Madison. Several letters to DeLeon during 1897 and 1898 contain interesting references to Eugene Debs.

Finley Peter Dunne *Mss*, Library of Congress. An undated birthday greeting to Mr. Dunne from Eugene Debs, Robert Hunter, and Mother Mary Jones.

Max Ehrmann *Mss*, possession of Mrs. Ehrmann, Terre Haute, Ind. About thirty letters from Eugene Debs to Mr. Ehrmann, 1905–1918, plus Mr. Ehrmann's valuable Notes (covering the period up to the Pullman boycott) for a biography of Eugene Debs.

H. O. Fuhrberg Collection, possession of Mr. Fuhrberg, Seattle, Wash. Scrapbooks of clippings, plus the correspondence of Mr. Fuhrberg and Theodore Debs.

Samuel Gompers Letter-Books, American Federation of Labor, Washington, D. C. Valuable correspondence with Eugene Debs, 1891–1895.

Walter Q. Gresham *Mss*, Library of Congress. Valuable on Pullman boycott.

Frederic Heath *Mss*, possession of Mr. Heath, Milwaukee, Wis. Important letters from Eugene Debs to Frederic Heath, H. L. James, and Miss Elizabeth Thomas, 1897–1905, including several in handwriting of Kate Debs.

Robert G. Ingersoll *Mss*, Library of Congress. Letters from Eugene Debs to Mr. Ingersoll and his family, 1879–1916. Also valuable for the Presidential campaign of 1896.

Joseph A. Labadie *Mss*, Labadie Archives, Ann Arbor. Thirty letters from Eugene and Theodore Debs to Mr. Labadie, 1905–1926.

Henry Demarest Lloyd *Mss*, Wisconsin Historical Society, Madison. Mr. Lloyd's correspondence with Eugene Debs, Victor L. Berger, Clarence Darrow, Isaac Hourwich, Florence Kelley, and Thomas J. Morgan is very valuable for the period 1894–1903.

Frank P. O'Hare *Mss*, possession of Mr. O'Hare, St. Louis, Mo. Important letters from Eugene Debs to Mr. O'Hare, 1917–1922. Kate Debs' letters to Mrs. O'Hare, 1921, are the only collection of her letters known to me.

Richard Olney *Mss*, Library of Congress. Valuable on Pullman boycott.

Daniel L. Powell, Jr., Scrapbook, Labadie Archives, Ann Arbor. Helpful on Socialist Party of Detroit.

James Whitcomb Riley *Mss*, possession of Miss Lesley Payne, Indianapolis, Ind. Six letters from Eugene Debs to Mr. Riley, 1882–1898.

George A. Schilling *Mss*, Illinois Historical Society, Springfield. A few scattered letters from Eugene Debs to Mr. Schilling and Clarence S. Darrow, 1895, 1896, 1924.

Shubert Sebree *Mss*, possession of Mr. Sebree, Terre Haute, Ind. Six letters from Eugene Debs to Mr. Sebree, 1916–1918. Also some valuable clippings.

Upton Sinclair *Mss*, possession of Mr. Sinclair, Monrovia, Calif. Thirty letters from Eugene and Theodore Debs to Mr. Sinclair, 1915–1926, including several which are very valuable.

Henry Vincent Scrapbooks, Labadie Archives, Ann Arbor. Collection of clippings and photographs relating to Eugene Debs' life in Girard.

Peter Witt *Mss*, possession of Mrs. Witt, Cleveland, Ohio. A few scattered letters from Eugene Debs to Mr. Witt, 1910–1924.

II. GOVERNMENT DOCUMENTS

Debs v United States, 73 Fed 1021, appeal to 7th Cir. Ct. App. N. Dist. Ill. (dismissed on consent of counsel), March 1896.

Eugene V. Debs v. United States, Transcript of Record. Supreme Court of the United States, No. 714, Filed October 24, 1918.

Debs v United States, 39 S. Ct. 252 (1919).

Illinois Bureau of Labor Statistics, Thirteenth Annual Report. *Coal in Illinois, 1894*. Springfield, Ill., 1895.

In re Debs, 159 US 251 (no opinion, petition for writ of error denied), January 1895.

In re Debs, 158 US 564 (petition for writ of habeas corpus denied), May 1895.

New York State Senate. *Revolutionary Radicalism: Its History, Purpose and Tactics*. Report of the Joint Legislative Committee Investigating Seditious Activities, Filed April 24, 1920. 4 volumes. Albany, 1920.

United States v Debs, 64 Fed 724, Cir. Ct. N. Dist. Ill. (text of the injunction), December 1894.

United States v Debs, Transcript of Record, Fed. Ct. N. Dist. Ohio, No. 4057 Criminal (September 1918).

United States Bureau of Labor Statistics, *Michigan Copper District Strike*. 63rd Congress, 2nd Session, House Document No. 741. Washington, 1914.

United States Commission on Industrial Relations. *Final Report and Testimony of the Commission on Industrial Relations*. Created by Act of Congress August 23, 1912. 64th Congress, 1st Session, Senate Document No. 415. 11 volumes. Washington, 1916.

United States Department of Justice. *US v Debs*, Bulletin No. 155 (1918).

United States Strike Commission. *Report of the Colorado Strike Investigation*, made under H.R.387. 63rd Congress, 3rd Session. Washington, 1915.

United States Strike Commission. *Report on the Chicago Strike of June–July, 1894.* 53rd Congress, 3rd Session, Senate Executive Documents, vol. II. Washington, 1895.

III. WRITINGS OF EUGENE V. DEBS

A. *Collections of writings and speeches*

Debs: His Life, Writings and Speeches, edited by Bruce Rogers, with a short biography by S. M. Reynolds. Girard, Kansas: 1908.

Labor and Freedom. St. Louis, Mo.: 1916.

Pastels of Men. New York: 1919.

Speeches of Eugene V. Debs, with a Critical Introduction, edited by Alexander Trachtenberg. New York: 1928.

Walls and Bars. Chicago: 1927.

B. *Periodicals to which Debs regularly contributed articles*

Locomotive Firemen's Magazine, 1878–1894.

Railway Times, 1894–1898 (name changed to *Social Democrat* in 1897, to *Social Democratic Herald* in 1898).

Social Democratic Herald, 1898–1905.

International Socialist Review, 1900–1918.

Appeal to Reason, 1906–1913.

New York *Call*, 1908–1926.

National Rip-Saw, 1913–1918 (became *Social Revolution* 1917).

American Socialist, 1915–1917.

New York *Liberator*, 1919–1924.

Debs Magazine, 1922–1923.

American Appeal, 1926.

C. *Articles in other periodicals. Since at least five thousand speeches and articles by Eugene Debs found their way into print, this list is highly selective. I have omitted all articles which appear in the periodicals or the collections listed above. From his remaining output I have chosen only those items which for various reasons seemed of particular interest.*

"The American University and the Labor Problem," *Adelbert*, (Cleveland, Ohio), 6: 167–169.

"Another Talk on the Chicago & Northwestern Conspiracy," *Switchmen's Journal*, August 1906, 563–574.

"Appeal of the Radical Parties," *American Affairs*, October 20, 1904, 485–486.

"Appeal to the Working Class," Terre Haute *Toiler*, February 7, 1902.

"Appeal to Young America," St. Louis *Labor*, July 1, 1905.

"The Barons at the White House," Terre Haute *Toiler*, October 10, 1902.

"Climax of Capitalism," San Francisco *Advance*, April 27, 1901.

"The Coming Labor Union," *Miners' Magazine*, October 26, 1905.

"A Convict's Christmas Offering," *Workers' Chronicle*, (Pittsburg, Kansas), December 25, 1914.

"Days of Long Ago" (a Letter), *Locomotive Firemen's and Enginemen's Magazine*, January 1912, 117.

"Debs, as Socialist, Denies that Congress is Representative," New York *World*, March 17, 1923.

"Eugene V. Debs on California Situation," Los Angeles *Social Democrat*, July 31, 1915.

"Diabolical Plot of Capitalists," *Industrial Worker*, (Joliet, Ill.), March 1906.

"Did We Vote for Municipal Mix-Up," Terre Haute *Post*, February 24, 1914.

"Duties of the Hour," *Industrial Worker*, (Joliet, Ill.), July 1906.

"Education of Locomotive Engine-men," *Locomotive Engineering*, January 1892, 12.

"Face to Face," *Wilshire's*, September 1904, 385–386.

"Getting Together," *Labor Herald*, April 1922, 3–4.

"Growth of Unionism in America," *A.L.U. Journal*, September 3, 1903.

"Harriman Railroad Strike," *Chicago Socialist*, October 10, 1911.

"Hulman & Co.," Terre Haute *Gazette*, September 29, 1893.

"Ingersoll," *Melting Pot*, April 1915, 14–15.

"Letter to the Editor," Terre Haute *Post*, May 11, 1915.

"Man and Mule," *Switchmen's Journal*, September 1906, 652–653.

"Max Ehrmann and His Work" (Debs Scrapbooks, IX, 305, Rand).

"Mooney Must Be Saved," *Pearson's*, May 1917, 434–435.

"Old Bill Robinson," New York *Evening Journal*, January 19, 1902.

"On the Death of Daniel DeLeon," New York *People*, July 11, 1914.

"Organization for Emancipation," *Industrial Worker*, (Joliet, Ill.), September 1906.

"Reminiscences of Myron W. Reed," New York *Comrade*, November 1903, 34–35.

"Riley, Nye and Field," *National Magazine*, January 1914, 611–617.

"Robert G. Ingersoll," *American Journal of Politics*, 2: 198–202 (1893).

"Royal Epidemic," Terre Haute *Toiler*, March 14, 1902.

"A Sentiment on Social Reform," *Masses*, January 1913.

"Social Democracy," *National Magazine*, October 1898.

"The Social Democratic Party," *Independent*, August 23, 1900, 2018–21.

"Socialist Ideals," *Arena*, November 1908, 432–434.

"Socialist Party's Appeal," *Independent*, October 15, 1908, 875–880.

"Socialist Unity," *Socialist Review*, June 1920, 15–16.

"Soldiers, Slaves and Hell," *Iron City Socialist*, (Pittsburgh, Pa.), March 14, 1914.

"Stray Leaves from the Note Book of a Labor Agitator," New York *Comrade*, June 1904, 187–189.

"Susan B. Anthony: A Reminiscence," *Socialist Woman*, (Girard), January 1909, 3.

"Three Letters from Debs to Frank Putnam, Houston, Texas, March 14–25, 1912," *Rebel*, (Hallettsville, Texas), April 6, 1912.

"To My Crawford County Comrades," *Workers' Chronicle*, (Pittsburg, Kansas), March 6, 1914.

"Warren and Gompers," *Miners' Magazine*, December 22, 1911.

"What Can You Do?" *Progressive Woman*, (Girard), June 1909.

"What's Wrong with Chicago," *Chicago Socialist*, August 22, 1911.

"Who Organized the B. of R.T.?" *Switchmen's Journal*, September 1906, 643–646.

"Woman's Day Is Dawning," *Justice*, (Bradford, Pa.) February 1911.

"Woman's Vote," *Minnesota Union Advocate*, August 30, 1901.

D. *Leaflets and pamphlets*

Coming Labor Union. Chicago: 1905.

Debs' Last Call to the Voters in 1920 and His First Call in the New Campaign. Chicago: [1920?].

14th Anniversary of the Birth of the Coming Nation. [Girard, 1907?].

Inside View of the Appeal to Reason. Girard: [1907?].

Mission of the Socialist Party. [1904 campaign leaflet].

Motherhood and Suffrage. [Chicago, 1915?].

Stupendous Achievement. [Girard, 1908?].

To the Women of America! [Chicago, 1920?].

Tribute of Love to His Father and Mother, at the Golden Wedding Anniversary of Jean Daniel Debs and Marguerite Bettrich Debs at Terre Haute, Indiana, September 13, 1899. Terre Haute [circa 1899].

Why Railroaders Should Be Socialists. Girard: [1912?].

Winning a World. New York: [1920's].

Woman—Comrade and Equal. [Socialist Party, no date].

IV. CONTEMPORARY ARTICLES IN PERIODICALS

(Selected)

Baker, Ray Stannard. "Organized Capital Challenges Organized Labor," *McClure's,* July 1904, 279–292.

Benson, Allan L. "The Socialist Candidates," *Pearson's,* August 1912.

Bicknell, George. "Eugene V. Debs at Home," *Twentieth Century,* August 1910, 390–397.

——"Eugene Victor Debs," *Bridgemen's Magazine,* February 1914, 67–75.

Callender, Harold. "The Truth about the I.W.W." *Masses,* November, December, 1917.

"Candidate Debs is a Beneficent Influence in Prison, but Still a Revolutionist," *Literary Digest,* October 23, 1920, 57–58.

Cannon, James P. "Revolutionary Heritage of Eugene Victor Debs," *Labor Defender,* December 1926.

"Eugene V. Debs," *American Railroader,* September 20, 1885, 1–2.

"Eugene V. Debs," *National Federationist,* October 15, 1891, 1–2.

"Debs—the Living Link," *Current Literature,* July 1908, 35–39.

"Mrs. Eugene V. Debs," *Socialist Woman,* October 1908.

Debs, Katherine M. "The Right of Women to Vote," Terre Haute *Post,* May 21, 1910.

Debs, Theodore. "Roosevelt and Beveridge," Terre Haute *Post,* July 18, 1910.

Eastman, Crystal. "Socialist Party Convention," *Liberator,* July 1920, 24–29.

Eastman, Max. "Chicago Conventions," *Liberator,* October 1919, 5–19.

——"A Christmas Party," *Liberator,* February 1923, 5–7.

Ely, Richard T. "Pullman: A Social Study," *Harper's,* February 1885, 452–466.

Engdahl, J. Louis. "Death of the Socialist Party," *Liberator,* October 1924, 11–14.

——"Racing toward Socialism," *Coming Nation,* April 27, 1912.

——"The Workers' Party is Launched," *Labor Age*, February 1922, 14.

——"Socialism versus Syndicalism," *Twentieth Century*, September 1912, 3–10.

England, George Allen. "Story of the Appeal," *Appeal to Reason*, August 30, September 6 and 13, 1913.

Foster, William Z. "Revolutionary Tactics," *Agitator*, (Home, Washington), April 15 to July 1, 1912.

Ghent, William J. "The Appeal and Its Influence," *Survey*, April 1, 1911, 24–28.

Gompers, Samuel. "Debs, the Apostle of Failure," *American Federationist*, September 1908, 736–740.

——"Lesson of the Recent Strikes," *North American Review*, August 1894, 201–206.

——"Organized Labor in the Campaign," *North American Review*, July 1892, 91–96.

Haldeman-Julius, Marcet. "The Funeral of Eugene V. Debs," *Haldeman-Julius Monthly*, December 1926, 3–16.

Hall, Covington. "Debs and Direct Action," *Solidarity*, March 23, 1912.

Hillquit, Morris. "American Socialists and Moscow," *Current History*, October 1920, 16–19.

Hunter, Robert. "The Socialist Party in the Present Campaign," *Review of Reviews*, September 1908, 293–299.

Karsner, David. "Debs in 1920," *Socialist Review*, June 1920, 19–23.

——"The Passing of Socialism," *Current History*, June 1924, 402–407.

Lloyd, Henry D. "The Populists at St. Louis," *Review of Reviews*, September 1896, 298–303.

McFeely, Otto. "Campaigning with Debs," *Wilshire's*, December 1908, 4–5.

Oneal, James. "Changing Fortunes of American Socialism," *Current History*, April 1924, 92–97.

Pepper, John. "The S.P.—Two Wings without a Body," *Liberator*, May 1923, 32–33.

Phifer, Charles Lincoln. "Appeal's Fifteenth Anniversary," *Appeal to Reason*, August 27, 1910.

Reed, John. "With Gene Debs on the Fourth," *Liberator*, September 1918, 7–9.

Ricker, Allen W. "An Attack on Debs," *Appeal to Reason*, May 20, 1911.

Roosevelt, Theodore. "Murder Is Murder," *Outlook*, December 16, 1911, 901–902.

Saposs, David J. "The Line-Up at Cincinnati," *Labor Age*, September 1922, 18–20.

Sinclair, Upton. "The Socialist Party," *World's Work*, April 1906, 7431–7432.

Slobodin, Henry L. "The State of the Socialist Party," *International Socialist Review*, March 1917, 539–541.

Steffens, Lincoln. "Eugene V. Debs on What the Matter Is in America and What to Do about It," *Everybody's*, October 1908, 455–469.

Sweeney, Charles. "The Uncaging of Debs," *Liberator*, February 1922, 22.

Varney, Harold Lord. "An American Labor Party in the Making," *Current History*, April 1924, 86–91.

Watkins, Gordon S. "Present Status of Socialism in the United States," *Atlantic Monthly*, December 1919, 821–830.

Willard, Cyrus Field. "The Social Democracy," *New Time*, October 1897, 240–243, and November 1897, 337–338.

V. CONTEMPORARY LEAFLETS AND PAMPHLETS

(Selected)

Clark, Evans, and Charles Solomon. *The Socialists in the New York Board of Aldermen*. New York: 1918.

Condo, Samuel S. *Memorial Lecture on Eugene Victor Debs*. Marion, Ind.: 1924.

Debs White Book. Girard: 1920.

Eastman, Max, and others. *Debs and the War*. Chicago: [1919?].

Engdahl, J. Louis. *Debs and O'Hare in Prison*. Chicago: 1919.

An Evening in Girard. Girard: 1908.

Foster, William Z. *Bankruptcy of the American Labor Movement*. Chicago: [1922?].

Gompers, Samuel. *Address* to the Arbitration Conference held at Chicago, Ill., December 17, 1900, under the Auspices of the National Civic Federation. Washington, D. C.: [1900?].

Hillquit, Morris. *Present Day Socialism*. New York: 1920.

Hollingsworth, J. H. *Eugene V. Debs—What His Neighbors Say of Him*. Terre Haute: 1916.

Holmes, John Haynes. *Debs—Lover of Men*. New York: 1927.

Hurt, Walter. *Eugene V. Debs—An Introduction*. Williamsburg, Ohio: [circa 1910?].

Nearing, Scott. *The Debs Decision*. New York: [1919?].

Pepper, John. *Underground Radicalism: An Open Letter to Eugene V.*

Debs and to All Honest Workers Within the Socialist Party. New York: [1923?].

Ruthenberg, C. E. *From the Third Through the Fourth Convention of the Workers (Communist) Party of America.* Chicago: [1925?].

Sinclair, Upton. *America's Greatest Newspaper.* Girard: [1910?].

Socialist Campaign Book, 1912.

Trachtenberg, Alexander, editor. *American Socialists and the War.* New York: 1917.

VI. CONTEMPORARY POLITICAL TRACTS

(Selected)

Altgeld, John P. *Live Questions.* Chicago: 1899.

Broun, Heywood. *It Seems to Me.* New York: 1935.

Carwardine, William H. *The Pullman Strike.* Chicago: 1894.

Cleveland, Grover. *The Government in the Chicago Strike of 1894,* (reprint of speech at Princeton, 1904). Princeton, N. J.: 1913.

Dyche, John A. *Bolshevism in American Labor Unions.* New York: 1926.

Foster, William Z. *The Great Steel Strike and Its Lessons.* New York: 1920.

Gompers, Samuel. *American Labor and the War.* New York: 1919.

——and William English Walling. *Out of Their Own Mouths.* New York: 1921.

Oneal, James. *American Communism.* New York: 1927.

Pingree, Hazen S. *Facts and Opinions; or, Dangers That Beset Us.* Detroit: 1895.

Social Democracy Red Book. Terre Haute: 1900.

Sullivan, J. W. *Socialism as an Incubus on the American Labor Movement.* New York: 1909.

Swinton, John. *Striking for Life; Labor's Side of the Labor Question.* New York: 1894.

White, William Allen. *The Editor and His People,* edited by Helen Ogden Mahin. New York: 1924.

VII. CONTEMPORARY AUTOBIOGRAPHIES, BIOGRAPHIES, AND COLLECTED LETTERS, THAT MENTION EUGENE V. DEBS

Ameringer, Oscar. *If You Don't Weaken.* New York: 1940.

Biographical Sketches of Members of the Indiana State Government, 1885. Indianapolis: [1885?].

Bloor, Ella Reeve. *We Are Many*. New York: 1940.
Buchanan, Joseph R. *The Story of a Labor Agitator*. New York: 1903.
Chaplin, Ralph. *Wobbly*. Chicago: 1948.
Commons, John R. *Myself*. New York: 1934.
Darrow, Clarence. *The Story of My Life*. New York: 1932.
Dell, Floyd. *Homecoming*. New York: 1933.
Eastman, Max. *Enjoyment of Living*. New York: 1948.
—— *Heroes I Have Known*. New York: 1942.
Flynn, Elizabeth Gurley. *Debs, Haywood, Ruthenberg*. New York: 1939.
Foster, William Z. *From Bryan to Stalin*. New York: 1937.
—— *Pages From a Worker's Life*. New York: 1939.
Goldman, Emma. *Living My Life*. New York: 1931.
Gompers, Samuel. *Seventy Years of Life and Labor*. New York: 1925.
Haywood, William D. *Bill Haywood's Book*. New York: 1929.
Hillquit, Morris. *Loose Leaves From a Busy Life*. New York: 1934.
Holmes–Pollock Letters, edited by Mark DeWolfe Howe, vol. II. Cambridge, Mass.: 1941.
Jones, Mary. *Autobiography of Mother Jones*. Chicago: 1925.
Karsner, David. *Debs, His Authorized Life and Letters*. New York: 1919.
—— *Horace Traubel: His Life and Work*. New York: 1919.
Kopelin, Louis. *Life of Debs*. Girard, Kansas: [1920?] (pamphlet).
Maurer, James. *It Can Be Done*. New York: 1938.
Poole, Ernest. *The Bridge*. New York: 1940.
Powderly, Terence V. *The Path I Trod*. New York: 1940.
Riley, James Whitcomb. *The Letters of James Whitcomb Riley*, edited by William Lyon Phelps. Indianapolis, Ind.: 1930.
Sanger, Margaret. *Autobiography*. New York: 1938.
Sinclair, Upton. *American Outpost*. New York: 1932.
Steffens, Lincoln. *Autobiography*. New York: 1931.
—— *The Letters of Lincoln Steffens*, edited by Ella Winter and Granville Hicks. New York: 1938.
Tumulty, Joseph P. *Woodrow Wilson As I Know Him*. New York: 1921.
Vincent, Henry. *The Editor With a Punch: Wayland*. Massillon, Ohio: 1912 (pamphlet).
Vorse, Mary Heaton. *A Footnote to Folly*. New York: 1935.
Waldman, Louis. *Labor Lawyer*. New York: 1944.
Wayland, J. A. *Leaves of Life*. Girard, Kansas: 1912 (pamphlet).
Young, Art. *Art Young: His Life and Times*, edited by John Nicholas Beffel. New York: 1939.
—— *On My Way*. New York: 1928.

VIII. CONTEMPORARY HISTORIOGRAPHY

(*Selected*)

American Federation of Labor. *Proceedings* of the National Conventions, 1890–1926.

American Labor Year Book, (published annually or biannually, 1916–1926). New York: Rand School.

American Railway Union. *Proceedings* of the First Quadrennial Convention, held in Chicago, June 12 to 23, 1894. Chicago: 1894.

DeLeon, Solon, editor. *American Labor Who's Who*. New York: 1925.

Industrial Workers of the World. *Proceedings* of the First Convention, Founded at Chicago, June 27–July 8, 1905. New York: [1905?].

Socialist Party of the United States. *Proceedings* of the National Conventions, 1904–1912.

Secondary Sources

Aldred, Guy A. *Convict 9653: America's Vision Maker*. Glasgow, Scotland: [1942?].

Barnard, Harry. *"Eagle Forgotten": The Life of John Peter Altgeld*. Indianapolis, Ind.: 1938.

Beffel, John Nicholas. "Four Radicals," *American Mercury*, April 1932, 441–447.

Browne, Waldo R. *Altgeld of Illinois*. New York: 1924.

Calverton, V. F. "Eugene V. Debs and American Radicalism," *Common Sense*, July 1933, 10–13.

Claessens, August. *Eugene Victor Debs: A Tribute*. New York: 1946.

Coleman, McAlister. *Eugene V. Debs: A Man Unafraid*. New York: 1930.

—— *Pioneers of Freedom*. New York: 1929.

Cox, Ora Ellen. "Socialist Party in Indiana since 1896," *Indiana Magazine of History*, June 1916, 95–130.

Destler, Chester McArthur. *American Radicalism: 1865–1901*. New London, Conn.: 1946.

Fine, Nathan. *Farmer and Labor Parties in the United States, 1828–1928*. New York: 1928.

Foner, Philip S. *Jack London: American Rebel*. New York: 1947.

Heritage of Debs: The Fight Against War. Chicago: 1935.

Hicks, Granville. *John Reed: The Making of a Revolutionary*. New York: 1936.

Holbrook, Stewart H. *Lost Men of ·American History*. New York: 1948.

James, Henry. *Richard Olney & His Public Service*. Boston: 1923.

Knoles, George H. "Populism and Socialism, with Special Reference to the Election of 1892," *Pacific Historical Review*, September 1943, 295–304.

LePrade, Ruth, editor. *Debs and the Poets*. Pasadena, Calif.: 1920.

Lewis, Arthur Morrow. *The Art of Lecturing*. Chicago: 1908.

Lindsey, Almont. *The Pullman Strike*. Chicago: 1942.

Lloyd, Caro. *Henry Demarest Lloyd*. New York: 1912.

Madison, Charles A. *Critics and Crusaders*. New York: 1947.

Milburn, George. "The Appeal to Reason," *American Mercury*, July 1937, 359–371.

Miller, Clyde R. *Process of Persuasion*. New York: 1946.

Morais, Herbert M., and William Cahn. *Gene Debs*. New York: 1948.

Nevins, Allan. *Grover Cleveland*. New York: 1932.

Painter, Floy Ruth. *That Man Debs and His Life Work*. Bloomington, Ind.: 1929.

Peterson, James. "Trade Unions and the Populist Party," *Science and Society*, Spring 1944, 143–160.

Pringle, Henry F. *Theodore Roosevelt*. New York: 1931.

Sandburg, Carl. *American Songbag*. New York: 1927.

Schnittkind, Henry T. *The Story of Eugene Debs*. Boston: 1929.

Shannon, David A. "The Appeal to Reason," (unpublished, 1947).

—— "Eugene V. Debs and American Men of Letters," (unpublished, 1947).

—— *Anti-war Thought and Activity of Eugene V. Debs, 1914–1921*. (unpublished Master's thesis, U. of Wisconsin, 1947).

Stolberg, Benjamin. "What Manner of Man was Gompers," *Atlantic Monthly*, March 1925, 404–412.

Yellen, Samuel. *American Labor Struggles*. New York: 1936.

INDEX

ABBOTT, Lyman, 145.
Adams, Samuel, 369.
Addams, Jane, 109, 332.
Akron *Times*, 333.
Altgeld, John Peter, 94, 124–5, 130, 133, 135–7, 138, 144, 145, 154, 155, 169, 170, 187–8, 190–1, 206, 252, 331, 425–6, 449.
American Appeal, 453–4. See Debs, Eugene V.
American Federation of Labor, 37–8, 41–2, 49–50, 90, 93, 107, 144, 148–50, 162–3, 182–3, 193, 214, 217–21, 236–7, 244, 248, 257–8, 259, 273, 284, 305, 332, 335, 338–40, 395–6, 426, 438, 447. See Gompers, Samuel.
American Labor Union, 219–21, 236–7.
American Legion, 441.
American Press Association, 70, 160.
American Protective Association, 68–9, 133.
American Protective League, 357, 363.
American Railway Union: reasons for its formation, 90–2, 156–7; initiating conference, 92–3; organizational principles, 92–3, 259; rejects Negroes, 92–3, 116; early strategy and actions, 94–5; Gompers criticizes formation, 95–6; successes, 97–8, 100–1, 107, 114; dispute on Union Pacific, 101–2; and Great Northern strike of 1894, 103–7; and Pullman boycott of 1894, 111, 116–51; first national convention, 114–20, 165; Debs re-elected president, 120; leaders indicted and tried for conspiracy, 146, 152–3, 164–6, 426; leaders jailed for contempt of court, 151–3, 164, 166–7; criticized by Federal Investigating Commission, 156; Debs mentions sacrifices for, 160, 359; routine of leaders while jailed at Woodstock, 168–70; attempts to rebuild, 172, 178–81; effects of its destruction, 181–3, 192, 241; merges into Social Democracy, 195; not a dual union, 257–8; Debs'

affection for members of, 270, 275; all debts paid by Debs, 179, 181, 322; its leaders criticized, 241, 379.
American Revolution of 1775–1783, 25, 65, 74, 369, 398.
American Smelting and Refining Co., 231.
American Socialist, 353.
Ameringer, Oscar, 269–70.
Anaconda Copper Co., 396.
Anarchists and anarcho-syndicalists, 45, 50–2, 238–9, 241, 255–6, 295, 307–9, 310, 311, 312.
Anthony, Susan B., 27, 105, 224–5, 300.
Appeal to Reason, 200–1, 231, 246–7, 249–50, 252, 254–5, 265, 270, 283–4, 285–6, 287, 289–95, 300, 303–6, 310, 312–13, 322, 334, 343, 427, 442.
Appleton's *Encyclopedia*, 25.
Arbitration of labor disputes, 80, 156, 169.
Arnold, Benedict, 144, 401.
Arnold, Frank, 30, 32, 33, 44, 45.
Arnold, J. W., 135, 138.
Arthur, Peter M., 46, 47, 56, 58, 66, 70, 81, 82, 121, 127, 141, 151, 159, 160, 180.
Atchison railroad, 129.
Atlanta, Ga., prison, 389, 390–414, 415, 416, 419, 422, 423–5, 428, 429, 430, 433, 441, 443.

BAER, George F., 217–8.
Baker, Charles, 344, 354–5.
Baker, Newton D., 363.
Bakers' union, 49, 444.
Baltimore & Ohio railroad, 24.
Barnes, J. Mahlon, 219, 244, 263–4, 268–9, 272, 273, 295, 310–1.
Baur, Arthur, 205–6, 312, 385, 410, 411, 422.
Baur, John Jacob, 35–6.
Baur, Mrs. John Jacob, 35, 61, 385, 411, 414, 422.
Baur, Oscar, Jr., 298–9.
Bell Syndicate, 423, 429.

Bellamy, Edward, 71–2, 97, 168, 200, 202, 223, 301, 313, 315.
Belmont, August, 218.
Benson, Allen L., 334, 337.
Bentall, J. O., 428.
Berger, Victor L., 173, 188, 192, 194–5, 197–9, 200, 210–11, 214, 219, 221, 238, 240–1, 244, 259, 260, 262–4, 271–2, 274, 295, 309, 311, 320, 342, 349, 350, 394, 398, 406, 420, 453.
Berkman, Alexander, 94, 392.
Beveridge, Albert J., 190–1.
Bible, 10, 286, 399.
Bicknell, George, 299.
Bisbee, Ariz., strike of 1917, 345, 351, 360.
Black, John C., 165.
Bland, Richard, 188.
Blatchford, Robert, 168.
Bloor, Ella Reeve (Mother), 292–3, 398.
Bly, Nellie, 170.
Bolsheviks of Russia, 324, 329, 338, 348–9, 355, 358, 369, 382, 383, 389, 394, 396, 398, 412–3, 419, 430, 431–2, 438–9, 445.
Bosch, Alfred, 388–9.
Boston & Maine railroad, 128.
Boudin, Louis B., 453.
Boyce, Ed, 193, 215, 221.
Bradstreet's, 98, 154.
Branstetter, Otto, 269, 406–7, 412, 429–30, 431–2, 439.
Brennan, John, 139.
Brewer, George D., 427.
Brewery workers' union, 92, 219.
Brooklyn Elevated Railway strike of 1887, 55.
Broun, Heywood, 268, 377–8, 458.
Browder, Earl, 439–40.
Brown, John, 8, 158, 202, 255, 282, 287, 323, 373, 445.
Brown, William M., 347–8.
Browne, Waldo R., 449.
Bryan, William Jennings, 188, 190–2, 200, 206, 211, 262, 272–3, 275, 284, 332, 449.
Buchanan, Joseph R., 56, 91, 163.
Buffalo switchmen's strike of 1892, 81, 84, 89, 114, 132, 163, 182.
Building trades' unions, 49, 343.
Burleson, Albert S., 400.
Burns, Robert, 26.
Burns, William, 195, 197, 204, 241.
Business unionism, 37, 49, 99, 220, 255–8, 451.
Byrne, Michael J., 399, 428.

Cabin Creek, W. Va., strike of 1913, 320–1, 336.
Cahan, Abe, 240.
Caldwell, Henry C., 102.
Callery, Phil H., 263.
Calumet, Mich., strike of 1913, 326.
Canton, Ohio, speech by Debs, 1919, 353–9, 360, 362, 365–7.
Carey, James F., 214.
Carmack, Edward W., 250.
Carnot, Sadi, 123.
Carpenters' union, 49, 219.
Carwardine, William H., 108, 109, 110, 113, 117.
Catholic Church, 6, 68–9, 133, 306, 399, 428.
Cedar Rapids federation of the Railroad Brotherhoods, 90–1.
Challenge, 443.
Chaplin, Ralph, 434, 444–5.
Chase, John, 253.
Chautauqua Society, 197, 223.
Chicago & Eastern Illinois railroad,16.
Chicago & Erie railroad, 123, 125.
Chicago & Galena railroad, 22.
Chicago & Northwestern railroad, 73–5, 132–3.
Chicago American, 211.
Chicago, Burlington & Quincy railroad, 129; Burlington strike of 1888, 55–8, 159.
Chicago Chronicle, 169, 176, 232.
Chicago Daily News, 436, 444.
Chicago Evening Post, 142–3.
Chicago Evening Press, 174.
Chicago Federation of Labor, 123, 128, 144–5, 175, 400.
Chicago Herald, 126.
Chicago Inter-Ocean, 142.
Chicago, Milwaukee & St. Paul railroad, 126, 165.
Chicago stockyards strike of 1885,49.
Chicago Times, 45, 142, 150.
Chicago Tribune, 94, 125–6, 130, 142, 150, 155, 163, 178, 245.
Children's Crusade for Amnesty, 428.
Christenson, Parley P., 407.
Christian Science Monitor, 403, 431.
Christian Socialist Fellowship, 268, 310.
Cigarmakers' union, 49, 219.
Cincinnati Enquirer, 169.
Civic Federation of Chicago, 109, 216.
Civil War, 7–8, 10, 18, 436.
Claessens, August, 433–4, 444, 452–3.
Clark, Buster, 424–5.
Clark, Edgar E., 160.

Class Struggle, 382–3.
Clay, Henry, 370.
Cleveland, Grover, 59, 87, 89, 128, 130–2, 134–7, 140, 144, 148, 151, 154, 162, 163, 187–8, 192.
Cleveland *Citizen*, 239.
Cleveland *Plain Dealer*, 174, 355, 359, 365, 379.
Clothing Workers, Amalgamated, 457. *See* Needle Trades' unions.
Coal strike of 1897, 196–7; of 1919, 395–6.
Cobb, Frank I., 344.
Coeur d'Alene, Idaho, strike of 1892, 88–9, 92, 114, 132, 162, 163, 182, 193, 214; of 1899, 245.
Collier's Magazine, 349.
Columbian Exposition of 1893 in Chicago, 98–9.
Coming Nation, 173, 200.
Commons, John R., 92, 114.
Communist Labor Party, 393–5, 397–8, 406.
Communist Party: formation in 1919, 393–5; Debs' views on, 397–8; practical illegality of, 404; Debs refuses conditional support from, 406; Debs' evaluation of, in 1921, 419–20; forms Workers Party, 420; relations with Debs after 1921, 431–3, 437, 438–40, 445–8, 456.
Communist (Third) International, 394, 419–20, 437.
Comrade, 443.
Conservator, 292.
Cook County, Ill., Jail, 152–3, 161, 173, 422.
Cooke, Jay, & Co., 16.
Coolidge, Calvin, 454.
Co-operative Colony of Liberty Jail, 168.
Co-operative Commonwealth, Brotherhood of, 193, 194, 195, 197–9.
Co-operative Dinner Club, 228-9.
Corneille, Pierre, 9, 17.
Cox, Ben, 206.
Cox, James M., 401, 403.
Cox, Jesse, 199.
Coxey, Jacob S., 114, 188.
Credit Mobilier, 16.
Cregier, DeWitt C., 133.
Cripple Creek, Col., strike of 1894, 214, 370.
Cunnea, William A., 362, 365.
Current History Magazine, 443.
Curry, Mabel D., 410.
Curtis, Jennie, 117.

DARROW, Clarence, becomes ARU attorney, 132–3; and People's Party, 163; defends ARU leaders, 164–6, 173, 188; Democratic nominee for Congress, 190–1; speaks in Terre Haute, 228; attorney for Haywood, 253; and McNamara trial, 305; services refused by Debs, 362; tries to win amnesty for Debs, 400–1, 407, 408.
Daugherty, Harry M., 407, 408, 412.
Debs, Emma, (Mrs. C. O. Maillaux), sister of Eugene, 11, 31, 69, 147, 157, 160, 204, 319.
Debs, Eugene V.: ancestry, 4, 25; influenced by Victor Hugo, 6, 14, 17, 63, 168, 192, 261, 301, 337–8, 388, 422; childhood, 6–11; religion, 6–7, 10, 68–9, 266, 287, 347, 399, 426–7, 459; influenced by John Brown, 8, 158, 202, 255, 282, 287, 303, 323, 373, 445; education, 8–10, 15–6, 17, 25; influenced by revolutionary traditions of Europe and America, 8, 9, 25–6, 71–2, 74, 192, 202, 230, 232, 301, 303, 304, 370; works as railroader, 11–9, 239, 241, 301; relations with Theodore Debs, 12–3, 25, 31, 32, 100, 225, 277–8, 289, 319–20, 380, 387, 399–400, 442; and neighbors in Terre Haute, 12–3, 15, 28–30, 42; as a craftsman, 13, 24–6, 225–6; as a cook, 13, 229, 286; influenced by parents, 13–4, 25, 40, 63, 68, 147, 170, 180, 194, 225, 229, 248–9, 374; literary tastes, 14, 15, 17, 19, 25, 63, 72, 80, 168, 202, 226, 292, 380–1, 382, 388–9, 425–6, 436, 456; reliance on rank and file, 16–7, 79, 151, 284, 308, 352, 360–2, 380–2, 386, 397, 430–1; relations with workingmen, 17, 19, 31–3, 53, 61, 70, 82–3, 178, 180, 183, 194, 264–5, 270–1, 275, 280, 287–9, 292–3, 302, 385, 388, 396–7, 458–9; works as billing clerk, 18, 20–3; and Negro problem, 19, 42–3, 63, 68, 259–61; a sentimental personality, 19, 29–30, 62, 174–5, 209, 294, 317–24, 441, 444–5; use of liquor, 19, 53–4, 63, 145–6, 164, 250–1, 287–9, 366, 373–5, 393, 452–3, 459; as a scholar, 19, 63, 91–2, 301, 317, 372–3, 396–7, 446; in Vigo Lodge of BLF, 21–3, 30; and force and violence, 24, 34, 106, 123, 124, 128, 140, 143, 254–5, 307–8, 327, 396,

402; as an orator, 24–8, 30, 98,
105–6, 115, 225–6, 229, 265–7, 371,
377, 453; friendship with Riley,
27–8, 53–4, 62–3, 80, 100, 171, 173,
206, 339; influenced by Ingersoll,
26–7, 63, 80; opposes strikes, 23–4,
34; supports woman suffrage, 27,
43, 224–5, 299–300, 303–4, 403–4;
prominence in Democratic Party,
28–30, 35, 41–3, 416; City Clerk of
Terre Haute, 29–32, 39, 321; and
prostitution, 29, 321–3; secretary-
treasurer of BLF, 30–4, 35, 40, 69,
82; editor of *Locomotive Firemen's
Magazine*, 31, 33, 38, 39, 40, 56, 64,
70, 74–5, 79, 80–2, 84, 89–91, 94,
96, 99; and arbitration, 34, 80,
148–50; largely responsible for
growth of BLF, 31–3, 39, 46–50,
52–3, 69, 77, 301; courtship of Kate
Metzel, 35–7, 40; contact slight
with AFL, 37–8, 41; promotes other
unions, 38–40; opposes militant
unionism, 34, 41, 54; promotes
unions in Terre Haute, 38, 226–7;
serves in Indiana legislature, 41–3,
192; marriage to Kate Metzel,
43–4; clashes with P. M. Arthur,
46, 58, 151, 159–60; calls for joint
action by Railroad Brotherhoods,
47, 55, 58, 64–8, 72–84; attacks
Pullman, 47–8; converted to business unionism, 49–50, 59, 255–6;
and Haymarket episode, 50–2,
93–4, 202, 246, 247; and Burlington
strike of 1888, 55–8; denounces
Pinkertons, 57; campaigns for
Cleveland, 59, 89; defends strikes,
60, 80; childlessness, 61; plans
new home, 61–2 affection for
children, 62, 280, 285–6, 298–9, 375,
428; spends leisure at home, 63;
dislikes writing, 63–4; and dual
unionism, 65–7, 73, 79, 218–21,
255–8, 298; leader of Supreme
Council, 66–8, 72–81; denounces
religious prejudice, 68–9; projects
labor journal, 69–70, 81; opposes
exploitation of consumers, 69–70;
offered job by American Press
Assn., 70, 160; and political reform
in 1890, 70; influenced by Laurence
Gronlund, 71–2, 156; influenced by
Edward Bellamy, 71–2, 168, 202,
223, 301; influenced by Utopian
socialism, 71–2, 91, 99, 156, 168,
195–9; and Debs Publishing Co.

80–1, 91, 223; advised by Gompers
to stay in BLF, 81; and Buffalo
strike, 81, 84; calls for labor unity
and political action, 89–90, 97–8,
115; helps to found ARU, 91–3, 96;
criticized by Gompers, 95–6; con-
tributes to growth of ARU, 95,
97–8, 101; influenced by Marxism,
99, 156, 173, 183, 192, 237, 287,
337, 446, 451, 459; denounces
labor injunction, 102, 177–8, 434;
expert management of Great Northern strike, 103–7, 303; urges delay
in Pullman strike, 112; investigates
dispute in Pullman, 112–4; keynote
speech at ARU convention, 114–5;
opposes boycott of Pullman cars,
117–8, 119; outlines strategy for
boycott, 120; drafted for re-election
as president, 120; asks aid from
other unions, 121–2, 124, 144; warns
against violence and disruption of
mails, 123, 124, 128, 140, 143;
responsible for direction of boycott,
126–8, 134, 140, 146–7; attacked by
newspapers, 130, 142, 145, 154–5,
180; hires Darrow, 132–3; attacks
use of Army, 137–8; seeks to rally
ARU members, 140–1; arrested
for conspiracy, 146; actions defended by Kate Debs, 147–8; seeks
to end boycott, 148–9, 150; asks
sympathetic strike by AFL, 149;
supports People's Party, 151, 162–3,
170, 174, 187, 188–92; jailed for contempt of court, 151–3; appeals to
his conscience to justify his actions,
153, 261, 331, 363, 368; testifies to
Federal Investigating Commission,
155–6; attacks policies of BLF at
1894 convention, 156–61; sentenced
to six months in jail for contempt,
164; trial for conspiracy dismissed,
164–6; jailed at Woodstock, 167–76;
attacks Federal judiciary, 164,
177, 291, 303–4, 384; a celebrity
while in jail, 169–70, 173–4; visited
by socialists, 173–4; honored on
release from jail, 175–7; pays all
ARU debts, 179, 181, 322; tries to
revive ARU, 178–81; and Abraham
Lincoln, 183, 230, 270, 287, 372–3,
400; refuses to run for President
in 1896, 188–90; summary of
career to 1896, 191–3; becomes
socialist, 192–3; aids WFM at
Leadville, 193–4; supports coloni-

zation, 194–6, 197; aids UMW in West Virginia, 196–7; theory of business cycles, 197; deserts colonization for class-conscious politics, 197–9, 200–1; opposes all reform parties, 199, 202, 258; asks aid from Rockefeller, 201; opposes Spanish-American War, 202–3; effect of socialist views on his personal friends, 204–6, 291–2; friendship with Reynolds, 206–8, 212, 227, 229, 232, 274, 293, 448; attacks Rochester faction and DeLeon, 210; runs for President in 1900, 208–12; shirks positions of leadership, 213, 230–1, 244, 295, 308, 386; advocates class-conscious, industrial unionism, 214–6, 218–22, 234–7, 240–2, 256–8, 297–8, 332, 335; helps to found American Labor Union, 218–21; careless of precise truth, 220–1, 225–6, 241, 317–20, 368, 426; and lecturing, 223–4, 227; runs for President in 1904, 230–3; supports IWW in opposition to right-wing Socialists, 237–44; defends Moyer and Haywood, 245–55, 289–90; and the *Appeal to Reason*, 200–1, 246–7, 249–50, 289–94, 303–4, 310, 322; and death, 248–9, 430, 435, 449; clashes with Roosevelt, 251–3; quits IWW, 255–6; runs for President in 1908, 262–84; clashes with reform wing of Socialist Party, 263–4, 271–2, 295–8, 307, 309–11, 331–2, 333–4, 335, 349–50, 357, 397–8, 438–9; clashes with anarcho-syndicalists in Socialist Party, 295–6, 298, 307–8, 332; refuses to remove from Terre Haute, 285; routine in Girard, 285–8; derides city-dwellers, 286; and prohibition, 286–7; clashes with Warren, 289–94, 303–4, 310; influenced by personal friendships in his political decisions, 295, 346, 398, 437, 443; and immigration, 297; helps young writer, 300–2; defends McNamara brothers, 304–6; runs for President in 1912, 308–12, 324; and Wayland's suicide, 312–4; and feud between Kate and Theodore Debs, 319–20; investigates Cabin Creek strike, 320–1, 336; retires, 322; and *National Rip-Saw*, 325, 328, 329, 333, 345, 349, 353, 426, 442; basis

of anti-war views, 324, 326, 328, 330, 340; denounces invasion of Mexico, in 1914, 325–8, in 1916, 333; and patriotism, 328, 329, 331, 339, 353; seeks to prevent U. S. involvement in World War, 328–40; not a pacifist, 331, 353; attacks pro-war socialists of Europe, 331–2, 348–9, 352; attacks IWW, 332; runs for Congress in 1916, 334–8; refuses to denounce right-wing Socialists, 342, 346, 406; angered by infringement of civil liberties, 345, 350–2; follows equivocal policy, 345–8; calls for world revolution, 349; motives in giving Canton speech, 353–4, 403; Canton speech, 353–9, 360, 362, 365–7; defends Russian Revolution, 355, 382–3, 396, 398, 401, 402, 439, 454; indicted under Espionage Act, 359–60; inspired by anti-war movement, 354, 360–2, 380–2; regards conviction and imprisonment as certain, 360, 362–3, 366, 368; Cleveland trial, 362–77, 423, 443; compliments prosecution, 365, 369, 374, 379–80; explains opposition to war, 368–71; angry at prosecutor, 373–4; convicted and sentenced, 373, 375–6; predicts triumph of socialism, 374–6; summary of career to 1918, 377–9; Supreme Court upholds conviction, 383–4; travels to Moundsville, 384–7; finds contentment at Moundsville, 387–9; transferred to Atlanta, 389; relation to other inmates, 390–3, 402–3, 424–5; calls for united revolutionary party, 396–8; runs for President in 1920, 398–404; the campaign for his release, 400–1, 404–9, 412–3; attacks League of Nations, 401; clashes with Wilson, 401–2, 405–6; and Communists, 406, 419–20, 431–3, 437, 438–40, 445–8, 456; attacks dictatorship in Russia, 412–3, 431–2; reactions to his pardon, 413–4; loses citizenship, 415, 440–1, 456; triumphant return to Terre Haute, 416–9; suspends judgment on political affiliation, 419–20, 429–30; attacks penal system, 422–3, 429, 433; complains about own condition, 421, 427–8, 430; calls for industrial unionism, 426, 434, 439–40, 450–1;

and coarse humor, 427; at Lindlahr
sanitarium, 431–6; rejected as
speaker by BLF convention, 434–5;
announces adherence to Socialist
Party, 436–7; not in full accord
with Socialist Party, 438–9; tours
for Socialist Party, 440–1, 449,
451–3; extremely ill, 392–3, 419,
442; gives library to Rand School,
442–3; becomes chairman of
Socialist Party, 446; and election
of 1924, 446–8; contrasts Altgeld
and Bryan, 449; defends Sacco
and Vanzetti, 451–2, 453, 455–6;
and *American Appeal*, 453–4; takes
wife to Bermuda, 454–5; final illness
and death, 455–8; summary of
career, 458–9.
Debs, E. V., Publishing Co., 80–1, 91,
223, 225, 319.
Debs, Eugenie, sister of Eugene, 11,
31.
Debs Freedom Monthly, 428–9.
Debs, Gertrude Toy, wife of Theodore, 199–200, 455.
Debs, Jean Daniel, father of Eugene,
3–11, 14–5, 20, 21, 25, 31, 36, 40, 63,
147, 170, 192, 194, 205, 225, 229–30,
248–9, 261, 292, 299, 323.
Debs, Katherine Metzel, wife of
Eugene: her character in 1882,
35–7; attitude toward social reform,
40; becomes engaged to Debs, 40;
marriage to Debs, 43–4; effects of
solitude on, 52–3, 56, 61, 69;
dislike of Debs' use of liquor, 53–4;
her sterility, 61; as a housekeeper,
61–2; and Debs, 64; manages Debs
Publishing Co., 91, 223, 319; new
home of, 61–2; entertains Riley
in 1893, 100; arrives in Chicago
during Pullman boycott, 147–8;
aids Debs in Woodstock, 173–6;
attitude toward socialism, 204–5;
management of finances, 53, 61–2,
206; edits Debs' speeches, 225–6,
317; at Co-operative Dinner Club,
229; nature of Debs' letters to,
225, 232, 413; tries to save Debs'
health, 234, 284, 285, 292, 299, 319,
322, 360, 422, 442; brother dies,
248; sole beneficiary of Debs' will,
249; missed by Debs, 250; attitude
toward children, 293, 298; espouses
socialism, 299, 323; advocates
woman suffrage, 299–300; feud with
Theodore Debs, 319–20; receives

tributes from Debs, 205, 322–3,
385, 421–2; urges Debs to retire,
336–7; supports Debs' views in
1916, 336–7; ill in 1917, 338;
possible influence on Debs in World
War, 347; not present at Debs'
trial, 363; sees Debs leave for
prison, 385; preserves letter attacking Debs, 409; fails to visit Debs
in prison, 409–10; rejects aid from
National Rip-Saw, 410–2; amused
at Debs, 425; called snobbish, 421;
chides Debs, 427–8; illness of,
422, 442, 453–4.
Debs Legend, 100, 267–8, 287–9,
294, 377–9.
Debs, Louise, sister of Eugene, 6.
Debs, Marguerite Marie Bettrich
(Daisy), mother of Eugene, 3–6,
10, 12–3, 25, 33–4, 36, 40, 147, 170,
194, 205, 248, 289, 374.
Debs, Marie Marguerite (Mrs. John
G. Heinl), sister of Eugene, 6, 15,
204.
Debs Rebellion, 108, 129, 151, 153.
See Pullman boycott.
Debs, Theodore, brother of Eugene,
11–13, 25, 31, 32, 36, 40, 43, 53, 100,
103, 122, 127, 134, 147, 157, 160,
176, 199–200, 205, 223, 225, 274,
276–8, 284, 289, 301–2, 319–20, 347,
380, 385, 387, 397, 399–400, 403,
404, 410, 420, 427, 429, 442, 449,
455, 457, 458.
Declaration of Independence, 355.
DeLeon, Daniel: quoted, 1; biography, 96–7; praises ARU, 97;
characterized, 182–3; attacks
colonization plan, 194; supported
by Debs, 202; splits SLP, 208;
attacked by Debs, 210, 256; co-
operates with Debs in IWW,
238–9, 241–3; praised by Debs,
331; and Communists, 420; also
212, 332.
DeLeon, Solon, 243.
Dell, Floyd, 318.
Democratic Party, 28, 41–3, 58–9,
71, 151, 162–3, 187–92, 211–2, 273,
336–7, 401, 416.
Denver & Rio Grande railroad, 100.
Denver *Post*, 324.
Department of Justice, U. S., 357,
359.
Depew, Chauncey M., 190.
Depression, of 1865, 10–11, 18; of
1873, 16–18; of 1885, 44–5; of 1893,

90–1, 98–9, 108, 118, 161, 187, 191; of 1907, 284; of 1913, 328, 338; of 1920, 441, 451.
Detroit *Free Press*, 196, 279.
Disabled American Veterans, 454.
Dixon, A. C., 130.
Dooley, Mr. *See* Dunne, Finley Peter.
Dual unionism: among the Railroad Brotherhoods, 65–7, 73, 79; and the ARU, 95–6, 149, 257–8; and the ST & LA, 183; and the American Labor Union, 218–21; and the IWW, 236–44, 255–8; attacked by Debs in 1010, 208.
Duke, 391–2.
Dumas, Alexander, 215–6.
Dundy, Elmer S., 101–2.
Dunne, Finley Peter, 142–3.

EAST St. Louis race riot of 1917, 345, 351.
East St. Louis strike of 1886, 45.
Eastern railroad, 128.
Eastman, Max, 364, 367, 372.
Eckert, George, 168–9, 172, 176, 283, 435–6. *See* Woodstock jail.
Edwards, A. S., 173.
Egan, John M., 146.
Ehrmann, Max, 300–1, 333.
Eight-hour day, 44–5, 49, 50–1, 70, 80, 81, 215.
Elderkin, Thomas J., 175.
Election, of 1888, 58–9; of 1892, 87, 89; of 1896, 187–92; of 1900, 208–12, 234, 454; of 1904, 230–4; of 1908, 262–84, 334; of 1910, 307; of 1912, 283, 310–2, 324, 334; of 1916, 334–7; of 1920, 397–406, 420, 437; of 1924, 446–8.
Ely, Richard T., 109.
Emporia *Gazette*, 418.
Engdahl, J. Louis, 386.
Erwin, Charles, W., 417–8.
Espionage Act of 1917, amended 1918, 349, 359, 362, 379.
Estes, George, 237.
Everybody's Magazine, 272, 278.

FABIAN socialism, 168.
Farmer-Labor Party, 407.
Federal Investigating Commission of 1894, 108, 100, 118, 155–6.
Federated Trades & Labor Council. *See* American Federation of Labor.
Federation of Railroad Brotherhoods, 47, 55, 58, 64–6, 158–60. *See* also Cedar Rapids Federation *and* Supreme Council.

Field, Eugene, 147, 171–2.
Foster, William Z., 395, 426, 433, 439, 446–8.
French Revolution of 1789, 4, 21, 398.
Frick, Henry C., 87–9, 94.

GABLE, William F., 291–2.
Gaylord, W. R., 309.
General Managers Association, 118, 121, 123, 124, 126, 128, 137, 141, 146, 156, 159–60, 166, 175.
General Nicholas, 392.
George, Henry, 71–2, 91, 96–7, 132, 168.
Gerber, Julius, 397.
Germer, Adolph, 320.
Gitlow, Benjamin, 395.
Goethe, Johann, 9, 19.
Goldman, Emma, 198.
Gompers, Samuel: character of, 37; philosophy of trade unionism, 37–8, 49, 50, 72; demands labor unity, 79; advises Debs to remain in BLF, 81; opposes Populists, 91, 162–3; describes formation of ARU, 95–6; defends business unionism, 99; analyzes Great Northern strike, 107; and Pullman boycott of 1894, 121, 122, 144; protests against class justice, 153–4; and coal strike of 1897, 196; estranged from Debs, 204; co-operates with National Civic Federation, 216–9; and Leadville strike of 1896, 193, 220–1; fights Socialists in AFL, 99, 221, 236, 257–8; fights IWW, 244; attacks Red Special, 273; attacked by Debs, 332, 335; supports World War, 339–40; and Steel Strike of 1919, 395–6; visits Debs in prison, 407–8; calls Debs a publicity-seeker, 416; attacked by Debs, 426; and Socialist Party, 439.
Goodwin, Roy M., 195, 197, 204, 241.
Gould, Jay, 70, 266.
Gould railway strike, of 1885, 45, 56; of 1886, 49, 124.
Great Northern strike of 1894: causes, 102–3; no violence or disruption of mails, 103, 104, 106–7, and Railroad Brotherhoods, 103–4; intervention by governor of Minnesota, 104–5; arbitration urged by St. Paul Chamber of Commerce, 105–6; outcome of, 106–7, 159–60; analysis by Gompers, 107; aid received from

non-members, 114; ARU lucky in, 118; not publicized in *Locomotive Firemen's Magazine*, 157; Debs recalls, 301, 303.
Greenback Party, 71.
Greenbaum, Leon, 213, 221.
Gregory, Stephen S., 164–6.
Gronlund, Laurence, 71–2, 156.
Grosscup, Peter S., 130–1, 132, 135, 136, 146, 164–6, 318.
Guthrie, William N., 229.

HAESSLER, Carl, 434.
Hagerty, Thomas J., 215–6, 237, 238, 241, 244.
Hanford, Benjamin, 230, 264, 274, 280, 380.
Hanna, Marcus A., 191–2, 217–8, 220, 221, 258.
Hannahan, John J., 54, 77, 78, 100.
Hapgood, Norman, 408.
Hapgood, Powers, 421.
Hardie, Keir, 173–4, 192, 324.
Harding, Warren G., 401, 403, 407, 408, 412, 413, 415.
Harper, Ida Husted, 27, 29, 31, 43, 44.
Harper, Thomas, 29, 31, 53, 132.
Harper's Weekly, 94.
Harriman, Job, 208–11, 262, 305–6.
Harris, Frank, 339, 425.
Harrison, Benjamin, 59, 87–9, 162.
Harrison, Carter H., 99, 152.
Hawthorne, Nathaniel, 3C3, 324.
Hayes, Max S., 208–10, 236, 238, 239, 262; 295.
Hayes, Rutherford B., 24.
Haymarket bombing of 1886, 50–2, 93–4, 133, 202, 246, 247, 255.
Haywood, William D., 215–6, 219–20, 237–9, 244–56, 263, 269, 283, 290, 295, 308, 332, 342, 358, 366, 370, 378.
Heath, Frederic, 199, 210, 214, 219, 231, 240–1, 262.
Heathcote, Thomas, 112, 151.
Heinl, John G., 15, 204.
Henley, William Ernest, 456.
Henry, Patrick, 25–6, 202, 253, 369.
Higgins, Jimmie, 230–1, 233, 269, 274, 295, 380–1.
Hill, James J., 102–7, 303.
Hill, John A., 66, 72.
Hillquit, Morris, 208-10, 219, 221, 239, 244, 253, 262–4, 281, 295, 297, 309–11, 330, 333, 341–2, 394, 406, 420, 440–1, 443, 447, 456.
Hoehn, G. A., 197.

Hogan, Dan, 270.
Hogan, James, 195, 197–8, 204, 241.
Hollingsworth, J. H., 336.
Holmes, Oliver Wendell, Jr., 383–4.
Homestead, Pa., strike of 1892, 87–9, 114, 132, 163, 182.
Hopkins, John P., 119, 130, 138, 148, 150.
Horthy, Admiral, 454.
Hourwich, Isaac, 196–7.
Houston *Chronicle*, 322.
Howard, George W., 65, 66, 67, 72, 77, 79, 92, 93, 95–6, 103, 104, 106, 112, 119, 122, 126, 134, 146, 169, 204, 241, 379.
Hubbard, Elbert, 443.
Hugo, Victor, 6, 9, 14, 17, 63, 168, 192, 261, 301, 337–8, 388, 402, 422.
Hulman, Anton, 206.
Hulman, Herman, 20, 22.
Hulman & Cox grocery house, 18, 20–23.
Hynes, William, 47.

ILLINOIS Central railroad, 124–5, 155.
Illinois Federation of Labor, 123–4.
Impossibilism, 212–3, 288, 394.
Indiana Federation of Labor, 450–1.
Indiana legislature of 1885, 42–3, 192.
Indiana State Teachers College, 228.
Indianapolis *Journal*, 28.
Industrial unionism: early examples, 92; the ARU, 92–3, 158, 181–2, 192; a central objective of Debs, 202, 379, 406; an issue in Socialist Party 214–5; and the American Labor Union, 218–21, 236–7; and the IWW, 236–44, 255–8; Debs' program wins partial endorsement by Socialist Party, 297–8, 308; new labor federation advocated by Debs in 1915, 331–2, 335, 338, 339–40; and railroad strike of 1922, 434; Debs co-operates with Trade Union Educational League, 437, 439–40, 445; advocated by Debs in 1925, 450–1.
Industrial Workers of the World, 236–44, 246, 255–7, 295, 331, 332, 345, 349, 351, 358, 360, 370, 439.
Ingersoll, Robert G., 26–7, 63, 80, 145–6, 191, 206, 339.
Intercollegiate Socialist Society, 268.
International Harvester Co., 231.
International Socialist Review, 220, 238, 242, 260, 264, 268, 296, 297, 327, 343, 351, 353, 442–3.

Iron and Steel Workers, Amalgamated Association of, 87–8.
Irons, Martin, 124.
Irwin, William, 132.

JEFFERSON, Thomas, 230.
Jesus, 10, 266, 267, 280, 287, 399, 426–7, 443, 459.
Jones, (Mother) Mary, 228–9, 237–9, 320, 336.

KAISER Wilhelm, 358.
Kangaroo socialists. See Rochester faction.
Kansas City & Fort Scott railroad, 129.
Karsner, David, 384–6, 388, 423–9, 436, 443.
Kautsky, Karl, 173, 301.
Kavanagh, Francis B., 365.
Keefe, Dan J., 217.
Keliher, Sylvester, 67, 92, 93, 112, 122, 126, 146, 195, 198, 204.
Kelley, Florence, 153, 175.
Keracher, John, 437.
Kerr, Charles H., 268.
Kirkpatrick, George R., 334, 337.
Kiwanis clubs, 441.
Knights of Labor, 37, 49–50, 56, 90, 93, 115, 123, 144, 148, 154, 162.
Kolchak, A. V., 401.
Kollontai, Alexandra, 336.
Kopelin, Louis, 294.
Kruttschnitt, Julius, 218.
Ku Klux Klan, 396.

LABADIE, Joseph A., 223–4, 242, 383, 447.
Labor and Freedom, 374.
Labor Defense Council, 448, 456.
Labor Herald, 440.
Labor injunction, 58, 101–2, 130–3, 134, 151, 166–7, 177, 181–2, 196, 395–6, 434, 451.
LaFollette, Robert M., 332, 446–8.
Lamont, Daniel S., 135.
LaMonte, Robert Rives, 234.
Larkin, James, 336.
Leach, Joshua, 21, 23.
Leadville, Col., strike of 1896, 193–4, 214, 220.
League of Nations, 401, 408.
Lease, Mary Ellen, 187.
Ledoux, Urbain, 415–6.
Lee, Algernon, 234, 453.
Leffingwell, Samuel J., 38.
Left-Wing Manifesto of 1919, 394.

Lenin, Nikolai, 324, 369, 382–3, 398, 432, 433, 438.
Lewis, John L., 395–6.
Lewis, Sinclair, 436, 457.
Liberator, 343, 360, 364, 382, 433, 438. See Masses.
Liebknecht, Karl, 329.
Lincoln, Abraham, 183, 230, 267, 270, 287, 331, 370, 372–3, 400.
Lindlahr Sanitarium, 431–6, 438, 444–8, 456–7.
Lloyd, Henry Demarest, 98, 153, 163, 168, 173, 175, 177, 188–90, 193, 195, 196, 258, 366, 443.
Lloyd, William Bross, 366.
Locomotive Engineers, Brotherhood of, 22, 24, 38–9, 45–7, 55–8, 65–7, 73, 90, 121, 141, 151, 159–60, 240.
Locomotive Firemen, Brotherhood of: prior to 1877, 21–5; Debs becomes leader of, 30–1; growth as fraternal society, 31–4, 35, 37–45; growth as trade union, 45–55; calls first strike, 55; loses Burlington strike of 1888, 55–60; and the Supreme Council, 64–84; Debs resigns as officer, 81–3, 148, 256, 301, 331; initiates Cedar Rapids federation, 90; and Great Northern strike, 103–4; and Pullman boycott, 122; Debs attacks policies of, 156–61; and conciliation employers, 22–3, 34, 41, 81–4, 103–4, 122, 159–60, 162; Debs recalls experiences in, 423; Debs keeps gift from, 426; Debs rejected as speaker by 1922 convention, 434–5.
Locomotive Fireman's Magazine, 24, 30, 31, 37–40, 43, 46, 47, 49, 50–2, 55, 56, 58, 63, 64, 69, 70, 71, 72, 74–5, 79, 80–4, 89, 91, 96, 98, 99, 114–5, 157, 180, 215, 221, 317, 442. See Eugene V. Debs.
London, Jack, 182, 268, 339, 425–6.
London, Meyer, 350.
Looking Backward. See Edward Bellamy.
Los Angeles Record, 457.
Los Angeles Times, 181, 232, 304–5.
Louisville & Nashville railroad, 55, 159.
Lovejoy, Elijah, 369.
Lovejoy, George, 144.
Ludlow, Col., strike of 1914, 326–8, 330, 370.
Lusitania sinking, 328, 329.

MACARTHUR, Robert S., 130.

Machinists' union, 343.
Madden, W. H., 124.
Maillaux, Mrs. C. Odilon. *See* Emma
Debs.
Mailly, William, 221.
Markham, Edwin, 226, 301–2.
Markle, Theodore, 20.
Marseillaise, 277, 386.
Marx, Karl. *See* Marxism.
Marxism, 96–7, 99, 156, 173, 182–3,
192, 195, 237, 273, 331, 337, 402,
446, 451, 459.
Masses, 311, 318, 343, 349, 353, 374,
441. See *Liberator.*
Masters, Edgar Lee, 457.
Maurer, James H., 416.
May Day, 50, 239, 343–4.
McBride, John, 121, 173.
McDonald, Dan, 237.
McGuire, Peter J., 38, 72.
McHenry County Jail. *See* Woodstock
Jail.
McKeen, Frank, 206.
McKeen, Riley, 24, 29, 31, 55, 206.
McKinley, William, 191, 200, 217.
McKinley Tariff Act of 1890, 87, 89.
McNamara, James B., 305–6.
McNamara, John J., 305–6.
McNamara case of 1911, 304–6, 313.
McParlan, James, 245.
Medical Review of Reviews, 435.
Mencken, Henry L., 425.
Meredith, George, 228.
Metal Workers, United, 237.
Metzel, Daniel, 35, 248.
Michigan Southern railroad, 22.
Milchrist, Thomas, 124–5, 126, 130,
135, 137, 165.
Miles, Nelson A., 135.
Miller, Clyde R., 354–5, 359, 365, 367,
379–80, 408.
Milwaukee *Leader*, 321.
Milwaukee *Vorwaerts*, 173, 200.
Mine Workers, United, 49, 92, 196–7,
219, 283, 320, 332, 343, 395–6, 400,
421.
Miners, Western Federation of, 92,
193, 214–21, 236–7, 245, 255, 295,
326–7, 332, 423.
Miners' Magazine, 243, 280.
Mitchell, John, 216, 218.
Mooney, Tom, 357–8.
Moore & Langen Printing Co., 31, 38,
179.
Moore, Mark, 38.
Moore, Thaddeus, 179.
Morgan, John Pierpont, 218.

Morgan, Thomas J., 148, 173–4, 181,
192–3.
Morgan, William, 40.
Morris, William, 200.
Morrison, Frank, 218, 416.
Moskowitz, A. W., 359, 388–9.
Moundsville, W. Va., prison, 387–9,
391, 410, 422, 423, 443.
Moyer, Charles, 237, 238, 244–54.
Moyer-Haywood-Pettibone case of
1906–1907, 244–56, 263, 289, 290,
305–6, 325, 378.
Mulford, E. M., 146.
Mussolini, Benito, 454.

Nation, 349.
National Civic Federation, 216–8, 220,
235, 242, 258.
National Rip-Saw, 325, 328, 329, 333,
345, 349, 353, 410-1, 426, 442.
Nationalist, 72, 443.
Needle trades' unions, 343, 439.
Negro problem, 19, 42–3, 63, 68, 92–3,
116, 215–6, 217, 257–61, 345, 378,
396.
Nelson, Knute, 104–5
New York *Call*, 268, 333–4, 353, 384,
397, 417, 423, 436–7.
New York *Daily Forward*, 200, 239,
343.
New York City Elevated Railways,
47, 159.
New York *Morning Journal*, 139.
New York *Sun*, 141, 183.
New York *Times*, 131, 145, 281.
New York *Tribune*, 154–5.
New York *Worker*, 255.
New York *World*, 145, 169, 178, 312,
344, 402.
Newport News & Mississippi Valley
railroad, 55.
Nineteenth Century Club of New
York, 197.
Norris, George W., 332, 340.
Northern Pacific railroad, 16, 159.
Nye, Edgar Wilson (Bill), 28, 63.

OCCIDENTAL Literary Club, 25–8.
O'Hare, Frank P., 250–1, 263–4, 269,
325, 333, 350–1, 353, 410–1, 417–8,
428.
O'Hare, Kate Richards, 314, 325, 344,
350–1, 353, 354, 362, 366, 370, 373–
4, 394, 410–2, 417, 428.
Ohio & Mississippi railroad, 47, 67.
Olney, Richard, 125, 126, 128–31,
134–7, 141, 146, 151, 171, 180.

Oneal, James, 353, 397, 421.
Orchard, Harry, 245.
Otis, Harrison Gray, 181, 232, 304–6.

PAINE, Thomas, 25, 26, 192, 202, 301, 331.
Panhandle railroad, 124–5.
Palmer, A. Mitchell, 405.
Palmer Raids, 396, 404, 410.
Park, Holmes, 107.
Parker, Harry, 274.
Parsons, Lucy, 238–9, 241.
Pearson's Magazine, 339.
Peffer, William A., 154.
Pennoyer, Sylvester, 154.
Pennsylvania railroad, 23–4, 32–3, 45, 47.
People, 97, 194, 195.
People's Party, 71, 89, 90, 91, 99, 115–6, 151, 162–4, 170, 174, 182, 187–92, 211.
Pettibone, George, 244–6, 254.
Phelps, Erskine, 148.
Phillips, Wendell, 27, 331.
Pillsbury, Charles, 106.
Pingree, Hazen Smith, 139–40, 148.
Pinkerton detectives, 24, 45, 57, 88, 235, 245.
Pittsburgh conference of 1881, preliminary to formation of AFL, 37.
Pollock, John C., 318.
Poole, Earnest, 281–2.
Populists. *See* People's Party.
Powderly, Terence V., 49, 72, 115.
Prevey, Marguerite, 347, 355–6, 359, 373–4, 386, 398, 410, 420.
Progressive Party, 446–8.
Proletarian Party, 437.
Pullman, George M., 47–8, 70, 109, 110, 112, 116, 117, 118, 137, 142–3, 150, 154, 156, 166, 171.
Pullman, Illinois, 48, 108–14, 150–1, 155.
Pullman boycott of 1894: cause of original strike, 108–12; Pullman employees join ARU, 111; strike called in Pullman, 112; strikers appeal to ARU convention, 116–7; efforts of ARU to negotiate settlement, 117, 118–9; boycott voted by ARU convention, 119; Debs' attitude toward boycott, 117–20; General Managers Association supports Pullman, 121, 123, 124, 126, 128, 137, 141; Railroad Brotherhoods oppose ARU, 121–2, 141, 151; all ARU lodges support boycott, 122; use of strike-

breakers, 123, 124; supported by other unions, 123, 127, 128, 137, 144–5, 148, 151, 153–4; violence and disruption of mails, 123, 124–5, 135–8, 138–40, 143, 144, 154, 165; most commercial newspapers oppose, 123, 125–6, 130, 131, 139, 141–3, 154–5, 203; Edwin Walker named special Federal attorney, 126; effectiveness of, 123, 127–8; use of U. S. Army, 129, 130, 134, 139–40, 144, 154; the injunction, 129–32; ARU resolves to ignore injunction, 132; Darrow named ARU attorney for, 132–33; character of Federal deputy marshals, 138–40; efforts to arbitrate, 144–5, 148, 149, 150; ARU leaders indicted for conspiracy, 146; Federal intervention endorsed by House of Representatives, 146; AFL rejects proposal of sympathetic strike, 148–50; ARU leaders jailed, 151; boycott ends, 151; Report of Federal Investigating Commission, 155–6; effects of defeat, 155, 163, 169–70, 181–3, 192, 206, 215, 256, 303, 451; conspiracy trial of ARU leaders, 164–6, 368; use of blacklist, 113, 155, 172, 178–80, 270; Debs ascribes defeat in part to rejection of Negroes, 259; recalled by Debs, 359, 370, 426, 434.

QUEEN & Crescent railroad, 66–7.

RACINE, Jean Baptiste, 9, 17.
Railroad accidents, 17–18, 22, 40–1, 42, 57.
Railroad Brakemen, Brotherhood of. *See* Railroad Trainmen, Brotherhood of.
Railroad Brotherhoods, 90, 91, 103, 107, 114, 116, 127, 144, 149, 156–61, 162, 180, 182, 204, 339–40, 434, 447. *See* Cedar Rapids federation; Supreme Council; and the specific Brotherhoods.
Railroad Conductors, Brotherhood of, 65, 66, 67, 72–80.
Railroad shopmen's strike of 1922, 434.
Railroad strike of 1877, 23–4, 57, 59, 134.
Railroad Trainmen, Brotherhood of, 38–9, 64–8, 73–80, 81, 90, 122, 141, 180.
Railway Car Men, Brotherhood of, 40, 67, 90, 97.

Railway Conductors, Order of, 22, 24, 38–9, 58, 65, 73, 78, 90, 104, 121–2, 127.
Railway Service Gazette, 72.
Railway Telegraphers, Brotherhood of, 67, 73.
Railway Telegraphers, Order of, 67, 73, 78, 90.
Railway Times, 101, 171, 173, 190, 195, 442.
Railway Workers, United, 237.
Rand School of Social Science, 442–3.
Ratchford, Michael D., 196
Red Special of 1908, 268–84.
Reed, John, 349, 360–1, 382, 388, 394–5, 398.
Reinbold, Phil K., 417, 418, 424.
Republican Party, 41–3, 59, 162–3, 190–2, 211–2, 217, 273, 275, 284, 336–7, 401, 404–5.
Reynolds, Jean, 207, 293.
Reynolds, Jessica, 206–8, 229, 293.
Reynolds, Stephen Marion, 206–8, 209, 212, 227–9, 232, 274, 276–8, 283, 293, 299, 448.
Richardson, E. F., 253.
Ricker, Allen W., 295.
Riley, James Whitcomb, 28, 35, 53–4, 62–3, 80, 100, 171–2, 173, 206, 339.
Riner, John A., 102.
Rio Grande & Western railroad, 100–1.
Robertson, Thomas S., 145.
Rochester faction, 208–13.
Rock Island railroad, 155, 164.
Rockefeller, John D., 201, 218, 266, 278, 327–8, 330.
Rockefeller, John D., Jr., 327.
Roderus, Frank, 294.
Rogers, Louis W., 67, 79, 92, 93, 101, 103–4, 106, 122, 126, 146, 169, 190, 204, 223.
Roosevelt, Theodore, 97, 190–1, 231, 251–3, 262, 272, 281, 304, 310, 312, 343, 358.
Root, Elihu, 346.
Rose Polytechnic Institute, 228.
Rousseau, Jean Jacques, 9, 17.
Ruskin, John, 200.
Russell, Charles Edward, 309, 330, 343, 346.
Russian Revolution, of 1905, 239; of March 1917, 342; of November 1917, 348–9, 355, 369, 382, 383, 396, 398, 406, 412–3, 430, 431–2, 437, 438–9, 443, 454.

Ruthenberg, Charles E., 342, 344, 354–5, 367, 395, 398.

Sacco-Vanzetti case of 1920–1927, 396, 451–2, 453, 455–6.
St. John, Vincent, 237–8.
St. Joseph's Cathedral in Terre Haute, 10.
St. Louis Anti-War Manifesto of Socialist Party, 341–2, 350, 352, 355, 359, 362, 367, 370–1.
St. Louis *Mirror*, 283.
St. Paul & Pacific railroad, 102.
St. Paul Chamber of Commerce, 105–6.
St. Stephen's Church in Terre Haute, 44.
Sandburg, Carl, 436, 444–5.
Santa Fe railroad, 100.
Sargent, Frank P., 45, 53, 76, 78, 93, 100, 103, 122, 127, 158.
Saunders, William, 40.
Schiller, Johann, 9, 14.
Schilling, George A., 178, 190, 449.
Schuhardt, Will, 417.
Schurz, Carl, 190.
Schwab, Charles M., 218.
Scott, Thomas A., 45.
Sedition Act of 1918. *See* Espionage Act.
Sebree, Shubert, 361–2, 381.
Seidel, Emil, 309.
Shakespeare, William, 63.
Sharts, Joseph W., 362, 431.
Shaw, George Bernard, 228.
Sherman, Charles O., 237–9.
Sherman, John, 110.
Sherman Anti-Trust Act of 1890, 110, 131, 135, 167.
Sherwood, Isaac R., 280.
Simons, Algie M., 238, 262–4, 268, 343, 443.
Sinclair, Upton, 228, 330, 380, 388, 398–9, 403, 408, 449.
Upton Sinclair's Magazine, 380.
Single-tax movement, 71–2, 258.
Slobodin, Harry, 343.
Smith, Jesse, 407–8.
Smith, O. J., 29.
Social Democracy of America: formed by leaders of ARU, 195; program combines colonization and political action, 195–6; the Utopians and Marxists split, 197–9; Debs comments on split, 199, 256.
Social Democrat, 195.
Social Democratic Herald, 200, 211, 231, 240, 243–4, 258–9, 273, 442.

Social Democratic Party: formed in 1898, 197–9; early growth, 199–201, 208–13; convention of 1900, 208–9, 214; in election of 1900, 208–12; merges with Rochester faction to form Socialist Party, 212–3.

Social Revolution. See *National Rip-Saw.*

Socialist Labor Party, 96–7, 182–3, 197, 202, 208, 210, 331, 338.

Socialist Party: formed in 1901, 212–3; policy divisions exist from origin, 213–4; dispute about American Labor Union, 219–21; convention of 1904, 230–1; in election of 1904, 230–3; Debs' program for, 234–6, 256–61; policies of reform wing of, 234, 236; split by IWW, 236–44; and Moyer-Haywood-Pettibone case, 248; opposes labor parties, 258; and Negro problem, 258–61; convention of 1908, 262–4; in election of 1908, 264–84; and expropriation of capitalists, 271–2; sectional divisions within, 288; Debs' attitude toward factions of, in 1910, 294–8; reformism within, 296, 307; and immigration, 297, 309; and industrial unionism, 297–8, 308; anarcho-syndicalism within, 307–9, 312; convention of 1912, 308–9; in election of 1912, 310–12; and Cabin Creek strike, 320–1; pre-1914 position on war, 324–5; opposes World War, 325, 329–30, 334–5, 341–2; trade union policy attacked by Debs, 335; proposed merger with Socialist Labor Party fails, 331, 338; new left-wing forms, 342; St Louis Anti-War Manifesto, 341–2, 350, 352, 355, 359, 362, 367, 370–1; splits on war issue, 342–3, 357; growth of pro-war sentiment among leaders of, 330, 342–3, 349–50; left-wing expelled in 1919, 383, 393–5, 396–8; in election of 1920, 397–405; weakened condition of, 404, 406–7; in amnesty campaign for Debs, 408; tries to win Debs' endorsement, 419–20, 429–30; Debs affirms allegiance to, 436–7; Debs not in full accord with, 438–40; Debs becomes chairman of, 446; in election of 1924, 446–8; convention of 1925, 447–8; Debs tours for, 449, 451–3; convention of 1926, 455.

Socialists of Europe, 324, 329–30, 338, 348–9, 445.

Socialist (Second) International, 324, 329–30, 331–2, 338, 371.

Socialist Trades & Labor Alliance, 183, 238.

Southern Pacific railroad, 123, 218.

Sovereign, John R., 115, 123, 137, 144, 196.

Spanish-American War, 200, 202–3.

Spargo, John, 262, 310–1, 343.

Stahl, Carl, 206, 319–20.

Stalin, Joseph, 369.

Standard Oil Co., 163, 218, 325, 328.

Standard Publishing Co. *See* Debs, E. V., Publishing Co.

Stanford University, 280.

Stedman, Seymour, 199, 262–4, 295, 362, 364, 365, 367, 368, 397.

Steel Strike of 1919, 395–6, 426.

Steffens, Lincoln, 270–2, 278, 305, 408, 412–3, 416, 432.

Steiner, Virgil, 365–6.

Stephens, Madge P., 410.

Sterling, Edward R., 366.

Steunenberg, Frank, 244–5.

Stevens, Samuel M., 30, 32, 33.

Stokes, J. G. Phelps, 343.

Stokes, Rose Pastor, 343, 346, 354, 362, 365, 370, 372, 373–4, 398, 431–2.

Sue, Eugene, 6, 168.

Sumner, Charles, 331, 370.

Supreme Council of the United Orders of Railway Employes, 66–8, 73–80, 81, 90, 442.

Supreme Court, United States, 166–7, 247, 250, 289, 357, 359, 379, 380, 383–4.

Swinton, John, 86, 154, 183.

Switchmen's *Journal*, 280.

Switchmen's Mutual Aid Association, 40, 56, 73–80, 97.

Taft, William Howard, 262, 272, 275, 282, 284, 304, 310, 343, 454.

Taylor, William S., 290.

Telluride, Col., strike of 1901, 214.

Terre Haute conference of 1881, preliminary to formation of AFL, 37–8.

Terre Haute *Daily News*, 70.

Terre Haute *Express*, 27.

Terre Haute *Gazette*, 29, 69, 264–5.

Terre Haute *Post*, 299, 322, 323.

Terre Haute street car strike of 1902, 226–7.
Terre Haute *Tribune*, 344, 348, 418, 449.
Terrell, Joseph Z., 387–8, 389, 391.
Tobin, Daniel, 340.
Trade Union Educational League, 439–40.
Traubel, Horace, 228, 291–2, 388, 425, 443.
Trautmann, William E., 237–8.
Triner, Joseph, 367.
Trotzky, Leon, 369.
Trumbull, Lyman, 163, 166–7, 175.
Tucker, Irwin St. John, 428–9.
Tumulty, Joseph P., 405.
Typographical Union, International, 38.

Union Pacific railroad, 47, 100–2, 159.
Union Reform Party, 202.
Unionism and Socialism, 234–6.
United Shoe Machinery Co., 231.
United States Steel Co., 218, 231, 306.
Unity Convention of Socialist Party in 1901, 212–3.
Untermann, Ernest, 238, 309, 379.

Vandalia railroad, 5, 24, 301.
Vanderbilt, William H., 34.
Versailles, Treaty of, 383, 408, 441, 453–4.
Vigo Lodge of BLF in Terre Haute, 21, 22, 40, 41, 157–8.
Villa, Pancho, 333.
Villard, Oswald Garrison, 349.
Voltaire, Francois, 9, 25, 192.
Voorhees, Daniel Wolsey, 7, 27, 59.

Wabash railroad, 55.
Wagenknecht, Alfred, 344, 354–5, 356, 386, 395, 398.
Wagner, Phil, 325.
Waite, Davis H., 134, 138, 177.
Walker, Edwin, 126, 129, 130, 131, 135, 141, 153, 165.
Walling, William English, 296, 343.
Walsh, Frank P., 443.
Wanamaker, John, 59.
Wanhope, Joshua, 253, 281.
Warren, Carl, 286.
Warren, Fred D., 246, 249–50, 265, 267, 270, 285–7, 289–91, 295, 300, 303–4, 309–10, 312, 378.
Warren defense campaign of 1909–11, 290–5, 303–4, 310, 317, 378.

Washington, George, 369.
Washington *Post*, 141.
Wayland, Julius A., 173, 200, 231, 246, 249–50, 265, 285, 294, 303, 310, 312–4, 322.
Webster, Daniel, 370.
Wertz, Edwin S., 371–2, 374–5.
Westenhaver, David C., 333–4, 367, 368, 369, 371, 372, 373, 375–6, 379–80.
Western Labor Union, 218.
White, Clarence H., 228.
White, William Allen, 418.
Whitlock, Brand, 139, 272, 280.
Whitman, Walt, 80, 228, 232, 292, 425.
Whittier, John Greenleaf, 202.
Wickes, Thomas H., 108, 111–2, 118–9, 145, 148.
Wilde, Oscar, 425.
Wilkinson, S. E., 64, 75, 79, 160, 180.
Wilson, Noble C., 338, 353, 381.
Wilson, Woodrow, 310, 312, 325, 327, 328, 333, 338, 339, 340, 344, 350, 353, 384, 395, 400, 401, 402, 405, 406, 407.
Wilson Tariff Act of 1894, 128.
Wisconsin legislature of 1923, 441.
Wisconsin, University of, 283, 441.
Witt, Peter, 317.
Wobblies. *See* Industrial Workers of the World.
Wolf, Morris H., 318, 320, 362, 363, 364, 366, 368, 369, 371, 373–4.
Woman suffrage, 27, 43, 224–5, 299–300, 403–4.
Wood, Charles, 402.
Woods, William A., 130–1, 132, 153, 164, 177–8.
Woodstock, Ill., Jail, 164, 167, 283, 422, 435.
Work, John M., 262, 448.
Workers' Chronicle, 427.
Workers (Communist) Party, 420, 437, 438.
World War I, 324 ff.
Wright, Carroll D., 155.

Young, Art, 265, 311–2, 360–1, 441.
Young Men's Christian Association, 197, 259.
Yung, J. Rudolph, 254–5.

Zenger, John Peter, 303.
Zerbst, Fred G., 391, 393, 397, 400–1, 402–3, 413, 414.